LEARNING, MEMORY, AND CONCEPTUAL PROCESSES

WALTER KINTSCH
University of Colorado • Boulder, Colorado

JOHN WILEY & SONS, INC.

New York · London · Sydney · Toronto

Library of Congress Catalog Card Number: 76-104189

Printed in the United States of America

10   9   8   7   6   5   4

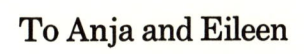

To Anja and Eileen

PREFACE

This book is concerned with how people learn: how they acquire new information, how information is retained, and how what a person already knows guides and determines what and how he will learn. For the most part the book deals with the area that is traditionally called *learning* or *human learning*. However, whenever it appeared appropriate material was introduced that belongs to *perception, problem solving*, or *thinking*. Results obtained in psychological laboratories are the main concern of this book; naturalistic observations, data obtained in actual educational situations, as well as neurological and physiological results concerning learning and memory are not discussed.

Chapter 1 presents a brief outline of the basic experimental procedures and results in the laboratory study of verbal learning. In Chapter 2 we turn to the problem of interpretation of experimental results of this type. In these two chapters some of the basic problems and approaches that will concern us throughout the book are outlined. Chapter 3 is fairly self-contained and presents an example of how a contemporary theory is developed and applied to a wide range of experimental topics. The next two chapters present a detailed examination of the research on memory: problems of short-term memory, the organization of memory, and the view of learning as a change in what is remembered from trial to trial are discussed by means of a large number of experimental studies. A final problem is taken up in Chapters 6-8: how do people learn to analyze a stimulus situation, and what principles and rules relate their responses to the stimulus-as-coded? In order of increasing complexity, such topics as discrimination learning, pattern recognition, concept formation, and the rules of natural language are discussed. Each chapter is provided with a summary.

Much of the research reported is recent. Some, in fact, is so recent that it is not at all sure whether it can stand the test of time and further research. However, I have tried throughout the book to relate current research problems to their historical roots. It is an unfortunate tendency among some psychologists to disregard everything but the very latest research on a problem. I believe that we can avoid much re-discovering and much re-entering of blind alleys if proper attention is given to the work of earlier generations of psychologists: their experimental methodology may be outmoded, but perhaps not their ideas.

This book is not committed to any particular psychological theory or viewpoint. In spite of this eclecticism the book is strongly theory-oriented. It is well known that experimental psychology possesses an extremely well-developed and sophisticated research methodology. In view of the difficulty of the subject matter that we have to deal with this is by no means a luxury but dire necessity. However, while concentrating upon methodology, experimental psychologists have not always paid sufficient attention to problems of data interpretation, i.e., theory construction. Recently many research workers have realized that theoretical questions must be taken just as seriously as methodological problems if we want to further our understanding of human behavior. I have tried in the present book to show how convincing this kind of argument is. In doing so many points of contact among seemingly disparate approaches could be pointed out. I have consciously stressed similarities and parallels, without, I hope, glossing over differential characteristics too cavalierly.

The student who studies this book will find that it can be read at various levels, depending upon how familiar he is with the area. Hardly any previous training in psychology is assumed, as the book is reasonably self-contained. The beginning student can obtain a general overview from it and should have no difficulty following the general argument, without, however, being able to fully appreciate all sections of the book and many of the minor details. Some mathematical background, especially an understanding of elementary probability theory —about at the level of a good modern statistics course—will be very helpful. However, the book is written in such a way that the reader without such training can omit technical sections without losing the train of the argument.

There is really more material in this book than can be covered in most one semester or quarter courses. As I have indicated above, the material is organized into reasonably independent blocks, so that the instructor can make selections appropriate for the nature of his course.

I am grateful for the many comments and suggestions that I have received from several people during the writing of this book. The editorial assistance of George Mandler is especially appreciated. My wife Eileen has read the whole manuscript and made numerous stylistic improvements and has diligently defended the English language from many atrocities. In addition, Section 3 of Chapter 8 is based directly and in part verbatim upon a literature review that she has prepared. It is a great pleasure to acknowledge my indebtedness.

My writing of this book has, of course, been profoundly affected by the way in which many interactions with past and present colleagues and students have shaped my view of psychology and, most of all, by the writings of the authors that are discussed here. I hope I have described their work fairly and accurately and that I have given credit to the proper individuals wherever credit was due.

WALTER KINTSCH

Boulder, Colorado
September 1969

CONTENTS

LEARNING, MEMORY, AND CONCEPTUAL PROCESSES

INTRODUCTION

Every reader of this book on learning is familiar with instances of learning, and indeed, he has been engaged in learning for a lifetime. In grade school we learn how to read and write, in graduate school we may learn how to make a clinical diagnosis; we learn to drive a car, and we acquire efficient study habits, or inefficient ones, as the case may be; we learn to behave appropriately at a party as well as in a classroom; we learn to be prejudiced, to be anxious and fearful, and some of us acquire pathologically maladjusted behavior patterns. Most of these learning situations have been studied in the laboratory by experimental psychologists. School learning has various counterparts in such verbal learning procedures as paired-associate learning, or serial learning. Medical diagnoses are essentially a problem in concept formation. Learning-to-learn effects have been explored with both animal and human subjects. Social psychologists have studied the acquisition of social attitudes and skills. Extensive work exists on the learning and unlearning of fear-responses and maladjustive behavior. Both the work on classical and instrumental conditioning of animals is relevant in this context.

What do all these situations have in common so that they can be listed under the topic of "learning"? The answer to this question turns out to be much more difficult than one might suppose. There is no really adequate definition of "learning." For instance, one might believe that learning always involves repetition. But a little reflection will show that repetition does not always produce learning—sometimes it merely results in fatigue. Or, consider the idea that learning implies improvement, or that it leads to some desirable consequence. Clearly, such a definition of learning is incomplete: it would exclude extinction and unlearning from the domain of learning, as well as the learning of maladjustive acts.

We shall not attempt a formal definition here. It is enough to define learning by pointing to commonly agreed instances. When a science is young and still in full development it is very hard to define its subject matter adequately. Not until it has reached maturity and its methods and results have become generally known and accepted is it possible to give a precise definition. The psychology of learning is still a long way from maturity. It has no generally accepted theories or research paradigms. It is still very much in a state of flux and resists explicit definitions. But it is not really necessary to define learning in order to study it. Everyone will agree that the behavior in certain situations should be called learning. Such situations can be taken as prototypes and as the topics of investigation for the learning psychologist. In other cases, there will be disagreement whether this or that should be called learning, or whether it should be assigned to motivation, perception, decision-making, or something else. There is no harm in such disagreements. In fact, it would be risky to restrict the topic of learning too severely without having a clear understanding of the consequences of such a restriction. It makes little sense to respect the borders between scientific domains too carefully until a science has reached a later stage of development than psychology has reached up to now. From the wide range of possible topics concerning learning a few have been selected for discussion in this book. It concentrates principally on human, rather than animal learning. Although much research in learning has used animals as subjects, this work appears to be quite distinct from the main concerns of workers in the field of human learning and will not be discussed here, except for a few cases where the relevance of the animal work is particularly obvious. Some justifications for the neglect of animal work are given in Chapter 2. Basically, it is argued that much animal work is primarily concerned with questions of motivation, rather than learning per se.

The topic of human learning is not treated comprehensively, however. Verbal learning receives the most attention, especially as it involves memory and the learning of concepts or rules. In Chapter 1 the most important experimental procedures in verbal learning are introduced and some basic experimental results are briefly presented. In the following two chapters the interest shifts to specific problems and issues of theoretical significance. These chapters build upon the earlier material, but new experimental evidence is continually introduced as the complexity of a problem unfolds and as theoretical analysis reveals what kind of experimental questions are fully relevant to an issue. A significant modern development is presented in Chapter 4: the interrelationship between learning and memory is explored, and verbal learning is considered as a change in the resistance to forgetting. The relevance of the classical work in memory to the understanding of verbal learning is discussed, as well as the more recent work on short-term memory, and models of learning which are primarily models of memory storage are described. Two further modern developments are the topics of Chapter 5. The crucial role which decision processes play in determining the performance of subjects in learning experiments is explored, primarily with respect to recognition learning. Secondly, the importance of organizational factors in memory and learning is discussed. Learning does not occur in a vacuum: the organization of the learning material with respect to what is already known by the learner is a crucial factor in learning and retention, which may not be neglected.

A somewhat different set of problems is treated in the remaining three chapters. The structure of the learning material, both perceptual as well as conceptual structure, is a major determinant of performance in discrimination learning, concept formation, and rule learning. The ordering here is in terms of increasing abstractness from discrimination learning to rule learning, but some similarity of processes seems to unite these topics. Chapter 6 deals with discrimination and generalization, and introduces the idea that subjects learn discriminations by responding according to strategies of stimulus coding. Material from animal learning, perception, and artificial intelligence is included to illustrate this point. Chapter 7 is much more specific: the popular experimental paradigm of concept identification is analyzed in some detail. This work provides a good example for the close interaction between formal theoretical work and empirical research. The last chapter raises the question of how much more complex concepts and rules are learned. Finally, the problem is investigated how knowing a set of rules—the rules of natural language—affect the learning of rule-structured material.

This book presents a set of ordered, meaningfully related problems in human learning. Materials have been selected that fit the overall progression of the argument. Its intention is to permit the reader to gain an understanding and appreciation of current research in human learning, rather than to provide a comprehensive treatise that would fulfill the functions of a handbook. Topics which are only incidental to the main concern of the book have been omitted. Among the most obvious omissions are motor learning and human classical and instrumental conditioning with their applications to social and behavioral control.

Before proceeding with the presentation, it is necessary to make explicit the beliefs concerning experimental methods and the tactics of scientific research which underlie much of the work reported here. Human behavior is always multiply determined. In every situation a variety of perceptual, motivational, and interpersonal factors are effective. The basic methodological precept of the learning theorist has always been to control these factors as well as possible, to keep experiments simple, to break down the complexity of human behavior into manageable subproblems. The traditional method of learning theory has been, and still is, to go from the simple to the complex, to analyze behavior in simple, controllable experiments in the belief that understanding gained from this analysis will prove relevant to the explication of human behavior in more complicated and socially relevant situations. Most of the work reported here must be understood within this methodological framework. Two comments about this research strategy are in order. First, although learning theorists are frequently concerned with quite simple laboratory situations, one must not forget that the human subject is an indivisible whole at all times and that behavior is not necessarily simple just because the experimental situation is so; conversely, the results of an experiment are not necessarily trivial just because the experiment is well controlled. Secondly, the record of learning theory with respect to the study of really complex and socially relevant problems must be defended. Learning theorists in the past have handed out some extravagant promissory notes which they were unable to cash. Watson's boast that he would make anyone into whatever he liked—"doctor, lawyer, artist, merchant-chief, and yes, even beggar-man and thief, regardless of his talents, penchants, tendencies, abilities, vocation and race of his ancestors"—will not be forgotten soon (Watson, 1924). There have been similar incidents since then, only a little less crude. Thus, the learning theorist today is somewhat in the role of the shepard who cried "wolf" too often. On the other extreme, for many learning theorists the study of paired-associate learning or maze learning has become a goal in itself; they refuse to be concerned with anything but well-controllable laboratory experiments. The patient and relatively risky work of extending learning theory to problems of more general interest has attracted only few research workers. Therefore, the "technology of learning" is still in its infancy. Applied problems will not be specifically considered in this book, but an attempt will be made to show how knowledge of human learning which can be obtained in well-controlled and simplified laboratory experiments can be used to understand more complex phenomena.

Throughout this book the relationship between theory and data will be a matter of serious concern. Not all learning psychologists will approve of the heavy emphasis upon explanation and theory. As a reaction against uncontrolled speculation psychologists have sometimes refused to theorize altogether and have insisted that empirical results should speak for themselves, that theory and model construction is merely a confusing and superfluous past-time. This is hardly the place to argue about the role of theory in psychology, but it will help the reader if the position taken here is made explicit right at the begining. This book is written with the conviction that empirical and theoretical investigations must complement each other if research is to be fruitful. Speculations without due regard for empirical results are an idle game and may indeed blind the investigator to the true features of his subject-matter. On the other hand, empirical data randomly gathered just because they are "facts" have no value in themselves and may obscure the relevant aspects of a problem just as much as theoretical prejudice. Data are made meaningful through theoretical interpretation; a theory is given substance through its empirical base. Neither can stand alone; understanding is the result of their continuous interaction.

As far as theories go, this book is entirely eclectic. Instead of supporting a particular point of view, much emphasis has been put upon alternative interpretations of a given set of data. There are usually many ways to talk about a phenomenon. Various theories or models may appear to be different, but it is often quite difficult to tell whether they make differential testable predictions, and what these are, or whether they are really saying the same thing in different languages as far as testable implications are concerned. Psychology has a long history of sloppy theorizing in this respect. In this book communalities between theories have been stressed, even if these theories seem to be greatly different at a vague verbal level. In order to differentiate theories they must be stated precisely and in a great deal of detail. If a problem is so poorly understood that it is not yet possible to state alternatives with the required specificity, then this fact is important in itself; it will not do to hide lack of understanding through vague use of language. Alternatives must be precisely formulated in order to determine what kind of data are necessary for a conclusive test of different interpretations. This, of course, requires a certain amount of mathematics. Mathematical formulations had to be resorted to throughout the book. In general the level of mathematics is kept very simple; a familiarity with the most elementary notions of probability theory is all that is required for most of the mathematical material in this book.

VERBAL LEARNING:
BASIC EXPERIMENTAL RESULTS

111111111111

1. PROCEDURES AND EXPERIMENTAL MATERIALS

There are a few basic experimental paradigms which are frequently employed in the study of verbal learning. Of course, numerous variations of these paradigms exist, and entirely new experimental designs are occasionally encountered. New designs and variants of old ones will be discussed whenever the occasion arises, but the classical procedures as well as the standard learning materials of verbal learning studies will be described first.

In the classical verbal learning experiment each subject learns a *list* of *items*. (For illustration see Table 1.1). Each *trial* involves a *study* phase and a *test* phase. Two major testing procedures are used. In the *anticipation* method on opportunity to study an item is given after each test; a trial thus consists of the sequential presentation of all items of a list for test and immediate study. In the *study-test* presentation method, on each trial all items are first shown one at a time for study, and then presented again for testing. Presentation rates are usually between 1 and 4 seconds per item, but in some experiments the rate of presentation may be treated as an experimental variable, and in others the subject may be permitted to pace himself. Learning trials are continued either for a predetermined number of trials or until the subject reaches some performance criterion, such as a trial on which all responses are correct. Various performance measures are used. For instance, two rather gross statistics are the total number of errors made by a subject in learning a list, or the number of trials required to reach criterion. Other more informative measures will be discussed below.

Procedures

A widely used procedure in verbal learning is *paired-associate learning*. In paired-associate learning the subject learns a list of stimulus-response pairs, a process similar to learning the vocabulary of a foreign language. A sample list is shown in Table 1.1. The first word serves as the stimulus for the recall of the second member of the pair, which is traditionally called the response word. There is an obvious parallel here between the conditioned stimulus and the conditioned response in classical conditioning: the subject learns to perform the conditioned response whenever the conditioned stimulus is presented; in paired-associate learning the subject learns to respond with the response member of an item-pair whenever the stimulus member is presented. There is some question whether this parallel is more than superficial, but this problem will be deferred until later. Several sub-problems of paired-associate learning may be distinguished. For example, an experimenter may study *stimulus discrimination* learning by varying the similarity of the stimulus terms in a list while keeping the response terms constant. A very useful distinction is the one between *response learning* and *associative learning* which is often made. In a paired-associate task the subject must learn two quite different

Table 1.1. *Paired-associate learning. (Each row is exposed for a brief period of time in the window of a memory drum. One presentation of this 8-item list constitutes a trial. The items are adjective-number pairs.)*

Anticipation Method		Study-test Method	
OVERT–?	(test)	OVERT–7	
OVERT–7	(study)	RURAL–6	
RURAL–?		CRINGING–2	
RURAL–6		RHYTHMIC–8	
CRINGING–?		SORRY–1	Study Phase
CRINGING–2		STRIDENT–5	
RHYTHMIC–?		FLABBY–3	
RHYTHMIC–8		UGLY–4	
SORRY–?		OVERT–?	
SORRY–1		RURAL–?	
STRIDENT–?		CRINGING–?	Test Phase
STRIDENT–5		RHYTHMIC–?	
FLABBY–?		SORRY–?	
FLABBY–3		STRIDENT–?	
UGLY–?		FLABBY–?	
UGLY–4		UGLY–?	

things: he must learn what the responses are, and then he must learn to associate each stimulus term with the proper response term. The experimenter may manipulate the difficulty of one of these subtasks while keeping the other constant. For example, if an experimenter employed unfamiliar meaningless letter combinations as responses, response learning will be difficult. The problem is one of *response integration* in this case. When familiar words are the response terms, response integration represents no problem since the responses, being familiar words, are already available. However, some response learning will still be required, because the subject must learn which of the many possible words are actually used in the experiment. Response learning may be eliminated completely by informing the subject beforehand which response terms are used in the experiment. This is easiest if a well-defined set of response terms is used, such as the numerals from 1 to 10. In the extreme case, when only two responses are used, such as 1 and 2, such paired-associate tasks resemble classification learning except that the assignment of stimuli to response classes is entirely arbitrary.

Both the anticipation method and the method of blocked presentations are used in paired-associate learning, with the anticipation method being favored by most investigators. List length is usually between 10 and 15 item-pairs. New random orders of presentation are used on each trial.

In *serial learning* each item serves both as a stimulus and as a response. Items are presented always in the same order and the subject learns to anticipate the next item of the list in response to each item. A special signal serves as a simulus for the recall of the first item of the list.

Table 1.2. *Serial learning. (Each item appears for a short time in the window of a memory drum during which the subject must anticipate the next item. The same presentation order is used on each trial.)*

---

*

OVERT
RURAL
CRINGING
RHYTHMIC
SORRY
STRIDENT
FLABBY
UGLY

*

In a typical *free-recall* experiment subjects are given a list of items, and are later asked to recall as many as possible. Usually from 20 to 40 items are presented, one at a time. Recall may be oral or in writing. Subjects are instructed to recall as many words as they can, without regard to the order in which the items have been presented. The recall periods vary from 30 seconds to 2 minutes. Order of presentation is randomized from trial to trial.

Table 1.3. *Free recall. (Each item appears for a short period of time in the window of a memory drum. After all items have been shown the subject is asked to recall as many of the words as he can. Different presentation orders are used on each trial.)*

---

*

OVERT
RURAL
CRINGING
RHYTHMIC
SORRY
STRIDENT
FLABBY
UGLY
*

recall

In a *recognition* experiment items are presented as in free recall experiments, but different testing procedures are employed. Basically, there are three types of recognition tests; all three involve the use of *distractor* items. The distractor items are selected from the same set as the learning items, and new distractor items are used on each trial in multitrial recognition experiments. In a single-item test, learning items and distractor items are presented one at a time in random order, and the subject responds with either "old" or "new" to each item. In a variation of this procedure, the subject is given a printed list of all learning and distractor items in random order and is asked to check those items which have been presented before. In a *multiple-choice* test each learning item is combined with several distractor items and the subject is asked to pick out the old item from each set of alternatives.

In *verbal discrimination learning* the subject is given a set of items (usually 2) and must learn to select one of the items which has been arbitrarily designated as correct by the experimenter. For ex-

Table 1.4. *Recognition learning.* (*Items are presented as in Table 1.3. After the study phase, subjects are given a test sheet and are asked to circle the items they were shown before.*)

---

*

OVERT
RURAL
CRINGING
RHYTHMIC
SORRY
STRIDENT
FLABBY
UGLY

*

Test sheet:

SORRY	NAIVE	SUBLIME	RHYTHMIC
TINY	RURAL	BLATANT	STRIDENT
HOSTILE	FLABBY	OVERT	CANDID
CRINGING	POLITE	UGLY	GOLDEN

---

ample, item-pairs printed one above the other are shown for about 2 seconds, during which time the subject must make his response; the correct item is then shown alone for study. List length is comparable to that used in paired-associate experiments.

Needless to say, there are many variations of these procedures. Perhaps the most important one which enjoys considerable popularity at present involves a *continuous* item presentation, rather than a list learning procedure. For instance, in a continuous recognition experiment several hundred items are shown one by one for a brief period of time. Some of the items are repeated, others are new; the subject's task is to respond with either "old" or "new" each time an item is shown. A similar procedure is frequently used with paired-associates: a particular item pair may be repeated for a while, and then dropped from the experiment; new pairs can be introduced continually. The advantage of continuous designs is that they make it possible to control the lag of an item, that is, the number of other items which intervene between successive presentations of a given experimental item.

The procedure most frequently discussed in Chapters 1-4 is paired-associate learning; however, these chapters are not exclusively concerned with paired-associate learning. In Chapter 5 some special characteristics of recognition learning and free-recall learning are explored. Also, at that point a systematic comparison of the various

Table 1.5. *Verbal discrimination learning. (Each row is exposed for a short period of time during which the subject chooses one item of the pair. A study-test procedure may also be used. Different orders are used on each trial, as well as different left-right positions for the members of each word pair.)*

OVERT	CANDID	(test)
OVERT		(study)
RURAL	NAIVE	
RURAL		
TINY	CRINGING	
CRINGING		
RHYTHMIC	HOSTILE	
RHYTHMIC		
POLITE	SORRY	
SORRY		
GOLDEN	STRIDENT	
STRIDENT		
FLABBY	BLATANT	
FLABBY		
SUBLIME	UGLY	
UGLY		

verbal learning procedures will be made. Some of the conclusions reached there may be anticipated. The various verbal learning procedures are by no means equivalent. Different procedures are used to explore different kinds of experimental problems, as will become apparent during the succeeding chapters. Also, there is considerable evidence that free recall, recognition, and paired-associate learning involve quite different psychological processes. The laws of verbal learning do not apply to all experimental procedures in the same way.

Materials

Learning items are usually words, numerals, line drawings, or arbitrary letter combinations. In most experiments standardized materials are being used. With words as learning material experimenters attempt to equate them on the basis of number of syllables, or grammatical classes, with some apparent bias in favor of adjectives and nouns. Extensive tables published by Thorndike and Lorge (1944) permit the selection of words according to frequency of usage in English. Thorndike and Lorge tabulated the frequency of occurrence of English words based upon a wide range of written materials. The number of occurrences of each word per million words was counted; words occurring more than 100 times per million were classified as AA words; words with a frequency between 50 and 100 per million were classified as A words; actual frequency counts were given for words occurring less than 50 times per million.

Letter combinations which do not form English words are also used as learning materials, usually in the form of consonant-vowel-consonant (CVC) combinations (the "nonsense syllable") or as consonant trigrams. Nonsense syllables were originally introduced by Ebbinghaus (1885), who needed a pool of learning items which was sufficiently large (this was very important as Ebbinghaus was his own subject in his experiments), and which was at the same time simple enough and supposedly homogeneous with respect to learning difficulty. Ebbinghaus objected to the use of words in verbal learning experiments because he had noted that some words were very much easier to remember than others, depending upon their meaning and familiarity. Later investigators, however, observed that the use of nonsense syllables provided only an incomplete solution to this problem. Some nonsense syllables are more nonsensical than others and Glaze (1928) and others actually measured the differences in meaningfulness among nonsense syllables. Glaze introduced the construct "association value" of a CVC which he operationally defined as the percentage of subjects who could provide a response on a brief association test, given the CVC: subjects were asked to respond with the first word that occurred to him. Glaze scaled 2000 CVCs this way. COL and WIS are examples of syllables for which all of Glaze's subjects reported an association, while GOQ and XUW are syllables which did not mean anything to his informants. Glaze's data are based upon only 15 subjects, but have proved to be very useful. A number of later investigators have repeated Glaze's procedures, refined them, and explored several interesting variations. A notable example is Noble's index of meaningfulness (Noble, 1952). Noble asked subjects to give as many free associations as they could within one minute in response to disyllable words, including both ordinary English words and artificial words. The mean frequency of associations in response to each item was taken as an index of meaningfulness, m. Thus GOJEY received an m-value of .99, FEMUR 2.09, and KITCHEN 9.61, for example. In other studies subjects simply rated the number of associations or ideas that they felt each stimulus item provided. Thus, scales of association value are now available for all CVC combinations (Archer, 1960).

The excessive use of nonsense syllables in verbal learning experiments has been criticized for a number of reasons. It is now well known that nonsense syllables are not a homogeneous set of items. On the contrary, variations in meaningfulness among nonsense syllables are greater than among words. In addition, most nonsense syllables do not have a unique pronounciation in English, and the number and kind of associations a CVC produces depend upon the way it is pronounced. To avoid this problem CVCs are almost always spelled in psychological experiments. Spelling, however, introduces new problems. The spelled CVC is no longer a unitary response, but a collection of letters. Thereby problems of response integration are introduced which often are quite incidental to the main concern of a study. Furthermore, in the typical learning experiment employing CVCs learning is slow and subjects become bored quickly.

2. TASK VARIABLES

The rate of learning in verbal learning experiments is in part determined by the characteristics of the learning material. Psychologists have studied extensively what happens when different groups of subjects are given lists to learn which differ in the nature of the learning material. With nonsense syllables, the meaningfulness of the syllables is an important factor. With words, the frequency of occurrence in the natural language is related to learning speed. A somewhat different problem concerns the interrelationship of the items within a list. No matter what the items are, the similarity among them is an important factor in learning. Similarly, the learning rate is affected if the items which make up a list are not independent, i.e., if one can predict what an item will be, at least in part, given the other items of the list. Some representative experiments which illustrate the nature of these effects will be described in this section.

Meaningfulness

There is little controversy about the effects of meaningfulness upon verbal learning: meaningfulness facilitates verbal learning. The exact nature of this effect depends somewhat upon the way in which meaningfulness is measured, as well as upon the learning task under consideration, but the over-all facilitative effect of meaningfulness has been demonstrated in many experiments. One of the first of these was a study by McGeoch (1930). McGeoch used a free recall procedure with 6 groups of subjects. Each group learned a list of nonsense syllables selected from Glaze's (1928) scale such that the association value of syllables within each list was the same but varied over the whole range from 0 to 100% between groups. The number of items recalled was a positive function of the association value of the items. This result has been replicated frequently and extended to other learning procedures such as serial learning and paired-associate learning. In paired-associate learning the effects of meaningfulness of items in the stimulus and response position can be distinguished. For instance, Cieutat, Stockwell, and Nobel (1958) selected items of high and low meaningfulness, both for the stimulus position and the response position. Four different lists of item-pairs were constructed in this way. A separate group of subjects learned each list. This factorial design permits one to study the effects of meaningfulness of stimulus items separately from the effects of meaningfulness of the response items. Figure 1.1 shows the results of this study. Meaningfulness was found to have an effect in both positions, but the effects of response meaningfulness were considerably larger than the effects of stimulus meaningfulness. The results of this experiment have also been replicated by later investigators.

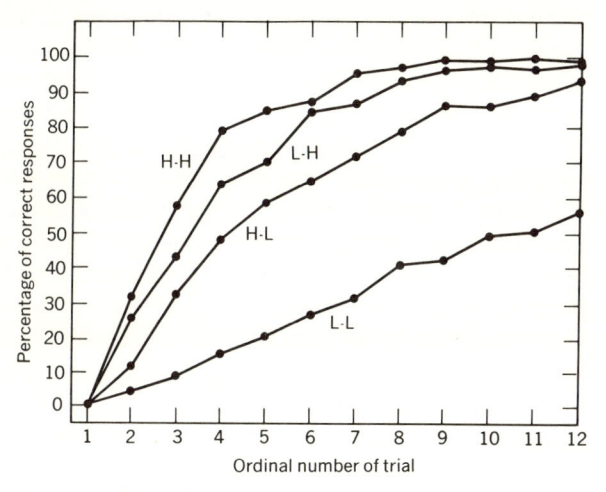

Fig. 1.1 *Acquisition curves for lists of 10 paired associates as a function of practice. The four* S-R *combinations of low (L) and high (H) meaningfulness* (m) *represent the parameter. Each curve contains 20* Ss. *(after Cieutat, Stockwell, and Noble, 1958)*

Frequency

While psychologists are almost unanimous about the effects of meaningfulness upon verbal learning, some controversy exists about the frequency variable. In a free-recall experiment by Hall (1954) the

Thorndike-Lorge frequency count was found to be an effective variable in recall. Four lists of 20 words each were constructed from words occurring once per million, 10 times per million, 30 times per million, and more than 50 times per million, respectively. After three presentations, more words were recalled from the lists made up of the more frequent words, although the effect was not very large: recall of the least frequent words was about 80% of the recall for the most frequent words. Similar results were obtained by several other experimenters, but a large scale study of the frequency effect failed to yield positive results (Underwood and Schulz, 1960). These authors found that the learning of a list of trigrams was not related to trigram frequency. Instead, they proposed that trigram pronounceability was critical for learning speed. Others (Johnson, 1962; Terwilliger, 1962) have argued against the way in which Underwood and Schulz measured trigram frequency. They did this by breaking down the natural word unit into successive overlapping letter triplets, and counting the frequency with which these triplets were obtained. Thus, the word "triplet" for instance would be counted 5 times: TRI, RIP, IPL, PLE, and LET. Such a procedure places undue stress upon written language. Frequency of use presumably refers to the frequency of the spoken word (but note that even the Thorndike-Lorge count is based upon written text!). Since there is no unambiguous relationship between letter triplets and the phonemes of the English language, the failure to obtain a relationship between frequency defined in this manner and learning is hardly critical. Some recent experiments have supported this position, especially an instructive study by Gibson, Bishop, Schiff, and Smith (1964). They showed that items which were both frequently used and meaningful are easiest to remember, irrespective of pronounceability. Three lists of trigrams were devised which contained the same letters rearranged as anagrams. In the first list meaningful trigrams such as AFL and TWA were used. These were rearranged so as to make them more pronounceable (FAL, TAW) for the second list. A third arrangement was used as a control with both meaningfulness and pronounceability absent (LFA, WTA). Retention, measured by both free recall and recognition, was best for the meaningful items and second best for the pronounceable items. Parenthetically, we might note the results of a perceptual recognition task which the authors also tried out with the same material. When items were flashed on a screen for a very brief period of time by means of a tachistoscope, recognition thresholds were lowest for the pronounceable items, followed by the meaningful items. This reversal illustrates a point which will be elaborated below, namely, that in order to understand the effects of an experimental variable, one must never lose sight of the actual task which the subject is asked to perform.

Imagery

When words are used as stimulus material the ease with which they arouse mental images is highly correlated with the ease of learning (Paivio, 1969). The image-evoking value (I) of a word is determined by methods similar to those used to determine its meaningfulness. Typically subjects are given a mimeographed booklet which contains the test words. The subjects are then asked to rate the words on the ease or speed with which they arouse an image from "very easy— image aroused immediately" to "very difficult—image aroused after long delay or not at all." Note that the I-values determined with this procedure are just as objective as meaningfulness values.

Learning materials vary widely in their image-evoking value from abstract nouns to concrete nouns to pictures and objects. As the concreteness of a learning item increases it becomes easier to learn. Interestingly enough, if the I-values of both the stimulus and response terms are controlled in paired-associate learning, variations in the I-value of the stimulus terms have a much more powerful effect upon learning rate than variations of the I-value of the response terms. Paivio (1969) argues that the stimulus member of a pair serves as a "conceptual peg" to which the response is connected during learning, and from which it can be retrieved on test trials. The more concrete a stimulus item is, i.e., the more likely it is to arouse an image, the better it will serve this function. A concrete stimulus readily elicits the compound image which was formed during learning and from which the response component may be retrieved. Note that the greater effect of imagery on the stimulus side rather than on the response side in paired-associate learning is exactly the opposite of the effects of meaningfulness. It has been shown above that stimulus meaningfulness plays a minor role compared to response meaningfulness.

The image-arousing potential of a word (I) and its meaningfulness (m) are of course highly correlated. However, the suspicion that I is effective only because items which easily arouse an image are also meaningful proves unfounded. On the contrary, Paivio (1969) reports that if one varies I independently of m, its effects upon learning are undiminished; if, on the other hand, m is varied but I is kept constant, the effects of m upon learning are reduced to zero. Thus it seems that concreteness is a more basic variable in learning than the traditional meaningfulness. Further experimental clarification of this issue will certainly be forthcoming in the next few years, but no matter whether effects of meaningfulness independent of imagery will eventually be demonstrated, it seems safe to predict that imagery (I) will stay with us as one of the most important task variables in verbal learning.

Intralist Similarity and Redundancy

Exactly what the subject is doing when he learns a list of words or CVCs appears to be the critical factor for understanding the effects of intralist similarity. A general statement that intralist similarity either helps or hinders verbal learning cannot be made. Different results are obtained for different learning tasks. We shall only review a few of the relevant experiments here, but this will be sufficient to illustrate the dilemma. Intralist similarity may be defined in several ways. When the experimenter uses nonsense syllables as learning material, the number of letters which are common to the syllables is taken as an index of intralist similarity. When words are employed, the criterion is usually similarity in their meaning. Letter-overlap is referred to as formal similarity; similarity in meaning as associative similarity.

Underwood and Richardson (1956a)—in an experiment which used 400 subjects—studied the effects of intralist similarity upon serial learning. CVCs served as learning material, and similarity was manipulated by letter overlap. In addition, syllables of high and low association value were used. More trials were needed to learn the lists with high intralist similarity. This was especially true with low association value syllables. Similar results were obtained in other experiments, including a study in which the high similarity list consisted of synonymous adjectives (Underwood and Goad, 1951). In paired-associate learning, the classic study of this variable was performed by Gibson in 1942. Gibson had subjects learn a 12-item list which consisted of simple figures paired with nonsense syllables. For different lists the difficulty of stimulus discrimination was varied systematically by making the figures which served as stimulus items more similar to each other. Intralist similarity hindered learning, as in the serial learning experiments reported above. A number of later studies were concerned with the locus of the similarity effect in paired-associate learning (e.g., Underwood, 1953). When similarity is increased in both stimulus and response pairs the difficulty of learning also increases. Increasing only stimulus similarity has the same effect, but increases in the similarity of the response members has complex effects upon learning. High similarity may help rather than hinder paired-associate learning in some respects. Note the relevance here of the distinction between response learning and the associative phase of paired-associate learning. At first, the subject simply has to learn what the response alternatives are; later, his task becomes one of hooking up or associating each stimulus item with its corresponding response. Underwood, Runquist, and Schulz (1959) have shown that high similarity among the members of the response set actually facilitates the response learning phase, even if the over-all effect of similarity is negative. Two lists of paired-associates were used with CVCs as stimuli for both lists. The responses were similar adjectives for one list and dissimilar adjectives for the other. Control subjects were given 16 paired-associate trials with both lists. In another experimental condition of interest, separate groups of subjects received from 1 to 13 regular paired-associate trials and were then stopped and asked to recall as many as possible of the adjectives which served as responses. While performance was better for the low-similarity list throughout the 15 trials of the experiment, subjects could recall more of the responses from the high-similarity list, at least for the first few trials of the experiment.

Several experiments have shown that intralist similarity facilitates free-recall learning. In one of these experiments (Miller, 1958) similarity was manipulated not by controlling the amount of letter-overlap in CVCs but by imposing constraints upon the learning material in the form of generating rules. Miller employed the mechanism shown in Fig. 1.2 to generate his similar stimulus lists. This mechanism is a finite state system which generates strings of letters (S, N, X, and G) of length 2 or more. An admissible string of letters is any

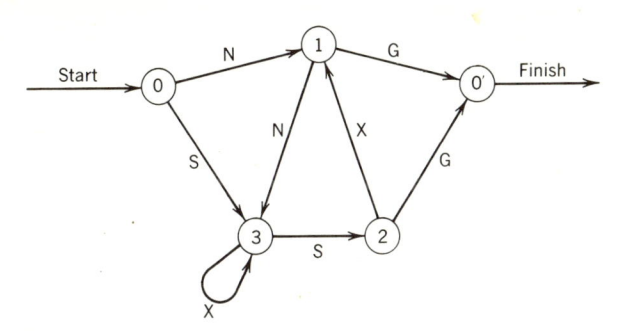

Fig. 1.2 *Diagram of the finite state generator of the redundant strings in Miller's experiment. An admissible string is any sequence of letters generated by starting in State 0 and ending on the first arrival at State 0'. (after Miller, 1958)*

sequence obtained by starting in State 0 and ending upon reaching State 0'. The system has three states, represented by the circles numbered 1, 2, 3. The permissible transitions are shown by arrows. Whenever a transition occurs the system generates as its output the letter shown next to the arrow. The reader can easily check the working of this mechanism by tracing out a possible path in Fig. 1.2, writing down the appropriate letter as each transition is made. One way of listing the total set of well-formed strings generated by this system which clearly shows the similarities that obtain within this set is achieved by using parentheses to denote optional symbols. All well-formed strings are variations of the following four basic strings: NG, NNSG, SSG, and SSXG. Embedded within these basic strings are loops which are optional: N(N(X)SX)G, N(N(X)SX)NSG, S((X)(SXN))SG, and S((X)(SXN))SXG. Of the 22 strings of length 7 or less Miller selected 9 as items for his similar list. A low similarity list was constructed by generating strings at random from the four letters S, X, N, and G, with the constraints that the list should have the same number of strings of each length as did the high similarity list. Because of the way in which the two lists were constructed, Miller speaks of a redundant list and a random list, rather than high and low similarity. Part of the results of Miller's free-recall experiment are shown in Fig. 1.3. It is obvious that the redundant list (high similarity) was much easier to learn than the random list. Subjects who noticed the similarity among the redundant

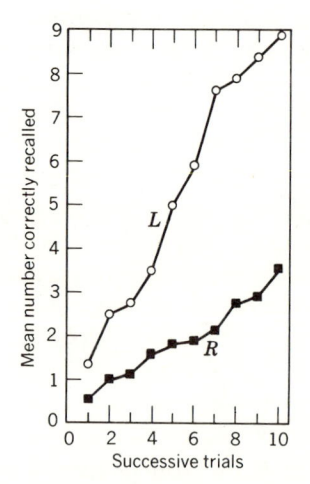

Fig. 1.3 *Mean number correct as a function of the trial number. L indicates a redundant list and R indicates a random list. (after Miller, 1958)*

strings had much less to remember than the subjects who had to memorize the random strings. Once one knows the rules for the generation of redundant strings, the pattern of each item becomes highly predictable; hence each item contains less information than a randomly generated item. Letter sequences in random items are unpredictable, that is, each letter must be memorized separately. This consideration shows that the results of the Miller experiment are not so unreasonable as they might have appeared at first in the light of the results of Underwood and Richardson (1956a) on the effects of intralist similarity in serial learning. Similarity in the Miller experiment is obviously confounded with information content. The higher similarity becomes, the less information is to be remembered.

Garner (1962) has pointed out a very important implication of experiments like the Miller (1958) experiment. What determines the difficulty with which an item will be learned is not so much a function of the characteristics of that individual item but rather of the internal structure inherent in the total set of items to be learned. In free-recall learning the task of the subject is to learn which subset of items out of the total set of all possible items make up the learning list. Garner hypothesized that the ease of free-recall learning is not a question of the characteristics of the individual items but of the structure of the subset which is to be learned and its relationship to the total set of potential stimuli. In a series of experiments by Garner and his coworkers evidence for this position has been obtained. In the first of these studies Whitman and Garner (1962) constructed an item pool of 81 figures by using three levels of values, each of four variables. The variables and their levels were shape (square, triangle, and circle), lines (0, 1, or 2) spaces (right, left or none), and dots (above, below, or none). Three subsets of 9 figures each were selected from the set of potential stimuli so that each level of each variable occurred equally often, but with different correlations between variable pairs. The three sets are shown in Fig. 1.4. Set *A* has no correlation between variable pairs (all variables are orthogonal); for set *B* one pair of variables is perfectly correlated, while the others are orthogonal, (shape and space covary: all squares have a space on the left, all triangles have a space on the right, and circles have no space); the maximum possible constraint is achieved in set *C*, where three variables are correlated and only the dot-variable is orthogonal. Separate groups of subjects learned each list with a typical free-recall procedure, after having been familiarized with the way in which the stimuli in this experiment were constructed. The median number of learning trials to criterion for the three subsets of stimuli were 19 for list *A*, 12 for list *B*, and 2 for list *C*, respectively. Thus, the list with

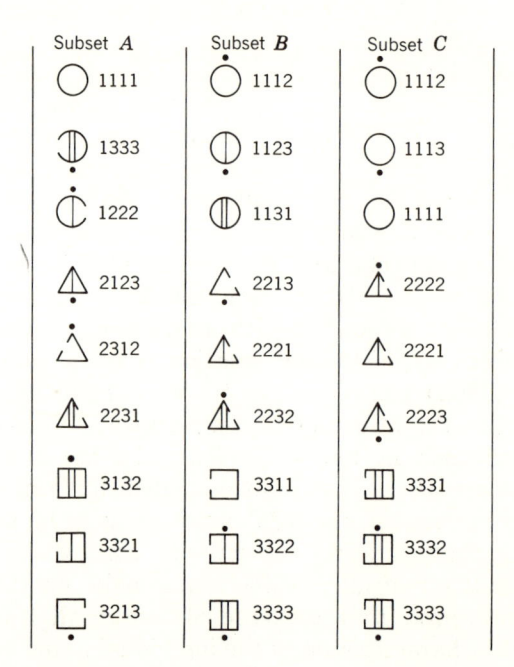

Fig. 1.4 *The three subsets of the stimuli used by Whitman and Garner. The number to the right of each figure provides the coded values for the four variables, in the order: shape, space, line, and dot. The coded values of the figures common to sets* B *and* C *are underlined. (after Whitman and Garner, 1962)*

the greatest intralist similarity was by far the easiest to recall. Note that three of the items in lists *B* and *C* are identical. In spite of this one-third overlap in items, learning rates for the two lists were widely different. In fact, when the proportion of correct responses for the items common to both lists *B* and *C* is plotted as in Fig. 1.5, the learning curves for these items are almost identical with the learning curves for the subsets within which they were contained and appear to be unrelated to each other.

The conclusions of Miller (1958) and Whitman and Garner (1962) were supported by the results of an experiment (Horowitz, 1961) in which a more conventional definition of similarity was employed—the extent to which trigrams in a list share the same letters. Horowitz constructed a low and a high similarity list by using 12 or 4 letters, respectively, to construct his trigrams. In one condition subjects were given standard free-recall instructions. Subjects recalled more from the high similarity list than from the low similarity list, at least on the first learning trials. What makes this study particularly interesting is that Horowitz also included a second experimental condition in which subjects were given an ordering task. On each test trial, subjects were given cards with the test items printed on them and were asked to put them into the correct order. Needless to say,

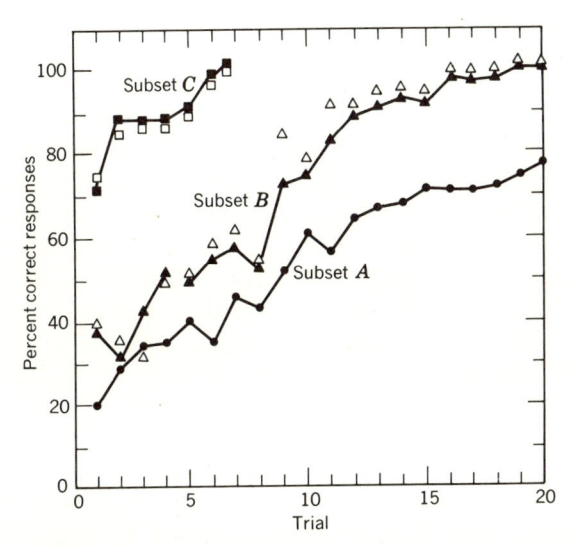

Fig. 1.5 *Percentages of correct responses as a function of number of trials for the various subsets of figures. The open points are data from just those three figures in subsets* B *and* C *which were identical. (after Whitman and Garner, 1962)*

items were presented in the same order on all trials in this condition. Contrary to the results with the free-recall procedure, but in agreement with the serial learning studies reviewed earlier, the high similarity list was more difficult to learn. Obviously the effects of intralist similarity depend upon the task given the subject. A larger parent population may be constructed from 12 letters than from 4 letters and hence the low similarity list is selected from a larger set of potential stimuli. Horowitz's free-recall results are exactly what one would expect if amount of information is a critical variable in learning: there is more information in the low similarity list and hence there is more to learn. Horowitz's ordering task, on the other hand, primarily involves discrimination between items. As Garner (1962) has shown, discrimination performance is optimal if each stimulus dimension provides as many discriminations as possible, and does not duplicate information provided by another variable—which is more nearly the case in the low similarity list than in the high similarity list.

Instead of studying the learning of artificially constrained item lists, the effects of the natural structure of language upon free-recall may be investigated. The speaker of English generates well-formed sentences just as the finite state mechanism of Miller (Fig. 1.2) generates well-formed letter strings. The rules according to which a speaker generates his sentences are the syntactic and semantic rules of the English language, and these are, of course, greatly more complicated than the transition rules in Fig. 1.2. However, one can approximate a natural language by means of finite state generators and one can distinguish between degrees of approximations depending upon the complexity of the generating mechanism (Shannon, 1948). Basically this is achieved by using actual word frequency statistics extending over word sequences of various lengths. A zero-order approximation is obtained by selecting words at random from a dictionary. Thus, one word is as likely to appear as any other, and there are no sequential dependencies among words. For a first order approximation words are again drawn at random, but with probabilities proportional to actual word frequencies in English. Still there are no sequential dependencies among the words which make up a string, but the more frequent words are more likely to be used. For second order approximations, word-pair probabilities of actual English are used. Thus, knowing a single word, one can guess to some extent what kind of word would follow it: for instance, after ARE, one would expect GIRLS, or LEARNED, or COLD, but not IS, or PERAMBULATE. A third order approximation is based upon the actual frequencies of word triplets, and in general, a k-th order of approximation takes into account the distributional statistics of k-tuplets of words. A finite state mechanism generating a k-th order approximation to English has as many states as there are different English word sequences of length $(k-1)$. For each state there exists a probability distribution over the set of all English words which determines the likelihood that a word will follow this particular string of $(k-1)$ words. Every word in the English language has a certain probability of occurrence after a particular string of $(k-1)$ words. For instance, after the string of length two, FAMILY WAS, such words as LARGE or MY have a relatively high probability of occurring as the third word, while DARK, IS, and CAME are unlikely in this position. The following two illustrations are taken from Miller and Selfridge (1950) and show word triplets and word quintuplets with frequencies representative of English:

a. Third order approximation: FAMILY WAS LARGE DARK ANIMAL CAME ROARING DOWN THE MIDDLE OF MY FRIENDS LOVE BOOKS PASSIONATELY EVERY KISS IS FINE.

b. Fifth-order approximation: ROAD IN THE COUNTRY WAS INSANE ESPECIALLY IN DREARY ROOMS WHERE THEY HAVE SOME BOOKS TO BUY FOR STUDYING GREEK.

It is important to understand the purpose of these statistical constructions. They are not presented here as a theory of language; more precisely, it is not maintained that a speaker of English generates sentences in the same way as the devices described above. This issue will be more fully discussed in Chapter 8, but at this point one can state that the rules of language are not finite state devices. Such devices are much too clumsy, even for relatively short strings; the number of different sequences that must be considered is extremely large; and, for each of these sequences, one would have to know the probability with which every word of the English language follows it. However, statistical approximations provide a very useful way of generating learning materials for psychological experiments in which some of the short-range relationships of the natural language are preserved, without encountering the full complexity of natural language material.

In practice, a technique taken from an old children's game may be employed to obtain a *k*-th order approximation quite readily. Speakers of the language know, by definition, what a well-formed word sequence is like. Suppose a speaker is presented with THE MIDDLE, is asked to guess the next word of the sentence, and responds with OF. Now the first word of the string may be deleted and the remainder is presented to another subject with the same instruction. This subject's response to MIDDLE OF may be MY. This procedure can be repeated any number of times, thus generating a third order approximation like the one presented above.

Miller and Selfridge (1950) obtained passages of 10, 20, 30, or 50 words for each order of approximation from 0 to 7, as well as English text. These lists were read to their subjects one at a time. Subjects were instructed to write down as many words as they could remember, preferably in the correct order, although order was not used as a criterion for scoring. The results are shown in Fig. 1.6. As in the experiments on artificial constraint, free recall was better with the more highly constrained lists. The absence of an improvement after about the 4th order approximation led the authors to conclude that the short-range, familiar relationships between words facilitate learning and that meaningfulness per se is less critical. Later investigators have shown this conclusion to be erroneous (Marks and Jack, 1952; Coleman, 1963). When order is used as a criterion in scoring and when prose and approximations are matched in syllabic length and word frequency, recall continues to be improved as the order of approximation increases, and text is recalled significantly better than the highest order of approximation studied. In fact, the greatest improvement in recall seems to occur between the highest order of approximation and text. This finding is, of course, in agreement with the statement made earlier that finite state devices (and the approximations generated by them) are insufficient as models of natural language. There is obviously something about natural language which facilitates recall above and beyond mere statistical redundancy.

A number of conclusions may be drawn from this review of experiments concerned with the effects of intralist similarity and redundancy. First, the importance of the total set of learning items must be stressed. Verbal learning is not a question of the acquisition

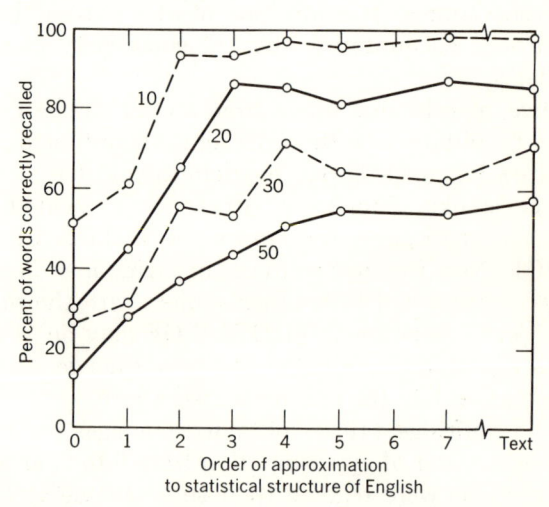

Fig. 1.6 *Percentage of words correctly recalled as a function of order of approximation to the statistical structure of English for lists of 10, 20, 30, and 50 words. (after Miller and Selfridge, 1950)*

of single items, but of sets of items. Whether an item is easy or hard to learn depends mostly upon the structure of the list (or sentence) in which it is embedded. This effect was most noticeable in free-recall experiments: the better structured the learning material is, the easier it is to recall it. However, the interrelationships of the items of a list are equally important in paired-associate learning: if the response set is coherent and highly available, response learning is facilitated; however, if the stimulus items are very similar to each other, stimulus discrimination is more difficult.

Secondly, a confounding of the two experimental variables, similarity and redundancy, is apparent. The two are obviously related, but it would be interesting to see whether similarity, defined either as letter overlap or semantic similarity, can be manipulated separately from the sequential constraints within a list. It is possible that the facilitatory effect of intralist similarity upon recall is entirely due to the confounding of similarity and redundancy which is present in all of the experiments described above. To appreciate the nature of this confounding, note that if only highly similar items are used to make up a list, there are in general fewer items to choose from than when all kinds of items are selected as list members. Hence, high-similarity lists are more redundant in a statistical sense.

Finally, it appears that an understanding of the effects of variables such as the ones discussed in this section can only come after a better understanding of the learning process itself has been achieved. The effects of task variables such as similarity and redundancy obviously depend upon the learning task. There is no such thing as verbal learning, only paired-associate learning, free-recall, or other such procedures. A much more detailed analysis of what the subject actually does while he learns a list of items is indicated.

3. TRANSFER AND RETENTION

In the previous section experimental variables which affect the learning of a single list were discussed, such as the nature of the learning material and the similarity of the items within a list. In the present section some studies will be described which show how the learning of one list affects the learning of another list, as well as the experimental variables which enter into this relationship. If a person is interested in the effects of learning one list upon the learning of a second list, the problem is one of *transfer of training:* if learning one list helps learning a second list, transfer is *positive;* if learning one list interferes with learning another, transfer is *negative.* Alternatively, one may inquire how learning a second list affects the *retention* of the first list. Two kinds of transfer must be distinguished: *specific transfer* is obtained if it can be shown that some particular aspect of one list causes the effects upon the second list (for instance, high similarity between lists); *nonspecific transfer* is the result of more general factors, such as warm-up effects, fatigue, or learning-to-learn.

Two experimental designs are used to study how the learning of one list influences what happens with another list. Müller and Pilzecker (1900) studied the *retroactive* interference effects of learning a second list upon retention of a first list by comparing an experimental group which learns two lists, A and B, in succession and is then tested for recall of list A with a control group which only learns list A and rests while the experimental subjects learn the second list. In the study of *proactive* effects the first list serves as the transfer-producing list, and learning (or retention) of the second list becomes the dependent variable of interest. The two designs may be outlined as follows:

Retroaction Paradigm:

Experimental Group:	Learn List A	Learn List B	Recall List A
Control Group:	Learn List A	Rest	Recall List A

Proaction Paradigm:

Experimental Group:	Learn List A	Learn List B	Recall List B
Control Group:	Rest	Learn List B	Recall List B

Specific Transfer

Note that in these experimental paradigms specific and nonspecific transfer effects are confounded. If learning two lists A and B is compared with learning only one list, sources of nonspecific transfer and the specific transfer from A to B are confounded. If one is interested in how the relationship between A and B affects learning, a more appropriate control group would be one where subjects learn two lists, first an unrelated list X and then B. In this case, the nonspecific transfer over tasks is controlled, and any differences between learning A-B and X-B may be attributed to the specific effects of A on B.

It is customary to express transfer effects by a percentage score. Suppose E is the total number of correct responses in the experimental group, and C is the total number correct in the control group. Then a measure of transfer is obtained by calculating

$$100 \times \frac{(E-C)}{C}$$

The sign of this measure indicates whether transfer is positive or negative. Percentage scores are usually calculated, rather than the simple difference score $(E-C)$, to facilitate comparison of transfer effects between different experiments, in which the over-all scores, and hence their difference, may vary over a wide range.

The experimental paradigm which is best suited to the study of transfer effects is paired-associate learning. In paired-associate learning an explicit distinction is made between stimuli and responses, and hence the nature of transfer effects may be explored more fully by studying various relationships between the stimulus and response terms of the two lists. In Table 1.6 the most basic transfer designs are shown, employing the customary notation. A capital letter refers

Table 1.6. *Basic transfer designs*

	List 1	List 2	Description
I	*A-B*	*C-D*	Basic control list
II	*A-B*	*A-C*	Different responses to the same stimuli
III	*A-B*	*C-B*	Same responses with new stimuli
IV	*A-B*	*A-B$_r$*	Stimuli and responses are re-paired

to either a stimulus or a response set, depending upon its position: $A = (a_1, a_2, \ldots, a_k)$, where a_i is the ith item in list A. Different sets of items are denoted by different letters. Thus in Transfer Paradigm I, a different set of items is used for the stimulus and response terms of the two lists. In the second paradigm, new response terms are used in the second list, but the stimuli of the first list are repeated. In the third paradigm response terms are retained but combined with new stimuli, and in the last paradigm both the stimulus and response terms of the first list are retained in the second list, but they are re-paired. These basic transfer paradigms can be varied in many ways by manipulating the relationship among the various terms. For example, suppose the second list in Paradigm II does not repeat exactly the same stimulus terms, but uses related, though not identical terms: for instance, if A is a set of nonsense syllables, a related set A' may be obtained, by changing the vowel of each syllable, leaving the consonants intact; if A is a set of nouns, a related set A' may be constructed by replacing each term in A by its synonym, and so forth. Different degrees of similarity between lists may be investigated in this way.

It is clear that the maximum amount of positive transfer is produced if both the stimulus and response terms of the two lists are identical; in this case subjects receive simply two learning trials with the same list. The conditions which produce maximal negative transfer, or inhibition, are not intuitively obvious. Early experiments were ambiguous. In some experiments moderate degrees of similarity resulted in maximum inhibition. In others retroactive inhibition increased proportionately to increases in similarity. In a very influential paper, summarizing the evidence available at that time, Osgood (1949) argued that interference effects depended upon the locus of the similarity between two paired-associate lists. According to Osgood's analysis, opposite effects will be observed, depending upon the relation between the response terms of two lists when the similarity between the stimulus terms of two paired-associate lists is increased from neutral to identical. If the responses are identical, increasing stimulus similarity will result in increasing facilitation, but if the response terms are unrelated or antagonistic, inhibition will be produced. The relationship between similarity and retroaction which Osgood hypothesizes is shown in Fig. 1.7, the transfer and retroaction surface.

In Fig. 1.7 stimulus similarity is represented by the width of the figure; it ranges from functional identity to neutrality. Response similarity ranges through identity, similarity, neutrality, opposition, and antagonism, as represented by the length of the figure. Identity is the point of maximum similarity in both dimensions, i.e., the upper left hand corner. The direction and degree of transfer and retroaction

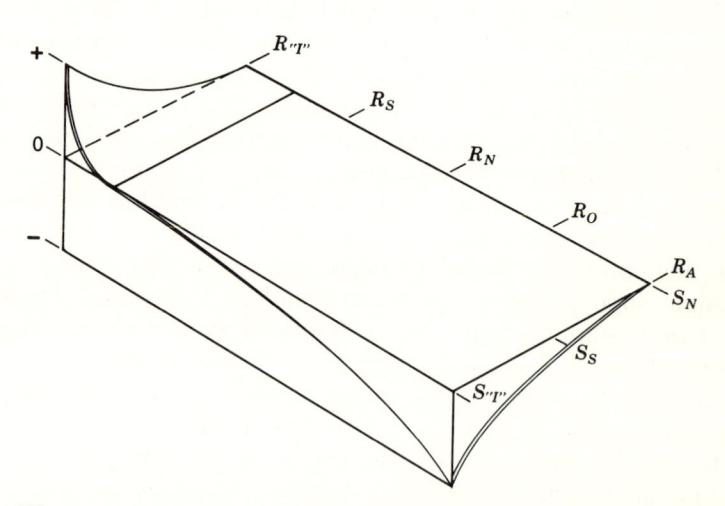

Fig. 1.7 *The transfer and retroaction surface: medial plane represents effects of zero magnitude; response relations distributed along length of solid, and stimulus relations along its width. (after Osgood, 1949)*

effects are shown by the vertical dimension. The median plane represents a zero effect; whenever the surface rises above, facilitative effects are expected; whenever it falls below, interference relations exist. For unrelated stimuli Osgood's transfer surface always implies zero effects; maximum interference is found when the same stimulus is paired with an antagonistic response; maximum facilitation occurs if the same stimulus response pair is repeated. Between these points Osgood drew a smooth, unbroken surface that represents the transfer effects for other stimulus and response relationships.

Osgood himself tested several points on the transfer and retroaction surface. He used two-consonant combinations as stimuli and adjectives as responses. Stimuli were identical for both the original list and the intervening list, but the response terms were varied in meaning. In the intervening lists, responses were either identical, similar, neutral, or opposite adjectives. Recall of the original list was best when the intervening list was identical, next best when similar responses were used; and worst for the neutral and opposite response conditions. No significant differences between the latter two groups were obtained, however.

A study by Bugelski and Cadwallader (1956) was designed as a more extensive test of Osgood's retroaction surface. Both the response and the stimulus similarity of the intervening list were varied in a 4×4 factorial design. Osgood's adjectives were used as response terms, and the nonsense figures of Gibson (1942) served as stimuli. Stimulus similarity was varied in four steps: identical, similar, less similar, and neutral. For identical stimulus terms manipulation of response similarity produced effects upon recall of the original list which are exactly opposite to Osgood's results: an intervening list with responses opposite in meaning to the first list responses produced less interference than either similar or neutral responses, which did not differ from each other. On the other hand, the effects of stimulus variability were in agreement with Osgood's hypothesis: as the stimuli became less similar to the original list, all effects decreased in magnitude. No significant differences among groups were obtained when the intervening stimuli were not at all related to the original list.

Both Osgood's and Bugelski and Cadwallader's studies used a retroaction design. A systematic investigation of the transfer surface using a proactive interference design was reported by Dallett (1962). With material similar to the two studies above, Dallett investigated the recall of a common paired-associate list as a function of different first list learning. The most striking result of Dallett's study is his failure to obtain interference effects at all: The only statistically significant effect obtained was a facilitation of second list recall when the first list had identical responses and similar stimuli.

Wimer (1964) made another attempt to explore similarity effects in a proactive inhibition design. Two hundred and fifty subjects were assigned to 25 groups according to a 5 × 5 factorial design. Adjectives served both as stimuli and responses, and were categorized into 5 degrees of similarity: identical, similar, unrelated, opposed, and antonymous. For instance, for the adjective "tense" the 5 similarity classes were tense, hard, basic, soft, and relaxed. Each group of subjects learned a different first list, and then a common second list. The dependent variable in this experiment was trials to learn the second list. After an adjustment for performance differences in first list learning, only one group showed a statistically significant effect: positive transfer was obtained when both stimuli and responses were identical with the first list. In particular, there was no evidence for inhibitory effects of meaningfully dissimilar material at all. If anything, antonyms tended to facilitate learning.

It is obvious that Osgood's transfer surface does not describe the data correctly. At this point it is worthwhile to consider how the transfer surface was derived in the first place. It was not based upon extensive theoretical notions; instead, it was a low-level empirical generalization, a simple and meaningful description of the data on transfer available to Osgood in 1949. Only two factors, the similarity between the stimulus and response terms of the two lists seemed necessary in order to account for the results of transfer experiments. The failure of subsequent research to conform to Osgood's generalization could be due to several factors. For one, other experimental variables may be important in transfer which Osgood did not account for. Secondly, it may be that Osgood's measurement of similarity was inappropriate. There is reason to believe that both these factors need to be considered. Several comments have already been made about similarity. The basic problem appears to be that the relevant similarity dimension does not go from same to neutral to opposite, but that opposite falls somewhere between the same and neutral points of the scale. Instead of similarity, the axes of the transfer surface could be relabeled as "relatedness" and thus would range from "same" to "unrelated". By definition, opposition implies some degree of relatedness. Thus, if one would place the data points from opposition relationships somewhere near "similar" on the transfer surface, some of the results of Bugelski and Cadwallader (1956) and Wimer (1964) could be accommodated within Osgood's framework.

Among the experimental variables which have been shown to be important in transfer studies, in addition to those considered by Osgood, are degree of learning, response meaningfulness, stimulus meaningfulness, and stability of the experimental environment.

Degree of learning of both the first and the second list significantly influences transfer of training. McGeoch (1929) studied the effects of this variable with a retroactive inhibition design. He varied degree of first list learning in 5 steps: subjects learned a 9-syllable list of either 6, 11, 16, 21, or 26 trials. All subjects were then given an interference list for 11 trials, and finally relearned the original list. Retroactive inhibition was found to decrease with greater amounts of first list learning. In a complementary study Melton and Irwin (1940) kept first list learning the same for all subjects but varied the amount of learning of the intervening list from 5 to 40 trials. They found that retroactive inhibition increased when more second list trials were given, at least up to a point. When the intervening list was learned very well (40 trials), retroactive inhibition of the first list actually decreased again.

Degree of learning affects proactive inhibition in a similar way, as an extensive study of Postman and Riley (1959) has shown. Postman and Riley's subjects learned serial CVC lists for either 5, 10, 20, or 40 trials of original learning. Then a second list was learned, again for either 5, 10, 20, or 40 trials. After a 20-minute rest, subjects relearned the second list. The more trials subjects were given on the original list, the more proactive inhibition was produced, at least up to a point. This result agrees with the retroactive inhibition studies just mentioned: as interfering responses increase in strength, retention decreases. When second list learning was varied, a more complex relationship was found: with very low and very high degrees of second list learning, proactive inhibition was found, but not with 10 or 20 learning trials. The significance of this result is unclear. If it should prove to be genuine, it might mean that at very high degrees of learning, factors other than interference among associations become important. Note, for instance, the reduction in interference which occurs when the interfering list is very well learned: if strength of association alone were the determining factor, this result would be quite inexplicable. Possibly high levels of learning result in a structure of the learning material which prevents it from interfering with other associations, as Mandler (1962) has argued.

Response meaningfulness, measured in any of the variety of ways that were discussed earlier, is another factor which must be considered in transfer studies. In general, increasing amounts of meaningfulness of the responses of the first list impede second list performance. An illustrative experiment is one by Merikle and Battig (1963). Merikle and Battig studied transfer in an *A-B, A-D* paradigm for three conditions of meaningfulness of the first list responses (*B*). Consonant trigrams were used as low-meaningful material, nonsense syllables as medium-meaningful material, and words as high-meaningful material. While strong negative transfer was obtained with the high-meaningful material, none was observed with low-meaningful material, with the nonsense syllables providing intermediate results.

Stimulus meaningfulness also has important effects on transfer of training. Negative transfer is increased when highly meaningful stimuli are used, but little or no transfer occurs when low-meaningful stimuli are used. A relevant experiment was reported by Martin (1968). Martin used 6-item, paired-associate lists, with either high-meaningful nonsense syllables or low-meaningful syllables as stimuli and the digits 1-6 as responses. Transfer was studied in an *A-B, A-B_r* paradigm relative to an *A-B, C-B* control group. Learning to re-pair the old stimuli and the old responses was very difficult for the group which had the high-meaningful syllables as stimuli, but not for the group which had the low-meaningful stimuli.

When the similarity of learning conditions in general was varied experimentally, stable results were obtained, in agreement with the proposition that anything that helps to differentiate the general conditions of learning of the original list and of the interfering list reduces interference. Postman and Postman (1948) report a study in which four groups of subjects learned two paired-associate lists by the method of anticipation and were tested for recall of the first list after a 15-minute rest interval. Lists were made up either of compatible word pairs (doctor-heal) or incompatible word pairs (war-peaceful). For Group I both lists consisted of compatible word pairs, and for Group II only incompatible pairs were used. For Groups III and IV the original list and the interference list were not both of the same kind. The results showed better retention for the latter two groups. Bilodeau and Schlosberg (1951) demonstrated a similar effect. They had three groups of subjects learn a paired-associate list in a messy storeroom. Then one group learned a second list in the same storeroom, a second group was taken to a cardroom which was quite different in appearance for second list learning, and a control group did long division in the storeroom. This last group retained the first list best, but of more interest here is the fact that the subjects who learned the second list in a different environment showed less interference effects than the subjects who learned both lists in the same environment.

A very large number of other studies could be described in this context. However, a continued accumulation of experimental results would only be confusing to the reader. Enough has been said to identify the principal experimental variables of interest. In order to understand how learning one list affects the learning of another list the following variables have been shown to be important: the similarity between the stimulus terms of the two lists; the similarity between the response terms of the lists; the meaningfulness of both the stimuli and the responses of the first list; and the degree of learning of the lists. All of these factors interact with each other, so that empirical relationships become quite complex. However, there is no need to abandon the effort to account for these complexities in some reasonably simple way. For instance, Martin (1965, 1968) has shown how some of the newer findings can be combined with the classical results of Osgood in quite a satisfactory manner. However, Martin's approach was theoretical rather than inductive, and will be discussed later. In fact, we shall return repeatedly in later chapters to aspects and portions of the rich mass of empirical results which have been described above. All theories of learning have something to say about transfer processes, and in discussing a particular theoretical problem it is often necessary to reconsider some of the empirical results which were mentioned here, thus permitting us to explore their meaning in a wider context.

Nonspecific transfer

Suppose a subject learns two unrelated lists in a verbal learning experiment. Frequently, he will find the second list easier to learn than the first, though this is not necessarily the case. If the lists are very long and very boring, he may be fatigued or lose his motivation to learn, and therefore perform more poorly on the second list. However, in general, subjects tend to get better as they gain more experience with learning lists in the laboratory. Two sources of nonspecific transfer have been identified: first there is a simple *warm-up* effect and secondly subjects learn how to learn. *Learning-to-learn* is an extremely important phenomenon. If subjects are given many lists to learn there may be continued improvement due to learning-to-learn, which poses some methodological problems in transfer experiments. As has been noted above, control groups in transfer experiments must be given experience with learning as many lists as experimental groups, otherwise there will be serious discrepancies between control and experimental subjects in their general learning facility.

Learning-to-learn has been studied in many experiments. An illustrative study is one by Postman and Schwartz (1964). These authors showed that the learning-to-learn effect is quite specific, and is maximized if the learning experience is with the same task and the same material as the criterion task. They trained subjects either with trigrams or adjectives, and with either a serial or a paired-associate task. Adjectives were used for the criterion task, which was paired-associate learning for half of the subjects and serial learning for the other half. Relative to a control group which learned only one adjective list, all experimental groups showed improvement. The biggest improvement occurred when the pretraining task and the criterion task were the same. Similarly, subjects pretrained on adjectives did better than subjects pretrained on trigrams on the criterion task, which, as will be remembered, involved adjectives. From this study, and others not reported here, one may conclude that subjects learn techniques of learning which at least in part are quite specific to the task and the learning material at hand.

SUMMARY

The most common experimental procedures, the standard learning materials, and the principal experimental variables in verbal learning experiments have been described in this chapter. The discussion was broad, with relatively little attention to detail. More explicit analyses will be presented later when attempts will be made to integrate this material into a wider framework.

Paired-associate learning, serial learning, free recall, recognition, and verbal discrimination have been briefly described. The importance of using carefully scaled learning materials was pointed out. Letter trigrams can be scaled in terms of meaningfulness, association value, and pronounceability. Words must be categorized according to their frequency of occurrence in the natural language, as well as syllabic length and grammatical class.

The discussion of experimental variables in verbal learning was divided into two sections. First, the learning of a single list was considered; secondly, interaction effects were discussed which occur when more than one list is learned. The meaningfulness of nonsense syllables and the frequency and image-evoking potential of words were shown to be important determinants of learning rate in verbal learning experiments. Of even greater importance is the relationship which exists between the various items of a list. Interitem similarity has different effects upon paired-associate learning depending upon its locus in a list: Similarity of the stimuli increases the difficulty of stimulus discrimination, but similarity of the response terms facilitates response learning. In general, it has been shown that similarity among items impedes learning if the task is one of discrimination between the items, but helps if the items have to be recalled. The latter effect is apparently caused by the fact that similarity is usually confounded with statisical predictability, or redundancy. The more redundant, i.e., the better structured, a set of items is, the easier it is to recall. This was demonstrated in several experiments, using geometric figures which varied along partly correlated dimensions, constrained letter sequences, or statistical approximations to English text as learning material.

It is of course trivially true that a subject never learns just one list, but that his learning experience is embedded in a continuous stream of such experiences. Interaction effects between different learning experiences constitute one of the main problems, perhaps the main problem, of the psychology of learning. In the laboratory experiments discussed here, the problem has been reduced to its simplest form: how does learning one list affect learning another list? Two aspects of this problem were discussed: the retention of the first list after a second list is learned; and the transfer of training from learning a first list to learning a second list. The experimental data in this area are quite complex, because there are a rather large number of relevant experimental variables that interact in a complex way. In paired-associate learning, the following variables are known to be important in transfer: the similarity of the stimulus terms of the two lists; the similarity of the response terms of the two lists; the meaningfulness of the first-list stimuli; the meaningfulness of the first-list response; and the degree of list learning.

Many of the topics described in this chapter will be taken up again in the context of more specific discussions of particular problems. The function of this chapter is to present an overview of what verbal learning is about and how experimenters go about their task. In order to tell what it all means, we must turn to somewhat different considerations. One must ask what the process of verbal learning is like, or rather what the various processes are like. If more is known about this question, it will be easier to bring some system and order into the mass of empirical results concerning task variables in verbal learning.

THEORIES AND THEORETICAL ISSUES IN VERBAL LEARNING

22222222222222

In this chapter three different, but not necessarily contradictory attempts to understand some of the phenomena of verbal learning will be discussed. The first is interference theory, which until recently has dominated research in verbal learning. This theory relates directly to the work described in the previous chapter. In fact, its ability to order and interpret this research, even if only in part, stands as the greatest achievement of that theory. The other two developments which will be taken up are not really theories of verbal learning, but rather methods and techniques which may be used for theoretical work. The utility of these methods will be illustrated by applying each to a particular theoretical issue. Mathematical models will be explored in connection with the question whether learning should be represented as a transition between discrete learning states (in the extreme, there would be just two states, so that learning would be all-or-none), or whether learning consists in the gradual, incremental formation of habit strength, or associative strength. It is not intended to decide this issue with a yes-or-no answer, but to show how detailed formal work can further the understanding of learning processes. The other recent development with respect to theory construction in psychology is computer simulation. It will be shown how a traditional verbal learning theory—Gibson's stimulus discrimination theory—can be restated and explored in new ways through computer simulation, opening some unexpected possibilities. Of course, the discussion of mathematical models and computer simulation given here is by no means exhaustive: The examples merely illustrate the power and elegance of these techniques. Further use will be made of these techniques in several other chapters of this book.

Before proceeding with these topics, another problem must be discussed, however. This is the relationship of the extensive research on animal learning to the understanding of human learning processes. Historically, much of the theoretical work on learning has been based on animal research. An explicit consideration of the relevance of this work to the important issues in human learning is therefore the first order of business in this chapter.

1. CONDITIONING AND THE ROLE OF REINFORCEMENT IN HUMAN LEARNING

Historically, the psychology of learning has had two immediate roots. One is Ebbinghaus' book *On Memory* in 1885. Ebbinghaus is truly the "father of verbal learning." His methods as well as his basic concepts still dominate the field. He introduced the nonsense syllable, the favorite stimulus material in verbal learning research for generations; he initiated the continuing concern with serial learning; and, finally, he gave verbal learning its theoretical base in associationism. There is no need to describe Ebbinghaus' contributions in more detail, because throughout this book we shall be dealing with work which grew out of this tradition, or we shall be struggling to relate developments from other sources to that tradition.

The second source from which most of the research on learning derives is Pavlov's work on conditioning (Pavlov, 1927; 1928). Like Ebbinghaus, Pavlov provided a whole subarea of psychology with its basic experimental methods and theoretical constructs. Much of animal learning can be regarded as a continuation and extension of Pavlov's work. The experimental paradigm which Pavlov introduced is today called *classical conditioning:* a stimulus which naturally elicits a certain response (as food elicits salivation) is paired with a neutral stimulus (e.g., a tone) which, through repeated pairings, comes to elicit the same response as the original stimulus, or a response very similar to it. The first stimulus-response pair is called the *unconditioned stimulus* (UCS) and the *unconditioned response* (UCR); the originally neutral stimulus is called the conditioned stimulus (CS); the CS evokes the *conditioned response*, or CR. A CS-UCS pairing constitutes a *reinforcement.* If reinforcement is withheld, i.e., if the CS is presented alone repeatedly, the CS loses its power to evoke the CR. This process is called *extinction.* If a stimulus which is similar to the CS, but not identical, is presented instead of the CS, the CR may still be evoked, but to a lesser degree and with a lesser probability; this is an instance of *generalization.* If two stimuli are presented to the organism one of which is always followed by the UCS and one of which is never followed by the UCS, the CR will occur when the reinforced stimulus is presented, but not when the non-reinforced stimulus is presented; the organism is said to have acquired a *discrimination* as a result of such training. Conditioning, extinction, generalization, and discrimination were all first studied by Pavlov.

A second kind of conditioning must be distinguished from Pavlovian or classical conditioning. In this case there is no unconditioned stimulus present which can be used by the experimenter to elicit the to be learned response. Instead, the experimenter must wait for a spontaneous occurrence of that response, or some rudimentary version of it. Once the desired response has been omitted, the experimenter can reinforce it by presenting a reinforcing stimulus. The reinforcement increases the likelihood that the response will be repeated. The prototype for this kind of conditioning is given by a hungry rat learning to press a bar which delivers a food pellet as reinforcement. The main difference between classical conditioning and this kind of *instrumental* conditioning is operational: in the former case the experimenter can evoke the response which is to be conditioned through presentation of the UCS, while in instrumental conditioning this degree of control is not available. Otherwise, conditioning, extinction, generalization, and discrimination apply identically to both types of learning. Whether classical and instrumental conditioning really represent two different types of learning is another question. The strongest evidence in favor of distinguishing two different types of learning is that some responses (e.g., visceral responses) can be conditioned classically, but not instrumentally. Recent work, however, has shown that many responses previously thought to be subject only to classical conditioning can be instrumentally conditioned (Miller, 1967).

Whatever their position regarding the two types of learning, learning theorists in the past have been largely concerned with problems of animal conditioning (Tolman, 1932; Guthrie, 1935; Skinner, 1938; Hull, 1943). Therefore, some defensive comments are in order in a book which is almost exclusively concerned with human learning. How can one talk about learning and neglect a large part of the research which has been done under that label in the last 50 years? The answer to that question is simply that the area of learning is so large that some selection is necessary, and, what is more germane, most studies of animal conditioning are concerned with problems which are not directly relevant to the study of human learning. Animal conditioning experiments are often addressed to motivational problems, rather than to learning per se. Of course, motivation is in itself a highly interesting and rewarding area of study and it can not always be cleanly separated from learning proper. Nevertheless, the results of most animal experiments seem to have little relevance for the understanding of human learning. The common terminology which has been used in both areas of investigation has sometimes obscured this fact and deceived learning theorists with misleading parallels between verbal learning and conditioning.

Central to the research on animal learning has been the concept of *reinforcement*. Different investigators agree quite well what a reinforcement is at the empirical level, but formal definitions and explanations depend upon the theoretical position of the experimenter. The "law of effect," as it was first formulated by Thorndike in 1931, maintains that a response is strengthened if it is followed by satisfying consequences and weakened if it is followed by dissatisfying consequences. The law of effect has since undergone numerous revisions. For Hull drive reduction was central to the problem of reinforcement (Hull, 1943); recently, Premack (1965) has argued that the more frequent responses reinforce less frequent ones. We need not be concerned with the theoretical controversies which surround the law of effect. Common to all nations of reinforcement is the idea that reinforcement has a direct and automatic strengthening effect upon a response. Most studies of animal learning are concerned with behavior changes which occur as a consequence of reinforcement. However, reinforcement seems to be primarily a matter of motivation, rather than learning, and for that reason studies concerned with reinforcement are not directly relevant to the psychology of human learning.

To make completely clear what is at issue here, we shall compare in detail the experimental procedures of verbal learning and animal conditioning. Their similarity is best illustrated by comparing the classical conditioning paradigm with paired-associate learning. In paired-associate learning an item (say, a word) is connected with an arbitrary response (say, a digit). The stimulus is presented first and the subject is given an opportunity to anticipate the response item. This is followed by a joint presentation of the stimulus-response pair, which serves as a reinforcement for the subject's response. The parallel between paired-associate learning and classical conditioning is obvious: in both cases a previously neutral stimulus comes to evoke a new response as a consequence of repeated CS-UCS pairings. However, this parallelism is based upon superficial features of the two experimental paradigms and is quite misleading. A reinforcement in paired-associate learning, as defined above, does not directly strengthen the stimulus response connection according to the law of effect. Rather, it serves as an occasion for the subject to acquire information about the association which is to be learned, and thereby determines the subject's future behavior. This viewpoint is, of course, entirely in disagreement with Thorndike (1931), as well as with many explicit and implicit beliefs long held by researchers in verbal learning. However, the evidence supporting it is quite convincing. Estes (1967) has discussed this problem recently, and we shall briefly outline his main conclusions here.

First, consider the evidence upon which Thorndike himself based his law of effect. Thorndike (1931) was quite aware of the alternative interpretation of reinforcement in terms of providing information about the environment. He called it the "representational" or "ideational" theory, but he rejected it for a number of reasons. Of those reasons, Estes finds only one convincing, namely, the greater effectiveness of saying "right" after a response than saying "wrong." The problem is this. It has been found by Thorndike and later investigators that if a response in a paired-associate experiment is called "right" the probability of repetition is increased; if a response is called "wrong" the probability of a repetition is correspondingly decreased, but not as much. Thorndike believed that his observation contradicts the representational theory of reinforcement: "right" and "wrong" both supply the same amount of information and should have effects of the same magnitude. However, Buchwald (1967) has pointed out that this conclusion is based upon a superficial analysis of the experimental situation. In the experiment the subject must remember two things: the stimulus-response relationship and the relation between that and the reinforcement. If the reinforcement is "right" both of these will tend to increase the probability of a repetition of the response. However, if the experimenter says "wrong," the two effects will oppose and partially cancel each other. If the subject remembers the stimulus-response association but forgets that the experimenter called it "wrong" he will tend to repeat the old response, and only if he recalls both the response and the reinforcement will the probability of a repetition be depressed. Thus, a reduced effect of "wrong" is precisely what an informational interpretation of reinforcement would lead one to expect. Hence one can not use this finding to differentiate between the law of effect and the representational theory. Thorndike's reasons for rejecting the informational interpretation of reinforcement were therefore insufficient.

In order to show that the law of effects is actually wrong and that reinforcement in human learning does not consist in an automatic strengthening effect of rewards (or a complementary effect of punishments) we shall consider the effects of amount of reinforcement and delay of reinforcement in human learning. Numerous studies have shown that magnitude of reward is positively related to learning rate in animal experiments and that as the delay of reward increases (beyond a certain point) learning is inhibited. These are some of the best established findings in animal learning (e.g., Kimble, 1961). If it can be shown that these variables have different effects in human learning, and particularly in verbal learning, the interpretation of verbal learning as a type of classical or instrumental conditioning will be in serious doubt.

In an experiment by Keller, Cole, Burke, and Estes (1965) subjects were given a list of 25 paired-associate items to learn. The 25 stimuli were paired with two responses which were rewarded differentially. On each trial of the experiment a stimulus item was presented and the subject selected his response. The experimenter rewarded the subject's response with a number of points which depended upon the item and the subject's response. The points were later used to determine the amount of money which the subject received for his participation in the experiment. The two responses were differentially reinforced for each item; for instance, one response might be worth 8 points and the other only 1 point for a particular item; another item might be assigned 2 versus 4 points, etc.

In one condition subjects were told only the number of points which they received for their response. In this condition the rate of learning depended directly upon the difference in the point values which were associated with each item. For instance, if 8 points were given for one response and only 1 point for the other, an item was learned much faster than when the correct response was reinforced with 4 points and 2 points were given for the incorrect response. This finding appeared to be a direct confirmation of the law of effect: the bigger the reward differential for the two responses, the faster the differential development of response strength. However, Keller *et al.* also ran a second group of subjects with a slight modification in procedure: instead of only telling the subject how many points his response was worth on each trial, they gave the subject complete information, both about the value of the response actually made and about the value of the alternative response. Under these conditions, there was no effect of rewards. Small reward differences were learned as fast as large differences when the subjects were given complete information on every trial. This finding, of course, raises the question about the earlier observation that learning rate was a direct function of reward magnitude when subjects were not given complete information on each trial. Can one consider this as evidence for a direct action of rewards upon learning? Keller *et al.* argued that this was by no means so, and attributed their finding to the subject's choice of strategies in those cases where they had learned an item only partially. Suppose a subject has learned that response A is worth x points for item i. If x is large the subject will then tend to choose response A, but if x is small he will choose the alternative response. Clearly, such a strategy will work best with items for which the two response alternatives receive rewards which differ greatly in magnitude. Thus, the results of Keller *et al.* are entirely in agreement with the idea that response-reward associations are something that must be learned just as other associations. Their finding that the reward magnitude had no effect if subjects were given complete information is hard to reconcile with the idea that the greater rewards have a greater strengthening effect. Apparently rewards have only indirect effects, in the sense that subjects select the response with the highest reward, if they know which one that is. Information seems to be the basic variable. This is also implied by another result of Keller *et al.*: their subjects who were given complete information on each trial learned twice as fast as the partially informed subjects. Of course, this experiment alone is hardly conclusive. Yet, it shows what kind of argument can be made. Other experimental results, which further support the representational theory of reinforcement as far as human learning experiments are concerned have been reported by Estes (1967).

Just like magnitude of reward, delay of reward also has quite different effects in human learning and animal conditioning. As has already been mentioned, learning is optimal in instrumental conditioning if the reinforcement follows immediately upon the response. Similarly, a very brief CS-UCS interval is optimal in classical conditioning; conditioning becomes almost impossible with even moderate delays. In paired-associate learning delay of reinforcement has no corresponding effect. Estes (1967) has reviewed the relevant studies in this area. The function of reinforcement seems to be to provide information rather than some kind of automatic strengthening of responses according to the law of effect. Under conditions which insure adequate information reception, delays up to 8 seconds between the subject's response and the experimental reinforcement have absolutely no effect upon the rate of paired-associate learning (Kintsch and McCoy, 1964). Similar findings have been reported for the learning of simple motor tasks (Bilodeau and Bilodeau, 1958) and concept formation (Bourne and Bunderson, 1963). However, human learning is a complex affair and it would be naive to expect that delay of reinforcement always has the same effect, or rather lack of effect, irrespective of experimental conditions. In some studies delay retards performance because the experimental conditions make it difficult for the subjects to retain the stimulus and their own response in memory sufficiently long for the reinforcement to be related to them (e.g., Saltzman, 1951). It is also possible to arrange experimental conditions in such a way that delay of reinforcement actually facilitates learning (e.g., Buchwald, 1967). However, the way to understand such results is to analyze each experiment in terms of the manner in which the subjects treat the relevant information rather than in terms of an automatic inhibitory effect of delay.

If reinforcement in human learning is not a matter of an automatic strengthening of a response, the neglect of animal studies in this book is understandable. Of course, this does not mean that these studies are uninteresting or unimportant in themselves—it simply means that the study of human learning might as well begin with the investigation of human learning proper, and that relatively little could be gained by approaching the subject matter via animal learning. Whenever animal studies seem to be directly relevant, such studies will be freely introduced. This is the case mostly in Chapter 6 which deals with discrimination learning.

2. INTERFERENCE THEORY: COMPETITION AND UNLEARNING

Among the inheritance which psychology received from philosophy was the doctrine of associationism. Ever since Ebbinghaus it has been widely accepted that what is learned in verbal learning are associations, and that interference between associations plays an essential role in forgetting. The theory of verbal learning was for a long time a theory of the formation and extinction of associative bonds. Today, this tradition is alive in the interference theory of verbal learning. Although one of the more successful and established theories in psychology, interference theory has undergone considerable changes in the last few years and continues to do so, moving farther and farther away from pure associationism.

Until the 1950's interference theory made do with an absolute minimum of theoretical machinery: stimulus, response, and association were the only constructs thought necessary. Learning consisted in a gradual strengthening of $S—R$ associations through reinforcement. This scheme received its first major change when Hovland and Kurtz introduced the concept of response learning in 1952. These authors observed that prefamiliarization of syllables in a serial learning task facilitated learning. This observation necessitated a distinction between response learning and associative learning. The concept of response learning was important because it marked the first deviation from a strict stimulus-response conception of verbal learning. Response learning does not involve the establishment of a stimulus-response bond. Psychologists found that they had to deal with responses for which there were no identifiable stimuli. Mandler (1967) refined the concept of response learning by pointing out a confounding in Hovland's original use of the term. In the Hovland and Kurtz experiment response learning involved both learning the identity of the set of experimental responses, as well as learning how to make the responses. Mandler suggested that the term response learning, or response integration, be reserved for learning how to make a response. Underwood and Schulz (1960) in their influential monograph have made extensive use of the concept of response learning. The recent concern with problems of response integration is also partly responsible for the preference of words over nonsense syllables as learning materials by contemporary experimenters. Words (at least high frequency words) are never learned in the sense of response integration. The subject merely learns that a particular word is a member of the response set, but he knows the word quite well before. Nonsense material, on the other hand, requires response integration, and therefore may introduce undesirable complexity into a learning experiment.

In recent years interference theory has shifted its focus of interest from a concern with the fate of individual associations to problems concerning the availability of the whole response set. Concepts like response availability and response selection are being given an increasingly important role within the theory.

Two-factor Theory of Interference

Classically, interference was considered to be a matter of response competition. If an association exists between two items a and b, the learning of a new association a—c interferes with a—b because at the time of recall, the responses b and c will compete with each other when the stimulus term a is presented (McGeoch, 1942). A study by Melton and Irwin (1940) on the effects of degree of learning upon retroactive inhibition (which was mentioned before in Chapter 1) provided an interesting if somewhat baffling analysis of recall errors. The concept of retroactive interference implies that forgetting occurs because the second-list associations interfere with the first-list associations. One might therefore suppose that a good deal of response competition between the associations from the two lists would occur, and that items from the second list would occur as intrusion errors when subjects try to recall the first list. However, Melton and Irwin report that second list intrusions were quite rare in their experiment. Total retroactive inhibition (and hence errors in recall) increased as a function of second-list trials. The number of intrusion errors, on the other hand, was higher when the interfering list was presented for only a few trials, and became quite negligible when the second list was learned well. Melton and Irwin concluded that response competition was only of minor importance in forgetting, and that most forgetting must be attributed to some "Factor X." They speculated that during the learning of the second list the first-list associations might actually be unlearned.

These two factors, response competition and unlearning of associations when successive lists involve conflicting associations, have become the principal mechanisms by means of which interference effects are explained. Underwood (1948) assumed that the mechanism of unlearning was that of experimental extinction: unreinforced elicitations of the S—R bond would weaken the association. An important consequence of this assumption was that unlearning should have the same characteristics as experimental extinction, in particular, spontaneous recovery of extinguished associations. Spontaneous recovery means that after a period of rest more associations are available than immediately after unlearning: some extinguished associations recover spontaneously. To test this prediction Underwood had subjects learn two lists of 10 adjective pairs in an A—B, A—C design and tested for recall after time intervals ranging from 1 minute to 48 hours. A modified free-recall test was used: subjects were shown the common stimulus word and responded with either the B or the C response, whichever they could remember. For brief retention intervals many more C-responses were given than B-responses. However, as the retention interval increased, the frequency of C-responses decreased sharply, while the frequency of first-list responses remained fairly constant. After 48 hours the original list and the interference list were equally well recalled. This finding means that there could not have been any unlearning of the first list. If the first list had been unlearned during acquisition of the second list, a more permanent superiority of second list recall over first list recall would be expected. There was, however, one way in which the unlearning concept could be saved, namely, by the assumption that the extinguished first list associations may recover spontaneously. The lack of a decrease in the recall of first-list responses agrees with such an assumption: spontaneous recovery runs counter to the usual forgetting over time, and the two processes apparently balanced each other.

Barnes and Underwood (1959) put the finishing touches on the two-factor theory of interference with their experimental demonstration of unlearning of first-list associations. They conducted two parallel experiments, one using an *A—B, A—C* transfer design, and one using the *A—B, A—B'* paradigm. All lists were constituted of 8 CVC-adjective pairs. In the *A—B, A—C* lists there was no apparent response similarity. Responses in the *A—B, A—B'* lists were similar in meaning, such as *insane-crazy*. All subjects learned the first list to a criterion of one correct anticipation and then were given either 1, 5, 10, or 20 trials with List 2. The recall test was a modification of Underwood's modified free-recall procedure: subjects were given a sheet of paper with the stimulus words printed on it and were asked to write down both responses. This procedure avoids the effects of response competition, or list differentiation, and provides a pure measure of the availability of the first- and second-list responses. The results for the *A—B, A—C* paradigm are shown in Fig. 2.1 as a function of trials on the second list. The interesting result is the decrease in recall of the responses from the first list with increasing List 2 learning. The decline in *A—B* associations seen in Fig. 2.1 was a genu-

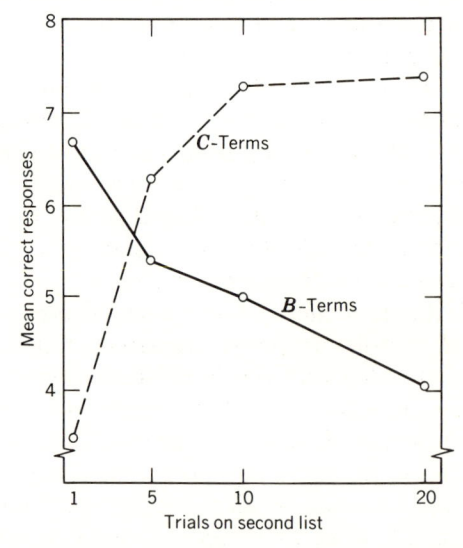

Fig. 2.1 *Mean number of responses correctly recalled and identified with stimulus and list in the* A-B, A-C *paradigm. (after Barnes and Underwood, 1959)*

ine unlearning effect attributable to $A—C$ learning rather than simple forgetting. Barnes and Underwood demonstrated this by means of a control group which learned the first list only and then rested for a period of time equivalent to that spent in learning the $A—C$ list by the group given 20 trials. Mean recall for this control group was almost perfect (7.75 correct).

While first-list associations became less available as second-list learning increased, no loss of differentiation was observed. The term differentiation, as used here, refers to the subject's ability to tell from which of the two lists a response comes.

With the $A—B$, $A—B'$ paradigm no forgetting of B was obtained. Instead, the learning of the second list was facilitated: after only one anticipation trial, recall of List 2 was nearly perfect. Barnes and Underwood interpret this result as evidence in favor of a mediational process. The subject learns a response chain $A—B—B'$. Thus, in the case of response similarity, an entirely new transfer mechanism is invoked. It is, of course, possible that the subject also tries to establish a response chain like $A—B—C$ in the $A—C$ paradigm, but fails because of the lack of association between B and C and finally extinguishes the $A—B$ connection through lack of reinforcement. An $A—B—B'$ chain on the other hand, will lead to correct responses and is thus likely to be established through reinforcement (Postman, 1961).

Interference at this point is regarded as an interaction between specific associative bonds, mostly in the form of extinction of old bonds during the learning of new ones, with response competition assigned a minor role. This conceptual system is supplemented by a few auxiliary terms, principally response differentiation and mediation.

Transfer

The results of Barnes and Underwood (1959) were extended to a number of other transfer situations by McGovern in 1964. To recapitulate, one of the conclusions of Barnes and Underwood was that first-list associations become extinguished during second list learning in the $A—B$, $A—C$ negative transfer paradigm. McGovern's strategy was to examine other transfer paradigms for the presence of $A—B$, $A—C$ extinctive relationships. Basic to her analysis is the distinction between an associative and a response learning phase in paired-associate learning. Thus, in learning an association between $S—R$, there are three different kinds of associations which must be considered: first of all the forward association $S{\rightarrow}R$, then the backward $R{\rightarrow}S$ association, and finally response recall. McGovern assumed that the stimuli in response recall are environmental stimuli (stimuli emanating from the room, the experimental equipment, the experimenter, etc). Thus, response recall represents an association between contextual stimuli and the response terms. When an extinctive relationship is present in a transfer experiment for any one of these three types of associations, negative transfer will be produced. Consider the standard transfer paradigms shown in Table 1.1 of Chapter 1. In the control group A—B, C—D the forward and backward associations between A and B in the first list will not be affected when the C—D list is learned; but new response terms (D) are learned in the presence of the contextual stimuli which are already connected to the first list responses (B), and therefore the associations between the contextual stimuli and the first list responses B will be extinguished. In the A—B, C—B design the only first list associations extinguished during second list learning are the backward associations $B{\rightarrow}A$ (new associations $B{\rightarrow}C$ are being acquired). On the other hand, in the A—B, A—B_r paradigm, both the forward and backward associations of the first list will suffer during second list learning. Finally, McGovern's model predicts that forward associations and contextual associations are subject to extinction in the A—B, A—C paradigm. Thus, an obvious prediction can be derived from the model: the paradigms in which two kinds of associations are being extinguished should produce more negative transfer than paradigms in which only one type of association is extinguished during second list learning.

McGovern tested this prediction in an experiment in which subjects learned two 8-item lists. The first list was learned to a criterion of one errorless trial, and after a 1-minute rest interval, 15 anticipation trials were given on a second list. Immediately afterwards a modified free-recall test was administered: the subjects were given the first list stimuli and were asked for the first list responses. The results are shown in Table 2.1, together with the transfer paradigms used and the theoretical predictions. The finding that much more negative transfer is obtained in the first two conditions where two associative bonds were involved than in the second two groups where only one type of bond was weakened is of course what would be expected from McGovern's analysis. It shows that looking at forward associations, backward associations, and response recall as separate sources of interference is very useful in understanding the results of transfer experiments. However, it does not prove McGovern's controversial hypothesis that response recall is based upon association to contextual stimuli.

Several studies have been reported in Chapter 1 in which the similarity between the stimuli and responses of two successively

Table 2.1. *A summary of McGovern's experiment.*

Training Condition		Mean Number of Correct Responses after Interpolated Learning	Nature of Extinctive Relationships
List 1	List 2		
A-B	*A-C*	4.79	Forward and contextual associations
A-B	*A-Br*	4.75	Forward and backward associations
A-B	*C-B*	6.42	Backward associations
A-B	*C-D*	6.54	Contextual associations
A-B	—	7.71	—

learned lists was varied. Osgood's attempt to order and interpret these results in terms of his transfer surface has also been discussed (Osgood, 1949). Osgood's transfer surface was essentially an empirical generalization, and it was shown that it fails to describe adequately the very complex pattern of results obtained in transfer studies since Osgood originally proposed it. In fact, the reader who recalls the section on transfer from the previous chapter will probably agree that there appears to be very little hope for any kind of simple generalization that can account for these exceedingly complex results. However, Martin (1965) has approached the problem quite successfully via a model that distinguishes between forward associations, backward associations, and response recall. A transfer surface can be drawn separately for each of these subprocesses. Total transfer can then be expressed as the sum of these three component transfers. Sources of positive and negative transfer can be combined in this way, and, depending upon the importance which is assigned to each component, most experimental results available can be accounted for. Additional experimental variables must be considered separately, however. The transfer surfaces take into account only the relatedness between the stimuli and response terms of the two lists. As has been shown in Chapter 1, the meaningfulness of both stimuli and responses, and the degree of learning play an important role in modifying transfer results.

Proactive Inhibition and Extra-experimental Sources of Interference

From the experiments already described it is clear that by introducing an interpolated interfering list marked forgetting can be produced in the laboratory. But how is the forgetting to be explained which occurs over, say, a week when the subject learns only one list? Traditionally this loss has been attributed to the interference from activities outside the laboratory during this week. This interpretation was never quite satisfactory. It meant stretching the interference hypothesis rather far to hold that the large amount of forgetting of a nonsense syllable list within a few hours was caused by interference from something which the subjects learned outside the laboratory, nonsense syllables still not being in common use. In 1957 Underwood remedied this situation by showing that most forgetting was produced by interference not from unspecified tasks learned outside the laboratory, but from tasks learned previously in the laboratory.

Figure 2.2 taken from Underwood (1957) shows that proactive interference plays a very important role in determining paired-associate recall. The very large differences in recall which were obtained in different experiments can be explained as proactive inhibition effects: the more lists subjects have learned previously, the poorer their recall. In constructing this figure, Underwood used the results from 16 published studies which fulfilled the following criteria: learning was to one perfect recitation of the list, retention was measured by a recall test after 24 hours, and finally, relatively massed practice was used during learning. The studies included had several different kinds of materials (geometric forms, nonsense syllables, words) and also differed in such factors as list length, and manner and rate of presentation. These factors are probably responsible for some of the remaining variance in Fig. 2.2, but the overwhelming effect of number

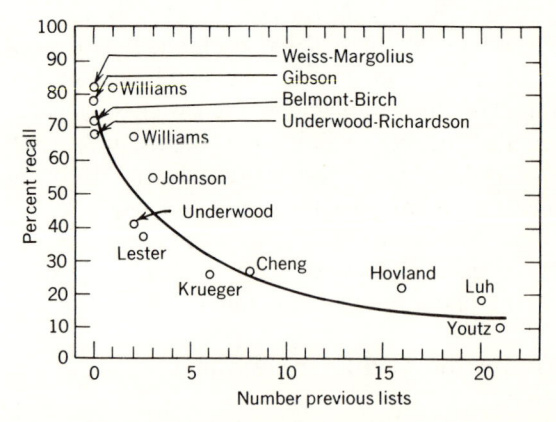

Fig. 2.2 *Recall as a function of number of previous lists learned from a number of studies. (after Underwood, 1957)*

of previous lists learned is clearly discernible. As Underwood points out, this makes the task of the theorist much simpler: after 24 hours the amount of forgetting still to be explained is only of the order of 25%, not around 75%, as one would conclude from Ebbinghaus' data, who, of course, had learned many previous lists.

The remaining 25% of forgetting were assigned their place within the framework of the interference theory of forgetting by Underwood and Postman (1960). The old hypothesis of extraexperimental sources of interference, which seemed a little overtaxed when it was used to explain all forgetting, now appeared sufficient for handling the reduced problem. Underwood (1957) had demonstrated the considerable power of proactive interference from lists not designed to be particularly similar to the test list. The extension from this result to forgetting without formal interfering tasks was not such a large step, especially since the interference effects of new learning during the retention interval (retroactive inhibition) could now plausibly be supplemented by the interfering consequences of previous extraexperimental learning (proactive inhibition).

The arsenal of interference theory already included sufficient mechanisms by means of which habits learned previously could interfere with present learning: learning a list requires the breaking or unlearning of previous associations, and these extinguished verbal habits may recover spontaneously in time, interfering with the retention of the to be learned list. Of course, if the extinguished habit is practiced again during the retention interval, its recovery would be facilitated and the interference would be maximal. One would speak of retroactive inhibition in this latter case. However, actual practice during the retention interval is not necessary, because extinguished verbal habits will recover spontaneously in the absence of practice. Underwood and Postman specified letter-sequence interference and unit-sequence interference as possible sources of extraexperimental interference. Letter-sequence interference refers to the associations which are established among letter sequences through ordinary language. Unit-sequence interference is produced by the preexisting associations among the words of a learning list. As an example, the authors say that if *over* is an item of a learning list, the association *over-there* must be extinguished before a new association can be established. But with the passage of time, the original association will recover and interfere with retention. Furthermore, should the subject use the expression *over-there* during the retention interval, the recovery of the association would be facilitated and interference increased. Some preliminary tests of this hypothesis provided positive results.

At this point interference theory was a comprehensive theory of forgetting, which adequately explained the major phenomena with which the laboratory study of forgetting had been concerned up to that time. However, the concept of interference from extraexperimental sources has recently come under attack, necessitating a restriction of the theory to formal retroactive and proactive inhibition designs.

The extension of interference theory to account for forgetting from extraexperimental sources of interference was made the subject of several experimental investigations. In general, the data have not supported the predictions from the theory. A study reported by Slamecka (1966) illustrates some of the problems which were encountered. Slamecka tried to show that preexperimental associations are unlearned during laboratory learning, just as Barnes and Underwood had shown that associations formed in the laboratory are unlearned after competing list learning. His experimental design utilized three groups of subjects and is summarized below:

Group	Preexperimental Associations	Learn List 1	Learn List 2	Recall	Recall
I	*A-P*	*A-B*	*A-C*	*A-P*	*A-B, C*
II	*A-P*	*A-B*	—	*A-P*	*A-B*
III	*A-P*	—	—	*A-P*	—

In the preexperimental association test the *A*-terms (two syllable nouns) were shown to the subjects who responded with the first association that occurred to them. The response terms during paired-associate learning (*B* and *C*) were unrelated nouns. For the recall tests the stimulus words were exposed on a memory drum and subjects were given unlimited time to recall their free associations, and one or both of the responses of the paired-associate lists.

Recall of first list responses was about 33% less for Group I than for Group II, indicating considerable unlearning of the prescribed responses (retroactive interference). However, there was no difference between the three groups in their ability to recall their free associations, whether measured by frequency of recall or by response latency. Thus the Underwood and Postman hypothesis that preexperimental associations are unlearned during laboratory learning was not supported by the data. The subjects in this experiment were very well able to differentiate between the responses of the paired-associate list and preexperimental associations. Apparently this differentiation process sets aside well-established associations and removes them from the possibility for unlearning. Anything that makes differentiation more difficult should produce unlearning and therefore interference. The results of the studies on environmental similarity between original learning and transfer tasks may be understood within this context.

Underwood and Ekstrand (1966) set themselves the task of exploring why extraexperimental associations do not seem to produce proactive interference and are so resistant to unlearning. They argued that the two most salient characteristics of associations learned outside the laboratory are a high degree of overlearning and distributed practice. They tried to simulate extraexperimental associations and the decreased proactive interference which they produce in the laboratory by having subjects learn a paired-associate list for many trials, and with distributed practice. More specifically, subjects were given either 12, 32, 48, or 80 trials on an *A—B* list either with massed practice (all trials on the same day) or with distributed practice (spaced over 4 days). Immediately after *A—B* learning, and *A—C* list was learned to a criterion of one correct anticipation. Twenty-four hours later, subjects were tested for the retention of the *A—C* list and then given a recall test. A sheet of paper was given to the subject on which all stimuli were listed and subjects were asked to write down the response terms from both lists into appropriate spaces.

The results for the recall of the *A—C* list were in agreement with earlier studies (Postman and Riley, 1959) when the original list had been learned with massed practice: as the number of trials with the *A—B* list increased, proactive inhibition effects became stronger, but only up to a certain point; with 80 trials on the original list, a reversal occurred. When the original list is very well learned, it interferes less with recall of a second list. With distributed practice, on the other hand, number of trials on the original list had no effect at all upon *A—C* retention, and, in fact, retention was always much better then with massed practice. Either no or very little proactive interference was produced with distributed practice. Similar results were obtained for the recall of the original list (*A—B*): recall was essentially perfect when original learning had been distributed over four days, irrespective of the number of learning trials. With massed practice, something resembling more the usual retroactive interference effects was observed: retention tended to improve as a function of amount of original learning (e.g., McGeoch, 1929).

The authors concluded that extraexperimental associations do not produce a significant amount of interference, and that distribution of practice is a major factor responsible for this lack of interference. But why does distributed practice reduce interference? As yet interference theorists have not come up with a satisfactory answer to this question. Underwood and Ekstrand indicate that the concept of association might be insufficient to provide a convincing answer. Perhaps properties of association other than just strength play a role in determining the amount of interference. The reduced interference with distributed practice surely can not be explained by any lack of strength of the habits learned in this manner. It may be necessary to introduce the concept of structure at this point: the associations developed in $A—B$ learning by distributed practice might in some way be structured differently so as to reduce interference effects (Mandler, 1962). The reduction in proactive interference with the massed practice groups between 48 and 80 $A—B$ trials also supports the concept of a structure which in some as yet unspecified way evolves in overlearning, or with distributed practice.

Spontaneous Recovery

Underwood's equating of unlearning and experimental extinction appears to be another weak point of contemporary interference theory. If unlearning is extinction, unlearned associations should recover spontaneously during the retention period, since spontaneous recovery is a well-established characteristic of experimental extinction.

The concept of spontaneous recovery was introduced to account for the observation that after longer retention intervals (24 to 48 hours) the first and second lists in an $A—B$, $A—C$ design are equally well recalled. At shorter retention intervals the second list is better recalled. Underwood (1948) suggested that the first list responses which have become unlearned when the second list was learned recover strength spontaneously, so that the second list loses its initial superiority. Alternative explanations of this finding are, of course, quite possible. In fact, negatively accelerated forgetting curves alone seem sufficient to handle Underwood's results. Koppenaal (1963) has argued that spontaneous recover is an unnecessary assumption and should be retained only if direct evidence for it can be obtained. He distinguished between absolute recovery and relative recovery of first list associations, only the first of which could be admitted as evidence for the existence of spontaneous recovery. Relative recovery refers to an increase in the availability of first list responses relative to second list responses. Negatively accelerated forgetting curves imply such a phenomenon. Absolute recovery refers to an increase in the absolute number of responses available to the subject at recall.

Koppenaal used an A—B, A—C design and a control group which learned only one list. Retention was tested after 1, 20, or 90 minutes, 6, 24, or 72 hours, or 1 week. Since it was important in this experiment to obtain a measure of response availability uncontaminated by other factors, the "modified-modified free recall" procedure of Barnes and Underwood was used for the recall test. Subjects were shown the stimulus words on a memory drum and were asked to give both responses without regard to order. At the shorter retention intervals, significantly more responses were recalled from the second list than from the first list. At longer retention intervals this difference disappeared. Thus, there was relative recovery of first list responses versus second list responses. But there was no absolute recovery: the frequency of first list responses decreased as a function of the length of the retentional interval.

The single-list control group recalled initially about as many words as the experimental subjects could recall from List 2, but as the retention interval increased it improved relative to List 2 recall. This is an interesting finding. It means not only that proactive inhibition effects are relatively permanent, but also that proactive inhibition actually increases with time: the superiority of the recall of the single list over the recall of the second list was most pronounced after a retention interval of one week. Since the two-factor theory of interference ascribes all interference effects to either unlearning or response competition, and neither of these effects could have been operative in the present situation, where did the inhibition of List 2 recall come from? (Response competition is presumably eliminated by the recall procedure used here, and since no other list was learned after List 2, no opportunity for formal unlearning existed.)

There are a number of other studies since Koppenaal's original report in which absolute recovery (in statistically significant amounts and with conventional scoring methods) could not be demonstrated either. The retention intervals used in these studies ranged from several hours to several days. If, however, much smaller intervals are used, an absolute rise in correct first-list responses is found. Postman, Stark, and Fraser (1968) had subjects learn two successive lists in an A—B, A—C paradigm; in the control condition a single list of paired-associates was learned. Each list consisted of eight CVC-adjective pairs. Recall tests for the first list were given either 8 or 26 minutes after the end of List-1 learning. Recall tests consisted of unpaced presentations of the stimulus terms A together with the second-list responses (C); subjects were required to supply the List-1 responses (B). This procedure was devised to minimize the possible effects of response competition, including variations in output order of the B

and C terms, which may still be affecting recall in the modified-modified free recall procedure (A is given, B and C are asked for).

Absolute recovery of unlearned associations could be demonstrated with this procedure: after 8 minutes, subjects could recall 4.0 items; after 26 minutes recall rose to 5.6 items.

This result is replicable, as Postman *et al.* have shown in a series of further studies. However, these studies also raised some questions as to the interpretation of the rise in correct responses as spontaneous recovery of extinguished associations, to which we shall turn below. On the whole, then, the evidence for spontaneous recovery is ambiguous: for the retention intervals commonly used it cannot be demonstrated, but a clear demonstration of absolute recovery exists for short retention intervals. Some intriguing questions remain as to the proper interpretation of this effect.

Associative Interference or Rules of Response Selection?

It is difficult and extremely risky to try to discuss controversies which are so young that neither all of the arguments nor all of the data are as yet available. However, some recent results of Postman concerning interference mechanisms are so interesting and potentially important that they will be described here anyhow.

The problem is to determine what is unlearned in negative transfer experiments. The classical answer of interference theory to this qustion is most clearly formulated in the McGovern study reported above: Specific associations—forward and backward associations between stimuli and responses, and associations between contextual cues and the response terms—are being unlearned. Postman, Stark, and Fraser, 1968; Postman and Stark, 1969) announced some serious doubts about this classical interpretation.

Consider the following experiment. One condition consists essentially of a replication of the McGovern experiment. Different groups of subjects learn two paired-associate lists each, according to the various standard transfer paradigms. Ten item lists of letter-adjective pairs were used. The first list was learned to a strict criterion, then the subjects received 10 anticipation trials on List 2, and finally a test of List 1 was administered. The test procedure was modified-modified free recall (MMFR). In the second condition the treatment was identical, except that both learning and test employed a multiple-choice method. On each trial the subject was shown four response alternatives, one of which was the correct one and the three others were taken from other items of the list. The reason for including this second condition was to provide a control for response recall: with a recognition procedure, response recall is not involved, and hence one would expect a somewhat modified pattern of results for the various transfer designs, using McGovern's arguments.

When learning was with the anticipation procedure and the MMFR test was given, typical transfer results were obtained; in other words, McGovern's results were replicated. However, for the recognition learning group none of the transfer paradigms produced negative transfer, except for some slight amount in the $A—B$, $A—B_r$ condition. Recognition of List-1 items was approximately the same in all other conditions, and equaled the performance of the control group. This is a very striking and important result: retroactive interference seems to be a matter of response availability! Specific associations seem to be highly resistant to unlearning. Thus, interference may not work on individual associations but rather on the entire repertoire of first-list responses; a process of response selection may be responsible for the results generally obtained in transfer studies.*

Postman offers the following outline of the operation of this hypothetical response selection mechanism. When the subject receives his instructions, a class of response terms is selected as appropriate for the list which is to be learned. Within the selected response class the availability of individual responses is governed by the "spew principle": the most frequent responses come first. When the response terms are changed, as they are in the transfer studies under consideration here, a new selection criterion must be adopted. The effectiveness of this criterion depends upon the distinctiveness of the new responses: the more distinct the two response sets are, the more effective will be the exclusion of the first-list responses. During recall subjects scan the available responses and match them against the criteria of selection; responses which fail this test will not be produced overtly. Thus most interference in transfer experiments remains covert. (The scanning of the response set and the editing of responses correspond to what is often referred to as list differentiation).

There is one more assumption which must be made, namely, that there is some inertia in the selector mechanism. If the subject is instructed to recall List 1 while the List-2 criteria are still dominant, he may experience considerable difficulty—depending upon the similarity

---

*There are several transfer studies in which retention was tested with a matching task, which did not involve response recall, as in the present study, but in which small amounts of interference were observed. However, in these studies response recall was involved in the learning phase, as learning was with the regular anticipation method. Therefore, these studies are difficult to interpret.

of the criteria—and he will need some time to change his set appropriately. But the important consideration is that interference is produced not by the individual List-2 associations, but by the dominance of the most recent criterion. The strength of the List-2 associations is quite irrelevant according to this way of thinking; what is important is the degree of criterion dominance.

The results on recovery of first-list associations which were reported in the previous section are in very good agreement with this hypothesis. Postman *et al.* performed a whole series of recovery experiments in which they systematically manipulated the expected dominance of the second-list criteria at the end of training. Obviously if the criteria appropriate to the second list are very strong at the end of training, the subject will do poorly if he is asked to recall the first list responses; after some 20 minutes, the second-list criterion will no longer be dominant, and the subject will now be able to recall more first-list responses than he could right after training. Therefore, recovery of first-list associations will be observed. On the other hand, if the second-list criterion is weak in the first place, no further changes will take place with time, and there should be no recovery of first-list associations. Postman *et al.* manipulated criterion strength in various ways. In the condition MMFR (1) subjects were given the stimulus terms together with the second-list responses and were asked to provide the first-list responses; these subjects were directly confronted with the second-list terms, which should lead to a persistence of the second-list criteria. In the condition MMFR (2) subjects were given only the stimulus terms and asked for both first and second list terms; under these circumstances the subject's set for recall of the second list responses did not receive external reinforcement since he is not confronted with these terms; hence it should be weaker, but it should still be present to some degree because of the instructions to recall both first and second list terms. In a final condition, subjects were asked to recall the first list terms only (as in the McGovern experiment); here set-produced interference should be minimized, and thus there should be no room for recovery of associations as a function of time. The experimental results of Postman *et al.* nicely confirmed these expectations: considerable absolute recovery of first list associations over a 24-minute interval was found with the MMFR (1) test, some with the MMFR (2) test, and none at all with the third recall procedure.

In conclusion, it seems that interference theory has come almost full circle: it started out with the notion that interference was produced by response competition; later, attention shifted more and more to unlearning as the basic mechanism of interference in transfer experiments; now Postman wants to reinstate response competition in the dominant role. However, response competition is back with a difference: 40 years ago, it was the competition between individual associations that was held responsible for intereference; today, generalized response competition is thought to arise as a consequence of the inertia of the response selector mechanism. No longer is it a matter of competition between alternative responses to the same stimulus but rather between alternative response systems.

3. MATHEMATICAL MODELS: DISCRETE LEARNING STATES OR INCREMENTS IN RESPONSE STRENGTH?

Traditionally, learning has been regarded as a process of gradual improvement. Learning curves which rise in small trial-by-trial increments have been reported in numerous studies, so that most psychologists did not even consider seriously the idea that learning might be anything but a gradual process. However, on closer examination the experimental evidence is not as tight as one might have supposed. The many learning curves which are obviously gradual functions rather than step functions can be discounted as evidence in this case. Typically, learning curves are based upon group averages. But consider what happens when many step functions are averaged for which the step does not occur on the same trial: the result will be a gradually rising curve just as if the individual learning curves had been gradual. In addition, the learning tasks studied by psychologists are often quite complex. For instance, paired-associate tasks may involve stimulus discrimination, response learning, and association as subtasks. Thus, even if the learning of each subtask is all-or-none rather than incremental, data based upon the whole process will be quite complex. In short, the problem is not so obvious as it first appears and deserves more detailed investigation. First of all, it is necessary to state precisely and explicitly what the theoretical alternatives are and what their implications are with respect to experimental data. Two mathematical models of paired-associate learning will be compared, one following from the basic axiom that learning is an incremental process, and one from the axiom that learning is all-or-none.

Before stating these models and deriving testable implications from them, it is necessary to be quite explicit about the boundary conditions of these models. They are not general models of verbal learning or even paired-associate learning. Instead, they apply only to a very specific kind of paired-associate experiment. The principal restriction is that response learning be eliminated from the paired-associate task; this is done by telling the subject beforehand what the responses are. Specifically, experiments will be discussed where there are only two responses, 1 and 2, and where the subject learns to classify all items as either 1 or 2. A second boundary condition concerns the stimulus material: items must be easily discriminated, so as to minimize problems of stimulus discrimination. What remains is a very simple paired-associate task, and the reader may protest against wasting much theoretical effort on such a trivial experimental task. However, it pays to investigate a problem in its simplest form first; once some understanding of the central issue has been obtained, the restrictions imposed here will be dropped one by one. Tasks with more than two known responses will be considered, and finally the model will be extended to cases involving response learning and stimulus discrimination. The strategy which is followed here is one of starting from the simplest, most manageable case, and making all extensions explicit.

The discussion which is to follow will be much clearer if the reader who is not familiar with the general approach described here takes a few minutes to look at some sample paired-associate data, the way they are coded, and the kind of summary statistics which are calculated from them.

The results from a paired-associate learning experiment are shown for one subject in Table 2.2. In this experiment subjects learned a 10-item list by the method of anticipation. The nonsense syllables which served as stimuli are shown in the table. Only two response alternatives were used (A and B). During a three-second anticipation interval the stimulus syllable was shown on a memory drum and the subject responded with either A or B. The subject was instructed to guess if necessary. The stimulus-response pair was presented jointly for two seconds. The items were presented in a new random order on every trial. The intertrial interval was 30 seconds. Learning continued until a criterion of two successive correct trials was reached. The subject's responses were recorded only as correct (0) or incorrect (1).

The second part of Table 2.2 shows a number of typical data statistics which may be used to evaluate the adequacy of a theory. Most of these are frequency distributions of one sort or other; for example, in Table 2.2(a) the distribution of the number of errors per item is shown. For each item, either 0, 1, 2, . . . errors occur. Table 2.2(a) is simply a count of the number of items in the data for which exactly 0, 1, 2, . . . errors occurred. Thus, in the sample data shown here, on exactly two items (LAM-A and PEB-B) the subject made one error. It is often convenient to summarize the information contained in a frequency distribution such as Table 2.2(a). The most important summary statistics are the mean, or average, and the standard deviation of the frequency distribution. Calculational formulas for both statistics are shown in the table. The interpretation of the other parts of Table 2.2 is generally obvious, but readers who are not familiar with the methods of data analysis described here should make sure that they understand how each statistic has been calculated from

Table 2.2. *The performance record of one subject learning a 10-item paired associate list to a criterion of two successive correct trials and some common statistical analyses of the data. Correct responses are denoted by 0 and errors by 1.*

Items	1	2	3	4	5	6	7	8	9	10	11	12	
MUC-*A*	0	0	0	0	0	0	0	0	0	0	0	0	
WAV-*B*	1	0	1	1	1	0	0	0	0	0	0	0	
CID-*B*	0	1	1	0	0	0	1	0	1	0	0	0	
LAM-*A*	1	0	0	0	0	0	0	0	0	0	0	0	
KOL-*A*	0	1	0	1	0	1	1	0	0	0	0	0	
DOR-*B*	0	0	0	0	0	0	0	0	0	0	0	0	
NAZ-*B*	1	0	1	0	0	0	0	0	0	0	0	0	
PEB-*B*	0	1	0	0	0	0	0	0	0	0	0	0	
HIG-*A*	0	0	0	0	0	0	0	0	0	0	0	0	
VEL-*A*	1	1	0	0	0	0	0	0	0	0	0	0	
Total errors	4	4	3	2	1	1	2	0	1	0	0	0	18
Proportion of errors	.4	.4	.3	.2	.1	.1	.2	0	.1	0	0	0	

(a) *Distribution of number of errors per item.*

Number of errors per item: k	Frequency: $f(k)$	Proportion: $p(k)$
0	3	.3
1	2	.2
2	2	.2
3	0	0
4	3	.3
	10	1.0

Mean number of errors per item: $M(k) = \dfrac{\Sigma k \, f(k)}{\Sigma f(k)} = \dfrac{18}{10} = 1.8$

Standard deviation: $s(k) = \dfrac{\Sigma (k - M(k))^2 f(k)}{\Sigma f(k)} = 1.7$

Table 2.2 (Continued)

(b) *Distribution of the number of errors before the first success.*

Number of errors before the first success: j	Frequency: $f(j)$	Proportion: $p(j)$
0	6	.6
1	3	.3
2	1	.1
	10	1.0

Mean number of trials before the first success: $M(j) = .5$
Standard deviation: $s(j) = .7$

(c) *Distribution of trial of last error.*

Trial of last error: n	Frequency: $f(n)$	Proportion: $p(n)$
0	3	.3
1	1	.1
2	2	.2
3	1	.1
4	0	0
5	1	.1
6	0	0
7	1	.1
8	0	0
9	1	.1
	10	1.0

Mean trial of last error: $M(n) = 2.9$
Standard deviation: $s(n) = 3.1$

(d) *Distribution of error runs of length i.*

Error runs of length i	Frequency	Number of runs per item
1	9	.9
2	3	.3
3	1	.1
	13	

Total number of runs per item: $R = 1.3$

the sample data. The examples shown here, of course, are not exhaustive; for instance, we could find the distribution of the number of errors between the first and second success, or any other pair, or we could look at some sequential statistics, like the number of times an error is followed by an error k trials later, without regard to intervening responses, which is the so-called auto-correlation of errors k trials apart. Some other sequential statistics which play an important role in evaluating the goodness of fit of a model will be introduced below.

A Comparison of Two Models

A model which is built upon the assumption that learning is an incremental process is the *linear model*. The alternative assumption that learning is a discrete process may be embodied in a *two-state Markov model*. Both models will be described here and differential testable implications will be derived.

In the simple linear model (Bush and Mosteller, 1955) learning is viewed as a continuous process. On each trial n the probability of the correct response (p_n) changes. It starts from some guessing level p_1 at the beginning of the experiment and increases to an asymptote of 1. Since in the paired-associate learning experiments to be discussed here reinforcement occurs on every trial (i.e., the stimulus-response pair is shown to the subject on every trial), every trial has the same effect, i.e., the same operator can be applied to the response probability on every trial. As the name of the model implies, this operator is linear: the response probability on trial n is related to the response probability on the next trial by a linear equation. Because of the restriction that the same operator be applied on all trials the model is called the single-operator linear model. The formal statement of the model is very brief:

> **Definitions:** For a single subject and item there exists a probability p_n that the subject will give a correct response on trial n. The presentation of the stimulus-response pair constitutes a reinforcement. The response probability on the first trial is p_1.
>
> **Learning axiom:** When a reinforcement occurs on trial n

$$(1) \qquad p_{n+1} = p_n + (1-p_n)\theta$$

The linear model generates a sequence of response probabilities $p_1, p_2, p_3, \ldots, p_n, \ldots$ which increase continuously. Errors become more and more rare as learning proceeds, but there is no "conditioning" state in which errors are impossible. As a sample-derivation, the mean number of errors per trial, i.e., the mean learning curve, will be derived from Eq. (1). Let q_n denote the probability of an error on trial n; since the probability of an error and of a success on a trial must sum to 1, we have $q_n = 1 - p_n$. Multiplying Eq. (1) by (-1) and adding 1 to each side we obtain

$$1 - p_{n+1} = 1 - p_n - (1 - p_n)\theta$$

Substituting q_n for $1 - p_n$

(2) $$q_{n+1} = q_n(1-\theta)$$

The mean learning curve can now be obtained by induction; start with q_1 and apply Eq. (2) repeatedly to compute successive q-terms and see what pattern emerges:

$$q_2 = q_1(1-\theta)$$
$$q_3 = q_2(1-\theta) = q_1(1-\theta)^2$$
$$q_4 = q_3(1-\theta) = q_1(1-\theta)^3$$

. .

. .

. .

(3) $q_n = q_1(1-\theta)^{n-1}$

The correctness of this conjecture can be verified by resubstitution into Eq. (2). Many other statistics could be derived for this model, but this one example will do for the moment.

The assumption that learning is all-or-none naturally leads to a two-state Markov model (Bower, 1961). Basically, the model assumes that an item can be in either one of two states: it is learned or it is not learned. On each learning trial there is a certain probability c that the item becomes learned, i.e., it leaves the initial state and enters the learning state. There is no provision for forgetting in this simple model (nor is there in the previous model); once an item is in the learning state, it remains there. If an item is in the learning state, a correct response occurs; if an item is in the initial state, a correct response occurs with probability $(1 - p)$ and an error occurs with probability p. The learning rate c and the probability of an error in the initial state p do not change over trials.

The axioms of the model may be stated formally as follows:

1. **State Axiom:** On each trial an item is either in the initial state I or in the learning state L.

2. **Learning Axioms:** On Trial 1 all items are in state I. Whenever a stimulus-response pair is presented jointly, the item may become conditioned to that response with probability c, i.e., it enters the learning state L. L is an absorbing state, that is, an item remains in L once it enters it.

3. **Response Axioms:** If an item is in state L the correct response is always made; if it is in state I, errors occur with probability p and successes with probability $(1-p)$.

4. **Constancy Axiom:** p and c are independent of the trial number n.

It is convenient to express these axioms in the form of a *transition matrix*. The rows of this matrix correspond to states L and I on trial n, the columns to the same states on trial $(n + 1)$; entries show the probability of a transition from the row state to the column state on any trial:

$$(4) \qquad \begin{array}{cc} & \begin{array}{ccc} \text{L} & \text{I} & Pr(\text{error}) \end{array} \\ \begin{array}{c} \text{L} \\ \text{I} \end{array} & \begin{bmatrix} 1 & 0 \\ c & 1-c \end{bmatrix} \begin{bmatrix} 0 \\ p \end{bmatrix} \end{array}$$

A *starting vector* [0,1] provides the information that items start with probability 1 in state I. Equation (4) is to be read as follows: the first row says that if an item is in L, it will always remain in L; the probability of an error on that trial is 0; if an item is in I, it will go to L with probability c and stay in I with probability $(1-c)$; the probability of an error in I is p.

This model is called a Markov model because, in general, processes are called Markovian if they have discrete states and transition probabilities between these states that depend only upon the state in which the process is at the moment.

In order to derive the predicted mean learning curve from this model, note that an error can occur on trial n only if the item is still in state I on that trial. The probability that an item does not leave state I on a trial is $(1-c)$, the probability that it is not learned on that trial. Hence the probability that an item is still in State I after $(n-1)$ trials is $(1-c)$ taken $(n-1)$ times, or $(1-c)^{n-1}$. If an item is in I, an error occurs with probability p. Hence the mean learning curve is given by

$$(5) \qquad Pr(\text{error on trial } n) = p(1-c)^{n-1}$$

Equation (5) is identical with Eq. (3), the mean learning curve for the linear model. This simply means, as was pointed out before, that as far as the distinction between incremental and all-or-none processes is concerned, mean learning curves are worthless. They do not differentiate between alternatives.

The models are clearly distinct with respect to behavior on trials before the last error. According to the two-state Markov model, errors occur only in the initial state I; hence at least up to and including the trial of the last error an item must have been in state I. (It is impossible that an item may have left I and later returned: once I has been left, return is impossible according to the model.) The important point now is that in state I the probability of an error is constant and does not depend upon the trial number. Thus, the all-or-none model predicts no improvement in response probability up to the trial of the last error. This prediction is called the *stationarity* prediction. According to the linear model, performance on trials before the last error is not stationary, since response probability rises continuously on every trial, and there is nothing special about the last error in any particular response sequence.

How can one test the stationarity prediction? The most obvious procedure would be to look at each item sequence separately and to determine whether response probability on trials before the last error is indeed a constant or not. However, in paired-associate learning typically only a few errors are made for each item; therefore not enough data are available from a single item to provide a serious test of the stationarity hypothesis. Thus, we depend upon proper averaging responses from many items but omitting the last error and all later responses, as shown in Table 2.3(a). If precriterion performance is stationary, no incremental trend should be present in data thus averaged. Alternatively, one can use the trial of the last error as a reference point to construct a backward learning curve, as shown in Table 2.3(b). The portion of the curve to the right of the last error is of course entirely an artifact of the averaging method employed, but stationarity may be examined on the trials before the last error. Suppes and Ginsberg (1963) have pointed to a possible source of confounding in this way of plotting learning curves. In a plot such as the one shown in Table 2.3(a) the number of data points upon which successive points are based decreases as more and more items are learned and are therefore omitted from the calculations. The last points of the curve are based upon those items which were learned last, i.e., the hardest items. It is conceivable that the later portions of the curve are depressed because they are based upon the most difficult items,

Table 2.3. *An analysis of the trials before the last error for the data of Table 2.1.*

(a) *Performance on trials before the last error.*

Items	1	2	3	4	5	6	7	8	9	10	11	12
1												
2	1	0	1	1								
3	0	1	1	0	0	0	1	0				
4												
5	0	1	0	1	0	1						
6												
7	1	0										
8	0											
9												
10	1											
Frequency of errors	3	2	2	2	0	1	1	0				
Total frequency	6	4	3	3	2	2	1	1				
Proportion of errors	.50	.50	.66	.66	.00	.50	1.00	.00				

(b) *The backward learning curve. Trials before the last error.*

Items	−9	−8	−7	−6	−5	−4	−3	−2	−1	Last Error
1										
2						1	0	1	1	1
3		0	1	1	0	0	0	1	0	1
4										
5				0	1	0	1	0	1	1
6										
7								1	0	1
8									0	1
9										
10									1	1
Frequency of errors		0	1	1	1	1	1	3	3	
Total frequency		1	1	2	2	3	3	4	6	
Proportion of errors		.00	1.00	.50	.50	.33	.33	.75	.50	

Table 2.3 (Continued)

(c) *The Vincent curve.*

Items	First Half					Second Half			
2		1	0				1	1	
3	0	1	1	0		0	0	1	0
5		0	1	0			1	0	1
7		1					0		
Frequency of errors		5					5		
Total frequency		10					10		
Proportion of errors		.50					.50		

and that therefore any incremental trends in the data are masked by this effect. The backward leaning curve is similarly confounded with item difficulty. Suppes and Ginsberg (1963) have suggested the construction of Vincent curves to avoid this confounding. In a Vincent curve each learning sequence contributes equally to each point of the curve irrespective of the length of the sequence. For instance, short sequences such as those obtained in paired-associate experiments may be divided into halves, and the number of errors and successes in each half may be counted and averaged over all sequences. Thus, each sequence contributes equally to both points of the Vincent curve. If sequences of sufficient length are available, they may be partitioned into 3, 4, or even 10 equal parts to yield Vincent curves of 3, 4, or 10 points, respectively. A chi-square test can be employed to test the hypothesis that the proportion of errors is the same for all points of the curve. The sample data of Table 1 are Vincentized into halves in Part (c) of Table 2.3.

In an experiment by Kintsch (1965) 32 subjects (college students) learned a list of 10 paired-associate items to a criterion of 2 errorless trials. Stimuli were high association value nonsense syllables, and the numbers 1 and 2 served as responses. The anticipation procedure was used. The average number of errors per item for all items and for only those items for which the last error had not yet occurred are shown in Fig. 2.3. It does not show the regular decrease of the mean learning curve but fluctuates around a line somewhat below $\frac{1}{2}$. The deviations from this line are not statistically significant ($\chi^2 = 4.68$, 5 *df*, $p > .30$). When the responses before the last error were divided into equal halves, values of .50 and .47 were obtained for the first and second half of the trials, respectively. With a chi-square of .53 for 1 *df*, these values are not significantly different from each other. The conclusion is therefore justified that in this experiment learning was not an incremental process, but occurred in an all-or-none manner.

There are a number of experiments in the literature which support this conclusion since the all-or-none model was first applied to paired-associate learning by Bower (1961, 1962). However, stationarity is observed only when the experiment is of the particularly simple type described here, that is, the stimuli are easily discriminable and, most importantly, there are only 2 response alternatives and the subject is told what they are.

Another prediction of the all-or-none model which may be easily examined also concerns performance on the trials before the last error. On those trials, an item is in the initial state I, and, according to the assumptions of the model, correct responses in this state occur with probability $(1 - p)$, whereas errors are made with probability p. Responses on successive trials are assumed to be independent, just as if they were determined by tosses of a biased coin which comes up "correct" with probability $(1 - p)$. More specifically, the conditional probability of a correct response on any trial n given an error on the previous trial $(n - 1)$ should be equal to the conditional probability

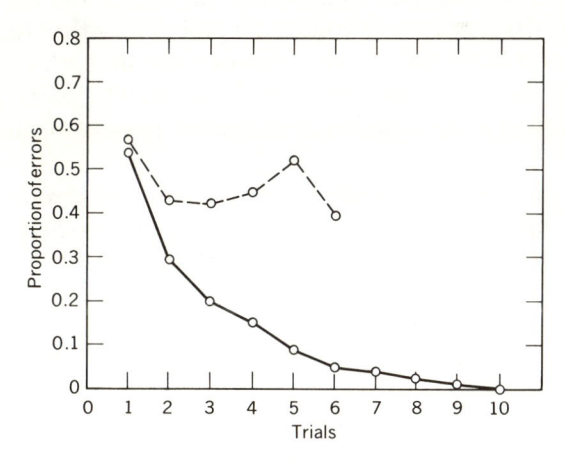

Fig. 2.3 *Proportion of errors on all trials and proportion of errors on trials before the last error.*

of a correct response on trial n given a correct response on trial (n − 1). Table 2.4 illustrates these calculations for the sample data provided earlier, the two desired statistics being 6/8 and 2/8, respectively. In the experiment mentioned above we obtain $Pr(0_{n+1} \mid 1_n) = .50$ and $Pr(0_{n+1} \mid 0_n) = .61$, where 0's and 1's denote correct responses and errors respectively. A statistical test shows that these two values are significantly different. Precriterion responses are therefore not independent, but successes tend to follow successes. This failure of the model need not deter us from further analysis. It is hardly likely that a model as simple as the present one can give a completely satisfactory account of paired-associate learning, but before one can make the model more realistic it is necessary to determine how far its simplest version can be pushed, and exactly where it breaks down.

Bower (1961) has derived many quantitative predictions from the simple all-or-none model for statistics such as the mean learning curve, the total number of errors per item, and others discussed above. A few derivations will be shown here as examples of the methods used.

The most informative statistic is the predicted distribution of the number of errors per item (sample calculations were presented in Table 2.2(a)). The derivation proceeds in two steps. First, we calculate the probability which we shall call b that no more errors will occur after a trial in state I. This can occur in several ways; first, if the item is learned, which has probability c; second, if the item is not learned on the first trial but a correct response occurs anyway, and the item is learned on the second trial—the corresponding probability is $(1-c)(1-p)c$; next we consider the probability that the item is not learned for two trials but correct guesses occur on both of these trials, and learning occurs on the third trial: $(1-c)^2(1-p)^2c$; in the same way, we consider the possibility that correct guesses occur on the first

Table 2.4. *Frequency of successes and errors after successes and errors on the previous trials for trials up to the last error.*

		Trial $n+1$		
		0	1	
	0	2	6	8
Trial n				
	1	6	2	8
		8	8	16

three trials and the item is learned on the fourth trial, and so on, *ad infinitum.* The total probability of no more errors after a trial in state I is then the sum of all these terms:

$$b = c + (1-c)\ (1-p)c + (1-c)^2(1-p)^2c + (1-c)^3(1-p)^3c + \ldots$$

$$= c[1 + (1-c)\ (1-p) + (1-c)^2(1-p)^2 + (1-c)^3(1-p)^3 + \ldots]$$

The term in brackets is simply the sum of an infinite geometric series and we obtain

$$(6) \qquad b = \frac{c}{1 - (1-c)\ (1-p)}$$

The theoretical distributions of errors per item can then be expressed as

$$(7) \qquad Pr(T=k) = (1-p)b \qquad\qquad \text{for } k = 0$$

$$= [1 - (1-p)b]\ (1-b)^{k-1}b \quad \text{for } k \geq 1$$

The probability that no errors are made is easy to understand: with probability $(1-p)$ a success occurs on the first trial, and with probability b no further errors occur; the second expression is to be interpreted as follows: the first term $[1 - (1-p)b]$ makes sure that at least one error occurs; the second term $(1-b)^{k-1}$ provides for the next $(k-1)$ errors; and the last term b insures that no further errors occur after that.

Equation (7) is important because it shows that the predicted error distribution for the all-or-none model is geometric: it has a maximum (depending upon the values of c and p) either at 0 or 1, and from there decreases by a fraction $(1-b)$ for every value of k. This is a general property of all-or-none models and reflects the constancy axiom in a quite direct way. Hence it is a very useful statistic for empirical tests of the model.

The mean number of errors per item can be obtained from Eq. (7) by standard methods. Alternatively, the same expression can be calculated by adding up the error proportions for all trials as given by Eq. (4):

$$(8) \qquad E(\text{errors per item}) = \sum_{n=1}^{\infty} Pr(\text{error on trial } n)$$

$$= \sum_{n=1}^{\infty} p(1-c)^{n-1} = \frac{p}{c}$$

Note that the summation above is taken over all values of n, while in any actual experiment only a finite number of trials can be given. However, once an item enters the learning state L no more errors occur and we assume that our learning criterion is sufficiently strict so that when a subject reaches criterion all items are in L.

Another useful statistic which can be easily derived from the model is the probability that the last error will be made on trial k, $Pr(n' = k)$. (Sample calculations are shown in Table 2.2(c).) Again, we make use of b, the expression for the probability of no more errors after a trial in state I. If no errors are made at all, we say that the last error occurred on Trial 0. For the last error to be made on the kth trial, we must make sure that the item has not left state I on the previous $(k-1)$ trials—which has probability $(1-c)^{k-1}$; then, an error must occur on the kth trial—errors in state I have probability p; finally, no more errors may occur after that trial—which is b, as calculated above. Hence we have

$$(9) \qquad Pr(n' = k) = (1-p)b \qquad \text{for } k = 0$$
$$= (1-c)^{k-1}pb \qquad \text{for } k \geq 1$$

It can be shown that the mean of the distribution of the trial of last error is

$$(10) \qquad E(n') = \sum_{k=0}^{\infty} k\,Pr(n'{=}k) = \frac{pb}{c^2} = \frac{1/c}{1+c(q/p)}$$

where $q = 1 - p$.

As a final example, we shall derive the predicted number of errors before the first correct response, $(Pr(J{=}k))$. The probability that the first success is made on trial 1 is $(1-p)$. If the first success occurs on trial k, three conditions must be met: an error must be made on the first trial (p); errors must be made on the next $(k-1)$ trials $[p^{k-1}(1-c)^{k-1}]$; and the sequence must be terminated by a success $[1-p(1-c)]$. Thus

$$(11) \qquad Pr(J{=}k) = (1-p) \qquad\qquad \text{for } k = 1$$
$$= p[p(1-c)]^{k-1}\,[1-p(1-c)] \qquad \text{for } k > 1$$

The mean and variance of this distribution can be obtained by standard methods (e.g., Atkinson and Estes, 1963, p. 135): The predicted mean is

$$(12) \qquad E(J) = \sum_{k=1}^{\infty} k\,Pr(J{=}k) = \frac{p}{1 - p(1 - c)}$$

If the predictions just derived from the model, as well as many others which are derived in the original report by Bower (1961), are to be compared with statistics calculated from experimental data, the parameters c and p must be estimated. There are a number of different techniques available in mathematical psychology for parameter estimation, differing greatly in sophistication, adequacy, and complexity (Atkinson, Bower, and Crothers, 1965). For present purposes a simple procedure will be used which is easy to understand, even if it has few desirable statistical properties. The parameter p may be determined *a priori:* there are two response alternatives in the experiment, hence the probability of an incorrect guess $p = \frac{1}{2}$. Alternatively, one might estimate p from the observed probability of an error on trials before the last error. For the data of Kintsch (1965) we obtain $p = .49$. The small deviation from the *a priori* value may be taken as a sampling error in the data. The estimate for c is obtained by setting the observed mean number of errors per item equal to Eq. (8) and solving for c: 1.39 errors were made per item on the average, therefore

$$1.39 = \frac{p}{c} = \frac{.49}{c}$$

and

$$c = .35$$

These estimates can be substituted into the expressions derived above as well as into other expressions presented in the original source. The numerical predictions obtained in this way are compared with the corresponding data statistics in Table 2.5 and Figs. 2.4-2.6. Obviously, the model fits the data quite well. A statistical test of the goodness of fit of the predicted distributions in Figs. 2.4-2.6 confirms this im-

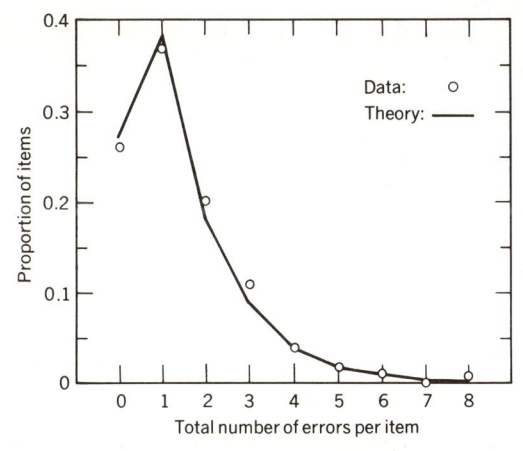

Fig. 2.4 *Distribution of the total number of errors per item.*

Table 2.5. *Paired-associate data and predictions from the all-or-none model.*

	Observed	Predicted
Mean number of errors	1.39	—
Standard deviation	1.11	1.40
Mean number of trials before the first success	.79	.79
Standard deviation	.95	.98
Mean trial of last error	2.05	2.07
Standard deviation	2.07	2.34
Total number of error runs	.96	.95
Error runs of length 1	.66	.65
Error runs of length 2	.21	.21
Error runs of length 3	.05	.05
Error runs of length 4	.02	.02

pression: in no case can the null hypothesis of no difference between observed and predicted values be rejected by the Kolmogorov-Smirnov test, the probability of differences as large or larger than that observed being at least .20. However, all predicted standard deviations are somewhat larger than the observed values, in spite of the adequate fit of the distributions.

Although the model is directly relevant only to the sequence of correct and incorrect responses of the subject, it seems reasonable to

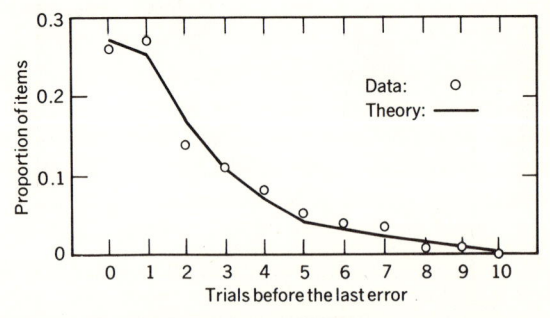

Fig. 2.5 *Distribution of trials before the last error.*

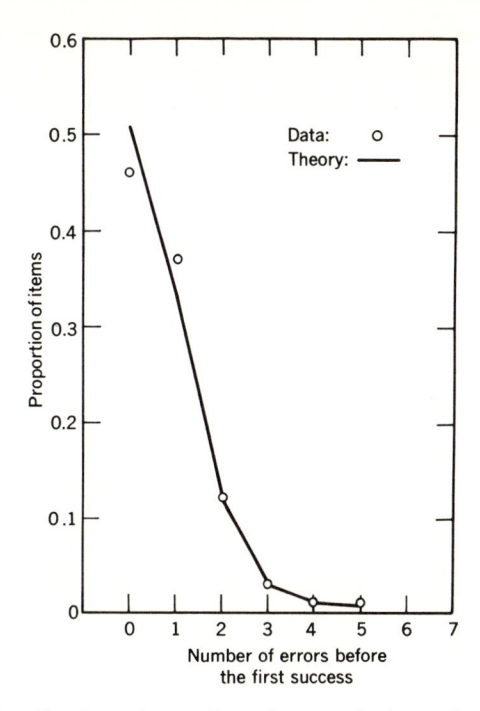

Fig. 2.6 *Distribution of number of errors before the first sucess.*

suppose that if the model reflects psychological reality, other aspects of the learning process might be correlated with the states and the transition between states postulated by the model. Millward (1964) has shown that response latencies in simple paired-associate learning do exhibit such a correlation. Millward plotted response latency in the manner of a backward learning curve. He obtained the average latency for the trial of the last error, for items 1, 2, . . . trials before the last error, as well as for items 1, 2, . . . trials after the last error. He found that on trials before the last error the latency was large and did not change much, but that after the last error, response latencies decreased rapidly to an asymptotic value. This finding has been replicated in a number of other studies. In addition, it has been observed that the maximum response latency occurs at the trial of the last error (Suppes, Groen, and Schlag-Rey, 1966, summarized several sets of relevant data). These findings clearly support the assumption of two distinct states. Latencies are high initially and stay high as long as the item is not learned. On the trial of the last error, which for many items is also the trial on which learning occurs, latencies increase sharply. Afterwards, latencies accelerate and finally reach an asymptotic value. The gradual decline of latencies after the last error is no embarrassment to the all-or-none model. Depending upon the exact assumptions which one makes about the latency mechanism, Markov models can very well account for such a decrease. However, there exists no logical necessity why continuous and discrete processes should not both be considered simultaneously: it is not unreasonable to assume that when an item is in the learning state as far as response probabilities are concerned, response latencies undergo a continuous decline. What is interesting, and what may be regarded as strong support for the all-or-none model, is that response probabilities and latencies change dramatically at the same point in the learning process—upon transition from an initial state to the learning state.

The galvanic skin response during paired-associate learning behaves in very much the same way (Kintsch, 1965). Whenever an alert subject is presented with a stimulus, he reacts to it with an orienting reflex (Pavlov, 1928). The orienting reflex is a nonspecific response, consisting of a number of components one of which is the galvanic skin response (Sokolov, 1963). One characteristic of the orienting reflex is that it habituates rapidly when the same stimulus is presented repeatedly. Repeated presentation of a stimulus is, of course, essential to a learning experiment and a question arises concerning the course of habituation of the orienting reflex during learning. It is possible that habituation is not at all affected by learning instructions. On the other hand, it seems more likely that some relationship between the two psychological processes exists. If so, the all-or-none model tells us how to look for such a relationship. In the experiment of Kintsch (1965) subjects learned to associate 12 nonsense syllables with the responses 1 or 2. Whenever an item was presented the temporary change in the subject's resistance level (GSR) was measured. When the average GSR was computed as a function of learning trials no particularly interesting effects emerged. However, when items were arranged before averaging with the last error as a reference point in the manner of a backward learning curve, an interesting relationship between the habituation of the GSR and learning could be observed. On trials before the last error, subjects reacted with a rather large GSR to the presentation of an item, and there seemed to be some tendency for the GSR to increase during those trials. After the last error, habituation set in and reactions declined in magnitude. These results parallel the latency data reported above. The postulated transition between learning states apparently represents an important reference point not only for response probabilities but also for other aspects of the total response of the subject, such as response latencies and the orienting reflex.

The all-or-none model for paired-associate learning is certainly one of the more successful theories in psychology: in several published experiments an impressive fit to the learning data has been demonstrated, and lawful relationships between latencies and orienting responses and the inferred structure of the learning process have been found. In spite of such achievements, the model is incomplete as a theory of paired-associate learning. Its range of applicability is restricted to a very simple experimental situation: item lists of moderate length with two response alternatives which are known to the subject beforehand. As soon as one goes beyond this restricted situation, the model is likely to fail. We have already stressed the need to keep the experimental task simple if one wants to observe all-or-none learning. In particular, it is necessary to exclude response learning, and in a number of tests of predictions of the all-or-none model this precaution has not been observed. Failures of the model in such cases are, of course, hardly instructive. However, even when subjects know the response alternatives but there are more than two responses the model can no longer adequately describe the learning data. Performance before the last error in paired-associate experiments with more than two known response alternatives is often not stationary (Suppes and Ginsberg, 1963; Atkinson and Crothers, 1964). A common observation, especially when Vincentized backward learning curves are considered, is that performance increases somewhat just before the trial of the last error. Binford and Gettys (1965) demonstrated that paired-associate learning is not all-or-none when there are more than 2 responses with a second-guess procedure. When subjects are permitted to make a second guess after every error, the all-or-none model predicts that second guesses should be no better than chance. This prediction was clearly wrong. Not only were second guesses correct with greater than chance frequency, but they improved during the course of learning from about chance level at the beginning of the experiment to around 90% correct just before the trial of the last error.

Possibly negative findings such as these mean that the model cannot be extended beyond a very simple situation. This would imply that the good results obtained in that situation were probably due to some trivial circumstance without general interest. On the other hand, a strong argument can be made that the model describes the basic learning process and that the failures of the model arise because the model is applied to situations where the learning process is not unitary, and hence not all-or-none. Such a viewpoint implies that one can show that learning can be decomposed into all-or-none subprocesses. Several recent attempts to analyze complex learning processes into elementary units have demonstrated the fruitfulness of this approach.

All-or-none Subprocesses of Complex Learning

The troublesome failure of the simple all-or-none model in the case of more than two response alternatives which are well known to the subject may be reconsidered in terms of the argument presented above. Perhaps it represents not a failure of the learning assumptions of the model but a poor analysis of the total learning situation. In such experiments a subject may be doing more than just acquiring correct associations. For instance, a subject who learned a list of common words paired one-to-one with the numbers 1-8 was observed using her fingers to mark whenever a particular response number came up on each trial. In this way, whenever she was uncertain she could try one of the responses not yet excluded, which markedly improved her chances of guessing correctly. Similarly, subjects may not use already learned response alternatives for guessing. Clearly, the chance level would increase during the course of an experiment if subjects use such a strategy, resulting in the nonstationary precriterion performance typically observed in these experiments. Suppose, therefore, that learning proceeds as postulated, but that when there are more than two response alternatives the subject may learn not only which response is correct, but also to eliminate incorrect alternatives. Millward (1964) and Nahinski (1967) have explored such error elimination models and concluded that by reanalyzing the situation, rather than the learning assumptions, models could be obtained which can account adequately for phenomena such as increases in precriterion performance, or second guess data.

The evidence for a distinction between a response learning and an association stage of paired-associate learning has already been discussed. Since the associative stage of learning may be described as an all-or-none model, it appears possible that a two-stage process of which each stage is an all-or-none step could account for the total learning process. Kintsch (1963) has developed such a model and shown that it fits the data quite well. His experimental data came from an 8-item paired-associate list with nonsense syllables as stimuli and two-place numbers as responses. Some response learning was thus required, because subjects had to learn which numbers served as responses in the experiment. As expected, the all-or-none model could not describe the data adequately. For instance, performance before the last error was not stationary. A two-stage model, on the other hand, did quite well. In this model items are thought to be in an initial state at the beginning of the experiment where neither responses nor associations are known. Therefore, the probability of a correct response is zero as long as an item remains in the initial state. The intermediate state is a partial learning state in which the response is available but not yet hooked up to the correct stimulus item. Correct responses occur with some probability $(1-p)$ in this state, and errors occur with probability p. The third state of the model is a learning state in which responses are always correct. Transitions between states occur with fixed probabilities and are independent of the trial numbers. Thus a three-state Markov model is obtained and predictions for various learning statistics may be derived in the same manner as for the two-state model. Note, for instance, that although performance before the last error is no longer stationary, stationarity should hold for performance in the intermediate state. A test of this prediction is obtained by computing Vincentized learning curves for the data between the subject's first correct response on a particular item and his last error on that item.

However, more interesting than a mere demonstration of the goodness of fit of the model was a successful application of the two-stage model to an experimental design introduced by Rock (1957). Rock had devised an ingenious experimental procedure for demonstrating all-or-none processes in paired-associate learning. He argued that if learning is all-or-none, replacing an item with a new one whenever an error occurs should not interfere with learning at all, and in fact he found that a paired-associate list was learned with such a substitution procedure just as easily as a control list in which the same items were presented on all trials. Although Rock's findings were replicated a number of times, his conclusions came under much attack (Williams, 1961; Underwood, Rehula, and Keppel, 1962; Postman, 1963). It could be argued that list difficulty was a source of confounding in this experimental design. Subjects tend to make errors on the most difficult items, which were then replaced with new items. On the average, new items will be easier to learn than the ones discarded and therefore subjects in the substitution group end up learning an easier list than subjects in the control group. A proper control subject would learn a list composed of the same items which were finally learned by a subject in the substitution group. Using such a control, it was shown that the substitution procedure actually did retard learning. In the same vein Battig (1962) showed that differences between a conventional control group and a substitution group could be detected if the learning material was carefully selected for homogeneity so as to minimize item-selection artifacts. This finding could be very serious for the concept of all-or-none learning, except for the fact that in the critical studies learning tasks involving both response learning and association were used. The all-or-none model is therefore not applicable, but the two-stage model correctly predicts the slower learning with the substitution procedure. Whenever an error occurs for an item which is already in the intermediate state, this item will be replaced by a new item, and hence a loss occurs. However, a mathematical model is not limited to such qualitative predictions. It is a simple task to rewrite the model taking into account the procedural change brought about by the substitution method and to derive exact quantitative predictions for the course of learning with this procedure. This can be done without estimating any of the model parameters from the data of the experimental group, because one should be able to transfer the parameter estimates obtained from control subjects learning the same kind of material with a regular paired-associate procedure. This was done in two experiments by Kintsch (1963). In both cases the retardation of learning with the substitution procedure could be predicted accurately from the two-stage model.

Although we have been talking about response learning and association stages, no direct experimental evidence exists which would permit an unambiguous identification of the two stages of the model in this manner. All that has been shown is that a two-stage model describes paired-associate learning better than a one-stage model when response learning is involved, and that, in addition, it can account for the results obtained with Rock's substitution procedure. It seems plausible, of course, to identify the two stages of the model as response learning and association, but such an interpretation would be strengthened if the two stages could be separated experimentally. This has not yet been done in the present case, but Polson, Restle, and Polson (1965) have reported a related experimental application of a two-stage model where such a separation was successfully achieved. In their experiment response learning was avoided by using a response set familiar to the subject, but a stimulus discrimination stage was added to the association phase of the experiment.

Polson, Restle, and Polson (1965) used a mixed list design. Sixteen simple line drawings served as stimulus material. Eight stimuli were unique and the others consisted of four confusable pairs, such as two slightly different diamonds, two Chinese characters with one small change, etc. Five common words were randomly assigned to these stimuli as responses with the restriction that twin items never received the same response. All subjects were familiarized with the five response words before the beginning of the experiment proper. Items were presented in random order for as many trials as necessary to reach a criterion of two successive correct trials.

Unique and confusable items were analyzed separately. Learning of the unique items was quite well described by the simple all-or-none model, except for a slight improvement in performance on trials before the last error, as is typically obtained with more than two response alternatives. The analysis of the confusable items was based upon a distinction between two kinds of errors. Since twin items never had the same response, confusion errors within stimulus pairs could be scored separately from nonconfusion errors. The nonconfusion errors represent failures of association. When a confusion error is made, the subject obviously has established an association between a stimulus pair and a response, but cannot yet discriminate between the two similar stimuli of the pair.

According to the two-stage model, since nonconfusion errors are made in the associative phase of learning, they should not be different from the errors made in the case of the unique items. Therefore it should be possible to predict the nonconfusion errors from the simple all-or-none model, using the parameter estimates obtained from the unique items. Indeed, Polson *et al.* have shown that such predictions fitted the data very well. As for the confusion errors, the authors could show by an analysis of the total number of confusion errors per item that they too were generated by an all-or-none process. On the other hand, when performance on the confusable items was analyzed without distinguishing between different kinds of errors, the all-or-none model was clearly inappropriate; for instance, it has been shown in (7) that the all-or-none model implies a distribution of errors per item which is geometric. The error data obtained here however, were clearly not geometric. A two-stage model was necessary to describe them.

A study by Bregman and Chambers (1966) which is somewhat different in approach and not directly concerned with paired-associate learning provides a third example for the technique of analyzing a complex learning process into all-or-none subprocesses. The authors start with the observation that when a recognition procedure is used in a paired-associate experiment (subjects are given all stimulus and response items on a test trial and asked to match them) subject's second guesses contain more information about the correct stimulus and response pairing than could be accounted for on the basis of random guessing. However, in studies showing this effect (Bregman, 1966) learning materials such as word pairs were used and it is possible that partial learning may have occurred. In support of this hypothesis the authors relate an observation by Bartlett (1932) who found that one of his subjects could remember that he had seen a head in profile rather than full face, but had forgotten whether it was in left or right profile. Apparently, such attributes of the stimulus as "profile" and "right" could be remembered independently of each other. Hence it is possible that attributes rather than the stimulus pair as such represent the primitive elements of memory which are learned in an all-or-none manner. Total learning would then be a gradual process, since ordinarily several attributes must be learned before a stimulus can be identified properly.

In an experiment to test this hypothesis Bregman and Chambers used stimulus material which consisted of geometric figures which differed along three dimensions, such as color, form, and borders. Seven different values were used for each dimension. In order for the experiment to succeed it was imperative that subjects actually perceive the stimulus material as intended by the experimenter. Hence subjects were given extensive pretraining before the beginning of the experiment proper: they were instructed about the three dimensions used in the construction of the stimulus material and what the values were on each dimension, and they learned to manipulate the material in several ways—all with the express purpose of biasing the subject in favor of encoding the stimulus material in the way suggested by the experimenter. After this, seven stimulus items were formed by randomly combining one color, one border, and one form for each item. Each item was presented to the subject for four seconds and then a test was administered by the method of reconstruction. The seven colors, seven borders, and seven forms were drawn on sheets of plastic and presented to the subject with the instruction to recombine the seven original items, guessing if necessary. Thus the subject assembled seven stacks of three plastic sheets, one from each dimension. After each test, the experimenter separated incorrectly assembled stacks and permitted subjects to make another guess. Finally, subjects were questioned as to how they perceived the stimulus material, in particular whether they used subcategories (such as "warm colors").

The principal results of this study concern the question whether or not second guesses were better than chance. To calculate guessing probabilities in this rather complex situation is by no means a trivial task, and the reader is referred to the original source for the method used. For those subjects who perceived the learning material in the way the experimenter intended, i.e., those who did not use idiosyncratic subcategories, second guesses did not differ from chance expectancy. On the other hand, subjects who violated the boundary conditions of the experiment, that is, subcategorizers, performed better than chance on their second guess. However, the authors could show that if the information about idiosyncratic subcategories is taken into account in calculating guessing probabilities, second guess performance again was random. These findings present impressive support for the notion that attributes are indeed the primitive elements of learning and are learned all-or-none. Note that great care must be taken before one can identify an attribute with some aspect of the physical stimulus, because each particular subject's perceptual and inferential biases must be considered.

A number of other attempts to break down complex learning processes into all-or-none subprocesses have been reported, both in paired-associate learning and related areas (Suppes and Ginsberg, 1963; Bower and Theios, 1964; Restle, 1964) and in the field of animal learning (Theios, 1963; Theios and Brelsford, 1966). This approach offers considerable promise, especially when the stages or subprocesses can be given a psychological interpretation. Further use will be made of the results of this section in later discussions. Thus, we shall rely heavily upon analyses in terms of Markov models when the interaction between learning and forgetting is taken up in Chapter 4. The idea that gradual learning may be broken down into all-or-none learning of components will appear again in connection with Bower's multicomponent theory of retention (Bower, 1967). Stage interpretations of paired-associate learning and recall are discussed again in Chapter 5. In Chapter 7 the two-state Markov model (Eq.(4)) is applied to concept learning. On other occasions, however, when learning situations appear to be more complex and are less easily analyzed into subprocesses, learning will be represented as an incremental process. The question posed initially, whether learning is all-or-none or incremental thus turns out to be badly put. The true problem seems to be: under what conditions should learning be represented as an all-or-none process, under what conditions can it be represented as the sum of several all-or-none substages, and under what conditions is a genuine incremental model appropriate?

4. COMPUTER SIMULATION OF STIMULUS DISCRIMINATION

Stimulus Discrimination Theory

In 1940 Gibson formulated a theory of stimulus discrimination which may be regarded as an application of Hull's theory to verbal learning (Hull, 1943). Gibson's theory was very influential for almost two decades, but then suffered some neglect. Underwood reviewed the theory in 1961 and concluded that it had lost its usefulness, partly because parts of it were shown to be empirically wrong, but mostly because the theory had become irrelevant for too many of the problems in the area of verbal learning. However, recent work on computer simulation of verbal learning has led to a renewal of interest in stimulus discrimination and differentiation and to a revival of Gibson's theory in modern form, or, rather, a new theory with stimulus discrimination as a central mechanism (Feigenbaum, 1963).

Gibson (1940) suggested that paired-associate learning may best be understood as a process of discrimination among the stimulus items which are to be learned. Stimuli are confused with each other because of stimulus generalization. If response R is associated with stimulus S, stimulus S', which is similar to S, will also elicit R because of generalization effects. The only way to discriminate between the stimuli is through differential reinforcement, i.e., by establishing a connection not only between S and R but also between S' and R'. Stimulus generalization takes place on a dimension of similarity. By not specifying the concept of similarity in terms of an underlying stimulus continuum, Gibson achieved considerable flexibility for the theory.

The theory also included a postulate concerning spontaneous recovery of generalization tendencies which will be neglected here since it is contradicted by the empirical evidence (Underwood, 1961). Instead, a number of predictions from the theory which do not involve this postulate will be discussed and some of the experiments performed to test these predictions will be described. A very obvious prediction can be derived from the theory concerning intralist similarity. Clearly, the greater the similarity, the stronger will be generalization tendencies. This prediction is in agreement with some experimental results which were reported earlier (Gibson, 1942; Underwood, 1953). However, as Underwood (1961) points out, even with perfect discriminability among stimuli, and hence no generalization at all, wide differences in learning occur as a function of other factors, such as differences in responses. The theory is therefore correct as far as it goes, but it is severely limited.

If a paired-associate list with stimulus terms A and responses B is learned first, and then a second list A'—B is learned, Gibson's theory predicts positive transfer as a function of the similarity between A and A'. If A' is similar to A, it will elicit the response B because of generalization even before the learning of the second list starts, and hence second list learning will be facilitated. A number of studies confirm this prediction, e.g., Bruce (1933). Bruce had three groups of subjects learn two paired-associate lists each. A control group learned two unrelated lists (A—B, C—D), one of the experimental groups learned two lists with common stimulus terms (A—B, A—C), and the other experimental group learned two lists with common response terms according to the paradigm under discussion here (A—B, C—B). When learning of the second list in the three groups is compared, it was found that common stimulus terms in the two lists made the list harder relative to the control group, but that common response terms led to much faster learning, in agreement with the prediction made above. Other evidence, including some studies where similarity between the two lists was varied systematically, is also in agreement with Gibson's prediction, but again the theory is not sufficiently complete: the facilitation of second list learning is most noticeable on the first trials of learning, while on later trials other factors, not accounted for by the theory, dominate the learning process (Underwood, 1961).

Bruce's group which learned two lists with identical stimulus terms but different responses illustrates another transfer paradigm which may be analyzed in terms of Gibson's theory. However, theoretical predictions in this case are somewhat ambigous, because the theory identifies two opposing effects, and it is not clear which influence would dominate in any particular case. On the one hand we expect negative transfer. In an (A—B, A'—C) design the B response appropriate to the A stimulus will generalize to the similar A' stimulus and interfere with second-list learning. In fact, this experimental paradigm is used to demonstrate proactive inhibition: learning List 1 interferes with learning List 2. On the other hand subjects who have leaned a list A—B will make fewer errors in learning a list A'—C which are due to intralist generalization because they have already learned to discriminate the A-items. This effect has been called stimulus predifferentiation and is exactly opposed to the effects of proactive inhibition. Attempts to demonstrate stimulus predifferentiation have been ambiguous. The effects of stimulus prefamiliarization should be purely positive if one can avoid attaching specific responses to stimuli during prefamiliarization which will later interfere with A—C learning. Gannon and Noble (1961) have reported that repeated presentation of the stimulus terms before paired-associate learning facilitates learning, but Underwood and Schulz (1960) did not obtain such an effect. In general, the experimental evidence in this area is confusing, which probably means that the relevant variables have not yet been identified. The theory's corresponding inability to specify when to expect positive transfer because of predifferentiation and when to expect negative transfer because of proactive inhibition illustrates the need for a more precise statement of a theory so that quantitative predictions are possible.

Computer Simulation

Recently Feigenbaum (Feigenbaum, 1963; Simon and Feigenbaum, 1964) has developed a theory of verbal learning which also places the main emphasis upon discrimination processes. However, apart from the concern with discrimination processes the work of Gibson shows little similarity to that of Feigenbaum. While Gibson came from the tradition of Hullian learning theory, Feigenbaum's orientation is toward cognitive psychology. He is concerned with the information processing characteristics of the human organism rather than with conditioning principles. And last but not least, the two authors chose completely different ways to state their theories. Gibson stated her theory verbally, in the form of a Hullian postulate system. The basic theory is contained in nine postulates, from which a number of experimental propositions are then derived and tested against whatever data were available at that time. Feigenbaum, on the other hand, states his theory in the form of a computer program. His computer program corresponds to Gibson's postulate set. But instead of deriving theorems from a postulate set, Feigenbaum lets the computer simulate human behavior. Essentially, the computer is used as a subject in verbal learning experiments. If the computer learns in the same way as human subjects do in a "real" experiment, we can conclude that the computer program (our theory) is adequate; if the computer does things differently than human subjects, we know that something is wrong in the instructions to the computer. Note that in computer simulation the interest is not in writing a program which permits the computer to learn, but in making the computer learn in the same way as people do, because the rules according to which the computer learns are to serve as a theory of human behavior.

Various versions of the verbal learning program exist, and it is being improved continually. We shall follow here the description given by Simon and Feigenbaum (1964). The program is called EPAM, for Elementary Perceiver and Memorizer. However, as yet the program has no perceptual system. The stimulus material has to be preanalyzed by the experimenter in terms of its attributes or distinctive features. In practice, this means that the computer treats syllables as lists of letters. It also treats complex stimuli in this way. For instance, the stimulus-response pairs in a paired-associate experiment are treated simply as lists of syllables. The program thus learns compound stimuli as lists, and it has no separate associative mechanism.

Two subsystems of EPAM may be distinguished, a performance system and a learning system. The performance system recognizes stimuli by sorting them through a discrimination net, that is, it asks a series of questions about the stimulus. Because questions depend upon the outcome of earlier questions it is convenient to diagram the hierarchy of questions in the form of a tree. Each node of the tree corresponds to a question and an item is sorted successively downward in the tree until it reaches a terminal node. At the terminal node some image (a description of a stimulus) is stored and the incoming stimulus item is recognized as belonging to the same class as the image in the terminal node. The learning system has the dual function of building the images in the terminal nodes of the tree, and elaborating the discrimination net itself. Suppose, for instance, that the discrimination net consists of only the very simple tree shown in the left part of Fig. 2.7 and that the syllable KAB is to be classified. KAB will be sorted down the left branch and compared with the image stored there, K—. Although this image is very incomplete, there is no positive difference between the incoming syllable KAB and K—, but merely a lack of detail. Through the process of image building the image might then be elaborated, with a possible result shown in the right half of Fig. 2.7. Discrimination learning occurs, when a stimulus is sorted to a terminal node which contains an image which is actually different, from the stimulus, as would be the case in the example shown in Fig. 2.7. The program compares KAW with K-B, detects the difference in the third letter and constructs a new test in order to discriminate between the two items.

It is impossible to describe the actual computer program in all its detail here. A working program needs many instructions, some of which are not particularly interesting from a psychological viewpoint, but are crucial for the actual performance of the program. In fact, the great deal of specificity which is necessary to obtain a program which actually works is one of the disadvantages of this method of theory construction. It is sometimes not quite clear why a program performs as it does, or fails to perform, whether it is because of some psychologically interesting feature of the program, or whether it is merely a consequence of a computer programming routine. However, the basic principles of the program are easy to comprehend, and instead of further elaborating the details of the program we shall report some simulations of the experiments described in connection with Gibson's theory.

It is quite obvious that EPAM would have more difficulty learning a paired-associate list with high intralist similarity than a list with low intralist similarity. Simon and Feigenbaum replicated, with

(a) Input: KAB

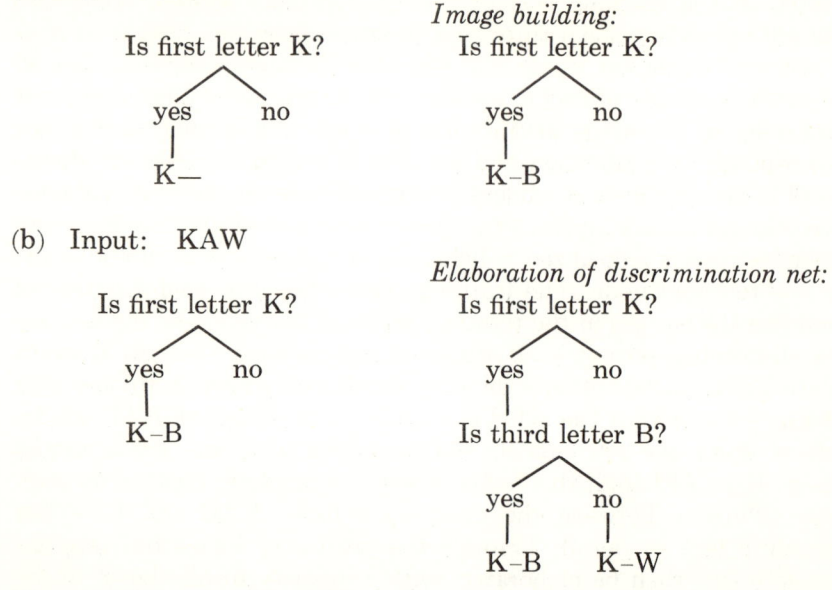

(b) Input: KAW

Fig. 2.7 *Two examples of discrimination nets; for explanation see text.*

EPAM as subject, the Underwood (1953) experiment, which is one of the classic experiments in the psychological literature demonstrating such an effect. It will be remembered that Underwood found (a) that similarity in the response terms had no effect upon learning difficulty, and (b) that as stimulus similarity increased from low to high, more trials were needed to reach a criterion (with their material, a 30% difference was observed). EPAM's performance exhibited both these effects: response similarity did not impede learning (in fact, a slight facilitation was obtained), but stimulus similarity retarded learning by about 40%, which compares fairly well with the experimental data.

The Bruce (1933) experiment on transfer effects as a function of interlist similarity was also simulated with EPAM. Compared with learning two unrelated lists (*A—B,C—D*) Bruce found positive transfer when the two lists had the same response terms (*B*): the number of trials to criterion was reduced to 75%. EPAM's simulation produced precisely this value. For the (*A—B, A—C*) paradigm Bruce found negative transfer: the number of trials to criterion increased to 130% of the control group. EPAM showed an increase of 112%.

Stimulus predifferentiation should clearly be beneficial for

EPAM. The size of the positive effect which is to be expected would depend, of course, upon the exact characteristics of predifferentiation training. If stimuli are merely presented for observation only a very rough discrimination net will be constructed and little positive transfer is expected. On the other hand, if the subject is forced to elaborate an extensive discrimination net, for instance, if he must learn to recall the stimulus items, later paired-associate learning would be greatly facilitated. Simon and Feigenbaum report an experiment with EPAM in which a positive effect of stimulus predifferentiation has been obtained.

To date, EPAM has not yet been applied to a sufficiently wide variety of problems to judge its ultimate usefulness. It can handle the effects of similarity in paired-associate learning quite well, as we have seen, and it has been successfully applied to a few other problems (mediation, serial position effect). However, the theory is intended as a comprehensive theory of learning. Further developments will show whether the theory can make contact in an interesting way with other problems in verbal learning and thereby justify its considerable complexity.

One problem with EPAM is that it is completely deterministic. If EPAM learns a list of paired-associates once, is then erased, and given the same list for learning again, it will learn the list in the same way as it did the first time. Also, whenever an error occurs, EPAM dutifully performs a correction. People do not seem to operate in this way, although this may be difficult to tell because one cannot erase people's memory. Certainly, when different subjects are given the same list to learn they do not learn it all in the same manner. For this reason group averages are usually taken in psychological experiments. With EPAM, there is no need to obtain a group average, since successive runs on the same problem are practically identical. Hintzman (1967) has developed a verbal learning program SAL (for Stimulus and Association Learner) which escapes this criticism. SAL's discrimination net grows according to stochastic rather then deterministic processes. There are other differences between EPAM and SAL as well, mostly because various attendant mechanisms of EPAM have been omitted to keep SAL as simple as possible. However, the most interesting difference is that SAL does not always construct a new test node when it makes an error, but does so only with probability a. With probability $(1-a)$ no learning occurs, in which case the old image is replaced by the new one (with probability b) or the old image is retained and the new information discarded (with probability $1-b$). Thus SAL has two parameters which must be estimated from a data: a, a measure of the learning rate, and *b* a measure of perseveration tendency. Hintzman has applied this model to an astonishingly large number of problems. He does not directly compare the model with experimental data (parameter estimation techniques have not yet been developed), but he observes the computer's performance in various experimental situations for trial values of *a* and *b*. This turned out to be a very interesting and useful exercise, since it showed how far the explanatory power of the concept of discrimination net could be pushed, and where and why it breaks down.

Certainly, as long as fascinating attempts like EPAM and SAL are in the making, it is too early to reject Gibson's postulate that discrimination processes are at the heart of verbal learning. However, regardless of the ultimate fate of this theory, it is clear now that stimulus discrimination is only one of the important mechanisms which must be considered in the study of learning and that an adequate theory of verbal learning cannot rely solely upon stimulus discrimination.

SUMMARY

In the first two sections of this chapter two classical approaches to theory construction in verbal learning were described. There have have been recurrent attempts to apply the theory of conditioning as developed in animal learning studies to verbal learning. However, these extensions from animal learning to human learning were rejected as ill-founded. This does not mean that it is improper to use terms such as stimulus, response, conditioning, or reinforcement; such terms are well defined in verbal learning (e.g., stimulus is the first member of a paired-associate, response is the second member, and reinforcement is the joint presentation of the two). The problem is rather that conditioning theories as developed in animal learning research imply a particular notion of reinforcement which can not be transferred to human verbal learning. In human learning, reinforcement does not have an automatic strengthening action, but rather serves to provide information to the subject, which the subject may employ to modify his behavior depending upon the characteristics of the experimental situation. Therefore, conditioning theories which imply an automatic effect of reinforcement are inappropriate to verbal learning. The question whether they are, indeed, appropriate for animal learning was not raised.

Interference theory is a theory in the tradition of associationism. An association between two verbal items *a* and *b* is formed through reinforcement, i.e., the joint presentation of the pair. If a new association a—c is established, it will interfere with the old one, because of response competition between b and c when stimulus a is presented. Much of the work reported in Section 2 concerned a second postulated mechanism of interference: unlearning of the a—b association, which occurs during the learning of the a—c association. Unlearning is thought to be a process comparable to experimental extinction. As such, it is subject to spontaneous recovery. Experimental evidence was described from transfer studies in which subjects learned two paired-associate lists successively. Finally, some recent theoretical developments were discussed which assign a central role not to interference between particular associations, but to a response selection mechanism.

The last two sections of the chapter are quite different in intent: their purpose is as much to illustrate modern techniques of theory construction as to discuss a specific theoretical problem. Mathematical models were used to explore the issue whether learning is a gradual process of strengthening of an associative bond, or whether it could be better represented as a transition from one discrete learning state to another. It was shown that in the case of paired-associate learning with two known response alternatives a model which distinguishes only between a learning state and a no-learning state could adequately describe the experimental data. Considerable attention was devoted to detailed data analyses and to the problem of obtaining statistics which actually discriminate among theoretical alternatives. Several studies were reported in which some success was achieved in extending the boundary conditions of the model to include two-stage learning processes, such as response learning and association, or stimulus discrimination and association.

Compared with mathematical models, computer simulation is a technique which can handle much more complex phenomena, but it is correspondingly harder to evaluate experimentally. Theories which stress the role of stimulus discrimination in verbal learning have long been known in psychology, but computer simulation has given new life and vigor to this approach. Unlike mathematical models, the computer simulation theory of stimulus discrimination is not merely descriptive, but it also specifies a hypothetical model of how this discrimination is achieved through the establishment of a discrimination net.

The techniques developed here with respect to both mathematical models and computer simulation will be used repeatedly in later chapters.

STIMULUS SAMPLING THEORY

3333333333333

The models which have been discussed in the previous chapter have all been very specific. For instance, the mathematical models of paired-associate learning apply to only a small section of paired-associate learning. With each model, specific and often quite narrow boundary conditions have been stated indicating the experimental situations which the model was designed for. This approach contrasts sharply with the way theories were employed in psychology some 30 years ago: at that time theories, or at any rate systems, were proposed which were global in intent. To explain all learning, and in fact behavior *in toto* was the declared aim of early psychological theories. However, global theories ran into more and more problems. They worked well in some experimental situations but failed in others and had to be modified with *ad hoc* arguments which became more and more strained. Today comprehensive theoretical systems play a much smaller role in the field of learning. Of the theories discussed in such texts as Hilgard's (1956) *"Theories of Learning"* perhaps the only one which shows definite signs of survival is the Skinnerian system. The once dominant Hullian system has dissolved into a point of view and into a number of miniature systems which apply to very specific experimental problems. Such miniature systems strongly predominate in learning theory today. There are some loosely organized super-systems which can be used to classify the present-day miniature models but, for the most part, these must be called points of view rather than explicit theories. The neo-behavioristic, neo-Hullian orientation has already been mentioned. The most important alternative to neo-behaviorism is what is beginning to be known under the name of information processing theories. The discrimination net models of paired-associate learning described in the previous chapter are examples of information processing models. Several other examples will be described later. Again, it is important to understand that this is a general point of view on how to construct models of human behavior; it is an orientation towards certain kinds of variables (information processing) and techniques (computer simulation), but it is not an explicitly formulated theory from which unambiguous consequences are derivable.

There is one broad theory active today in the psychology of learning which is more specific: the stimulus-sampling theory of Estes (Estes, 1950; Neimark and Estes, 1967). Stimulus-sampling theory is a supertheory in the sense that it specifies a set of basic terms and processes which are to be applied to specific problems. It is really a collection of miniature models, just like the other super-systems mentioned above, except that its basic assumptions can be stated more precisely than is the case with other approaches.

On a continuum from strict behaviorism to information-processing models stimulus-sampling theory falls somewhere in between. Its basic terms are stimulus, response, and reinforcement, and thus it is an S-R theory. On the other hand, it contains some features of information processing models. It is not necessary in stimulus-sampling theory that responses be directly determined by S-R connections, but S-R connections may be treated as "information" upon which the subject may base his response. Thus stimulus-sampling theory may be well suited to form a bridge between the divergent approaches which characterize the field of learning today—especially because it is stated in precise mathematical language so that it is possible to separate the really substantial issues from those which merely reflect the semantic difficulties of translating one theoretical language into another.

The general scheme of stimulus-sampling theory will be outlined first and then some representative applications of the theory to particular problems will be discussed. We begin by defining the relationship between stimulus-sampling theory and the mathematical models of paired-associate learning described in the last chapter. This discussion will touch upon one of the main problems of the theory, that is, the question of when stimuli are sampled as elements and when a situation is perceived as a whole, as a stimulus pattern. This problem will be considered in more detail in the following section, with examples from paired-associate learning as well as discrimination learning. Finally, some applications of stimulus sampling models to probability learning experiments will be described, as well as some extensions which take into account the amount of reward and interpersonal interactions and illustrate how decision processes which intervene between direct S-R connections are handled within the theory.

In an article summarizing the work on stimulus-sampling theory

Estes (1959a) mentioned Skinner, Guthrie, and Hull as the classical learning theorists who influenced the development of stimulus-sampling theory most strongly. Guthrie (1935) contributed the stimulus-response contiguity principle as the basic mechanism of learning, as well as the analysis of gradual learning in terms of all-or-none conditioning of stimulus elements. The influences of Skinner and Hull are less specific, but equally important. From Skinner (1938) comes the behavioristic approach, the rejection of cognitive as well as physiological terms and the emphasis upon the analysis of functional relationships between experimentally defined stimuli (i.e., classes of environmental events) and responses (i.e., classes of behavioral events). Hull's application of mathematical methods to psychology demonstrated the enormous promise of a formalistic approach and served as the immediate stimulus for Estes' work.

Stimulus-sampling theory does not at all resemble a single theory in the classical sense. It is more like a collection of many miniature theories, unified through some common principles. A few recurrent themes (S-R conditioning, stimulus sampling) provide a common core around which specific models are built. Every application of the theory to a new situation constitutes a separate model. The theory thus escapes the main criticism leveled against the classical learning theories—of forcing an infinite variety of problems into the Procrustean bed of a few invariant laws. On the other hand, it invites a new charge, that it is an endless proliferation of models. It is surely true that in applying a theory to an experimental situation the particular characteristics of that situation must be taken into account. On the other hand, it seems quite meaningless to construct a new theory for every problem, even if it is only a miniature theory. Stimulus-sampling theory avoids this criticism, because the various stimulus sampling models all remain within a common framework and use the same explanatory constructs, and only the way in which these constructs are used is allowed to vary according to the demands of a problem.

It is important to realize that the stimuli in stimulus-sampling theory are hypothetical constructs and cannot be identified directly with environmental events. There are a number of ways in which an experimental situation can be represented in terms of stimuli, and furthermore, there are a number of ways in which the organism can sample these stimuli. Depending upon the specific assumptions which are made in this respect, one or the other stimulus-sampling model is obtained. The experimental situation sometimes suggests a particular stimulus representation, or a particular sampling process, but this is not generally the case. Often more than one approach is possible, and stimulus-sampling models compete with each other.

An experimental situation may be represented by a large number of stimulus elements, some of which are sampled by the subject on each trial. Depending upon the way in which this sampling occurs, three classes of models may be distinguished (Estes, 1959b). Suppose that the total number of stimulus elements is finite and that on each trial of a learning experiment each stimulus element has probability θ of being included into the subset of elements sampled by the subject, and probability $(1-\theta)$ of not being sampled. The number of elements sampled on each trial is therefore a random variable, with a mean of $N\theta$, where N equals the total number of stimulus elements. At any time each stimulus element is connected to one of the response alternatives. The probability of a given response is determined by the number of elements in the sample which are connected to that response, divided by the total number of elements sampled. Learning trials normally terminate with a reinforcement for one of the response alternatives, and it is usually assumed that the effect of a reinforcement is to condition all elements sampled on that trial to the reinforced response. Models of this type are called "fixed sampling probability models," or "fixed θ models," and were introduced by Estes and Burke (1953).

Fixed sample size models (e.g., Estes, 1950) employ a different sampling rule. Suppose that there are N stimulus elements, and that the subject responds to a random sample of size s on each trial. The response and conditioning assumptions are the same as above. The ratio $s/_N$ determines the rate of learning in this case.

Corresponding to the two finite N models considered above, an infinite case can be obtained which has the same set of responses and reinforcement probabilities and a single free parameter which corresponds to θ and $s/_N$ above. This model may be regarded as a limiting case obtained by letting $N \rightarrow \infty$, and keeping θ or $s/_N$ fixed, or as a special case of Bush and Mosteller's linear model (Bush and Mosteller, 1956; Estes and Suppes, 1959).

The three classes of models described above have in common the assumption that a stimulus situation is represented by a large number of stimulus elements. Estes calls such models component models, to distinguish them from pattern models in which stimulus situations are conceived as wholes. Mathematically the pattern model can be regarded as a special case of the fixed sample size model, obtained by letting $s=1$, and N be a small number or 1 in the simplest case, as in the one-element pattern model. Psychologically, the transition from component to pattern models presents a more profound change in that under some circumstances stimulus situations may act as wholes, or as patterns, rather than as collections of elements. Suppose an experimental situation is represented by N patterns (N being a small number). Each pattern is connected to one of the experimental responses. On each trial the subject samples one pattern at random and performs the response connected with this pattern. When the experimenter reinforces a response other than the one performed, the pattern sampled on that trial may change its conditioning state to the reinforced response with probability c. If $N = 1$, learning is all-or-none, because the correct response either *is* or *is not* connected to the stimulus pattern. If $N \neq 1$, the response probability can assume the values, $1/_N$, $2/_N$, ... $N/_N$, depending upon the number of stimulus patterns which are connected with the correct response.

The basic types of stimulus-sampling models can be combined and varied in many ways. For instance, Atkinson and Estes (1963) have found a mixture between component and pattern models useful for certain problems arising in discrimination learning and transfer. Although a subject might respond to stimulus patterns during discrimination learning, when new stimuli are presented in a transfer test which are partly identical with the stimuli used during discrimination learning, subjects analyze the stimulus into components and base their responses upon the conditioning states of these components. This work is discussed in the next section. Multiple-process models have also been developed within the framework of stimulus-sampling theory, in particular, a model for discrimination learning which distinguishes between the acquisition of observing responses and discriminative responses.

The concept of stimulus fluctuation provides another powerful extension of the theory. The basic idea is that the availability of stimulus elements may change spontaneously as a function of time (or other variables, such as deprivation state). The relevance of such a mechanism to problems of forgetting, spontaneous recovery, or distribution of practice is obvious (Estes, 1955a, 1955b). Related developments are a model with neutral elements (LaBerge, 1959), and a two-process theory for discrimination learning with a special mechanism for the adaptation of irrelevant stimuli (Restle, 1955).

Another interesting modification of stimulus-sampling theory involves changes in the conditioning assumptions of the theory. Suppose one permits conditioning to be determined not only by the reinforcement delivered by the experimenter but also by other factors, such as the subject's response on that trial, or on the immediately preceding trial, or perhaps upon the previous reinforcement. One can use this technique to explore what the important events are during learning: if certain contingencies are included in the model, one can determine whether they result either in an over-all improvement in goodness of fit of the model or perhaps in a suggestive pattern of parameter estimates. In this way the relevance or irrelevance of various learning events for the effectiveness of a reinforcement may be studied. Suppes and Atkinson (1960) and Suppes and Schlag-Rey (1962) have obtained some promising results with this technique. For instance, it has been observed that concrete objective features of the reinforcement in a probability learning experiment (such as the arm of a maze which is reinforced, the particular response which occurred, etc.) are much less important than subjective, relational aspects (such as confirmation or disconfirmation of a response, alternation, perseveration, etc.).

Both the all-or-none model of paired-associate learning and the linear model may be identified with particular stimulus-sampling models. All-or-none learning arises when a stimulus situation is represented by a single pattern; the linear model corresponds to sampling from a large population of stimulus elements. Thus, the discussion of mathematical models of paired-associate learning in the previous chapter could be translated into the terminology of stimulus-sampling theory. Different stages of learning could be accounted for in terms of different stimulus propulations which must be conditioned.

The problem remains, however, to determine under what conditions an experimental situation is represented by stimulus patterns, and under what conditions it must be represented by stimulus elements. Of course, this kind of restatement of a problem solves nothing in itself, but it does suggest that the question of all-or-none learning of paired-associates is merely a part of a much larger problem which one can expect to encounter in various forms in different learning situations.

1. THE EFFECTIVE STIMULUS: SELECTION OF ELEMENTS OR PATTERN FORMATION?

In many experimental situations the subject neither responds to patterns as a whole nor samples elements at random from the total population; rather, he selects components or aspects of the stimuli which then become the functional stimulus for him. Thus an interesting question arises. When does a subject respond to the total experimental situation, and when does he respond to selected components only?

It should be noted that this problem is not one created by stimulus-sampling theory. It is a very real psychological question that is at issue here—stimulus-sampling theory merely provides a convenient framework. In fact, the first studies demonstrating stimulus selection which will be described here have nothing to do directly with stimulus-sampling theory.

A review of studies dealing with stimulus selection in paired-associate learning is given by Underwood (1963). In general, these studies show that if the stimulus terms in a paired-associate experiment consist of several unrelated components, only some of these components become functional as a consequence of a paired-associate learning. The subject selects components of a complex stimulus and learns only the associations between these selected components, the functional stimulus, and the response. Underwood, Ham, and Ekstrand (1962) performed an experiment in which the probability was manipulated that a particular component would be selected by the subject as the functional stimulus. Subjects in their experiment learned 7-item paired-associate lists with digits as responses. The stimulus terms of one list were nonsense trigrams and color combinations. A second list used word-color combinations as stimuli. It was hypothesized that in the first list subjects would pay attention primarily to the color cues and tend to neglect the nonsense trigrams, while in the second list subjects might find it easier to attend to word meanings and neglect the color cues. This hypothesis was evaluated by a transfer test after each subject had learned to a criterion the list to which he was assigned. Three kinds of transfer tests were given: under one condition, subjects were tested with the complete stimulus terms, as during original learning, in a second condition subjects were tested with the color cues only; in the third condition subjects were tested with the words or trigrams only. The results of Underwood *et al.* strongly confirmed the hypothesis of stimulus selection. The subjects tested with the trigrams and color recalled on the average 5.5 digits. However, subjects tested with the color alone were quite as good and recalled 5.4 digits on the average. Omitting the trigram from the stimulus did not interfere with recall, presumably because subjects had learned color-digit associations. On the other hand, when the color was omitted from the stimulus terms and testing was with the trigrams only, recall was clearly depressed (2.7 digits). Subjects had relied more upon the color than upon the trigrams during learning, and insufficient trigram-digit associations had been formed. For the subjects learning word-color items, the results were almost reversed. Words were a more prominent cue than color and the average recall for words plus color, words alone, and color alone was 6.3, 5.0, and 3.8 digits respectively.

Although the Underwood *et al.* experiment, and others of its kind reviewed by Underwood (1963) clearly demonstrate that stimulus selection occurs during paired-associate learning they raise some questions which cannot be answered on the basis of these experiments because of a methodological limitation in their design. Average transfer data do not indicate how stimulus selection takes place. Underwood (1963) considered three possible ways in which selection could operate. A subject may learn items either by words alone or by color alone, with more items being learned by words alone than by color alone. Alternatively, a subject may learn all items in the same way, paying attention to either color or words, with most subjects preferring word-coding to color-coding. Finally, it is possible that a subject learns about both components of an item, with the word-component being somewhat stronger than the color-component. The only way to decide among these possibilities is to study transfer results of individual subjects rather than group averages, and to give more than one kind of transfer test to each subject.

Trabasso and Bower (1968) have reported a paired-associate experiment designed to study stimulus selection in more detail. Sixteen subjects learned an 8-item paired-associate list with the numerals 1 and 2 as responses and color-syllable combinations as stimuli. After reaching a criterion subjects received 4 transfer tests on color alone and 4 tests on syllable alone for each item. No feedback was given during the transfer tests. The over-all proportions correct were .93 for syllables and .68 for colors. Thus the syllables were the more salient cues in this experiment.

To obtain more detailed information about the stimulus selection process, each item was classified according to the results of the 8 transfer tests. If all responses on the 4 test trials with color-only were correct, but at least one error occurred when syllables were tested, the item was classified as learned on the basis of a color code. Conversely, if all responses to syllables only were correct, but one or more errors occurred on the color-tests, an item was classified as a syllable-type. Finally, if the responses to both the color and syllable components of an item were correct, the item was classified as a both-type. This classification revealed that most items were learned on the basis of both cues (57 subject/item sequences), and that almost as many items were learned on the basis of syllables only (52); solutions on the basis of color were much rarer (10). The interesting question, of course, concerns the way in which individual subjects learned the 8 items. In particular, does a subject use the same selection strategy for all items, or does he respond to color cues for some items and syllable-cues for others? The latter appears to be the case, as only one subject used a consistent strategy, in that he learned all items on both components. All other subjects tended to employ more than one solution strategy. Most frequently, subjects learned some items on the basis of both cues and attended to syllables only for other items. On the basis of a statistical analysis of their data Trabasso and Bower (1968) concluded that subjects distributed their items over solution-types proportional to mean frequencies. Thus, selection effects in this type of experiment occur because subjects select either one or the other cue as their functional stimulus with unequal selection probabilities, but little or no inter-item dependencies exist.

The stimulus selection experiments in paired-associate learning show that if offered a chance, subjects select among the components of a stimulus and thereby simplify the task for themselves. However, under some conditions subjects respond to all components of a stimulus situation, so that the question arises which experimental conditions favor pattern formation rather than some form of stimulus selection.

Studies in which subjects coded the stimulus in terms of patterns have been reported, among others, by Binder and Estes (1966), Friedman (1966), and Friedman, Trabasso, and Mosberg (1967). A design characteristic common to all these experiments is that at least some of the stimulus items among which subjects are asked to discriminate have common components. Consider, for instance, Experiment I of Binder and Estes (1966), the design of which is shown in Table 3.1.

Table 3.1. *Design of Experiment I of Binder and Estes (1966).*

Training		Testing syllable combinations
Syllable combinations	Responses	
ab	R_1	ae
ac	R_2	be
de	R_1	ad
df	R_3	dc
		bc
		cf

The letters in Table 3.1 stand for different nonsense syllables. During the first phase of the experiment subjects learned a 4-item paired-associate list, with overlapping pairs of nonsense syllables as the stimuli and the numerals 1, 2, and 3 as responses. The order of the two components of each stimulus pair was randomized over trials. Note that in order to learn this list successfully, a subject had to attend to both members of a stimulus pair. He had to form patterns—selection strategies could not work in this case. After a fixed number of learning trials subjects were given transfer tests with new compounds which consisted of recombinations of the components of the items already learned. The testing syllable combinations are also shown in Table 3.1. The transfer results in this and the other experiments referred to above clearly indicate that, during the training phase, component-response associations had been formed as part of the pattern-response learning. A few simple principles permit us to account for most of the transfer data in the Binder and Estes experiment, as well as in the other experiments mentioned above. One is the *additivity rule*. It is easiest to illustrate this rule with an example. Suppose a subject has learned to associate the compound *abc* with response 1 and *def* with response 2. If he is now tested with a new compound *abd*, the additivity rule predicts that the probability of a 1-response will be $\frac{2}{3}$, that is, the probability of a response will equal the proportion of cues present that are conditioned to it. This rule is the basic response rule in stimulus-sampling theory. Atkinson and Estes (1963) report an experiment in which this particular prediction was tested: their observed proportion of 1-responses was .669. The second rule needed to predict transfer results in this kind of experimental situation is the familiar *probability matching rule*. This rule says that the probability of a response is proportional to the frequency of reinforcement. For instance, if twice as many learning trials are given for the association ac—1 than for ad—2, the probability of a 1-response when *a* alone is presented for a test should be twice as great as the probability of a 2-response. In an actual experiment Binder and Feldman (1960) observed 36 one's versus 16 two's in a situation like this.

A number of supplementary principles have also been identified in transfer studies. Binder and Estes (1967) observed that the *novelty* of some cues must sometimes be taken into account in predicting transfer. Of even greater interest in the present context is the *validity-principle* which was established in the study by Friedman, Trabasso, and Mosberg (1967), because it shows how selection effects may arise in learning. Friedman *et al.* found that subjects gave more weight to valid cues than to invalid cues in determining their responses on a transfer trial. In order to understand this notion better, Table 3.2 reproduces the training and test lists used in the Friedman *et al.* experiment. Note first that because of component overlap the only way this list can be learned is by paying attention to both stimulus components, except for the control items (hi) and (jk). Secondly, note that the letters used to construct the first 7 items differ in validity: some letters (a, e, g) are completely valid in the sense that they are associated with only one response. Others (c, d, f) are completely invalid, and the element (b) is partially valid, since it appears with R_2 twice as often as with R_1. On transfer tests subjects proved to be biased in favor of the more valid letters, i.e., they tended to base their responses more upon the more valid elements, rather than choosing among the letters of a test pair with equal likelihood. In other words, there was a tendency to select the more valid components of the stimulus in the Friedman *et al.* study.

When do subjects select the components of a stimulus and when do they form patterns based upon the total stimulus situation? From the experiments reviewed above the answer seems to be that subjects select components if the experimental design permits it, but that in the presence of component overlap among the stimuli the coding process uses all the information available in the stimulus. Indeed, from the results of Friedman *et al.* it appears that as long as some component overlap exists within a list all items within that list are coded as patterns, even if for some items stimulus selection would have been possible. In Table 3.2 items (hi) and (jk) could have been learned

Table 3.2. *Experimental design of the experiment by Friedman et al. (1967).*

Training lists	Transfer test lists
$ab - R_1$	ad, ae, af, be, df, bg,
$ac - R_1$	bi, bj, ce, cf, df, dh, fk
$bd - R_2$	—
$bc - R_2$	a, b, c, d, e, f, g, h, i, j, k
$cd - R_3$	
$ef - R_3$	
$fg - R_1$	
$hi - R_3$	
$jk - R_2$	

even if only one letter would have been selected as the functional stimulus, but subjects transferred the correct response nearly perfectly to either element alone. Thus selection effects did not occur in this case, even though such effects would have been possible. Subjects adopted a strategy of pattern coding for all items in the list once they realized that such a strategy was necessary for at least some of the items.

Further studies of stimulus selection and pattern formation are needed before one can specify the processes involved in sufficient detail, and with more confidence than is now possible. At the present stage of understanding, though, it appears that subjects start with some simple selection strategy. If the problem is such that simple strategies do not work, more complex and richer codes are tried, until a solution can be achieved. The limited information-processing capacity of subjects restricts them to trying only one or at most a few coding operations simultaneously. Truly complex problems, which unlike most laboratory studies have no well-defined solution, probably involve decision procedures which permit the subject to combine and weigh the output of several parallel operations. Probably the set of coding responses which the subject has available is structured in some way. There may be a hierarchical structure from simple to complex operations in terms of the number of stimulus components which are being considered, or in terms of abstract-concrete and absolute-relational dimensions. There are no reliable answers yet available to these important questions. However, some related problems will be taken up in Chapter 6, which deals with coding processes in discrimination learning.

2. PROBABILITY LEARNING

The basic experimental design of probability learning is simple: on each of a long sequence of trials one of two lights is turned on by the experimenter according to some prearranged schedule, and it is the subject's task to predict which light will come on. A random schedule determines which light is turned on on each trial; hence the name probability learning. This experimental situation is of interest for several reasons. For one, it provides a good example to illustrate the principles of stimulus-sampling theory. Second, it is a problem interesting in its own right: early workers, for example, Humphreys (1939) believed they had found in probability learning an experimental design ideally suited to study effects of reinforcement or information feedback in an experimental situation analogous to classical conditioning. Today, largely through the sophisticated analyses made possible through the use of mathematical models, we know that Humphreys was but partially right: when proper care is taken, probability learning may indeed be looked upon as a simple conditioning task, but under other conditions human behavior may be surprisingly complex, even in this super-simple experimental task. This is especially true when explicit rewards are introduced, when trial sequences differ from randomness, or when the experiment is turned into a two-person game. Stimulus-sampling theory provides a baseline against which these higher-order effects may be explored. Extensions of the theory are often possible; additional processes can sometimes be specified which modify the basic conditioning model. A particular example to be discussed below is the scanning model which describes how subjects make decisions in experiments of this kind if differential rewards are employed and how this decision process interacts with the conditioning process.

Consider a simple probability learning experiment, such as the one introduced by Humphreys (1939) and Grant, Hake, and Hornseth (1951). The task of the subject is to predict which one of two (or sometimes more) events will occur (e.g., whether a light will be turned on or not). After the appearance of a pilot light, which signals the start of each trial, the subject makes one of two possible prediction responses, usually a key press. Then the experimenter provides some feedback to the subject, that is, he turns a light on, or does not turn it on. The light serves as a reinforcement for the subject's response. In most experiments to be discussed here, the experimental events are not contingent upon the subject's responses. Before the experimental session the experimenter decides for each trial whether or not the light will be turned on, e.g., by flipping a coin. In this case the experimental events form a random sequence, with the probability of "light on" being .5. Estes and Straughan (1954) have introduced a modification of this basic experimental paradigm which has been widely accepted: In order to make the symmetry between the two responses and the two events on each trial more explicit, they used two event lights, one corresponding to each response. This experimental arrangement is familiar to many students of psychology as the "Humphreys Board": two telegraph keys for the two response alternatives, a pilot light above each key for the two feedback events, and a pilot light in the middle of the board to indicate trials.

Some standard notation is needed at this point. Call the two response alternatives A_1 and A_2. Let $P(A_i)$ denote the proportion of A_i

responses during an experimental session, or during a block of trials, where $i = 1,2$. The two events are designated by E_1 and E_2. For the moment we shall only consider event sequences which are randomly generated and not contingent upon the subject's responses. Let π be the probability of the event E_1. By the symmetry of the situation, E_2 must then occur with probability $1—\pi$. The value of π is the most important independent variable in probability learning experiments. Note, that as far as the subject is concerned, there is no "solution" to the experimental situation. The subject is asked to predict whether the E_1 or the E_2 light will come one, but what really happens has been determined by a random choice. The only thing the subject can do is to learn something about the relative frequencies of E_1 and E_2 (i.e., the π -value) and adjust his behavior accordingly.

The outcome of probability learning experiments which has excited most interest is the fact that subjects, in general, do adjust their responses to the relative frequencies of the experimental events E_1 and E_2. There are other features of the data which are at least equally important, but we shall neglect them for the time being, until we have developed a theoretical framework within which they can be studied.

During the first few trials of a probability learning experiment subjects choose the two response alternatives equally often, but as training continues they start to predict the more frequent event more often, in fact the frequency of prediction E_1 matches the frequency of the occurrence of E_1. This probability matching is, of course, irrational: if subjects were concerned with maximizing their number of correct predictions over a block of trials, they would always choose the more frequent event. Instead, after some training $P(A_1) = \pi$, which is not a maximizing strategy. A numerical example will demonstrate this: suppose the experimenter presents E_1 on random 70% of the trials, i.e., $\pi = .7$. By always making response A_1, a subject can therefore be correct 70% of the time; if, however, a subject probability matches, $P(A_1)$ will be .7, and the expected number of correct trials will be 70% of the A_1 responses and 30% of the A_2 responses, i.e., $P(\text{correct}) = (.7)(.7) + (.3)(.3) = .58$, which is less than what a maximizing strategy can achieve. Of course, subjects do not always probability-match. In some experiments subjects were found to maximize instead and in others subjects perform somewhere between these two: They overshoot the matching value without going to the extreme of always predicting the same response. As Estes (1964) has concluded in a recent review, experimental results are widely discrepant, but the data are not unsystematic. Estes notes that probability matching is found in experiments in which the subject is led to concentrate upon every trial. This is sometimes achieved by asking the subject to state his expectation on each trial (e.g., Estes and Straughan, 1954; Friedman, Burke, Cole, Estes, Keller and Millward, 1964), or by simulating a psychophysical or problem—solving situation (e.g., Goodnow, 1955). Overshooting occurs when subjects are instructed to maximize successes over blocks of trials (Das, 1961) or when the random character of the event sequence is specially stressed (e.g., Edwards, 1961). Estes points out that these findings help to indicate the boundary conditions within which matching behavior is obtained. For the time being we choose to stay within these conditions and investigate the phenomenon of probability matching, but we shall return to the interesting question of when matching holds and when it does not.

Although deciding whether or not probability matching occurs appears to be a straightforward empirical problem, Estes (1964) notes that actually there exist quite complex questions concerning the interpretation of probability matching data. Matching is supposedly a property of "asymptotic behavior", a stable performance level which is reached after an initial learning phase. In the early probability learning experiments, subjects appeared to reach a stable level after about 80 trials. This level was used as an estimate of asymptotic performance. It soon became apparent, however, that when the experiment was continued for many more trials (say for 300 trials, or up to 1200 trials) further changes occurred, i.e., performance was not "really asymptotic." But it is impossible to maintain that these further changes which occur with prolonged training are due to learning effects as conceptualized by the model. Learning is only one factor which determines behavior and one can hardly suppose that, if there is a stable performance level due to learning effects, it will be maintained forever. People get tired, lose interest in the experiment, or simply get bored and want to try something new. In fact, as Estes notes, the instructions given to the subjects often preclude stable performance for long periods of time: Subjects are often urged to do their best, and thus the lack of improvement associated with stable performance level will be interpreted by the subject as a sign of failure, and this becomes a reason to vary his behavior. Thus asymptotes in a probability learning experiment are inherently unstable. Apparently the subject has several response systems available in this experimental situation, and he will choose among them depending upon instructions and other experimental conditions. One mode of response, and it appears to be the dominant one, leads to the phenomenon of probability matching.

Two Models

The two most obvious models which can be obtained from stimulus-sampling theory both predict probability matching. These are, of course, the pattern model and the linear model. Let us begin by applying the one-element pattern model to the probability learning experiment. As in previous applications, we assume that the experimental situation is represented by one stimulus pattern. There are two conditioning states: The pattern may be conditioned to response A_1 or to response A_2. On each trial that response to which the pattern is conditioned occurs. If the experimenter reinforces the response that occurred the pattern does not change its conditioning state; however, if the opposite response is reinforced the pattern may change its conditioning state with probability c.

Note that this model is exactly the same as the one applied to paired-associate learning earlier, except that the conditioning states now correspond to the two response alternatives, and that neither response is consistently reinforced: response A_1 is reinforced (i.e., the light E_1 is turned on) with probability π, and response A_2 is reinforced with probability $1-\pi$.

Figure 3.1 shows the four possible outcomes that can occur on

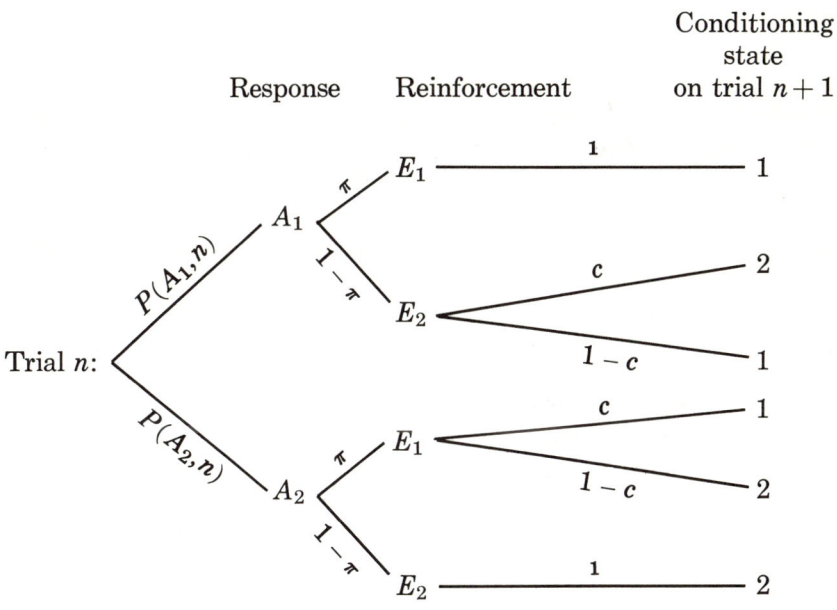

Fig. 3.1 *Response-event-conditioning sequence according to the one-element pattern model.*

a learning trial according to the pattern model. On any trial the pattern may be in one of two states: conditioned to A_1 (State 1) or conditioned to A_2 (State 2). Denote the probability that on the n-th trial the pattern will be in State 1, or State 2, respectively, by $P(A_{1,n})$ and $P(A_{2,n})$. On each trial the experimenter presents one of the two experimental outcomes with probabilities π and $1-\pi$, respectively. If the subject's response is A_1 and E_1 occurs, the pattern remains in State 1. If, however, E_2 occurs, the pattern may change its conditioning state with probability c. The probability that the disconfirmation will remain ineffective and the pattern stays in State 1 is, of course, $1-c$. Figure 3.1 shows the probabilities of the three experimental outcomes so far discussed: a stay in State 1 because the response has been confirmed, which occurs with probability π; change to State 2 because of a disconfirmation, $(1-\pi)$ times the probability of a change c; and remain in State 1 in spite of a disconfirmation, $(1-\pi)$ times the probability of no change $(1-c)$. If the subject makes response A_2 on trial n, three similar outcomes result, as shown in the lower branch of Figure 3.1. The diagram in Figure 3.1 may be summarized in the transition matrix shown below:

$$
\begin{array}{c}
\text{Trial } n+1 \\
\begin{array}{cc}
\text{State 1} & \text{State 2}
\end{array}
\end{array}
$$

$$
(1) \qquad \text{Trial } n \quad
\begin{array}{c}
\text{State 1} \\
\text{State 2}
\end{array}
\left[
\begin{array}{cc}
\pi + (1-\pi)\,(1-c) & (1-\pi)c \\
\pi c & \pi(1-c) + (1-\pi)
\end{array}
\right]
$$

The first row of this matrix shows the probabilities of transitions between State 1 on trial n to States 1 or 2 on the next trial. For instance, the first entry in the matrix is composed of the first and third branch in Fig. 3.1, since there are two possible ways in which a subject can stay in State 1 from one trial to the next. The other entries are similarly obtained from Fig. 3.1.

The transition matrix Eq. (1) specifies what happens from one trial to the next. If we assume that on the first trial the subject starts out with $P(A_1) = P(A_2) = \frac{1}{2}$, which is reasonable at least for a group average, we can easily write down an expression relating the probability of an A_1 choice on two successive trials. From Eq. (1) we know already the probability that the subject makes an A_1 response on trial $(n + 1)$, given that on the previous trial he had chosen A_1 or A_2, respectively. Since by definition the expected proportions of A_1 and A_2 choices on trial n are $P(A_{1,n})$, and $P(A_{2,n})$, we may write

$$
(2) \quad P(A_{1,n+1}) = P(A_{1,n})\,[\pi + (1 - \pi)\,(1 - c)] + P(A_{2,n})\,\pi c
$$

Equation (2) is a difference equation, and there are simple mathematical techniques available with which such equations can be solved (Atkinson, Bower, and Crothers, 1965). A solution of (2) consists in expressing $P(A_{1,n})$ as a function of π, c, and the initial condition, $P(A_{1,1})$. By letting n vary in this equation, the mean learning curve predicted by the model can be traced out. However, our main interest lies in asymptotic behavior, and it is not necessary to obtain an explicit solution of (2) in order to obtain asymptotic predictions. By definition, asymptotic performance is stable performance, i.e., there are no more changes in the mean response rates per trial: mathematically, this means that $P(A_{1,n+1}) = P(A_{1,n})$. Thus, the trial subscript can be dropped and, noting that $P(A_2) = 1 - P(A_1)$, we have

$$P(A_1) = P(A_1) \left[\pi + (1 - \pi)(1 - c) \right] + [1 - P(A_1)] \, \pi c.$$

Rearranging terms, we find the expected asymptotic response probability to be

$$(3) \qquad\qquad P(A_1) = \pi$$

That is, the pattern model predicts the characteristic experimental outcome of probability matching.

Note that (3) does not depend upon the parameter c of the model and is completely determined by the experimental conditions. Other features of the learning process, such as the nonasymptotic portion of the mean learning curve, are different in this respect, because the model does not specify them uniquely until the parameter c has been estimated. The model generates a whole family of mean learning curves, all of the same structure, (and, as has just been shown, all having π as asymptote) but their rate of approach to this asymptote depends upon the general term c. The parameter c summarizes the effectiveness of a disconfirmation in the present model, and it cannot be specified beforehand by the experimenter. It must be estimated from the data of a specific experiment.

In the linear model learning is seen as a trial-by-trial increment in the probability of the to be learned response, rather than a transition between discrete states. Learning in the sense just described occurs on every trial, depending only upon the outcome which the experimenter chooses to present on that trial. If the experimenter presents E_1 this event serves as a reinforcement for the A_1 response, that is, $P(A_1)$ receives an increment. By the symmetry of the situation, whenever $P(A_1)$ increases, $P(A_2)$ must decrease correspondingly. Similarly, the event E_2 serves as a reinforcement for A_2. Note that this is quite different from the assumptions of the previous model: learning, that is a change of state, could occur only when the subject made an error of prediction; no changes were assumed to occur after successful predictions.

The name linear model specifies the manner in which response probability is assumed to change from trial to trial. The difference between the response probabilities on two successive trials is assumed to be given by the following linear transformation:

if E_1 occurs on trial n,

(4a) $$P(A_{1,n+1}) = P(A_{1,n}) + [1-P(A_{1,n})]\theta$$

if E_2 occurs on trial n,

(4b) $$P(A_{1,n+1}) = P(A_{1,n}) - \theta P(A_{1,n})$$

This formulation possesses two very desirable features: it is the simplest possible one mathematically, and it can be given an intuitively appealing interpretation. Equation (4) expresses the assumption that the change which occurs on a learning trial is proportional to the maximum possible change on that trial. If A_1 is reinforced on trial n, the maximum possible increase for A_1 equals $(1-P(A_{1,n}))$, and the actual increase will be a fraction θ of this. If A_1 is not reinforced on trial n, i.e., if E_2 occurs and A_2 is reinforced, $P(A_1)$ is assumed to decrease by a fraction θ of the maximum possible decrease, $P(A_{1,n})$.

The average change in the probability of the A_1 response from one trial to the next can easily be obtained by noting that increases will occur with probability π (whenever E_1 is presented) and decreases will occur with probability $(1-\pi)$, whenever E_2 is presented. Thus,

(5) $$P(A_{1,n+1}) = \pi[P(A_{1,n}) + [1 - P(A_{1,n})]\theta] + \\ + (1 - \pi) [P(A_{1,n}) - \theta P(A_{1,n})]$$

In order to find the solution of this difference equation at the asymptote of learning, we let $P(A_{1,n+1}) = P(A_{1,n})$. Dropping the now unnecessary trial subscript and rearranging terms we arrive at

(6) $$P(A_1) = \pi.$$

Thus the linear model predicts the same terminal performance in a probability learning experiment with noncontingent reinforcement as the pattern model, in spite of the vastly different assumptions upon which the two models are based.

Sequential Data

The pattern model and the linear model differ in their predictions concerning sequential behavior: given a particular response and reinforcement on one trial, what will happen on the next trial? Inspection of Fig. 3.1 shows that the pattern model makes very strong predictions in this respect. The model requires that subjects always make an A_1 response if they had made this response on the previous trial and if this response had been reinforced through the occurrence of E_1. Formally this can be expressed as $P(A_{1,n}|E_{1,n-1}A_{1,n-1}) = 1$. Even without looking at any experimental data it is clear that this prediction must be wrong. People simply are not that consistent. Experimental data completely support our intuition here: the required probability is not even close to 1 in most experiments. Thus, the one-element pattern model is clearly wrong and must either be discarded or modified. However, before continuing with the comparison between the linear model and the pattern model we must examine a difficulty shared by both models.

Both of these models, as well as other reinforcement theories, predict that on any trial a subject should be more likely to perform a response A_i, the more E_i events have immediately preceded that trial, i.e., $P(A_{i,n}) \leq P(A_{i,n}/E_{i,n-1}) \leq P(A_{i,n}/E_{i,n-1}, E_{i,n-2}) \leq \ldots \ldots \leq P(A_{i,n}/E_{i,n-1} \ldots E_{i,n-j})$, etc. This follows because reinforcement theory assumes that reinforcement strengthens a response. In one of the early experiments on probability learning Jarvik (1951) noted that this was not true and that, in fact, subjects tend to behave in exactly the opposite way: The longer a run of any particular event, the more likely the subject is to predict the opposite event. This phenomenon has been called the "gambler's fallacy", and has been replicated in a number of later experiments. Such a finding is, of course, sharply critical of reinforcement theory. As mentioned above, reinforcement theory predicts positive recency curves (increases in response probability as a function of number of reinforcements), while negative recency curves are observed (subjects become less likely to predict an event after it has occurred several times in a row). To be more precise, most empirical recency curves are not strictly negative: they increase at first, pass through a maximum after one or two reinforcements and then decrease (see Estes, 1964 for a review of the relevant experiments). A completely satisfactory explanation for this finding is not available at the present time, but Estes (1964) makes a strong argument that it might be merely an experimental artifact. The subjects in a probability learning experiment are not entirely naive with respect to the experimental procedure, but have some extraexperimental experience with gambling situations and the like. Habits from such extraexperimental situations will generalize to the experimental situation and may be responsible for the bow-shaped recency curves which have been observed. It is possible that people are not used to very long runs of the same event in a gambling situation, and hence, when such a run occurs, they tend to predict the opposite event because they feel it is time for a change. All this would mean is that people have a poor understanding of the concept of probability, because long runs do occur in a random sequence, although not very frequently. The term "gambler's fallacy" seems to imply that this kind of maladaptive behavior may be observed outside the laboratory. In the laboratory the "gambler's fallacy" should extinguish through lack of reinforcement, just as other extraexperimental habits extinguish, and should be replaced by the appropriate prediction behavior characterized by a positive recency effect. Estes' explanation implies that when training is extensive, or when practiced subjects are used in an experiment, the negative recency effect should disappear. In experiments by Anderson (1960) and Edwards (1961) precisely this observation was made.

The reasoning outlined above motivated the probability learning experiment of Friedman, Burke, Cole, Keller, Millward, and Estes (1964). The goal of these authors was to collect data really relevant to the theoretical issues under consideration. Observations are not scientifically relevant merely because they have been made, even when they are careful and well controlled observations. At each stage in the development of a science only certain observations are important, while others, which are just as "empirical" and just as "true", are irrelevant because they do not further our understanding of the issues with which we are concerned. Of course, the observations with which no one knows what to do today may be the crucial data of tomorrow, but in the regular day-to-day progress of science, where issues are well defined, data are most useful when they are theory-oriented.

The procedure used by Friedman *et al.* (1964) is essentially the one introduced by Estes and Straughan (1954) which was discussed above. Their main innovation was the use of well practiced subjects; 80 subjects served in three experimental sessions each. The first two sessions were comparable. Each consisted of 8 blocks of 48 prediction trials. The reinforcing events E_1 and E_2 occurred with probability π and $1 - \pi$, respectively. On odd trial blocks, π was always equal to .5. On even trial blocks, different π-values were employed, ranging from .1 to .9, but not including .5. In effect, subjects were thus given experience with many different reinforcement probabilities but were retrained under the neutral $\pi = .5$ condition after each nonsymmetric condition. The third session of the experiment also contained 8 blocks of 48 trials each. For the first and last block π was .5, while for the 288 trials in the middle of the session a π-value of .8 was used. The results of primary interest concern this last series of trials, where subjects were no longer naive, and where any preexperimental habits had been given sufficient opportunity to extinguish. Figures 3.2 and 3.3 show the mean learning curve during the $\pi = .8$ series, as well as the recency curves computed from the last half of the $\pi = .8$ series. Clearly, probability matching obtains, and, more importantly, the recency curves are positive, as required by reinforcement theory. Predictions derived from the linear model are also shown in Figs. 3.2 and 3.3 and are in good agreement with the data. Thus, the hypothesis offered by Estes that the negative recency effect is not an intrinsic property of the data but arises through generalization from preexperimental response tendencies is supported by the outcome of the experiment. Even more direct evidence in favor of this hypothesis is provided by a comparison of the recency functions in the beginning of the experiment and at the end of the experiment. The first session started with a $\pi = .5$ series, and the third session ended with such a series. Recency functions were computed separately for both series. In the latter case an increase in the probability of a response as a function of consecutive reinforcements was observed, as in Figure 3.3. This, however, was not the case for the data from the beginning of the experiment. The recency function based upon that portion of the data was flat, i.e., the subject's responses were independent of the length of the run of the preceding reinforcements. Why the subjects in the Friedman *et al.* study started out this way while the recency curve

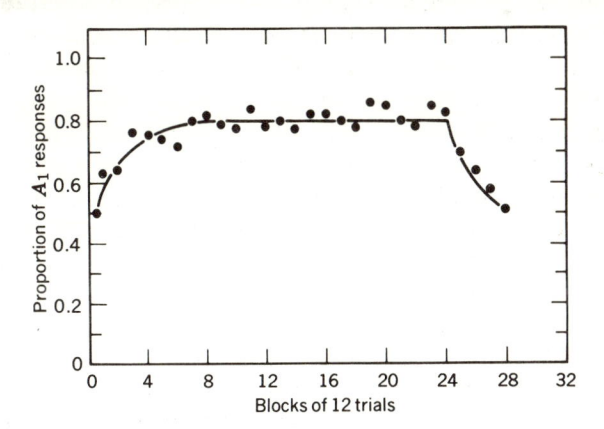

Fig. 3.2 *Observed and theoretical (linear model) proportions of* A_1 *reponses per 12-trial blocks during* $\pi=.8$ *series and following* $\pi=.5$ *series. (after Friedman* et al., *1964)*

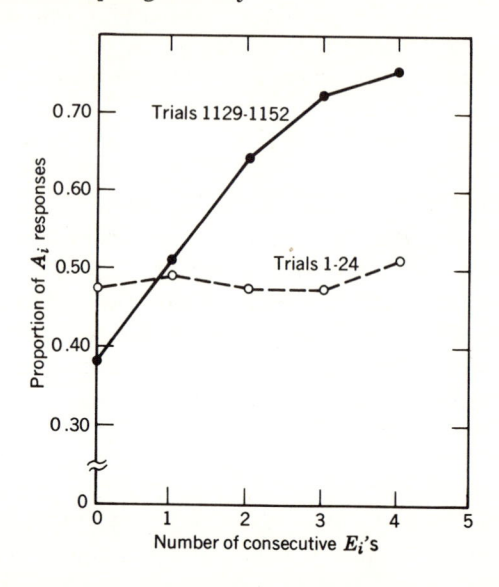

Fig. 3.3 *Recency curves for initial and terminal* $\pi = .5$ *blocks. (after Friedman* et al., *1964)*

for the subjects in other experiments actually decreases is not clear, and further study of the changes in the recency function during the course of learning would be desirable.

On the whole we may concur with Estes and maintain that the recency functions are in agreement with reinforcement theory, at least qualitatively, when interfering preexperimental guessing habits are extinguished. With respect to the linear model an even stronger statement may be made, since it was shown in Figs. 3.2 and 3.3 that the quantitative predictions of the model are quite adequate. The one-element pattern model, on the other hand can not account for the sequential data as was shown above. However, a small change in the model can overcome the difficulty. It will be remembered that in general a stimulus situation can be represented by any one of N mutually exclusive stimulus patterns. We have, up to now, only considered the case $N = 1$ and found it wanting. If N is treated as a free parameter the pattern model can account for the sequential data just as well as the linear model. Relevant data from the Friedman *et al.* experiment are shown in Table 3.3. In Table 3.3 the relative frequency of all possible response-reinforcement-new-response sequences are pooled over the last half of the $\pi = .8$ experimental condition. The predictions made by the linear model and by the pattern model are also shown. Detailed derivations for sequential predictions from the linear model may be found in Estes and Suppes (1959); corresponding derivations for the pattern model are given in Estes (1959b). It is clear that both models describe the sequential data very well.

The predictions of the linear model and of the general pattern model shown above may be used to calculate the predicted value of the probability of an A_1 response on trial n, given an A_1 response and an E_1 event on trial $n-1$. This is obtained simply by using the basic rule for conditional probabilities:

$$P(A_{1,n}|A_{1,n-1}E_{1,n-1}) = \frac{P(A_{1,n},E_{1,n-1},A_{1,n-1})}{P(E_{1,n-1},A_{1,n-1})}$$

The resulting values are .828 for the linear model and .826 for the general pattern model. Both of these values differ from the observed statistic (.829) only in the third decimal place. It is perhaps a little disconcerting that two models which are based upon very different learning assumptions should produce such similar predictions. The linear model assumes that learning occurs on all trials, while learning takes place only on correction trials according to the pattern model. However, this difference is more apparent than real, as Estes has pointed out (Estes, 1964). In the linear model the increment on each trial is proportional to the maximum possible increment (Eq. 4). When $P(A_{1,n})$ is small (and hence A_2 is likely to occur) a disconfirmation has a relatively great effect, but when $P(A_{1,n})$ is large (and the response A_1 tends to be made) the effects of a confirmation are neces-

Table 3.3. *Observed and theoretical proportions of response-reinforcement-new-response sequences for Trials 97-192 of the* $\pi = .8$ *series of Friedman et al. (1964) (after Estes, 1964).*

A_{n-1}	E_{n-1}	A_n	Observed value	Linear model	Pattern model
1	1	1	.562	.560	.662
1	2	1	.116	.116	.118
2	1	1	.103	.106	.104
2	2	1	.021	.021	.020
1	1	2	.081	.082	.082
1	2	2	.043	.045	.044
2	1	2	.054	.052	.053
2	2	2	.019	.019	.019

sarily restricted. Thus, both models predict learning mainly after errors, and the similarity of their predictions is not as unexpected as it appeared. Note that the prediction that either all or most learning occurs on error trials is counter to the assumption that satisfying aftereffects, or confirmation of expectancies, play an important role in learning. In fact, Estes shows that a model which assigns a crucial role to such effects can not account for the pattern of response probabilities in Table 3.3 at all. The model he discusses assumes that the response A_i is incremented on trial n whenever $A_{i,n}$ and $E_{i,n}$ occur, while disconfirmations leave response probabilities unchanged.

Concerning a General Theory of Choice Behavior

The excellent agreement between theory and data which was obtained in the Friedman *et al.* experiment shows that the models discussed above are able to provide a detailed and accurate explanation of probability learning, as long as the design of the experiment observes the boundary conditions of the theory. The latter restriction is important not only because it limits the range of the available models, but also in a broader sense since it shows what one may expect to achieve in psychology, and what goals seems to be out of our reach at present. We certainly do not have a general theory of probability learning, or of choice behavior in general. We do not seem to be close to such an achievement, either. Adult human subjects offer a problem of much greater complexity than psychological theories can cope with. But the model or models for choice behavior discussed above are adequate explanations for human behavior under circumstances which are very restricted, but nevertheless clearly specifiable. Note that even in the Friedman *et al.* experiment the models do not predict sequential behavior at the beginning of the experiment and apply only after presumed extraexperimental guessing habits have become extinguished. Anderson (1964) suggests that the effect of the prolonged training in this experiment is not to train out interfering response tendencies, but rather to train in the behavior to be described by the model. Whichever way one chooses to look at this problem, the result is always the same: under certain conditions the model describes what people do and is therefore an adequate theory, but it fails as a general theory of choice behavior. A general theory of choice behavior probably should be hierachical. At one level the theory should specify exactly what the experimental conditions are for the application of a particular model. Thus, a general theory would state the conditions under which choice behavior is to be described by stimulus-sampling theory (random event structure, instruction to predict correctly on every trial, experienced subjects, etc.) and presumably would give some reasons why this theory is relevant. For other experimental conditions, other models would apply, such as the maximizing strategy discussed earlier, or other versions of learning theory. In other words, the rules which govern a subject's behavior in a probability learning experiment depend upon the conditions of this experiment. Under different experimental conditions different models will be applicable, or, as Herman and Bahrick (1966) express this idea, "the basic problem for a subject in choice situations is the selection of decision rules rather than of decision alternatives."

Although we do not have at this time a general theory of choice behavior in the sense outlined above and most of the work in learning theory has been concerned with the trial-and-error learning approach, a few alternatives have been explored. Consider an experimental design which lies outside the boundary conditions of the models discussed so far because the occurrence of the experimental events E_1 and E_2 is not randomly determined but depends upon events on previous trials. For instance, imagine an event sequence which is constructed so that E_1 and E_2 occur with equal frequency ($\pi = .5$), but where the probability of a repetition is .75. Hake and Hyman (1953) have introduced this experimental design and have shown that subjects learn to adjust their predictions to contingencies of this kind. If the probability of a repetition is actually zero not even rats have much difficulty with the resulting alternation schedule, and college students easily learn a double alternation of the form 11001100 . . . (Schoonard and Restle, 1961). Even when much longer and considerably more complicated subsequences are repeated, subjects will eventually learn the pattern involved (e.g., Galanter and Smith, 1958). In fact the search for patterns appears to be one of the first strategies which subjects employ in a probability learning experiment (Jarvik, 1951; Feldman, 1963). Galanter and Smith not only demonstrated that subjects can respond to event patterns but also attempted to determine the experimental conditions conducive to such behavior. They stressed the role of instructions and other motivational conditions. Subjects memorized patterns when such a strategy appeared to them worthwhile in terms of increased monetary gain. The authors made a similar observation with regard to maximizing in random event sequences when subjects were paid for being correct. Several of their subjects realized quite suddenly that maximizing was the best strategy in this situation and started to predict the more probable event on all trials.

It is clear that any explanation of the behavior observed in experiments employing a conditional probability schedule must take into account the factor of memory which was neglected in the models discussed above. Subjects are not simply responding to the outcome of each trial in isolation, but they remember longer outcome sequences and adjust their behavior to the regularities in such sequences. Two alternative theories have been suggested which can account for this phenomenon. The first is a straightforward extension of stimulus-sampling theory (Burke and Estes, 1957; Restle, 1961). Suppose subjects have a memory span for k trials. The stimulus sample to which a subject responds then includes stimulus traces from the last k events, plus whatever background stimuli are present. Obviously, such a theory can describe the learning of event patterns up to length k, although, if k is even moderately large, learning ought to be fairly slow since so many different samples must be conditioned. For $k=7$ a subject would have to keep tract simultaneously of the conditioning states of 128 event patterns. An alternative model with reduced demands upon subject's memory load is based upon the observation made by Hake and Hyman (1953) that the event patterns which subjects appear to remember best are uninterrupted runs of the same event. Suppose therefore that the subject does not memorize all possible event patterns but merely remembers how many times the same event has occurred in a row. On any given trial such a subject would know that the outcome on this trial has occurred $0,1,2,....,k$ times before, and would predict whether the same event will occur on the next trial or not on the basis of his knowledge of the lengths of event runs in the experiment. Choice probabilities are therefore a direct function of the run structure of an experiment. Goodnow (1955) has proposed this model, and Restle (1961) has given it a quantitative formulation.

It should come as no surprise that experimental attempts to distinguish between these alternative explanations were inconclusive (Rose and Vitz, 1966). We have stated above our belief that models of choice behavior are not necessarily mutually exclusive, but that depending upon the characteristics of an experimental situation behavior follows one or another set of rules. We had reason before to deplore the lack of a general theory of choice behavior which would tell us exactly what the relevant characteristics are and why, and the experiment by Rose and Vitz serves to stress the seriousness of this deficiency. These authors constructed event sequences which observed certain regularities but were carefully balanced with respect to the unconditional probabilities of experimental events and even the probabilities conditional upon the preceding one, two, or three events. Some of the regularities employed were, for instance, that no run of length 3 was permitted, or that no run was longer than 4, or that sequences of the form 1101 were always followed by a 0 while 0010 sequences led to a 1. Their subjects readily learned these rules, although they had some difficulty with the more complex patterns. The authors concluded that, in general, their results favored the run hypothesis rather than the k-trial memory span model: not only was the former a better predictor, but many subjects also reported that they were attending to runs. However, subjects also learned rules such as the one mentioned above (1101→11010), which they could not do if they were merely remembering the event run in progress. Apparently, subjects can assume both modes of operation. They usually prefer the much simpler run strategy, but under as yet poorly understood conditions will respond to more complex patterns. The authors observed that subjects found it especially easy to observe complex regularities in the event sequence if they occurred after long runs.

There is another aspect of the results of the Rose and Vitz (1966) experiment which has far-reaching implications. The authors report that errors occasionally occurred in the application of rules like 011111→0111110, and that these errors often were accompanied by comments such as, "I must have miscounted." Observations such as this imply that a theory which assumes that subjects respond to runs (or to any k-tuple, for that matter) is unrealistic: Subjects do not always remember correctly, and a more adequate learning theory would have to take into account performance limitations due to the properties of the subject's short-term memory. Similarly, the study of Herman and Bahrick (1966) which was quoted above shows that the kind of display provided to the subject and the instructions given to him significantly influence the manner of information encoding, and, as a consequence, the selection of a decision rule. It therefore appears likely that further progress towards a general theory of choice behavior will depend upon a better understanding of such processes as short-term memory and information encoding. But before turning to a consideration of these processes in Chapter 4 the descriptive methods discussed above will be applied to a few more problem areas where they have yielded interesting results.

Two-person Interactions

The probability learning experiment has some interesting implications for the experimental study of games. Depending upon the constraints which the experimenter imposes in a game situation, a number of different types of experimental games may be distinguished. There exists a voluminous literature on this subject, of which only a few examples will be treated here, all pertaining to the simplest class of games.

An experiment by Suppes and Atkinson (1960) shows the manner in which experimental games are related to the probability learning experiment. Indeed, their experiment is nothing but a probability learning experiment for two persons, and not yet a game at all, but the extension to more truly game-like situations is obvious. The subjects in the Suppes and Atkinson experiment were run in pairs and were seated at opposite ends of a table. In front of each subject were two response keys with their associated event lights, and a signal lamp which indicated the trials of the experiment. In other words, the experimental setup was identical to the one used in probability learning experiments, except that a pair of subjects was run simultaneously. In the experiment to be reported first, subjects were even told that they were participating in a probability learning experiment, and that they only served in pairs because the equipment was designed in this way and because running pairs of subjects was a more economical procedure. However, the actual experimental design differed greatly from the noncontingent reinforcement procedure of the conventional probability learning experiment. Whether a subject's response was right or not (this was indicated by momentarily lighting a lamp above one of the subject's response keys, just as in a regular probability learning experiment) depended upon which response he had made and, in addition, upon which response his partner had made. This double contingency is expressed by a payoff matrix which gives the probabilities that the response of subject A will be called right on any given trial, depending upon the responses made by the two subjects:

			Response of player B:	
			B_1	B_2
(7)	Response of	A_1	.50	1.00
	player A:	A_2	.50	.25

Player B was correct whenever player A was not. Hence the entries of the reinforcement matrix for player B will be 1 minus the reinforcement probabilities for player A which are shown above:

		Response of player B:	
		B_1	B_2
Responses of	A_1	.50	.00
player A:	A_2	.50	.75

A different group of subjects played the game defined by the following payoff matrix (from now on only player A's payoff matrix will be shown):

(8)

	B_1	B_2
A_1	.33	1.00
A_2	.50	.17

Probably one should not use the terms "game" and "player" at all in this particular context: Suppes and Atkinson intentionally designed the experiment as a hybrid of a true experimental game and the conventional probability learning experiment. There are at least three elements missing from a true game situation: subjects were not informed of the payoff matrix, nor were they told about the responses of the other player; in fact, as has been mentioned before, they were led to believe that they were not interacting at all. But for precisely those reasons the experiment is sufficiently close to the probability learning paradigm so that attempts to apply the learning theories developed in the previous section should find optimal conditions.

Forty subjects each played the games (7) and (8). Two hundred trials were given in a continuous sequence. The data of primary interest concern asymptotic performance. Mean proportions of A_1 and B_1 responses during the last 60 trials of the experiment are given (together with their standard deviations) in the last four columns of Table 3.4.

Of the two kinds of predictions shown in Table 3.4 the ones labeled "game theory" should hardly be called "predictions" at all, for the reasons mentioned above. Yet they are of considerable interest, because they point up very important features of the experiment. However, before turning to a consideration of game theory, the learning theory predictions for the two-person interaction experiment will be outlined briefly. The simplicity of the one-element pattern model makes it a good starting point, although we already know that the model is too simple to give an account even for the conventional probability learning experiment. Suppose we have a two-person game with a symmetric payoff matrix, so that one person's loss is always the other's gain. In general, the reinforcement probabilities for player A are

(9)

	B_1	B_2
A_1	a_1	a_2
A_2	a_3	a_4

Table 3.4. *Predicted and observed asymptotic response probabilities for two experiments (Suppes and Atkinson, 1960, Chapter 3)*

	Predicted				Observed			
	Markov model		Game theory		Mean		s.d.	
Response:	A_1	B_1	A_1	B_1	A_1	B_1	A_1	B_1
Payoff Matrix (7)	.67	.61	1.00	1.00	.67	.60	.08	.06
Payoff Matrix (8)	.60	.63	.33	.83	.60	.65	.08	.09

Remember that the pattern model assumes that a subject always responds according to the conditioning state of the stimulus pattern which he samples. In the present experiments, responses are therefore determined by the conditioning states of two stimulus patterns, one of which is sampled by player A and the other by player B. Since the conditioning states of the two patterns are independent of each other, the four response combinations (A_1,B_1), (A_1,B_2), (A_2,B_1), and (A_2,B_2) result. The transition probabilities among these four response combinations are easily obtained by the application of the conditioning rules of the model: whenever a response is reinforced, the stimulus pattern remains conditioned to that response; whenever a response is made but the other response alternative is reinforced on that trial, the stimulus pattern changes its conditioning state to the reinforced response with probability c. For the present we shall assume that both subjects have the same conditioning rate c. This is not a necessary assumption, but it simplifies the presentation somewhat (see Suppes and Atkinson, 1960, Chapter 1, for further details). Suppose, that on some trial n the stimulus pattern of player A is conditioned to response 1 while the pattern B is conditioned to 2. According to the assumptions of the model, the response pair on that trial will be A_1,B_2, as shown in Fig. 3.4. The payoff matrix (9) shows that in this case player A will be correct (and B incorrect) with probability a_2, i.e., both players receive an E_1 reinforcing event. Therefore, the conditioning for player A will not change, while the stimulus pattern sampled by player B might become conditioned to B_1 with probability c (upper branch of Fig. 3.4). If both players receive an E_{2-} reinforcement, on the other hand, nothing will change for player B (his response was correct), but player A will change to A_2 with probability c. Note an interesting property of the tree in Fig. 3.4: no matter what happens,

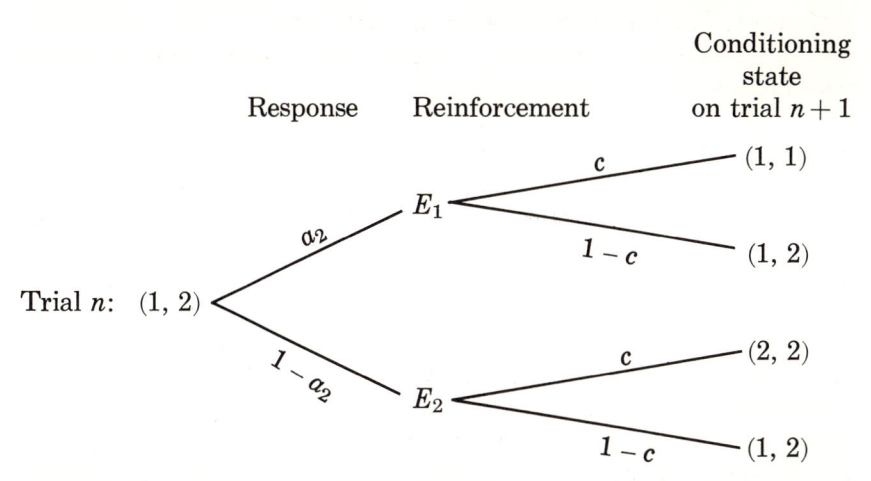

Fig. 3.4 *Response-event-conditioning sequence for a two-person inter-action experiment, given State (1,2).*

it is impossible that both players change conditioning states on the same trial, i.e., there is no branch which leads from A_1,B_2 to A_2,B_1. The transition probabilities from the other states may be similarly obtained and are summarized in the following matrix:

		(1,1)	(1,2)	(2,1)	(2,2)
	(1,1)	$(1-c)$	a_1c	$(1-a_1)c$	0
(10)	(1,2)	a_2c	$(1-c)$	0	$(1-a_2)c$
	(2,1)	$(1-a_3)c$	0	$(1-c)$	a_3c
	(2,2)	0	$(1-a_4)c$	a_4c	$(1-c)$

It is well known that for matrices of the above type, stable asymptotes exist and are independent of the initial probability distributions of the states. However, since the actual derivation requires familiarity with the elements of matrix algebra, only the result will be presented here. At asymptote,

$$(11) \qquad P(A_1) = \frac{a_1+a_2+a_3+a_4-a_1a_3-a_2a_4-2a_3a_4}{2(a_1+a_2+a_3+a_4-a_1a_2-a_1a_3-a_2a_4-a_3a_4)}$$

$$P(B_1) = \frac{a_1+2a_2+2a_4-2a_1a_2-2a_2a_4-a_3a_4}{2(a_1+a_2+a_3+a_4-a_1a_2-a_1a_3-a_2a_4-a_3a_4)}$$

Thus, asymptotic response probabilities depend only upon the reinforcement probabilities but not on the learning rate c, and a parameter-free prediction can be made before the experiment is actually performed. The predictions shown in Table 3.4 were obtained in this way, and correspond extremely well to the observed data for both experiments.

As in the noncontingent probability learning experiment for a single subject the simple pattern model makes very good predictions of asymptotic performance. But here, as well as there, the model fails to describe sequential behavior. In the case of a single subject the model implied that if a subject makes a response and this response is reinforced, he will always repeat that response on the next trial. The data were not at all in agreement with this deterministic prediction; nor do they agree with the corresponding predictions in the two-subject case. According to transition matrix (10) all transitions which involve a change in the conditioning states of both subjects have probability zero. However, actually observed values range from .11 to .32. Double state changes on the same trial are therefore not at all rare, as one might have expected. Just as in the previous section, the model may be changed so as to avoid this unrealistic prediction by relaxing the restriction that each subject samples only one pattern. Suppes and Atkinson (1960) have investigated some of the sequential predictions of the multielement pattern model with varying success. One of the problems which they encountered concerned the rather formidable mathematical complexity of the multielement model when it is applied to two-person games.

As was the case with the simple probability learning experiment, the theoretical alternative to learning theory is represented by a version of decision theory. The branch of decision theory which deals with conflict of interest situations of the type encountered here is called game theory. Game theory is a normative theory. It consists in the specification of strategies which a rational subject should follow in situations where the outcome is jointly dependent upon the decisions of two or more interested parties. We shall discuss game theory only in the briefest outline and only insofar as it is relevant to the two games described above. Both of these games are instances of a class of simple games, called two-persons zero-sum games, for which game theory provides a clear and compelling criterion of rationality. The term zero-sum refers to the property of payoff matrices such as (9) that one person always wins as much as the other loses. The criterion of rationality is the minimax principle of von Neumann and Morgenstern (1944), which states that each player should minimize his maximum loss. For the payoff matrix (7) the minimax principle leads to a very simple and intuitively quite compelling strategy: both players should always choose the first response. This is entirely clear for player A: no matter what his opponent does, an A_1 response will always be at least as good as A_2. For player B the situation is not clear and we must invoke the minimax principle. Since the maximum loss for a B_2 response is greater than the loss for a B_1 response, player B optimizes his winnings by always choosing B_1. Thus, games like (7) have a stable solution, and for rational opponents, such games will be quite boring to play since there is no uncertainty at all involved in the outcome. The equilibrium point of such games is called a saddle point in the terminology of game theory. In general, a saddle point will be an entry which is the smallest in its row and the largest in its column. The rational solution to such games appears to be quite compelling and one would suppose that intelligent subjects would soon find this solution. The failure of the subjects in the Suppes and Atkinson experiment to do so is, of course, not critical in this respect, because their subjects were kept from the possibility of a rational solution by the design of the experiment (they were not even told that they were playing against each other). In an experiment under conditions which were designed to favor rational strategies Lieberman (1960) concluded that except for deviations largely due to the boredom of repeated identical choices college students do employ a minimax strategy, at least on the final trials of his 200-trial experiment. Lieberman's subjects played a game with a saddle point in which both players could choose among three response alternatives. The subjects received or lost a small amount of money on each play.

For games like matrix (8) which do not have a saddle point von Neuman and Morgenstern proved that there exists a probability distribution over the response alternatives which maximizes the resulting expected value of the game for each player. In other words, there exists a mixed strategy which assures each player of a gain which is as large as possible under the constraints of the experiment. Note that the argument now depends upon the concept of expected value, i.e., the player employing a minimax strategy is assured of being rational only in the long run. The proof of this theorem requires some sophisticated mathematical concepts and will not be given here. In fact, even the method of determining a mixed minimax strategy for a particular payoff matrix is sufficiently complex so that we shall refer the reader to other sources (Luce and Raiffa, 1957; Suppes and Atkinson, 1960). The mixed minimax strategy for payoff matrix (8) is given in Table 3.4. The failure of the data to come anywhere near these predictions is irrelevant for the reasons mentioned above. Another game reported by Suppes and Atkinson is more interesting in this respect. In this experiment subjects were informed of the true character of the situation, and in fact, the payoff matrix which controlled wins and losses for each player was actually displayed to the subjects during the experiment. The payoff matrix for player A is shown below:

	B_1	B_2
A_1	.3	.8
A_2	.4	.1

This is a two-person zero-sum game without a saddle point. Player A's minimax strategy is to respond with A_1 with probability .375; player B should choose B_1 with probability .875. Before turning to the results of this experiment it is interesting to compare this rational solution with learning theory predictions, which can be calculated from Eq. (11). According to the one-element model, asymptotic choices of A_1 and B_1 should be .589 and .607, respectively. Observed were $P(A_1) =$ .691 and $P(B_1) = $ .684 for the last 60 of 200 experimental trials. These values differ markedly from the asymptotic predictions generated by the one-element model, but for A_1 the deviation was not even in the direction of a minimax strategy. We have thus a very illuminating result: when the properties of a two-person game are made quite explicit to the subject, he no longer behaves according to the rules of learning theory, but appears to strive for more optimal strategies, even though these strategies are not minimax strategies. The first conclusion agrees with our discussion of probability learning: depending upon instructions and other features of the procedure, subjects can be induced to behave rationally, or at least to adopt decision rules which are different from the ones predicted by the learning model. The second conclusion comes as no surprise if one considers the difficulty of arriving at a mixed strategy. It is clearly too much to expect that subjects should arrive at a strategy which was judged too complex to be presented here in detail within the 200 experimental trials, given human limitations of memory load and computing ability. Apparently, subjects tried to optimize their behavior, but some intuitively obvious characteristics of the payoff matrix may have misled them. For example, Suppes and Atkinson suggest that one reason for player A's ill-considered preference for A_1 was that it was not much worse than A_2 if B selects B_1, but greatly superior to A_2 if B selects B_2.

Rapoport and Orwant (1962) have reviewed a number of zero-sum two-person games without saddle points and have also concluded that it is difficult for subjects to arrive at a minimax solution, although subjects do attempt to optimize their behavior. In fact, the kind of solution subjects arrive at are often only very little inferior to true minimax solutions. This is true also in the game described above, and might be a further reason for subjects' failure to find a minimax solution.

The Scanning Model

Most of the experimental games discussed in the Rapoport and Orwant review (1962) involve monetary rewards to subjects, not just differential reinforcement probabilities as in the examples given here. However, before discussing the role of monetary payoffs in two-person games, it seems appropriate to study the effects of monetary rewards in a simple two-choice experiment. Suppose a subject can make one of two responses A_1 or A_2. On each trial the subject wins or loses 5 cents. Let π_i be the probability of a win. In general, $\pi_1 \neq \pi_2$. A theoretical treatment of this experimental paradigm within the framework of stimulus sampling theory has been provided by Estes (1962). Estes observed that the familiar probability learning experiment is embedded within this choice situation. He assumes that on each trial of the experiment the subject predicts the reinforcement for each response, and then, on the basis of his predictions, selects a response. The subject's predictions are governed by the same processes as in a conventional probability learning experiment. In particular, as we shall be concerned here only with asymptotic performance, the over-all frequency with which a subject predicts reinforcement after responses A_1 and A_2 will come to match the actual reinforcement probabilities π_1 and π_2, respectively. Thus, the probability of predicting reinforcement for both responses will be $\pi_1.\pi_2$. In general, the probabilities that a subject will predict the four possible outcome combinations on trial n (for large n) are:

	Prediction	Probability of prediction
	$A_1 A_2$	$\pi_1 \pi_2$
(12)	$A_1 \bar{A}_2$	$\pi_1 (1-\pi_2)$
	$\bar{A}_1 A_2$	$(1-\pi_1) \pi_2$
	$\bar{A}_1 \bar{A}_2$	$(1-\pi_1)(1-\pi_2)$

where the bar over a response alternative denotes that the subject expects no reward for this response on this trial. If the subject expects either the second or the third of these outcome combinations, his decision rule is obvious: he will always choose A_1 (or A_2 in case of the third outcome), since he prefers winning to losing 5 cents. On the

other hand, if the subject predicts reward for both or for neither of
the two response alternatives, his decision rule is less obvious. One of
the possibilities which Estes has explored is that in case of a tie the
subject chooses a response with a probability equal to its current
choice probability on all types of trials, i.e., A_1 is selected with probability $P(A_1)$ and A_2 is chosen with probability $P(A_2)$. With these
assumptions, the asymptotic probability of an A_1 choice may be expressed recursively as

$$P(A_1) = \pi_1 \pi_2 . P(A_1) + \pi_1(1-\pi_2).1 + (1-\pi_1)\pi_2.0 +$$
$$(1-\pi_1)(1-\pi_2)P(A_1)$$

$$(13) \qquad = \frac{\pi_1(1-\pi_2)}{\pi_1 + \pi_2 - 2\pi_1\pi_2}$$

Estes shows that Eq. (13) predicts asymptotic performance quite
well for three groups of subjects in an experiment by Atkinson (1962).
Atkinson's subjects were asked to press one of two response keys for
340 trials. When they were correct, they received 5 cents, when they
were incorrect they were fined 5 cents. The three different reinforcement schedules which were used in this experiment to determine
whether a response was correct or not are shown in Table 3.5, together with the observed choices on the last block of trials and the
predictions calculated by Eq. (13). Note that the predictions are
truly *a priori*, in that no part of the data had to be used for parameter
estimation. Table 3.5 also summarizes the relevant features of an experiment by Siegel and Abelson (Siegel, 1961). In this experiment,

Table 3.5. *Predicted and observed asymptotic A_1 choice proportions for
two experiments with response contingent reinforcement.*

	π_1	π_2	A_1 choice Predicted	A_1 choice Observed
Atkinson (1962):	.6	.5	.600	.601
	.7	.5	.700	.685
	.8	.5	.800	.832
Siegel (1961):	.75	.25	.900	.929
	.70	.30	.846	.850
	.65	.35	.775	.753

as in the previous experiment, subjects could win or lose 5 cents on each trial; 20 subjects were run for 300 trials for each condition.

Observed and predicted values in Table 3.5 are quite close, thus lending some support to the notion that subjects scan the response alternatives on each trial, generate a prediction of the reward that will be received for each response, and then choose a response accordingly. The scanning model is further supported by some data reported by Lieberman (1962). In this experiment the amounts won and lost were not the same for both response alternatives as was the case in the previously reported experiments. Lieberman played a game with his subjects in which both the experimenter and his subject held cards with a 1 or 2 on it and each placed one card face down on a table. After both had made their choices the two cards were turned up, revealing their choices and determining the outcome of the play according to the following deterministic payoff matrix:

	E_1	E_2
S_1	3	-1
S_2	-9	3

If $S_1 E_1$ occurred the subject received three cents from the experimenter. If $S_1 E_2$ occurred the experimenter received one cent from the subject, and so on. Subjects were given \$2.50 at the start of the game and played for 300 trials. The experimenter's choices were all fixed in advance. For one group of 10 subjects the experimenter reinforced S_1 responses with probability .25 and S_2 responses with probability .75 (Group O). A second group of subjects was rewarded 50% of the time, no matter which response a subject made (Group N). Predictions for subjects' asymptotic choices may be derived from the scanning model by considering the four outcome possibilities on each trial and the probabilities of the subject's predicting each outcome, as in (12):

Outcome: (Gain for subject)		Probability of prediction:
3	3	$\pi_1 \pi_2$
3	-9	$\pi_1 (1 - \pi_2)$
-1	3	$(1 - \pi_1) \pi_2$
-1	-9	$(1 - \pi_1)(1 - \pi_2)$

If the subject expects any one of the last three outcome combinations his decision rule is unambiguous, since he prefers winning to losing, or losing one cent to losing 9 cents. If the subject expects on any trial that both responses will be rewarded, we shall assume as before that he will choose response S_1 with the overall probability of that response. Hence, for asymptotic performance,

$$P(S_1) = \pi_1\pi_2P(S_1) + \pi_1(1-\pi_2) + (1-\pi_1)(1-\pi_2)$$

$$= \frac{1-\pi_2}{1-\pi_1\pi_2}$$

Substituting $\pi_1 = .25$ and $\pi_2 = .75$ (Group O), we obtain $P(S_1) = .31$, which is not too far off the observed asymptote of .38. For Group N the model predicts an asymptote of .67, which is identical with the observed proportion of S_1 choices over the last 50 trials of the experiment.

Lieberman has also presented game theory predictions for this experiment. The game is a zero-sum game without a saddle point, and the minimax behavior for the subject is to choose S_1 with probability .75. The minimax strategy for the experimenter is the one employed against Group O (choose E_1 25% of the time). The strategy employed against Group N ($\pi_1 = \pi_2 = .5$) is non-optimal. The results for Group O are in agreement with the evidence reported above that subjects are generally not able to perceive and play a mixed minimax strategy. Group N seems to approach rational behavior more closely, but note that the subjects in this group did not attempt to exploit the experimenter's weak play, as they could have by making more than 75% S_1 responses. Clearly the scanning model gives a better and more parsimonious account of the results of this experiment.

Before concluding this discussion a serious deficiency of the scanning model must be mentioned. As Estes has pointed out, the model is only concerned with a subject's preference for one of the two response alternatives but does not handle different absolute payoff values. As long as one outcome is preferred to the other, the model always makes the same predictions no matter what the degree of preference may be. Obviously this is a serious failure of the model, because it seems unlikely that subjects behave in the same way when the payoffs are 1 cent and 5 cents, or 1 cent and $100. An experiment by Siegel and Goldstein (1959) supports this common sense expectation. The authors observed three groups of 36 subjects for 300 trials in a prediction experiment with a π-value of .75. No payoffs were given to the first group of subjects. Group II was a reward group: subjects received 5 cents for each correct response and were not punished for errors. In Group III subjects also received 5 cents for correct predictions but were fined 5 cents when incorrect. The observed proportion of A_1 choices were .75, .86, and .95, respectively, for trials 281-300.

Applying Eq. (13) we predict an asymptote of .90 for both Groups II and III. Although this prediction is not far off the observed values, it fails to reflect what is presumably an important difference in the outcome for the two payoff combinations.

The extensions of the probability learning experiment to two-person interactions and differential rewards have been presented here in order to demonstrate the considerable explanatory power of contemporary learning models, and in particular of stimulus-sampling theory. At the same time, the discussion has emphasized the lack of an adequate and complete theory of human choice behavior. It is true that stimulus-sampling theory describes the behavior of subjects in a number of different experimental situations. The description is accurate, at least as far as the coarser aspects of the data are concerned, and the range of applicability of stimulus-sampling theory is quite broad. Yet it is clear that subjects do not always adjust to the experimental situation in the trial-by-trial manner characteristic of the learning process. In some situations subjects attempt to find rational strategies, and their behavior resembles problem solving rather than learning, even if subjects are usually unable to find optimal solutions in any but the least complex experiments. More work is necessary to determine the factors which control this difference, and to find out exactly what goes on in experiments which are outside the boundary conditions of learning theory. Such information presumably would reflect back on our understanding of the learning process itself. The studies mentioned in this chapter, especially those dealing with games and differential rewards, are not more than a fraction of the current work in this area, but they fairly represent the achievements as well as the problems encountered in the study of that deceptively simple experiment, probability learning.

SUMMARY

Stimulus-sampling theory presents a conceptual framework within which specific models may be developed for specific experimental problems. The basic terms of the theory are stimulus (S), response (R), reinforcement, conditioning, and stimulus sampling. Unlike some other S—R theories it does not insist on direct S—R connections which are automatically strengthened through reinforcement. Subjects may be viewed as scanning several S—R connections and deciding among them on the basis of the information provided by the experimental reinforcement. Thus, the range of applicability of the theory is not restricted to simple conditioning situations.

The central assumptions of the theory specify the sampling process. Depending upon how stimulus sampling is assumed to work, different classes of models are obtained. In particular, subjects may either sample elements or patterns. If they sample from a large population of stimulus elements, learning is gradual because on each trial only a small proportion of the stimulus elements can become conditioned. On the other hand, if the total stimulus situation is represented by stimulus patterns learning is a discrete process, because patterns are conditioned as units. It was shown that the models of paired-associate learning which were discussed in Chapter 2 could be given a stimulus-sampling interpretation. The problem discussed there can be expressed within stimulus-sampling theory as conditioning of stimulus elements versus conditioning of a pattern as a whole.

A related problem concerns stimulus selection. If subjects sample elements they restrict themselves sometimes to a subset of the elements present, which then becomes the functional stimulus for them. Through transfer tests the experimenter can determine which aspects of the stimulus were functional for a given subject and which were not. The importance of stimulus selection was demonstrated with several experiments from the literature on paired-associate learning. Other studies were discussed where selection apparently did not occur, but where subjects responded to patterns and transferred to components of the stimulus in a manner predictable from the pattern model. Conditions under which pattern formation rather than stimulus selection occurs were tentatively identified.

In the second half of the chapter implications of stimulus-sampling theory with regard to sequential choice behavior were discussed. In the "probability learning" experiment subjects predict for many trials in succession which of two lights is going to come on. The lights are actually turned on according to a random schedule, so that the subjects can learn only the probabilities with which the lights are being turned on. Models derived from stimulus-sampling theory predict that the subject's response frequencies will come to match the frequencies with which the experimenter turns on the corresponding lights. In addition, predictions were derived from the models concerning the trial-by-trial dependency of the subject's response upon his immediately preceding response and the preceding reinforcement. Relevant data with respect to both predictions were discussed. It was concluded that models exist which describe the subject's behavior quite well in some clearly circumscribed situations. However, subjects can assume many different modes of behavior and one would need a superordinate theory which indicates when and why a particular model is to be applied to an experimental situation. Details of the experimental condition, particularly instructions, perceptual lay-out, and memory load appear to be critical, but their effects are not yet fully understood.

Extensions of the theory to two-person interactions and to experiments with monetary rewards were described. Predictions from learning models were contrasted with rational or optimal modes of behavior.

MEMORY

44444444444444

Memory is of obvious significance for learning. Behavior changes in a learning experiment represent a balance between the processes of acquisition and forgetting. Immediately after presentation of a paired-associate item the probability of a correct response is close to unity, if certain precautions have been taken to insure adequate perception of the stimulus. Since in almost all verbal learning experiments perceptual conditions are very favorable, the question arises why learning is usually so slow, since directly after each item presentation items are always "learned." Similarly, if only one item were used in a paired-associate experiment it would practically always be learned in one trial; only with longer lists do subjects need many learning trials.

Such observations suggest that forgetting between presentation of an item and its test is an important factor in learning. Acquisition processes and memory interact to cause the trial-to-trial changes which are investigated in most verbal learning experiments. Acquisition (learning proper) depends upon variables operating at the time of item presentation, or prior to it. Forgetting depends upon the conditions during the retention interval. One way to describe the performance changes during a learning experiment would be to say that items become more resistant to forgetting as learning proceeds. This does not mean that learning is nothing but increased resistance to intertrial forgetting, as there are other factors (e.g., stimulus encoding, subjective organization) which play an equally significant role in verbal learning.

The interaction between memory and acquisition processes in verbal learning has long been recognized (McGeoch, 1942), but has been regarded as little more than a truism. Only recently, stimulated by the findings of experiments on short-term memory, has its profound significance been appreciated.

Murdock (1963a) demonstrated the close relation between short-

136

term memory experiments and paired-associate learning. In a short-
term memory experiment, which also can be regarded as the first trial
of a regular paired-associate study, subjects were presented with lists
of common word pairs. After the presentation of each list, retention
was tested by presenting the first member of each pair alone. The
results are shown in Fig. 4.1 for lists 2-5 pairs long. Strong forgetting
effects are apparent: probability of recall is a decreasing function of
the number of subsequent pairs in the list. The last item in each list,
for which little opportunity for forgetting existed, was almost always
"learned." The less than perfect performance for the last item might
have been caused, at least partially, by Murdock's procedure, because
in some instances recall tests of other items intervened between the
presentation of the last item of a list and its test. In any case, subsequent list pairs clearly lead to much forgetting, although the effect
seems to level off with about 3 intervening pairs in this experiment.
Thus Fig. 4.1 suggests two performance components: a short-term
memory factor which is especially prominent when the retention interval is brief, and a second factor which accounts for the performance
with longer retention intervals. This second factor seems to be independent of the number of subsequent list pairs, but is influenced
by list length.

Tulving (1964) has also argued that some of the phenomena of
learning and memory may be identical. He developed a method for

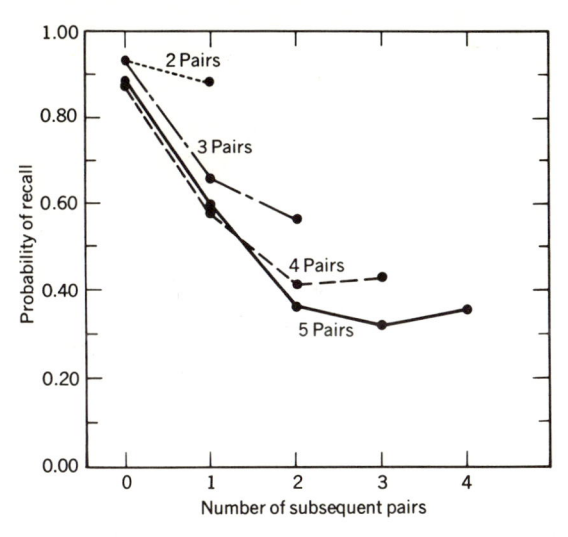

Fig. 4.1 *Probability of recall for lists of 2-5 pairs. (after Murdock,
1963)*

the analysis of free-recall data which permits tracing the course of forgetting throughout a multi trial experiment. Instead of merely plotting the average number of correct responses or the number of incorrect responses per trial, Tulving distinguishes four (noninde-pendent) categories of responses on each trial: recall of an item which was also recalled on the previous trial $(C_{n-1}C_n)$, recall of an item which was not recalled on the previous trial $(N_{n-1}C_n)$, nonrecall of an item which was recalled on the previous trial $(C_{n-1}N_n)$, and nonrecall on two successive trials $(N_{n-1}N_n)$. Data from an experiment in which subjects learned to recall a 22-word list are shown in Fig. 4.2. The usual mean learning curve is the sum of two of the components from Fig. 4.2, intertrial retention $(C_{n-1}C_n)$ plus intratrial retention $(N_{n-1}C_n)$. Of these, only the former shows an increase as a function of learning trials. Intratrial retention actually decreases. However, Tulving argues that this decrease is an experimental artifact caused by the fixed list length used in his experiment, and that without this restraint intratrial retention does not change over trials. The increase in intertrial

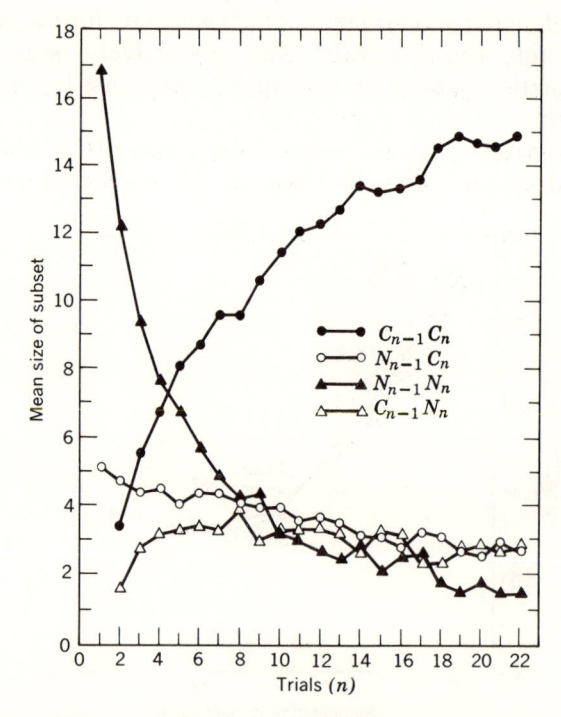

Fig. 4.2 *Four different components of performance derived from trial-to-trial analysis of recall data. (after Tulving, 1964)*

retention was found to be correlated with a tendency of the subject to group the words in the recall list into higher order subjective units.

These results suggest two subprocesses of learning: intratrial forgetting or short-term memory processes, and more long-term changes which have something to do with the subject's organization of the learning material. With this as a working hypothesis concerning the basic processes involved in verbal learning, we shall turn towards an examination of the phenomena of memory.

The classical studies of memory were performed by Ebbinghaus (1885). Ebbinghaus estimated memory losses by means of a savings procedure. He learned a list of nonsense syllables, waited a certain number of hours, minutes, or days, and then relearned the list. The time which relearning took was compared with the original learning time, and the savings calculated in percent were used as estimates of retention. Figure 4.3 shows the forgetting curve that resulted from Ebbinghaus' pioneering work. The curve is negatively accelerated: most forgetting occurs during the first few hours after learning; after that the rate of forgetting decreases greatly.

At the time of this investigation, Ebbinghaus (who served as his own and only subject) was about forty years old. Each day he learned 8 lists of 13 nonsense syllables to a criterion of two successive correct trials. Whenever he was conscious of an uncertainty or hesitation, a trial was not accepted as correct. The total time needed to learn the 8 lists was then compared with the relearning time after retention intervals ranging from 20 minutes to 31 days. During the course of the experiment, Ebbinghaus learned and relearned more than 1200 different lists. Ebbinghaus was a very careful worker and having noted that learning time depended upon the time of the day (he was 12% slower around 7 p.m. than at 10 a.m.), he adjusted his results for diurnal variations. For instance, with an 8-hour retention interval, original learning and relearning necessarily had to be conducted at different times of the day.

Mathematically, Ebbinghaus' forgetting curve can be closely approximated by an exponential function

$$(1) \qquad\qquad Y = ab^{-t}$$

where Y is a measure of the amount retained, a and b are constants, and t is the retention time. Taking logarithms, we obtain

$$(2) \qquad \log Y = \log a - (\log b) \cdot t = a_0 - a_1 t,$$

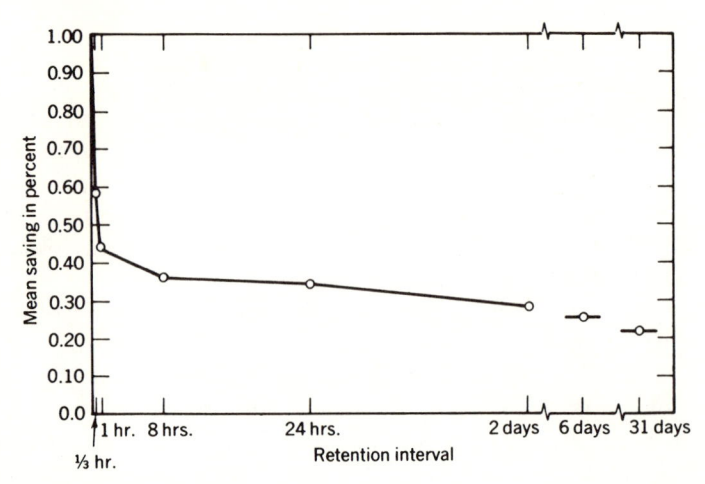

Fig. 4.3 *Retention of lists of nonsense syllables as determined by the savings method. (after Ebbinghaus, 1885)*

such that $\log a = a_0$ and $\log b = a_1$. Equation (2) implies that amount retained in memory is linearly related to the logarithm of retention time. Hence, if plotted on semilogarithmic paper, the retention function should be a straight line. The slope of the line is determined by the constant b, while a is the Y-intercept of the line. Figure 4.4 shows a plot of Ebbinghaus' data in semilogarithmic form. It is obvious that a straight line provides a fairly good description of the data points. In addition, the results of a number of other investigators are shown in Fig. 4.4. With the exception of the uppermost curve, all other curves are based upon memory for lists of nonsense syllables using the savings method. Ebbinghaus' original results are amply confirmed by these data. Straight lines can be fittted to all curves. The fact that these curves show somewhat better retention throughout seems to be the only difference between Ebbinghaus' data, based upon one subject learning many different lists, and the other sets of data shown here which give averages for groups of subjects learning a single list. The curve showing retention for poetry is the only one where memory does not decrease monotonically. However, these results are questionable since the experimenter did not exclude the possibility of voluntary or involuntary rehearsal during the interval between learning and retention test, as Woodworth and Schlosberg (1961) point out, from whom this figure has been taken.

Various other retention tests have provided similar results. Although estimates of the amount retained depend greatly upon the exact testing procedure which is employed, the exponential shape of the forgetting curve seems to be quite independent of these factors. Thus, recognition tests tend to give much higher estimates of amount retained than recall tests. However, in both cases the typical negatively accelerated forgetting curve has been obtained. An interesting consequence of this shape of the forgetting curve is known under the name of "Jost's law" (Jost, 1897). When two associations are of equal strength but of different ages, the older one will lose strength more slowly with the further passage of time. If strength of an association is identified with the ordinate of Figs. 4.3 and 4.4, the law follows, since a relatively old association will have reached a flatter part of the forgetting curve, while the newer association is still at a point of the curve where considerable forgetting occurs.

Many early experimenters believed disuse to be the primary cause of forgetting. However, what the subject does during the retention interval was soon shown to be a crucial factor in forgetting. Jenkins and Dallenbach (1924) demonstrated that if the subject sleeps during the retention interval forgetting is markedly reduced relative to a waking control group. In their study subjects learned a list of 10 CVCs and were tested for recall after 1, 2, 4, and 8 hours of ordinary waking activity or sleeping. For all retention intervals recall was much better after sleep. The effect was quite strong: for example, after 8 hours sleep about 6 syllables could be recalled, while after the same time spent awake only about 1 syllable was recalled. This and related findings prompted McGeoch to attack the view that disuse is a major

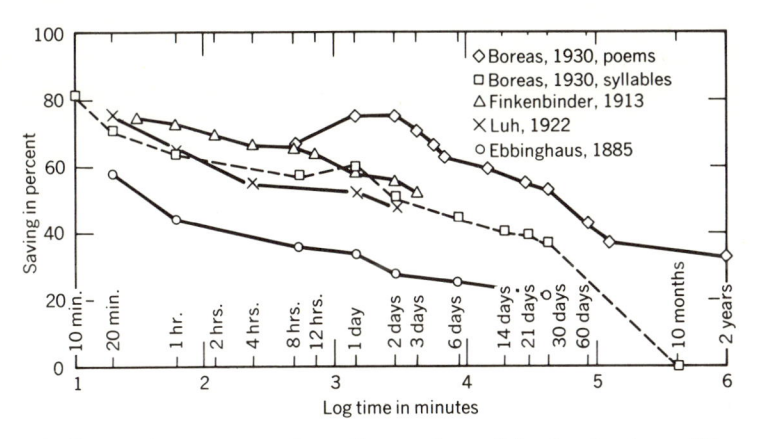

Fig. 4.4 *Retention curves plotted on a logarithmic abscissa. The materials were nonsense syllable lists except for the uppermost curve. (after Woodworth and Schlosberg, 1961)*

factor in forgetting (McGeoch, 1932). He maintained that time per se has no effect, but that the events which occur in time are important. Iron does not rust because of the passage of time, but because of certain chemical reactions which take place in time; similarly, forgetting is not a passive decay process, but is determined by the environmental events occurring during the retention interval. New activity during the retention interval interferes with what has been learned before, thus producing forgetting. Memory would be perfect if the retention interval were completely devoid of activity.

The interference theory of forgetting discussed in Chapter II originated from observations such as those reported above. Thus, this theory is a direct outgrowth of the work of Ebbinghaus and his followers. A characteristic of all this work is that it is concerned with rather long retention times. Forgetting is tested hours or even days after learning. Only recently have psychologists begun to study systematically much shorter retention periods. This work has considerably affected our picture of memory.

To lend some order to the discussion in this chapter we shall at this point present a brief overview, anticipating the main results to be discussed below. We shall distinguish three separate memory stores, although this is by no means generally accepted among psychologists. We present this distinction as a working hypothesis; in the remainder of the chapter supporting evidence will be cited which attests to its reasonableness, even if it may not be possible to prove it to everyone's satisfaction. We assume that information first enters a *sensory memory*, which is a large-capacity store from which information is lost rapidly unless it is attended to and transferred to primary memory. *Primary memory* is a kind of working memory with a limited capacity from which information is lost within about 15-20 seconds, although it may be retained in primary memory for more extended time periods through rehearsal. Information selected for more permanent storage enters *secondary memory*. Secondary memory has an essentially unlimited capacity. Forgetting from secondary memory is relatively slow; it takes two forms: actual loss of information and inability to retrieve information which is nevertheless still in storage.

The terms *short-term memory* and *immediate memory* are often used to designate memory for short retention periods, which is based mostly but not necessarily upon primary memory. The term *long-term memory* corresponds to secondary memory and contrasts with short-term memory. The reader should be specifically warned that the term long-term memory will frequently be applied to situations where retention periods are "long" only in contrast with the few seconds for which information is held in primary memory.

A diagram showing the relationships among the three memory components is shown in Fig. 4.5, which will serve as a guide for the further discussion of memory in this chapter. In Fig. 4.5 a distinction has been made between *structural components* of memory and *control processes*, following Atkinson and Shiffrin (1968). The structural components are the three memory stores: sensory memory, primary memory, and secondary memory. Forgetting may occur from each one of these stores but the rates of forgetting are different and the causes of forgetting may also be different. The control processes regulate what information is selected from sensory memory, what gets rehearsed, and what gets stored in memory. Other control processes concerning retrieval from long-term memory will be discussed in Chapter V.

Short-term Memory

The distinction between a short- and long-term memory store is by no means new, although its full significance has not been appreciated until recent years. James (1890) first distinguished between primary and secondary memory: information in primary memory has never left consciousness; information in secondary memory has been absent from consciousness for some time. Recall from primary memory is easy and effortless, while active search processes often characterize retrieval from secondary memory. For an item to enter secondary mem-

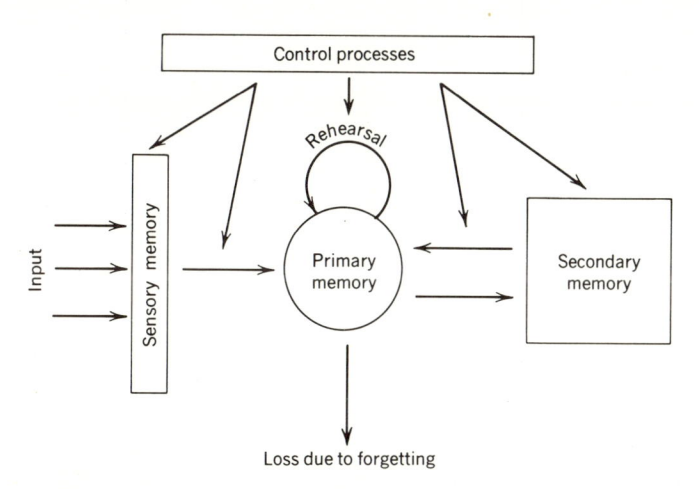

Fig. 4.5 *A schematic outline of the memory system.*

ory, stimulation must exceed some minimum duration, otherwise it will fail to "set" in secondary memory. Stern (1938) made a similar distinction in terms of immediate and mediate memory. He also discussed sensory memory stores, which do not involve subject's central processing capacities but consist in the continued excitation of the sense organ itself.

Ebbinghaus (1902) himself had noted that two different processes seemed to be going on when material within the span of immediate memory or when material exceeding that span was learned. There is a sharp discontinuity between memory for six nonsense syllables and memory for 12 syllables. While the former could almost always be recited correctly after just one presentation, only very few syllables, perhaps not more than the first and last, could be retained when 12 CVCs were presented. The results of an experiment, with Ebbinghaus as the only subject, which shows the relationship between the number of repetitions necessary to learn a list of CVCs to a criterion of one correct recitation and the length of the list are reproduced in Fig. 4.6. Only one presentation is necessary as long as the list is within the capacity of immediate memory, which is here about

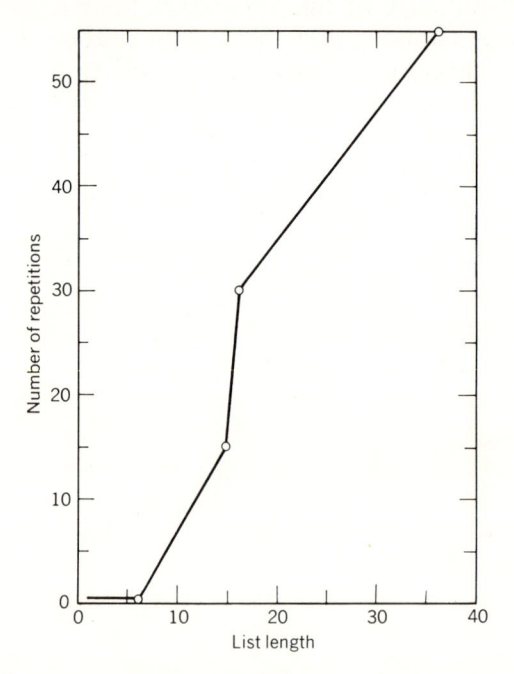

Fig. 4.6 *Number of repetitions necessary to learn a list as a function of list length. (after Ebbinghaus, 1902)*

six items. After that, it took Ebbinghaus approximately 2 repetitions per added item in order to learn the list, i.e., in order to store the added items in secondary memory.

Although short-term memory has a sharply limited capacity, this limitation appears to be primarily in the number of items which can be held, but not in the size and information content of these items. This important aspect of short-term memory has been stressed by Wundt (1905). Wundt observed that the capacity of immediate memory was restricted to about 6 items when the learning material consisted of items taken in isolation, such as random letters, digits, or isolated lines. However, if these elements were grouped into larger units (e.g., grouping letters so that they form a word) many more elements could be retained in immediate memory because the subject remembered about as many words as he could remember single letters. Müller and Schumann (1894) have investigated some of the conditions which determine the size of units in immediate memory.

In spite of these promising beginnings, the study of immediate memory progressed very little between the First World War and the late 1950's. This probably occurred because the earlier studies had relied upon introspective methods, at least in part, and when introspection became unfashionable with the advent of behaviorism, psychologists rejected the problem together with the methodology. That is, the importance of the problem was fully recognized: learning theory found some kind of short-term memory mechanism essential in order to explain the effects of reinforcement in establishing an $S—R$ bond when reinforcement was delayed. Both Pavlov (1928) and Hull (1943) postulated a stimulus-trace mechanism, so that retroaction did not have to be invoked to explain the effects of delayed reinforcement. However, they were not particularly interested in this mechanism *per se*. Hull and his followers gave the stimulus trace concept the lofty status of an intervening variable, and turned to other problems. Nor did psychologists interested in verbal learning and memory do much more to further our understanding of immediate memory, or to follow up the interesting suggestions of pre-behavioristic psychology. Most of their efforts went into two problems: the relationship between different experimental conditions and the length of the series which could be retained after one presentation (the memory span), and the distribution of errors in different serial positions.

Contemporary work on immediate memory received its impetus from a number of different sources. Neurological discoveries and theories indicated the existence of two different memory stores; information theory provided a means of dealing with the capacity of immediate memory; and the close relationship between perception and learning came to be realized. Suddenly, immediate memory turned out to be a central problem in psychology. The work and the theories of Hebb (1949) and Broadbent (1958) were especially important in stimulating this interest in immediate memory. The theoretical impetus also brought about methodological innovations. Beginning with the work of Peterson and Peterson (1959), several objective procedures have been developed for the experimental study of short-term memory.

Hebb (1949) was concerned with the physiological basis of memory. Memory, as it is usually understood, involves some structural change within the organism, the nature of which need not concern us here. Such a structural change requires an appreciable amount of time, and Hebb found it necessary to postulate some sort of a mechanism to carry memory until the structural change occurs. Anatomical and physiological evidence for such a mechanism was already available. Lorente de Nó (1938) had described fibers which were arranged in closed, potentially self-exciting circuits. Thus, a short-term memory mechanism based upon a reverberating stimulus trace seemed to be both a possible as well as a necessary inference. Hebb postulated two kinds of memory: long-term memory, which is based upon a structural trace and is permanent except for interference from other long-term traces; and short-term memory, based upon an activity trace. Short-term memory is subject to autonomous decay. Hebb pointed out two possible reasons for this inherent instability of short-term memory: the cells in a closed, reverberating cell assembly may become refractory, or interruption through external events may occur. Activity traces are transformed into structural traces when the stimulus is presented repeatedly, or simply through consolidation: if an activity trace is not interfered with but is allowed to run its course, a stable structural memory trace is established.

Quite different considerations motivated Broadbent's distinction between a temporary and a more permanent memory store (Broadbent, 1958, 1963). Broadbent tries to infer the flow of information in the human perceptual and memory system from purely behavioral data. He does not concern himself with neurological detail, but at the same time he is not satisfied merely with a description of behavior. Just as one can describe the working of a computer in terms of a flow-diagram which identifies the function of the various subsystems without giving much thought to the electrical engineering details, one can construct and test a rough model of information processing within the organism. Broadbent's model clearly shows his interest in perceptual problems. Studies of multichannel listening have led him to stress the concepts of perceptual filter and channel capacity. If information is presented to a subject over several sensory channels simultaneously, the typical subject is able to pay attention to only one channel at a time. Subjects have a limited capacity for information processing. Information which has been processed is stored in short-term memory, where it will be lost rapidly unless it is rehearsed. Rehearsal means repeated passage through the same limited-capacity channel. Therefore, if the capacity of this channel is taken up either by new input or by any other interruption, forgetting will occur. In addition, of course, information may be stored in a more permanent manner in long-term memory.

Broadbent illustrates this model by pointing to our everyday experience with memory for telephone numbers. Most of us can recall our own telephone number and a few others whenever we are called to do so. On the other hand, when we look up a new number in the telephone book, memory is very frail. We can keep the number in mind as long as we need, if we can repeat it to ourselves silently. However, should we be distracted before we reach the telephone we are likely to forget our number unless we can periodically rehearse it. On the other hand, suppose we hear a new number which we want to remember and we cannot write it down. Then we try to memorize this number by some means or other. This we shall refer to as long-term storage.

The reason why Broadbent distinguished a separate short-term memory store was his belief that forgetting in short-term memory followed quite different rules than the forgetting of old-established memories.

Apart from a separate short-term memory store, Broadbent also distinguished a sensory memory store. He found that sensory information could be kept in a sensory store without being analyzed for a period of a second or so. The capacity of this store is large relative to the capacity of short-term memory, but forgetting is very rapid. Material in the sensory store decays with time and is not dependent upon interference.

Brown (1958) obtained some experimental results which he interpreted as evidence for spontaneous decay in short-term memory. In one of his studies, he employed a retention interval of approximately 5 seconds which was either filled with a digit reading task or empty and thus could be used for rehearsal. From one to four serially presented consonant pairs were to be remembered. He found that when rehearsal was permitted almost no forgetting occurred, except when 3 or 4 consonant pairs were used. On the other hand, when rehearsal was impossible (or at least made difficult) much less material was recalled. This result was interpreted to mean that short-term memory decays rapidly, unless it is continually reinstated through active rehearsal. Brown also found that recall was inversely proportional to the amount of material which was to be recalled.

These findings were soon extended. Peterson and Peterson (1959) provided the first systematic study of retention time in short-term recall and devised an experimental procedure for the study of the recall of single items. On each trial a consonant trigram was presented, followed by a three-place number. Subjects were asked to count backwards by threes from this number until a light appeared. The subject then attempted to recall the consonant trigram. Retention intervals of 3, 6, 9, 12, and 18 seconds were studied. The results of the experiment are shown in Fig. 4.7. In the same figure, the results of a replication of the Peterson experiment by Murdock (1961) are also shown, as well as a repetition of the experiment using one or three common words instead of consonant trigrams. Note that the forgetting curves in Fig. 4.7 have the same shape as Ebbinghaus' curve, although the retention interval is only a few seconds. Immediately after presentation, recall is almost perfect. The few errors which did occur would normally be called errors of perception rather than memory, but the distinction between perception and immediate memory is not as clear

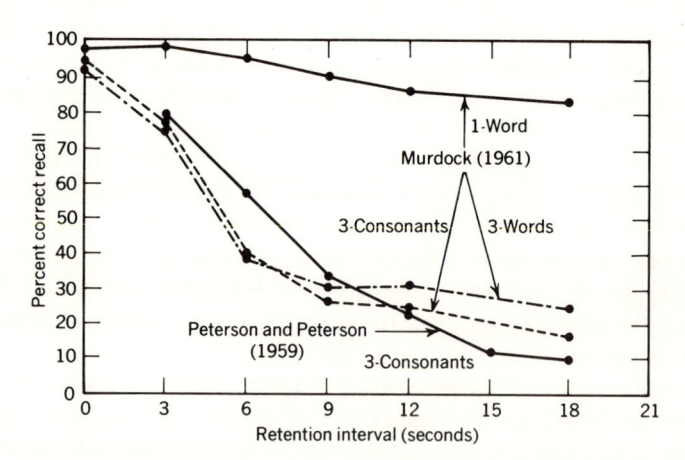

Fig. 4.7 *Percentage frequency of completely correct recall of three-consonant trigrams (Peterson and Peterson, 1959; Murdock, 1961), and one-word and three-word units (Murdock, 1961). (after Melton, 1963)*

as psychological terminology implies, as is nicely illustrated by Broadbent's results. Only 18 seconds after presentation, recall drops to about 20% for trigrams or three-word groups. No important differences are apparent in the recall of three words or three consonants. If only one word is to be remembered, forgetting is much less, but some forgetting is clearly present, even in this case. Evidently, it is the number of units or "chunks" (Miller, 1956) which determines the rate of forgetting rather than the number of physical elements within an item, such as letters, or information units.

The experiments described so far obviously do not prove that there are distinct memory stores. It may very well be that there are no functional distinctions between short-term memory and long-term memory and that forgetting always follows the same laws, regardless of time intervals. Melton (1963), for instance, has argued in an influential review paper that all memory traces are structural and therefore permanent and that all forgetting is due to associative interference. However, without prejudging this issue, we shall accept the distinction between sensory memory, primary memory, and secondary memory as a useful heuristic hypothesis, and proceed to examine the relevant experimental data. First, we shall briefly describe some of the characteristics of sensory memory. In the following two sections the basis for the distinction between primary memory and secondary memory will be examined more thoroughly and some experiments will be discussed which elucidate the nature of short-term forgetting. In the final section of this chapter we shall return to the topic of learning and shall show how the newly gained understanding of short-term memory explains the effect of temporal variables in paired-associate learning.

1. SENSORY MEMORY

When a stimulus acts upon the nervous system and is terminated suddenly some information continues to be available for a brief period of time. Stimuli like a click or flash elicit electrical activity in both the receptor and the sensory projection area of the brain which persists briefly after the termination of the stimulus itself. At a more behavioral level, such phenomena as visual after-images are well known. Although sensory after-effects belong more to the realm of perception than memory proper, they are important for our understanding of the operation of the total memory system.

When subjects are shown tachistoscopically (say for 50 milliseconds) a display of letters or digits they can identify approximately

4-5 items. This is a long-established result in psychology (Cattell, 1885; Erdmann and Dodge, 1898). Recently it was shown that the number of symbols perceived is underestimated with this technique. The limit is imposed by the subject's processing capacities but not by what he can see. Sperling (1960) demonstrated this with a partial report procedure. Subjects were presented 12 letters or digits arranged in three rows of 4 items each. Exposure duration was 50 milliseconds. Immediately after the stimulus presentation one of three signal tones (high, medium, low) instructed the subject which one of the three rows he was to report. Subjects recalled correctly 76% of the items. Since they did not know in advance which row to recall this must mean that subjects had available 76% of the 12 items, i.e., 9.1 symbols, which is appreciably more than they ever could report directly. However, if the signal tone was delayed for only one second, performance dropped to 36%, i.e., to 4.3 symbols, which is within the range of the results normally obtained with the report procedure.

Sperling interpreted these results as evidence for a visual storage system which decays rapidly, but from which the subject can extract information as long as it is available. Two kinds of evidence exist for the peripheral nature of this storage system. The first is based upon the introspection of experimental subjects who often report that the physical stimulus is gradually fading out, and that they are reading items off the diminishing stimulus trace (Sperling, 1963). Secondly, Averbach and Sperling (1961) conducted an experiment in which they showed that when the visual trace was erased, no improvements in report were possible. In this experiment 18 letters were exposed for 50 milliseconds. These letters were arranged in 6 rows and 6 different signal tones were employed to tell the subject which letters were to be reported. The experimental variables of interest were delay of the signal tone (up to 5 seconds) and brightness of the pre- and post-exposure field. If the pre- and post-exposure fields are dark, sensory after-images may persist for several seconds; on the other hand, a light field interferes with after-images. Figure 4.8 shows the results of the experiment. Estimates of the capacity of visual storage are now increased up to about 16 symbols. More important is the striking difference between the effects of light and dark post-exposure fields. It is quite obvious that a light post-exposure field severely interferes with the accuracy of partial reports. Therefore, it seems highly probably that the effect is based upon a persisting visual trace.

Estes (Estes, 1965; Estes and Taylor, 1966) has used a forced choice technique for estimating the number of elements perceivable from a display of very brief duration. Sets of printed symbols in ran-

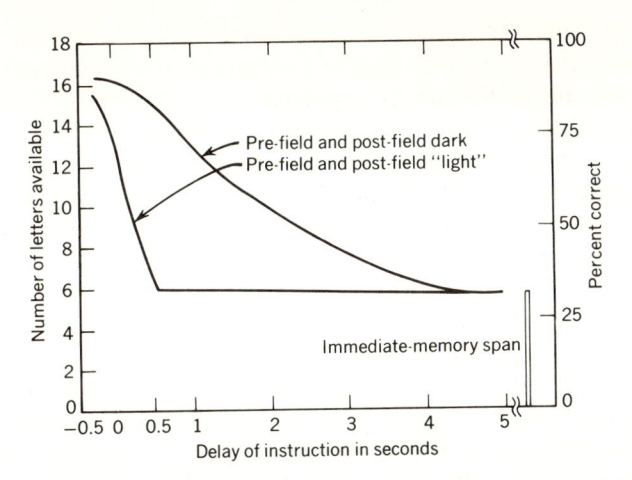

Fig. 4.8 *Information available to one observer from two kinds of stimulus presentations. The right ordinate is the average accuracy of partial reports; the left ordinate is the inferred store of available letters. Average immediate memory span for both presentations is indicated at right. (after Sperling, 1963)*

dom arrangements contained either one of two critical symbols, *A* or *B*, plus noise elements. Following a 50-millisecond exposure of each set the subject had to say whether an *A* or a *B* had been included. For a display of size *D* the probability of a correct response corrected for guessing is given by

$$P_c = \frac{K}{D} + \left(1 - \frac{K}{D}\right)\frac{1}{2}$$

where *K* is the number of elements effectively processed. Since the critical elements are placed at random somewhere in the display, the probability that the critical elements is among the *K* processed elements is *K/D*. The second term in the equation is the correct for guessing: if the critical element is not detected, the subject has probability 1/2 of guessing correctly. By equating P_c with the proportion of correct detections observed in an experiment with display size *D*, and rearranging terms we obtain an estimate of the number of elements processed by the subject:

$$K = (2P_c - 1)D$$

For instance, for a 16-element matrix one subject responded correctly

85% of the time. This implies a K-estimate of 11.3 elements perceived for display. Again we find that subjects can perceive many more elements than normally can be reported.

Estes was not only interested in the mean number of elements which the subject can perceive, but also in the manner in which subjects scan a display. He found that elements are processed serially, one-by-one, rather than in parallel, but that such factors as density and location of elements in the display must also be considered.

Most of the characteristics of the visual information store are incidental to its visual nature. An essential difference from short-term memory is that it is not subject to the same capacity limits as short-term memory. In Fig. 4.8, which is based upon partial reports from an 18-symbol display, capacity estimates of over 16 symbols were obtained, and there is no reason to believe that this is an absolute maximum. Some of Broadbent's observations indicate that there may be a corresponding auditory information store which is not affected by the severe capacity limitations that affect short-term memory proper, (Broadbent, 1958). In a multichannel listening experiment subjects typically attend to only one channel at a time. However, when subjects shift attention to a previously rejected channel, they are able to retrieve some of the information which has been presented over this channel during the last second or two. Just as in the visual case, the subject seems to be able to take advantage of a persisting sensory trace, which, however, decays very rapidly.

Broadbent reports a series of experiments which are concerned with the ability to shift attention when information is presented over more than one sensory channel simultaneously. In one experiment he presented a digit sequence such as 723 to the right ear of a subject, and simultaneously another sequence such as 945 to the left ear. As long as the presentation rate was less than 1 second per digit-pair, subjects were able to shift from one ear to the other and to reproduce the digit sequence in the correct temporal order. When the presentation rate was increased (to 2 digits per second on each channel) subjects reported first all digits presented to one ear and then all those presented to the other. This observation is interesting as it suggests limits on the human ability to shift attention, but in addition it implies the existence of a sensory memory store in which information can be retained at least for as long as 1.5 seconds without being processed at all.

In another experiment Broadbent studied the performance of subjects when two different messages were presented simultaneously, one to each ear. Each message had its particular call-sign and subjects were instructed to report as much as they could remember from the message designated by the call-sign. When the call-sign for the non-attended message was presented subjects shifted attention immediately and were able to retrieve the last items from the previously rejected message. This finding provides further evidence for a sensory memory store, since the information in the unattended channel must have been preserved in some way until the subject started to process it.

The results reviewed so far are sufficient to indicate the essential features of sensory memory. Sensory memory seems to be a large-capacity store where information is held for brief periods of time. Only a fraction of the available information in sensory memory is attended to and selected for further processing. We shall examine next the fate of the information that is transferred to a more permanent memory system.

2. THE DISTINCTION BETWEEN PRIMARY AND SECONDARY MEMORY

Both behavioral and neurological data may be cited in support of the distinction between primary and secondary memory. Milner (1967) reported an intriguing case of a specific memory deficit observed in a brain-damaged patient. A patient with hippocampal lesions suffered from an inability to form new long-term memory traces. At the same time the patient's immediate memory as well as his long-term memory appeared to be quite normal. He performed well on intelligence tests, and on other tests involving previously acquired knowledge his motor skills were normal; there were no apparent personality changes as the result of the brain damage. However, he could not remember any new information for long. He behaved normally as long as information was held in immediate memory, but no long-term traces were formed. As soon as his attention was distracted, the contents of primary memory were lost. These observations of Milner (1967), which have since been confirmed in other cases, strongly suggest that the neurological basis for immediate memory and long-term memory are quite distinct, as Hebb has hypothesized.

Quite apart from this neurological evidence, there are many purely behavioral results which seem to require a distinction between immediate memory and long-term memory. None of these experiments is crucial in itself, but their cumulative effect strongly supports the two-store hypothesis.

If subjects are given a list of words to recall, the last items of the list, i.e., the ones most recently presented, will be recalled best. This is called the "recency effect" in free recall. If one wants to attribute the recency effect to retrieval from primary memory, the question arises whether there are experimental variables which affect recall of the most recent items but have no effects upon the retention of earlier items, or vice versa. Glanzer and Cunitz (1966) have shown that presentation rate is such a variable. They had 240 subjects learn eight 20-word lists with presentation rates per word of 3, 6, or 9 seconds. The proportion of recall is plotted against the serial position of the words in Fig. 4.9. Statistical analysis supports the conclusion that rate of presentation had no effect upon the most recently presented items, but giving subjects more time with each word clearly had a beneficial effect upon recall of the first 15 words in the list.

Quite similar results are obtained when frequency of the words to be recalled is varied. Sumby (1963) asked subjects to recall lists of 15 unrelated words, which were either high frequency or low frequency words from the Thorndike-Lorge count. Over-all recall was better for the high frequency words, but the interesting result is the interaction between serial position and frequency which Sumby observed: Recently presented words were recalled equally well, irrespective of frequency (on the average, high frequency words were recalled better by one-half word in the second half of the list); the difference between the recall of high and low frequency words came primarily from the first half of the series (2.4 words in favor of high frequency lists).

When two messages are presented to a subject simultaneously, subjects do better if they are told beforehand which list is to be recalled (Brown, 1954). If a subject does not know which list is to be recalled, first-item recall is depressed, but not the recall of the last items.

An experimental variable which has opposite effects, i.e., it changes the recall probability of the most recent items, but leaves the earlier items unaffected, is delay after presentation. Glanzer and Cunitz (1966), in the study already referred to, reported a condition in which subjects were shown a 15-word list, but recall was not attempted until an interval of 0, 10, and 30 seconds after the end of the presentation of the list. The delay interval was filled with a counting task.

Figure 4.10 shows the results of this experiment. While the usual recency effect was obtained for 0 delay, the effect is attenuated for 10-second delay and completely absent when a delay of 30 seconds intervened between the end of presentation and the beginning of recall. Essentially identical results were obtained in an experiment by

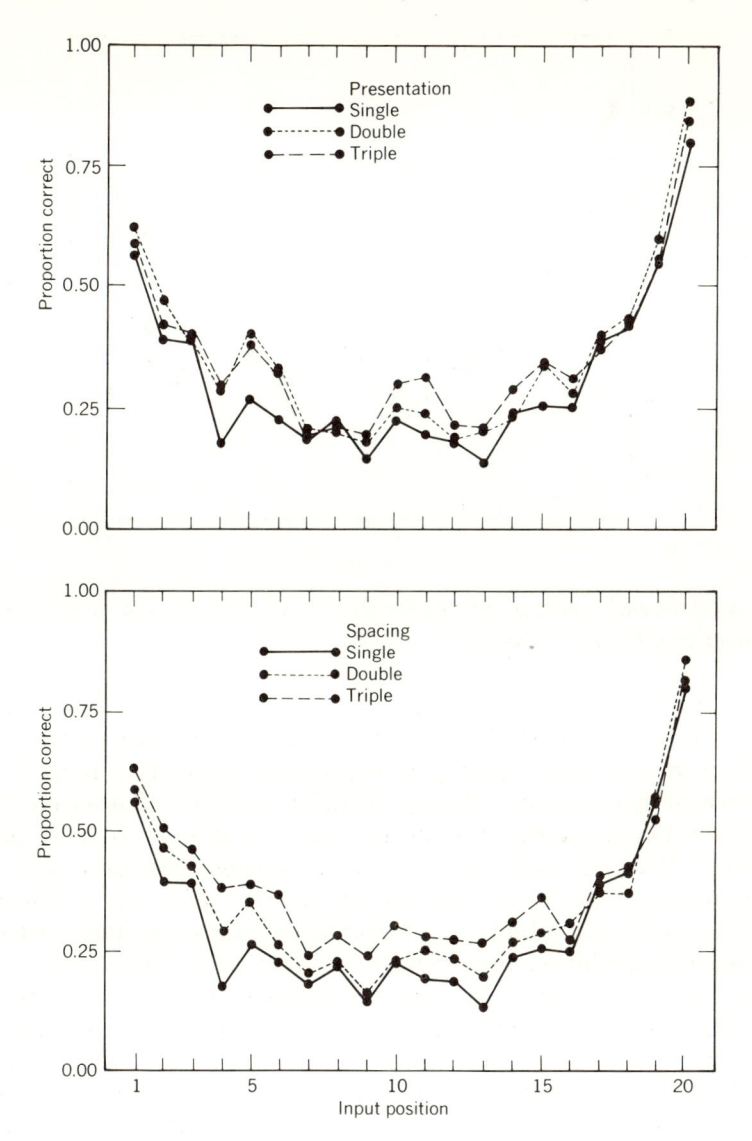

Fig. 4.9 *Serial position curves for single (1S/P) double (2P), and triple (3P) presentation above; for single (1S/P), double (2S), and triple (3S) spacing, below. (after Glanzer and Cunitz, 1966)*

Postman and Phillips (1965). However, instead of interpreting this result in terms of short-term forgetting during the delay interval, Postman and Phillips interpret it as evidence for an increase in pro-

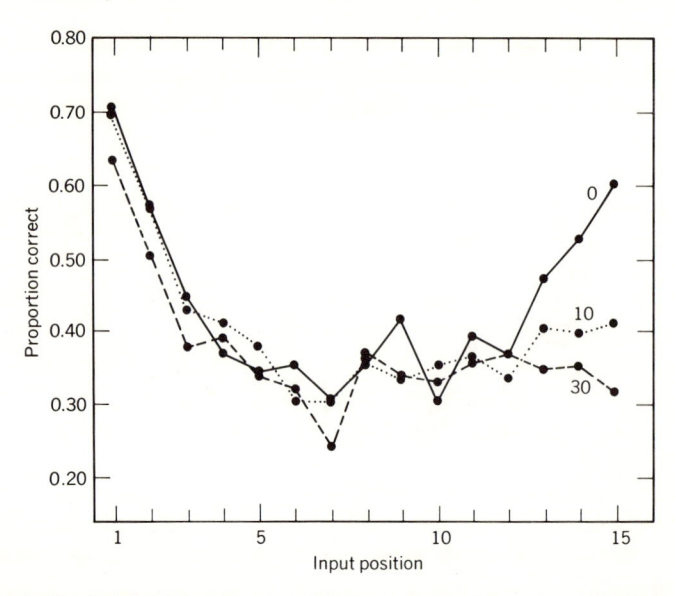

Fig. 4.10 *Serial position curves for 0-, 10-, and 30-second delay. (after Glanzer and Cunitz, 1966)*

active inhibition after the end of learning. The associations which were established when the first items of the list were learned and which were unlearned during the acquisition of the later items of the list recover spontaneously during the delay interval and interfere with the retention of the items which were learned last. Thus, as so often happens, the same observation serves to support two quite different interpretations. However, Glanzer and Cunitz point out a difficulty with the proactive inhibition interpretation: for every item lost due to proactive inhibition a recovered early item should be recalled in the delay conditions. But no such recovery of early items was obtained.

When subjects recall a list of items in a experiment, the order of recall determines to a large extent what kind of a serial position curve will be obtained. Several experimental studies are available (Raffel, 1936; Deese, 1957; Murdock, 1963c; Tulving and Arbuckle, 1963, 1966) which all show that if the recall of the last items of a list is delayed by making the subject recall the early items of the list first, the usual recency effect is not obtained or at least is strongly diminished. The early and middle items of the list, which do not depend upon short-term memory, are not affected by order of recall. The experiment of Tulving and Arbuckle (1963) nicely illustrates this point. In this experiment subjects learned a 10-item paired-associate list, with the numbers 0-9 as stimuli and nonsense syllables as responses. The order of presentation and test was arranged so that each item with a given input position was recalled in every output position. Their results are shown in Fig. 4.11. Output interference does not seem to operate on recall of early and middle input items. The first items are recalled much better than the middle items. This primacy effect is characteristic of most free-recall and paired-associate data, except when subjects are instructed to concentrate upon each item as it is presented and not to rehearse earlier items (Raffel, 1936; Waugh and Norman, 1965). Recall of items 9 and 10 depends upon how long the recall attempt is delayed: recall is very good immediately after the end of presentation, but rapidly approaches the level of items 5 and 6 if it is delayed by recall attempts of other items.

The evidence from the studies reported above strongly supports the hypothesis of two different memory mechanisms, a short-term memory which contributes to recall if the retention time is relatively brief, and a more permanent memory which is less sensitive to retention time but depends upon such variables as rate of presentation, word frequency, etc.

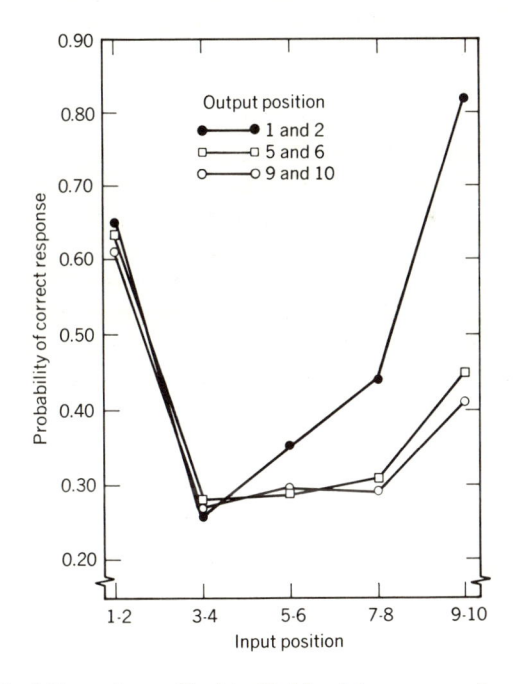

Fig. 4.11 *Probability of recall of individual items as a function of input position as parameter, for ordered input lists. (after Tulving and Arbuckle, 1963)*

Waugh and Norman (1965) formulated a simple quantitative model for the distinction between short-term and long-term memory. Following James (1890) they use the terms primary and secondary memory instead of short- and long-term memory. The general scheme of the model is essentially that of Fig. 4.5 except that they are not concerned with sensory memory. Primary memory is a limited capacity system. As new items enter, old ones are displaced and lost permanently. Items in primary memory may be rehearsed. Rehearsal may be overt or implicit: what is meant by rehearsal may best be described as keeping attention on a particular item. The effects of rehearsal are twofold: it reenters items in primary memory and it may lead to storage in secondary memory. Two kinds of interference cause forgetting from primary memory: input interference, which is determined by the number of new items which have been perceived during the retention interval, and output interference, which depends upon how many old items have been recalled between the presentation and test of the item under consideration. Thus, if an item appears in position n from the end of the list, and the subject attempts to recall this item after recalling m other items, the total number of interfering units is $i = n + m$. Adding n and m implies that output interference is equally as strong as input interference. This assumption is supported by the studies of Murdock (1963c) and Tulving and Arbuckle (1963), while in a later study Tulving and Arbuckle (1966) report input interference to be more disruptive than output interference. The assumption is acceptable as a first approximation, though a more complicated weighting of the relative contributions of n and m could probably improve the model somewhat.

According to Waugh and Norman, the probability of recalling an item which has been followed by i inputs or attempts to recall is given by the probability that the item can be retrieved from primary memory, secondary memory, or both. Assuming that these probabilities are independent, we have

(3) $$R_i = P_i + S_i - P_i S_i$$

where R_i is the probability of recalling the item in serial position i, P_i is the probability that it is in primary memory, and S_i the probability that it is in secondary memory. The concept of short-term memory implies that P_i is a monotonically decreasing function of i and that

$$\lim_{i \to \infty} P_i = 0$$

On the other hand, secondary memory is supposed to be relatively permanent within the experimental condition considered here. Hence we may assume that secondary memory is independent of the serial position i of an item, i.e.,

$$S_i = S$$

The value of S may be estimated from the asymptote of short-term forgetting curves. Whether or not S is in fact constant and independent of i may be determined from inspection of the recall probabilities for sufficiently large i. In general, the probability of recall is fairly constant after about 12 intervening items, except for the primacy effect which is characteristic of most free-recall studies. However, for the time being, we shall neglect this effect, and concentrate upon the properties of primary memory.

Rearranging the terms of Eq. (3), and dropping the unnecessary i-subscript in the case of secondary memory, we obtain

$$(4) \qquad P_i = \frac{R_i - S}{1 - S}$$

Equation (4) makes it possible to estimate the contribution of primary memory to total recall from experimental data, since R_i, the recall proportion of item i, and S, the asymptotic recall proportion, are directly observable quantities.

The value of Waugh and Norman's model is that it provides an analytic method for the separation of primary and secondary memory and thereby permits the direct comparison of short-term memory data from different experiments, irrespective of procedural differences which determine total recall. Waugh and Norman present some normative data for primary memory which were obtained in an experiment using a probe procedure. Subjects listened to test lists of 16 single digits which were read at a constant rate (either 1 or 4 digits per second) over earphones. No digit was repeated more than twice. The last digit was identical with one of the digits presented and served as a cue for recall of the digit that had followed it initially. This digit was the probe digit and was accompanied by a high frequency tone. Positions 3, 5, 7, 9, 10, 11, 12, 13, and 14 of the presentation series were tested ten times each during an experimental session. Four subjects served in 12 sessions each. From the results, estimates of the probability that an item was in primary memory were obtained. The broken lines in Fig. 4.12 show the 90% confidence limits for these estimates.

If the model is correct, data from other experiments under quite different experimental conditions, when transformed by Eq. (4) and

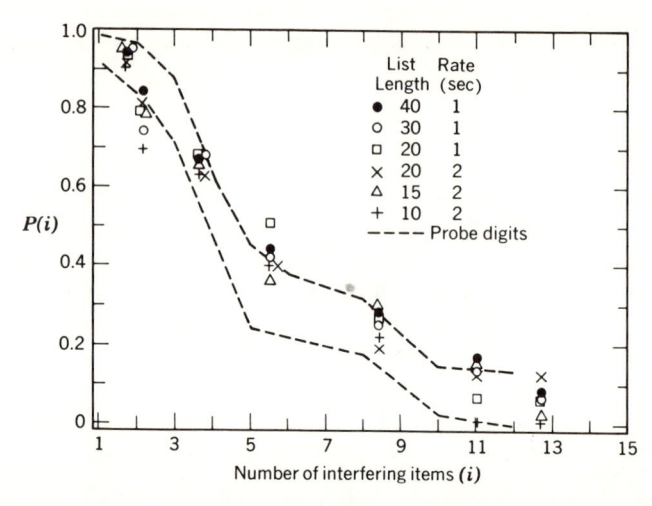

Fig. 4.12 *Free recall data from Murdock (1962) corrected for asymptote and response interference. (after Waugh and Norman, 1965)*

plotted against the number of interfering items *i*, should fall within these confidence limits. Waugh and Norman have analyzed 24 different sets of results, taken from five published reports by different experimenters, and have found that, indeed, primary memory estimates show great consistency. Most of the data fell right between the confidence limits, and no evidence for a seriously deviant trend was found. The data analyzed came from both free-recall and paired-associate experiments, but primary memory estimates conformed quite well to the function which was obtained with the probe-procedure. As an illustration, one of the figures from Waugh and Norman is reproduced here (Fig. 4.12). The data are from a free-recall experiment by Murdock (1962) in which list length and rate of presentation were varied. Note that primary memory appears to be independent of list length, as postulated. Secondary memory, on the other hand is an orderly function of such variables as list length or presentation time. In the present case, for instance, estimates of S varied from .12 for the 40-item list to .45 for the 10-item list, as can be seen in Fig. 4.13, where the untransformed recall data are plotted as a function of serial position and list length.

One feature of the conceptual scheme employed here which often tends to be neglected is that an item may be recalled from both primary and secondary memory. In fact, Eq. (3) assumes that whether or not an item enters secondary memory has absolutely no effects upon forgetting from primary memory. This point is quite crucial in evaluating studies which are concerned with the primary-secondary memory distinction. It means that experimental data are never pure indicators of short-term memory processes. This considerably complicates the task of the experimentalist, but nothing is gained by not facing this difficulty. At least, the analytical tools of Waugh and Norman are available to indicate to what extent experimental data are influenced by each factor. Hebb (1961) has performed an important experiment which gives some direct support for the hypothesis that whenever a short-term memory trace is established, there exists at least the possibility that the material will also be stored in long-term memory. Hebb had originally thought that the repetition of a digit in a memory span experiment is a pure example of an activity trace. In fact, he used the example of a calculating machine where the second string erases the first. However, an experiment which he performed showed that this comparison was not justified. Subjects listened to 9 digits, presented at a rate of 1 per second; 24 such trials were given. On every third trial the same string of digits was repeated. The results showed that performance on new strings did not change as a function of trials, but recall of the repeated series improved steadily. This improvement is only understandable if one assumes that some sort of a structural memory trace had been formed. Hebb's result illustrates

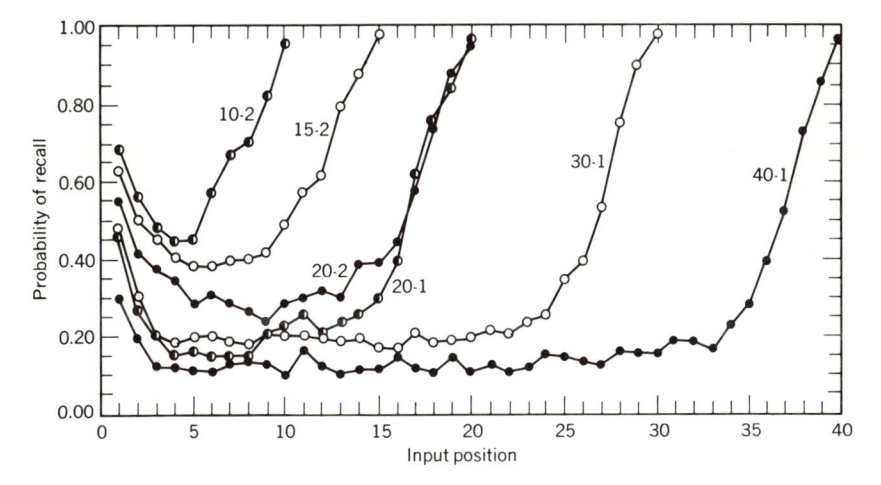

Fig. 4.13 *Serial position curves for six different groups with lists of unrelated words varying in presentation time and list length. (after Murdock, 1962)*

the possibility implied by Eq. (3) of joint storage as activity trace (primary memory, short-term memory) and structural trace (secondary, long-term memory).

In this connection it is most interesting to note what happens when the Hebb experiment is performed with patients with hippocampal lesions. It will be remembered that such patients have a very specific memory deficit: the clinical evidence indicates that both their primary and secondary memories are intact, but that they are unable to store new information in secondary memory. Hence, if Hebb's experiment is repeated with such patients, no improvement over repeated series is obtained (Caird, 1964). Using a clever experimental procedure, Buschke (1968) also confirmed that patients with bilateral hippocampal lesions suffer from a learning deficit but have normal immediate memory. Buschke used a missing-scan procedure: subjects were read 12 randomly selected numbers from the set of numbers 1-16 and had to report which numbers were *not* read to them. Some numbers were read only once and some were read twice. The brain-damaged subjects performed as well as a control group when the numbers occurred only once, but they did significantly poorer than normals with the repeated numbers. Buschke's results nicely confirm the interpretation of the Hebb data that the improvement which occurred when items were repeated was due to storage in secondary memory—something the brain-damaged subjects could not do.

Talking about short-term memory and long-term memory as two different "stores" may have misleading semantic implications. It should not be understood to mean that items are being kept in two physically separate bins. A subject who is given a list of words to memorize in a free-recall experiment does not learn these words *de novo*, or store their codes in short- or long-term memory. The words are already part of the subject's total store of knowledge, they have their meaning and emotional connotations, they belong to an extensive network of associations and are categorized in various ways. The subject merely tags a word which is already available in some way so that it can be identified later as a member of the learning list. The evidence just presented indicates that there are two ways to do this: one temporary method which requires continued rehearsal to prevent loss, and a relatively permanent method which does not, but which is not always effective. In any case, a word is always understood as such, that is, it is identified as a particular member in the subject's memory structure, whether it is held in short-term memory or long-term memory.

3. THE NATURE OF FORGETTING IN SHORT-TERM MEMORY

An enormous burst of research activity in the past ten years has provided us with much information about the characteristics of short-term forgetting. Without attempting a comprehensive review of that literature it is the purpose of this section to explicate the principal features of short-term forgetting by means of selected experimental studies.

Explicit rehearsal and verbal labeling which presumably facilitate rehearsal should improve short-term retention according to the scheme outlined so far. The relative importance of decay and interference as causes of short-term forgetting can be investigated by means of experiments in which the rate of presentation is varied. As will be shown, these experiments on the whole disagree with the notion that spontaneous decay is the primary mechanism of forgetting from short-term memory. However, exactly what causes interference in primary memory is another question which is not easy to answer. Several experiments relevant to the various aspects of this problem will be discussed. One of the most important characteristics of short-term memory is its restricted capacity. We shall explore in some detail the capacity limitations of short-term memory and how they can be overcome through "chunking." Finally, experiments concerned with acoustic encoding in short-term memory will be described.

Rehearsal

We have ascribed a two-fold effect to rehearsal: it keeps items in primary memory and it affords an opportunity for storage in secondary memory. Thus, the more rehearsal is permitted, the more likely it is that an item will be stored in long-term memory. A study by Howe (1967) illustrates this. Howe presented to his subjects strings of 9 consonants, three at a time for 3 seconds each. Half of his subjects were instructed to rehearse the consonant triplets by reading them out loud repeatedly during the presentation interval. After the presentation of the 9 consonants, a digit-reading task provided for some interference. For those subjects who were not especially instructed to rehearse, interference had its biggest effects upon the recall of the last items, in agreement with the results of the delayed recall experiments discussed above (Glanzer and Cunitz, 1966; Postman and Phillips, 1965). However, in the rehearsal condition the effects of interference were the same for all items: presumably items were stored in long-term memory and hence were equally vulnerable to interference effects, while under standard conditions the most recent items which are stored in short-term memory suffer most when recall is delayed.

Bernbach (1967) studied the effects of labels upon short-term memory for colors with school children. He showed his subjects 8 different color cards, which were placed face down in a row before the subject. Then a test card was shown, and the subject had to select the original card which was identical with it. Bernbach had noted that the serial position function obtained with this procedure was different for adults and children, apart from the obviously better performance of the adults. Both curves showed nearly perfect retention for the most recent item, but while the serial position function for children decreased monotonically, the adult function looked more S-shaped. It was also characterized by a strong recency effect, but in addition a somewhat smaller primacy effect was present, which was absent in the data from children. Bernbach argued that this primacy effect resulted because adults rehearse the first few items, while the children, being unfamiliar with the names of the colors used, were unable to rehearse. To test this hypothesis, he taught the children a label for each color before starting the experiment proper. His hypothesis was completely confirmed. The children's short-term memory function showed a primacy effect, and became just like that of the adults, except at a much lower level. Thus, letting the children rehearse items by providing them with verbal labels improved their recall by raising the probability that early items were stored in long-term memory.

Rate of Presentation

By varying the presentation rate in short-term memory experiments one may hope to obtain data concerning the nature of forgetting from short-term memory. If forgetting is a process of spontaneous decay, the duration of the retention interval per se should be a significant variable, and hence one would expect recall to be superior with a fast presentation rate rather than with a slow rate of presentation. On the other hand, if the main source of forgetting in short-term memory experiments is interference, a fast rate of presentation should not facilitate short-term memory. The problem is complicated by the fact that experimental data are always to some extent jointly determined by recall from both memory stores.

Some experimental data concerning rate of presentation have already been discussed (Glanzer and Cunitz, 1966; see Fig. 4.9). They illustrate the interaction of presentation rate with serial position. The early part of the list is improved by slower presentation, which is just what would be expected since that part of the list is supposedly re-called from long-term memory, and giving subjects more time to memorize material improves long-term memory. The most recent items, on the other hand, are not affected by presentation rate. Thus, short-term memory is not a function of rate of presentation. In Fig. 4.13, recall of a 20-word list presented at rates of one or two seconds per word (Murdock, 1962) is shown. The effects of rate upon the early part of the list only is again obvious.

The conclusion that short-term memory is not dependent upon presentation rate contradicts the assumption of spontaneous decay in short-term memory. The experiment of Waugh and Norman (1965) discussed above provides additional evidence against decay theory. In their experiment two presentation rates (one and four digits per second) were used. This variable had no effect upon recall (and hence Waugh and Norman chose the number of interfering items rather than time per se as the independent variable in their model for primary memory). However, Waugh and Norman did not observe an inter-action between rate and serial position comparable to the results dis-cussed above, probably because they used a shorter list length. There-fore, the contribution of long-term memory to their data was relatively small.

The experimental literature on the effects of rate of presentation on short-term memory is unfortunately much more confusing than the results reported so far imply. Indeed, Aaronson (1967) in a recent review concluded that the effects of rate upon immediate recall are only very poorly understood. Pollack, Johnson, and Knaff (1959) performed one of the early experiments in this area using a running memory span paradigm with rates ranging from .125 to 4 items per second. Their subjects performed better at slow rates, a finding which is characteristic of most other studies, too (see Aaronson, 1967). Since rate-serial position interactions are not reported in most of these studies, it is possible that at least some of these findings are caused by the effects of rate upon long-term memory and hence do not contradict the generalization presented here. However, in three experiments better performance is reported with fast rates of presen-tation than with slow rates (e.g., Conrad and Hille, 1958), support-ing a decay interpretation of memory. All of these studies were con-cerned with the recall of a series of 8 digits, presented at rather fast rates (from 30 to 120 per minute). It is not at all clear, what the causes for these divergent findings are. Order of recall plays an im-portant role in these studies: Posner (1964) found no rate effects when subjects recalled the last half of an 8-digit series first, while in the same experiment performance was better for the fast rate when recall order was the same as input order.

Not all the important variables in immediate memory experiments in which rate of presentation is varied have as yet been identified. The need for great care in interpreting the respective contributions of short- and long-term memory in any given set of experimental data has already been pointed out. Non-memory factors also seem to play an important role. Especially when presentation rates are quite fast, as is the case in many of these experiments, perceptual factors cannot be neglected. Certainly in at least some of the studies in which an overall superiority of slow rates of presentation was observed, these effects may have been due to differential acquisition levels, rather than to retention. Norman (1966) showed that such indeed was the case in an experiment which he performed using the probe-procedure. He presented 15-digit lists at rates of 1, 4, 7, or 10 digits per second. Presentation was either visual or auditory. When his results are presented as in Fig. 4.14, forgetting seems to be dependent upon rate of presentation: the faster the rate of presentation was, the more forgetting was observed. However, Norman argues that this difference reflects a difference in the initial acquisition level rather than differential rates of forgetting. If the curves of Fig. 4.14 all have the same rate of forgetting, they are different only because they start at a different level. If they are shifted along the horizontal axis, without any change in their vertical values, the overlapping curves of Fig. 4.15 are obtained. Obviously, the only differences among these curves are in their initial values. Figure 4.15 also shows that mode of presentation primarily affects acquisition and not the rate of forgetting. The one digit per second visual results have been superimposed upon the auditory results, and, again, no differences in rate of decay are apparent. A probable interpretation of these results is that with fast rates, presentation outpaces encoding. In agreement with this interpretation, Norman observed in another part of his experiment that the deleterious effects of high presentation rates are most noticeable at the end of long lists. A similar conclusion was reached by Buschke and Lim (1967). They used the missing scan procedure: a series of digits (1-13) is presented in random order with one of the digits missing. The subject's task is to tell which one of the digits was missing. Since he is forced to guess if he is not sure, all errors are intrusion errors (one of the digits actually presented is called missing). Rate of presentation was varied between 1 and 4 items per second. The results showed that errors increased linearly as a function of rate increases. An analysis of the serial position of errors led

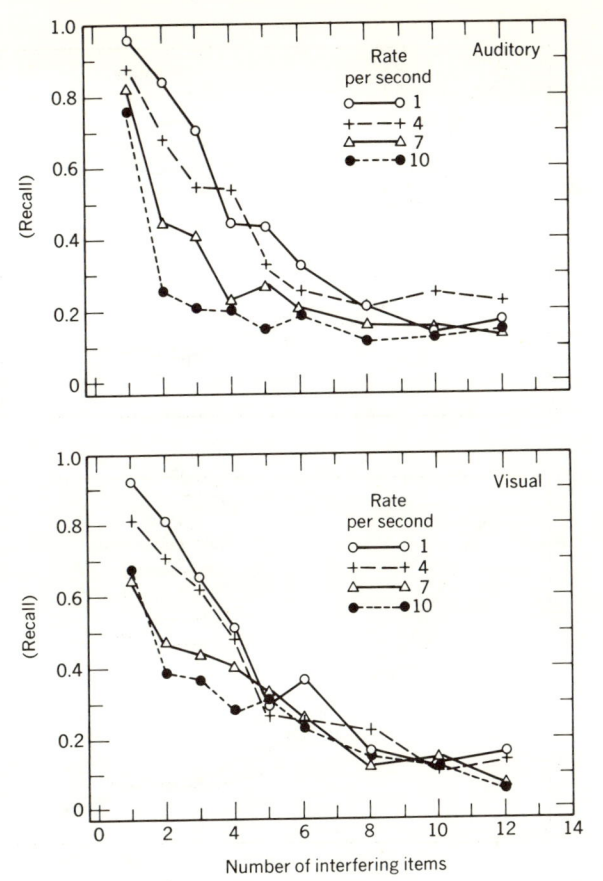

Fig. 4.14 *Relative frequency of correct recall in the probe-digit experiment. The abscissa is the number of digits presented between the critical digit and its test—counting the probe. (after Norman, 1966)*

to the conclusion that with fast rates of presentation perceptual encoding is less effective for the later items.

On the whole, then, the data support the generalization offered above that rate of presentation does not affect short-term memory. Most of the divergent results can be explained as perceptual effects or are confounded because primary and secondary memory have not been distinguished explicitly.

The Nature of Interpolated Activity

If short-term forgetting is not a matter of spontaneous decay it becomes especially important to study how forgetting is affected by the

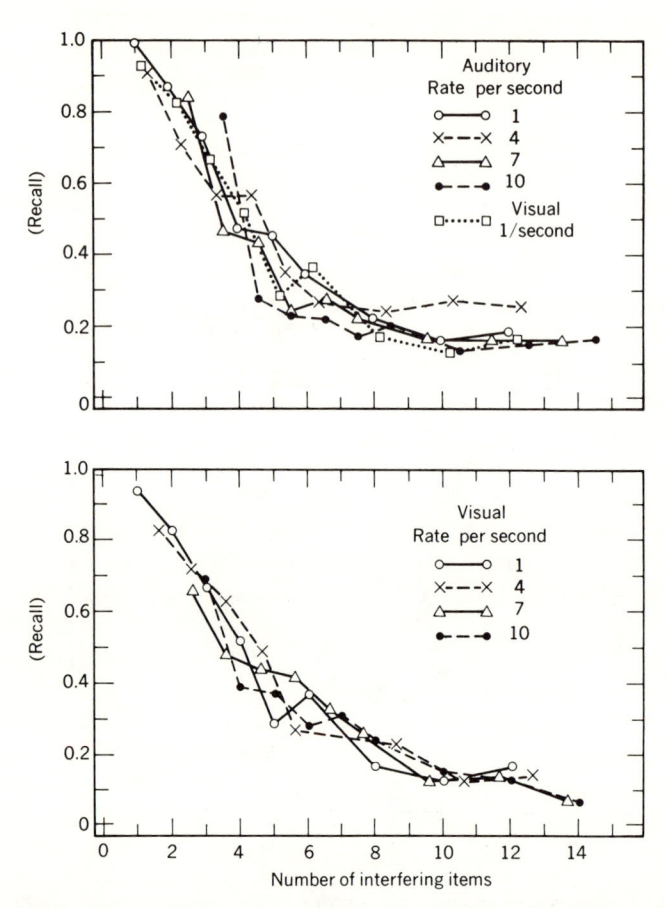

Fig. 4.15 *Data from Fig. 4.14 shifted along the abscissa so that the rates of forgetting can be compared. (The abscissa values are correct only for the data presented at the rate of one digit per second). (after Norman, 1966)*

nature of the material which is interpolated between presentation and test. We know (Brown, 1958) that when no activity at all is demanded from the subject during the retention interval, very little forgetting occurs. Therefore, interpolated tasks are used in studies of short-term memory. These may or may not involve new learning. An example of the first kind is the probe-procedure of Waugh and Norman (1965). The original study of Peterson and Peterson (1959) is an example of the second kind; the interpolated task in this case involves presentation of categorically dissimilar (mental arithmetic) material which will not be tested later. Murdock (1967a) has suggested the name "distractor" technique for this experimental procedure. He has also argued convincingly that there is no essential difference between the results obtained with the distractor and probe techniques. Results obtained with these two techniques are not numerically identical, in the sense that the rate of forgetting as well as the asymptotic value may differ, but the shape of the retention function itself, and the psychological processes which it reflects, appear to be the same, no matter what the nature of the interpolated material is.

A systematic exploration of different interpolated tasks in a short-term memory study has been provided by Neimark, Greenhouse, Law, and Weinheimer (1965) who showed that the similarity of the interpolated material and the learning material affected retention. As learning material they used 16 CVCs of either high or low association value. Retention intervals of 0, 3, 9, and 18 seconds were studied. During the retention interval subjects spelled aloud at a fixed rate nonsense syllables of either high, medium, or low association value, or three-digit numbers. The high association CVCs were recalled very well and no clear effects attributable to the similarity of the intervening material were found. However, for low association value syllables, recall was best when the interpolated task involved the most dissimilar materials (numbers, and high association value CVCs), and decreased as the interpolated material became more similar to the learning material.

This result, is, of course, in agreement with the interference theory of memory. However, the authors point out another possible interpretation of the data. Pillsbury and Sylvester (1940) have held that the difficulty of the interpolated material affects retention independent of other factors. It is possible that reading unfamiliar syllables was a more difficult task than reading high association value syllables and served better to prevent rehearsal. An experiment in which the difficulty of the interpolated activity was varied independently of similarity has been reported by Posner and Rossman (1965). In their main experiment, subjects listened to an 8-digit series and performed a "transformation" task before attempting recall of the series. The transformations involved either 0, 1, 2, or 3 digit pairs in the 8-digit series, but never the first two digits. The transformations which subjects were required to perform were reversal (writing down a pair of digits in the opposite order from their presentation), addition (two adjacent digits are added and the sum is written down), 2-bit classification (classifying each pair of numbers into above or below 50), and 1-bit classification (the subject records A if the pair is high and odd or low and even, B for the reverse). These tasks were graded in difficulty according to the amount of information reduction involved. Reversal involves no information reduction at all and is the easiest of the tasks, while the 1-bit classification requires the most information reduction. The results are based entirely upon the analysis of the recall of the first digit pair, which was never itself transformed or recorded and was always recalled first by the subject. Thus the first digit pair was treated identically under all conditions, and only the nature and number of the transformations which intervened between the presentation of the first digit pair and recall distinguished the experimental conditions. The results are shown in Table 4.1. It is apparent that both the nature and the number of transformations performed during the retention interval strongly affected recall. The difficulty of the intervening activity does affect short-term retention, even when similarity effects are absent. In fact, in the present experiment the influence of task difficulty quite overwhelmed and reversed any effects due to similarity: according to the Neimark *et al.* study, one would suppose that writing down digits would interfere more with the retention of digits than the writing of letters. However, the only tasks which involved the writing of numbers were the reversal and addition tasks, which produced the least amount of interference.

In two follow-up experiments Posner and Rossman (1965) explored the interaction between the difficulty of interpolated activity and the length of the retention interval. In one experiment the total

Table 4.1. *Total errors in the first pair of digits after Posner and Rossman, (1965).*

Task	Number of pairs transformed				
	0	1	2	3	Total
Reversal	22	26	31	50	129
Addition	44	62	56	104	266
2/Bit	29	50	71	114	264
1/Bit	28	62	94	108	292
Total	123	200	252	376	

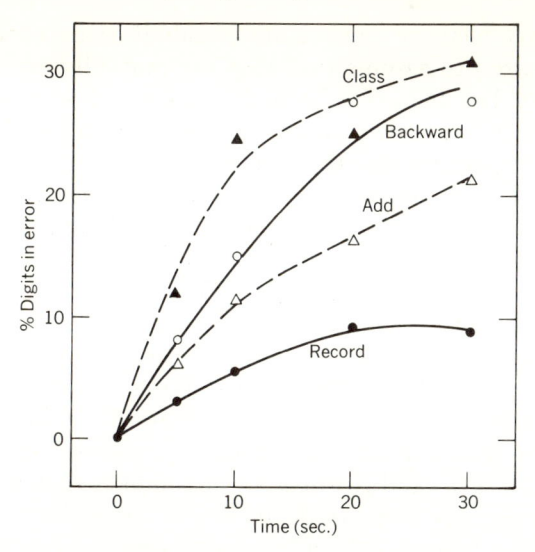

Fig. 4.16 *Percentage recall as a function of time for various size transforms. (after Posner and Rossman, 1965)*

interpolated time was kept constant, but the effects of task difficulty were still obtained. In a second experiment, retention time was varied systematically. The results are shown in Fig. 4.16. Effects upon recall caused by task difficulty were observed for every retention interval.

Posner and Rossman interpret their results in terms of rehearsal. There is a limited central processing capacity available for the rehearsal process, and the more of it that is taken up by intervening tasks, the more forgetting will occur. A number of other experimental studies support the idea that short-term memory is a limited capacity system (Miller, 1956; Broadbent, 1958). For instance, Murdock (1965a) has shown that the difficulty of a subsidiary task which subjects perform while listening to a list of words affects recall. He used card sorting tasks of various levels of difficulty and found that the number of words recalled decreased as the card sorting task became more demanding.

The results described above need to be looked at in terms of the distinction between primary and secondary memory. It is not quite clear whether such variables as the similarity of the interpolated material with the learning material, the difficulty of the interpolated material, or the difficulty of a distracting task actually influence the rate of forgetting from primary memory, or whether their effects are upon secondary memory alone. Both possibilities are conceivable and there is no reason to assume that they are mutually exclusive. If primary memory has indeed a limited capacity, it is possible that a difficult interpolated activity requires a larger portion of this limited capacity for its performance than an easy activity and hence displaces more items from primary memory. On the other hand, capacity problems may arise in the transmission of material from primary memory to secondary memory. This transmission makes demands upon a subject's central processing capabilities. The more of these needed for the performance of interpolated tasks during the retention interval, the less remain for the task of storing the to be remembered items in secondary memory. This is the same as saying that active rehearsal is required for storage in secondary memory and that the difficult tasks interfere more with the necessary rehearsal process than easy tasks. The model of Waugh and Norman (1965) implies such a process: forgetting from primary memory depends only upon the number of perceived items and recall attempts which occur during the retention interval, while storage in secondary memory requires rehearsal. The model does not have a specific mechanism to deal with the effects of the difficulty of the interpolated activity upon primary memory, which is assumed to be a function merely of the number of interpolated perceptual acts. The notion of perceptual act is not as clear as one would wish it to be: four digits, letters, or unrelated words presumably correspond to four perceptual acts, but how many perceptual acts does a four-word sentence involve? More precisely, what is the unit of interference in primary memory? Is it simply the total number of interpolated items, no matter what these are? Or is the number of different items the proper measure of interference? Or are there some higher order units that must be taken into account? This problem has been systematically investigated by Waugh and Norman (1968). Their general procedure consisted of constructing strings of items according to certain constraints which will be explained below. Subjects listened to a string and immediately following the last item, one that had appeared earlier was repeated accompanied by a tone. This was the probe item. Upon this signal the subject was instructed to report the item that had followed the last occurrence of the probe item. The strings were constructed so that they differentiated among a number of possible hypotheses concerning the nature of interference effects in primary memory. For instance, consider the hypothesis that the total number of intervening items is important, no matter what these items are, versus the alternative hypothesis that the number of different items determines interference and that items occurring twice in immediate succession function as a unit. Under the first hypothesis the following two strings should be equivalent:

... 7, 3, 8, 8, 4, 4 Probe: 7 Correct Response: 3,
... 7, 3, 8, 5, 9, 2 Probe: 7 Correct Response: 3.

In each case 4 digits follow the test item. According to the hypotheses that only different items count, the first string should be recalled much better than the second string, because there are only 2 different items intervening. In this manner Waugh and Norman investigated several different hypotheses concerning the effective unit of interference in primary memory. In addition to the two hypotheses already mentioned they explored the idea that items may function as a unit of interference only if they are not currently stored in primary memory, as well as a few other possibilities. We need not describe these in detail, since they all were counterindicated by their results. The only hypothesis which could account for their data was that the unit of interference is determined by a subject's expectancies: any newly presented item can displace an earlier item from primary memory as long as it is not redundant. A redundant item is one which the subject expects to occur at a given place in a series, e.g., a 5 is expected after 1234-, or a 4 is expected after 77711199944-. Thus, regularly occurring highly predictable items do not interfere with other items stored in primary memory.

Let us look at the converse of this finding. We have just seen that the newer, the more unexpected an item is, the greater is its interference potential upon other items in primary memory. It is also true that the newer an item is, i.e., the more different it is from whatever preceded it, the more likely it is to be retained. It has been mentioned before that when a list of items is presented in a short-term memory experiment a primacy effect is typically obtained: The first few items in the list are better retained than later items (except for the very last ones, which still are in primary memory). The new items at the beginning of a list are the ones which are best recalled. As more and more items of the same kind are presented, retention quickly reaches a state of equilibrium. After at most 3 or 4 items newness seems to wear off and performance becomes stable. In general, very little forgetting occurs on the first trial of short-term memory experiments, but after just a few further trials stable conditions develop (e.g., Murdock, 1964). However, if after a few items the nature of the material is suddenly changed, the new material is retained almost as well as the items at the very beginning of the experiment. After a few trials with the new material performance returns to the old level. This effect was demonstrated first by Wickens, Born, and Allen (1963) and has been repeated with different types of materials since. Wickens *et al.* found that when a letter is tested after a series of digits, performance is as good as on the first trial of the session, but that performance deteriorates rapidly when several trials with the same learning material are given.

There are two prominent explanations for this phenomenon. One is in terms of proactive interference: the more items of the same kind presented, the more proactive inhibition builds up, and the poorer will be retention. The difficulty with this interpretation is that it fails to explain why performance becomes stable after only a few trials; one would expect proactive inhibition to accumulate throughout the experiment and that there would be a progressive performance decrement, which is not what has been found in the large majority of experiments. An alternative explanation would be in terms of perceptual factors. It may be that new items—items either at the beginning of a list, or following a change in the material—are always attended to. Such items enter short-term memory, but once short-term memory is filled to capacity with items of a kind, further items may not always be processed. The subject may prefer to rehearse the items he already has in short-term memory, rather than to attend to another item, unless that other item is distinct perceptually. If something new comes up he drops what he has been doing and responds to the new stimulus. This hypothesis may also explain the von Restorff effect: If an item in an otherwise homogeneous series is in any way outstanding—it may belong to a different class of stimulus materials, or it may merely be colored red—the likelihood that it will be recalled increases considerably (von Restorff, 1933).

What, then, may one conclude from the evidence reviewed here as to the nature of interference in primary memory? First of all, it is clear that interference is of crucial importance in short-term retention, in that what happens during the retention interval clearly affects the likelihood of retention. However, interference effects in short-term memory do not appear to be identical with the interference between specific associations postulated by classical interference theory. The main variable in classical interference theory is the similarity among associations, but similarity is overshadowed in importance by other factors as far as short-term retention is concerned. The amount of work involving short-term memory that the subject is asked to do during the retention interval seems to be more predictive of short-term forgetting than the similarity of his activity to the item which is to be retained. Thus, backward counting interferes with the retention of nonsense syllables, and long-division interferes even more. Similarly, interference is increased if much processing is required during the retention interval because new and unexpected items are presented, but it will be minimal if highly predictable items are presented. It seems that the capacity of primary memory is quite small and that anything that takes up some of this limited capacity interferes with the contents of primary memory. Items which are distinct perceptually for some reason or other, perhaps because they are the first ones in a list, are much more likely to enter into primary memory than items which are embedded in a homogeneous list, and therefore they are better retained and interfere more with other items in primary memory.

Chunking and the Capacity of Short-term Memory

In this section we shall review attempts to measure the capacity of short-term memory and the related problem concerning the proper unit of measurement of information in short-term memory.

The short-term memory function for consonant trigrams is almost identical with that for word triplets. The study by Murdock (1961) upon which this conclusion is based has already been referred to and the relevant data are shown in Fig. 4.7. Obviously, separate letters are not the appropriate unit for short-term memory. When letters form a meaningful word, they are treated as a whole, so that three words are not harder to remember than three unrelated letters. Psychologists have long known that subjects group single letters, digits, nonsense syllables, or even words into clusters, which then act as units in memory. Miller (1956) has named such groupings chunks. When presented with a meaningful sequence of letters, subjects perceive words, not separate letters, and words are stored in short-term memory. The perceptual processing which takes place when these chunks are formed is quite automatic and seems to require a minimum of time and effort. In fact, one of the main differences between short- and long-term memory appears to lie in the way in which material is encoded for storage. Chunks are stored in both short- and long-term memory, but the chunks of short-term memory are the result of very superficial perceptual processing, while the units of long-term memory are based upon higher level analyses, which require time and often considerable effort.

Chunking is the result of the subject's perceptual coding processes. The experimenter may influence these by arranging stimuli in ways which favor the formation of particular chunking patterns. The principles of perceptual organization are not completely understood yet, but Koffka's "law of Prägnanz" (1935) is a good description of these phenomena. The law says, briefly, that perceptual organization tends to move in the direction of a regular, simple, meaningful, and stable percept. This formulation explains little, for what will happen depends entirely upon the prevailing conditions. We do not yet know exactly which principle to evoke in any given situation, as the various tendencies implied by the law of Prägnanz might well be in conflict with each other. Nevertheless, perceptual organization does occur and the factors described certainly are relevant.

Experimental investigations of chunking are rare. Müller and Schumann (1894) showed that chunking can be induced by reading a series of nonsense syllables in a rhythmic manner. Chunks formed through an arbitrary reading rhythm can be very powerful factors in memory and may even overshadow the effects of serial associations. Visual groupings of unrelated items have similar effects. McLean and Gregg (1967) taught subjects random sequences of letters which were presented visually in groups of 1, 3, 4, 6, or 8. When a subject could recall the series perfectly, inter-response times were recorded and used to assess chunking. If a subject formed chunks of a certain size, the times between the letters belonging to the same chunk ought to be shorter than the times between letters belonging to different chunks. On the basis of this principle, McLean and Gregg could provide unambiguous evidence not only for chunking but also for the proposition that subjects use a chunk size which corresponds to the grouping used in the presentation of the learning material. Thus, most subjects who were shown letters in groups of 6, formed chunks of that size in recall, etc. Subjects who were shown the letters singly also formed chunks, but different subjects chose different chunk sizes. Again, as in the case of Müller and Schumann's results, the chunk proved to be a stronger bond than associative relations across chunks. For instance, when the (randomly chosen) letters of two adjacent groups happened to form a meaningful syllable, inter-recall times were determined by the presentation group rather than the meaningful unit.

Perceptual organization is not something which is fixed once and for all. One can learn principles of organization and use them for chunking previously unorganized material. Miller (1956) describes the case of the apprentice telegraph operator, who at first hears each "dit" and "dah" separately. Then he learns to organize the sound patterns into letters, and finally into words and whole phrases. He can form larger and larger chunks as he learns more about the telegraphic code. This is greatly to his advantage because the larger the chunk which he can deal with as a whole the more information he can handle in memory.

In a demonstration experiment (Miller, 1956) subjects were taught to recode sequences of binary digits (1's and 0's) into larger chunks and thereby to increase the amount of material which could be remembered. People can repeat back about nine binary digits if each digit is treated as a chunk and remembered separately. But suppose subjects are taught to recode a sequence of binary digits in terms of digit pairs: 00 is renamed 0, 01 is renamed 1, 10 is renamed 2, and 11 is renamed 3. If the subject translates a string of zeros and ones into this new code, his memory load is reduced by half. One can devise even more efficient codes in terms of triplets, quadruplets, or even quintuplets. There are $2^5 = 32$ different quintuplets and the subject must learn to give a different decimal digit name to each pattern. Once he has mastered this code he can store binary digit sequences in chunks of size five, thereby greatly increasing the capacity of his immediate memory. Miller has shown that subjects can actually use such a recoding scheme. However, it turned out that a great deal of practice was necessary before the more complicated recoding procedures could be used efficiently. It is not sufficient merely to understand the coding principles. The recoding must be almost automatic, or the subject will lose part of the next group while he is trying to remember the proper label for the last group. A well-practiced subject was able to repeat back up to 40 binary digits, by using a 4:1 or 5:1 encoding ratio.

The span of immediate memory is about 7, plus or minus 2, chunks, and is quite independent of the size of these chunks. This is a very important and curious result. It is implied by the discussion above, but there are a number of direct experimental tests which establish its validity beyond question. Wundt (1905) found the span of immediate memory to be about 6 "simple impressions", which may be isolated lines, digits, letters, words, or arhythmic metronome beats. He pointed out in this connection that the touch alphabet of the blind is limited to six binary symbols. However, the capacity of immediate memory can be greatly enlarged through suitable grouping of elements: While only six isolated letters may be kept in consciousness at one time, up to 10 letters can be retained if they are presented as CVCs, and from 20-30 letters if they form part of a sentence. In studies of subjective grouping of metronome beats six groups of beats could be retained when beats were grouped in patterns of two; when patterns of four beats were formed, 5 of them could still be retained simultaneously; practiced subjects managed to handle as many as five beats of size eight, for a total of 40 beats! Wundt's studies depended heavily upon the introspective report of his subjects, and it is interesting to note their substantial agreement with modern findings obtained with objective methods, such as those of Miller (1956). Miller's results (shown in Fig. 4.17) demonstrate the constancy of the memory span when the size of the chunk is varied in terms of information content. To understand this figure, a brief digression into information measurement is necessary.*

Information is measured in terms of uncertainty. In a situation where many different alternative outcomes are possible and we have no idea which one to expect, uncertainty is very great, and an observed outcome is very informative, in the sense that it reduces much uncertainty. On the other hand, if there are only a few alternatives possible, or if one has good reason to expect the occurrence of one particular outcome anyway, uncertainty and hence the information value of the expected outcome is low. Telling you that it will be sunny tomorrow is not very informative when it is summer in California and anything else would be quite a surprise.

The conventional unit of information measurement is in terms of bits. A bit is the uncertainty which exists when two outcomes are possible, each with equal likelihood, as for instance in the toss of an unbiased coin. Four equally likely outcomes represent an uncertainty of two bits, 8 equally likely alternatives amount to an uncertainty of three bits, and so on. In general, if there are n equal alternatives the logarithm to the base 2 of n indicates how many bits of information are obtained if one of these alternatives occurs.

Suppose a subject recalls the following string of 0's and 1's: 0110010. Since at each position in this string there is a choice between exactly two alternatives (0 or 1), each such choice is worth one bit of information; there are seven choices, so that the total amount of information retained is 7 bits. Now suppose a subject is given the string 6379528 and he recalls this one, too. In the construction of this string a choice was made at each position among 10 alternatives, the digits 0-9. In terms of information, we have at each position $\log_2(10) = 3.3$ bits, and hence a total of $7 \times 3.3 = 23$ bits which have been retained in memory. It is clear that a string of decimal digits is much richer in information than a string of 0's and 1's. Hence, since subjects are about equally capable of recalling either one, the capacity of short-

---

*Excellent and clear discussions of information theory in psychology are available (e.g., Garner, 1962); we shall only attempt to introduce the basic principles of information measurement here.

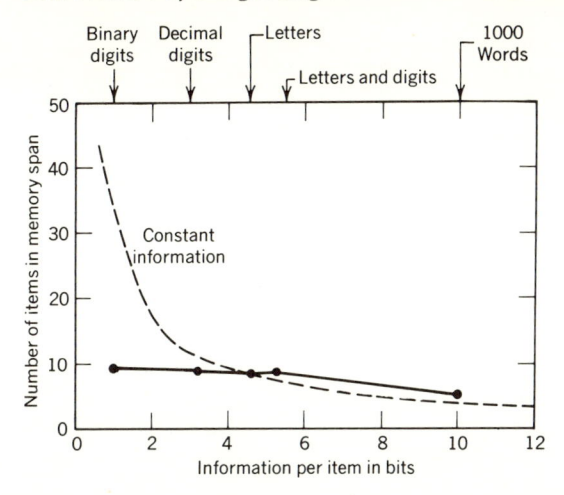

Fig. 4.17 *The span of immediate memory plotted as a function of the amount of information per item in the test materials. (after Miller, 1956)*

term memory is by no means constant if measured in terms of amount of information. If amount of information measured in bits were a critical variable in short-term memory recall of seven 0's or 1's should imply that only a little more than two decimal digits could be recalled, since 2 decimal digits amount to 6.6 bits! Instead, the capacity of short-term memory is measured in terms of "chunks" which may differ widely in their information content; let us consider Miller's (1956) evidence.

In Fig. 4.17 the number of items which a subject can repeat after one presentation is shown for different item populations. The population size increases from 2 (binary digits) to 1000 (words), the information per item increases correspondingly from 1 bit to 10 bits, but the memory span hardly changes at all. The number of chunks is what matters in immediate memory, but not the information per chunk. Figure 4.17 is based upon an experiment using a standard memory span procedure. Lists were read aloud at a rate of one item per second and subjects were given as much time as needed for recall. The number of items which a subject could always recall plus a weighted average of the longer sequences that were recalled only occasionally were used to obtain an estimate of memory span.

Pollack's work, which is summarized in Fig. 4.18, confirms the independence of chunk size and memory span (Pollack, 1953). The amount of information retained after one presentation increases al-

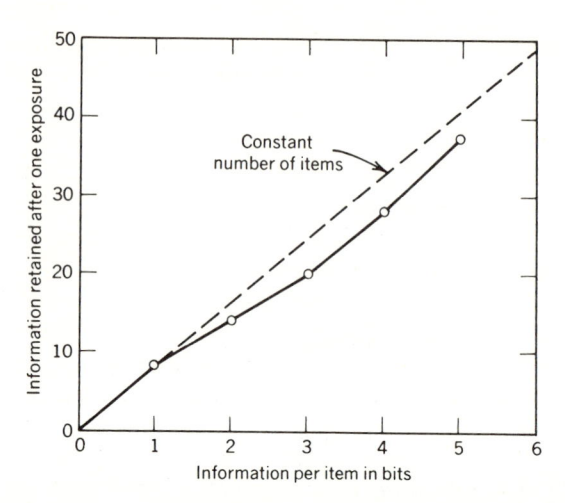

Fig. 4.18 *The amount of information retained after one presentation plotted as a function of the amount of information per item in the test material. Data from Pollack (1953), (after Miller, 1956)*

most linearly with chunk size, which implies that the number of chunks remembered was constant, irrespective of information per chunk. Note that this conclusion with respect to the span of immediate memory is at variance with the findings concerning long-term memory. In Chapter 1 we reviewed several studies which show that, in general, free recall of lists which exceed the immediate memory span improves as redundancy increases. Redundancy is a term from information theory and it refers to the difference between the actual information in a message, or any kind of learning sequence, and the maximum possible amount of information. For instance, the maximum uncertainty of a 27-letter alphabet (26 letters plus space) is 4.75 bits. However, in normal English text a letter contains only about 2 bits. Thus letter redundancy in English is nearly 60 percent. The reason for this redundancy is that the letters in English text are to a certain extent predictable; we are much more likely to expect an H after a T than a Q, and so on. Redundancy is therefore absence of uncertainty, or information, and the studies reviewed earlier imply that the less information in supra-span sequencies, the better recall is. This statement needs to be qualified, because it has been shown earlier that the rate of learning is determined not only by the amount of redundancy, but even more by the exact nature of the structure which causes the redundancy. Adelson, Muckler, and Williams (1955) have reported an experiment in which subjects learned lists of alphabetic letters. All lists contained 15 letters, but the information per letter was varied by changing the number of different letters used in the list, and by introducing sequential dependencies into the list. Figure 4.19 shows that their results agree fairly well with the conclusion that information in bits divided by the number of trials to criterion is a constant for learning sequences longer than the span of immediate memory.

Thus, we have here an interesting contrast: the span of immediate memory is approximately constant if measured in terms of items, but not in terms of information content; the span of long-term memory is approximately constant if measured in terms of information. Even if the latter conclusion must be qualified because other variables are often more important than merely the total amount of information, this observation adds to the growing body of evidence that short-term memory and long-term memory have quite different operating characteristics.

Encoding in Short-term Memory

In most of the experiments on short-term memory discussed here the learning material consisted of words, letters, digits, or perhaps nonsense materials. There are two things common to these materials: they can be pronounced, and they have meaning, although both the degree of meaningfulness and pronounceability may vary somewhat. The question we want to address ourselves to now is, how such material is coded in short-term memory. It is known that meaning is the most important principle of organization in long-term memory (Chapter 5). Short-term memory is different in this respect: the code employed is more primitive and meaningfulness plays a much lesser role than the gross sensory characteristics of the stimulus material. Obviously, words retained in short-term memory are understood, and letters are named—they are not simply meaningless sounds. However, their acoustic properties rather than their meaning appear to determine their fate in primary memory. There are two lines of converging evidence for this assertion. One group of studies shows that people can readily control what to attend to on the basis of physical characteristics of the stimulus material, but that they cannot disregard irrelevant parts of a stimulus in the absence of distinguishing

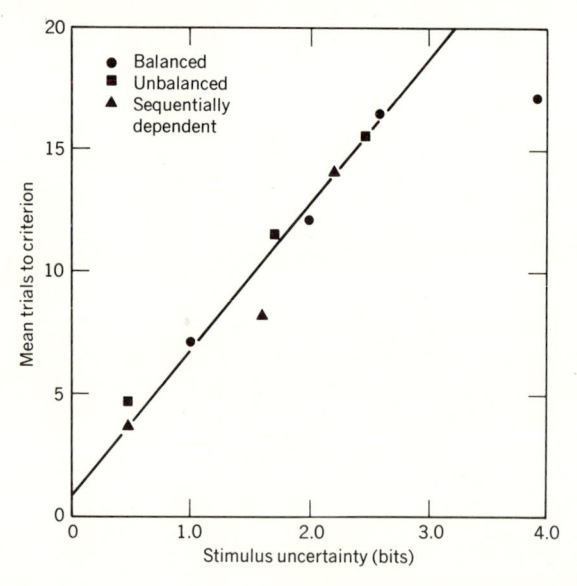

Fig. 4.19 *Mean trials to criterion in learning lists of letters as a function of the uncertainty of the list. (after Adelson, Muckler, and Williams, 1955)*

physical characteristics. Secondly, there is much evidence that most confusion errors in primary memory occur because two like sounding letters or words are confused while words alike in meaning are not subject to confusion.

Broadbent (1958) has reviewed some studies which show that subjects can attend selectively to one sensory channel and neglect messages arriving simultaneously on other sensory channels. For instance, in dichotic listening experiments the subject receives two messages simultaneously, one for each ear. Typically, the subject listens to one message at a time and shifts between channels, trying to catch as much of each message as possible. Moray (1959) has studied the fate of the rejected message and concluded that it gets lost completely. Once a message is filtered out, it cannot be recognized later. However, the perceptual filter does not reject messages without analyzing them in a superficial way. For instance, Moray pointed out that when the subject's name is included in a message which is to be rejected, the subject does react to it. Similarly Treisman (1964) has found that a subject does retain some information about rejected messages. Subjects can tell whether it was a man's or a woman's voice, and other such gross physical characteristics. The important point is that the analysis of the stimulus input is halted relatively early, prior to the analysis of verbal meaning. This conclusion was confirmed in a study by Bartz, Satz, Fennel, and Lally (1967). These authors presented strongly associated word-pairs simultaneously in a dichotic listening task, e.g., FOOT to the right ear, and BALL to the left ear. Their subjects did not use these associations, but reported the words which were presented to one ear first, and then the words from the other ear.

Other experiments show that once a subject attends to a particular channel, the total input is stored in short-term memory, and knowledge that part of this input is irrelevant and should be disregarded is of no help as far as short-term retention is concerned. Selzer and Wickelgren (1963) presented subjects either with 12 digits or with 16 digits and instructed them that in each case only 12 digits need be recalled; when subjects were tested for recall, they were given the 1st, 5th, 9th, and 13th digits of the 16-item list. In spite of that, subjects made twice as many errors with the 16-item list than with the 12-item list. Obviously, what determined recall was the number of items presented, not the number of items to be recalled. Similarly, Wickelgren (1964) found that subjects who were instructed to recall only the initial consonant of either a consonant-vowel pair, or a consonant-vowel-consonant syllable, did better in the first case than in the latter. Instructions to ignore everything after the first consonant apparently were of little help to subjects. They were unable to filter out the unnecessary letters, and stored the whole syllable in short-term memory, filling it up with irrelevant material.

Studies by Dallett (1964, 1965) lead to identical conclusions. Dallett tested subjects' recall after presenting them a list of 8 non-redundant digits, or lists of 7 digits plus a redundant zero prefix. Recall was the same under the two conditions. In later studies the position of the redundant zero in the digit sequence was changed. Still, subjects were unable to take advantage of their knowledge that a zero occurs in a particular position and improve their recall by devoting their total capacity to the seven remaining digits.

Whether or not a redundant prefix will interfere with the recall of a digit sequence will depend to a large extent upon the precise experimental conditions. Dallett's results are probably dependent upon a rather fast presentation rate. If the subject is given enough time, he will try to organize the sequence, find relevant associations, or employ some other mnemonic device: he will store the material in long term memory. If he is not given a chance to do so, he must rely upon short-term memory alone, using what Mackworth (1965) has called an "echo-technique."

What is stored in primary memory appears to be a description of the acoustic properties of a stimulus. If a sensory input other than an acoustic one is involved it is translated into an acoustic code and stored as such. It is easy to guess why the acoustic code should be prevalent. Rehearsal is necessary to keep an item in short-term memory, and most people find it hard to rehearse images, while verbalizations are easy enough to rehearse. Although it is doubtful that the short-term memory code is always acoustic, a number of studies indicate that an acoustic code is employed under a wide variety of conditions. Three different lines of experimental evidence converge to this conclusion: studies which show a relationship between the rate of naming and memory, studies of the interference effects of acoustically similar material, and studies of confusion errors in short-term recall.

Glanzer and Clark (1963) let subjects describe verbally a set of 8 geometric shapes which were either black or white and then tested for recall by the method of reproduction. Subjects were given the figures and indicated whether they were black or white in the original string. A high negative correlation ($r = -.80$) between the number of words used to describe the string of figures and the accuracy of reproduction was found. This led Glanzer and Clark to put forward the "verbal loop hypothesis": a subject translates visual information into a series of words, retains the verbalization, and bases his final response upon it. If there is either a short exposure time or a long retention time, those stimuli that require a long string of words for an adequate description will be handled less accurately than stimuli which may be described in just a few words. A rather similar result was obtained by Mackworth (1963) with a standard memory span procedure. She showed subjects either 9 or 10 items for 5 seconds and instructed them to try to recall in the correct order as many of the items as possible. The items were digits, letters, colors, or shapes. Before the experiment, subject's reading speed for each kind of material was determined. For the four materials reading speeds in items per second were 3.4, 3.0, 2.1, and 1.8, respectively. The average number of items correctly recalled for the different materials were 7.6, 5.7, 5.0, and 4.4 items. Thus, the faster the reading speed, the better recall was. This finding can be explained if we assume that subjects translate the visual material into acoustic form: they read it into the short-term memory store. The greater the reading speed, the more material can be coded during the exposure time. It is also possible that the rate of rehearsal in short-term memory is limited by reading speed, and that items which can be read faster can be rehearsed more.

The effects of acoustic similarity in short-term memory are very much like the effects of general similarity in long-term memory. If interitem similarity is high, learning is retarded; this result has been found in many verbal learning studies. Conrad and Hull (1964) have shown that the same is true for short-term memory. They determined the memory span of subjects for lists in which the acoustic confusability among the items was varied systematically. Lists in which the letters were acoustically distinct were retained better than lists with confusable items. Similar results are obtained when the effects of acoustic similarity are studied with a retroactive inhibition design (Dale, 1964; Wickelgren, 1965a). In the experiment of Wickelgren subjects were read 4 letters at a rate of 2 per second. Then, a tone followed by an interference list of 8 letters was presented. After that, subjects were asked to recall the original 4 letters. When the interference list was similar in pronunciation to the original list, greater retroactive interference was produced than when the letters of the interference list and the letters of the original list were very different in pronounciation.

The most significant evidence which shows that representation in short-term memory is through an acoustic code comes from the study of confusion errors in recall. Conrad (1964) argued that intrusion errors in immediate recall are systematic; memory traces may decay partially, and therefore similar traces are more likely to be confused with each other than dissimilar traces. The relevant dimension of similarity along which such effects are to be expected is acoustic similarity. Conrad's experiment contained two parts. At first, he obtained a confusion matrix for the letters B C P T V F M N S X presented auditorily over noise to 300 subjects (Table 4.2). The rows of this matrix represent the input letter; columns show the subjects' response; entries are the frequency of each response, given that the row-stimulus was presented. Next, Conrad constructed a memory confusion matrix based upon the recall intrusions from 387 subjects. Subjects were presented visually with a 6-letter sequence and tested for recall immediately. The same 10 consonants were used. A careful scoring system was employed in order to avoid including random guesses and other noise into the data: Only those sequences were scored which contained a single substitution error. In this way it was possible to maintain without ambiguity that the subject had confused a particular pair of letters. Table 4.3 shows the memory confusion matrix. The error pattern in Tables 4.2 and 4.3 is remarkably similar. The rank order correlation between the two tables is .64. It appears that although the letters were presented visually in the memory experiment, the subject recoded them acoustically, so that when a letter was partially forgotten, errors occurred which were characteristic of auditory confusions.

Conrad's results were replicated by Wickelgren (1965b) with auditory presentation of the recall lists. In addition, Wickelgren made

Table 4.2. *Listening confusions (after Conrad, 1964).*

					Stimulus letter					
	B	C	P	T	V	F	M	N	S	X
B	—	171	75	84	168	2	11	10	2	2
C	32	—	35	42	20	4	4	5	2	5
P	162	350	—	505	91	11	31	23	5	5
T	143	232	281	—	50	14	12	11	8	5
V	122	61	34	22	—	1	8	11	1	0
F	6	4	2	4	3	—	13	8	336	238
M	10	14	2	3	4	22	—	334	21	9
N	13	21	6	9	20	32	512	—	38	14
S	2	18	2	7	3	488	23	11	—	391
X	1	6	2	2	1	245	2	1	184	—

Table 4.3. *Recall confusions (after Conrad, 1964).*

	B	C	P	T	V	F	M	N	S	X
				Stimulus letter						
B	—	18	62	5	83	12	9	3	2	0
C	13	—	27	18	55	15	3	12	35	7
P	102	18	—	24	40	15	8	8	7	7
T	30	46	79	—	38	18	14	14	8	10
V	56	32	30	14	—	21	15	11	11	5
F	6	8	14	5	31	—	12	13	131	16
M	12	6	8	5	20	16	—	146	15	5
N	11	7	5	1	19	28	167	—	24	5
S	7	21	11	2	9	37	4	12	—	16
X	3	7	2	2	11	30	10	11	59	—

subjects copy the lists as they were presented, so that perceptual errors could be excluded from the analysis. In later studies, Wickelgren (1965c, 1966) showed that the confusion effect may be predicted from the linguistic structure of the different letters. Before we can understand these studies it is necessary to introduce some basic concepts from the linguistic characterization of speech sounds.

Linguists analyze the flow of sounds in natural speech into phonemes. A phoneme is a class of sound patterns, among which the native speaker of a language does not distinguish in the sense that two sounds belonging to the same class are never used to carry a difference in meaning. The smallest difference between two sound patterns which suggests to the hearer different contents is the difference of a single phoneme. By this criterion, the /r/ in *rat* and the /k/ in *cat* are two different phonemes. Sounds in the same phoneme class are acoustically similar but by no means identical. Thus there are obvious differences in the /k/ in *key*, *ski*, and *caw*, but these are merely free variations within one phoneme. There are 46 phonemes in English.

The phonemes of a language may be described by means of a distinctive feature system. Each phoneme can be encoded or decoded by a number of simple operations, corresponding to its distinctive features. It is somewhat arbitrary which operations are selected to describe the phonemes of a language. However, a distinctive feature system should be constructed so that a minimum number of dimensions are needed to identify each phoneme. A classification system based upon the features of the articulatory system is frequently used and is shown in Table 4.4, which is reproduced from Miller and Nicely (1955). Most of the features used are self-explanatory and their articulatory origin is obvious. Duration is perhaps the least intuitive feature. Note that most features are binary except for place of articulation, which is trinary (front, middle, and back). An alternative distinctive feature system is that of Jakobson and Halle (1956) who use a system of 9 binary dimensions. These dimensions were selected on the basis of more abstract and general considerations than English articulation. For instance, they use features such as vocalic-nonvocalic, grave-acute (which differentiates /o/, /u/ versus /e/, /i/, and compact-diffuse (e.g., /o/ versus /u/). We are in no position here to comment on the advantages of one system over another, but the distinctive feature analysis in general has very important consequences for our understanding of both perception and memory.

Miller and Nicely (1955) performed a study of perceptual confusions among English consonants. Sixteen consonants were presented under conditions of frequency distortion and noise. Subjects were instructed to guess at every sound. An analysis of the confusion errors showed that these were highly systematic. The more distinctive

Table 4.4. *Classifications of consonants in a distinctive features system (after Miller and Nicely, 1955).*

Consonant	Voicing	Nasality	Affrication	Duration	Place
p	0	0	0	0	0
t	0	0	0	0	1
k	0	0	0	0	2
f	0	0	1	0	0
θ	0	0	1	0	1
s	0	0	1	1	1
ʃ	0	0	1	1	2
b	1	0	0	0	0
d	1	0	0	0	1
g	1	0	0	0	2
v	1	0	1	0	0
ð	1	0	1	0	1
z	1	0	1	1	1
ʒ	1	0	1	1	2
m	1	1	0	0	0
n	1	1	0	0	1

features two consonants had in common, the greater the likelihood of a confusion. In Fig. 4.20, the data from one of the conditions (S/N ratio of -6 db) of the Miller and Nicely experiment were plotted as a function of the number of distinctive features in common between the stimulus letter and the letter given as a response by the subject. For instance, if the letter p was presented and the subjects gave p as a response, an entry is made under Distance 0. Responses t, k, f, and b are entered under Distance 1, r would be counted under Distance 2, n as 3, and z as 4, depending upon the number of distinctive features in Table 4.4 which are different from the stimulus letters. As Fig. 4.20 shows, the effect of similarity upon perception is a very strong one. However, not all features are equally affected by distortions or noise. Miller and Nicely have shown that voicing and nasality are perceived accurately even under quite adverse conditions, while place of articulation is severely affected by noise. They concluded that the perception of any of these five features is relatively independent of the perception of the others. Perception of consonants operates more like a 5-channel system than as one single complex channel.

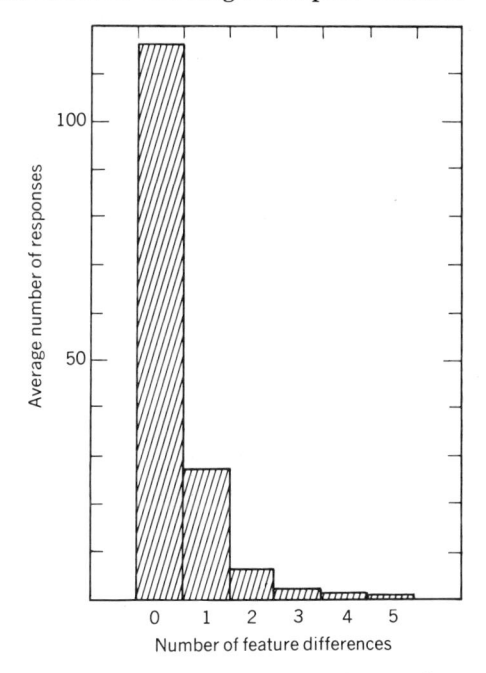

Fig. 4.20 *Perceptual confusions as a function of the number of different features between consonants. (after Table III of Miller and Nicely, 1955)*

Wickelgren (1965c, 1966) has shown that the same holds true for short-term memory. Indeed, one can analyze the memory confusion data of Conrad (1964) shown in Table 4.3 in the same way as described above for the perceptual confusion data of Miller and Nicely (1955). Figure 4.21 shows that the result of this analysis is almost the same as that obtained for perceptual confusions. The figure is due to Murdock (1967b) who suggested this kind of analysis. Obviously memory for English consonants is not all-or-none. However, the regularity of the confusion data suggests that forgetting may be all-or-none at the level of distinctive features.

While the studies reviewed above do indeed demonstrate that short-term memory uses an acoustic or articulatory* coding system under the conditions of these experiments, it is conceivable that other

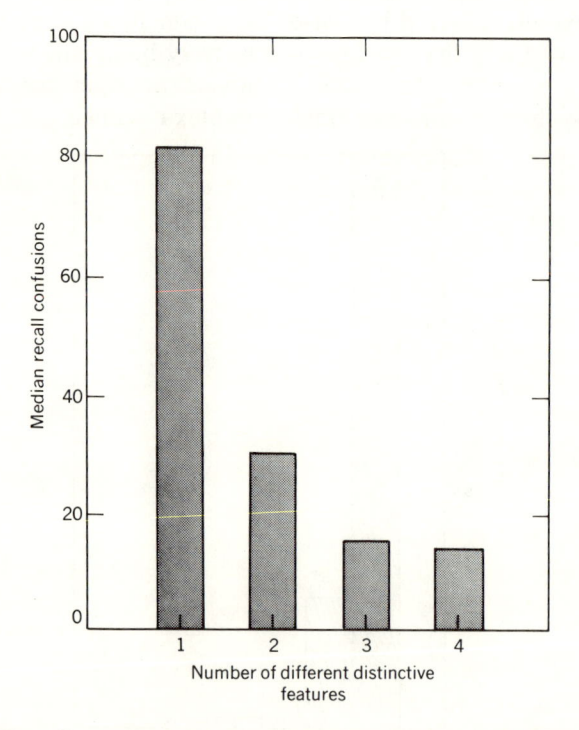

Fig. 4.21 *Recall confusions as a function of the number of different distinctive features. Data from Conrad (1964). (after Murdock, 1967)*

*Note that in all the studies described above acoustic and articulatory features were completely confounded. We are therefore unable to distinguish whether the short-term memory code is acoustic or articulatory.

codes may be used under different conditions. We know that what is stored in short-term memory is not bits of information, and that it is not even proportional to this measure (Miller, 1956). Visual similarity likewise seems to play no role in short-term retention. Calfee (1966) studied recognition memory for visually confusing letters (BCDGOQRU), acoustically confusing letters (BCDEPTVZ) and neutral letters (ADHIMQYZ). Reaction time was used as a dependent variable in this study. A large effect of acoustic similarity was obtained, but none of visual similarity. In a similarly designed recall experiment Cimbalo and Laughery (1967) obtained the same result.

Language factors also appear to be ineffective in short-term memory, or at least, are overridden in importance by acoustic confusions. The studies dealing with this problem are difficult to interpret. It is well known that factors like meaningfulness, redundancy, or semantic similarity influence long-term retention. Since one cannot exclude the possibility of long-term storage in experiments designed to study short-term memory, how should a small effect of semantic similarity in a short-term memory experiment be interpreted? It may be evidence of semantic coding in short-term memory, but it may have nothing to do with short-term memory. Conrad, Freeman, and Hull (1965) studied the retention of 6-letter sequences in which statistical predictability and acoustic confusability were controlled. The latter produced the expected large effect, while predictability had little influence upon recall (about 1/15 of the acoustic factor). Baddeley and Dale (1966) and Baddeley (1966) report experiments in which the effect of semantic similarity upon short-term retention is explored. In the first study no such effect was observed; in the second a small influence of semantic similarity was present. Dale and Gregory (1966), on the other hand, reported significant effects of semantic similarity in an experiment using a retroactive interference paradigm. Semantic similarity between the original learning material and the interpolated material increased the number of intrusions from the interpolated material. Laughery and Pinkus (1967) report an experiment similar to the Gibson *et al.* (1964) study which was reported in Chapter 1. Gibson *et al.* presented subjects 12 trigrams, varying meaningfulness and pronounceability of the trigrams. Meaningfulness was found to be more helpful to recall than pronounceability. Laughery and Pinkus presented only 4 trigrams and these letter by letter before testing for recall, and obtained the opposite result. If we assume that because of the length of the list and manner of presentation Gibson *et al.* were primarily measuring long-term memory, while Laughery and Pinkus dealt with short-term memory, the different outcomes can be explained.

The studies mentioned above suggest that secondary memory is primarily sensitive to semantic similarity and primary memory to acoustic similarity. However, in all of these studies primary and secondary memory effects were confounded, which probably explains the somewhat ambiguous results obtained. Kintsch and Buschke (1969) took advantage of the procedure developed by Waugh and Norman (1965) to separate primary and secondary memory. Their learning material consisted of strings of 16 words. After the 16 words were presented, one of them was repeated and subjects were asked to respond with the word that had followed the repeated word originally. There were three types of strings in this experiment: some consisted of 8 pairs of synonyms in random order (POLITE-COURTEOUS), others consisted of randomly ordered homophone pairs (NIGHT-KNIGHT), and the third type were strings of unrelated words which served as controls. The results were broken down into separate primary- and secondary-memory components according to the model of Waugh and Norman (1965), as described in Section 1. As hypothesized, acoustic similarity and semantic similarity had quite different effects upon primary memory and upon secondary memory. Acoustic confusability significantly interfered with primary memory, but had no effect upon secondary memory. The opposite was true of semantic confusability. It produced significant interference in secondary memory, but primary memory estimates were quite the same whether subjects learned unrelated words or synonyms.

The two most salient features of the short-term memory trace are a low level of processing and a preference for the aural dimension. However, not all short-term storage is acoustical, although this is difficult to establish because of the omnipresent confounding of short-term and long-term storage in psychological experiments. Certainly, storage in long-term memory is multidimensional, and it is possible that subjects simply prefer the acoustical dimension for storage in short-term memory because it is easy to rehearse material by speaking to oneself. It is equally certain, that there is no compulsory auditory encoding. Gibson and Yonas (1966), and Kaplan, Yonas, and Shurcliff (1966) have demonstrated that subjects do not use an auditory encoding strategy in a visual search task. Their findings suggest that auditory encoding is used only when necessary, namely when rehearsal is required. When a subject is looking through a column of letters to find, say, an E, there is no need for rehearsal and hence no auditory encoding.

More direct evidence for nonacoustic short-term storage comes from studies of motor responses. Rapid forgetting over short time intervals characterizes motor responses just as it does verbal responses (Adams and Dijkstra, 1966; Posner and Konick, 1966). Posner and Konick had subjects move a lever which was concealed from sight to a certain position and then tested for retention of this motor movement after intervals ranging from 0 to 30 seconds. Tasks differing in difficulty filled the retention interval (rest, copying, addition, or classification of digits). As in experiments with verbal material, substantial short-term forgetting was observed. Verbal mediation could be excluded, because the authors showed that subject's verbal codes were much too vague to account for the accuracy of the motor results when such codes were reported at all. However, unlike verbal experiments, the difficulty of the activity during the retention interval had no effect upon retention of the motor movement. Thus, although short-term motor memory has been demonstrated, it may be quite a different psychological process than short-term memory for verbal material. Certainly, implicit rehearsal presents problems in motor tasks which do not exist in verbal tasks.

4. MODELS FOR SHORT-TERM MEMORY AND LEARNING

The distinction between short-term memory experiments and learning experiments is somewhat arbitrary. The convention observed here is to talk about short-term memory experiments whenever items are given only one study trial. Repeated presentations and tests characterize learning experiments. In most verbal learning experiments the retention interval for a given item is not explicitly controlled by the experimenter as it is in short-term memory experiments. However, it is quite obvious that the methodology of short-term memory experiments can be adjusted to permit repeated presentations of the same items.

In a typical paired-associate experiment using the anticipation procedure each item is presented once for a presentation and test on every trial. If items are presented in random order the number of other items intervening between two presentations of any particular item will equal $(m\text{-}1)$ on the average for a m item list and may range from 0 to $2(m\text{-}1)$. One may expect the number of items intervening between presentation and test to play a very important role. Therefore in many recent learning experiments the interval between presentations has been controlled. This is easiest to do in a continuous paired-associate task: A stimulus-response item is introduced at some point, and after k presentations and tests of other items, the stimulus alone is shown for a test and followed by the joint presentation of the stimulus response pair. This cycle may be repeated as often as required. The number of intervening events between presentations can be kept constant or can be varied systematically. It is also possible to separate tests and reinforcements with this procedure. An item may be tested after k other items have been shown (we shall call this a test with lag k) but the reinforcement, that is, the joint presentation of the stimulus-response pair, may be delayed by j more presentations or tests of other items.

What kind of results should be expected in such an experiment? Clearly, the first test should give results identical with those obtained in comparable short-term memory experiments: Retention should be nearly perfect for an immediate test, but should decrease as a function of lag to an asymptotic value, the long-term memory component. But what are the effects of repeated presentations upon this short-term memory function? We know that subjects eventually learn to respond perfectly in most learning experiments. Therefore, after sufficiently extended training, one may expect the probability of a correct response to be one, or close to one, independent of lag. During intermediate periods of training the short-term memory function increases from the value characteristics for only one presentation until it eventually becomes uniformly one.

There are no data showing precisely such an effect, but whatever data are available certainly agree with the expectation expressed above. Hellyer (1962) studied the recall of consonant trigrams after 3, 9, 18, and 27 seconds as a function of the number of presentations of the trigrams. His subjects read aloud the trigrams either 1, 2, 4, or 8 times. The retention interval was filled with digit naming. His results are shown in Fig. 4.22. For one presentation Hellyer's results resemble those obtained in comparable experiments, as can be judged from the data of Peterson and Peterson (1959) and Murdock (1961) which are also included in Fig. 4.22. As the number of presentations increase, the short-term memory function becomes flatter. Presumably, after several more presentations no more short-term forgetting would have been observed at all.

There are two ways in which the improved retention after repeated presentations can be interpreted. The rate of short-term forgetting may decrease as a function of repetitions. If learning consists in the gradual build-up of associative strength, items which have been presented repeatedly would have acquired more associative

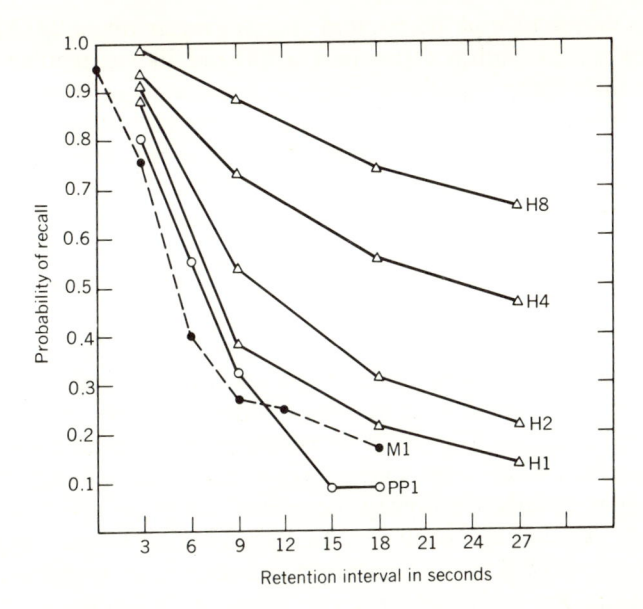

Fig. 4.22 *Probability of recall as a function of the length of the reten-*
tion interval and number of repetitions. After Hellyer (1962); data for
one repetition from Peterson and Peterson (1959) and Murdock
(1961) are also shown.

strength and forgetting would be slower. Alternatively, the phenomenon could be ascribed entirely to the greater likelihood that an item
presented repeatedly resides in secondary memory while short-term
forgetting may be independent of repetitions. The view of learning as
a discrete process naturally leads to this second interpretation.

Existing evidence favors the second alternative. Several relevant
studies will be discussed later, but an experiment by Bjork (1966)
illustrates the nature of this evidence more clearly than any other
single study. Bjork used a paired-associate task with a modified anticipation procedure. He constructed presentation sequences in such a
way that all interpresentation intervals from 1 to 40 were equally
likely to occur. There were 21 items with CVCs as stimuli and the
digits 3, 5, and 7 as responses. A different presentation sequence was
constructed for each item. All subjects received the same sequences
but with different items to counterbalance for interitem differences,
so that 21 different learning curves could be obtained, each one giving the probability of a correct response as a function of trials for a
particular sequence of interpresentation intervals. The shortest se-

quence involved 12 repetitions, and the longest involved 29. From the standpoint of the subject the task appeared like a regular paired-associate task except that items were not grouped in trial blocks but were presented continuously, and both very short and very long interpresentation intervals were unusually frequent. The subjects responded by pressing one of three buttons. The continuous nature of the task made the use of error elimination strategies by the subject rather difficult and hence one can expect to obtain data which are in essential agreement with the all-or-none learning model described in Chapter 2.

Bjork's 21 mean learning curves do not look like proper mean learning curves: they are much more irregular, in spite of the fact that 50 subjects had served in his experiment. However, the irregularity is not random: Whenever there is a short interval between successive presentations the performance curve jumps up, but the improvement is only temporary, especially when there is a relatively long wait until the item comes up for its next trial. In the top panel of Fig. 4.23 the first three presentation sequences are reproduced from Bjork's data. For example, only one other item intervened between the third and fourth presentation in sequence 3, and all subjects responded correctly. However, the improvement was clearly due to short-term memory rather than real learning as can be seen by the drop in performance on the fifth trial which came after 29 intervening items.

The over-all increasing trend of the learning curves reproduced here does not permit us to settle the question whether the rate of short-term forgetting changes during learning. However, if the trial of the last error is noted for each subject-item sequence and only performance before the last error is analyzed it becomes possible to look at short-term memory data unconfounded by long-term memory effects. The argument used here is identical with the one used previously in connection with the all-or-none learning model. We assume that if an item is in long-term memory recall will be perfect and no forgetting will occur within the experimental session. Hence presentations before the last error provide a pure measure of short-term memory. The first three of Bjork's presentation sequences are reproduced here as illustrations of the kind of performance changes which were observed on trials before the last error (lower panel of Fig. 4.23). The short-term memory effects here are even more pronouncd than in the mean learning curves. For brief interpresentation intervals performance tends to be elevated due to short-term memory effects. Otherwise, the curves do not increase as a function of trials but hover

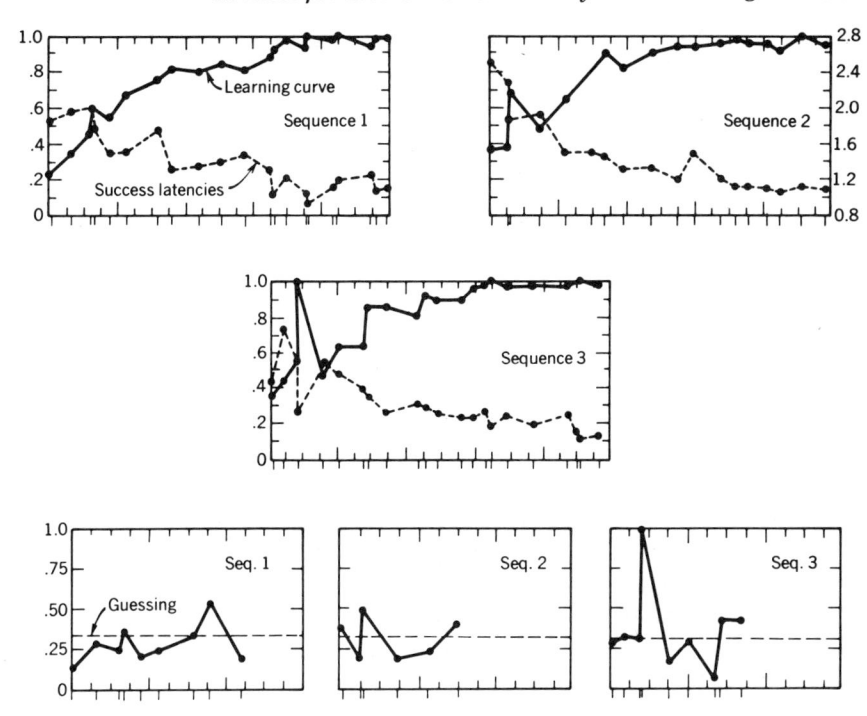

Fig. 4.23 *Mean learning curves and mean success latencies for three presentation sequences (above); proportions of correct responses on presentations prior to the last error for the same items (below). The hash marks below each abscissa designate the trials of the experiment on which the presentation occurred. (after Bjork, 1966)*

right around the guessing level of ⅓. Precriterion performance is stationary but differs from pure guessing because of the possibility of correct responses from short-term memory if the interval between presentation and test is not too long. In Fig. 4.24 data from all sequences prior to the last error were plotted as a function of interpresentation interval. For short lag, performance is much better than chance, but if about 20 items intervene between successive presentations subjects receive no more benefit from short-term memory and precriterion performance is not different from chance. Thus, for sufficiently long interpresentation intervals learning appears to be truly all-or-none. For short intervals the simple all-or-none model must be modified. Items always enter short-term memory when presented, but are likely to be forgotten before they are tested. Figure 4.24 gives the forgetting probability as a function of time since presentation.

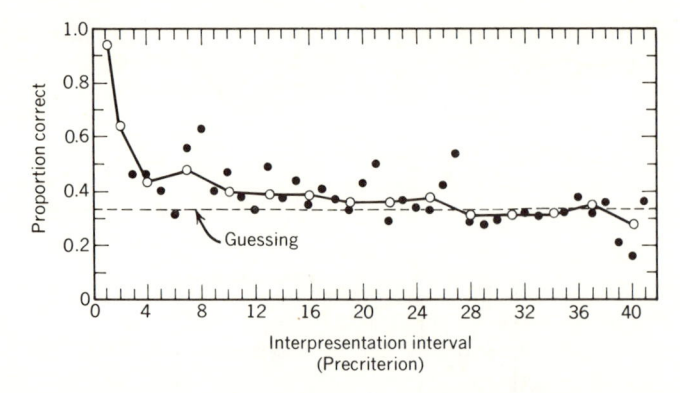

*Interpresentation interval
(Precriterion)*

Fig. 4.24 *Forgetting curve prior to the trial of the last error. (Open circles are the average of three successive points.) (after Bjork, 1966)*

Performance on trials before the last error will therefore not be at the guessing level but at a level jointly determined by the guessing probability and short-term memory.

Bjork's data beautifully illustrate the role of short-term memory in paired-associate learning. The interpresentation interval, however, affects not only short-term memory but also long-term memory. The probability of storage in long-term memory depends strongly upon the length of the interval between two presentations of a paired-associate. An experiment by Greeno (1964) demonstrates this point. Greeno arranged his items in blocks of 30 trials. Distributed items were presented once in each block; each massed item was presented twice in each 30-trial block, with either zero or one item between the two presentations. Thus, massed items were presented twice as often as spaced items. In spite of that, performance on spaced items and on the first presentation of massed items in each block of trials was practically equal, as Fig. 4.25 shows. Performance on the second presentation of the massed items was very good, of course. But this effect was transitory. The second presentation, following immediately after the first, seemed wasted as far as later performance was concerned. The effectiveness of a study trial depended upon the length of the presentation interval. If two study trials followed each other closely they were hardly more effective than a single trial.

Several studies in which continuous paired-associate tasks have been used, instead of list learning as in Greeno's experiment, confirm and extend this finding. Word-digit pairs were presented twice with either 0, 1, 2, 4, 8 or 16 other pairs between the successive presentations in a study by Peterson, Wampler, Kirkpatrick, and Saltzman

(1963). Eight filler items followed the second presentation, and then the word was shown alone for a test. All items were presented at a 2-second rate. In Fig. 4.26 the results of this experiment are shown. Greeno's results are confirmed insofar as an interpresentation interval of about 8 items was considerably more beneficial than very brief intervals. However, the probability of a correct response does not increase monotonically with the length of the interpresentation interval but shows a definite drop for very long intervals. Young (1966) has replicated all essential features of the Peterson *et al.* experiment as part of a larger investigation. His results are also shown in Fig. 4.26 and are almost identical with those of Peterson *et al.* Therefore, it seems quite certain that the decrease with very long interpresentation intervals is more than just a sampling error which we may comfortably neglect. Note also that Young's subjects remembered as much after just one presentation as after two massed presentations.

The efficiency of learning can be further manipulated through the interspersing of test trials between presentations. This was first noted in an experiment by Izawa (1966). Two of her experimental conditions were as follows. In the first condition nonsense syllables paired with two digit numbers were presented for a study trial and then the nonsense syllables were shown alone for a test trial on which no

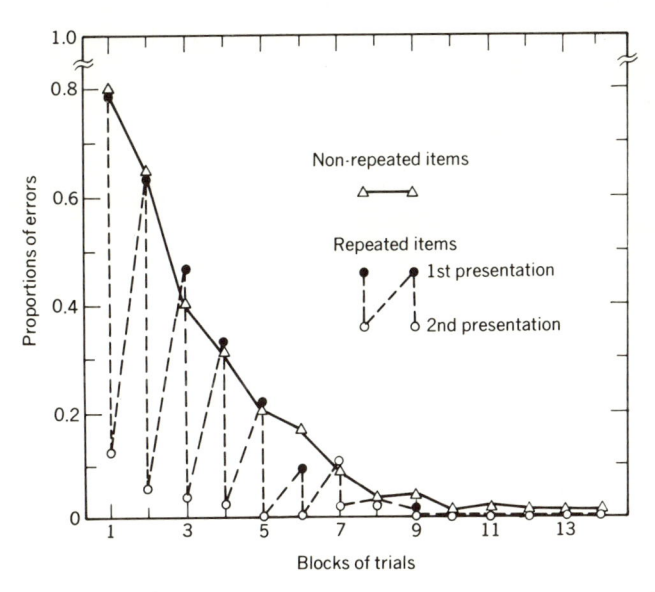

Fig. 4.25 *Mean learning curves for repeated and non-repeated items.* *(after Greeno, 1964)*

knowledge of results was given. Reinforcement-test cycles were repeated until each subject reached a criterion. In the second condition each cycle included three trials: a reinforcement, i.e., the joint presentation of the stimulus-response pairs, and two test trials. Izawa's main interest was in finding out whether performance on tests given successively without intervening reinforcement produced significant changes in the correct response probability. She found no such changes, suggesting that neither learning nor forgetting occurred on test trials in her experiment. Nor was there any tendency towards increased stereotypy of whatever responses happened to occur on the test trials. However, something of importance evidently did occur on test trials, because interspersed test trials increased the effectiveness of subsequent study trials. Subjects learned considerably faster when two test trials were given between study trials than when only one test trial was given. Of course, the number of intervening test trials and the length of the interpresentation interval were confounded in Izawa's experiment, and in view of the results just discussed it is not clear which variable was responsible for her results. In the experiment already mentioned Young (1966) separated the two variables experimentally and concluded that the introduction of a test trial between two study trials does facilitate recall over and above the effect which an additional test trial necessarily has upon the interpresentation interval. Something happens on a test trial which helps subsequent learning.

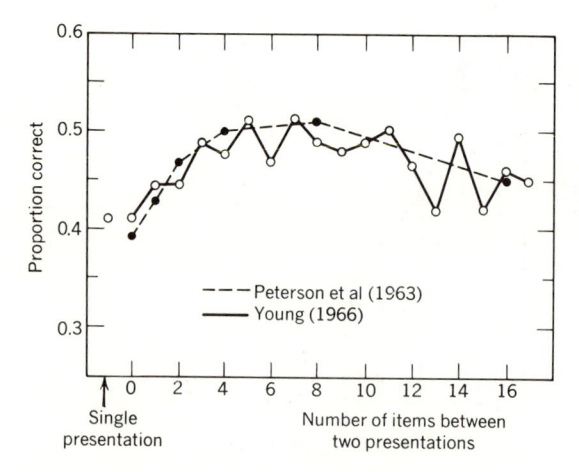

Fig. 4.26 *Recall as a function of the lag between two presentations of an item. (after Peterson et al., 1963, and Young, 1966)*

In the following sections we shall explore several alternative interpretations of the data just described. Intentionally, the data have been outlined in rather more detail than usual in this book; now we shall see what theoretical notions are needed to account for this quite complex set of empirical results. We shall first discuss various attempts to incorporate short-term forgetting notions into the all-or-none model for paired-associate learning. Next a model will be considered in which rehearsal in short-term memory plays a central role. In these models items are treated as a unit and forgetting is all-or-none; a final model will be described which is concerned with partial forgetting. Taken together these models should give the reader a fairly good idea how models are constructed, and how they are modified in interaction with empirical results.

Forgetting Models for Paired-associate Learning

In Chapter 2 we concluded that the simple one-element model provides a reasonably accurate description of paired-associate data as long as learning does not involve a succession of stages, such as response learning, associative learning, or stimulus discrimination. On the other hand, it is obvious from the preceding discussion that a model as simple as the one-element model cannot account for the rather complex relationships which are discovered when one looks at the learning process with the techniques of short-term memory studies. However, the phenomena of short-term memory can be incorporated quite well into the general framework of this model.

It is easy to see how the one-element model can be modified so that it will account for short-term forgetting. Remember that the basic assumption of this model was that learning may occur with probability c whenever an item is presented for study. Once learning has occurred, the subject will always respond correctly; as long as an item is unlearned the subject may "guess" correctly with some probability q. Without a change in the learning assumptions which the model makes, one may introduce a short-term memory state in addition to the unlearned state in the following way. Whenever an item is presented and the subject pays attention to it it enters short-term memory; in addition, with probability c, it may also be stored in long-term memory. Items in short-term memory may be forgotten with probability f. Note that learning is still a discrete event in this model, but it makes little sense to say that it is "all-or-none." Performance before the last error will still be stationary, at least after the item has been shown once. But the probability of a correct response on trials before the last error now depends upon the length of the retention interval, and will in general be higher than what could be expected purely on the basis of guessing. Indeed, the ability of the forgetting model to account for data such as those in Figs. 4.23 and 4.24 was the reason for constructing it in the first place.

It is important to state the forgetting model a little more precisely if we want to see whether it predicts correctly the more intricate relationships which we have found in the data (Figs. 25 and 26), or if we want to see what modifications are necessary before these phenomena can be described. Equation (5) is a formal statement of the model. It is due to Atkinson and Crothers (1964), who called it the LS-2 model.

$$(5) \quad \begin{array}{c} \\ L \\ S \\ F \end{array} \begin{array}{cccc} L & S & F & Pr(\text{correct}) \\ \begin{bmatrix} 1 & 0 & 0 \\ a & (1\text{-}a)(1\text{-}f) & (1\text{-}a)f \\ a & (1\text{-}a)(1\text{-}f) & (1\text{-}a)f \end{bmatrix} & & & \begin{bmatrix} 1 \\ 1 \\ g \end{bmatrix} \end{array}$$

Equation (5) shows the transition probabilities between the three states which the model assumes. Each element of the matrix denotes the probability of entering the state designated on the top of its column on a learning trial, if on that trial an item is either in the learning state L (top row), the short-term memory state S (middle row), or the forgetting state F (bottom row). The transition probabilities reflect the learning and forgetting assumptions of the model. On each trial an unlearned item may be learned with probability a. If the item is not learned $(1\text{-}a)$, it still enters short-term memory, and may be forgotten with probability f or remains there with probability $(1\text{-}f)$. If an item is either learned or in short-term memory, a correct response will be given. If an item is forgotten, a correct response can occur only when the subject guesses correctly (g). Items which are presented for the very first time are equivalent to forgotten items.

For the sake of comparison, the transition matrix which defines the one-element model is reproduced below:

$$(6) \quad \begin{array}{c} L_{(\text{learned})} \\ U_{(\text{unlearned})} \end{array} \begin{array}{ccc} L & U & Pr(\text{correct}) \\ \begin{bmatrix} 1 & 0 \\ c & (1\text{-}c) \end{bmatrix} & & \begin{bmatrix} 1 \\ q \end{bmatrix} \end{array}$$

It can be shown mathematically, and it makes sense intuitively after some reflection, that the states S and F in Eq. (5) may be lumped into a common state SF, if at the same time the probability of a correct response in this common state is adjusted in the following manner:

$$
(7) \quad \begin{array}{c} \\ \text{L} \\ \text{SF} \end{array}
\begin{array}{cc} \text{L} & \text{SF} \\ \begin{bmatrix} 1 & 0 \\ a & (1\text{-}a) \end{bmatrix} \end{array}
\quad \begin{array}{c} Pr(\text{correct}) \\ \begin{bmatrix} 1 \\ 1 - (1\text{-}g)f \end{bmatrix} \end{array}
$$

Equations (5) and (7) are equivalent in the sense that they describe exactly the same process, except for the very first trial, for which an additional response rule is needed if Eq. (7) is used, since all items have probability g of being correct if they are presented for the first time.

By rewriting the forgetting model in the form of (7) the close relationship between the forgetting model and the one-element model becomes apparent. Equations (6) and (7) are obviously equivalent, with $c = a$, and $q = 1 - (1\text{-}g)f$. The reason for pointing out this relationship in such detail is to make clear that the inclusion of a short-term memory mechanism does not simply invalidate everything that was said and done before about models of paired-associate learning. It represents an important change in how we formulate the laws of learning, but it involves a modification and reinterpretation of earlier results, rather then their rejection.

Atkinson and Crothers (1964) have applied the forgetting model along with several other comparable models to 8 different paired-associate experiments. In all of these experiments the anticipation procedure was used, but the experiments differed in list-length (9-18), and in the number of response alternatives (3 or 4). Over-all goodness of fit was evaluated by a chi-square test, and was found to be quite good for the LS-2 model, and indeed better than for most of the competing models. Some systematic deviations from the data need not concern us here, because in spite of the good fit of the model obtained by Atkinson and Crothers, the model must be revised extensively before it can account for more than the bare minimum of the empirical results reviewed in the preceding section.

First of all, several studies have shown (e.g., Fig. 4.25) that the learning probability depends upon the intertrial interval. Equation (5) fails to predict this effect. The reason for this failure is apparently the assumption that learning is equally effective from states F and S. Suppose this assumption is relaxed, and a different learning probability, b, is assumed for items which are held in short-term memory. If $b << a$, items are much more likely to enter the learning state from the initial state than from short-term memory. Take, for instance, the case $b = 0$, i.e., no learning occurs from short-term memory: the shorter the interpresentation interval the more likely an item is to be in short-term memory, and the less likely it is that learning occurs. Results such as the saw-tooth learning curves in Fig. 4.25 imply that b equals zero, or is close to it.

By assuming different learning rates for states S and F one can account for the increase in the probability of a correct response as a function of the preceding interpresentation interval, but in actual fact this increase is followed by a decrease if the interval is very large (Fig. 4.26). A relatively innocent oversimplification in the model appears to be at the root of this problem. The model assumes a "long-term memory state" from which no losses can occur. We have pointed out previously that "long-term memory" is surely a misnomer. The duration of an experimental session is usually less than one hour and the paired-associates learned to criterion during that session are surely not stored in the long-term memory which contains a person's vocabulary, concepts, response programs, and whatever else makes up his store of experiences. The long-term state is so called simply because it is long-term relative to the time intervals involved in most paired-associate studies. Rate of loss in the long-term state is small, and in the order of minutes, while in the short-term state rate of loss is larger and in the order of seconds. However, the assumption that the rate of loss is actually zero from the long-term state is certainly not more than a convenient oversimplification. If one permits loss from state L, the concave shape of the curves in Fig. 4.26 can be explained. When the interpresentation interval is too long, the additional advantage because of short-term forgetting is small (most items in state S are forgotten by that time anyway), but forgetting from state L becomes a problem, leading actually to a downturn in the curves in Fig. 4.26.

These extensions of the forgetting model leave only the facilitative effects of test trials unaccounted for. There is an obvious *ad hoc* assumption which solves that problem (even if it does not explain it): permit learning to occur also in unreinforced test trials, albeit with a much lower rate, because the observed effects are generally quite small (Young, 1966).

The reason for these successive modifications of the forgetting model are not that the model must by all means be saved in the face of contradictory evidence. That certainly would not be worth the trouble. On the other hand, by modifying and changing the model in response to new data one can come to a better understanding of the data. One can get some idea what a particular result implies, and whether it really involves an interesting substantive issue, or is merely a consequence of some trivial circumstance. For instance, if it turns out that there is forgetting from the long-term learning state, no one will be much surprised; if anything else has been maintained it was merely for reasons of mathematical convenience, and because there were no empirical results which demanded that additional complication. Figure 4.26 shows that one can not get by without assuming forgetting from long-term memory, but this is hardly a very significant finding. On the other hand, the implication that the learning rates from short-term memory and the initial state must be unequal is of considerable interest. Whether or not short-term memory is some sort of a dead-end road where items may remain for a while but are not further processed is certainly not obvious.

Although the modified forgetting model can account reasonably well for the empirical results under consideration it is not the only adequate theory for paired-associate learning. The same formal framework can be given quite a different psychological interpretation.

Suppose that paired-associate learning involves the construction of memory codes for the learning items. A code is an internal representation of an item. A good code differentiates an item form all the other items. Recall for such an item will be perfect or close to perfect, so that one may say that this item is in the "learning state." However, it will often happen that the subject constructs a poor code which does not differentiate the item sufficiently well. Even a poor code will support retention for a short time, but as more and more other items are presented confusions occur which result in recall failures.

The coding hypothesis implies a learning model which is almost equivalent to Eq. (5). If a code is sufficiently good to preclude later confusions, an item is in state L; an insufficient code may support recall in state S with probability $(1-f)$ when other items intervene between the presentation and test of an item. Note that in this model the difference between the states L and S is not in terms of two distinct storage mechanisms, but depends upon the goodness of the memory code.

The coding theory has one big advantage over the forgetting model stated earlier. It implies that the learning rates from states S and F should not be equal. The forgetting model had to be modified in order not to contradict the finding that the efficiency of learning is a function of the interpresentation interval. It was necessary to assume that the probability of entering state L was greater when an item was new or forgotten, than when an item was being held in short-term memory. This assumption was forced upon the model by such findings as those of Figs. 4.25 and 4.26. The coding theory has a natural interpretation here where the forgetting model had to do with an *ad hoc* assumption. Whenever the subject studies an item which he does not yet know, he tries to find a memory code for it and he has probability a of finding an adequate code. However, if he sees an item for which he already has a code and is able to give a correct response to it on the basis of that code, he does not search for a new code, even if his code turns out to be inadequate in the long run and breaks down on some later trial. Therefore, the probability of entering the learning state L from state S, where the subject responds correctly but has only a temporary code, is zero. Even if one assumes less consistent subjects, that probability should be small and much less than the learning probability for items for which the subject does not have a code at all, either because they are new or because the code that had been constructd proved to be inadequate.

Of course, all the other modifications which were necessary for the forgetting model can be made equally well for the coding model. More specifically, one would have to make some provision for the fact that even good codes may break down eventually.

The coding theory is due to Restle (1964) and Greeno (1967). Among its ancestors one must mention Gibson's discrimination hypothesis (Gibson, 1940). In both theories the learning process is basically one of establishing discriminations among items. A more immediate predecessor is Restle's cue selection theory (Restle, 1962), which included the notion that no learning occurs on trials on which a correct response occurs even if it was made on the basis of a cue which may prove to be inadequate later.

The forgetting model and the coding model are closely related formally, but they are based upon very different assumptions. On the one hand the evidence discussed earlier strongly supports a distinction between primary and secondary memory and it is tempting to identify these with the short-term and learning states of the forgetting model. On the other hand, the coding hypothesis has some implications which agree very well with the data and which can only be included into the forgetting model in an *ad hoc* manner. Perhaps one should also point out that the short-term forgetting which plays such an important part in all of these models looks a little different from the decay functions for primary memory. According to the forgetting model we have to assume that primary memory extends over as much as 20 intervening items (see Fig. 4.24) — which is rather unlike previous results (e.g., Fig. 4.12). Thus it is quite possible that the intermediate state in Eq. (5) reflects primarily the effects of bad codes and is not identical with primary memory. The exact role which primary memory plays within the coding model remains to be worked out.

An alternative framework in which the relation between short-term forgetting and the learning process may be expressed is provided by stimulus-sampling theory. The application of this theory to the phenomena of short-term forgetting is based upon the notion of stimulus fluctuation which was developed by Estes (1955 a, b). Either stimulus-component or pattern models can be applied to the present problem. However, in previous chapters we found the pattern model to be particularly promising in applications to verbal learning and therefore we shall discuss here only the pattern-fluctuation model.

In previous applications of the pattern model it has always been assumed that patterns are sampled randomly on each trial. More specifically, it has been assumed that the probability of sampling any given pattern on a trial when the stimulus is presented equals $1/N$, where N is the total number of patterns needed to represent this stimulus. This assumption is changed in the fluctuation model: we assume that there is a positive correlation between the patterns sampled on successive experimental trials. If on any trial n stimulus A was represented by pattern j, the probability that the same pattern j will be re-sampled when item A is presented on trial $(n+1)$ is larger than $1/N$. Estes has suggested that the mechanism which introduces such a correlation is stimulus fluctuation. Suppose that the N stimulus patterns are not all available on any given trial but may be divided into two subsets. One set of patterns is available to the subject, and on each trial the subject samples a pattern at random from this set of available patterns. Obviously the probability of sampling the same pattern on successive trials is higher than $1/N$ and depends upon the number of patterns in the available set, which may be only one as in the case described below. The crucial idea is that the subsets of available and unavailable patterns may exchange members: patterns may fluctuate between the two sets as a function of time or as a function of interfering events.

If the retention interval is very short, little fluctuation can have occurred, and the subject very likely samples the same pattern which had become conditioned on the previous trial and hence will give a correct response. On the other hand, if the retention interval is very long, repeated transitions between the available and the unavailable set will have occurred, and the two sets will be in equilibrium: the expected proportion of conditioned and unconditioned patterns will be equal in the available and in the unavailable set after sufficient fluctuation. Thus we have two kinds of mechanisms in this theory: stimulus fluctuation which corresponds to short-term forgetting, and conditioning which corresponds to the more permanent kind of learning.

The fluctuation model has been applied to data from short-term memory experiments by Young (1966), and in slightly different form by Izawa (1966) and Rumelhart (1967). We shall not present any formal derivations from the model but shall attempt to show informally how the pattern fluctuation model can account for the data reported earlier in very much the same way as the other models discussed here.

To begin with, consider the basic phenomenon of short-term forgetting. The model correctly implies a response probability of near unity right after the presentation of an item if patterns are always conditioned when they are sampled on a study trial. Because the conditioned item may fluctuate into the unavailable set, rapid short-term forgetting is also predicted. A stable asymptote of short-term retention is implied because after sufficient fluctuation the probability that the conditioned pattern is in the available set will no longer decrease and will equal the proportion of conditioned patterns in the unavailable set.

Of course, perfect learning is possible in this model in spite of stimulus fluctuation. Once all patterns are conditioned, recall will be perfect. The relationship between the efficiency of learning and the length of the intertrial interval is also predicted fairly accurately by the model, at least qualitatively. The model implies that the probability of a correct response after two reinforcements should increase to some asymptote as a function of the length of the interval between the reinforcements. If two reinforcements follow each other too soon, the pattern available on the second trial is likely to be conditioned already and the second reinforcement is wasted. As the intertrial interval increases the likelihood that an as yet unconditioned pattern may have fluctuated into the available set increases, and hence the effectiveness of the second reinforcement increases. The model fails to predict the decrease in the response probability after two reinforcements which occurs when the interval between the two reinforcements is too long (see Fig. 4.26). The model shares this failure with all other models discussed here which do not have a mechanism for long-term forgetting. In this case, we must postulate some kind of mechanism which permits conditioned patterns to revert to the guessing state as a function of time, or as a function of interfering events.

Another result which the model as stated here can not account for is the observation that the probability of a correct response after two reinforcements is greater when a test trial intervened between the reinforcements than without a test trial (Young, 1966). As with all other models, an assumption that some learning occurs on test trials can readily solve this difficulty. Of course, such an *ad hoc* assumption which is not motivated by the general theory is more a stop-gap than a real solution and explains nothing. However, the same problem was encountered by the other models discussed here.

A Model with a Rehearsal Buffer

Atkinson and Shiffrin (1968) have developed a model with an explicit rehearsal mechanism. They assume that primary memory storage in itself, without rehearsal, plays a negligible role and show that rehearsal strategies may under certain conditions become the dominant features of the learning process. Their model, which assumes that learning occurs when an item is rehearsed, can account for most of the empirical phenomena discussed earlier.

The importance of rehearsal will depend upon the experimental conditions. Atkinson and Shiffrin designed their experiments so as to maximize the utility of rehearsal. They used sets of 4 to 8 two-digit numbers as stimuli and the letters of the alphabet as responses. Stimuli and responses were re-paired at random throughout an experimental session and the subject's task was to remember which response a given stimulus was paired with when it was presented last; 220 trials were given per session. Reliance upon long-term storage is obviously a poor strategy in this experimental situation. On the other hand, short-term memory itself decays too fast to be of much use here, since each trial (test-study-blank) took 11 seconds. This rather slow presentation rate provided ample opportunity for rehearsal.

The over-all structure of the buffer model is outlined in Fig. 4.27. The basic assumption which Atkinson & Shiffrin make is that subjects use a rehearsal buffer of fixed size. This simply means that subjects keep rehearsing a fixed number of stimulus-response pairs throughout the experiment. Changes in the pairs which are being rehearsed occur according to the following rules: When an item is already in the buffer and it is shown again re-paired with a new response, it is always entered into the buffer in place of the old stimulus-response pair. This assumption is necessary, otherwise subjects might be rehearsing incorrect pairs. When an item is presented which is not being rehearsed it will be entered into the buffer with some probability a, replacing one of the items in the buffer at random. There may be several reasons

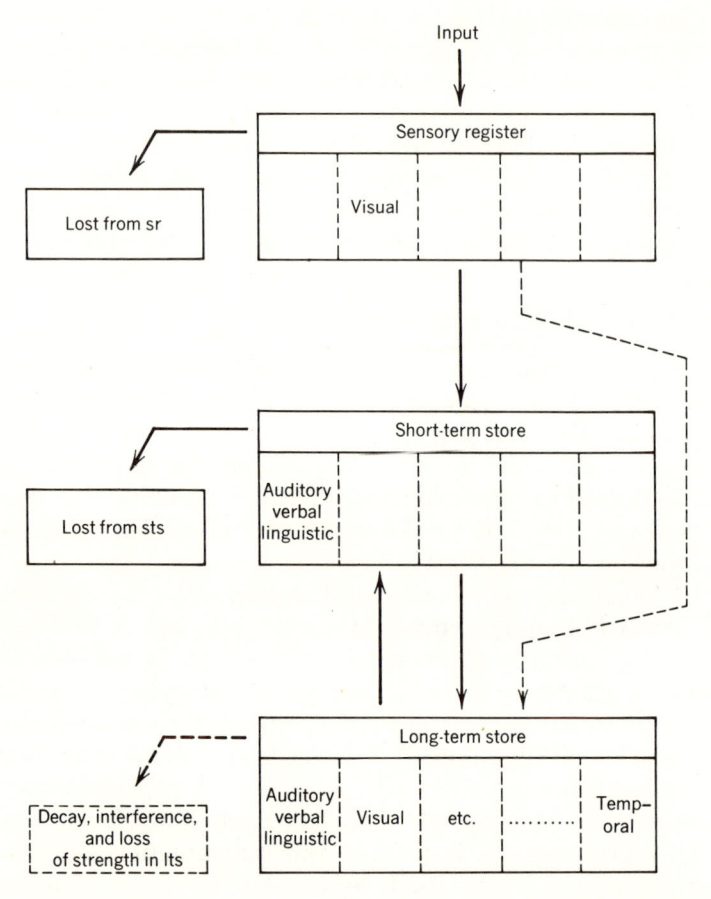

Fig. 4.27 *Structure of the memory system. (after Atkinson and Shiffrin, 1968)*

why not every new item is entered into the buffer. Reorganization of the buffer costs time and effort, and the subject may be reluctant to give up a combination of items which is particularly easy to rehearse.

While the subject relies mostly upon short-term rehearsal, more permanent information will also be stored. Atkinson and Shiffrin assume that when an item is first presented and whenever it is rehearsed later some information about it is transferred into a long-term store. This implies that the probability of retrieval from the long-term store increases monotonically as a function of the length of the time an item spends in the rehearsal buffer. Unlike other models, a provision for loss from long-term store is also made: as soon as an item leaves the rehearsal buffer, the information in the long-term store about this item begins to decrease.

The response rule for this model is simple: if an item is in the rehearsal buffer at the time of the test, the correct response will be given. If the item is not in the buffer, a search of the long-term store will be made. The probability of retrieving the item from the long-term store is an increasing function of the number of times the item had been rehearsed and a decreasing function of the number of trials since the item has left the rehearsal buffer.

This model has been applied to a number of different experiments all of which were performed with the general experimental paradigm discussed earlier. The assumptions of the model have generally been supported by these experimental tests, in particular those concerning the rehearsal buffer. In one experiment the authors investigated the probability of a correct response as a function of the length of the retention interval for intervals ranging from 0 to 17 intervening items. A short-term memory function was obtained which showed a regular decrease in performance as a function of the number of intervening items. The buffer model described this function quite well, but more than that, it predicted an interesting effect which one probably would not have noticed in the data without the model as a guideline. Let us take the case where a stimulus is re-paired with a new response whenever it is presented. Suppose an item is presented for study on trial n, and is shown for a test for the first time on trial $n + j + 1$. The buffer model predicts rather large differences in retention depending upon the nature of the j items which filled the retention interval. Suppose all j items are different. In this case the likelihood is very large that the item which was shown on trial n will be kicked out of the buffer. Each of the j items may interfere with the item to be remembered. On the other hand, suppose that the retention interval was filled with j presentations of the same stimulus which was re-paired with a new response on every presentation. According to the model, once an item enters the buffer every succeeding item with the same stimulus stays in the buffer automatically. Thus, there exists only one chance that the item to be remembered will be kicked from the buffer if the intervening items are all the same and, therefore, much less forgetting should occur in this case. This prediction of the model was confirmed by the data. The probability of a correct response as a function of lag was higher throughout when all intervening items used the same stimulus than when every intervening item used a different stimulus.

There is another implication of the buffer model which is quite counter-intuitive, but which is confirmed by the data. It too depends upon the property of the buffer that once an item is in it, it will stay there when its stimulus is paired with a new response. Consider a sequence of j consecutive trials all involving the same stimulus, but where a new response has been introduced in the study phase of each trial. Notions such as proactive inhibition would lead us to believe that recall on trial j should decrease as a function of the length of the preceding sequence. However, the actual data show the opposite trend (Fig. 4.28). The predictions generated from the buffer model are shown as a smooth line. It is clear why the model predicts an increase in Fig. 4.28: the more often the same stimulus has been presented in succession, the more likely it is to be held in the rehearsal buffer, thus assuring its rehearsal when the response pairing is altered.

In other experiments of the same general design Atkinson & Shiffrin have presented the same stimulus response pair more than once and thus could study learning effects proper. Consider the probability of a correct response for items which have been presented twice and are tested n trials after the second presentation. Results reported earlier (see Fig. 4.26) would lead us to expect this value to depend upon the interval between the first and second presentation of the item. Very short and very long intervals are poorest and an intermediate interval is optimal. Atkinson & Shiffrin's data completely confirm these expectations, and they show furthermore that the same kind of function, except at different absolute levels, is obtained for different lengths of the retention interval (n).

The over-all fit of the buffer model is good, and some striking predictions have been derived from it. Nevertheless, the model is not

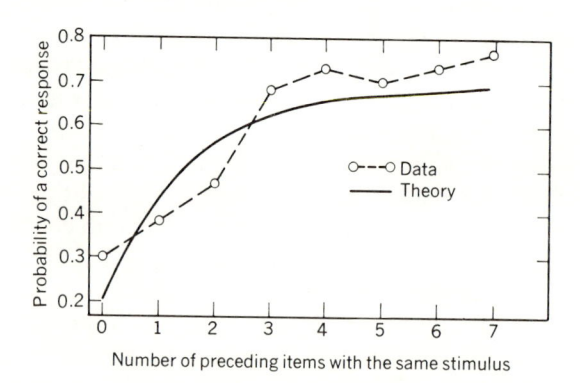

Fig. 4.28 *Observed and theoretical probability of a correct response as a function of the number of consecutive preceding items using the same stimulus. (after Atkinson and Shiffrin, 1968)*

perfect and several improvements could be made. For example, as the model is stated now, no provision is made for competition between responses in the long-term store. Occasional intrusion errors in the data suggest that such competition does occur, however. Atkinson and Shiffrin have also observed that the function relating the probability of a correct response to the length of the retention interval is often S-shaped. The probability of a correct response decreases only slightly over very brief intervals, but drops sharply afterwards. The model predicts the most rapid decline in response probability at the briefest retention intervals. The feature of the model which seems to be at fault in these cases is the assumption that when an item replaces another item in the buffer it knocks out one of the items at random. If instead one assumes that the probability of losing an item from the buffer is proportional to the length of the time an item has been in the buffer, the model correctly predicts an S-shaped lag curve. Atkinson and Shiffrin have shown that one condition under which the subject resorts to the strategy of replacing the older items first occurs when the buffer must be reorganized on every trial. By forcing the subject to read aloud each item as it is presented this condition may be approached. If he must make an overt response the subject apparently finds it easiest to enter all items in the buffer as they come, at the same time showing a bias towards kicking out those items which have been in the buffer for the longest time. In fact, this strategy may simply be an adjustment to the particular conditions of the Atkinson and Shiffrin experiment, in which short retention intervals were much more frequent than long intervals, and hence it did not pay to keep an item for too long. The subjects may have noticed this feature of the procedure and adjusted their rehearsal strategy accordingly.

A Multicomponent Theory of the Memory Trace

In most models considered so far, forgetting has always been considered to be an all-or-none process. The unit of analysis in these models was an item, i.e., a stimulus-response pair. An item was said to be stored in memory, or to have been lost from memory. All of the information about an item was assumed to be tied together, and an item was learned and forgotten as a unit. That such models could account for the data rather well implies that this assumption can not be completely unfounded, and that it makes sense, indeed, to regard items as the units of learning, at least with the simple kind of materials used in the experiments discussed. However, we have seen in Chapter II that this assumption will ultimately be a source of difficulty. When one is dealing with anything but the simplest learning tasks the possibility of partial learning must be considered. One way of approaching this problem is by treating the different attributes of a stimulus separately: although learning of an item may not be all-or-none, the different attributes or components of the item may be learned in that manner.

One model reported so far which is sufficiently complex to deal with gradual forgetting is stimulus-sampling theory. The one-element pattern theory assumes that learning is strictly all-or-none while the N-element pattern model, which has been discussed above, assumes that learning occurs in discrete steps. Finally, stimulus component models permit gradual learning. Thus, it is not always clear *a priori* how to represent a stimulus situation in the theory. At this stage of knowledge in psychology this indeterminancy may be an advantage. However, it also shows that stimulus-sampling theory is still incomplete: We do not know, until after the fact, how a stimulus in a learning experiment is to be represented in terms of the theoretical stimulus elements.

An alternative model which permits gradual forgetting has been outlined by Bower (1967). Bower assumes that subjects code a stimulus in a learning experiment as a list of attributes. These attributes may refer directly to the psychophysical properties of the stimulus material, or to the verbal label which the subject uses to identify the stimulus. Whatever the nature of the code for each attribute, information about each attribute can be formally represented by a vector of ordered components. Suppose an item has N binary attributes. Then a complete description of this item amounts to a listing of the value which this item has on the first attribute, on the second attribute, and so forth until all N attributes have been enumerated. The result is a vector of N binary digits. The restriction to binary digits is not serious. It is obvious that attributes with more than two values can be transformed into a larger number of binary attributes.

Suppose that loss of information in any component is all-or-none. The loss of information in the over-all trace will be determined by the number of component losses, and will itself be gradual. The basic parameter of the model is the probability that a particular component retains its value over a retention period of length t, denoted by $r(t)$. It is easy to show how an expression can be derived for the probability that after time t exactly i of the N components have retained their value. The value of that expression depends, of course, upon $r(t)$.

If a subject retains i out of a total of N components, what will the probability of a correct response be? In order to answer this question, further assumptions have to be made in the model, for instance, that the subject guesses whenever he forgets a component. In that case the probability of a correct response if i components are remembered is simply the probability that he guesses correctly on the forgotten ($N-i$) components.

Bower compared the forgetting functions implied by such a model with those predicted by the simple all-or-none model. Of the two the multi-component model provides the better fit to actual data.

One can regard $r(t)$, the probability that a particular component is retained after time t, simply as an empirical function and attempt to estimate it from the data. Alternatively, one can postulate some rational $r(t)$ function, and test to see how adequately this function describes the empirical function. An idea borrowed from stimulus-sampling theory provides an interesting rationale for a theoretical $r(t)$ function. Suppose that the value of each component may spontaneously change from the correct value to the null value, and vice versa, just like stimulus elements may fluctuate in and out of a set of available elements. Let f be the probability that the value changes from correct to null, and let c be the probability that a forgotten component resumes its correct value during a brief retention interval $\triangle t$. With the restriction that at time 0 all components had their correct value, the probability that a component has its correct value at time t can be derived. It is an exponential decay function of time with an asymptote determined by the ratio

$$\frac{c}{c + f}$$

The effects of repeated learning trials are represented by "trace multiplexing" in the multicomponent theory. This idea is somewhat different from the other learning mechanisms discussed so far. Usually learning is thought to make a memory trace stronger or more resistant to forgetting. Such a mechanism could certainly be developed for the multicomponent theory. For instance, subsidiary assumptions could be made which describe how $r(t)$ changes as a function of repeated learning trials. Instead, Bower suggested a multiplexing mechanism. He assumed that repeated trials lead to storage of several copies of the same memory trace, or multiplexing of the trace. Suppose one complete copy of a trace is stored on each trial, and that different copies fade out randomly and independently. The probability of retention of a single copy is $r(t)$. If z copies of a trace have been made, the probability of retention of this component after an interval of length t equals the probability that at least one copy is retained, viz.,

$$p_z(t) = 1 - \{1-r(t)\}^z$$

It is obvious that the assumption that exactly one copy is made on every trial can be relaxed by permitting learning failures, or, if the rate of presentation is slow and rehearsal plays a role, by allowing more than one copy per trial. The mathematical derivation of the equations relating probability of a correct recall to trials in a multiplexing system is too lengthy to reproduce here. Suffice it to say that Bower generates theoretical recall functions which look very much like the empirical functions reproduced in Fig. 4.22.

Serious quantitative tests of the model have not yet been reported. However, it appears that the model could account at least qualitatively for most features of learning data. For instance, the beneficial effects of overtraining on retention can easily be explained. Even after response probability has achieved unity, additional copies continue to be produced and retention is therefore improved. Some additional assumptions are needed, on the other hand, to describe the effects of intertrial interval in paired-associate learning. If the retention interval is short, the subject may recognize that the task is easy and fail to produce additional copies because he regards them as unnecessary. If the retention interval is long, the subject may add copies because he feels that extra copies are needed. Such auxiliary assumptions, or similar ones, could turn the multiplexing model into a serious competitor of other learning models.

We probably shall hear more about multiplexing models in coming years because there is some reason to believe that the nervous system actually uses such a scheme for establishing reliable memory traces. The nervous system and complex machines have at least that much in common, namely, that both must find some kind of a solution to the problem of how to make performance reliable when every component is inherently unreliable. Both electrical switching units and neurons do not operate with 100% accuracy. Occasional malfunctions at the component level can not be avoided. Every day several thousands of neurons die in the adult human brain. These neurons are not replaced and represent a source of error in all further calculations involving them. The reason why the total system continues to function in spite of component breakdown seems to lie in the extensive use of multiplexing. There are several mathematical models which show that one can achieve arbitrary accuracy from unreliable components. Multiplexing was the first technique suggested for this purpose by von Neumann in 1956. Von Neumann proposed to replace each component of an automaton by a bundle of n components. In addition, he used a "restoring organ" in the following way: suppose that k of the n copies give an output of 1, and the rest an output of zero. Instead of transmitting simply this information, the restoring organ increases the value of k if it is greater than some critical value k_c, and decreases it if it is less than the critical value. The reason for this operation is that if the input actually was a 1, a few malfunctions might occur, but most components will operate properly and give an output of 1. Hence, if most components are observed to give an output of 1, this is likely to be the correct output, and increasing k in this case will help reduce errors. In the most extreme case k_c could be regarded as a threshold: if more than k_c components give an output of 1, the total system puts out a 1; if fewer than k_c components give an output of 1, the total system puts out a 0. Von Neumann has shown that a system employing such a multiplexing scheme can be made arbitrarily accurate simply by increasing n, the number of redundant components. Since von Neumann's pioneering work much more efficient multiplexing schemes have been devised. For a brief review of error-correcting codes see Arbib (1964).

The important lesson for the learning theorist contained in this work is that the way in which actual systems assure perfect performance is by introducing redundancy and not by direct changes in the parameters of forgetting or acquisition processes. One may of course argue that learning models do not have to describe the actual mechanisms by which learning occurs. For instance, in the forgetting model discussed above, repetition has the effect of making entry into the "learning state" more likely. This model may be a good functional model, but it probably is a poor structural model. Rather than entering items into a learning state, the structural models of the future may deal with the construction of redundant networks. However, the development of an adequate functional model of learning and memory is neither a useless nor a trivial goal, and it is probably the best one can hope for, given our present understanding. Nevertheless, learning theorists will look closely at models which incorporate multiplexing schemes because such models might be more realistic in terms of what we know about the operation of the nervous system.

SUMMARY

Many psychologists distinguish between sensory memory, primary memory, and secondary memory. Of these, sensory memory has received only little attention here, since this topic belongs perhaps more properly to perception rather than learning. However, a fairly thorough account was given of the phenomena of short-term memory which have been so intensively explored in recent years. It was argued that a distinction between primary and secondary memory is useful because the two are affected differently by experimental variables; for example, rate of presentation or word frequency affects primarily the likelihood of storage in secondary memory but has no effect upon the recall of the most recently presented items, which may be attributed to primary memory. On the other hand, a short delay between presentation and test may strongly interfere with primary memory, but leaves unchanged the recall of the early and middle items of a list, which presumably is based upon secondary memory.

The discussion of the nature of short-term retention was concerned primarily with three topics: with the way interference works in short-term memory, with "chunking" and the unit of measurement in short-term memory, and with the role of acoustic encoding. Interference seems to be less a matter of specific associations than of total work load. It appears that primary memory has a limited capacity and that anything that takes up part of this capacity interferes with its contents. A very important point is that the capacity of primary memory is to be measured in terms of "chunks" of information. One can hold in immediate memory only a few chunks, but the chunks themselves may be very rich in information. Exactly what will form a chunk in any particular context depends upon a person's strategies for perceptual encoding. Verbal materials appear to be encoded acoustically in short-term memory, independent of their manner of presentation. Acoustic encoding presumably facilitates rehearsal in the form of implicit speech. Encoding in secondary memory, unlike primary memory, is not predominantly acoustic, and considerations of meaning play an important role.

Short-term memory experiments suggest looking at learning in a new way: learning may be considered as an increase in resistance to forgetting which occurs during multiple presentations of the same material. The first trial of a learning experiment is comparable to a short-term memory experiment. If the test follows immediately upon presentation, an item is practically always "learned" in the sense that it is retained in short-term memory. However, it usually requires several presentations of an item before it is learned more permanently. Studies concerned with the interaction of short-term memory and learning were reported in considerable detail. There are several different ways to include short-term memory mechanisms into existing learning models or to develop new models for these phenomena. The all-or-none model for paired-associate learning can be quite naturally extended to include a short-term memory state and a long-term memory state. Other approaches were also discussed which result in formally similar models but which are based upon a different psychological rationale. This work was described quite extensively both because of its intrinsic importance—all future learning theories will have to deal with the problem of short-term memory—and also because it provides a good case history of how models of learning are developed and modified in response to new experimental findings, and how they in turn stimulate new experimental explorations.

DECISION PROCESSES AND ORGANIZATIONAL FACTORS IN MEMORY

55555555555555

While the previous chapter was mostly concerned with problems of short-term memory and its interaction with more permanent memory, we shall concentrate in this chapter upon some more general aspects of memory. Specifically, we shall be concerned with the organization of the memory store and with variables which affect retrieval from this store. It is clear that some things are much easier to remember than others, and we shall argue that how easy something is to remember is at least in part determined by how well it is organized and how well it fits into the existing structure of the memory store, either through associative bonds, categorical relationships, or other types of relationships. Storage in long-term memory, therefore, is like a problem-solving task: the subject must find out in which way the to be learned material is organized, and how this organization is related to what is already stored in his memory; retrieval from memory, correspondingly, appears to be a problem of successfully exploiting the organizational structure of the memory store. We shall discuss these problems in the context of free-recall learning, since organizational factors appear to be most prominent in this learning paradigm. In the final section of this chapter, however, we shall show how organizational factors affect other learning paradigms and we shall attempt to compare and contrast the different verbal learning paradigms in this respect.

Another problem which has been remarked upon several times in previous chapters concerns the role of decision processes in memory. To a considerable extent subjects can control the processes of storage and retrieval in memory. Within the limits of experimental constraints subjects can decide what and how much to rehearse, how to organize material, how to go about searching their memory, and whether or not to make an overt response in the case of uncertainty. We shall examine this latter problem in the context of recognition learning: how does a subject decide to say "yes, I have seen this item before" or "no, this is a new item," if he is not sure what to say? In a later section we shall take up the somewhat more general problems concerning the subject's control processes in recall.

1. RECOGNITION

In a recognition experiment a number of study items are presented on every trial and subsequently tested by showing the study items together with distractor items and asking the subject to identify the old items. We shall be concerned here solely with item recognition, as distinguished from class recognition. In item recognition, or individual recognition, study and distractor items belong to the same set of homogeneous items. In class recognition the study and distractor items come from different sets. It is obvious that if the study items are words and three-place numbers are used as distractors on the recognition test, the subject will perform on a completely different basis than if both the study items and the distractors are three-place numbers. In more subtle cases it might be less obvious that the subject is either wholly or in part responding on the basis of class recognition. For instance, if all the words used as study items are associatively related (say they are associates of HOSPITAL), and unrelated words are used as distractors, class recognition and item recognition would be inextricably confounded. Class recognition may present quite different problems from item recognition; it may be more related to concept identification and will not be discussed here further.

In all recognition tests the similarity between the learning items and the distractor items is a very powerful variable. Underwood and Freund (1968) have shown that if subjects are given a multiple-choice recognition test consisting of the correct word, a high associate of the correct word, a formally similar word, and a neutral word, the high-associate words provide the major source of errors. Similarly, Anisfeld and Knapp (1968) have demonstrated that in a yes-no recognition task in which subjects were shown words which had been presented before, words which were common associates or synonyms of preceding words, and neutral control words, subjects made more false-recognition responses to common associates and synonyms than to control words.

In recognition tests it is often possible to recognize an item correctly on the basis of some remembered detail; in recall, on the other hand, memory for an isolated detail is usually less helpful. The nature of the learning material determines how important part-recognition will be. If the learning material is poorly integrated, for instance if consonant trigrams are to be studied, part-recognition may be quite effective, depending upon the confusability of the distractor items used in the experiment.

The most striking characteristic of experiments on recognition is the high level of performance which subjects achieve. In paired-associate experiments subjects need several trials before they master lists of only 10 or 12 pairs. In recognition experiments subjects can recognize almost perfectly several hundreds of items after only one presentation under suitable conditions. An experiment by Shepard (1967) is instructive in this respect. Shepard selected 300 frequent and 300 infrequent words from the Thorndike-Lorge count (Thorndike and Lorge, 1944). Of these 540 were shown to subjects as study items. The remaining 60 words together with a random subset of 60 of the words previously selected were used as test items. An old word and a new word were shown together and the subject had to indicate which member of the pair he believed to be the old word. Subjects identified correctly 88% of the words, on the average. Since the test items were randomly selected from 540 study items, one must suppose that subjects had retained about 475 words after a single exposure.

In passing, a curious phenomenon concerning the recognition of frequent and infrequent words should also be noted. Half of Shepard's words occurred frequently (CHILD, OFFICE) and the other half occurred very infrequently in the Thorndike-Lorge count (JULEPT, WATTLED). The infrequent words were recognized better than the frequent words. This is an interesting finding, because when subjects have to recall a word, rather than merely to recognize it, they perform better with frequent words (see the discussion in Chapter I). Later we shall comment more explicitly upon this difference between recall and recognition.

Shepard reported two more experiments which resulted in even higher retention scores. The procedure in these experiments was similar to the one just described. In the first experiment subjects were shown an inspection series of 612 sentences. The recognition score was 89%. Two cooperative subjects who agreed to undertake the boring task of studying 1224 sentences performed about as well as the subject given the standard inspection series (88% correct). In a final experiment the stimulus material consisted of colored pictures which were selected for high individual saliency and low confusability. Again an inspection series of 612 items was used. Retention tests in the usual manner were given immediately after inspection, and in addition a second test (constructed with different test pairs) was given either 2 hours, 3 days, 1 week, or 4 months after the first session. Percent correct recognitions on the immediate test was 97%. Scores on the delayed tests were 100%, 92%, 87%, and 58% for the four conditions described above. Thus, even after a delay of 7 days recognition was extremely good. After 4 months, on the other hand, the mean percent correct was not significantly different from chance.

We do not know the basis for this remarkable ability of subjects to recognize stimuli. Most of the laboratory work which has concentrated upon elucidating the mechanisms for recognition memory has used different stimulus materials. Highly confusable letter and digit combinations have been the standard materials in recognition studies. Such material is not at all suitable for studying the upper limits of recognition performance, but it is more convenient for studying the effects of other experimental variables in the laboratory. Because errors in recognition occur quite frequently with such stimulus material, the effects of experimental variables such as delay between presentation and test, or repetition of an item can be investigated.

Several procedural variations must be distinguished among recognition experiments. Some experiments use a list-learning procedure. A list of study items is presented to the subjects, usually one by one, either visually or auditorily. It is then followed by a test. For a yes-no recognition test the study items plus a number of distractor items which were selected from the same item pool as the study items, but which have not been shown before, are presented in random order and the subject is asked to tell whether each item is old or new. For a multiple-choice test each study item is paired with one or several distractor items, and the subject is asked to select the old item. The Shepard (1967) experiment just discussed used a list-learning procedure, together with a two-alternative multiple-choice test, except that only a subset of the study items was tested. In experiments on recognition learning several study and test trials may be given with the same list of items. To avoid learning distractor items, new distractor items are introduced at each test trial.

In the steady-state procedure study and test trials are combined and items are introduced and dropped continuously. The experimenter presents items one at a time from a pool of homogeneous items. Some items are repeated and the subject's task is to judge whether an item has been shown before or not. Shepard and Teghtsoonian (1961) have introduced this procedure. An adaptation to study forced-choice recognition memory under steady-state conditions has been described by Shepard and Chang (1963). In their experiment items were always presented in pairs after the first few trials. One item of each pair was an old item (i.e., it had been presented as a member of an earlier pair) and the other member was a new item. The subject's task was twofold: first he had to judge which item was the old item, and then he had to memorize the newly presented item for a later test trial.

The experiment of Shepard and Teghtsoonian (1961) provided some of the basic data concerning short-term recognition memory. Items were randomly selected from the set of all 3-digit numbers and were presented exactly twice per session. All items were printed on 3×5 inch cards. The subject was given a large deck of cards (200 in most conditions) and was asked to go through the deck at his own rate, noting on a record sheet for each item whether or not he had seen the number on an earlier card of the deck. No feedback as to the correctness of the response was provided. The experimental variable of principal interest was the lag between the first and second presentation of an item. The experimental results in terms of the probability of an "old" response to an old item as a function of the number of intervening presentations during the retention interval are shown in Fig. 5.1. The short-term memory function for recognition is remarkably

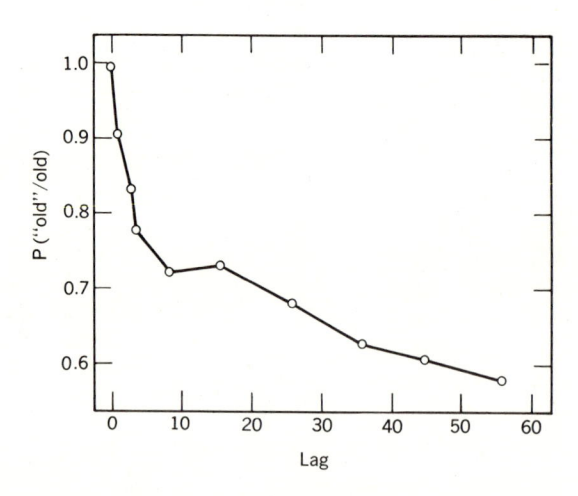

Fig. 5.1 *The probability of an "old" response to old items as a function of the number of intervening presentations since the last presentation of a stimulus. (after Shepard and Teghtsoonian, 1961)*

similar to that for recall. Even for the longest delays the probability of a correct recognition is well above the probability of a false recognition. The last point in Fig. 5.1 for a lag of 50 to 60 was still about .57, while the probability that a new number was classified as old averaged only .22. A completely steady state was not achieved, though. In this, as in all later experiments using the same procedure, the false recognition rate was not constant but increased throughout the experimental session. However, after the first 40 cards the increase was very small.

The effects of repetition upon recognition memory appear to be quite similar to the repetition effects observed earlier with paired-associate procedures. Kintsch (1966) modified the steady-state recognition procedure by repeating some of the items several times, but keeping the number of items intervening between successive presentations constant. Two groups of repeated items were used, one with lag 1 and one with lag 10. The probabilities of recognition failures for the first five repetitions are plotted in Fig. 5.2 for one of the conditions of Kintsch's experiment. The open triangles are for items repeated after only one intervening item, and the open circles are for items repeated after 10 intervening items. Evidently, performance is much better when items are presented with a lag of one, but considerable improvement as a function of trials occurs even with a lag of 10. Figure 5.2 also shows subjects' performance on items which were repeated three times with a lag of 1, and then two more times with a lag of 10, and items which were first presented with a lag of 10 and then shifted to a lag of 1. Of particular interest are the results for the items which were shifted from a short lag to a long lag: subjects made significantly more errors for such items than for control items for which 10 other items intervened between successive presentations from the very beginning. The "overshooting" of error probabilities after a shift from short to long interpresentation interval was replicated in two other experiments and appears to be a reliable phenomenon. It indicates that massed recognition trials are not as effective as spaced trials, just as in paired-associate learning. Indeed, it appears that paired-associate learning and recognition learning are identical as far as the effects of massing and spacing of trials are concerned. Therefore the forgetting models of paired-associate learning which were described in the previous chapter can be applied to recognition learning data with very little modification (Kintsch, 1966; Olson, 1969). However, a problem of interpretation still remains, because one can look at these models as describing a process of short- and long-term forgetting, or as a process of constructing memory codes which differ in adequacy. These alternative interpretations have been discussed extensively with respect to

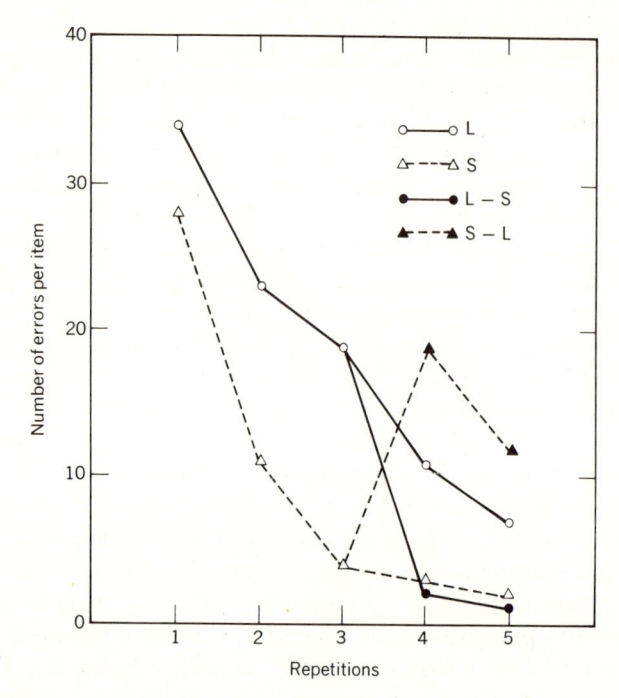

Fig. 5.2 *Proportion of items which were not recognized as a function of long and short retention intervals and changes in the retention interval. (after Kintsch, 1966)*

paired-associate learning in the previous chapter. Essentially the same issues arise in the interpretation of models for recognition-learning. Kintsch (1966) argued that memory codes could be classified in terms of their goodness of fit on a continuous scale; exactly how good a code had to be in order to support recognition reliably appeared to depend upon the demands of the task. Even poor codes might be sufficient if the retention interval is short, but they could not guarantee recognition after longer retention intervals.

Decision Processes in Recognition

So far we have not discussed efforts to deal directly with subject's response biases in recognition. The model of Kintsch (1966) does not have an explicit mechanism for this purpose: if a subject is biased towards "new" or "old" responses this is duly noted and incorporated as a parameter estimate—the probability of saying "old" if an item has never been presented before (the g of Eq. (5) in Chapter 4). However, the model has really nothing profound to say about response biases, changes in bias, or the dependence of bias upon experimental conditions. What is needed, then, is a more systematic treatment of response biases in recognition.

A subject can easily identify all old items correctly, simply by saying "old" whenever a stimulus is presented. Or he can be sure of never making a false recognition if he responds "new" all the time. Usually a subject chooses a bias somewhere between these two extremes. As already mentioned, learning models deal with response biases by means of the parameter g, the probability of responding "old" when an item is in the initial state. The false recognition rate can serve as an estimate of this probability. A subject may increase his hit rate by responding "old" on a proportion g of all trials on which he does not recognize the stimulus as such. Such a guessing strategy will, of course, indiscriminately increase the hit rate and the false recognition rate.

Models with such a guessing mechanism are called high-threshold models. The assumptions which high-threshold models make are briefly these. There exists a state (or several states) in which recognition of an item which has been presented before is perfect. Let the probability that an item is in this state be p_s. If an item is not in this state, and hence is not truly recognized, the subject can still guess that it is an old item with probability g. For new items there is a corresponding probability p_n of identifying the new item as new. If the new item is not recognized as such, a false identification will occur on a proportion g of trials, because the subject is assumed to guess "old" with probability g whenever he can not identify an item. If we let $P(\text{"old"}/\text{old item})$ and $P(\text{"old"}/\text{new item})$ be observed proportions in a recognition experiment, the assumptions of the high-threshold theory may be expressed more formally as follows:

(1a) $\qquad P(\text{"old"}/\text{old item}) = p_s + g\,(1\text{-}p_s)$

(1b) $\qquad P(\text{"old"}/\text{new item}) = g\,(1\text{-}p_n)$

Egan (1958) has discussed two special cases of Eq. (1) which have been implicit in much work on recognition memory. In the first case, we assume that $p_n = 0$, in spite of the fact that this assumption is somewhat counterintuitive (it implies that subjects can never recognize new items as such). Solving for $P(\text{"old"}/\text{new item})$ in Eq. (1b) and substituting into Eq. (1a) we have

(2) $\quad P(\text{"old"}/\text{old item}) = p_s + (1\text{-}p_s)\,P\,(\text{"old"}/\text{new item})$

Equation (2) says that the two observable variable $P(\text{"old"}/\text{old item})$ and $P(\text{"old"}/\text{new item})$ are linearly related. The line passes through the points $(0, p_s)$ and $(1,1)$: for $P(\text{"old"}/\text{new item}) = 0$, $P(\text{"old"}/$ old item) becomes p_s, and for $P(\text{"old"}/\text{new item}) = 1$, $P(\text{"old"}/\text{old}$ item) becomes 1. The function relating $P(\text{"old"}/\text{old item})$ and $P(\text{"old"}/\text{new item})$ is called the memory operating characteristic in analogy to psychophysical terminology, or isomemory function because all points on this function have the same memory strength p_s and differ only in the subject's guessing strategy. A family of curves for different memory strengths are shown in Fig. 5.3(a). If $p_s = 0$, all the subject can do is guess and his performance will fall on the main diagonal. If $p_s = 1$, the operating characteristic will be the upper boundary in Fig. 5.3(a). Three intermediate conditions are also shown.

A more realistic threshold model would assume that subjects can sometimes recognize the new stimuli as new, i.e., $p_n \neq 0$. Suppose we let $p_n = p_s$. In this case we obtain

(3) $$P(\text{"old"}/\text{old item}) = p_s + P(\text{"old"}/\text{new item})$$

by combining Eq. (1a) and (1b). The true recognition probabilities can be estimated from Eq. (3) as

$$P_s = P(\text{"old"}/\text{old item}) - P(\text{"old"}/\text{new item})$$

which is the traditional correction for guessing (Woodworth and Schlosberg, 1954, page 700): The operating characteristics implied by Eq. (3) are shown in Fig. 5.3(b) for several values of p_s.

It might seem more appropriate to consider a third case intermediate between Case I and Case II, where p_n is larger than zero, but not as large as p_s. As Egan (1958) has shown, the operating characteristic for such a case is still a straight line, but with an intermediate slope as in Fig. 5.3(c).

Curved operating characteristics are obtained from assumptions similar to those of the theory of signal detectability. Suppose that subjects can evaluate each item in a recognition task on a scale of familiarity. Because of stimulus generalization effects items which have never been presented before do not all have the same familiarity value but are characterized by a distribution of familiarity values $f(s)$. The familiarity values of items which have been shown once before are distributed according to another probability distribution $g(s)$, but are on the average higher than the familiarity values of new items. Figure 5.4 illustrates the familiarity distributions of old and new items. Note that in general there will be some overlap between the two distributions. Suppose that the subject's recognition response is completely dependent upon the familiarity value of the item which

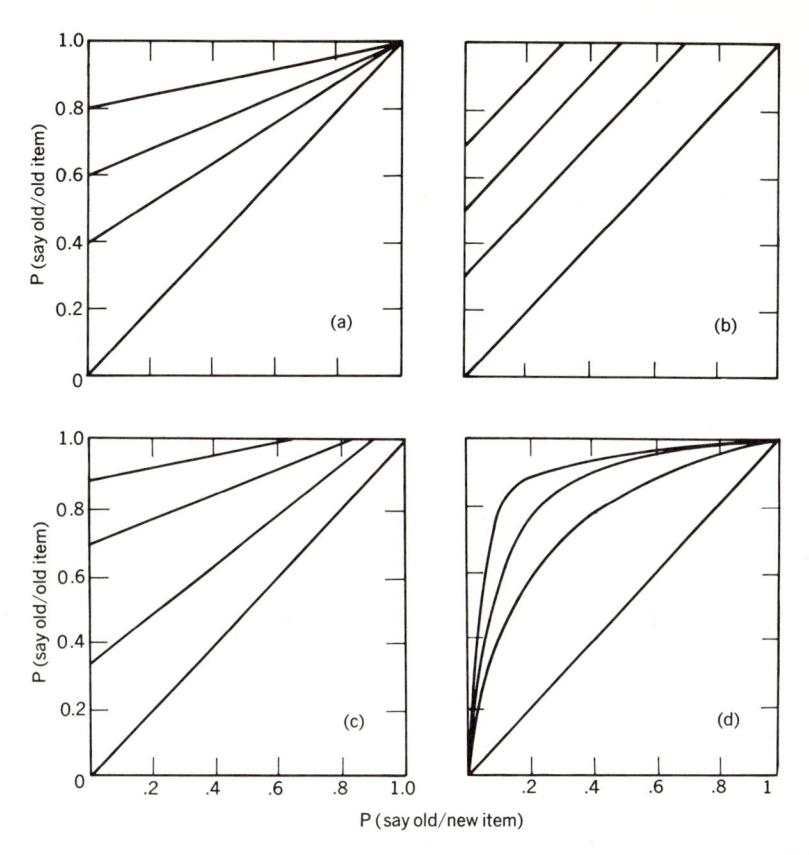

Fig. 5.3 *Memory operating characteristics according to four models.*

is being tested. If the value is high enough, the subject will respond "old"; if the value is low, the subject will respond "new." If the two distributions overlap, perfect responding is impossible. The best decision rule for the subject to follow is to fix a cut-off point c so that misses and false recognitions are balanced at some acceptable level, given the constraints of the situation. The area to the right of c under the curve $g(s)$ gives the probability of a hit; the area to the right of c under $f(s)$ gives the probability of a false recognition which is associated with the cut-off point c. Bias changes in this model imply a curved operating characteristic as shown in Fig. 5.3(d): as a very strict criterion (a c-value in the extreme right in Fig. 5.4) is progressively relaxed, large increases in the hit rate occur first, accompanied by only minor increases in the false recognition rate; as the criterion

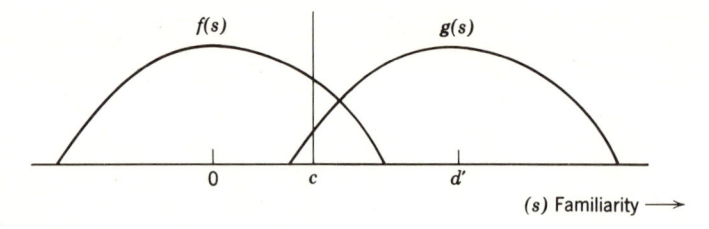

Fig. 5.4 *Familiarity distributions of new items (f(s)) and old items (g(s)).*

assumes lower and lower values, the gains in the hit rate become smaller and are paid for with disproportionately large increases in the false recognition rate.

Before we can turn to experimental results an alternative method of constructing operating characteristics must be mentioned. Most operating characteristics in psychophysical tasks have been obtained by inducing the subject to assume different criteria through variations in instructions, pay-offs, or the frequency of signal trials. Typically, a whole experimental session is run under one experimental condition, and the data from this session provide one point on the operating characteristic. A much more efficient method of data collection based upon confidence judgments has been suggested by Egan, Schulman, and Greenberg (1959) and Pollack and Decker (1958). An adaptation of the latter method is generally used in studies of recognition memory. The method relies upon the assumption that subjects can assume multiple criteria on a single trial. Instead of merely asking the subject for a binary recognition response, the subject also gives a confidence judgment. With confidence judgments on a four-point scale, we have effectively 8 different response categories, ranging from "certainly a new item" to "certainly an old item." The frequency of each response category is recorded separately for old and new items, as shown in Table 5.1. Normally the data provide only one point on the operating characteristic: the proportion of "old" responses given a new item, and the proportion of "old" responses given an old item is plotted. This corresponds to the cut-off between New-1 and Old-1. In our example the estimated hit rate corresponding to this cut-off point is $Pr(\text{"old"}/\text{old item}) = 200/300 = .67$ and the estimated false recognition rate is $Pr(\text{"old"}/\text{new item}) = 110/300 = .37$. Now suppose we repeat our calculation, but place the cut-off between Old-1 and Old-2. In effect we are saying that if the subject had used a stricter criterion he would have called "new" those items which he did call "old" but was least confident about. In this case we obtain as a second point on the operating characteristic $Pr(\text{"old"}/\text{old item}) = 160/300 = .53$ and $Pr(\text{"old"}/\text{new item}) = 80/300 = .27$. A similar argument can be made for the placement of the criterion between any of the other categories, and in this manner one can generate seven points from one set of data. It has been shown that operating characteristics based upon confidence ratings give comparable results to more conventional procedures. However, the two are not equivalent for all purposes. At this time, work on memory has almost exclusively relied upon confidence ratings.

An example of an empirical memory operating characteristic is shown in Fig. 5.5. This figure is taken from Egan (1958). Egan's subjects studied a list of 100 words and were then tested for recognition with a list containing the 100 study words plus 100 distractor items. Subjects used a 7-point rating scale, where a 1 meant "certainly old", a 4 meant "pure guess", and a 7 stood for "certainly new". The results shown in Fig. 5.5 are data from 4 subjects in Egan's first experiments. Egan grouped his 16 subjects in groups of 4 according to their performance; the data shown here are for the upper middle quarter. The other subjects produced comparable operating characteristics, with the faster learners tending more towards the upper

Table 5.1. *Hypothetical data to illustrate the construction of operating characteristics from confidence judgments: response frequencies for eight response categories from New-4 ("certainly a new item") to Old-4 ("Certainly an old item") for both new and old items.*

Old items			Response						
		New				Old			
	4	3	2	1	1	2	3	4	
Observed frequency:	10	20	30	40	40	50	50	60	(300)

New items			Response						
		New				Old			
	4	3	2	1	1	2	3	4	
Observed frequency:	80	40	40	30	30	30	30	20	(300)

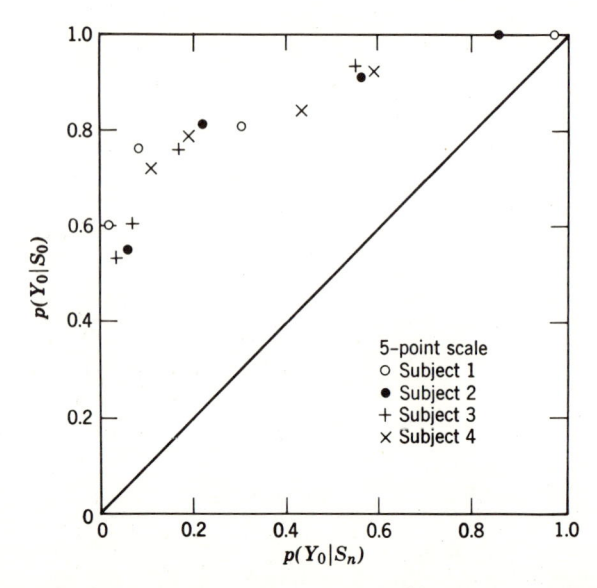

Fig. 5.5 *Operating characteristics for four subjects (the upper middle quarter of 16 subjects). A list of 100 old words was presented once and then a 200-word recognition test was administered. (after Egan, 1958)*

left in Fig. 5.5, and the slower learners regressing towards the main diagonal. It is certainly clear that the memory operating characteristics in Fig. 5.5 are not straight lines. Instead they look rather like the operating characteristics derived from signal detection theory. In fact, Murdock (1965b) reported some memory operating characteristics which could be well fitted by assuming that the familiarity distributions of old and new items are normal with equal variance and differs only in that the distribution of old items is d' units (measured in terms of the common standard deviation) higher. The data of Egan (1958), Murdock (1965b), and others to be discussed below clearly exclude all models which require straight-line operating characteristics, and hence all high-threshold theories of recognition memory. The learning model discussed in the previous section, as well as the conventional correction for guessing, are therefore contraindicated by this analysis.

The measure d', the mean familiarity difference of the old and new items, is an unbiased indicator of memory strength. The placement of the criterion c is influenced by factors only partially under the control of the experimenter. Parks (1966) has studied the question where subjects set their criterion. He hypothesized that subjects match their response probability to the proportion of repeated items in the experiment. In other words, subjects choose a criterion in such a way that the over-all probability of saying old is directly proportional to the probability that a test item is actually old. Parks analyzed several sets of recognition data and found them to be in good agreement with this matching hypothesis.

The d'-measure has been used to obtain unbiased estimates of the temporal decay of recognition memory. It is, of course, an old finding that the probability of a correct response decreases as a function of the length of the retention interval. However, it is impossible to determine the exact nature of the decrease in memory strength as a function of time from such data alone, because there is no guarantee that the subject's criterion remains constant over time. The traditional correction for guessing is based upon an unacceptable model for recognition memory, and may seriously distort the data. The signal detection model provides a much more satisfactory correction formula for recognition data. The mean difference d' between the familiarity distributions of old and new items is an unbiased estimate of memory strength. This difference is easily determined from the observed hit probability and false recognition probability. Suppose a subject correctly identifies 84% of all old items, and makes false recognition responses on 23% of all new items. Remember that we are assuming both $f(s)$ and $g(s)$ in Fig. 5.4 to be normal, and we shall select our scale in such a way that the common standard deviation is 1. For the area under the curve $g(s)$ to the right of c to equal .84, the cut-off point must be one z-unit below the mean of $g(s)$, as reference to a table of areas of the normal curve readily reveals. On the other hand, a false recognition rate of 23% implies that the area under $f(s)$ to the right of c equals .23, and hence that the cut-off point is .75 z-units above the mean of $f(s)$. Therefore, the total difference d' between the familiarity distributions of old and new items equals $1.00 + .75 = 1.75$ standard deviation units.

Wickelgren and Norman have reported a number of studies which use the analysis outlined above to investigate the decay of recognition memory (Wickelgren and Norman, 1966; Norman, 1966; Wickelgren, 1967). They find that recognition memory as estimated by d' decreases exponentially as a function of the number of intervening items between presentation and test. The following equation gave a good fit in their studies of recognition memory:

$$(4) \qquad d(i) = \alpha \, \Phi^i + \lambda \qquad , \qquad 0 \le \alpha, 0 \le \Phi \le 1, 0 \le \lambda$$

$d(i)$ is the mean difference between the familiarity distributions of old and new items, and i is the number of items presented during the retention interval. The α parameter is an acquisition parameter: when an item is presented its familiarity increases by an amount α. Φ is a forgetting parameter: each intervening item decreases familiarity by this proportion. λ is a long-term memory component which may be zero in some memory tasks. In one of his experiments Norman (1966) used three different types of material: single digits, paired digits, and nonsense sounds (digits played backwards through a tape recorder). Lists of 15 items were constructed from each type of material and spoken to the subject. After each list a probe word was spoken, and the subject had to tell whether or not the probe had been a member of the immediately preceding list. Two subjects participated in a large number of experimental sessions. $d(i)$ values were estimated for each subject, and for each serial position in the 15 item list which was tested. When the $d(i)$ values were plotted against i, the number of interfering items, exponentially decreasing curves were obtained which could be well fitted by Eq. (5.4). Large differences in recognition performance were obtained between the three experimental conditions (single digits, double digits, and nonsense sounds). However, in each case the decrease in $d(i)$ could reasonably be regarded as exponential. In fact, the rate of decrease was the same for all three conditions, and only the acquisition parameter depended upon the type of material.

Wickelgren (1967) also found that recognition memory as measured by d' decreases exponentially as a function of the number of subsequent items. He showed his subjects a sequence of 12 digits at a fairly rapid rate. After each sequence a recognition test was administered by presenting a digit pair and asking the subject whether or not the second item in the pair was an immediate successor of the first item in the list just presented. Subjects always responded yes or no and indicated their confidence in their decisions. The more items followed the test pair in the original list, the poorer recognition was. Estimates of d' decreased more or less exponentially as a function of the number of subsequent items, just as in the previous study. Another finding in Wickelgren's study points out a very significant property of recognition performance, namely independence from irrelevant alternatives. Suppose we have two study lists. In the first list a digit pair A-B is presented and followed by i other digits, none of which is an A. In the second list, the A-B pair is also followed by i other digits, but an A-C sequence is also presented somewhere in the second list. The test pair for both lists is either A-B (correct answer is "yes") or A-D (correct answer is "no"). In the second list an irrelevant association A-C is formed which could be expected to interfere with memory A-B. Many studies have reported such interference in recall. However, in recognition no such interference occurs. The d' estimates for the two lists were not systematically different in Wickelgren's experiment. This is a very interesting result. Recognition and recall are obviously quite different in this respect. Response competition plays an important role in recall, but in recognition subjects respond to the familiarity of an association with respect to a criterion, and the familiarity of that association relative to other associations to the same stimulus seems to be irrelevant.

One of the most powerful variables in recognition experiments is the nature of the recognition test. The proportion of correct responses in a yes-no recognition test are not directly comparable to that in a multiple choice test. If a multiple-choice test is given, the probability of a correct response is inversely proportional to the number of distractor items (e.g., Postman, 1950). The traditional correction for guessing does not remove differences between testing conditions with different numbers of alternatives. However, we already know that this correction is based upon some false premises, and it is still possible that differences between testing conditions could be predictable from more adequate theories of recognition performance if conditions of acquisition are controlled. For instance, the signal detection model permits the strength of memory to be estimated independently of testing conditions in terms of d', and specifies rules which govern a subject's performance in various recognition tests.

A relevant experiment has been reported by Kintsch (1968). He observed 4 subjects for 11 sessions each. Each session comprised 30 trials. A trial consisted of the presentation of 5 meaningless letter combinations, a delay of 20 seconds filled with a subtraction task, and a test. Five types of test trials were used: one of the study items was presented and the subject was asked to respond with either "old" or "new"; an item not shown before was presented and again the response was either old or new; or one of the study items was shown together with 1, 3, or 7 distractor items which had never before been presented and the subject had to select the old item. During the study period the subject did not know which testing condition was to be used on that trial. Subjects gave confidence judgments with their responses.

Figure 5.6 presents the most interesting results of this study. The data are shown separately for each subject, as well as a group average. 95% confidence intervals around the data points are also given. Note that large differences were obtained when a single item was presented for test, depending upon whether this item was new or old. Three subjects had a bias for saying "new", while the other subject responded

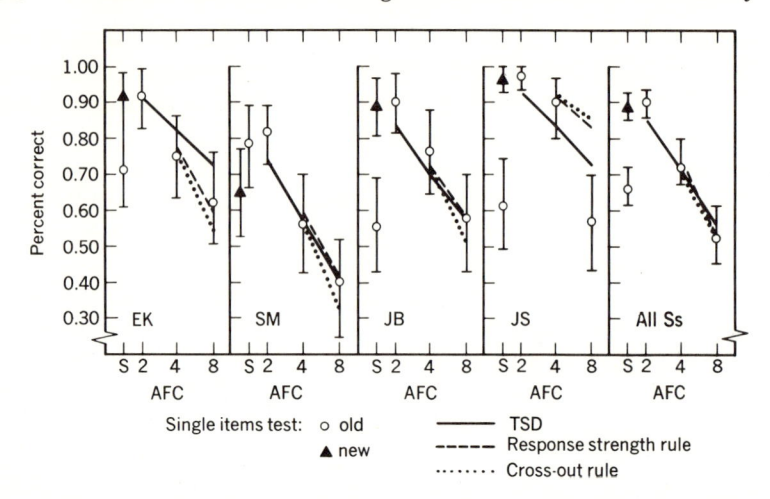

Fig. 5.6 *Proportions of correct responses under the five experimental conditions (single item tests with old and new items, and 2, 4, and 8 alternative forced choices) with 95% confidence intervals and theoretical predictions. (after Kintsch, 1968a)*

with the opposite bias. For all subjects the probability of a correct response decreased as the number of alternatives on the multiple choice test increased. The predictions labeled TSD for the multiple-choice performance were obtained in the following way. A memory operating characteristic was constructed on the basis of his performance in the yes-no condition. From this operating characteristic d' was estimated by standard methods. This estimate of d' was then used to predict subject's behavior under the multiple choice conditions. For this purpose it was assumed that in a k-alternative forced choice task the subject selects that alternative which has the highest familiarity value. Mathematically this means that the probability of a correct response is given by the probability that the correct item has a higher familiarity value than any of the $(k\text{-}1)$ distractor items. Tables prepared by Elliott (1964) make such computations very easy. Except for one subject, the predictions obtained in this way agreed with the data quite well. Note that these predictions are truly *a priori*, since no part of the multiple-choice data has been used for parameter estimation.

In spite of the successful predictions in Fig. 5.6, one should be wary of accepting the analogy to signal detection theory as a satisfactory theory of recognition performance. There are other models of choice behavior which describe the multiple-choice data in Fig. 5.6

almost as well. There is, for instance, the cross-out rule, suggested by Murdock (1963e) and Bower (1967). This rule assumes that a subject crosses out all alternatives which he thinks are wrong and chooses randomly among the remaining alternatives. Another decision rule which may be used is the Bradley-Terry-Luce choice theorem (Bradley and Terry, 1952; Luce, 1959). Suppose that old items have response strength $s(o)$, and that new items have response strength $s(n)$. Then, by the choice theorem, the probability of a correct response in a k-alternative recognition test is

$$P(C) = \frac{s(o)}{s(o) + (k\text{-}1)\, s(n)}$$

Predictions from both the cross-out rule and the choice theorem are also shown in Fig. 5.6*. In both cases the data from the two-alternative forced-choice condition were used to estimate the model parameter. It is quite obvious, that all three sets of predictions are about equally good, and that we are in no position at this time to decide in favor of one or the other choice model. However, the successful prediction of recognition performance in multiple-choice tests has surely reinforced the general position taken throughout this section that memory and decision processes in recognition must be clearly distinguished.

Models of Recognition Memory

The high-threshold theory as well as the signal detection theory have already been discussed in the previous section. In the high-threshold model, which is implied by the traditional correction for guessing, a two-valued memory trace is assumed: items are learned, in which case they are always recognized correctly, or items are not learned, in which case the subject can guess. We have seen that this model fails to predict empirical operating characteristics correctly. The second model, the signal detection model, assumes that the memory trace has a continuous representation and that the subject bases his response upon a criterion rule. Actually, this model has two distinctive components. One is the assumption of continuous, overlapping familiarity (or strength) distributions for old and new items. Psychologists concerned with psychophysical discrimination and measurement have often assumed that there is some intrinsic variability in an

---

*The choice axiom actually implies the cross-out rule. The proof is due to Marley (1965).

organism's response to a physical stimulus. Thurstone (1927) introduced the concept of discriminal dispersions: when the same physical stimulus is presented repeatedly an organism's responses to it will not all be identical but are normally distributed around some mean value. The "law of comparative judgment" is based upon the assumption that the choices which a subject makes are determined by this normal probability function. Thurstone's discriminal dispersion and the familiarity distributions for old and new items described above are formally equivalent. The second component of the signal detection model comes from modern statistical decision theory (Wald, 1950), which specifies the optimal decision rules under uncertainty.

Many empirical operating characteristics are not symmetrical, as required by the signal detection model so far discussed. As an example, three curves from an experiment by Norman and Wickelgren (1965) are reproduced in Fig. 5.7. A probe procedure was used in this experiment. Subjects listened to a series of digits and were then tested for recognition with either a single digit or a pair of digits. Memory operating characteristics were constructed from subjects' confidence ratings. The single digit results could be adequately described by a signal detection model with two overlapping normal distributions with equal variance. To fit the results for digit pairs several modifications of signal detection theory had to be explored because of the asymmetry of the operating characteristics. For example, if it is assumed that the means and variances of the underlying normal distributions are proportional, asymmetrical curves will result. Alternatively, one could have assumed that the probability distributions of new and old items are not normal, but are exponential distributions, or Raleigh distributions (Green and Swets, 1966). Norman and Wickelgren (1965) suggest still another mechanism to account for the observed asymmetry of the operating characteristics for digit pairs in Fig. 5.7. Their suggestion is not merely a formal improvement in the model without a psychological rationale, and is therefore particularly interesting: they propose that failures of attention may be causing the asymmetrical operating characteristics in Fig. 5.7. Suppose that $f(s)$ is the distribution of strength for the new items, and $g(s)$ is the distribution of strength for the old item, just as in Fig. 5.4. When an item is presented it does not always receive an increment in strength, as assumed previously, but only on a proportion p of the trials. With probability $(1-p)$ the memory strength (or familiarity) of an item remains the same when it is presented for study. Thus old items have a bimodel distribution: a proportion p of them have response strengths

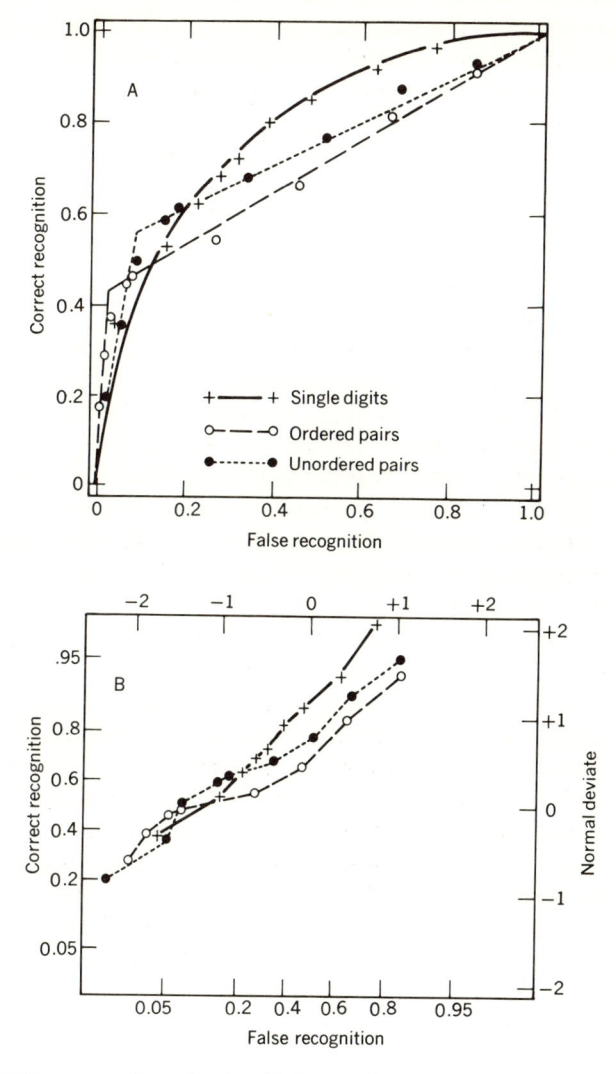

Fig. 5.7 *MOC curves for single digits, ordered pairs, and unordered pairs. The data are plotted on regular coordinates in A and on normal-normal probability coordinates in B. In A the smooth curve is the best fitting prediction from signal detection theory to the data for the single digits, and the straight line functions are best-fitting predictions of the Norman and Wickelgren model to the data for pairs. (after Norman and Wickelgren, 1965)*

distributed according to $g(s)$, and a proportion $(1-p)$ of them have response strengths distributed according to $f(s)$. If $p = 1$, the signal detection model and symmetrical operating characteristics result. If $p \neq 1$, asymmetrical operating characteristics are predicted, as required by the two curves for digit pairs in Fig. 5.7. Thus, the simple psychological assumption of learning failures can account for both sets of results.

The model of Norman and Wickelgren (1965) can be combined with the forgetting assumptions of Wickelgren and Norman (1966), and one can attempt to build a theory of recognition learning and recognition memory on this basis. Recognition learning could be incorporated by the assumption that repeated study trials result in successive increments in response strength, just as intervening trials produce more and more forgetting. Learning as well as forgetting in such a model would be conceptualized as a continuous process. Alternatively, one might want to retain the discrete learning models discussed earlier, and try to find a synthesis between Markov learning models and the decision processes which obviously play such an important role in recognition performance. Kintsch (1967) has shown that such a synthesis is quite feasible.

A slightly more general version of the three-state Markov model (Eq. (5) in Chapter 4) can be combined in a natural way with the assumption of an underlying familiarity continuum. The Markov model distinguishes a learning state and an intermediate state, in both of which the subject gives the response "old"; the difference between these two states is that forgetting is possible out of the intermediate state, but not out of the learning state; a third state, the initial state, was also assumed, which contains new and forgotten items. We shall generalize this model slightly by lifting the restriction that the transition probabilities in the intermediate state and in the starting state are proportional. In effect, this amounts to adding one more parameter to the model. The revised model is no longer a high-threshold model, as is shown by the following informal argument. Suppose there exists a continuous familiarity scale. Whenever a subject perceives an item he assigns to it some value s on that scale. New items are assigned values according to the probability distribution $f(s)$, old items are assigned values according to $g(s)$, as in Fig. 5.4. The subject's responses are determined by a criterion c, such that if $s > c$, $P(\text{old}) = 1$, if $s < c$, $P(\text{old}) = 0$. Note that the learning assumptions specify a discrete process: whenever an item is studied its familiarity changes from $f(s)$ to $g(s)$. We now add the assumption that learned items may be forgotten, and in particular that the forgetting probability depends upon how well the item was learned. If an item was assigned a very high familiarity value, say above a critical point λ, it will not be forgotten within the limits of the experimental session. On the other hand, if an item is assigned a familiarity value less than λ, it may be forgotten, in which case it is reassigned a familiarity value according to $f(s)$. Let f be the average probability that an item below λ is forgotten between presentation and test. This parameter obviously depends upon the length of the retention interval, just as the corresponding forgetting probability in the Markov model. One can now define three discrete states as regions on the familiarity scale: if $s>\lambda$, an item is in the learning state; if $c<s<\lambda$, an item is in the intermediate state; if $s<c$, an item is in the initial state. Figure 5.8 shows a diagram of this model and points out the parallels between the discrete version of the model and its reinterpretation with an underlying familiarity continuum. When repeated trials are presented the subject's action depends upon the familiarity value of the item studied. If this value is greater than λ the item is not further processed. If the familiarity is less than λ, the subject attempts to learn the item again, i.e., he reassigns it a new familiarity value from the probability distribution $g(s)$. The probability of entering the learning state in the Markov model is therefore equal to the probability of s being greater than λ, i.e., the area under $g(s)$ to the right of λ. A more formal statement of the equivalence between the two versions of the model can be found in Kintsch (1967).

Empirical memory operating characteristics were compared with predictions derived from this model. The empirical curves were based upon confidence judgments which were obtained in an experiment using a steady state design. In the same experiment, some items were repeated several times, always with a constant lag. Data from these items were used to estimate the parameters of the model. Essentially this amounts to obtaining probability values for all transitions between the states of the model, i.e., for all arrows in the upper part of Fig. 5.8. From these estimates the corresponding estimates for the reinterpreted model (lower part of Fig. 5.8) were computed. Memory operating characteristics could then be predicted by moving the cutoff point c from left to right in Fig. 5.8 and calculating the probability of hit and false recognition for every position of c. Predictions and obtained curves agreed fairly well, considering that the predictions were based upon the learning data only and were independent of the confidence judgments.

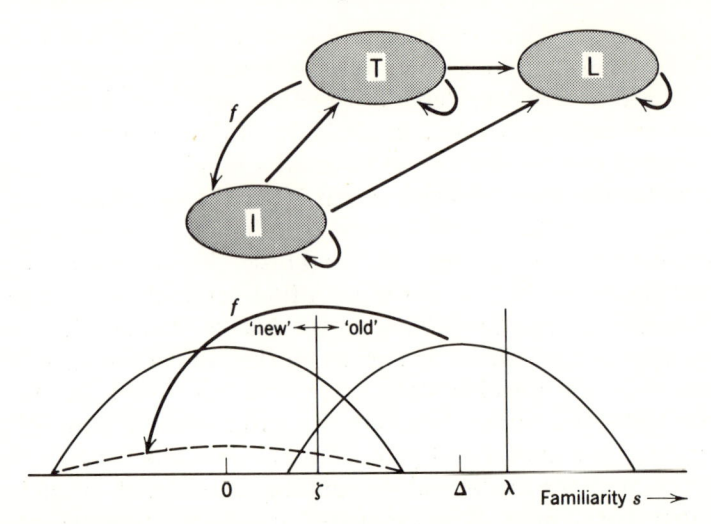

Fig. 5.8 *Two representations of a three-state Markov model for recognition learning. (after Kintsch, 1967)*

The model of Kintsch (1967) summarizes the present state of our knowledge about recognition learning. It combines familiarity distributions for old and new items, response rules from statistical decision theory, and the discrete state theory of the learning process. Its advantage is that it provides a framework in which a great many phenomena about recognition memory can be understood, from memory operating characteristics to the complex effects of the intertrial interval in recognition learning. Its disadvantage is its lack of uniqueness. Several of the component assumptions of the model could probably be exchanged for others, without affecting the over-all predictions of the model. In particular, we have no assurance that the representation of the memory trace is really continuous. A discrete state theory after Luce's psychophysical detection theory is not excluded by the available data (Luce, 1963). Similarly, we have no way of rejecting the various alternative formulations for the learning process. The model described here is closest to the coding theory of paired-associate learning. There are obvious parallels between the goodness of a mnemonic code and the familiarity of an item. However, alternative learning models could be formulated, just as in the case of paired-associate learning. Still, this is progress: at least one can now specify the over-all formal properties of the learning process and some of its components, and can show one possible way in which this process could work.

2. ORGANIZATIONAL PROCESSES IN RECALL

Free-recall learning presents a much more complex problem to the investigator than recognition learning. In recognition one has to deal only with two factors: the familiarity of the memory trace itself, and the operation of response biases. The familiarity value of an item together with the subject's decision criterion completely determine the recognition response. Thus no need exists to consider relationships between the items being learned. Recall learning is quite different in this respect: relationships among items are all-important in recall. The characteristics of a list as a whole rather than the characteristics of individual items determine recall performance. Recall involves a search and retrieval process, the efficiency of which depends upon how well the learning material has been organized in memory. The structure of the learning material itself and its relationship to the subject's existing store of knowledge in turn determine how successfully it can be stored in memory. We shall first discuss some experiments which are concerned with the effects of associative and categorical organization of the learning material. After that, the role of control processes in free-recall learning will be examined. Subjects can control what and how they want to store in long-term memory, they can direct the search of memory during retrieval, and they may edit implicitly retrieved responses before making an overt response.

Associative Relationships

Several studies concerning the effects of objective organization of the learning material upon free-recall learning were described in Chapter I. It is sufficient merely to mention these studies here and to restate their conclusions. They were all concerned with demonstrating that the more redundant a list is, the easier it is to recall. Miller (1958) constructed a set of meaningless letter combinations according to simple generating rules and showed that these rule-generated items could be recalled better than random combinations of the same letters. Garner (1962) and Whitman and Garner (1962) presented systematic investigations of the effects of statistical redundancy upon free recall. They showed that not only the amount of redundancy but also the exact nature of the redundancy affect recall. Simple contingencies are much easier to learn than complex interactions. Finally, a number of studies, starting with the classical paper of Miller and Selfridge (1950), provided evidence that the more a string of words approaches the statistical structure of English, the easier it is to recall the string.

Another important determiner of recall is the associative structure of a list of words. It is well known that if a large group of subjects is asked to give a free association to a stimulus word there will be a high degree of communality in the response. Kent and Rosanoff (1910) have collected the associations of 1000 adult subjects to 100 familiar English words. They instructed their subjects to respond with the first word that occurred to them, other than the stimulus word itself. The resulting tabulation of response words provided the basis for most work on the effects of associative structure in recall. For each stimulus word Kent and Rosanoff reported the number of subjects who responded with a particular word. For instance, for the stimulus word NEEDLE the three most frequent responses were THREAD, PIN, and SHARP with frequencies of 160, 158, and 152, respectively. Examples of associations given only once in response to the stimulus word NEEDLE are DILIGENCE, PINCUSHION, and WOMAN. Palermo and Jenkins collected extensive word association data in 1964, and most recent workers have used their tables.

Jenkins and Russell first investigated associative relationships in recall (Jenkins and Russell, 1952). They used a list of 48 words which consisted of 24 highly associated word pairs. The words were presented in random order, except that response words were not permitted to immediately succeed their respective stimulus terms in the presentation sequence. An immediate recall test was given. A high degree of associative clustering was observed in the recall protocols: associated word pairs tended to be recalled together. In fact, about half of the total recall could be accounted for by the association between words. Jenkins and Russell did not use a control group which learned a list with low associative strength between word pairs, but it has been shown in several later studies that associative interrelations in a list increase total recall. In one such study Jenkins, Mink, and Russell (1958) systematically varied the strength of the relationship between word pairs in a list. Four groups of subjects were each given a list of 12 different word pairs. The response communality for the pairs in List I was 71% (that is, 71% of the subjects in a free association task made the same response when the stimulus word was presented—these are highly related word pairs such as man-woman), and for Lists II, III, and IV response communality was 47%, 30%, and 14%, respectively. The order of presentation was random. Recall of the four lists depended upon the strength of the associative relationship between word pairs: an average number of 19, 18, 17, and 14 words was recalled, respectively. The recall protocols were analyzed for both forward and backward associations (a backward association was defined as a response word preceding the stimulus word). The number of both forward and backward associations increased as a function of response communality on the free association test, although forward associations were more frequent than backward associations under all conditions.

The investigation of associative relationships in recall has been extended to a more general case in the work of Deese (e.g., Deese, 1961; 1965). Instead of merely working with associatively related word pairs, Deese calculated the average relative frequency with which all words in a list tend to elicit each other in free association tests. This index can be obtained from a matrix such as that of Table 5.2. This table shows the associative relationships among the 15 words of one of Deese's lists. All of the words in this list happen to be high associates of BUTTERFLY. However, they are quite highly related to each other, in addition, as the table shows. Rows in Table 5.2 give the stimulus words, and columns give the response words. Entries are the percent of subjects who gave the column word as a free associate to the stimulus word. Since subjects may respond with associates which are not members of the list, the percentages in each row do not have to add up to 100%. Deese suggests as a measure of the strength of the associative interrelationships in a list the index of interitem associative strength; this index is simply the mean of the column sums in Table 5.2. In practice the index has a maximum around 30%. Therefore, the list shown in Table 5.2 has a relatively high interitem strength.

Deese constructed 18 different lists of 15 words each and computed their interitem associative strength. Associative frequencies were obtained from a sample of 50 subjects. A different group of 48 subjects then studied and recalled each list. The obtained recall scores correlated very highly with the index of interitem associative strength: $r = .88$. The more the items of a list tend to elicit each other, the better the list can be recalled. Deese also observed that the stronger the interitem associations were, the fewer recall intrusions occurred: $r = -.48$. In another experiment Deese (1959) showed that intrusions can be predicted quite accurately from the associative structure of a list. Suppose we want to predict the probability that BUTTERFLY occurs as an intrusion error in the recall of the word list shown in Table 5.1. The average of the frequencies with which each word of the list elicits BUTTERFLY may be used to predict its intrusion probability. The average associative strength of an intrusion, as defined above, correlated .87 with observed intrusion frequencies across 36 different lists in Deese's experiment.

Associative relationships not only predict total recall and intru-

Table 5.2. *Interitem associative matrix for fifteen high-frequency associates of BUTTERFLY (after Deese, 1961).*

	Moth	Insect	Wing	Bird	Fly	Yellow	Net	Pretty	Flowers	Bug	Cocoon	Color	Stomach	Blue	Bees	Average
Moth		2	2		10				2	10						
Insect	4				18					48						
Wing				50	24											
Bird			6		30									2		
Fly		10		8						18						
Yellow									3			11		16		
Net	2	2		2												
Pretty																
Flowers						2						2		2	2	
Bug	2	36		2	4										4	
Cocoon	16	6		4						10						
Color														20		
Stomach																
Blue												10				
Bees				15					5							
	24	56	8	81	86	2	0	0	10	86	0	23	0	40	8	28.3

sions, but also can account for some of the sequential phenomena which are observed in a free-recall experiment. It has already been mentioned that Jenkins and Russell could predict clustering from measures of interword association. Similarly, Rothkopf and Coke (1961) reported that if two words were recalled in sequence, the second word tended to have many associations with the first word. In Rothkopf and Coke's experiment both the probability of recall and the sequence of recall could, to some extent, be predicted from word association measures.

The studies discussed so far have only been concerned with the associative relationships among items of a list. It may happen, however, that items of a list are not associated with each other, but nevertheless cluster in recall because they all are associated with a word which itself is not a list member. For this situation Deese (1962) has devised his Index of Associative Meaning. This index is not restricted to the words appearing in a list, but is a count of the number of associates which any two words of the list have in common. For instance, none of Deese's subjects gave SYMPHONY as a response to PIANO, but the two words are still associatively related because both are associated with NOTE, SONG, SOUND, MUSIC, NOISE, and ORCHESTRA. The index of associative meaning does not predict the tendency of two words to elicit each other as does the index of inter-item associative strength, but it measures the likelihood that words are being used in the same linguistic environment. The index of associative meaning is therefore closely related to our next topic, the role of conceptual categories in recall. An experiment relating associative meaning and recall will be discussed below (Fig. 5.9).

Categorical Relationships

In 1953 Bousfield described a phenomenon which he labeled category clustering. Bousfield studied the recall of subjects who learned a 60-word list which was composed of 15 instances of each of four conceptual categories. The categories were animals, names, professions, and vegetables. The words were presented one by one in random order at a 3-second rate. Unlimited time was given for recall. Bousfield observed that words belonging to the same category tended to cluster together in the subject's output. The number of repetitions which a subject made in his recall was taken as a measure of clustering. A repetition was counted when a subject recalled two instances of the same category in succession. Bousfield's subjects made many more repetitions than would be expected on the basis of chance. They clearly were grouping words according to category in their output.

Bousfield had selected the words for his categories according to his best judgment. Most later investigators have made use of norms collected by Cohen, Bousfield, and Whitmarsh (1957)*. These authors compiled responses from 400 subjects to 43 categories, such as FISH, SHIP, BUILDING, VEHICLE, etc. Their subjects were told to write down the first four specific instances they could think of for each category. The responses for each category were then tabulated according to the frequency with which they occurred. For instance, TROUT, BASS, and PERCH were the three most frequent responses in the FISH category, with frequencies of 174, 124, and 101, respectively. TURTLE, SOLE, and CLAW give some idea about the words which occurred only once in this category. Bousfield, Cohen, and Whitmarsh (1958) have used these norms to investigate category clustering. They compared a highly organized list (15 frequent responses in each of four categories) with a low-organization list (15 infrequent responses in each of four categories). Words were presented in random order. Lists with high probability category members were recalled better, and clustering was more pronounced.

A number of empirical relationships concerning category clustering have been investigated so that we now have a fair amount of empirical knowledge about the recall of categorized word lists. Bousfield and Cohen (1953) have studied clustering as a function of repeated study trials. From 1 to 5 trials with a 60-word, four-category list were given to independent groups. Total recall improved from 24 words recalled after one trial to 38 words after 5 trials. At the same time, the number of repetitions doubled.

Cofer, Bruce, and Reicher (1966) have reported that recall of a categorized word list is better if all the items from the same category are presented in blocks than when the presentation sequence is completely random. In the same study recall improved and clustering increased when the subjects were given more time to study each item.

It seems that categorized word lists are recalled better because categorized words are somehow more available. This conclusion is suggested by the observation of Bousfield *et al.* (1958) that lists composed of high-frequency category members are recalled better than lists composed of low frequency category members—a result which has been replicated repeatedly (e.g., Cofer *et al.*, 1966). Note that words which are available (say because they are high-frequency members of a given conceptual category) are not therefore automatically produced:

---

*Recently such norms have been made available by Battig and Montague (1969).

the subject controls which of the available words are produced and rejects inappropriate words. We shall examine this editing process in more detail below.

Further supporting evidence for the availability hypothesis has been provided by Dale (1967a) who demonstrated that response availability within a single category correlates highly with recall. Dale assessed response availability by asking subjects to enumerate a category. More specifically he had subjects write down all English county names which they could remember and then selected 10 names in approximately equal steps of availability, starting with counties which everyone knew to names only rarely remembered. Different subjects were then shown the 10 words and asked to recall them. The probability of recall turned out to be a function of response availability. The more available a name was, the greater the likelihood of recall.

If the response availability of category instances is more or less controlled, most of the variance in recall of categorized word lists can be attributed to category recall, rather than to forgetting of category instances. Cohen (e.g., Cohen, 1966) has shown that if at least one word is recalled from a category, subjects recall a fairly constant percentage of the words remaining in the category under a wide variety of conditions. For instance, in one of his experiments Cohen manipulated list length. He had lists of 10, 15, and 20 categories, each composed of 3 or 4 words. If a category was recalled at all, i.e., if at least one word was recalled per category, the mean number of words recalled per category was around 60% and apparently invariant with respect to list length. In another experiment no differences in mean words per category were found when the rate of presentation was varied. How many words a subject recalls is primarily dependent upon how many categories he can remember. Subjects either recall a high percentage of the words in a category or none at all.

From the foregoing discussion one may well conclude that the unit of recall is not a word but rather a category. However, such a conclusion would be premature, because it is possible that purely associative mechanisms could account for the phenomena of category clustering described above. Category members are usually associated with each other and possibly subjects do not use categories at all in recall, but simply profit from the associative relationships present in a categorized list. Cofer (1965) has reported an experiment which was designed to separate the respective contributions of category and associative factors in recall. The study involved 6 groups of subjects. Each group learned a different word list. The six lists differed in associative meaning: the total number of associations which any two words in each list had in common varied from 0 to 40. In addition to variations in associative meaning, half of the words of each list consisted of conceptually related word pairs (e.g., bed-chair) while the other half were unrelated conceptually (e.g., bed-dream). Thus the two factors, associative meaning and conceptual relation, were varied orthogonally in this experiment and could therefore be evaluated independently. The results of the experiment are shown in Fig. 5.9. Clearly, both associative and conceptual organization affect clustering in recall. In addition an interaction between associative meaning and categorization was found. Categorization had large effects upon clustering at low values of associative meaning, but at high values of associative meaning categorization increased the tendency to cluster only very little above its already high value. No data are reported concerning the number of words which were recalled from the different lists. However, data from a later experiment with a similar procedure (Marshall, 1967) show that clustering scores and recall scores are positively correlated.

Although category clustering and associative clustering often are confounded, the results just reported indicate that it is not possible to explain one in terms of the other. All we can say at this point is that if the material is organized recall is better and clustering tends to occur. It does not seem to matter whether the organization is in terms of associations among the items of a list, superordinate categories, sequential dependencies of a statistical nature, or what else. In all of these cases the organism is somehow able to take advantage of the structure which is present in the learning material. Logically there are two ways in which this may happen: Perhaps organized material is easier to store in memory, or perhaps organization of the material facilitates the retrieval process. The two possibilities are not mutually exclusive, of course. In fact, it is clear that both are important in recall. We shall first discuss experiments which demonstrate the existence of a retrieval problem: sometimes more may be stored in memory than can be retrieved without special measures. On the other hand, it can also be shown that how the learning material is organized at the time of storage is crucial: in order to be effective, a retrieval strategy must be related to the organization of the learning material at the time of storage.

If a categorized list is learned by two groups of subjects under identical conditions, storage should be equal for the two groups. But suppose one of the two groups is given the category names as recall cues while the other group is simply asked to recall as many words as

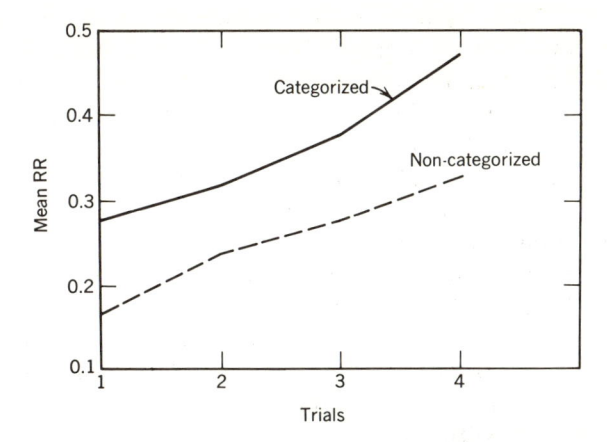

Fig. 5.9 *Mean ratio of repetition scores for recall at each of four successive trials for pairs with equal associative overlap, but classified as either categorized or non-categorized. (after Cofer, 1965)*

possible, without any cues. It is known that the first group recalls more words than the second group, and hence we may conclude that the cues facilitate retrieval.

The data alluded to above come from an experiment by Tulving and Pearlstone (1966). They constructed 9 categorized word lists which differed in length (12, 24, and 48 words) and in the number of words per category (1, 2, and 4). Items in each category were grouped together and each group of items was preceded by its category name. The lists were read to subjects and subjects were told to memorize the words, except for the category names which did not need to be memorized. For the recall test half of the subjects were asked to write as many words as they could remember on a blank sheet of paper, while the other half of the subjects were given a recall sheet with all of the category names printed on it. Afterwards, a second recall attempt was made, for which all subjects were given recall cues. The results were clearcut: The cues greatly facilitated recall. As an illustration we shall use here the results of the 48-item list which consisted of 12 categories of 4 words each. With cues subjects recalled about 30 words. Without cues recall was only 20 words. However, when the subjects who received no recall cues on the first test were given recall cues on their second attempt, they could retrieve about 28 items. These additional items were clearly "there", but the subjects needed some help before they could find them. In this context it is interesting to note that merely forcing the subject to recall more items is of little use. Cofer (1967) reported some experiments in which subjects were given 15-word lists to recall. If they could not recall all words they were told that so-and-so many words were missing and to write down additional words as well as they could to fill up the list. Cofer's subjects performed rather poorly in this forced recall.

The improved recall in Tulving and Pearlstone's cue-condition was entirely due to better category recall. For instance, for the 48-4 condition subjects on the average recalled words from 11.4 categories when they were given the cues, but only from 7.3 categories when they were not. However, if at least one word from a category was recalled a constant proportion of the remaining words was recalled. The mean number of words recalled per category was 2.61 for the cue-condition, and 2.65 for the no-cue condition. These data are, of course, in complete agreement with the results of Cohen (1966) which were discussed above, and imply that there are two rather different processes in recall. One has to do with the accessibility of higher order memory units, categories in this case; the other deals with the retrieval of items within these higher-order units. The latter process seems to be largely independent of the experimental variables which were manipulated in the studies discussed here.

Psychonanalysts have long known that one way to retrieve a person's repressed experiences is through the use of free associations. Free associations may also be used to recover otherwise unavailable memories in laboratory experiments, as has been demonstrated in a long series of studies going back about 40 years. We shall briefly outline a recent report by Haber and Erdelyi (1967) which included better controls than earlier studies. A fairly complex picture was shown briefly and the subjects were asked to recall its contents immediately. Some prompting was used to make sure that subjects reported everything they knew about the picture. The subjects in the experimental condition were asked to give free associations to the picture for 35 minutes. Subjects in the control group played darts during this time. A second recall trial concluded the experiment. The recall protocols (the subjects drew pictures together with identifying labels) were rated as to their over-all correspondence to the original picture. In immediate recall there were no significant differences between the reproductions of the experimental and control groups. However, after free associations subjects were able to recall significantly more details and came closer to the theme of the picture than on their first recall trial, while subjects in the control group could not improve their scores. This result was not merely a consequence of a tendency on the part of the experimental subjects to add highly probable but unperceived detail, or of indiscriminate embellishment as a result of the free associations. A second control group excluded that possibility: subjects in this group were never shown the original pictures at all, but instead were given the first drawing of a yoked subject in the experimental group. Otherwise these subjects were treated exactly like experimental subjects. No significant change in the recall scores following free associations occurred for these control subjects. Therefore Haber and Erdelyi concluded that free associations alone are ineffective; but if something has been perceived more is stored in memory than the subject can retrieve under ordinary circumstances, and free associations can help the subject to recover initially unavailable material.

The studies reviewed here point to the importance of processes occurring at the time of retrieval. When subjects are given retrieval cues they can recall things which they could not otherwise. However, what happens at the time of storage is equally important. Retrieval presupposes storage: a retrieval cue will only help if the material had been organized appropriately at the time of storage. Tulving and Osler (1968) have demonstrated this important point. Their subjects recalled 24-word lists. During presentation the words were shown either alone or together with a retrieval cue which was a weak associate of the to be learned word. With these two training conditions two methods of testing were combined factorially: Half of the subjects were given the retrieval cues and half were not. The results of the experiment were quite unambiguous: Retrieval cues facilitated free recall if and only if they were present both at the time of storage and at the time of recall. Cues present only at the time of storage or only at the time of recall did not improve performance; if anything they resulted in somewhat lower scores.

Thus, one can conclude that retrieval cues in recall are effective in the sense that they help subjects to recall items which they could not have recalled otherwise, but only if these cues are relevant to the way in which the subject had stored the learning material. Information about the retrieval cue must be stored with the information about the learning material.

Another well-known finding attests to the importance of storage processes: When a categorized word list is presented so that words from the same category are adjacent (blocked presentation) recall is much better than when the presentation order is random. Apparently the storage of learning material is facilitated by presenting similar items together, probably because it is easier for subjects to determine the relevant principles of organization.

Subjective Organization

In the previous section we have seen that if the learning material is organized in some way the subject uses this organization in learning to recall. This manifests itself in two ways: organization facilitates recall and leads to clustering in the subject's output which corresponds to the input organization. In this section we shall show that even if the input material is not organized by the experimenter, the subject imposes his own organization upon it in learning to recall. It appears that the major problem which a subject is faced with in a free recall learning experiment is to organize the material for himself so that it can be retrieved later. If a list is already objectively organized the subject's task is facilitated, but in either case long-term recall presupposes organization of the learning material.

The first experiment which showed that subjective organization occurs in the learning of a list of unrelated items was reported by Tulving in 1962. Tulving defined subjective organization as the tendency to recall words in the same order on successive learning trials, even if there are no experimentally manipulated sequential dependencies among the words of a learning list. For his experiment he used a list of 16 disyllabic nouns which were not related to each other in meaning, according to the best judgment of the experimenter. Each subject was given 16 recall trials, with a different order of presentation on each trial. The presentation rate was one word per second, and the recall period was 90 seconds. This rate is rather fast so that subjects did not have time for elaborate processing. The average number of words recalled as well as an index of the amount of subjective organization are shown in Fig. 5.10. The index is a measure based upon information theory which depends upon pairwise dependencies in successive recalls. If the index is low the order of recall from one trial to the next is unrelated. The statistical subjects whose "data" are also shown in Fig. 5.10 serve to show how much organization may be expected on the basis of chance alone. The increase in the subjective organization index which characterizes the performance of the actual subjects means that recall order became more and more stereotyped from trial to trial. As the figure shows, total recall and subjective organization correlate highly.

Instead of Tulving's information theoretic measure Bousfield, Puff, and Cowan (1964) suggested a different kind of index for subjective organization. They counted the number of words which were recalled in the same order on successive recall attempts and based a repetition index on this count. This index behaves very much like

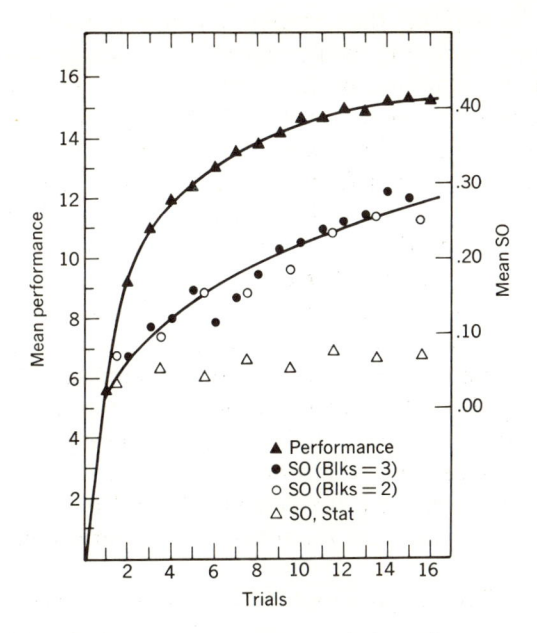

Fig. 5.10 *Mean performance (upper curve) and mean subjective organization (lower curve) as a function of trials. Mean subjective organization for blocks of 2 trials from 16 statistical subjects are shown for comparison, open triangles. (after Tulving, 1962)*

Tulving's subjective organization index. Both increase with trials and are correlated with total recall. Neither index is totally satisfactory, because both merely give an over-all measure of subjective organization and do not actually show how a list is organized. Furthermore, both indices take into account only the tendency of items to occur exactly in the same order from trial to trial, thereby underestimating the actual degree of organization in a list. One often finds tight clusters of words in subjects' recall protocols, but within each cluster words do not have a fixed order.

Considering the high correlation between subjective organization and recall the hypothesis suggests itself that organization is not merely an epiphenomenon of recall learning, but that there is actually a causal relationship between recall learning and subjective organization. Of course, in order to demonstrate that one learns to recall because material is organized subjectively, more than a correlational analysis is necessary. Tulving (1966) has performed some interesting experiments which strongly support this hypothesis. In one of his experiments he showed that merely repeating words over and over again does not facilitate memorization. Two groups of 12 subjects each learned the same list of 22 common nouns. The groups differed only with respect to the treatment which they received immediately prior to the learning of the experimental words. In one group (prior experience) the 22 nouns from the experimental list were shown 6 times on a memory drum and the subjects were asked to read the words as they appeared on the drum. In the control group (no prior experience) subjects read a list of 22 names for the same number of trials. Thus, at the beginning of training subjects with prior experience had seen the words to be remembered 6 times, while the control subjects had responded to the same number of unrelated items. Nevertheless, free recall performance was identical for the two groups of subjects. On the first trial the prior-experience group had a non-significant advantage over the no-prior-experience group in the mean number of words recalled (10.4 versus 9.2), but from the second trial on there were no consistent differences in the performance of the two groups.

While the above experiment shows that mere repetition does not facilitate free-recall learning when well-integrated items are used, Tulving's next experiment demonstrated that inappropriate organization can actually hinder learning. In this experiment two groups of 24 subjects each were given a list of 9 words to recall. Twelve learning trials were given. After learning the 9-word list, all subjects were given 12 learning trials with a second list of 18 words. In one condition the second list was composed of new words. In the other condition it included the 9 words already learned, randomly interspersed with 9 new words. Thus, in this group subjects had 12 free-recall trials with half of the list at the beginning of learning of the final list. If free-recall learning consists in the accrual of habit strength separately for each item whenever it is presented, a great deal of positive transfer must be expected from part-learning to whole-learning in this situation. If, on the other hand, free-recall learning is mainly a matter of subjective organization, the subject's organization of the 9-word list need not be the most appropriate one for the whole list. While the subject could simply attempt to add new subjective units to what he already has, he might find it necessary to reorganize the whole list and form new subjective units. Therefore, prior learning of a part of the list of unrelated words may have very little facilitating effect on the learning of the whole list. Indeed, Tulving's results show even a slight inhibitory effect (Fig. 5.11). The part-learning group started at a higher level, but after 7 trials the subjects who learned a completely new list sur-

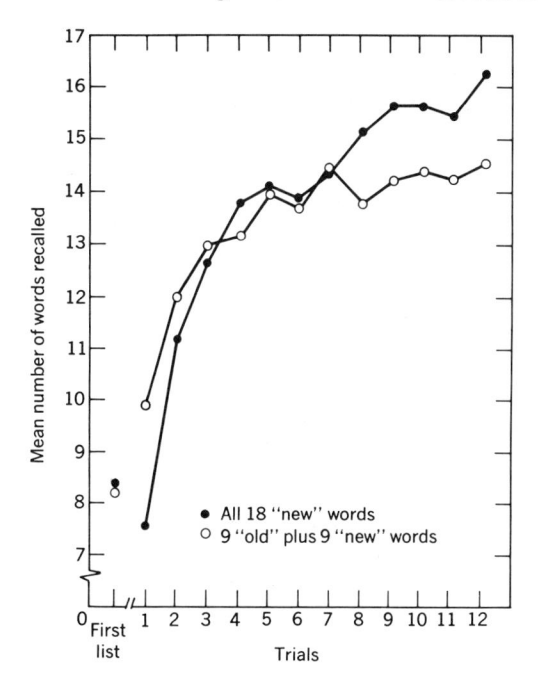

Fig. 5.11 *Learning curves for two groups of subjects on a whole list of 18 words. One group (open circles) had learned half of the whole list before learning the whole list, the other group (filled circles) had learned an irrelevant list. (after Tulving, 1966)*

passed it. Tulving argues that the subjects who learned part of the list first were unwilling to abandon or modify non-optimal subjective units acquired during part-learning, and that this inappropriate organization interfered with the learning of the whole list.

Strong interference effects due to inappropriate subjective organization have also been observed in an experiment by Bower, Lesgold, and Tieman (1969). Bower presented a list of 24 unselected nouns in 6 groups of 4 words each. Each group of words was shown for 12 seconds and subjects were told to make each four-tuple into a visual image. For one group of subjects the same four-tuples were presented on each of 4 trials; for another group of subjects the four-tuples were changed from trial to trial so that no two words appeared in the same four-tuple more than once. Bower points out that if free-recall learning is a process of conditioning of each item by itself, no differences between the groups should be expected. If free recall depends primarily upon the number of associations existing between items, the second group might be expected to perform better than the first group. The total number of associations is greater for this group, although the associations are less strong, because they received only one reinforcement. The results of this study are shown in Fig. 5.12. They strikingly agree with the expectations based upon a theory which stresses organizational factors in free recall. When the subjects were not permitted to form stable organizations hardly any improvement at all occurred from trial to trial. Interference with a subject's subjective organization negates learning effects, just as in the Tulving experiment discussed above. However, Bower's results are not necessarily critical of association theory. One might, for instance, argue that although many associations were formed when the four-tuples were changed on each trial, most of these were too weak to exceed a threshold necessary for recall, while repetition of the same four-tuple from trial to trial produced fewer but sufficiently strong associations. A purely associative interpretation of Tulving's result is less obvious.

Another demonstration of the importance of subjective organization for free recall has been reported by Mandler and Pearlstone

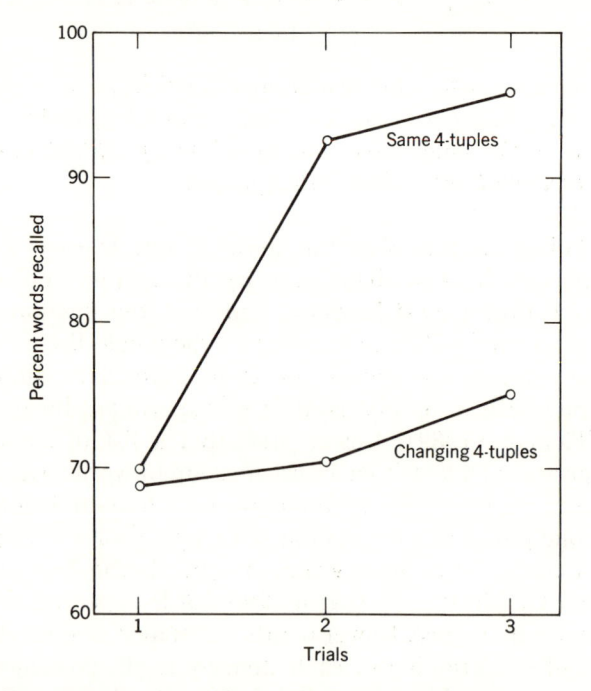

Fig. 5.12 *Percentage of words recalled with constant or with changing four-tuples. (after Bower, Lesgold, and Tieman, 1969)*

(1966). The principal purpose of their study was to study free versus constrained conceptualization. Subjects were given a deck of 52 cards, each of which had a word printed on it, and were told to sort these cards into from 2 to 7 categories according to any system they wished. They were also told that they will be given sorting trials with the same deck of cards until they achieve a stable organization, i.e., until they sort the cards in exactly the same way twice in a row. Mandler and Pearlstone called this a free concept-utilization task: subjects could use any basis they cared to for their sorting, but some kind of stable system had to be achieved. A second group of subjects was given a constrained conceptualization task: these subjects had to sort the 52 cards according to an experimenter-defined scheme, which is the usual procedure in concept formation experiments. In order to equate the difficulty of the sortings made by the free and constrained groups each subject in the constrained group was yoked with a free subject. The constrained subject's task was to sort the cards in the same way as the yoked free subject. Immediately after reaching the criterion of two identical sortings subjects in both groups were asked to recall as many of the words which they had just sorted as possible.

Not unexpectedly, the free subjects needed fewer trials to reach a stable sorting than the constrained subjects. Indeed, the latter took twice as long as the subjects who could choose their own basis of classification. In spite of this difference, the subjects in the two groups could recall an about equal number of words. The constrained subjects had twice as many sorting trials and hence twice as many opportunities to learn, but they were able to recall only 20 words on the average, just as the free subjects. Therefore, it is not the number of learning trials which matter for free recall, but the level of organization which is achieved on these trials. Both groups reached the same sorting criterion and hence recall was identical, although one of the groups needed twice as many trials to reach criterion than the other.

While trials to criterion in the sorting task were not related to free recall, the number of categories used in sorting was highly correlated with recall ($r = .95$). This relationship is shown in Fig. 5.13 for the 10 free subjects. Total recall is a direct function of the number of categories used in sorting. The subjects in Mandler and Pearlstone's experiment remembered a little over 5 words for each category. This relationship between the number of categories used (C) and recall (R) can be expressed formally by fitting a linear equation to the data. The best fitting equation is also reproduced in Fig. 5.13, together with the scatter diagram of the data. Mandler (1967b) has explored the category-recall relationship in a series of other experiments. In all

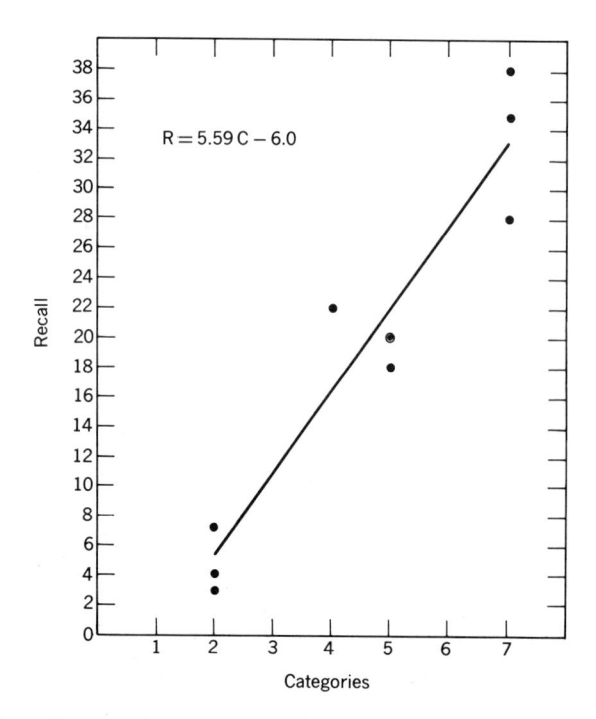

Fig. 5.13 *Recall as a function of the number of sorting categories. (after Mandler, 1967b)*

of these, a high correlation between the number of categories used in sorting and total recall was obtained (median $r = .70$). On the other hand, trials to criterion in the sorting task and recall did not correlate significantly (median $r = .16$), and the category recall relationship remained essentially the same when the number of sorting trials was controlled through partial correlation (median $r = .73$). Thus it is clearly the number of categories, not the number of trials, which determines recall performance in Mandler's experiments.

A similar finding has been noted above: when they are given a categorized word list subjects seem to recall the items in each category quite well if they recall a category at all. Certainly there must be experimental limits to this category-recall relationship, but these have not yet been explored adequately.

Mandler (1967b) also showed that sorting instructions and recall instructions are approximately equivalent for the task described above. In one of his experiments all subjects received 5 sorting trials, so that any differences in recall between the different groups used in this experiment must be caused by factors other than the number of trials. Half of the subjects received recall instructions, and half did not. Both groups were further subdivided according to their instructions for the sorting task: half of the subjects were asked to sort into from 2 to 7 subjective categories, as described above, while the other subjects were merely instructed to place the words one after the other into 7 columns. Subjects who received either organization or recall instructions, or both, recalled about equally many words. Subjects who were not instructed to recall, nor forced to organize the material, recalled significantly fewer words. Thus instructions to recall and instructions to organize had equivalent effects, in agreement with our hypothesis that free-recall learning essentially involves subjective organization of the learning material.

The above experiment illustrates a general principle in incidental learning experiments: intent to learn per se has no significant effect upon learning, but it is necessary that the subject make the right responses to the learning material (Postman, 1964). In the case of free recall, the right response is some kind of organization of the material, as we have just seen. In the case of other learning procedures, different responses are appropriate. Any kind of discriminative response appears to be adequate for recognition learning (e.g., Estes and DaPolito, 1967). In paired-associate learning the critical response seems to involve the establishment of some kind of relation between the stimulus and the response term. For instance, Bower (1968) has shown that instructions to form a mental image which includes both stimulus and the response term, or to form a sentence or phrase which connects the two terms are just as effective as regular paired-associate learning instructions when both the stimulus and response terms are concrete nouns.

Reconstructive Processes in Recall

We have maintained that in attempting to recall the subject searches for the superordinate units into which he has organized the learning material, and then retrieves as much as he can from each subjective chunk. There is another aspect of the retrieval process which has not yet been emphasized, namely, that subjects not only reproduce material from storage, but that they frequently reconstruct material on the basis of only partially retrieved information.

The reproductive character of free recall is especially pronounced when subjects are not given unrelated word lists to recall, but stories or pictures. Bartlett (1932) has conducted extensive investigations of how people recall meaningful stories. In one series of experiments he read his subjects a short story (about the length of a paragraph) and then had them recall it at various later dates. In analyzing the recall protocols of his subjects Bartlett noted two main features. First, memory for even the simple stories used in this experiment was extremely inaccurate. Often not more than the outline of a story was remembered, while details as well as the style of the story changed greatly, usually in the direction of becoming more stereotyped. Secondly, Bartlett was impressed by the large amount of construction which he could observe in the subjects' response protocols. Subjects often did not remember more than a vague impression or attitude, but proceeded to construct a story around it. Some subjects might remember nothing but an isolated detail, but then invent a plausible story as a rationalization for this detail.

In some of Bartlett's experiments subjects were tested repeatedly for recall of the same story. This procedure rapidly produced profound changes in the story. Proper names and titles were altered; individual characteristics were lost; the story tended to become abbreviated and more concrete. But the most interesting phenomenon which was observed in serial reproduction was the subjects' tendency to rationalize, to give the story some meaning or coherence, even when memory had become quite distorted. Sometimes elaborate connections were invented when some unfamiliar or improbable detail was remembered; at other times descriptions of a familiar setting and incidental features were deleted. Bartlett's subjects were clearly not reporting just what they could recall about a story, but they were making up the story as well as they could from the often meager information which they had been able to retain.

Similar observations have been made in studies of memory for form. In an influential experiment Wulff (1922) showed his subjects line drawings of abstract forms. The subjects were asked to draw the figures as they recalled them 30 seconds after presentation, and again after 24 hours, after a week, and two months later. Wulff analyzed the reproductions and identified several systematic changes in the drawings. Subjects either exaggerated characteristics of the original figure, which he called sharpening, or they neglected individual peculiarities, which he called leveling. Furthermore, Wulff found that these changes were progressive. Small errors on the first reproduction tended to become larger on successive reproductions. Wulff believed that he could identify three causes for the changes which he observed in his subjects' recall protocols. One was a tendency to normalize, i.e., to make the reproduction look more like a familiar object. This occurred especially often when subjects remembered a name or a verbal description of a figure. The second cause of errors of memory was a tendency to overemphasize a single notable feature of a figure. Both of these errors have their counterpart in Bartlett's descriptions of the distortions which occur in memory for stories. Wulff also reported an autonomous change of the memory trace as a function of time in storage. The memory trace itself was supposed to change gradually into a more simple and regular pattern. This third proposal attracted a great deal of interest in Wulff's experiment. In the more than forty years since Wulff's original study many experimenters have tried to test the hypothesis of autonomous change in memory with increasingly sophisticated techniques. Their efforts remained unsuccessful, because Wulff's hypothesis is stated so vaguely that it simply is not testable. It has never been specified with sufficient clarity exactly what changes are to be expected under what conditions. Riley (1962) has described this interesting episode of psychological history, which combines great sensitivity to methodological problems with completely inadequate theorizing. However, if we disregard the hypothesis of autonomous change in memory, Wulff's experiment and the many succeeding studies serve quite well to demonstrate the reconstructive character of recall. Leveling and sharpening seem to be characteristic of free-recall performance for both pictures and stories.

Wulff had already noted that verbal labels have a strong effect upon the recall of pictures. Carmicheal, Hogan, and Walter (1932) conducted a study to assess the importance of this effect. Their test figures are shown in Fig. 5.14. One group of subjects received Word List 1 together with these figures, and one group received Word List 2. A control group was given no labels at all. Two judges rated the deviations from the stimulus figure in the subjects' reproductions. They found that about three-fourths of the major changes were in the direction of the verbal label. For instance, subjects who were told that the first figure was a diamond in a rectangle tended to close the figure at the bottom, while subjects who were told to remember this as a curtain in a window tended to draw it more like a curtain.

The experiment of Carmicheal *et al.* leaves one important point unclear: when do the changes in the figure occur, at the time of perception, during memory storage, or at the time of reproduction? That the perception of a figure is in part determined by its name, its context, and the subject's expectancies is of course nothing new and it is possible that the Carmicheal *et al.* experiment could be entirely explained by perceptual factors. Hanawalt and Demarest (1939) have shown that this is not so, but that changes occur at the time of repro-

Stimulus Figures

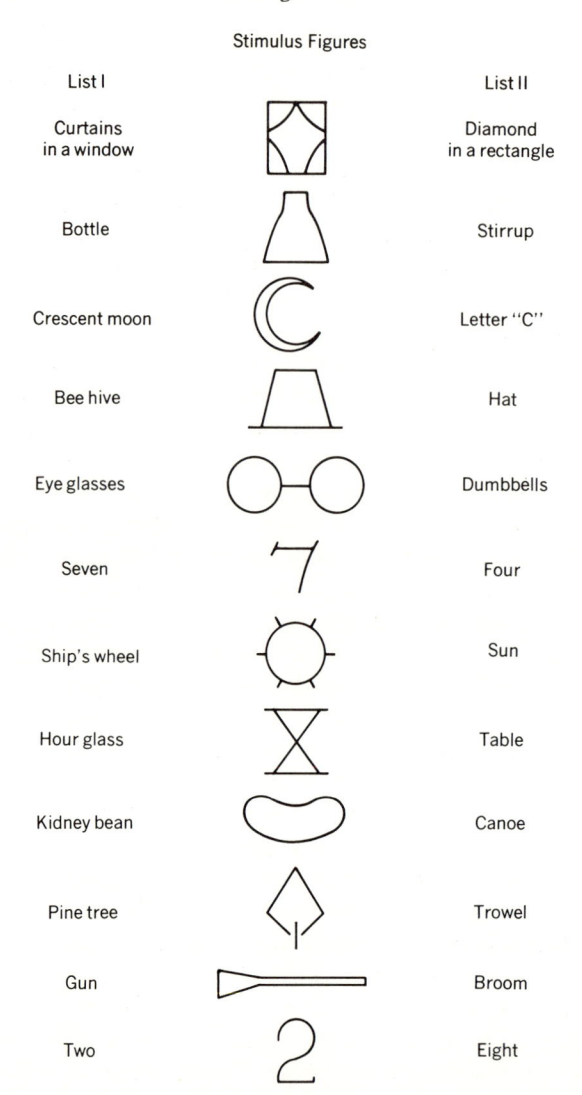

List I		List II
Curtains in a window		Diamond in a rectangle
Bottle		Stirrup
Crescent moon		Letter "C"
Bee hive		Hat
Eye glasses		Dumbbells
Seven		Four
Ship's wheel		Sun
Hour glass		Table
Kidney bean		Canoe
Pine tree		Trowel
Gun		Broom
Two		Eight

Fig. 5.14 *Figures and labels for the study of the effect of language on the reproduction of visually perceived forms. (after Carmicheal* et al., *1932)*

duction, independent of how a subject perceived the figure originally. Their method is a simple modification of the procedure of Carmicheal *et al.* Instead of giving subjects the verbal labels along with the stimulus figures, the figures were shown alone and labels were supplied only at the time of recall. Thus the labels could not have a systematic influence upon perception, although subjects will, of course, sometimes use their own labels. Effects upon the material stored in memory are also excluded, and changes which occur in the direction of greater similarity of the reproductions with the figures suggested by the labels must be caused by processes occurring at the time of reproduction. Hanawalt and Demarest found that the subjects' reproductions were indeed partly determined by the suggestions given at that time. Not surprisingly, this effect was strongest at the longest retention interval (7 days in their study).

Apparently what happens in recalling pictures or stories is that the subject remembers an over-all theme and then reconstructs the rest. Details, single features of a story or of a drawing, are easily forgotten, but the theme of a story is much less susceptible to forgetting.

Bower and Clark (1969) have shown how one can use the fact that the theme of a story is relatively easy to remember to dramatically improve memory for single words. He gave subjects 10 unrelated nouns and asked them to weave a story around these words, using every one of the 10 nouns. This task was self-paced and subjects took about $2\frac{1}{4}$ minutes, to make up their stories. Control subjects were given the same nouns for the same amount of time with instructions to memorize them for later recall. An immediate recall test was given at the end of the $2\frac{1}{2}$ minutes, and all subjects in both the experimental and control groups recalled perfectly. Twelve such lists were given in succession. After the 12th list, subjects were unexpectedly asked to recall all 120 words. The subjects who simply memorized the 12 lists in succession did very poorly. As one would expect, the effects of retroactive interference were powerful: they recalled only 14% of the words. On the other hand, subjects who made stories recalled 93% of the words, that is 6 times as much as the control subjects. Organizing the 10 nouns into a story, however artificial and silly it might be, apparently protected the words from retroactive interference, and since subjects could fairly easily recall the themes of their stories they thereby gained access to the individual words of each list.

Reconstructive processes in the recall of single words have been studied by Brown and McNeill (1966) by means of the "tip-of-the-tongue" phenomenon. The phenomenon itself is familiar to everyone from his own experience: a word of which one has knowledge can not be recalled. The evidence of knowledge is either an eventual successful recall or prompt recognition if the word is provided by some other means. If a word which a subject has not been able to recall is given to him, the subject often recognizes the word without any additional training. In the same vein, if a wrong word is given to the subject, he is frequently able to reject it, and may even be able to tell how similar it is to the target word. Brown and McNeill have shown that when complete recall is impossible but is felt to be imminent the subject can often recall the general type of the word, its meaning, its sound pattern, or the correct number of syllables. They did this by reading dictionary definitions of relatively uncommon words to a large number of subjects and asking them to provide the corresponding word. By this means they elicited several hundred instances of the tip of the tongue phenomenon. Whenever such an instance occurred the subject wrote down all words which he believed to be similar in sound or meaning to the target word, and also guessed the number of syllables in the target word and its initial letter. Unambiguous evidence for partial recall was obtained. Subjects could indeed recall the first letter, or the number of syllables of a word which was on the "tip-of-the-tongue."

This finding is important. It throws new light on the characteristics of the retrieval process. Even single words are not necessarily recalled as units, but as a bundle of different aspects which are only loosely tied together, such as general meaning, sound pattern, first letter, etc. When a sufficient number of aspects are retrieved the word is reconstructed—not very different from the manner in which a word or a picture is reconstructed at the time of recall. In the tip-of-the-tongue phenomenon the missing aspect refers to the pronounciation of the word in question: the subject knows what he is searching for but he can not find access to the necessary phonetic information to produce the word. The phonetic information must exist somewhere in his memory because he will recognize the correct word immediately if it is presented; however, for some reason which is not yet understood it is temporarily unavailable.

Before proceeding with a new topic we shall briefly summarize the results of this section. It has been shown that whenever the to be learned material is organized or structured in some way—associatively, conceptually, or statistically—recall is facilitated, and that the subject's output order tends to mirror the organization in the learning material. Furthermore, when a list of words has no detectable structure at all subjects impose on it some kind of ideosyncratic organization. Experimental manipulations which help the subject in this task facilitate recall; manipulations which interfere with it also interfere with recall. Thus, the conclusion was reached that subjective organization is a necessary and sufficient condition for free recall. The reason why organization is so important for recall is that it makes retrieval possible. Retrieval, as we have just seen, is not simply a process of reading off whatever can be found in storage, but a reconstruction of a plausible or probable response on the basis of whatever information is accessible. In the next sections we shall be concerned with the subject's control over the retrieval process. At first we shall turn to the question how the subject finds the right list of words, or the right story when he is asked to do so, rather than one of the many others which are also stored in memory. Secondly, we shall investigate the role which decision processes play in the subject's recall and how they keep the subject's reconstructive efforts within acceptable bounds.

3. CONTROL PROCESSES IN RECALL

It is apparent from the foregoing that long-term memory can not be compared with a storehouse or a dump in which experiences are dropped without regard to organization. Rather, it resembles a carefully arranged dictionary, full of cross-references, where each incoming bit of information is recorded in its proper place and connected with the existing body of knowledge. Each person has his own and unique organization of memory, depending upon his genetic endowment and the experience of his lifetime. This view of memory is not a new one. In the 19th century Herbart based his widely influential theory of pedagogy upon such a view of memory. He distinguished between perception and apperception, following the philosopher Leibnitz. Apperception is the assimilation of a new idea to the totality of a person's store of knowledge and experiences, which Herbart called the "apperceptive mass." While the details of Herbart's theory—a rather interesting mechanism for the interaction of ideas or memory traces, mainly by inhibition and disinhibition of each other (Boring, 1950)—are no longer important today, the concept of apperception certainly resembles "storage in long-term memory" as it has been used here, and apperceptive mass is not an unsuitable term for a person's organized store of experiences. Wundt (1905) has used the term extensively. Bartlett (1932), as well as Koffka (1935), also stressed that memory is organized, and that this organization is subjective. Bartlett's term for the product of the organization of past experience was "schema." He maintained that schemata do not persist as isolated members, but form part of a unitary, organized mass.

How does a subject ever find a particular item in the apperceptive mass, even if it is well organized? More precisely, what do we know about the subject's control and direction of search processes in long-term memory? This important question has received little attention in modern times. However, we shall briefly report here whatever information can be obtained from older sources concerning this problem, because we believe that the question is a significant one and should no longer be neglected.

Suppose a subject has learned a list of animal names, and then learns a second list consisting of names of cities. When the experimenter asks him to recall the first list, the subject will do so without giving any intrusions from the second list. We say that the subject has a set for recalling animal names, and therefore avoids inappropriate intrusions. Experimental investigations of the concept of set have frequently been reported in association experiments, reaction time experiments, and in studies of problem solving and thinking, but in the area of memory they have been rare.

Müller (1913) believed that the role of set in memory can be explained in purely associative terms. The task establishes a set or constellation which favors one association over the other. The general constellation determines the particular constellation: a cue like "large" may evoke "elephant" in the context of animal names, but it will evoke something like "Los Angeles" in the context of city names. Bühler (1908) pointed out that semantic meaning is often a more powerful determinant of retrieval than association by contiguity. In remembering sentences the particular words in which a sentence was expressed are easily lost while the meaning of the sentence is still retained. Subjects often can reproduce the meaning of a sentence correctly without using the words which were employed in the previous formulation of the sentence. There is of course no reason to suppose that association by contiguity and meaning mutually exclude each other as regulators of the reproductive process. What seems to be important are the instructions which a subject receives. The subject normally obeys the instructions which the experimenter gives him and searches his memory along whatever lines are indicated. Thus, he may try to remember the meaning of a sentence, or he may try to recall the particular words which were used to form the sentence. Ach (1910) has introduced the term "determining tendency" to designate the control which instructions and task characteristics exert over a subject's behavior. If a subject in a typical memory experiment has learned a list of paired-associates, like DUS-NEF, and is then given the stimulus terms of the pairs, he is set to reproduce the corresponding response members. However, the experimenter may change the determining tendency which controls the subject's behavior by giving him different instructions. Suppose the experimenter asks the subject to reverse the consonants in each syllable as it is presented instead of reproducing the associated syllable. Thus the proper response for the stimulus DUS would be SUD, rather than NEF. Obviously subjects will be able to comply with such instructions, even after strong associations between DUS and NEF have been formed. It is not the strongest association that occurs in a given situation, but that response which is appropriate to the subject's set. A parallel distinction is familiar in learning theory (e.g., Hull, 1943, and others). The reaction potential of a response is determined not only by habit strength, i.e., associative strength, but also by motivational factors, which bias the organism in a certain way. Corresponding biases are exerted by the instructions given to the subjects and by the properties of the learning task itself in the learning and memory experiments which are being discussed here.

An experimental investigation of set in in an experiment involving memory was undertaken by Ach (1910). Ach not only demonstrated the importance of determining tendencies but also suggested an operation to measure their strength. One of his subjects was taught three sequences of 8 nonsense syllables. The first sequence consisted of unrelated syllables; the second sequence was constructed so that all even members of the sequence rhymed with the preceding odd syllables; in the third sequence the even items were obtained by inverting the consonants of the preceding syllables. These three sequences were presented 70 times each, distributed over 6 days, thereby insuring that the subject had learned them very well. On days 7 to 14 only the odd members of the sequence were shown and the subject was asked either to reproduce the first word coming to his mind in response to each syllable, or to invert the syllable, or to find a rhyme for it. Different tasks were given on separate days. A number of new syllables were also included in the test period. The basic measure of the experiment was the subject's reaction time. Median reaction times are shown in Table 5.3, together with the percent correct reactions. Apart from the fact that the activity of inverting was obviously much easier than rhyming, both with respect to speed of reaction and correctness, Ach manages to demonstrate his point: when the association acquired during the six days of training agrees with the determining tendency established by the instruction, errors are rare and reactions are fast. When the response set and the previous association disagree, errors occur more frequently and the reaction times become longer. Responses to new syllables tend to have a rather long reaction time, but were always correct.

Ach's results are interesting: they identify an important problem

Table 5.3. *Median reaction times in seconds and percent correct reaction; Subject A (after Ach, 1910).*

	Construction of the four syllable pairs:			
Task	Rhymed	Inverted	Unrelated	New series
Reproduce	.87	.77	.88	1.08
Rhyme	.78	.89	1.13	1.05
	(83%)	(25%)	(75%)	(100%)
Invert	.80	.66	.84	.83
	(50%)	(100%)	(92%)	(100%)

and suggest an experimental method to study it. However, a replication of his experiment, using modern principles of experimental design and statistical analysis is absolutely necessary before one can draw any safe conclusions about the operation of determining tendencies. In particular, his suggestion to measure the strength of a set by placing it into conflict with a set-to-associate which has been established in the laboratory and is therefore under the control of the experimenter deserves some systematic study.

Not only Ach's experimental methodology, but also his theoretical concepts have been subject to criticism. Lewin (1917) objected to Ach's use of association as a baseline in his experiments. Rightfully, Lewin argued that there is nothing automatic about the tendency to reproduce the response member of a syllable pair when the stimulus syllable is presented, but that the subject is simply behaving under the control of the experimental instructions to associate, just as he does when the instructions are to rhyme, or to invert. The tendency to associate is therefore just as much a set as other response sets are. Nevertheless, this tendency has a peculiar characteristic which makes it particularly interesting: the experimenter can vary the strength of an association very easily by controlling the number of learning trials.

A deeper reason for the neglect of the concept of determining tendency or set by experimental psychologists in recent years lies in the vagueness and inherent difficulty of the concept. What is a tendency? What do we mean when we say that there is a tendency to respond with THREAD, PIN, and SHARP to the stimulus word NEEDLE, other than that these words frequently occur as responses to NEEDLE? Does an airplane have a tendency to fly with the utmost possible speed and noise? Problems like these are responsible for the preference of many experimental psychologists to regard the concept of determining tendency (or set) as a rather loose analogy, which may best be avoided. However, there is really nothing mysterious about the determining tendency. It plays in human behavior very much the same role as an executive program does in the operation of a computer. It performs essentially a message switching and control function. Depending upon the high level goals and policies of the organism it controls the input which the organism receives, and calls up the appropriate subroutines for processing it. "Calling up a subroutine" is computer-language, and merely another language, but one which helps to understand the functioning of determining tendencies. Depending upon task characteristics, instructions, and motivation a subject predetermines his response. For instance, the memory system associated with the concept ANIMAL may be searched, rather than CITIES. Or, the subject instructs himself to rhyme by making those areas of his memory accessible in which his previous experiences with the activity of rhyming are stored.

In Chapter 4 a diagram was presented which summarized current ideas about the memory system. It is time to have another look at this diagram (Fig. 4.5). There is no need to reiterate at this point what has already been stated in the discussion of this figure about the functional character of the diagram, or about the relationship between short- and long-term memory. But this is a good occasion to comment on the box labeled "Control Processes" in Fig. 4.5. It symbolizes the multiple control processes which are necessary for the functioning of memory. In order to recognize sensory stimuli, they must be compared and matched with stored codes of previous stimuli; the subject's response set will in part determine this match. The operations of short-term memory also must be controlled in several ways: the input is filtered and selected, part of it is coded for storage in long-term memory, and other parts are kept available temporarily through rehearsal. Finally, the executive controls the search of long-term memory when such a search is required. All this is done not by a little homonculus who hides in the "Control" box, but through instructions and feedback from other parts of the system. The experimenter's instructions, the inherent properties of the task, and the organisms own rules and intentions determine the set which governs his behavior. The determining tendency controls what is retrieved from memory, but what is retrieved in turn modifies the determining tendency. The feedback system which connects the boxes in Fig. 4.5 is extremely labile and of course open to influences from other parts of the brain. It may be interrupted at any time if emergencies occur: when the subject's chair collapses, instructions to rhyme will momentarily be cancelled.

Response Sets and Interference

The discussion of response sets and the determining tendency is reminiscent of the reinterpretation of interference theory recently offered by Postman which was presented in Chapter 2. Postman is concerned with the interference effects observed when subjects learn two or more related paired-associate lists. There is no need to describe Postman's experiments again (Postman, Stark, and Fraser, 1968; Postman and Stark, 1969) but we shall repeat his main conclusion in order to point out the close relationship which exists between his proposal and the work which has just been discussed.

Postman concluded that the mechanism responsible for unlearning in transfer experiments operates upon entire response sets rather than upon individual S-R associations. Following Underwood and Schulz (1960) Postman labeled this mechanism the response selector. He assumed that during the learning of a first list the selector mechanism activates appropriate responses and suppresses inappropriate ones. This is done primarily on the basis of relative recency, but may also occur on the basis of class recognition. When a subject learns a second list which requires a different set of responses, new selection criteria are established. Clearly, the more alike the two response sets are the harder it will be to discriminate them on the basis of class recognition, and the harder it will be to learn the new list. As errors occur the new criteria must be made more and more specific, so that the first-list repertoire becomes effectively suppressed. Finally, Postman argues that the selector mechanism is characterized by a certain amount of inertia. If he has just learned to suppress first-list responses, the subject finds it difficult to shift criteria quickly when he is asked to recall the first-list responses. This accounts for the reduced availability of first-list responses right after interpolated learning.

The reader might want to refer to the section in Chapter 2 where Postman's theory was presented in more detail. All we want to achieve here is to point out the correspondence between selector mechanisms and determining tendencies. It is most interesting to see that modern interference theory assigns such an important function to the action of response sets. Apparently, developments from different quarters are beginning to converge.

Editing of Implicitly Retrieved Responses: Decision Processes in Recall

Subjects do not respond with everything that comes to their mind when trying to recall a word. When an inappropriate word is implicitly retrieved the subject often knows that it is the wrong word and suppresses it before an overt response is made. Indeed, overt intrusions are quite rare in most free recall experiments. This is so only in part because the subject's retrieval system is so efficient that he only retrieves appropriate words. Subjects also screen words before actually making a response. Müller (1913) theorized that recall is a two-stage process. In the first stage memory traces are made available and in the second stage a decision is made on the basis of the familiarity of the traces. If a memory trace appears familiar, an overt response is made; if not, the trace is rejected and the search of memory is continued. In a free-recall experiment which is concerned with the learning of a list of items this means that a subject recognizes an item as a member of the list or rejects it.

The two-process theory is strongly favored by introspective reports. James (1890) has vividly described the search and decision processes which occur in trying to recall a forgotten name. Müller (1913) has provided systematic accounts of how subjects accept, reject, and edit ideas which come to their mind during recall, and has investigated the criteria which determine a subject's decisions. Such descriptions are useful, at least as a starting point for further research. However, introspection has its familiar problems: observers can't seem to agree. Bartlett (1932), for instance, thinks that judgmental processes are not generally a part of recall. Therefore introspective reports will not settle the question whether recall involves a recognition phase.

Peterson (1967) has shown that a large number of experimental observations can be explained by taking into account decision processes and response competition in recall. In experiments to study proactive and retroactive inhibition subjects learn two lists *A* and *B* in succession, and are then tested on one of them. Much of the forgetting which occurs is caused by response competition between the items of the two lists at the time of recall. Competition may result in overt intrusions or in the rejection of items from the irrelevant list. In fact, the number of intrusions is relatively small and decreases with degree of learning of the second list (e.g., Melton and Irwin, 1940). In agreement with this observation the hypothesis has been suggested that subjects learn to recognize to which list each item belongs. Indeed, subjects rarely give as an intrusion error a response which has occurred only recently in a different context and can still be recognized as belonging to that context (Peterson, 1967). If the items of two lists *A* and *B* belong to different categories response competition is markedly reduced through class recognition.

Peterson (1967) also attributed proactive inhibition in short-term recall experiments to the effects of response competition. The performance decrement which occurs during the first few trials of such experiments is correlated with an increase in the difficulty of the subject's decision problem. Few response alternatives must be considered at the beginning of an experiment, but as trials continue more and more alternatives accumulate. A study by Wickens, Born, and Allen (1963) is instructive: performance is almost perfect on Trial 1 but decreases over the next few trials, in part presumably because the problem of item recognition becomes more difficult. However when the experimenter changes the learning material, e.g., by presenting letters instead of digits, class recognition excludes the former responses and performance is raised again to the level of the first trial. The relatively fast build-up of proactive inhibition on such experiments can also be explained by Peterson's hypothesis: old responses are forgotten rapidly as others are acquired and a steady state in which the number of available response alternatives remains relatively constant is reached in just a few trials.

Experimental procedures such as modified free recall (Underwood, 1948) and modified-modified free recall (Barnes and Underwood, 1959) have been developed to study the effects of response competition and response availability separately in *A-B*, *A-C*, *A*-test designs. In the former the subject is asked to give the first response which occurs to him, in the latter the subject may give both the *B* and *C* responses. These procedures give evidence that at the time of recall the subject has more responses available and must make a selection on one basis or another. For instance, it is by no means so that the first response which occurs to the subject will always be given. Right after the learning of the *A-C* list the *C*-response may be much more available than the previously learned *B*-response, but if instructed the subject can often give the *B*-response, either alone or in combination with *C*.

While these studies show that response competition is an important factor under some experimental conditions, it is difficult to prove that response competition occurs as an integral part of every recall attempt, even when it is not built in by the experimental design.

Of course, in many instances only one response will be retrieved, recognized as correct, and given. It is in cases where errors occur that one can observe the working of the decision mechanism. For instance, in an experiment by Brown (1965) subjects were asked to make another attempt at recall when they made an erroneous response. A list of 21 words was presented and retention of successive words was tested by permitting subjects up to three recall attempts. Subjects were also asked how confident they were of their responses. The result of interest here is the following. When subjects made an error on their first recall attempt, it was often observed that their confidence in their response on the second attempt increased. Whenever this occurred subjects were actually correct almost half of the time on their second try. On the other hand, whenever a subject's confidence rating on his second attempt was lower than on his first, the *a posteriori* probability of being correct on that trial dropped to .13. Clearly, the subjects had judged a few responses as likely to be correct; when they were told that one of these was wrong, they were even more sure of the remaining alternatives. They also were able to recognize when they had run out of likely alternatives.

Very little research has been reported on how a subject goes about selecting one of a possible number of alternatives as his response in recall. One may hypothesize that this process is essentially the same as when a subject is required to select a response from a set of alternatives in a conventional recognition experiment. Each implicit response alternative has a familiarity value associated with it, and the subject makes his decision according to this familiarity value. In the case of overt response alternatives one may think of this familiarity as the result of a match between the perceptual trace of the physically present stimulus and a memory trace. In the present case one must assume that a subject implicitly retrieves an item and then treats it in the same way as an external stimulus, i.e., information about the item as a whole as well as about some of its characteristic features is sent back into the memory store for a check. The extent to which this information is compatible with the information which was stored about the learning material during the acquisition phase of the experiment is what has been called here the familiarity of the item. After a check is completed the subject makes an overt response if the familiarity exceeds a criterion, or he rejects the item otherwise. While in recognition experiments the subject always rejects on the basis of familiarity this is not necessarily so in recall. When recalling a list of words the subject's task is to decide whether or not an implicitly retrieved item was or was not a member of the learning list, just as in the case discussed above. However, when the subject is trying to recall a forgotten name, or the word which corresponds to a dictionary definition as in Brown and McNeill's (1967) experiment, the subject checks not the familiarity of a retrieved response alternative, i.e. its "oldness," but rather its appropriateness. A word must "fit" the definition and the recalled name must have all the proper associations before it is accepted as correct. Obviously, "appropriateness within a particular context" as well as "perceived oldness" may serve as the basic datum for a subject's decisions.

The characteristics of the retrieval process itself may also be used as decision criteria (Müller, 1913). If an item is retrieved promptly, subjects may use that as an indication that it is correct. A high correlation between confidence ratings and response latencies (as reported by Peters, 1910) does not prove that subjects use latency as a criterion in their confidence judgments, but it is certainly in agreement with such an hypothesis. In Peters' study differences in latency are much more impressive as a function of a subject's confidence in his response than as a function of the objective correctness of that response. Similarly, subjects report that they tend to be cautious if many alternatives suggest themselves, but are likely to assume that a response is correct if it is the only one they can think of, especially if that response is rich in associations or arouses a detailed and vivid image (Kuhlmann, 1907).

Not all of these decision criteria are effective in every recall attempt. Subjects may not attend to every relevant feature which they might use in selecting the best response, or the task characteristics might bias the subjects towards particular criteria. The problem has as yet been insufficiently explored. One should also note that once a particular decision criterion is chosen it may change during the course of an experiment, or as a function of experimental conditions. Müller and Pilzecker have described criterion changes as early as 1900: their subjects used a more lax criterion when recall occurred after 24 hours than when recall occurred soon after learning. The determinants of criterion changes are quite incompletely understood, in spite of the long history of the problem. Only recently have some promising starts been made in this direction. Murdock (1966) reported some striking criterion changes in short-term recall. In the immediate recall of five word pairs the subjects' criterion became stricter as the retention interval increased. Items in serial positions 1 and 2 were much less likely to be recalled correctly than items in positions 4 and 5, but at the same time fewer intrusion errors occurred and the confidence subjects had in their responses were not different when items 1 and 2 or

4 and 5 were tested. The strictness of the criterion in this study was correlated with the ratio of errors to correct responses: the more likely a correct response, the more lax the criterion. Subjects were apparently using the error/correct ratio in a similar manner as the proportion of noise-to-signal trials is used by subjects in a psychophysical detection task.

4. A COMPARISON OF EXPERIMENTAL PARADIGMS IN VERBAL LEARNING

As our discussion has amply demonstrated, there are important differences between what the subject does when he learns to recognize, or when he performs in a paired-associate experiment, or when he is simply asked to recall a list of words without regard to order. It makes little sense to lump all these together and talk about the "laws of learning" in general. Although we do not know very much at present about the relationships among these different learning processes, we shall attempt to compare them, especially with respect to organizational processes and decision processes as discussed earlier in this chapter. The reader will do well to keep in mind the tentative character of what can be said, given the rather severe limitations of knowledge which still exist in this area.

Recognition and Recall

It is often assumed that recognition and recall provide alternative measures of habit strength or associative strength in verbal learning and memory experiments. Recognition is thought to be the more sensitive measure of the two, and a response threshhold is invoked to account for this difference (Postman, Jenkins, and Postman, 1948; Bahrick, 1965). However, the empirical evidence for this one-process hypothesis is not very compelling.

It is true that most experimental variables affect recognition and recall in similar ways, but exceptions have been reported. While it is known that high-frequency words tend to be recalled better than low-frequency words (Hall, 1954) the opposite relationship holds for recognition (Schwartz and Rouse, 1961; Gorman, 1961; Shepard, 1967). A similar reversal was observed for disyllable meaningfulness by McNulty (1965a). Intentional and incidental learning instructions also have differential effects upon recall and recognition. Only instructions which insure that the subject organizes the material are effective for recall, but almost any instruction is adequate for recognition, as long as the subject makes some kind of a differential response to the learning items. For instance, Estes and DaPolito (1967) tested the retention of paired-associates after incidental and intentional instructions by both recognition and recall. In the incidental condition the subjects were asked to abstract the principle by which specific numbers were paired with specific nonsense syllables. Subjects who received intentional recall instructions were significantly better than subjects with incidental instructions, but no corresponding difference was obtained in recognition performance.

It is also true that recognition is usually superior to recall, but again this is not always so. Bahrick and Bahrick (1964) and Bruce and Cofer (1967) have shown that the usual superiority of recognition over recall depends upon experimental conditions and may be reversed by making the distractor items on the recognition test highly similar to the study items. In fact, the design of most recognition and free-recall experiments makes it likely that at least some of the recalled items will not be recognized. In free recall the subjects frequently start their report with the last items presented, thus taking the maximum possible advantage of their short-term memory store. In recognition experiments the order of testing is experimenter-determined and an item in short-term memory is likely to be forgotten by the time it comes up for a test. For instance, in one of the experiments by Schwartz and Rouse (1961) a recall test was given immediately after the presentation of a word list and then followed by a recognition test. They found, as have others, that a few of the recalled items could not be recognized; almost all of these items came from the end of the list.

Even if the usual result (much better recognition than recall) is obtained, there are difficulties with its interpretation. In commenting upon one of the early studies (Fischer, 1909) which described the superiority of recognition over recall, Müller (1913) pointed out that it is inadmissible to compare the two procedures directly, because we have no way of knowing the size of the set of alternatives which the subject considers in free recall, and we know that the number of alternatives is a powerful determinant of performance in tests of recognition. Attempts to circumvent this problem by estimating the amount of information transmitted in recall and recognition experiments have produced contradictory results (Davis, Sutherland, and Judd, 1961; Field and Lachman, 1966). They involve unconvincing estimates of the size of the set of items under consideration in recall, as well as unwarranted assumptions about the nature of errors in a recognition task (Dale and Baddeley, 1962). If the size of the subject's set of response alternatives in recall is known with some confidence (e.g., in the paired-associate task with the digits 1-8 as responses, as in the experiment by Estes and DaPolito (1967), or in an experiment by Dale (1967b) where the stimulus items were 15 two-digit numbers selected from the set of all possible two-digit numbers) the probability of a correct recall tends to equal the probability of a correct recognition, after correction for guessing. In such a case the subject probably actually converts the recall task into a recognition test in which he generates his own distractors.

Probably the most significant difference between recall and recognition lies in the fact that associative interference plays a major role in recall but not in recognition. Relevant experimental studies have already been reviewed (Postman and Stark, 1969; Wickelgren, 1967) and it is sufficient to remind the reader of the conclusions reached: the single item, or the single memory trace, appears to be the appropriate unit of analysis in the case of recognition memory, while recall is determined by interrelationships among items both within a list and between different lists.

The one-process hypothesis can perhaps be modified to account for the differences between recognition and recall which have been reviewed above, but it, as well as the attendant concern with the question of which is better, recognition or recall, has not yet proven to be very illuminating. Dual-process theories seem to hold more promise at this time. But before we discuss dual-process theories another important difference between recall and recognition must be mentioned.

Beginning with Hollingworth (1913) it has been accepted that part of the usually observed superiority of recognition over recall is due to recognition on the basis of partial cues. In order to recall an item correctly all of it must be stored in memory, or at least enough of it to permit reconstruction. On the other hand, it is possible to recognize an item correctly by responding to partial cues. McNulty (1965b) has recently demonstrated the importance of partial cues in recognition. With verbal stimulus material differing in the order of approximation to English, McNulty found that the superiority of recognition over recall was most pronounced at low orders of approximation. As responses became better integrated, the difference between the two procedures decreased. Yet, even at the text level a difference remained.

There is no doubt that response integration contributes to the difference between recognition and recall. However, this is not the only difference between the two procedures, and not the most basic one. The importance of the response integration factor arises partly from the use of artificial, poorly integrated learning material in many psychological experiments.

Dual process theories hold that there is a qualitative difference between recognition and recall. Estes and DaPolito (1967) assume that their intentional learning instructions facilitated rehearsal, and hence retrieval and take the lack of a difference between their incidental and intentional instructions in recognition to mean that retrieval processes are unimportant in recognition. The interaction between word frequency and testing procedures (recall and recognition) which has been observed in several studies can be interpreted in a similar way. High-frequency words are easier to associate and categorize than low-frequency words, and hence are easier to organize and recall; unfamiliar words are more distinctive and are less easily confused, and hence are easier to discriminate and recognize (Garner, 1962).

Some fairly direct evidence that the difference between retrieval processes in recall and recognition necessitates a dual-process interpretation of recognition and recall comes from studies by Dale (1967a, b), Cofer (1967), and Kintsch (1968b). The study by Dale (1967a) has already been reported in which response availability was found to be highly correlated with recall; in a second study Dale (1967b) replicated this result and, in addition, showed that response-availability measures and the probability of correct recognition did not correlate with each other. Cofer (1967) demonstrated that when subjects are given 15-word lists which are composed either of highly associated items, weakly associated items, or unrelated words, they could recall better from the high-association lists, but that there was no difference in recognition performance. For the recognition test subjects were given a printed sheet containing the 15 learning items and 15 distractors which were selected from words given as intrusion responses in previous recall experiments with the same lists. Kintsch (1968b) explored a further implication of the dual process theory. If retrieval and recognition processes can be separated as neatly as the dual process theory implies, organization of the learning material can have no effect upon recognition, since organization facilitates retrieval and retrieval in recognition is trivial. In his first experiment lists of 40 words, 10 each from four conceptual categories, were used as learning material. A high-organization list was constructed from the most frequent responses in the Cohen, Bousfield, and Whitmarsh (1957) norms, and a low-organization list was constructed from the least frequent responses. On a recall test subjects recalled 22 words from the high-organization list, but only 15 from the low-organization list. This difference was highly significant statistically. When a recognition test was given memory strength as estimated by the d' statistic was nearly identical for the two lists. In a second experiment the learning material consisted of CVCs which were constructed so that letter combinations were highly predictable in one condition (High-Structure) and unpredictable in the other (Low-Structure). In addition, intra-list similarity was varied by using either 5 or 10 different consonants to construct the set of CVCs. The results of the experiment are shown in Fig. 5.15. High intra-list similarity decreased performance for both recognition and recall, but did not interact with list structure. List structure significantly facilitated recall, but had little effect upon recognition. The data are clearly in agreement with the hypothesis that recall involves a retrieval phase and that an organized list is easier to retrieve than an unorganized one, but that recognition does not require retrieval and is therefore independent of list organization. A procedural detail of these experiments should be noted, however. When a study list consisted of high-frequency words from each of four conceptual categories, the distractor items were also high-

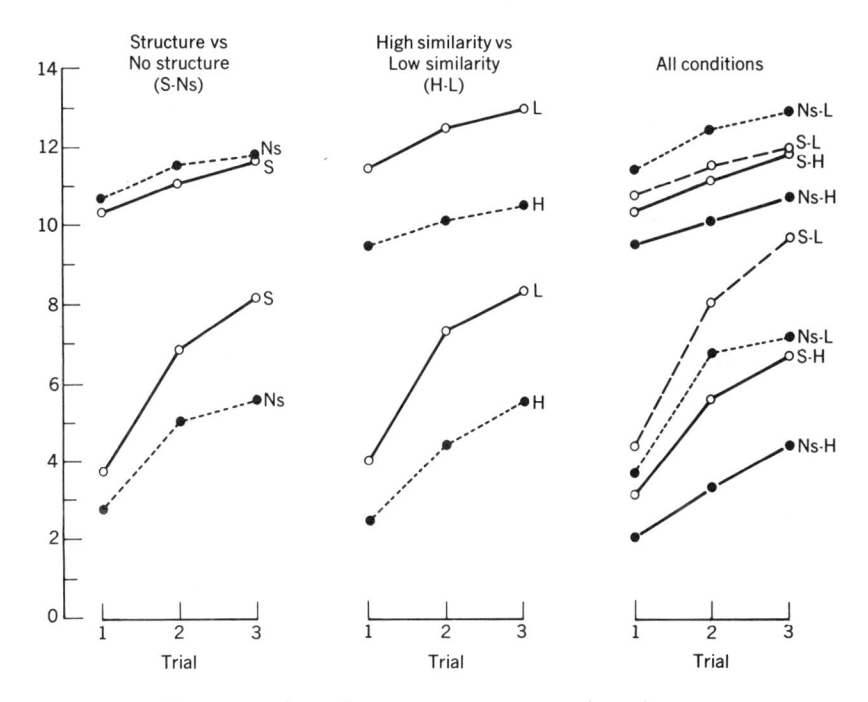

Fig. 5.15 *Mean number of correct responses minus incorrect responses. The upper curves refer to recognition, the lower to recall. (after Kintsch, 1968b)*

frequency words from the same four categories. If unrelated distractors had been used an effect of organization due to class recognition would certainly have been obtained. However, as long as one is concerned with item recognition proper organization of the learning material is an unimportant variable.

Dual-process theory merely maintains that recognition and recall are qualitatively different processes. The two-stage theory of recall, in addition, assumes that in recall responses are first retrieved implicitly, and then recognized as appropriate or inappropriate (Müller, 1913; Peterson, 1967). The evidence for this theory has been summarized in the previous section. The two-stage theory provides a psychological interpretation for a mathematical model of recall learning which has been proposed by Kintsch and Morris (1965), Evans and Dallenbach (1965), and Estes and DaPolito (1967). On the basis of purely formal analyses of the learning data these authors concluded that recall is a two-stage process and that recognition is a one-stage process. Kintsch and Morris also showed that recognition is a subprocess of recall. Subjects learned a list of CVCs to criterion by the method of recognition, and then were given additional learning trials until they reached a recall criterion. Recall learning after recognition learning appeared to be a one-stage process. Therefore it was argued that under normal learning conditions the first stage of recall learning consists in learning to recognize the items. However, these models provide no more than a very rough description of recall learning. A more adequate theoretical treatment of recognition learning and the decision procedures for choosing a response in a recognition task is given in Kintsch (1967). Satisfactory models of the retrieval process have not yet been proposed. In particular, it is not clear whether learning to retrieve an item is an all-or-none process like recognition learning. It may be so at the level of single cues, attributes, or aspects of an item. However, learning to retrieve an item as a whole may be quite a complex process. Furthermore, it has been stated repeatedly in this chapter that a model of the retrieval process must be inadequate as long as it treats the individual item as the unit of learning. A way must be found to deal with the facilitation of retrieval through organization of the learning material, as well as with the subjective organization which a list undergoes during free-recall learning.

Serial Recall

In many situations recall must be ordered rather than free. The extreme situation is serial learning in which each item serves as the recall cue for the next. Since the days of Ebbinghaus a large number of experimental studies have been concerned with the way in which order information is retained. Are items linked together through associations in a chain-like manner? Is each item associated with its place in the total series? Or does a subject organize a sequence of items into related clusters, thereby preserving order information? Very likely, serial learning consists of a mixture of these processes, with one or the other dominating depending upon the exact experimental conditions. However, instead of discussing the laboratory studies concerned with these problems (which, by the way, have failed to produce conclusive results to date), some interesting applications of serial-learning principles in practical situations will be described.

Since so many real-life situations demand that material be retained in its proper serial order, it would seem logical that people prepare themselves and have ready some organizational scheme for sequential learning. One might think that a good procedure would be to number the to be learned items sequentially. People certainly know the number sequence very well, and in this way could base their retrieval strategy upon it, going from one number to the next and recalling the item associated with each number. To some extent people actually follow such a strategy: experimental subjects sometimes associate each item with its place in the series. However, a series of numbers is quite inefficient as a principle of serial organization. It is too abstract and not well suited to the way in which human memory works. People remember concrete things much better than abstractions. Human memory is quite unlike a computer memory in this respect: not logical simplicity but concreteness counts! Thus an efficient system for serial organization should not be in terms of a number series, but should be defined in terms of an actually experienced, concrete sequence of visual images. This was very well known to the orators in classical Greece and Rome, who were called upon daily to perform what we would consider today prodigious feats of memory. Lacking paper to write notes on, speeches for all occasions had to be given from memory. In the ancient schools of rhetoric orators were specifically trained in the "art of memory." This training is very interesting because it was based upon rather profound insights about the nature of memory. First the orator was told to provide himself with a system for serial organization. Specifically, he was asked to visit a large house with many and varied rooms and to walk through it in a particular order. In each room a few easily discriminated objects were noted, also in a particular order: a windowsill, an arch, or a statue. The rooms and the objects in the room were committed to memory through much exercise until the whole series was mastered completely, forwards, backwards, and from any arbitrary starting point. When something was to be memorized the orator went in his mind through his house, depositing at each place an image constructed from the to be learned material. Upon recall, he revisited in his mind the places in the house in their proper order, retrieving from each the image which had been left there. The fixed sequence of places prevented him from forgetting his position in the sequence.

It was considered absolutely necessary that images be constructed from the learning material, because the Greeks knew that images could be retained much better than words or sentences. The more concrete, the more vivid, and the more affective these images were, the better. Indeed, the orator was advised to choose his "places" carefully; the light there should be neither too dim nor too glaring, so that it would not distract from the clarity of the images which were to be deposited.

Yates has written a fascinating and scholarly book on the art of memory from classical antiquity to its late bloom during the renaissance (Yates, 1966). The interested reader is referred to this source. Here we merely wish to note this historical curiosity and to point out how thoroughly "modern" the Greek view of memory was. In order to recall topics in their order, a system of serial organization is required; for this system to be effective it should be based upon concrete visual imagery, not upon abstract thought, words, or even sentences. This is in excellent agreement with the experimental research on memory as discussed previously.*

Paired-associate Learning

Paired-associate learning has traditionally been regarded as the ideal paradigm to study the formation of associative connections between the two items comprising an individual pair. Organizational processes between pairs have frequently been ignored—one simply assumed that such higher-order processes were not involved in paired-associate learning. Battig (1966) has convincingly demonstrated how unfounded such an assumption is. He showed that organizational processes involving inter-pair relationships were very important in paired-associate learning, and that they in fact always occurred, even when all conceivable precautions were taken to prevent their occurrence.

---

*Tests of the theory employing modern experimental methods are just beginning to appear, e.g., Crovitz (1969).

If all other cues are lacking, subjects still can use the state of learning of an item-pair as a basis for grouping. Battig's subjects performed significantly better in paired-associate tasks when he provided them with special cues as to the learning state of each item. For instance, Battig constantly varied the serial position of each item, except that once a correct response had occurred the serial position of that item was kept constant. Thus, constancy of serial position served as a cue indicating the learning state of the item. This procedure significantly facilitated paired-associate learning. The same effect was obtained when the serial position of an item was kept constant until the first correct response occurred; then the serial position of the item was varied randomly. This procedure too facilitated learning, showing that it is not constancy or variation *per se* that is important here, but the possibility of grouping items together. Battig reasoned that this grouping helped subjects to reduce inter-pair interference.

Nevertheless, in paired-associate learning the subject's task is merely one of establishing an association between the stimulus and the response term, either directly or through verbal mediation, or by forming an image which connects the two terms. Thus the retrieval process in paired-associate learning is simpler than in free recall. As in free recall, the subject presumably edits and controls implicitly retrieved responses, overtly performing only those which pass a test of familiarity. In fact, several of the studies used in the previous discussion of decision processes in recall actually employed a paired-associate procedure.

There is, however, one additional factor in paired-associate learning which has not yet been considered. Before a subject can retrieve the appropriate response in a paired-associate test he must be able to recognize the stimulus term. Several experiments have shown that recognition of the stimulus term is a necessary condition for the establishment of a stimulus-response connection (Bernbach, 1967; Martin, 1967a, b). As an illustration we may take a study by Martin (1967a) in which subjects learned 8 trigram-number pairs. Study trials and test trials were alternated, and on each test trial the subject had to make two responses: a yes-no recognition response, and recall of the response digit, guessing if necessary. On test trials the 8 stimulus items were shown together with 16 distractor items in random order. Some of Martin's results are shown in Fig. 5.16. When the recognition response was correct, the probability of recall increased over trials as a learning curve should; when the recognition response was incorrect, no recall learning occurred, and the probability of recall oscillated around the value of 1/8 expected by chance. Even more

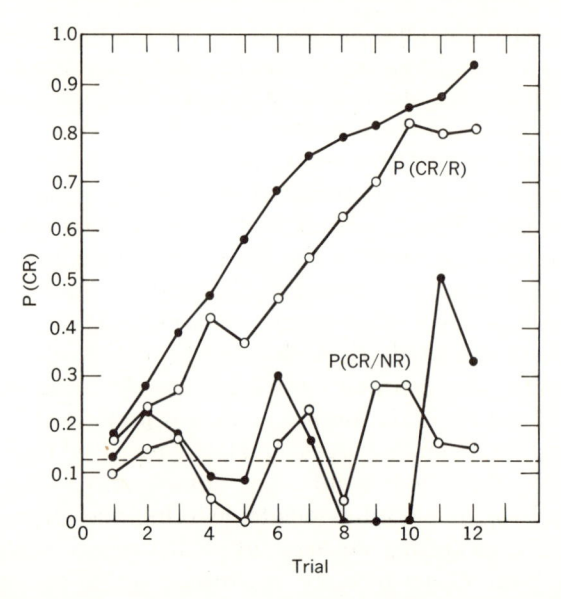

Fig. 5.16 *Proportion of correct responses (CR) given recognition (R) and nonrecognition (NR) of high- (full circles) and low-meaningful stimuli (open circles). The dashed line is the chance level. (after Martin, 1967)*

impressive is the finding that it does not matter how often the subject has already given a correct recall response to a particular item on previous trials: if he fails to recognize it recall performance on that trial is at the chance level. Similarly Bernbach (1967) has reported that it make no difference how often a subject has already correctly recognized an item previously: as long as he does not recognize it on a given trial, recall performance is no better than chance.

Not only is it empirically true that recognition is a prerequisite for associative recall, as we have just seen; it has also been argued for a long time that stimulus recognition is a logically necessary step in recall (Höffding, 1891; Köhler, 1949). The fact that an item pair *A-B* is associated means that there exists a memory trace *a-b*; if the stimulus term *A* is presented as a recall cue, somehow contact must be established between *A* and the memory trace *a*. Once the memory trace *a* is reached the response *B* can be produced on the basis of the associated trace *b*. However, somehow the stimulus *A* must be recognized as belonging to the memory trace *a*. How this is done has not yet been discussed (very little is known about the mechanism of recognition anyway, but we shall have occasion to discuss this problem a little more fully in the next chapter). Here it is sufficient to note that Höffding's philosophical problem has been turned into an empirical question concerning the stages of paired-associate learning in present-day research on verbal learning.

The mathematical models of paired-associate learning discussed in previous chapters may easily be extended to incorporate a stimulus discrimination stage. In fact, a special case where confusable stimulus pairs were used to study stimulus discrimination within this framework has already been described in some detail (Polson, Restle, and Polson, 1965). In most cases, however, it is simply not necessary to distinguish a separate stimulus discrimination stage. In paired-associate tasks with lists of moderate length and reasonably distinctive stimuli subjects learn to recognize the stimulus items so quickly that the neglect of this process in the formal models has no serious consequences. In the studies reported above in which the importance of stimulus recognition for the learning of paired-associates has been demonstrated, consonant trigrams with considerable letter overlap have been used as stimulus material. Stimulus recognition, then, is an important factor only if the items are relatively hard to discriminate.

On the whole paired-associate learning appears to require a fairly complex mechanism. Like free recall it involves retrieval and decision processes (which, however, may be simpler than in the case of free recall), and in addition there is a stimulus recognition stage.

Optimal Presentation Sequences

The differences and similarities which exist among the various verbal learning paradigms have interesting consequences when it comes to finding schemes which optimize learning. At the same time, the different optimization procedures will throw further light upon the characteristic features of the various experimental paradigms.

Suppose we have a list of m items (in the case of paired-associate learning each item is a stimulus-response pair) and are allowed to present each item n times. After the $N = nm$ presentations retention is tested on all items. How should one present the items so as to maximize performance on the test trial? For instance, we might have three items i_1, i_2, and i_3, and two reinforcements apiece. One presentation sequence might then be (i_1, i_1) (i_2, i_2) (i_3, i_3). In this case we say that items are presented in blocks of size 1, or that the block size $k = 1$. The largest possible block size with three items is $k = 3$ which is exemplified by the presentation sequence (i_1, i_2, i_3) (i_1, i_2, i_3). In general $1 \leq k \leq m$. The question which we want to address ourselves to concerns the optimal block size k.

Data have already been reported with implications for the case of free recall. Tulving (1966) has shown that a list of unrelated items is learned best if the subject is permitted to see all items before repetitions occur. This finding is in agreement with the theory that in free recall the learner must find a subjective organization of the list. If he is not given a chance to experience the whole list, inappropriate organizations will be formed which interfere with further progress.

In paired-associate learning the situation is more complicated. An extensive investigation of this problem has been reported by Crothers and Suppes (1967). These authors predicted optimal presentation orders from a simple mathematical model of the learning process and then checked these predictions against experimental data. The model which they used is the single-operator linear model, which, as will be remembered, was not one of the more successful models in describing paired-associate learning data. However, the general inadequacy of the linear model does not particularly concern us here, because all we are concerned with in this optimization problem is the mean learning curve. We want to find an arrangement of the learning items such that after a fixed number of trials the average probability of an error over the set of m items and the set of all subjects is a minimum. We know that a broad class of models predict equivalent mean learning curves and since the mean learning curve is all that matters here, the simple linear model is as good for our purposes as more complicated models with more realistic learning and forgetting assumptions.

Suppose that whenever item i is presented for study the probability of an error for item i decreases by some fraction α. In addition, whenever one of the remaining $(m - 1)$ items of the list is presented the probability of an error for item i increases by some fraction β. This second assumption simply says that while other items are being learned, item i may be forgotten. Crothers and Suppes have shown that if $\alpha > \beta$, the block size k should be chosen as large as possible in order to maximize learning. Therefore, if the rate of learning is greater than the rate of forgetting, choose $k = m$. On the other hand, if learning is slower than forgetting, i.e., $\alpha < \beta$, the smallest possible block size should be chosen in order to maximize learning ($k = 1$). Normally one would assume the learning rate to be greater than the forgetting rate and hence present n cycles of the whole list of m items, which is of course the usual presentation sequence in paired-associate experiments. Crothers and Suppes have investigated block sizes of

18, 36, 108, and 216 in studies in which single Russian words played over a tape recorder served as stimuli and their English orthographic representations as responses. Test probabilities increased monotonically over block sizes in their experiments when the learning task was made easy by using a multiple-choice recognition test. In other experiments a recall test was substituted for the recognition test, and only limited time was given for a response in order to increase the difficulty of the learning task. In agreement with the model, smaller block sizes were more efficient in the latter case. When easy and hard items were considered separately it was found that the larger block size was more efficient for the easy items, but that small block sizes were better for hard items, again confirming the theoretical predictions. However, none of the differences observed by Crothers and Suppes as a function of presentation sequence were very large.

When the items of a learning list are related to each other in some way the problem of optimizing the presentation sequence becomes somewhat more complicated. It is known that categorized word lists are easier to recall if all items which belong to one category are presented before items from the next category are introduced (e.g., Cofer, Bruce, and Reicher, 1966). Blocked presentation probably helps the subject to recognize the category membership of the items and to make use of it. Quite dramatic effects of presentation order in free recall of a categorized list have been reported by Bower, Clark, Lesgold, and Winzenz (1969). Bower's learning list consisted of 112 words which were organized into four hierarchies. An example for one of his word hierarchies is shown in Table 5.4. In the control condition (random-all words) the 112 words were presented in random order for

Table 5.4. *The hierarchy for "minerals" from the list of Bower et al.* (*1969*)

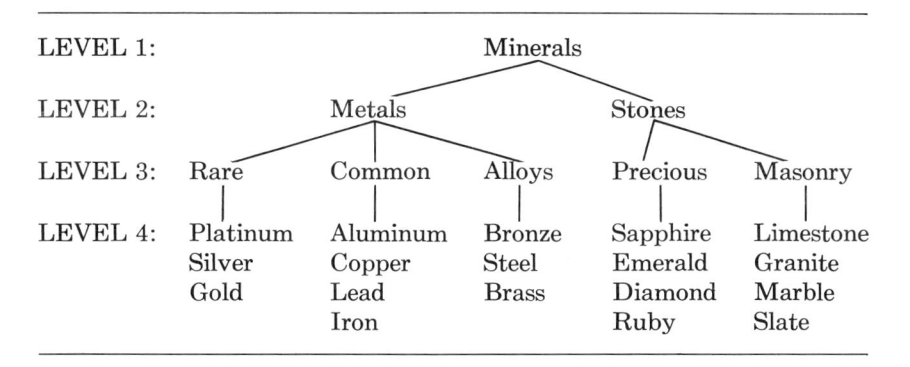

LEVEL 1:			Minerals		
LEVEL 2:		Metals		Stones	
LEVEL 3:	Rare	Common	Alloys	Precious	Masonry
LEVEL 4:	Platinum	Aluminum	Bronze	Sapphire	Limestone
	Silver	Copper	Steel	Emerald	Granite
	Gold	Lead	Brass	Diamond	Marble
		Iron		Ruby	Slate

four trials. In the experimental group only the level 1 and 2 words were shown on the first study trial. On the second study trial these subjects received the level 1, 2, and 3 words, and only on the last 2 trials were all words presented. Thus, subjects first learned the superordinate category labels before studying the category members. Note that the level 4 words (there were 74 of them) were given four reinforcements in the control group, but only two in the experimental group. A second control group (random-progressive) received the same number of words on each study trial as the experimental group, but these words were randomly selected from the total word pool. The average number of level 4 words recalled per trial is shown in Fig. 5.17. Obviously, teaching the subjects how to organize a list first by presenting a hierarchy of category labels into which later items may be fitted is much more effective than merely showing the items themselves. We may conclude, therefore, that in free recall the optimum presentation schedule is one which maximizes the probability that the subject utilizes whatever objective organization or structure exists in the learning list.

For the case of paired-associate learning Crothers and Suppes (1967) have obtained theoretical predictions through a slight extension of the model discussed above. If a paired-associate list is categorized it is reasonable to assume positive transfer among the items in the same category. Thus, three effects must be considered: learn-

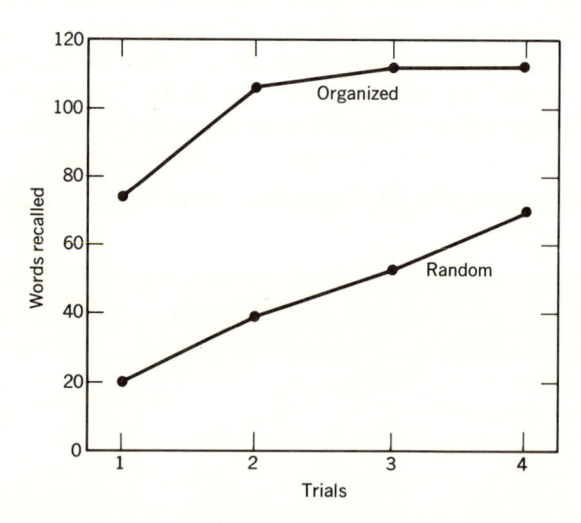

Fig. 5.17 *Mean number of words recalled from a 112-word list as a function of ordered, hierarchical presentation or random presentation. (after Bower, 1968)*

ing when an item is presented for study, forgetting of that item when other items are being learned, and positive transfer on trials with other items which belong to the same category as the original item. The presentation schedule which minimizes the expected number of errors depends upon the parameter values which are assumed for these three processes. The presentation of all items in each category in blocks is most efficient when there is little positive transfer. When positive transfer is large it seems best to present first one exemplar from one category, followed by the first exemplar of each of the other categories in turn, and then to recycle through all categories in the same order with the second exemplar from each, and so forth. There are several experiments in the literature in which the efficiency of learning is studied as a function of the presentation schedule. However, estimates of the learning, forgetting, and transfer rates in these experiments are not available and hence they do not provide an adequate test of the theoretical predictions. In most but not all studies, blocked presentation of items in the same category was most effective.

The problem of finding the most efficient presentation sequence in learning experiments deserves to be investigated much more fully than has been done so far. The work discussed here merely scratches the surface of a very rich problem. Further results of interest have been reported recently by Karush and Dear (1966). Basing their theoretical analysis upon the one-element model these authors found that the expected level of achievement in a paired-associate experiment with m items and a fixed number N of trials can be optimized by choosing on each trial that item for which the likelihood that it already has been learned is least. Optimization problems will probably receive much more attention in coming years as a technology of instruction based upon learning theory is developed.

SUMMARY

Two important aspects of long-term memory have been examined in this chapter: decision processes in recognition and free recall, and organizational processes in memory, primarily with respect to storage and retrieval in recall.

The manner in which decision processes enter into a subject's recognition performance appears to be relatively straightforward. If the familiarity value of a test item is greater than some critical value, the item will be recognized as old; if the familiarity value of an item falls below a criterion it will be called new. Items which have been presented repeatedly have on the average a higher familiarity value than new items. However, because familiarity values are only probabilistically determined there will generally be some overlap in the familiarity distributions of old and new items.

Control processes in recall are more complex. First of all, there appears to be an editing of implicitly retrieved responses on the basis of familiarity or the like, as in recognition. In addition, there are decision processes which direct the subject's search of memory. These have been discussed in the psychological literature under such names as determining tendency, generalized response sets, or selector mechanism.

The main part of the chapter was concerned with a discussion of the interdependencies which exist among the structure of the learning material, the organization of memory, and the subject's storage and retrieval processes. It was pointed out that organized lists are easier to learn in free recall experiments, whether the organization be in terms of inter-item associations, conceptual categories, or other rules. Furthermore, related items cluster together during recall. The mechanism which is responsible for both the facilitation of recall of structured materials and for the clustering during output operates both at the time of storage and retrieval. If at the time of recall retrieval cues are given to a subject, his performance can be significantly improved over unaided recall, which implies that often more may be stored in memory than can be retrieved. However, in order for retrieval cues to be effective their relationship to the to be learned material must be have been noted at the time of storage; only appropriately organized material can be retrieved.

The organization of memory is basically subjective. Even in the absence of an objective structure subjects impose their own organization upon the learning material. In fact, subjective organization appears to be a necessary and sufficient condition for the recall of a word list.

At the time of learning subjects seem to be engaged in finding some sensible principle of organization for the learning material. At the time of recall they are searching their memory, using whatever interitem relationships they have detected during storage as their guides. However, recall is not just a matter of reporting what has been retrieved; it also has many features of a reconstruction process. Subjects try to reconstruct acceptable answers from partially retrieved information.

In the last section of the chapter an attempt was made to compare the various verbal learning procedures, viz., free recall, recognition, paired-associate learning, and serial learning. It was argued that an important difference between recall and recognition exists in that retrieval presents a major problem in recall but not in recognition. It was also pointed out that organizational processes in paired-associate learning should not be neglected. In addition, the role of stimulus discrimination in paired-associate learning was emphasized. Serial organization together with image construction was described as an interesting mnemonic technique. Finally, a question was raised as to the optimal learning procedures for the various paradigms discussed here, given the differences in the learning processes involved.

DISCRIMINATION LEARNING

6666666666666666

On a screen before a subject two small disks of light appear briefly. The lights are carefully calibrated so that they are identical in every respect, except that one of them is brighter by a small amount than the other. The subject's task is to identify which of the two lights is the brighter one. If he performs correctly, he demonstrates that he can discriminate between the two lights. Experiments like this are called *discrimination* experiments. The procedure just described would be called simultaneous discrimination because the two stimuli which were to be discriminated were presented simultaneously. In a successive discrimination problem the stimuli appear one after the other, but the subject's task remains the same. Now consider a slight modification of this experimental procedure. Instead of asking the subject to tell which stimulus is brighter, one stimulus, called a standard stimulus, is shown first and the subject is asked to tell whether or not test stimuli are different from the standard.

Stimulus generalization is said to occur if the subject responds with "same" to stimuli which are actually different. Obviously, discrimination and generalization are closely related procedurally: discrimination implies differential responding; generalization implies lack of discrimination. The operational definition of concept learning or classification learning is identical with that of generalization: in a concept identification experiment the subject learns to make the same response to all instances of a concept. Membership in a concept class may be defined in terms of a common physical attribute (e.g., *blondes*) or in terms of abstract rules or relationships (e.g., *bachelor*). In either case instances of a concept may differ widely in characteristics which are irrelevant to the defining property. A distinction between concept formation and generalization is generally made in experimental psychology in spite of the lack of operational justification. This distinction appears to be historically determined: the term generalization is applied if the stimuli are relatively simple and their variability is restricted to a single known psychophysical dimension. Pure tones of different frequency, colors, or lights arranged in certain spatial patterns are typically used in both human and animal experiments on generalization. When the stimuli are somewhat more complex (words, line-drawings, pictures) and human subjects are used, the experiments have traditionally been labeled as concept formation. However, this difference reflects common usage more than any essential operational difference. Certainly, animals can learn concepts, as for instance Herrnstein and Loveland (1964) have shown. Herrnstein and Loveland taught pigeons the concept of the human figure using highly complex color photographs as their stimulus material.

The next chapters will be devoted to an analysis of discrimination and concept formation. First, following the traditional bias of learning theory, stimulus generalization and discrimination will be investigated in simple experimental situations.

The term stimulus generalization was introduced by Pavlov (1927) who repeatedly observed instances of stimulus generalization in his laboratory. For instance, salivary responses conditioned to a pure tone of 1000 cps occurred in response to tones of different frequencies, or even to the sound made by the experimenter's footsteps, or the rattle of his key chain. Pavlov investigated generalization systematically and found that the less similar a stimulus was to the conditioned stimulus, the less likely it was to elicit the conditioned response, and the smaller the magnitude of the conditioned response became if it occurred at all. Indeed, there appeared to be a regular, monotonically decreasing gradient of generalization around the value of the conditioned stimulus. Early in training Pavlov's dogs responded to a wide range of stimuli around the CS. After extended training responsiveness became more restricted to the vicinity of the reinforced stimulus. For Pavlov stimulus generalization was one of the basic phenomena of conditioning. He attempted to explain it in terms of irradiation of neural excitation.

Hull adopted Pavlov's thesis, minus the neural theory, and introduced a distinction between primary and secondary stimulus generalization which was subsequently to become very influential. Primary stimulus generalization is essentially identical with the Pavlovian concept. It is an automatic increment in response strength to stimuli which are physically similar to the conditioned stimulus. Secondary stimulus generalization occurs through mediating responses. If the similarity between stimuli is not physical (i.e., defined in terms of common elements, or of a common dimension, such as loudness or frequency in the case of tones) generalization may occur via a common mediating response. In this manner Hull could account for what he called logical or abstract similarity. We shall use the term generalization here in the sense of primary generalization at first and defer a discussion of mediation.

Stimulus generalization permitted Hull to solve what he considered a fundamental problem in learning theory. Given the variability of the human environment, two stimuli are hardly ever identical in all physical details. How, then, can a response ever become conditioned to a stimulus through repeated pairings with it, when the "same" stimulus is never repeated? Hull called this the stimulus equivalence problem, and suggested primary generalization as a way out of the dilemma. Because of generalization, small variations in the conditioned stimulus nevertheless permit the build-up of habit strength to some average value.

Hull's view of the role of generalization in learning has been vigorously attacked, most notably in a famous paper by Lashley and Wade (1946). Lashley and Wade argued that generalization is nothing but lack of discrimination. They maintained that Hull's stimulus equivalence problem was a paradox only for the learning theorist, but not for the learning organism. Variability in the physical stimulus *per se* is relevant only if the organism actually registers this variability. At the beginning of training an organism simply does not discriminate the conditioned stimulus very well. Therefore Pavlov's dog salivated to the CS of 1000 cps, to tones of similar frequency, and even to quite unrelated noises. As training progressed salivation to noises and other tones remained unreinforced and hence extinguished. In Lashley and Wade's view the empirical generalization gradients which are generally observed, are due to the inability of organisms to discriminate precisely among stimuli, and it is not necessary to postulate a special and basic process called generalization.

Quite the opposite approach has been taken by Spence in his elegant and very successful theory which explained discrimination learning in terms of generalization (Spence, 1937). Spence assumed that, in accordance with the views of Pavlov and Hull, a symmetric gradient of habit strength is established around the positive stimulus in a discrimination experiment, and that a similar gradient of inhibition is established around the negative stimulus. Performance is then determined by the algebraic sum of the two gradients. An example from Spence (1942) will illustrate the theory. Suppose an organism has been trained in a size discrimination task. A number of reinforcements to the positive stimulus (160 sq cm) have established a certain habit strength to that stimulus which generalizes to stimuli of similar size as shown in Fig. 6.1. Extinction trials with the negative stimulus (100 sq cm) have established a gradient of inhibition around that stimulus value, also shown in Fig. 6.1. The total response strength for each stimulus value is determined by subtracting the inhibitory tendency associated with it from its habit strength. The theory makes a number of interesting predictions. For instance, note that the maximum difference occurs at a point to the right of the S^+. Therefore, the maximum response rate in a generalization test under the present conditions should be displaced from the S^+, away from the S^-. This phenomenon has frequently been observed and is known under the name of peak-shift in the literature on discrimination learning.

Observe that in Spence's theory the effective stimulus is a concrete physical object: the subject learns to discriminate a square of 160 sq cm from a square of 100 sq cm. Positive habit strength is built up to the former, inhibition to the latter. On the other hand, one could maintain that what the subject really learns is to pick the larger of the two squares, rather than the particular square of 160 sq cm. In other words, the effective stimulus might be a relationship (e.g., larger) rather than a concrete physical object as Spence maintains. This notion is supported by an observation which has been termed transposition: if, after training to discriminate the two squares of size 160 and 100 sq cm, the subjects are given two stimuli of size 160 and 256 sq cm, they will choose the 256 sq cm stimulus figure, i.e., the larger one, rather than the former S^+! Offhand, the fact that transposition occurs seems to offer decisive evidence in favor of the relational hypothesis. However, Spence was able to show that

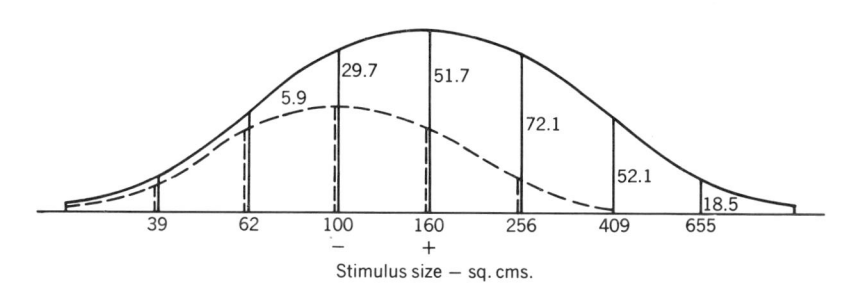

Fig. 6.1 *Hypothetical generalization gradients for habit strength after training on a positive stimulus of 160 and inhibition after training on a negative stimulus of 100. The difference between habit strength and inhibition is indicated numerically at several points. (after Spence, 1942)*

the theory summarized in Fig. 6.1 is in complete agreement with the experimental facts regarding transposition. The theory predicts, as is seen in Fig. 6.1, that the subject will respond more to the stimulus of 256 sq cm, which has never been experienced before, rather than to the S^+, since the habit differential is greater (72.1) for the larger stimulus than for the conditioned stimulus itself (51.7). In fact, Spence's theory wins out over the relational argument, because of another interesting implication which also can be read from Fig. 6.1. Suppose we present the 256-square and the 409-square for a transfer test. Relational theory must stick to its prediction that the larger of the two stimuli will be chosen, but from Fig. 6.1 the opposite prediction can be derived. The habit differential is larger for 256 sq cm than for 409 sq cm and hence the subject should not show transposition with the present stimulus pair. In addition, suppose we present two stimuli which are very large, so large that neither habit nor inhibition will generalize to them. For such a stimulus pair Spence's theory predicts random responding, while relational theory still would predict that the subject chooses the larger of the two stimuli. Empirical results support Spence in both cases: it is indeed true that transposition breaks down when the test stimuli differ greatly from the training stimuli, and that responding becomes completely random with stimuli very far removed from the training values.

Note that Spence's theory accounts for the surprising facts of transposition without invoking any new principles. Responses are still directly conditioned to the physical stimulus, and the summation of habit and inhibition gradients is all that is involved in transposition. However, one must realize the limitations of this theory. First of all, it is clear that humans can respond to relations. Relevant experimental studies will be discussed throughout the following chapters, especially in Chapter 8. However, even if we restrict ourselves to infra-human organisms, the victory of the absolute over the relative position is not as decisive as the discussion above may lead one to believe. Even rats can learn to respond to relational cues under appropriate conditions, as was shown by Lawrence and DeRivera (1954). It does not appear very fruitful to argue about whether organisms respond to relations or to a particular concrete stimulus. A relation between stimuli can be as good a cue in discrimination learning as more concretely definable attributes of a stimulus. This is obviously true for human subjects, while animals, especially lower ones, may be more tied to concrete objects.

A second, and even more severe limitation of Spence's theory lies in its restriction to nonverbal organisms and to experimental situations which insure that the animal is exposed and responds to all aspects of the stimulus situation. However, as will be demonstrated shortly, the most pervasive phenomenon of discrimination learning is that the subject responds selectively to different aspects of the stimulus. Coding operations and stimulus selection appear to be the central problem of discrimination learning. No satisfactory theory of discrimination learning can neglect these phenomena.

Spence postulates a theoretical process called *generalization* and explains with it such empirical phenomena as generalization and discrimination. Lashley attempts to explain the same set of empirical data by means of a theoretical construct *discrimination*. Note that in either case one member of the empirical pair discrimination-generalization is given a basic theoretical status and used as an explanatory mechanism. A third approach has sometimes been applied to the problem of generalization and discrimination: to investigate the empirical relationship between generalization and discrimination on an atheoretical level (Brown, 1965). The question then becomes whether one can predict a subject's generalization gradient for a particular set of stimuli, knowing his ability to discriminate among the members of that particular set, and vice versa.

Before taking up this question in detail we shall describe a typical experiment on generalization with human subjects, which will put our problem into better perspective. The "classical" experiment in this area is one by Brown, Bilodeau, and Baron (1951). The stimuli in their experiment were lights arranged in a row. One of the lights was designated as the CS and the subjects were instructed to respond by pressing a response key when that light was lit, but not to respond when another light was lit. Subjects were told to react as quickly as possible and not to be unduly concerned about false responses. Gradients of response frequency were found as a function of the spatial separation of the lights. The farther away a lamp was from the CS-lamp, the less likely a response was. This experiment—and several others like it—pose a serious problem in that generalization occurred to lights several inches away from the CS. Lamps separated by such distances are perfectly discriminable.

Why, then does generalization occur? There are other experimental studies which demonstrate that it is possible to directly relate discrimination and generalization, at least under some experimental conditions. Before returning to the problem raised by the Brown *et al.* experiment, a few such studies will be described. The first was performed by Guttman and Kalish (1956) with pigeons. It was a failure in the sense that the predictions of generalization gradients on the color dimension from the discrimination function were not adequate. The upper part of Fig. 6.2 shows the result of this experiment and helps to understand the experimental design. Pigeons were trained to peck a disk if it was illuminated with a color of a certain wave length. After training was completed, the disk was illuminated with colors of different wave lengths and the pigeon's response rate to stimuli different from the training stimuli was recorded. During these generalization tests an intermittent reinforcement schedule on the original training stimulus helped maintain responding to that stimulus. The training stimuli and the resulting generalization gradients around them are shown in Fig. 6.2. In the center part of Fig. 6.2 the discrimination thresholds for colors of different wave lengths are plotted for both pigeons and humans. If generalization is simply lack of discrimination it follows that generalization gradients should be flat where discriminability is low, and steep where small discrimination thresholds permit the subject to make very fine discriminations. A comparison of the two parts of Fig. 6.2 reveals no such relationship. For instance, for a CS of 560 mμ a markedly asymmetric generalization gradient must be predicted on the basis of the discrimination data: for wave lengths higher than 560 mμ discrimination is very good and hence only few confusions should occur, while for smaller wave lengths discrimination becomes quite poor, implying high confusability between stimuli and hence flat generalization gradients. The pigeon data, however, show no systematic relationship at all between generalization and discrimination.

While the pigeon data thus present an as yet unsolved puzzle, the data for human subjects come much closer to our expectations. An experiment which demonstrates the expected inverse relationship between discrimination and generalization was performed by Kalish (1958). Kalish's subjects were seated in front of a screen with an illuminated disk. A color was presented on the disk for 1 minute and the subject was told to try to keep it in mind, as he would be asked to identify it later. During the test period 9 colors, the training stimulus and four test values in steps of 10 mμ on either side of the training stimulus, were presented at a fairly rapid rate. Each stimulus was presented six times and order of presentation was random. The subject was instructed to release a telegraph key as rapidly as possible if the color shown was the same as the training stimulus. The stimulus values used and the results of the experiment are shown in the lower part of Fig. 6.2. Unlike the pigeon data, the generalization gradients for human subjects are inversely related to the discrimination function. Asymmetries in the generalization gradients occur where they are

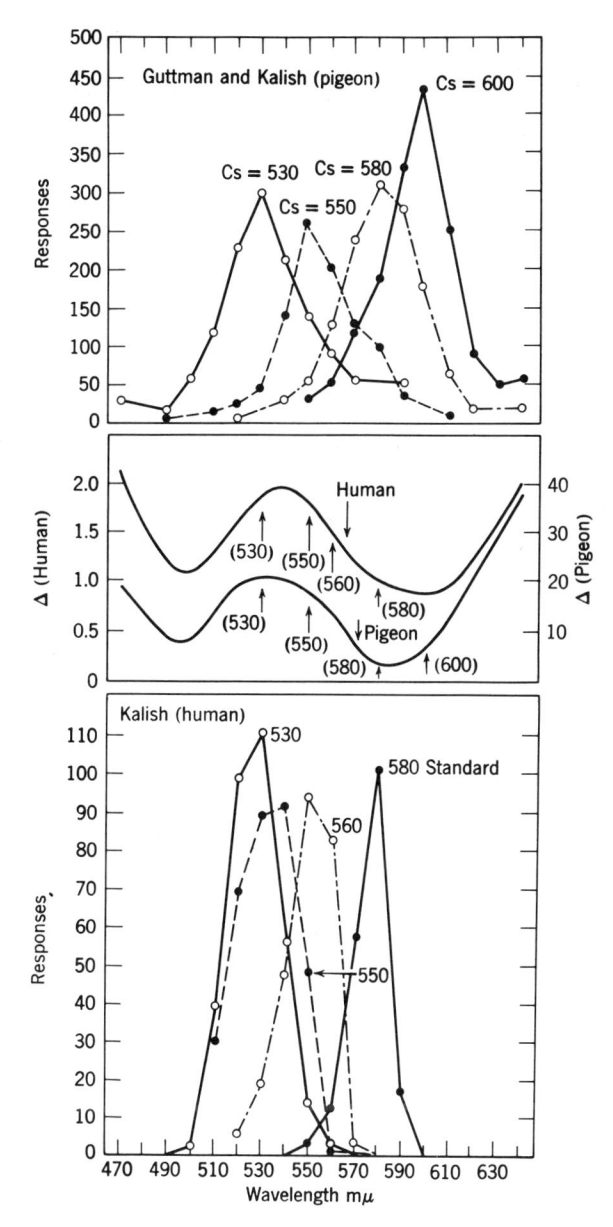

Fig. 6.2 *Upper: Mean generalization gradients for pigeons. Middle: Hue discrimination as a function of wavelength for pigeons and humans. Lower: Mean generalization gradients for human subjects. (after Kalish, 1958)*

predicted by the discrimination function. For the stimulus of 560 mμ the locus of maximum responding has actually shifted from the training value to the next lower value, which is in the region of greatest difficulty of judgment. Perhaps the only result which is somewhat discrepant with the expectations based upon the discriminability function is the symmetry of the gradient around 530 mμ. Since discrimination thresholds become smaller for lower values in this case, one would expect an asymmetry in the gradient in the direction opposite to the other gradients, which, however, failed to materialize. Nevertheless, Kalish's data clearly imply that discrimination and generalization are fundamentally dependent upon the characteristics of the underlying stimulus continuum, and are inversely related to each other.

The second experiment which successfully related generalization and discrimination used quite a different procedure. Discrimination learning was predicted from information about generalization gradients (Shepard and Chang, 1963). Eight Munsell color chips varying in brightness and saturation were the stimulus material in this experiment. In the first part of the experiment generalization gradients were obtained. Subjects were taught an identifying response to each color chip, learning, in effect, an 8-item paired-associate list with colors as stimuli and 8 different responses. From this experiment a confusion matrix was obtained, showing how often during the course of learning each response occurred as a confusion error for each stimulus. Each row of such a matrix is comparable to a generalization gradient, except that in the present experiment the stimulus material varied along two dimensions rather than only one, and hence the conventional way off plotting generalization gradients would be inapplicable. The second part of Shepard and Chang's experiment comprised several classification learning tasks. The set of 8 stimuli was divided into two subsets of 4 stimuli and subjects learned to discriminate between the two subsets. The generalization data were used to predict the difficulty of discrimination learning. For any given classification the number of times each stimulus was confused during the identification task with a stimulus which was assigned to the opposite subset in classification learning was used to predict the number of errors during classification learning. These predictions were quite successful. Figure 6.3 shows the correlation between the observed and predicted error scores for the various classifications. Seventy-eight percent of the error variance in classification learning could be accounted for by pairwise confusions among the stimuli as determined earlier in identification learning.

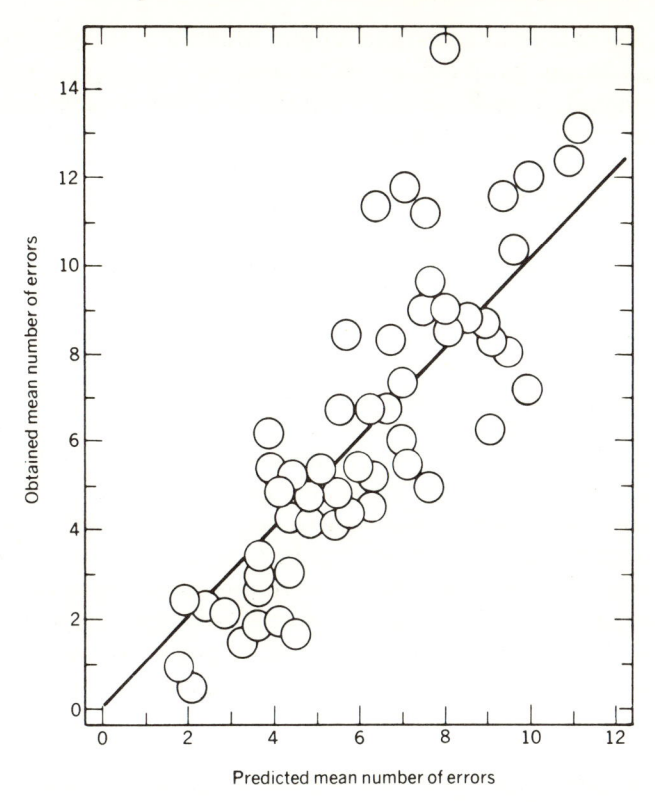

Fig. 6.3 *The mean number of errors per stimulus per subject are plotted for each classification against the corresponding numbers predicted from the earlier identification experiment. (after Shepard and Chang, 1963)*

1. RESPONSE BIASES IN GENERALIZATION EXPERIMENTS

The experiments just discussed show that at least under some conditions it is possible to predict generalization gradients from discrimination thresholds and discrimination learning from generalization errors. But they do not help to explain the discrepant results of experiments such as that of Brown *et al.* (1951), where generalization was observed to spatial positions several inches apart, so that inability to discriminate can hardly be taken as a reasonable explanation. The reason for such findings probably lies in the differential pay-off which is used in generalization and discrimination experiments and in the different response strategies and biases which are thereby induced, rather than in any basic differences in the processes of generalization and discrimination itself. In a typical discrimination experiment two stimuli are presented, either simultaneously or successively and the subject is asked to choose one. There usually are no asymmetrical pay-offs, or instructions which stress the importance of one kind of choice over the other. Generalization experiments are different in this respect. First of all, the subject is trained to respond to one stimulus (or in the human case told to do so) and then he is tested with several stimuli. His response is *same* or *not same*, and he is frequently impressed with the importance of responding correctly to the training stimulus. He may also be asked to respond as fast as possible and not to be too concerned about false identifications. Such instructions amount to asymmetric pay-off conditions: the subject is led to believe that it is very bad if he misses the correct stimulus, while errors of the second kind, *same*-responses to stimuli which differ from the training stimulus, are less objectionable. Certainly the instructions in the Brown *et al.* experiment which were described above could have led subjects to be strongly biased towards *same*-responses. This bias could have caused the large number of responses to stimuli which under optimal conditions and for an unbiased subject are clearly discriminable.

An experiment specifically designed to test this interpretation of stimulus generalization in the absence of discrimination problems has been reported by Zinnes and Kurtz (1968). This experiment will be discussed in some detail here, both because of its bearing on the present problem and also because it provides a good illustration of how intimately intertwined a subject's response biases and decision strategies are with his discrimination performance. We have already seen the importance of such factors for the understanding of recognition memory and probability learning experiments. The same concepts which proved to be useful in these earlier contexts can now be applied to the analysis of discrimination learning.

Zinnes and Kurtz studied discrimination and generalization with light paterns of varying size. In all tasks a pattern of 9 lights served as the standard stimulus (S_0). Different groups of subjects were assigned to different comparison stimuli (S_j) in order to study systematically the effects of stimulus discriminability. Three conditions of discriminability were used: light patterns consisting of 10, 11, or 12 lamps, henceforth called S_1, S_2, and S_3. In the discrimination experiment two light patterns, one of them the standard and the other one of the comparison stimuli, were presented successively and the subject had to identify the standard. In the generalization experiment, a stimulus pair was presented on each trial which could be either two standards (S_{00}), two comparison patterns (S_{jj}), or a standard-comparison pair as in the discrimination condition $(S_{0j}$ or $S_{j0})$. The subject's response was always *same* or *different*. In addition, asymmetric pay-offs were introduced explicitly. Three pay-off conditions were investigated, with different degrees of emphasis upon the importance of misses according to the following pay-off matrix:

$$
\text{Stimulus pair:} \quad
\begin{array}{c}
S_s(S_{00} \text{ or } S_{jj}) \\
S_d(S_{0j} \text{ or } S_{j0})
\end{array}
\overset{\displaystyle\text{Response}}{
\overset{\displaystyle same \qquad\qquad different}{
\left[
\begin{array}{cc}
0 & -1, -5, \text{ or } -10 \\
-1 & 0
\end{array}
\right]
}}
$$

Thus calling a "same" stimulus *different* cost subjects one point in one condition, 5 points in the second condition, and 10 points in the third condition. Otherwise pay-offs were the same. Subjects did not actually lose money in this experiment but were merely given "negative points."

The results of the experiment are shown in Fig. 6.4. In the upper part of the figure the probability of the *same* response is shown as a function of stimulus conditions and pay-offs. It is clear that emphasizing the importance of hits by making subjects lose more points when they miss a stimulus pair which was actually identical induced a bias towards saying *same*. On the other hand, the probability of saying *same* to a "same" stimulus pair was almost independent of stimulus discriminability, with the exception of one point (S_3 and pay-off 1). The lower part of Fig. 6.4 shows the probability of a *same* response when the two stimuli are actually different, and it is therefore a plot of generalization gradients, or rather the upper half of the gradients. Again the bias for saying *same* induced by the asymmetric pay-off is very noticeable, but equally apparent is a strong tendency towards fewer *same* responses with increasing stimulus differences, which is characteristic of generalization gradients in general. Also included is the discrimination performance for the same stimulus pairs. A comparison between generalization and discrimination performance is quite instructive; obviously discrimination was superior to generalization, and furthermore, the more asymmetric the pay-off for generalization responses, the more accentuated the difference between the two conditions became. For instance, if misses in a generalization experiment were punished by ten points, subjects made generalization responses 50% of the time to a stimulus of 12 lights when the standard stimulus contained only 9 lights. At the same time confusion errors with a discrimination procedure were only 5% for the identical stimulus pair. Thus, the finding that generalization occurs readily where discrimination is almost perfect is replicated here, and the importance of response biases for this phenomenon has been demonstrated.

Although Fig. 6.4 suggests that response bias may be a source of many apparent differences between generalization and discrimination, we have not yet proven that this factor alone can account for all of the observed differences. In fact, such a proof can only be attempted when we are willing to assume a specific model for both the subject's discriminative processes and for his decision strategies. The

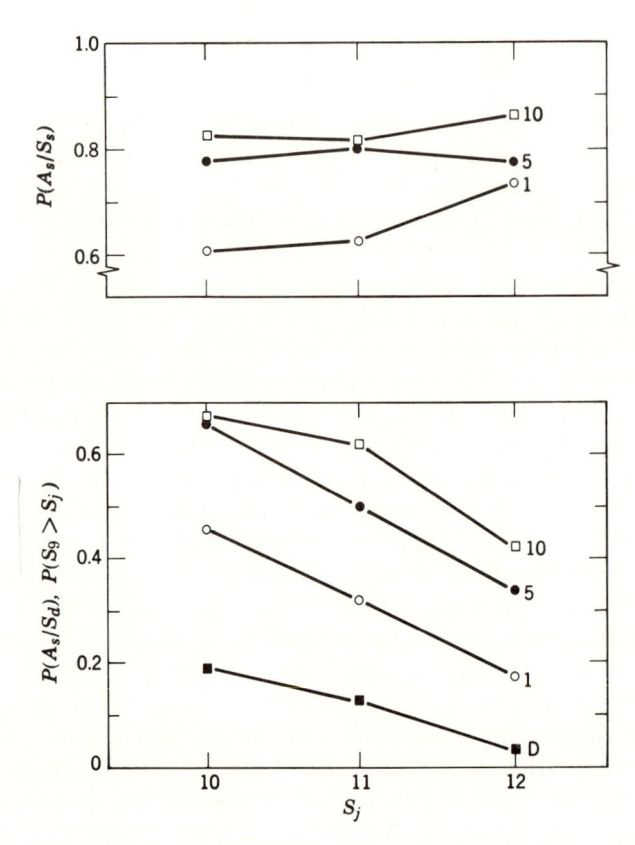

Fig. 6.4 *Observed proportion of* A_s *responses. Upper plot is based upon* S_s *trials, lower plot on* S_d *trials. The D curve in the lower plot is based upon the proportion of times* S_9 *was judged greater than* S_j *for j=10, 11,12. The three payoff conditions are indicated by 1, 5, and 10. The abscissa in each plot indicates the number of lights in the larger pattern. (after Zinnes and Kurtz, 1968)*

question is simply this: Can the data in Fig. 6.4 be accounted for quantitatively by a theory with a common mechanism for both generalization and discrimination but which permits differences in response strategies to operate in the two cases? Obviously this question is meaningful only within the framework of a formal model. But what is such a model to look like? At this stage of ignorance it seems best to explore several of the more reasonable candidates for a model, trying to get an idea about the performance of alternative schemes, rather than relying entirely upon one particular model. We shall start with two models using some ideas from signal detection theory.

A Thurstonian Model for Discrimination

Assume that the sensory representation of a stimulus is probabilistic. To each stimulus S there corresponds a probability distribution of sensory events, which Thurstone (1927) called discriminal dispersion. In particular, assume that the standard stimulus S_0 when presented repeatedly gives rise to sensory values x_0, which are normally distributed with mean 0 and standard deviation 1, as shown in Fig. 6.5(a). Correspondingly, the comparison stimulus S_j is represented by a distribution of x_j values which are independent of the x_0's and normal with mean d_j and standard deviation 1. On each discrimination trial the subject makes two observations, one of them corresponding to S_0 and one of them corresponding to S_j. His task is to identify the standard stimulus. Obviously the most reasonable decision rule in this situation is to say that the observation which produced the smaller x-value corresponds to S_0. Most of the time the x_0 will be smaller than the x_j, as Fig. 6.5(a) shows, and hence a correct response will be made. However, it is possible that merely by chance $x_0 > x_j$. In this case the subject will make an error. From Fig. 6.5(a) it is apparent that the smaller d_j, the greater the likelihood of an error. If we let $\phi(x;m,s)$ denote the normal density function with mean m and standard deviation s, and let $\Phi(x;m,s)$ be the corresponding cumulative probability function,

$$\Phi(x;m,s) = \int_{-\infty}^{x} \phi(x;m,s)\,dx$$

we have for the probability of an error in condition j

(1) $$Pr(x_0 > x_j) = \int_{-\infty}^{\infty} \phi(x;0,1)\,\Phi(x;d_j,1)\,dx$$

Equation (1) is to be interpreted as follows: $\Phi(x;d_j,1)$ is the probability of obtaining an x_j-value less than x, which is then weighted by the probability that the standard stimulus produces a sensory representation x_0 of magnitude x. Tables for Eq. (1) may be found in Elliott (1964). From these tables one can immediately read off the value of d_j which corresponds to any observed error rate in a two-alternative forced-choice discrimination experiment.

Thurstonian Models for Generalization

There are various possibilities for the formulation of a Thurstonian model for *same* and *different* judgments. First, rememmber the experimental task: the subject is shown two stimulus patterns successively, and has to judge whether they were the same or different. The stimulus pairs fall into two classes: same (S_{00} and S_{jj}) and different (S_{0j} and S_{j0}). We shall first assume that the subject responds to the size of the difference between the sensory representations of the two stimuli (see also Sorkin, 1962). If this difference is larger than some critical value c_k, which will be in part determined by the pay-off conditions which are in effect, the subject judges a stimulus pair as different; if this difference is below criterion, he says *same*. Figure 6.5(b)

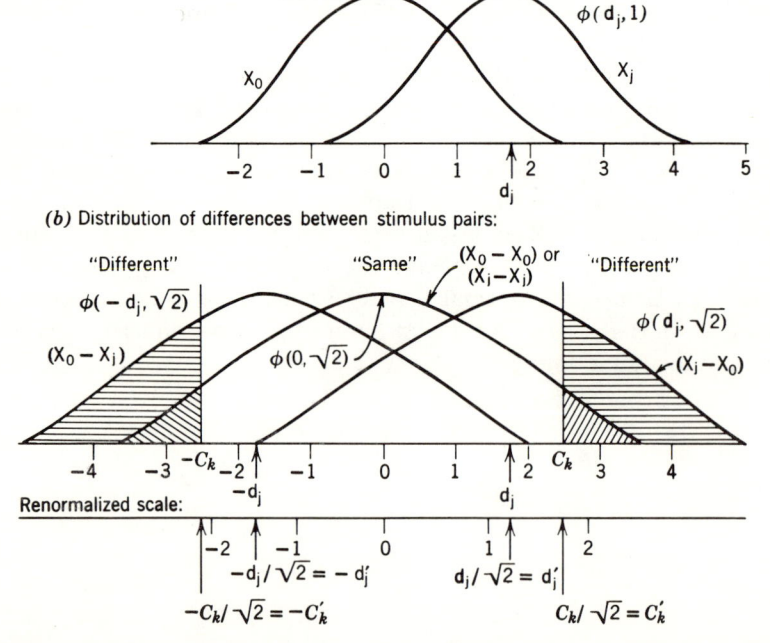

Fig. 6.5 *A Thurstonian model for discrimination and generalization.*

shows the distribution of the differences for both same and different pairs. Denoting responses by A and stimuli by S, and letting s stand for same and d for different, we have from Fig. 6.5(b) for the probability of saying *same* to a "same" stimulus pair

$$(2) \qquad Pr(A_s\, S_s) = \int_{-c_k}^{c_k} \phi(x;0,\sqrt{2})\,dx$$

The standard deviation of the distribution of the differences follows from a well-known statistical theorem which says that the variance of the difference between two independent random variables equals the sum of the variances. Next we shall transform all scores into standard scores (which is done by subtracting the mean of the distribution—0 in the case of the "same" distribution, d_j in case of the "different" distribution—and dividing by the standard deviation) and express Eq. (2) in terms of cumulative probability functions. The appropriate relationships may be read directly from Fig. 6.5(b):

$$(3) \qquad Pr(A_s\, S_s) = \phi(c_k/\sqrt{2}) - \phi(-c_k/\sqrt{2})$$

Note that nowhere in Eq. (3) does the term d_j appear. Hence the difference model predicts that the probability of *same* responses when the stimuli are actually identical is independent of discriminability. The data in Fig. 6.4 are not completely clear on this point. For pay-off conditions 5 and 10 $Pr(A_s\, S_s)$ was indeed independent of the particular stimulus used, but for pay-off condition 1 performance was better with the 12-light comparison than with the other two. Since all points in Fig. 6.4 are based upon more than 1000 observations, practically all differences between points are statistically significant, so that the deviations observed here can hardly be attributed to chance fluctuations.

The probability of saying *same* when a stimulus pair is actually different can also be read from Fig. 6.5(b). Using the same kind of notation as above we obtain (because of the symmetry of the figure)

$$(4) \qquad Pr(A_s|S_d) = \int_{-c_k}^{c_k} \phi(x;d_j,\sqrt{2})\,dx$$

$$= \Phi(c_k - d_j/\sqrt{2}) - \Phi(-c_k - d_j/\sqrt{2})$$

The three equations (1), (3), and (4) may be used to predict the data of the 9 generalization groups and the three discrimination groups in the Zinnes and Kurtz experiment. In order to do this 6 parameters must be estimated: d_1', d_2', and d_3' for each of the stimulus conditions S_1, S_2, and S_3, and three values c_1, c_2, and c_3 for each of the three pay-off conditions used in the experiment. However, we do not estimate parameters separately for the discrimination and generalization conditions, since we want to test the hypothesis that these conditions differ only in response strategies but are otherwise dependent upon the same processes. The parameter values which provided the best fit to the data as measured by a chi-square test were obtained by means of a computer search, and predictions using these values were calculated. The predictions fitted the data quite well, with the exception of the one deviant point already mentioned.

Although the difference model seems reasonable and, what is more, fits the data quite well, alternative theories must be explored. For instance, instead of assuming that the subject responds to the difference between stimuli, it is just as reasonable to assume that the subject classifies each stimulus as S_o or S_j and responds *same* or *different* depending upon whether or not the two stimuli on a trial were put into the same category. It turns out that this classification model is not nearly as adequate as the difference model discussed earlier. The minimum chi square is over twice as large for the classification model than for the earlier model, and it does not adequately predict the apparent independence of $Pr(A_s \mid S_s)$ from the size of the comparison stimulus which was observed for at least two of the pay-off conditions in Fig. 6.4.

In the models just discussed the sensory representation of a stimulus was continuous. A model which separates the stimulus and decision aspects of a discrimination task can also be obtained when a discrete representation of the stimulus is postulated. Suppose that corresponding to the two stimuli S_0 and S_j there are two perceptual states D_0 and D_j. Each stimulus is perceived correctly (it produces its corresponding perceptual state) with some probability p; with probability $1 - p$ a stimulus is misperceived (i.e., the stimulus S_0 produces the sensory state D_j, or S_j produces D_o). Further, we assume that subjects have response biases, so that their overt responses do not necessarily correspond to their perceptual states. Such a model is called a low-threshold model. It has been proposed by Luce (1963a) and has been applied extensively to psychophysical detection problems. The extension of Luce's model to the present problem is quite straightforward. However, Zinnes and Kurtz have shown that the low-threshold model does not fit their data very well. In fact, it is substantially poorer than either one of the previous models. The main problem is that the model cannot describe the discrimination data in Fig. 6.4 adequately. However, modifications of the model are possible which improve its fit.

A single instance of good (or poor) fit of a model is not very important. It is important, however, that one is aware of the range of possibilities which exist for theories of discrimination and generalization. The first of the theories discussed here (continuous representation of the stimulus together with a difference criterion) was most successful in providing an explanation for the Zinnes and Kurtz data. However, much more research is needed before the other alternatives, or modifications thereof, can be discarded. At this point we can hardly do more than provide reasonable working hypotheses to guide further investigations.

The problem is not so much whether one particular model is right and another model not, but rather whether we can account quantitatively for the results of generalization and discrimination experiments on the assumption that generalization and discrimination are inversely related and are like the two sides of the same coin, and that apparent discrepancies are merely the result of response biases. As far as this question goes, the answer seems to be "yes"; at least one of the quantitative formulations which have been tried above gave a good account of both the discrimination and generalization data from the Zinnes and Kurtz (1968) experiment, and other experiments, which cannot be analyzed formally, are at least qualitatively in agreement with this conclusion (e.g., Brown *et al.*, 1951). However, not too many suitable experimental studies are available. For example, all the generalization experiments using the galvanic skin response (GSR) as a dependent variable are inappropriate for present purposes (e.g., Hovland, 1937). If the GSR is conditioned to a stimulus (such as a 1000 cps tone) with shock as an unconditioned stimulus, and generalization is tested by presenting tones of different frequency on trials on which no shock is given, the GSR which occurs as an integral part of the orienting response to new stimuli (e.g., Sokolov, 1963) is confounded with the generalization effects.

2. THE ROLE OF STIMULUS CODING

The experiments on discrimination and generalization which have been discussed so far have without exception used very simple stimulus materials, such as rows of lights, random patterns of lights, or color chips differing in saturation and brightness. Performance in these experiments could be accounted for in terms of a perceptual process which is tied directly to the physical stimulus and which is modified by response biases. However, the usefulness of this approach is severely limited because with anything but the simplest stimulus materials discrimination performance does not directly depend upon the physical stimulus, but upon the way in which the subject has coded this stimulus. Many characteristics of learning and performance in discrimination experiments are consequences of this coding process.

The objective, physical stimulus which is directly under the control of the experimenter must be clearly distinguished from the stimulus which is actually effective for the subject. The first is the same for all observers; it is part of what we call the real world. Koffka (1935) called it the distal stimulus; Underwood's term for it is nominal stimulus (Underwood, 1963). The distal stimulus affects the organism through a series of transformations. For instance, the visual information about a distal object is first transformed into a pattern of light waves (Koffka's proximal stimulus), then into a retinal firing pattern, and finally into patterns of neural excitation which have a most complex relationship to the distal stimulus. Thus, the effective, functional stimulus is the product of many transformations, some of which may be deterministic and one-to-one, while others are subjective in the sense that they depend upon the momentary state of the perceiving subject; some transformations may be probabalistic and some may destroy or distort the original information, or add to it from memory. More concretely, when the experimenter presents three small green circles as the positive stimulus in a discrimination learning experiment the functional stimulus will generally not be "three small green circles," but some coded version thereof. Some obvious possibilities in the present case would be "green," or "green circles" or other such selective responses, but some subjects may employ a purely idiosyncratic code. Such codes may be verbal, but need not be.

Thus subjects do not discriminate distal objects directly, but the coded representations which they have constructed. Information in the distal stimulus which is not used in coding is lost, as far as the subject is concerned. Therefore, whenever a subject's coding response distorts the distal stimulus, attempts to explain discrimination learning solely in terms of the properties of the distal stimulus are misdirected. Excepting the few cases in which the stimulus material (and the experimental conditions) are such that the subject's coding responses mirror the relevant physical properties, the mediating role of coding responses in discrimination learning must be explicitly considered. Indeed, the main problem in discrimination learning and concept learning lies in the acquisition of appropriate coding responses which permit the necessary distinctions to be made.

In the previous section the effects of differential pay-off conditions or instructions upon discrimination and generalization were discussed. In the present section variables which influence the subject's perception of the stimuli will be considered. First, some experiments will be described which demonstrate the effects of verbal labeling in generalization experiments. Next, the role of coding processes in discrimination learning will be examined by means of three widely different examples: a classical experiment by Lawrence with rats which initiated the present concern with coding processes in discrimination learning; studies concerning the effects of shifts in simple concept identification experiments; and an experiment on the discrimination of letter-like stimuli. All these studies can only be understood if the mediating role of coding responses is taken into account. Finally, the question of how coding responses affect the relationship between discrimination and generalization data will be taken up. Depending upon the task characteristics coding processes may have essentially parallel effects upon generalization and discrimination, or quite different coding strategies may be used in generalization and discrimination experiments, thus making it impossible to predict one from the other.

In a series of studies Thomas (Thomas and DeCapito, 1966; Doll and Thomas, 1967) has shown that the concept of primary generalization, as Hull had used it, can hardly be applied to experiments with human subjects. Generalization depends upon the subject's coding responses, so that one is dealing with secondary or mediated generalization rather than primary generalization. Experiments have already been discussed in which subjects were shown a color and were then tested for generalization along the color dimension (e.g., Kalish, 1958). The results of these studies have sometimes been taken as indicating primary generalization gradients which were directly related to the physical stimulus continuum (wave length). However, even in this simple experimental situation the subject's coding processes cannot be disregarded, as Thomas and DeCapito (1966) have demonstrated. Like Kalish, they showed their subjects a color of a certain wave length and then tested for generalization by instructing them to lift a finger whenever the original color was shown, but not to react when a different color was shown. For one group of subjects the standard stimulus was a color of 490 mμ, which is a hue somewhere between blue and green. One third of the subjects were given the label "green" with the color, one third were given the label "blue," and the last third of the subjects served as a control group without labels. On the generalization test the first group of subjects responded more to higher wave lengths (greener colors), the second group to shorter wave lengths (bluer colors) and the control group was intermediate.

The same kind of confounding of generalization gradients via labeling was obtained when a different standard stimulus was used (548 mμ with labels "orange" and "yellow").

Another experiment which demonstrates the influence of coding via verbal labels upon discrimination performance was reported by Doll and Thomas (1967). Using the same procedure as in the experiment just discussed, these authors determined generalization gradients around a light of 530 mμ by the usual procedure of generalization trials without information feedback to the subject. However, some subjects received discrimination training before the generalization test with 530 mμ as the S^+ and either 540, 550, or 590 mμ as S^-. The results of this experiment, which are shown in Fig. 6.6, are quite interesting. First of all, note the flat generalization gradient after discrimination training with an S^- of 590 mμ. It appears that learning this discrimination induced the subject to form a very broad equivalence class: 530 mμ is green and 590 is orange, and hence the subject never learned to make fine discriminations in the neighborhood of 530 mμ. Now consider the subjects who were trained with an S^- of 540 or 550 mμ. In agreement with earlier results, and results from the animal literature reported in connection with Spence's theory of discrimination learning, these subjects show a peak-shift: the point

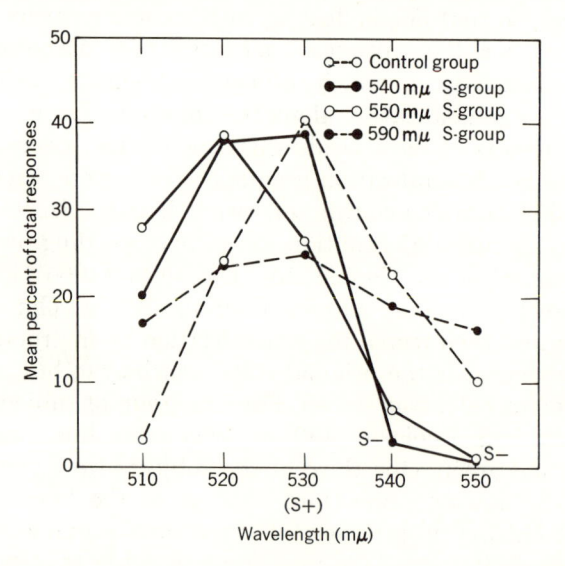

Fig. 6.6 *Mean generalization gradients for four groups of subjects which differ in the nature of previous discrimination training. (after Doll and Thomas, 1967)*

of maximum responding is moved away from the S^+ to the side opposite the S^-. However, unlike the animal data, the peak-shift is larger when the S^- was at 550 mμ than when it was closer to the S^+ at 540 mμ. The interpretation of this puzzling finding lies probably in the way subjects labeled the stimuli: 530 mμ and 540 mμ are so similar that subjects may not have used differential labels, so that the effects of the S^- were diminished.

The point of these two experiments is that even apparently simple generalization studies cannot be understood unless one is aware of the role of coding processes. The same is true of discrimination learning experiments. Convincing evidence for this assertion comes from transfer studies. First the pioneering experiment by Lawrence (1949) which was mentioned above will be described, and then we shall turn to similar experiments in human concept and discrimination learning.

Lawrence demonstrated that a good part of the difficulty in a discrimination task lies in finding the right cues to respond to. He first taught three groups of rats a simultaneous discrimination problem involving either a black-white discrimination, a discrimination between rough and smooth floors, or a discrimination between narrow and wide alleys. Then all rats learned a new discrimination problem, namely to choose one arm of a black T-maze, but to choose the other arm if the maze was white. T-mazes with both rough and smooth floors were used, but this cue was not correlated with reward. For the group trained initially on the black-white discrimination this task proved to be quite easy. Color-cues were relevant in both tasks, and therefore these subjects started the second problem with the appropriate coding responses. The problem was much more difficult for the other two groups of subjects, who at the start of the second learning task were making either inappropriate coding responses (smooth and rough floors) or were trained with an irrelevant problem (alley width no longer varied in the second problem). Since these two groups learned about equally slowly, the main difficulty seems to have been to establish the response to the color cue, which had been extinguished in the first training problem for at least some of the subjects, rather than in abandoning the inappropriate coding of the stimulus in terms of rough or smooth floors.

Similar results are obtained in studies of human concept formation (e.g., Kendler and Kendler, 1962). The learning materials in such experiments are usually drawings of simple figures, which may vary along such dimensions as shape (circle, square, and the like) or color, size, number, etc. Assuming binary dimensions the simplest kind of concept which can be defined with this stimulus material is of the form "All red cards belong to class A, all green cards belong to class B." In this case, color is called the relevant dimension, and shape, size, and numerosity are irrelevant dimensions. Once such a concept has been learned, as evidenced by a large number of correct classifications, the experimenter may change the basis of classification and begin reinforcing the subject according to a new scheme. Two kinds of changes must be distinguished: in a reversal response assignments are simply switched (red is B and green is A), but color remains the relevant dimension; in an extradimensional shift a new dimension is made relevant (e.g., large is A and small is B).

Consider a theory of discrimination learning which, like Spence's theory, assumes that during training habit strength is being built up to the S^+ while inhibition develops to the S^-. Reversal should be a much harder task to learn than an extradimensional shift according to such a theory. If an extradimensional shift involves stimulus values which are sufficiently dissimilar from the original training stimuli, few generalized response tendencies will have been formed during training and therefore interference from inappropriate responses during the learning of the shift problem should be a less serious problem than in a reversal. The results of many experiments, some of which are summarized in Kendler and Kendler (1962), indicate exactly the opposite: reversal shifts are easy to learn for adult human subjects, but extradimensional shifts may be very hard to learn. Apparently we are dealing here with the same kind of phenomenon as in the Lawrence (1949) experiment which has just been reviewed. Subjects learn a particular way to code a stimulus and base their response upon the coded stimulus. When the experimenter reverses the response assignments, the coding response of the subject remains appropriate, and all the subject has to learn is to switch responses. In an extradimensional shift, on the other hand, the problem is greatly more complicated. The old coding response is now irrelevant. The subject must learn to abandon it and to acquire a new coding response. Sometimes the now-correct coding response may have already been tried during the first learning stage. Since it was inadequate then it may have become extinguished, so that the likelihood that this coding response will be evoked after a shift may be quite small.

The theoretical alternatives at this point are between theories in which there is a direct connection between the discriminative stimulus and the response and theories in which some process which is partly under the control of the subject intervenes. Various investigators have used the terms coding response, mediating response, or attention for this intervening process. A discussion of the relative merits of these terms can be deferred until the need for some such term has been unequivocally established.

Predictions from theories which assume direct connections between stimuli and responses for reversal and extradimensional shifts are complicated by the fact that the old response receives partial reinforcement after an extradimensional shift: although *red-A* is no longer correct after a shift to *small-A*, some *small* items will be *red*, and thus the subject's responses will sometimes be reinforced even though they are based upon incorrect coding responses. It is well known that partial reinforcement retards extinction, and it is possible that the poorer performance after an extradimensional shift is due to this factor rather than to the need of finding a new coding response (Buss, 1953). It was a very difficult methodological problem to design experiments in which an extradimensional shift was not confounded with partial reinforcement, without introducing some other confounding factor. However, several experimenters eventually managed to show that the superiority of reversal over nonreversal performance is retained when partial reinforcement effects are eliminated (e.g., Harrow and Friedman, 1958).

The coding responses which are employed in the simple concept formation experiments under discussion are predominantly verbal. This is implied by a series of informative developmental studies. Both rats and nursery school children find a nonreversal shift easier than a reversal shift (Kelleher, 1956; Kendler, Kendler, and Wells, 1960). Kindergarten children have about equal difficulty with reversal and nonreversal shifts (Kendler and Kendler, 1959), and college students can handle reversal problems with great ease. The more verbal an organism becomes, the easier it becomes for him to execute a reversal shift, presumably because he codes the stimulus material verbally. Kendler and Kendler (1962) have some fairly direct evidence for the importance of verbalization in explaining the developmental results. They made 4-year old children verbalize aloud all stimuli in a concept identification experiment. One group of subjects was asked to tell the experimenter which was correct, the "large" one or the "small" one of a stimulus pair. Another group of subjects learned to say "black" or "white" in a similar way, and a control group was not required to say anything. When the cue which subjects were trained to verbalize was the relevant cue, performance was best. When an irrelevant cue was verbalized, the mean number of errors to criterion was about twice as high. The control group performed at an intermediate level. Obviously verbalization strongly influenced concept learning. The same experiment was also performed with 7-year-old children, but with somewhat different results. The interfering effect of irrelevant verbalizations was even more powerful than before, but no facilitative effect of verbalizing the relevant cue was found this time. Presumably 7-year-olds are capable of making the relevant verbal coding responses themselves, and outside help is of little importance to them.

One must not conclude from these examples that all coding responses are verbal. Verbal coding responses are certainly important, but coding responses may be of a much more general nature and need be neither verbal nor conscious. The concept of coding responses is needed to explain the results of many animal discrimination learning experiments as well (e.g., Lawrence, 1949; Sutherland, 1959). Although rats have more difficulty with a reversal shift than with a nonreversal shift, previous experience with reversal shifts leads to a marked improvement in their ability to execute reversal shifts in a T-maze (Krechevsky, 1932; Dufort, Guttman, and Kimble, 1954). A similar improvement over successive reversals has been demonstrated by Harlow (1949) for monkeys. Harlow's monkeys were given a choice between two stimulus objects differing either in size, color, or shape. The monkeys learned discriminations such as "the banana is under the barrel-shaped object." Over 300 such problems were learned in succession. The performance of the monkeys improved greatly from problem to problem. For the last 100 problems the monkeys chose almost always correctly after only one learning trial. Harlow described this improvement in the ability to learn as learning-to-learn. Using the present terminology one would say that the monkeys acquired appropriate coding responses which permitted them to disregard irrelevant cues (e.g., cues associated with spatial position) and to respond quickly to changes in the correlation between the relevant cue and reinforcement.

Another significant characteristic of coding responses in discrimination experiments is that coding responses are in general not a sensitization to particular stimulus values but refer to broad classes of cues which have some common discriminative property, i.e., to attributes or stimulus dimensions. Shape, color, and size, as well as other such simple attributes, are normally used in concept formation experiments. However, attributes are not necessarily restricted to variations in a single modality (Lawrence cites as a pleasant example the dryness of a wine), nor is it necessary that there be a correlation with some physical dimension (e.g., friendliness). Simple attributes like size are used merely because they are easy to control experimentally, not because they have a status of logical priority.

An experiment which demonstrated that coding responses are not specific to particular stimulus values (*red, green*), but refer to attributes (*color*) has been reported by Johnson (1967). Johnson compared extradimensional shift and reversal shift with an intradimensional shift. In order to achieve this, Johnson used stimulus cards which consisted of two figures, each varying in four dimensions, two of which, color and form, were four-valued. One figure on each stimulus card was either red or green, the other yellow or blue. After learning the original problem (red vs. green), subjects were divided into three subgroups. One group received a reversal shift (green vs. red), one group received an intradimensional shift (yellow vs. blue), and the third group was shifted to a new dimension (square vs. triangle). As in other studies, the extradimensional shift was much harder to learn than the reversal shift. However, there was no significant difference in learning the reversal and the intradimensional shift. Johnson's interpretation of these findings is that in both cases subjects could retain their coding responses (which therefore must have been something like "pay attention to color") and merely had to change the coding stimulus—overt-response connection. The reason for using two figures on each card in this study was that this permitted an intradimensional shift without suddenly introducing completely new stimulus values. If this precaution is not observed, novelty effects may distort shift performance, as they had in several previous studies of intradimensional shifts.

The experiments discussed so far were either animal experiments or simple concept identification experiments. However, as far as the importance of coding processes is concerned very much the same results are obtained in other types of discrimination experiments. An interesting study of what is learned when children are taught to discriminate letter-like stimuli shall serve as a final example. The study has been reported by Pick (1965).

Pick employed a transfer design in which subjects were first trained to discriminate a set of letter-like stimuli from a second set of items which were obtained by transformation of the standard items. Among the transformations used were such operations as changing lines into curves, right-left reversal, or size transformations. In the second stage of her experiment, subjects (kindergarten children) were given a new discrimination task. In the Experimental Group I the same set of standard items was used as before, but the transformations which generated the distractor items were changed. Thus, if the children had learned particular stimulus values during Stage 1 strong positive transfer would be expected. The subjects in Experimental Group II were given new standards, but the same transformations which were employed in Stage 1 were retained to produce distractor items. Thus, if the children had discovered how the forms differed in Stage 1, positive transfer would result. Finally, Pick used a control group which received both new standards and new transformations during the second stage of the experiment. Her results are shown in Table 6.1. Subjects made the fewest errors in Stage 2 when the dimensions of difference were the same in both parts of the experiment ($E2$). However, subjects who had to learn new coding responses to familiar standards ($E1$) still outperformed the group given both new standards and new transformations to learn (C). Therefore, one may conclude that coding is mostly a matter of discovering relevant dimensions of difference, although the superior performance of Group $E1$ over the control subjects shows that some coding was specific to particular letter shapes.

Coding and the Relationships Between Discrimination and Generalization

What happens to the complementary relationship between generalization and discrimination results, if coding processes are effective? We have already seen how this relationship may be modified through differential pay-off, and it would seem likely that the manner in which the subject responds to the stimulus might have similar effects. This is indeed true; in some cases subjects code the stimulus in the same way in generalization and discrimination experiments, so that it is possible to predict performance on one quite well from performance on the other; in other cases, the demands of the task are

Table 6.1. *Number of errors made in transfer stage by groups with three types of training (after Gibson, 1965).*

Group	Type of Training		Errors
	Standard	transformation	
$E1$	Same	Different	69
$E2$	Different	Same	39
C	Different	Different	101

such that different coding strategies are employed in discrimination and generalization experiments, which may produce completely dissimilar results in the two kinds of experiments. First some particularly spectacular examples from speech perception will be described in which the parallelism between generalization and discrimination results is preserved in spite of stimulus coding.

Consider the way people code the acoustic stimulus in speech perception. Speech perception is categorical, i.e., within a rather wide range acoustic stimuli are all assigned to the same response class and heard as the same phoneme. Stimuli within such equivalence classes are not discriminated even though relatively large differences in the physical stimuli may exist. On the other hand, physical differences of very small magnitude are discriminated if they separate two stimuli which belong to different classes, as has been convincingly demonstrated by Liberman, Harris, Kinney, and Lane (1961). Liberman *et al.* have synthesized speech stimuli which varied continuously from /do/ to /to/. In Part I of their experiment they obtained the identification functions shown in Fig. 6.7. Each stimulus was presented separately and the subject was asked to identify it as either /do/ or /to/. Note that although the physical stimulus varied in small steps, the subjects responded in an all-or-none fashion. Each stimulus was assigned to one of the two phonemes /d/ or /t/, with few exceptions. There certainly was no gradual change in response probabilities corresponding to the gradual changes in the acoustic stimuli. In Part II of the experiment discrimination functions were obtained. The method employed was the ABX procedure in which a stimulus pair is presented and followed by a test stimulus which is identical to either the first or the second member of the pair. Failure to discriminate with this procedure results in 50% choices. The functions shown in Fig. 6.7 show that subjects could not discriminate between stimuli in the same response class, but that they did very well with stimuli which belonged to different response classes. Predictions from a model which simply assumes that subjects discriminate only when the two stimuli are assigned to different classes work very well, as is shown by the broken lines in Fig. 6.7. Cross and Lane (1962) have recorded response latencies in the same experimental situation. They found that responses were made with short latencies when both stimuli belonged to the same class. If, however, the stimulus pair was so constructed that it crossed class boundaries response latencies were significantly lengthened. It appears therefore that subjects encoded the stimuli used in this experiment as either /do/ or /to/. The exact physical properties of the stimuli were unimportant and were, in fact,

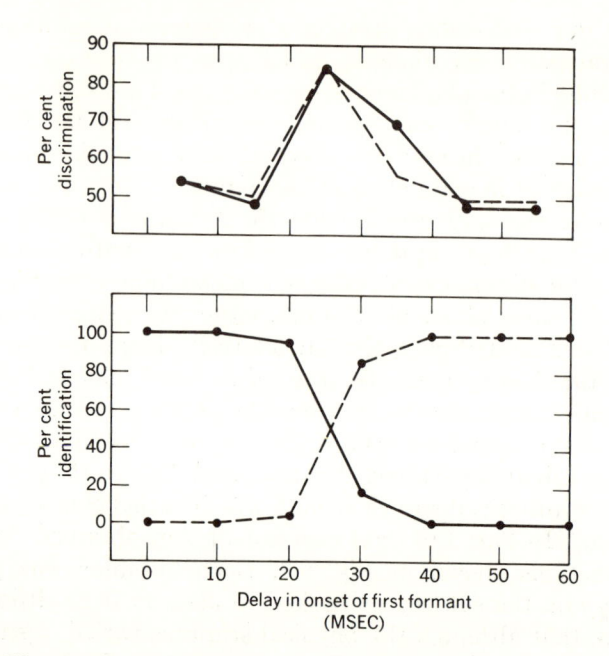

Fig. 6.7 *Observed distribution of discrimination and identification responses for the /do/-/to/ continuum in the experiment of Liberman* et al. *(1961). (after Lane, 1967)*

not perceived. Subjects were sensitive to physical properties only at phoneme boundaries.

The results shown in Fig. 6.7 and similar results obtained in other experiments form the basis for the motor theory of speech perception, which holds that speech sounds are encoded in terms of the articulatory processes which are used to generate them. One particular articulatory movement corresponds to a phoneme, but it produces a wide range of acoustic stimuli. However, this variability in the acoustic stimulus is not perceived, because the articulatory movement is used as a coding or mediating response.

Speech perception, of course, involves enormously overlearned coding responses. However, Lane (1965, 1967) has shown that rather similar coding responses can be taught in the laboratory quite easily. In one experiment Lane (1965) distorted the acoustic stimuli used by Liberman *et al.* by inverting their spectogram so that they were no longer perceived as speech. Then Lane used the two stimuli on the end of the continuum in a discrimination learning paradigm: the distorted /do/ was paired with the response *do*, and the distorted /to/ was paired with the response *to*. Finally subjects were given identification tests and discrimination tests with the full range of stimuli as in the previous experiment. The results were very similar to those shown in Fig. 6.7. Identification was again categorical and discrimination was best at the category boundary. Predictions from the labeling model which assumes that discrimination only occurs when stimuli were given different labels were again fairly successful. Lane (1967) has also reported similar results with visual stimuli and nonverbal responses. In all cases the discrimination and generalization data were related as in Fig. 6.7.

The arbitrary nature of coding responses has been impressively demonstrated in an experiment on color labeling in different cultures by Kopp and Lane (1968). Kopp and Lane started from the well-known fact that different cultures have different ways of partitioning the color continuum, just as within the same culture a color name may come to denote different parts of the spectrum as a result of historical change. If people code a color in terms of its conventional name the ability of humans to discriminate among colors should be culturally dependent. Figure 6.8 shows the results of an experiment which was performed to test this hypothesis with two American and two Tzotzil speakers. Tzotzil is a Mayan language. Five English and four Tzotzil color names were used which partition the hue spectrum in rather different ways, as is shown in Fig. 6.8. However, for all speakers the identification responses showed the wide plateaus and sharp drops characteristic of categorical responding. Discrimination was good at the category boundaries and at chance level within categories. Predictions of the discrimination data from the identification results by the labeling hypothesis are not as good as in previous two-response experiments, but there is some qualitative agreement between predictions and data in that the peaks and valleys of the discrimination function are usually correctly predicted. The latency data also confirm earlier results, showing pronounced peaks at category boundaries. The most interesting result is of course that the color discrimination functions for English and Tzotzil speakers are quite different, and that these differences can be predicted from the way the color names are used in the two languages.

When stimulus materials vary along several relevant dimensions differential coding operations may destroy the correspondence between discrimination and generalization. In such cases subjects may select some aspect of the stimulus in generalization experiments, but

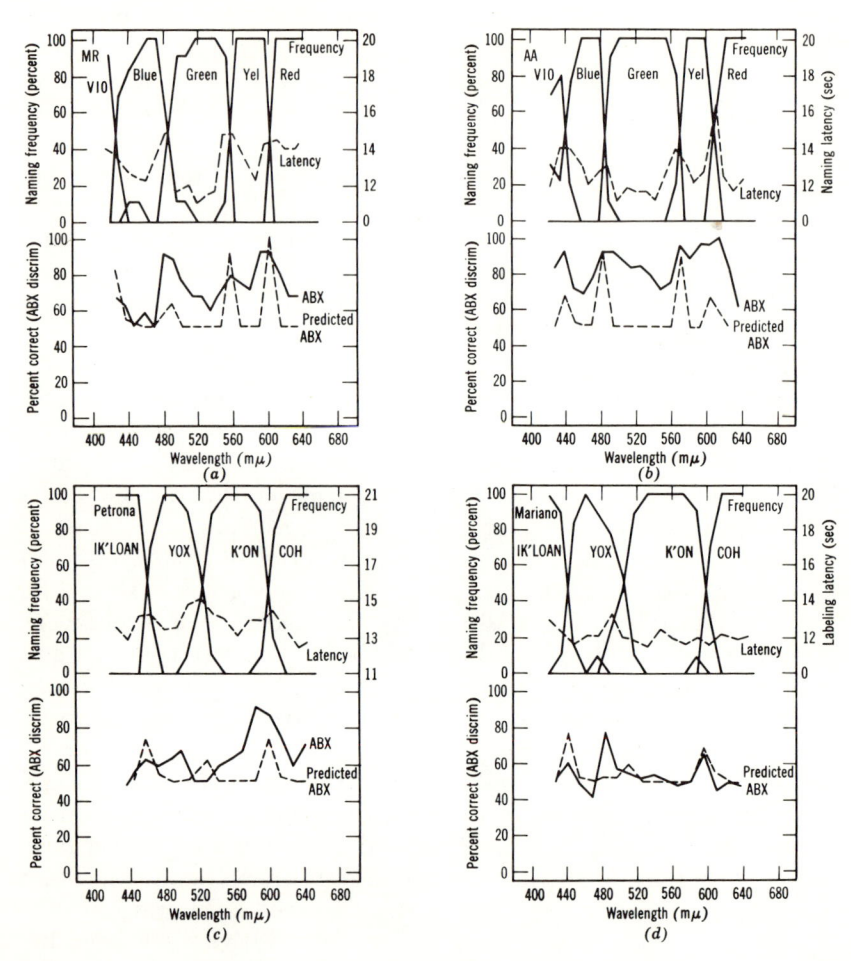

Fig. 6.8 *Identification probability, identification latency, and ABX discrimination measures as a function of wavelength for two English (MR and AA) and two Tzotzil (Petrona and Mariano) speakers. (after Kopp and Lane, 1968)*

may respond to a different aspect in discrimination experiments, so that it may no longer be possible to predict the discrimination data from generalization results as has been done above.

A study by Shepard, Hovland, and Jenkins (1961) illustrates this problem. The authors worked with sets of 8 pictorial stimuli which varied along three binary dimensions. In one part of their experiment they paired the 8 stimuli with 8 distinct responses and obtained the frequency with which each stimulus was confused with all other stimuli during paired-associate learning (generalization gradients). In the second part of the experiment the 8 stimuli were divided into two sets of 4 and subjects were taught the various classifications. There were 70 possible classifications, but not all of them needed to be examined separately, for they fall into 6 groups. The 6 different classifications were not all equally difficult to learn. Simple concepts such as "all triangles form one class, squares the other" were much easier to learn than other classifications for which the values of two or three stimulus dimensions jointly determined the class membership of an item. The ease of classification learning could not be predicted from the pairwise confusions during paired-associate learning. The relevant results are summarized in Fig. 6.9. Predictions were obtained by counting the average number of confusions made during identification learning for stimulus pairs which were assigned to different classes. From Fig. 6.9 it is obvious that these predictions were completely unsatisfactory. Too many errors were predicted for most classification conditions. During paired-associate learning the subject had to code each item individually; during classification learning he could get away with much simpler codes in many cases (e.g.,

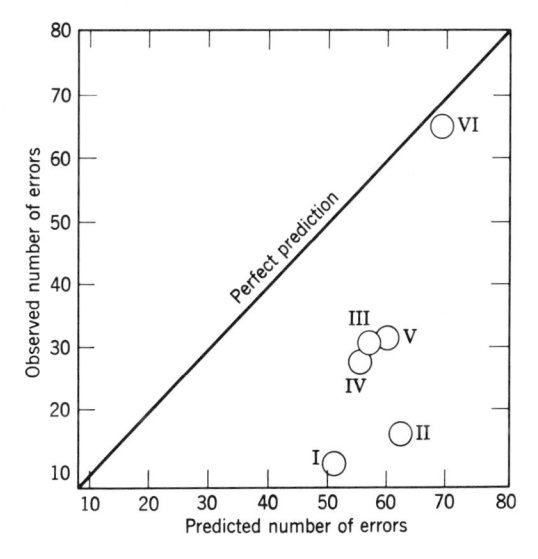

Fig. 6.9 *Mean number of errors made when each type of classification was learned for the first time, plotted against the number of errors predicted from identification learning. (after Shepard, Hovland, and Jenkins, 1961)*

classifications of the type "all triangles in one group", which is point I in Fig. 6.9). Thus, the match between discrimination and generalization data is destroyed. Contrast this result with Fig. 6.3 which reports data from a parallel experiment in which relatively unanalyzable stimulus materials were used, patches of color differing in saturation and brightness. There, the problem of differential coding was avoided, perhaps because language does not have enough expressions for small differences in saturation and brightness, and predictions of classification learning from identification data were quite successful.

3. MODELS OF DISCRIMINATION LEARNING

The various experimental results discussed in this chapter show two things very clearly: a model of discrimination learning must have some mechanism to deal with stimulus coding, and there must be some way to represent response biases due to differential pay-off conditions. Approaches to the latter problem have already been considered and we shall now describe efforts to deal with the problem of stimulus coding.

The idea that subjects code the stimuli in discrimination learning and respond on the basis of the stimulus-as-coded has been incorporated more or less explicitly in several theories of discrimination learning. Hull (1943) acknowledged the problem and tried to deal with it by postulating a mechanism of "afferent neural interaction." Guthrie (1959) insisted that "what is being noticed becomes a signal for what is being done." The ethologists (e.g., Tinbergen, 1951) have provided some beautiful demonstrations of the way in which coded stimuli control the behavior of animals in their natural environment. However, only in recent years has the central importance of coding processes in discrimination learning been fully recognized.

Orienting Responses

Historically, learning theory has had a strong bias for explanations which involve only directly observable events. Therefore the suggestion that coding is mainly a matter of orienting responses is not a surprising one. The subject may modify the proximal stimulus through orienting behavior and receptor adjustments. There can be no doubt that such behavior occurs and plays a significant role in discrimination learning. Watching a rat vacillate at the choice point of a T-maze, or a person looking back and forth between the stimuli in a simultaneous discrimination task is sufficient to demonstrate this point. On the other hand, orienting responses cannot possibly be the whole story: no overt receptor adjustment can explain how the pitch of a tone, rather than, say, its loudness can become a functional stimulus. The proximal stimulus is quite independent of the subject's orienting responses in this case, or in the case of tachistoscopically presented visual stimuli, and yet stimulus coding is observed.

Mediating Responses

Theories using the concept of a mediating response have been more successful. They avoid tying responses directly to the proximal stimulus by assuming that the proximal stimulus gives rise to a mediating response. The overt response is then connected with the covert stimulus consequences of this mediating response. Schematically, we have

$$S \rightarrow r \text{ - - - } s \rightarrow R.$$

The mediating responses transforms the nominal stimulus S into the functional stimulus s. Mediating responses are learned just as overt responses. A mediating response that is consistently reinforced because it produces a functional stimulus which is correlated with reward becomes dominant during training, i.e., it becomes associated with the proximal stimulus. When this stimulus is presented the mediating response is aroused and produces the appropriate functional stimulus. It is clear how such a theory can account for the experimental results described in the previous section. For instance, a reversal-shift is clearly less complicated than a shift to a new dimension:

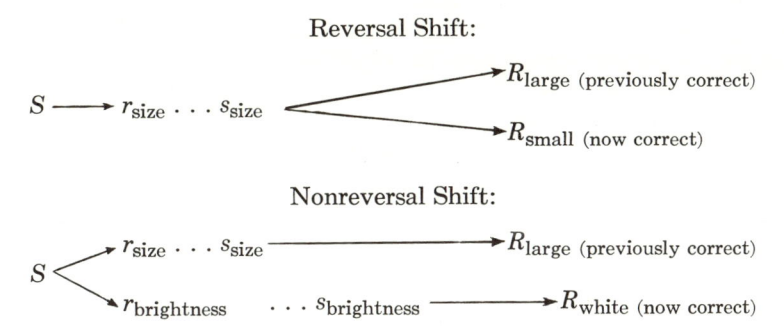

Reversal Shift:

$$S \longrightarrow r_{size} \cdots s_{size} \begin{cases} R_{large} \text{ (previously correct)} \\ R_{small} \text{ (now correct)} \end{cases}$$

Nonreversal Shift:

$$S \begin{cases} r_{size} \cdots s_{size} \longrightarrow R_{large} \text{ (previously correct)} \\ r_{brightness} \cdots s_{brightness} \longrightarrow R_{white} \text{ (now correct)} \end{cases}$$

The mediating response concept is related to stimulus coding. However, it is not as general as is required for the explanation of discrimination learning. The problem has been succinctly stated by Lawrence (1963). Mediating responses are the product of learning, and they are tied to the proximal stimulus so that, given that a certain mediating response has been acquired, a particular functional stimulus will always result until the mediating response is unlearned. It is difficult to understand the role played by sets, instructions, and attitudes within this framework. For instance, one can tell a subject (or one can teach him) to respond to the pitch of a tone and ignore its loudness. If one then instructs him to respond to loudness and ignore pitch, his behavior will change abruptly. Obviously, how a subject codes a stimulus is dependent upon such factors as set and instructions, and is not simply a function of a mediating response which is elicited by the stimulus itself.

The term mediating response carries with it the suggestion that the coding process is stimulus-determined, i.e., that a mediating response is elicited by the nominal stimulus and produces the functional stimulus. A term which stresses more the contribution of the state of the perceiver would be preferable. "Coding" seems to be the most suitable term. Several authors have suggested this term. For example, according to Lawrence (1963) a sensory input is transformed by coding operations into the stimulus-as-coded, or s-a-c. The s-a-c is a product of both the sensory input and organismic factors such as the conditioning state of the organism, the set, or the instructions given in the experiment. The s-a-c is then associated with overt behavior.

An Attention Model for Discrimination Learning

Several models of discrimination learning have been suggested which may be classified as attention theories: the subject pays attention to a particular aspect of the stimulus, i.e., he codes or analyzes the stimulus in a certain way. Which aspect he attends to depends upon such factors as instructions, previous experience, and the nature of the stimulus material. Sutherland (1959), Mackintosh (1965), and Lovejoy (1968) have worked out such models for animal discrimination learning. For human discrimination learning a model of this kind has been proposed by Zeaman and House (1963). The experimental task to which this model is applied is discrimination between geometric figures which vary along a number of well-defined dimensions, such as shape, color, and the like. The experimenter selects one dimension as relevant and reinforces responses according to the value of the relevant dimension. Thus it is a simple concept identification task. In describing this model the terminology of Zeaman and House has been slightly altered in order to relate it more closely to the present discussion, hopefully without doing violence to the intention of the authors.

Figure 6.10 outlines the model for the case of four binary stimulus dimensions with *Color* being the relevant dimension. Whenever an

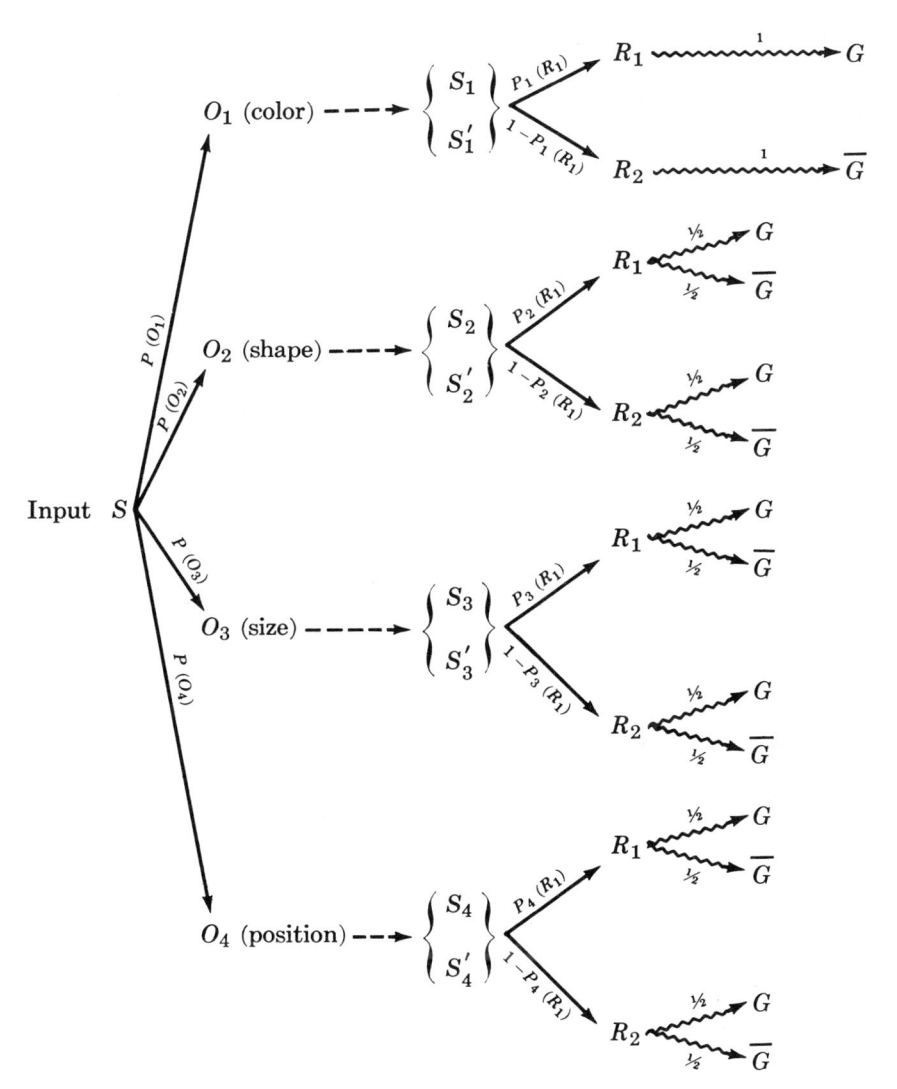

Fig. 6.10 *Outline of a model for discrimination learning. (after Zeaman and House, 1959)*

item is presented one of the four coding responses $O_i (i = 1,2,3,4)$ is elicited. Which one, depends upon previous experience, instructions, and the kind of stimulus material used in the experiment. A coding response produces the stimulus as coded s_i or s'_i, depending upon the value of the stimulus attribute. The stimulus as coded elicits the classification response R_1 with some probability $P(R_1)$. The effects of set or instructions can be represented within this framework as a bias for or against a particular coding response O_i. The effects of cue saliency can also be incorporated into the $P(O_i)$'s: dimensions which are very noticeable have high $P(O_i)$ values, dimensions which are less prominent have lower values. Finally, the model allows for the modification of both the coding responses and the overt classification responses as a function of experience. Whenever the response R_j based upon code i is reinforced, both $P_i(R_j)$ and $P(O_i)$ increase by a fraction θ, or θ' respectively, of the maximum possible increase. Whenever the response R_j is made and not reinforced, both probabilities decrease by a corresponding fraction. In other words, Zeaman and House assume that on each trial both $P(O_i)$ and $P_i(R_j)$ change as a function of reinforcement according to the "linear model." Note that if a subject makes an incorrect coding response the probability that his overt classification response will be reinforced will be $\frac{1}{2}$, no matter which response he makes if the stimulus items have been selected at random. This is like a probability learning situation with noncontingent reinforcement and $\pi = \frac{1}{2}$. We know from the results discussed in Chapter 3 that response probabilities will come to match reinforcement probabilities in such situations. Hence $P_i(R_j)$ for $i \neq 1$ should go to $\frac{1}{2}$ during training, no matter what the subject's initial biases may have been. Thus, subjects will respond with $P(R_1) = \frac{1}{2}$ as long as they persist in making incorrect coding responses. Once O_1 occurs, it will be consistently reinforced and $P(O_1)$ increases. Thus, the model predicts a sharp rise in the probability of correct responses after an initial period of responding at chance level.

A study of discrimination learning in retarded children provided the data which were used to test this model. Children were presented with a tray with two stimulus objects, drawings of the kind described above. One of the stimuli was baited with a piece of candy. For instance, the experimenter might have decided to put the piece of candy always under the red stimulus; drawings of a different color were never baited with candy. The retarded children had a very hard time with such problems, some taking over 100 trials to learn, thereby providing the experimenter with a great deal of information about presolution performance. In Fig. 6.11 backward learning curves are

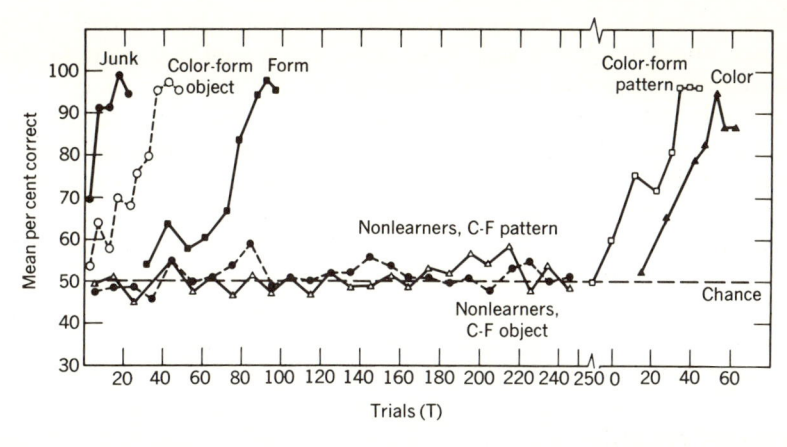

Fig. 6.11 *Backward learning curves for the discrimination of several kinds of stimuli. (after Zeaman and House, 1963)*

shown separately for fast and slow learners. It has been explained in Chapter 2 how such curves are constructed: the trial of last error is taken as a reference point and the average probability of correct responses is plotted on trials before the last error, indexed backwards. The curves in Fig. 6.11 are quite striking: slow learners show no improvement at all over 80 trials; once they start improving, they learn quite quickly. Fast learners learn at about the same rate as slow learners, the difference in the two groups lying in the much shorter time during which they remained at chance level. In terms of the model, the difference between slow and fast learners in this experiment is in the rate of acquisition of the proper coding response. Once subjects start making the correct coding response they all improve at the same rate. This result strongly supports the two-process notion of discrimination learning and would be very difficult to explain for theories which do not include some kind of coding mechanism.

It is easy to see how the model of Zeaman and House can explain the results obtained when a classification is suddenly reversed, or shifted to a new basis. The dominant coding response is still appropriate after a reversal or after an intradimensional shift, and unlearning of the overt responses to the stimulus-as-coded commences immediately. In the case of an extradimensional shift a new coding response must be learned before the actual classification learning can even begin.

One of the virtues of the Zeaman and House (1963) model is the clear distinction made between the acquisition of coding responses and the classification response proper. The model has several short-comings, though. The formal structure of the model is so complicated that one cannot derive explicit expressions and must completely rely upon computer simulation, which greatly increases the difficulty of arriving at strict tests of the model. Secondly, and more significantly, one would like a theory which makes more specific statements about the psychological processes involved in selecting one coding response rather than another, or about the relation between the information which the experimenter presents on a learning trial and the subject's learning processes. In Chapter 7 some similar models for concept identification will be described which are simpler mathematically and more amenable to psychological interpretations.

Pattern Recognizers

It is interesting and instructive to compare the functioning of artificial discrimination devices with models of human discrimination learning. Such devices are essentially computer programs written to solve specialized discrimination problems. Compared with the standard laboratory problems, the discriminations which are required are extremely complex. Perceptual as well as conceptual patterns have been studied by means of such "artificial intelligence" programs. It is important to realize that these programs are not trying to simulate human discrimination learning, but that they are designed to solve problems of the same kind as human subjects are asked to do in discrimination learning experiments, or in real life situations. It is by no means necessary that they should attempt to solve these problems in the same way as people do, but in several cases the design of pattern recognizers strikingly resembles the principles of stimulus coding described in the previous section. A brief look at the problems that arise when one attempts to translate these principles into a working program will therefore be quite informative.

Of the many proposals for pattern recognizers we shall consider the Pandemonium of Selfridge and the Concept Learner of Hunt (Selfridge, 1959; Selfridge and Neisser, 1960; Hunt, 1962; Hunt, Marin, and Stone, 1966). Both programs operate according to the principles of the coding theory of discrimination learning. The input is coded in terms of a set of features or attributes, and responses are connected with particular patterns of features. Furthermore, both programs assume that the set of features used to code the input is available at the outset. The only thing these pattern recognizers do is to learn to connect a particular output to the coded version of the stimulus. They do not generate their own coding responses; the dimensions used to analyze the stimulus must be provided by the programmer (but note that not much is known about how people detect or invent dimensions either). Except for this general scheme the two programs differ widely in how they go about solving their problem. Pandemonium is designed to recognize handprinted letters and processes information in parallel. The Concept Learner receives its input in verbal form ("Large black bear") and is concerned with finding classification rules ("dangerous" and "not dangerous") by building a sequential decision tree. The distinction between sequential and parallel processing is illustrated in Fig. 6.12. Whether sequential or parallel processing is used in artificial intelligence programs in mostly a matter of convenience. If processing capacities are restricted, se-

(a) Sequential pattern recognized:

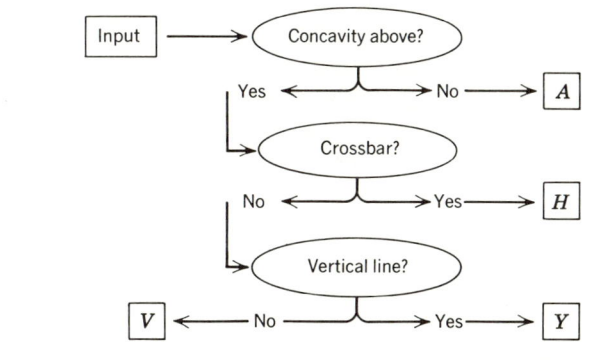

(b) Parallel pattern recognizer:

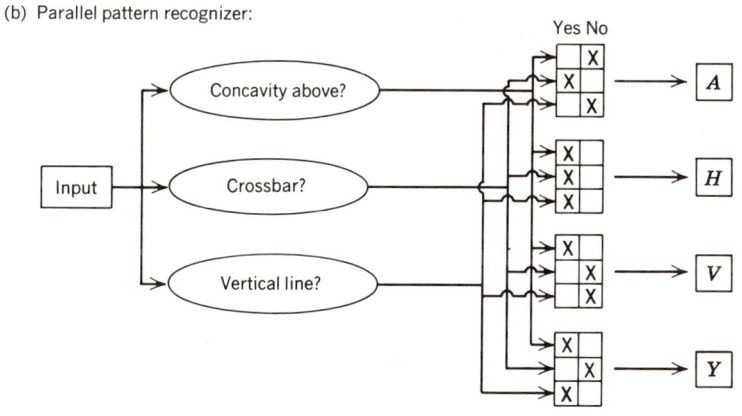

Fig. 6.12 *Serial and parallel processing of letters. (after Selfridge and Neisser, 1960)*

quential operations are indicated. If a system has sufficient capacity for parallel operations, greater speed can be gained by parallel processing.

Hunt's Concept Learner will be considered first. As mentioned before, the coding of the stimulus is done by the experimenter. The experimenter inputs the data in the form of an attribute matrix. Each column of the matrix corresponds to a different attribute of the stimulus. Each row corresponds to a different stimulus item. The entries in the matrix are the values of the row-item for the attribute designated at the top of each column. Figure 6.13a shows an example where the stimulus population consists of imaginary insects which differ along four dimensions: they have either 4, 8, or 12 legs; they can be red, yellow, or grey; they are large, small, or medium size; and they live in the forest, the desert, or in the water. Some of the insects are poisonous and some are not. How does the concept learner go about learning this classification?

As a first try the Concept Learner inspects all instances and counts whether there is an attribute value which is present in all poisonous insects and absent in all nonpoisonous insects, or vice versa. In the present example this search fails, as the reader can very easily

(a)

	Attribute 1 (No. of legs)	Attribute 2 (color)	Attribute 3 (size)	Attribute 4 (environment)
	four	red	small	forest
	twelve	yellow	large	desert
Poisonous	four	red	medium	water
Insects	twelve	grey	large	forest
	eight	yellow	large	desert
	twelve	red	small	water
	eight	grey	large	water
	twelve	yellow	small	water
	twelve	grey	small	desert
Nonpoisonous	four	grey	medium	desert
Insects	eight	red	large	forest
	twelve	yellow	medium	forest
	four	red	large	water
	four	red	large	forest

Fig. 6.13 *Illustration for the Concept Learner of Hunt, Marin, and Stone (1966).*

(b)

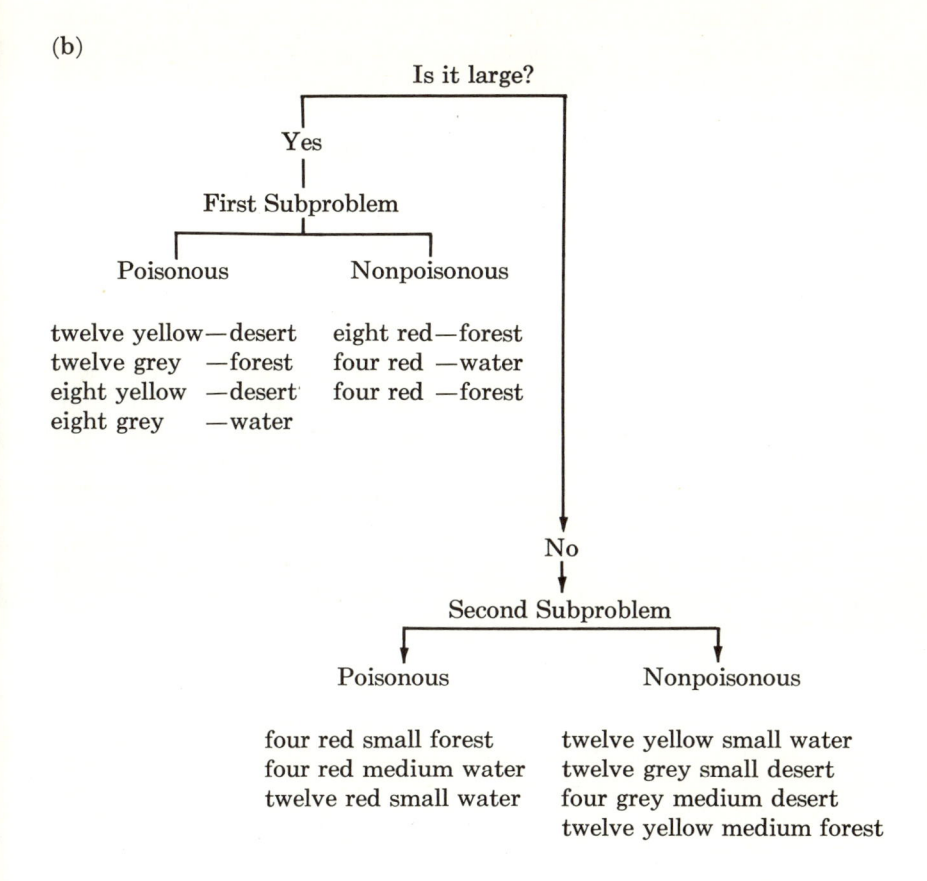

Is it large?

Yes

First Subproblem

Poisonous

Nonpoisonous

twelve yellow—desert   eight red—forest
twelve grey   —forest   four red —water
eight yellow —desert   four red —forest
eight grey   —water

No

Second Subproblem

Poisonous

Nonpoisonous

four red small forest   twelve yellow small water
four red medium water   twelve grey small desert
twelve red small water   four grey medium desert
                         twelve yellow medium forest

(c)

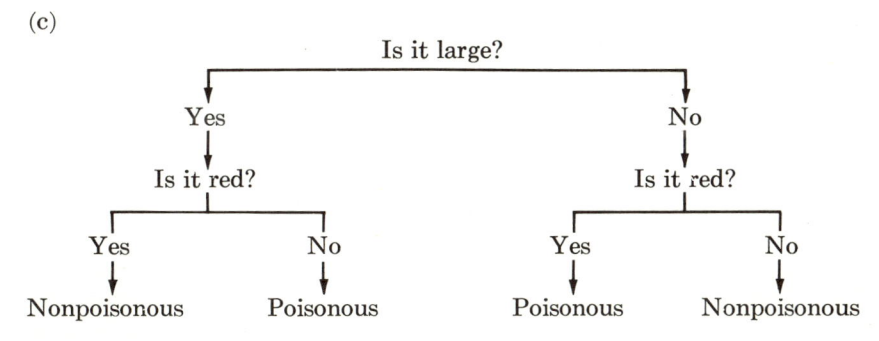

Is it large?

Yes   No

Is it red?   Is it red?

Yes   No   Yes   No

Nonpoisonous   Poisonous   Poisonous   Nonpoisonous

Fig. 6.13 *(Continued)*

ascertain by scanning the columns in Fig. 6.13a. Next, the program tries to break down the problem into manageable subproblems. This is done by counting the frequency with which characteristics appear in the description of positive instances and choosing the most frequent characteristic to form the first test question. In our example the most frequent characteristic of the poisonous insects is LARGE; hence the set of items will be divided into two subsets, LARGE and NOT LARGE, as shown in Fig. 6.13b. Subproblem 1 can be solved quite easily now by noting that the characteristic RED is present for all nonpoisonous insects but never appears among the poisonous insects. Thus a second test question can be constructed. Subproblem 2 can be solved by the same method, only that this time all the poisonous insects but none of the nonpoisonous insects are RED. The complete decision tree is shown in Fig. 6.13c. It represents the end-result of the discrimination learning process for the Concept Learner: given any member of the set of stimulus items the Concept Learner can tell to which category it belongs by asking two questions as in Fig. 6.13c.

The reader who is interested in the kind of problems which the Concept Learner can solve, how fast it solves these problems, and with what kinds of solutions it comes up, is referred to Hunt, Marin, and Stone (1966). All we wanted to do here is to illustrate the technique employed in one quite successful contemporary pattern recognizer. It should be especially noted that the kinds of operation which the concept learner performs are extremely simple: it merely counts characteristics, asks simple questions, and sorts items.

Now consider a completely different task, in which nevertheless some of the same general principles are employed, that of mechanical letter recognition. It would be an easy problem if all letters were printed alike and presented in a standard orientation. Quite simple schemes could surely be invented to recognize letters reliably. Indeed, that is exactly what is being done routinely in identifying check numbers: most bank checks bear an identification number in a standardized and simplified alphabet which can be recognized by quite uncomplicated pattern recognizers. Obviously, people can do much more than that. They can recognize an *A* if it is written in many different styles, positions, sizes, and even if it is partly erased. No mechanical pattern recognizer has been designed so far that can match the human ability to recognize patterns of all kinds. An interesting and instructive effort which has at least some of the capacities of the human is Selfridge's Pandemonium (Selfridge, 1959). Pandemonium has several levels of operations. First there is the level of the feature analyzers: the computational demons code the input data and transmit the coded data to the cognitive demons at the next higher level. The cognitive demons correspond to response alternatives. They collect all the information in their favor which is being offered to them by the computational demons and start shouting with a loudness proportional to the amount of evidence which they were able to amass. A decision demon then selects the response advertized by the loudest cognitive demon.

An example given by Selfridge and Neisser (1960) shows how this picturesque system learns to discriminate between ten handprinted characters. First, a 32×32 matrix is superimposed upon single handwritten letters. Each element of this matrix is scanned and the information whether it is black or white constitutes the raw data for the computer. Before Pandemonium actually starts to work on the data it uses a subprogram to clean up the data: it eliminates gaps and smoothes out contours and thereby gets rid of some of the noises introduced when the handprinted character was transferred to the input matrix, or which may have been caused by sloppy handwriting. Next, the program inspects the features of the input data. This is the stimulus coding process: 28 separate tests are carried out, and the results of these tests constitute the stimulus-as-coded. Examples of the kinds of tests used are measurements of the length of different edges, or the number of intersections which are obtained with standard horizontal test lines, etc. The stimulus coded in terms of the 28 features is then compared with the features of the letters which the program has learned before, and the probabilities are computed that the particular features which have been observed belong to each of the possible characters. The character with the highest probability is then chosen as output.

The program learns which features are characteristic of each letter by taking a census during its learning phase. For instance, for the feature "number of intersections with standard horizontal lines" the program observed that in 330 samples the event "three intersections" occurred 72 times: 6 times for A, 5 for E, 18 for M, 25 for N, 7 for O, 4 for R, 7 for T, and for no other letters. Hence the probability that, if three intersections had been observed, the letter was an A can be estimated as $6/72 = .083$. Similar computations can be made for all other features, and finally the estimated "posterior probabilities" can be combined and the most likely letter determined. There are quite sophisticated statistical techniques available for these computations, but they need not concern us here. Note, however, that the actual learning operations of the program are exceedingly simple. They consist in keeping a record of how often each feature value appeared. The program does not generate its own features, nor does it learn to concentrate upon features which actually discriminate between characters and neglect those that don't.

Artificial intelligence programs address themselves to problems that are much more ambitious than the standard laboratory experiments on discrimination. In the typical laboratory experiment on human discrimination learning or concept identification there is always a correct solution to the problem. No matter how obscure the solution may be, there is always some cue or principle which, when finally found, will permit a perfect solution of the problem. It would be trivial to build a pattern recognizer which would perform perfectly with such problems, simply by incorporating into the program the experimenter's rule or principle. Pattern recognition is difficult for an artificial intelligence device only when the problem is not well defined. There simply is no reliable cue to tell when a handwritten *A* is an *A*. There is no well-defined way to discriminate between actual and simulated suicide notes. Which symptoms are really relevant for the diagnosis of a particular disease? Such problems have motivated the work in artificial intelligence. The standard laboratory experiment on human discrimination learning looks modest indeed compared with such problems. However, it has been the traditional strategy of investigators interested in learning to look for basic principles in greatly simplified experimental situations which can then be used to obtain a better understanding of complex problems. As we have seen, some progress has been made along these lines, but the day has not yet arrived when artificial intelligence programs will be based upon the principles of discrimination learning derived from psychological laboratory experiments.

Innate Stimulus Analyzing Mechanisms

In his studies of discrimination learning in the octopus, Sutherland (1959) observed that the octopus had only a very restricted repertoire of coding responses, or stimulus analyzers as he preferred to call them. If the experimenter selected, as the relevant cue in a discrimination task, a stimulus dimension which is in the octopus' repertoire, the octopus would learn the discrimination; e.g., horizontal vs. vertical lines could be discriminated, as well as deviations from horizontality. On the other hand, such cues as right vs. left-sloping lines could not be detected. Sutherland concluded that discrimination learning in the octopus proceeded by attaching responses to the output of stimu-

lus analyzers; if the appropriate analyzer was missing in the repertoire of the organism, the problem could not be solved (although
later studies have shown the octopus' perceptual system to be somewhat more complex than Sutherland had originally supposed).

Sutherland believed that analyzers which permit the octopus to
code certain classes of stimuli but not others are innate. Humans
certainly depend upon coding responses which have been acquired on
the basis of experience. However, it is not clear to what extent analyzers are innate in the human case. Analyzers are clearly innate when
one can specify a particular perceptual mechanism, such as in the
case of color perception. When the physiological mechanisms which
perform the coding operation are unknown, or when a peripheral
mechanism does not exist, the distinction between innate and learned
stimulus analyzers becomes more difficult to make. As a concrete
example, do people learn to perceive a straight line, or are there innate mechanisms which permit us to perform this task? This problem
is somewhat outside the main concern of this book, but since it is of
considerable importance for the understanding of discrimination learning it will be outlined briefly.

Theories have been proposed which rely largely upon the effects
of experience. An important theory of this type is Hebb's (1949).
Hebb's organism starts out, like John Locke's famous empty tablet,
with a huge neural network with random interconnections. Repeated
stimulation of groups of neurons leads to the formation of "cell assemblies." Once formed, cell assemblies perform as stimulus analyzers and
permit the organism to solve more complex discrimination problems
by becoming combined into "phase sequences." Without getting too
involved in the details of Hebb's brain model, two features of this
model can be pointed out: first, that Hebb was one of the first theorists
explicitly to include coding notions in his treatment of discrimination
learning, and second, that he tried to do this by stressing the effects
of learning. Comparable with Hebb's brain theory in this respect are
some attempts to build pattern recognition devices which also start
out with a random net with rich but unstructured connections which
are then modified by reinforcement (e.g., the Perceptron of Rosenblatt, 1958).

There are at least two kinds of arguments against random net
theories. First, the mathematical probabilities that an initially random
net can ever find enough properties which are correlated with reinforcement to solve nontrivial discrimination problems seem to be dis-
concertingly small. Secondly, evidence has been obtained from physio-

logical studies of the perceptual system of animals which suggests that specialized innate stimulus analyzers play an important role in discrimination performance.

The lower an organism, the more specialized are its abilities for life and survival in a particular environment. A frog, for instance, appears to receive only very limited information about the surrounding world from his eyes, although the eyes are the frog's most important means of establishing contact with his environment. Modern science paints a rather dismal picture of a frog's life: the frog can do little more than sit on his lily-pad, snap at bugs which fly past, or jump into the water when an enemy approaches. At least that is what Lettvin, Maturana, McCulloch, and Pitts (1959) say that the frog's eye tells the frog's brain. Lettvin *et al.* came to this conclusion in a series of intriguing studies during which they presented various stimuli to the frog in a controlled experimental situation while recording the activity of single cells in the frog's optic tract. They observed that the information transmitted from the frog's retina to the brain was not about the point-by-point distribution of light and dark in the retina, but about qualitative features of the stimulus. Some cells were boundary detectors, others responded to moving curvatures, changes in contrast, or dimming. The different types of cells fell into anatomically distinct classes. Thus, the frog learns about small curved objects which move in its environment and are probably edible, and about large moving contours which may be a threat to him. His coding mechanisms limit him to information which is directly relevant to his survival. The interesting point about this is that this information was not extracted in the brain from some kind of "picture" transmitted from the retina, but was recorded only a few way stations behind the retina itself in the optic nerve.

Similar observations were reported by Hubel and Wiesel (1962) who studied the perceptual system of the cat. Hubel and Wiesel recorded from cortical locations and were able to discriminate among several types of cells which were concerned with the orientation of lines. Certain cells responded to lines in a particular orientation in the visual field, with some higher order cells responding to more general classes of lines. Hubel and Wiesel specifically note the much greater versatility of the cat's visual apparatus as compared with the frog's. In the frog very specialized processing occurs at a low level, while specialization in the cat's brain is postponed to a higher level and is carried out by a much larger number of cells.

The results of Lettvin *et al.* as well as those of Hubel and Wiesel show that innate stimulus analyzers play an important role in determining coding operations in the frog and in the cat. This finding has no direct implications for the human case but, together with the difficulty of conceiving of a random mechanism on purely formal grounds, it reinforces the notion that the human brain may possess much richer and more intricate innate structure than random net theories suppose.

The Fate of Nonattended Information

Coding frequently takes the form of some kind of stimulus selection. Typically a coding response could be described as paying attention to some particular stimulus dimension and rejecting others. Thus the question arises: What happens to the rejected information? In the case of lower animals which can code only a few stimulus dimensions, surplus information is presumably lost, but what happens with human subjects who could code a given stimulus in many ways? Broadbent (1958) was the first to concern himself with the fate of nonattended features. He thought that sensory filters, corresponding to stimulus analyzers, can be tuned in on a particular stimulus dimension, accepting information from this channel and rejecting all information on other channels. The stimulus dimensions which Broadbent was particularly concerned with were position in space of a speech source, voice qualities, sensory modality, and the like. The reason Broadbent thought the organism attends to only one channel and filters out all the rest, was the well-known capacity limitation of human information processing. Some aspects of this problem were discussed in Chapter 4 in connection with other experiments on short-term memory.

The filter theory is somewhat too strong, as a number of critics have pointed out. For instance, Moray (1959) showed that if a subject attends to a message which is presented to him over one ear, he normally does not react to messages sent to the unattended ear, nor does he remember anything about such messages, just as the filter theory would have it. However, the unattended message was not simply rejected, because if the subject's own name is spoken to the unattended ear, he hears it! Several findings like this led Treisman (1964) to propose a modification of the filter theory: unattended information is not rejected but attenuated. When a particular coding response is selected, other coding responses are not completely turned off but still perform at some minimal level. Although one can quite well restrict attention at a noisy cocktail party to one particular voice and not hear a word from the buzz around, one continually processes some information about it, though in rudimentary form. A person would very likely respond if the people behind started talking about him, or even if they discussed a topic which was of great interest to him. In the same vein, one can pay attention to a conversation while walking across a busy campus, without losing the way and without bumping into obstacles.

SUMMARY

The experiments on discrimination learning and generalization which were discussed here have two important implications. First it was shown that instructions and experimental pay-offs may introduce response biases that play a significant role in determining experimental results. Secondly, the way the subject perceives a stimulus was found to be an extremely important factor in discrimination and generalization experiments. Studies were discussed in which verbal labels were used to code the stimuli in generalization experiments, and several experiments were described in which stimulus coding was investigated by means of transfer experiments. First, subjects were induced to employ a particular coding strategy, and in a later stage of the experiment a transfer task was given such that the previously acquired stimulus coding was either relevant or irrelevant. For rats learning a T-maze and human subjects learning simple geometric concepts or discriminations among letter-like figures, performance on the second task depended crucially upon the relevance of the coding operations which were learned in the first stage of the experiment.

Generalization and discrimination are closely related operationally: generalization implies lack of discrimination, and vice versa. This inverse relationship has been demonstrated experimentally in some studies, but in others there seems to be no obvious correspondence between generalization and discrimination data. It was shown that in some cases differential response biases induced by instructions may lead the subject to make errors of generalization when virtually no discrimination errors occur. In other experiments, especially when highly analyzable stimulus materials are used, subjects may employ different coding strategies, depending upon the nature of the experimental task: some particularly simple ways to code the experimental stimuli if the task is one of classification or generalization may be inappropriate if the task is one of identification or discrimination. With other kinds of stimulus material subjects employ identical coding operations whether the task is one of classification or of identification, so that a person can very well predict the result of one task from the results of the other. Some experiments concerning the discrimination of speech sounds provided an illustration for the latter case.

Models of discrimination learning were discussed in the third section of the chapter. On the basis of the data reviewed earlier it was concluded that a model of discrimination learning must have the following features: it must make a distinction between learning to code the stimulus and associating the stimulus-as-coded with the response alternatives, and it must have a decision mechanism which selects among the response alternatives and is sensitive to pay-off and biases. Models in which stimulus coding is attributed to overt orienting responses were found to be insufficient. Mediation models were also rejected because they tie the mediating response too closely to the stimulus, making it difficult to deal with the effects of instructions and biases. A coding response appears to be a set to deal with the experimental stimulus in a certain way, rather than a mediating response evoked by that stimulus. An example of a coding or attention theory of discrimination learning was described, and some comments about the nature of coding responses were made. Finally, two artificial pattern recognition devices were described and their relationship to the coding theory of discrimination learning was discussed.

CONCEPT IDENTIFICATION

7777777777777

In a concept identification experiment the subject is confronted with a carefully constructed set of stimuli which are divided into two or more classes by the experimenter. It is the subject's task to identify the experimenter's classification rule. Frequently the experimental stimuli are simple line drawings which vary along such *dimensions* as shape, color, size, numerosity, presence and position of additional lines, dots, etc. Each dimension may have two or more *values*; for instance, shape may be either square, circle, or triangle, size may be large or small, etc. The concept is arbitrarily defined by the experimenter in terms of some stimulus characteristic. In the simplest case the experimenter chooses one dimension, say size, and assigns items to classes on the basis of their values on this dimension (e.g., all large figures are class A, all small figures are class B). Oviously, more complex concepts can be formed with stimulus materials of this type, but for the most part this chapter will be concerned with the very simplest kinds of concepts.

It is clear that concept identification is a particularly simple kind of discrimination learning. Thus, what was said about discrimination learning in general applies to concept learning. Most importantly, stimulus coding is central to concept identification: once the subject starts responding to the relevant stimulus dimension, the problem is as good as solved. Therefore, concept identification, especially the identification of very simple concepts, may be considered primarily as a problem of selecting the right stimulus dimension.

Concept identification is the most thoroughly investigated and best understood topic among those reviewed in the previous chapter. It is probably not the problem of greatest practical importance, but the methods used for its investigation and the results obtained should be useful in similar investigations of more complex phenomena. There-

344

fore, a rather detailed account of recent work on concept formation will be presented in this chapter.

1. PAIRED-ASSOCIATE LEARNING AND CONCEPT IDENTIFICATION COMPARED

The brief description of concept learning tasks given above makes it obvious that paired-associate learning and concept identification are closely related. Investigations which are concerned with the difference between the two provide a good starting point for our discussion, and serve to relate the material on concept identification to the work discussed in earlier chapters.

The experimental comparison between paired-associate learning and concept identification was initiated with a series of studies by Reed (1946). The stimuli in Reed's experiments were composed of four words, one of which was an instance of the concept to be learned (e.g., "vegetable," "color"), and three were dummies. The responses were nonsense syllables. Subjects learned by the anticipation method a list of 42 items, seven instances of six different concepts. The results were presented in terms of two measures of learning: the total number of errors made before reaching criterion, and the subject's verbal report. Subjects who could verbalize their solution were said to have acquired a "consistent" concept. Subjects who could not verbalize their solution or who stated it incorrectly were said to have learned an "inconsistent" concept.

In Experiment I Reed investigated the role of instructions which the subjects received. Subjects who were given regular paired-associate instructions made more errors (41) than subjects who were given concept learning instructions (31). Even more significantly, subjects who were given concept learning instructions were more likely to achieve a consistent solution than subjects who were given rote learning instructions (86% for concept learners versus 67% for paired-associate learners). In Experiment II Reed varied list length. Subjects were given lists of 24, 42, or 60 items, which means that the 6 concepts were represented by 4, 7, or 10 instances, respectively. Increases in list length had only a very small effect upon the total number of errors which subjects made in learning the list, in contrast with the strong effect which similar increases have in paired-associate learning. Indeed, increasing the list length actually facilitated learning if learning was measured by the proportion of subjects who achieved a consistent solution. Less than half of Reed's subjects (42%)

could verbalize the solution if each concept was represented by only 4 instances, while 86% correctly verbalized their solution if 7 instances were given for each concept, and almost all subjects (95%) achieved a consistent solution if given 10 instances for each concept. In a third experiment Reed confirmed the intuitively reasonable hypothesis that increasing the number of dummies on each stimulus card retards the process of concept acquisition.

Reed's studies clearly show that in spite of procedural similarities there are important differences between paired-associate learning and concept identification experiments. In particular, the observation that instructions to learn concepts facilitated learning indicates that there is a difference in the learning processes in the two tasks. Note that Reed's task is actually quite complex in that it draws upon the subject's pre-existing acquaintance with concepts such as animal, vegetable, and the like. One would suppose that the better established these concepts are, the easier it would be to identify them in experiments like Reed's. For instance if BED, FUR, and PILLOW are instances of the concept SOFT learning should be more rapid than when the same concept is represented by three words which are less strongly connected with it, such as PUDDING, LIPS, and SHEEP. Underwood and Richardson (1956b) were the first to investigate this problem. They collected normative data on the strength with which instances are related to conceptual classes. Controlled associations to 213 nouns were obtained from 153 subjects. Subjects wrote down the first sense impression which entered their mind as each stimulus word was presented; 6 seconds were given for each noun. Responses which were given by many subjects were called high dominant for that word; responses given by few subjects, but still more than 5%, were called low dominant. Examples of stimulus words for which the response SOFT was high and low dominant were given above. From these results Underwood and Richardson constructed lists of 24 nouns which were composed of 4 instances of each of 6 concepts such that two of the concepts had a high, two a medium, and two a low dominance level. Items were presented on a memory drum and the experimenter informed the subject on each trial whether he was right or wrong. The right answers were always the corresponding concept names. Three different instructions were given in this experiment in order to study the effect of restricting the response set. In the first condition subjects were merely told that the correct responses are free associates of the stimulus word. In the partially restricted condition subjects were told that all responses were sense impressions, and in a final condition subjects were given the actual response words. Both dominance level and instructions affected performance. The higher the dominance level the better performance, and the more information the subjects were given concerning the concepts to be learned, the better they did.

Underwood and Richardson's extension and simplification of the Reed experiments shows very clearly that we are dealing here with a very intricate process: subjects must search for the correct response, either explicitly as in the Underwood and Richardson experiment or implicitly as in Reed's, whereby the likelihood that each instance elicits the correct response depends upon its dominance level. This is an interesting problem, but it is too complicated for the initial comparison between concept learning and paired-associate learning. Simpler tasks with more easily controlled stimulus properties would seem to offer a better means to explore this difference. However, after we have achieved a better understanding of the basic process involved in concept identification we shall return to the experimental paradigm with which the comparison between paired-associate learning and concept identification historically began.

The principal difference between paired-associate experiments and concept identification tasks is that in paired-associate learning the only way to specify the stimulus-response connections is to list them. In concept formation, on the other hand, one does not need to list all stimulus-response connections: instead there exist general principles which are sufficient to specify all possible stimulus-response connections. In the experiments just discussed, these principles depended upon word meanings (e.g., "classify all vegetables together," or "all soft objects"). In many experiments described in the previous chapter and in most of the ones to be discussed here, concepts are defined by some common element or attribute (e.g., "all red objects belong to the same response, and all green and yellow objects to the other"). Finally, concepts may be defined through relationships among stimulus elements, or through rules. Two particularly simple examples of this kind of concept will be discussed below, and other studies will be taken up in Chapter 8.

Suppes and Ginsberg (1962, 1963) described an experiment which, like Reed's, lies halfway between paired-associate experiments and concept learning tasks. They taught children the numbers 4 and 5 in binary notation by using three different stimulus displays for each number. In the binary number system a 4 is denoted by 100 and a five by 101. The three displays for each number involved different objects, but they were all of the form *abb* for the 4 and *aba* for the 5. The child was shown each stimulus separately and responded by placing a card with either a 4 or a 5 printed on it upon the stimulus card.

The experimenter told the child whether his response was correct or not. The 6 stimuli were presented for 16 trials.

Suppes and Ginsberg wanted to classify their subjects as consistent and nonconsistent solvers after the manner of Reed, but instead of relying upon verbal reports they gave transfer tests with new stimulus material forming either *abb* or *aba* patterns. Children who responded correctly on the transfer tests were said to have learned the concept. Children who did not, but who had mastered the original task, must have learned associations between the 6 stimulus displays and the response cards, without evolving a general principle. Only a few subjects performed correctly on the transfer task, which means that most subjects learned the task by rote rather than by acquiring the concepts *abb* and *aba*.

The learning data obtained by Suppes and Ginsberg (1962, 1963) could be described quite well by the one-element model which was discussed in detail in Chapter 2. Let us merely review here the principal assumptions of the model. The unit of analysis for the model is a single stimulus-response conception or item. The item is unconditioned at the beginning of learning. Whenever it is presented it may become conditioned with probability c. As long as the item is unconditioned the probability of a correct response stays at some constant value p. Once an item is conditioned a correct response is always given.

As applied to the present instance the model has only one parameter, the conditioning probability c. The probability of a correct response in the unconditioned state here equals $\frac{1}{2}$ because of the symmetry of the experimental situation. Suppes and Ginsberg found that the one-element model fits their data quite well. In particular, the proportion of correct responses on trials before the last error remained constant at about $\frac{1}{2}$, as the model requires. An indication that the model was too simple was obtained, however, when the response sequences before the last error were divided into quartiles. The proportion of errors was more or less the same for the first three quartiles but dropped sharply in the last quartile. This drop was highly significant statistically.

When Suppes and Ginsberg applied the one-element model to their data, they used single items as a unit for those subjects, who, on the basis of the transfer test after learning, were classified as paired-associate learners. The data from these subjects were treated as if they came from a 6-item paired-associate list. However, as far as the concept learners were concerned, all items of the type *abb* were equivalent and all items of the type *aba* were also equivalent. Thus, these subjects learned in effect a two-item problem, which must be considered in the application of the model. The unit of analysis for the model then becomes not an item, but a concept. All items which are instances of the same concept are treated as equivalent. This is very important when one deals with pure concept learning tasks, instead of the mixture between concept learning tasks and paired-associate tasks which can be learned either way. In a pure concept learning task a particular stimulus display is never repeated. Subjects are thus forced to learn concepts, since the problem can not be solved through simple stimulus-response associations in the manner of paired-associate learning. Subjects learn a response to a stimulus class rather than to particular instances, and the theoretical unit of analysis shifts accordingly from the single item to the set of items which defines a concept.

In such an experiment Suppes and Ginsberg (1963) taught first grade children the concept of identity of sets. The stimuli in this study were sets of 1, 2, or 3 elements. Two stimuli were displayed on each trial and the children were simply asked to press one button when the stimuli were "the same" and another button when they were "not the same." The results were analyzed with the one-element model. On each trial the subject's response was treated as either correct (C) or incorrect (I). Thus, each subject's data were represented as a string of C's and I's, and the one-element model was used to investigate the statistical structure of these sequences. Independence of successive responses on trials before the last error and stationarity of the error proportions before conditioning were observed in their data, as predicted by the model. However, some evidence for non-stationarity was present in the fourth quartile of the Vincent curves, as in the previous experiment. Predictions of the distribution of the trials of the last error were moderately successful.

In summary, the experiments reviewed so far demonstrate that paired-associate learning and concept identification involve quite different processes and they give some indication as to the locus of that difference: a single item pair must be taken as the unit of analysis in paired-associate learning, but a whole class of equivalent items is the appropriate unit for concept learning.

2. TASK VARIABLES IN CONCEPT IDENTIFICATION

There are a number of experimental variables which are important in concept identification experiments. These are variables which are effective in discrimination learning in general, but the concept identification paradigm presents a particularly good opportunity for their investigation. However, in order to stress the importance of these task variables to stimulus coding operation in general, examples from outside the area of concept identification proper will be introduced whenever they appear to be relevant and instructive.

Cue Saliency

Subjects do not choose randomly among all possible cues. Both a subject's set and the characteristics of the stimulus material affect his choices. Psychologists have long been concerned with the properties of a cue which determine its salience or attention value.

A prominent hypothesis, which has its roots in the tradition of introspective psychology, holds that the more concrete a stimulus characteristic is, the more likely it is to be employed by subjects in a discrimination task, and the more abstract a characteristic is, the more difficult it is to use. In a series of monographs Gelb and Goldstein (1925) and Goldstein and Scheerer (1941) compared the sorting behavior of normal persons with that of brain-damaged patients. Goldstein and his co-workers used simple drawings as stimulus material, which were to be sorted according to the experimenter's instructions. A concrete sort involved sorting the drawing into object classes (e.g., "houses"); an abstract sort involved sorting according to formal similarity (e.g., "red objects"). The principal result of these studies was that brain-damaged patients were deficient in tasks which involved abstract classifications, but not in sorting on the basis of concrete attributes. Furthermore, the patients exhibited a peculiar inability to shift coding responses: once they had classified a set of items in one way they found it very difficult to re-sort the same items in any new way whatsoever.

Goldstein and Scheerer (1941) distinguished between concrete and abstract behavior as if the two were clearly separable and distinct classes. However, their data do not warrant such a clear distinction. Concrete and abstract seem more like end points on a continuum rather than discrete classes. Furthermore, these behaviors are hierarchically related to each other: an "abstract" sort (e.g., angular vs. rounded) presupposes that the subject disregards some concrete characteristics in assigning clocks to *round* and roofs to *angular*. Thus, it would probably be better to talk about higher and lower order categories. Abstract and concrete are terms with much surplus meaning and may be used in many different ways. It might be best to avoid these terms at present.

Similar comments apply to Heidbreder's suggestion that the

salience of a cue is determined by its "thing character" (e.g., Heidbreder, 1946). Heidbreder performed many experiments on concept identification in which the stimuli were line drawings and the experimenter selected such dimensions as objects, form, color, or numerosity to define the to be learned classification. Her results showed that subjects found it easiest to learn concepts defined on the basis of object classes, with more and more difficulty being encountered when the concepts were defined on the basis of form, color, or numerosity. She concluded that the thing character of cues influences concept acquisition: the more concrete cues are easier to learn than the abstract ones. However, abstractness is again confounded with complexity: in order to learn a classification based upon form, the subject must see clocks and wreaths as circles, i.e., he must learn to disregard the objects depicted by the drawings and respond to cues which are less obvious perceptually. In order to respond to numerosity, which was the hardest of Heidbreder's classifications to learn, subjects must learn to disregard not only the objects depicted, but also their forms and colors.

It seems more appropriate to assume that perceptual complexity is the basic variable in Heidbreder's experiments rather than the ill-defined thing-character. Baum (1954) has observed that in experiments like those of Heidbreder the drawings used as stimuli vary systematically in discriminability in a manner that corresponds closely to the ease with which concepts are learned when these stimuli are used as learning material. Indeed one of Heidbreder's own studies demonstrated that perceptual distinctiveness rather than thing-character determines the speed of concept acquisition. In this experiment color was preferred by subjects over form (Heidbreder, 1949). This was achieved by coloring the whole stimulus card instead of merely the drawing itself as in the earlier experiment. Heidbreder herself noted in the discussion of this experiment that not dominance of thing-character but perceptual factors influenced the ease of concept acquisition. She also remarked on the role of verbal coding: the easier it was for the subject to refer to the critical features in the experiment with a verbal phrase, the more efficient learning was. This, of course, is reminiscent of Glanzer's "verbal loop" hypothesis which had been encountered in a completely different context before (Glanzer and Clark, 1963; discussed in Chapter 4): in both rote verbal learning and concept learning the difficulty of learning is correlated with the difficulty of verbally describing the relevant features of the stimulus.

The role of perceptual factors in determining cue saliency has been clearly demonstrated in a study by Shepp and Zeaman (1966).

Shepp and Zeaman argued that the attention value of a cue is determined by the size of the perceptual differences involved. More specifically, a brightness cue should have higher attention value if the attributes used are black and white than if black and grey are employed; similarly, a size cue which contrasts large differences (72 mm vs 20 mm circles diameter) should be more salient and hence lead to faster concept acquisition than a small contrast (23 mm vs 20 mm). The authors tested this prediction with retardate children and fully confirmed it. When the relevant cue involved a small perceptual difference, a long period of no improvement preceded the learning of the discrimination task. When large differences were involved, the initial period of no improvement during which the subject presumably searches for the right coding response was greatly abbreviated.

Emphasis on the Relevant Cue

The hypothesis that perceptual factors determine the attention value of a cue receives further support from the findings of several studies in which perceptual emphasizing of the relevant cue facilitated concept learning. For instance, Hull (1920) showed that emphasis of the common element in the Chinese letters which constituted the stimulus material in his experiment increased the rate of concept acquisition. Hull's method of emphasizing the relevant cue consisted in coloring it, thereby making it stand out from the rather complex stimulus figures. Hull's results have been replicated and extended by Trabasso (1963). Trabasso's stimulus materials were line drawings of flowers. When the relevant cue was the size of the angle which was formed by the flower stem and the leaves, subjects found the problem quite hard to learn. Apparently, more salient cues were considered first, such as the shape of the flowers or the shape of the leaves, and the angle-cue was investigated only after these more obvious cues failed to lead to a solution. However, by emphasizing the angle cue—either by increasing the angle size or by coloring the angle red—performance could be considerably improved. Coloring the angle green had no emphasis effect: red flower stems attract the subject's attention, but green ones don't.

Another finding of Hull (1920) was that when subjects learned several concept learning problems in succession, learning was facilitated when the problems were presented in simple to complex order rather than in complex to simple order. This observation is closely related to the results on stimulus emphasis. Anything that will induce the subject to use the right kind of coding response will facilitate learning. An impressive demonstration of the importance of this factor has been provided by Zeaman and House (1963) in their report on discrimination learning by retarded children which has already been referred to before. The authors tried to teach a discrimination between line drawings of a red cross and a blue triangle to 15 retarded children. Only four of the children learned this discrimination in 500 trials. However, when actual objects of the same kind were substituted for the line drawings, thus emphasizing the relevant stimulus dimensions, 13 out of another group of 19 children learned the task. More importantly, all those who learned the object discrimination readily transferred to the picture discrimination. The results of this experiment are quite spectacular and have strong implications as to how one should go about teaching discrimination effectively. Figure 7.1 shows the backward learning curve for the few subjects who learned the original picture discrimination, and also includes the data from two groups of subjects who were first trained on a discrimination between real objects before learning to discriminate pictures. The learning curve labeled $O_1 \rightarrow P_1$ shows the transfer behavior from objects to pictures which has just been discussed. The second curve $O_2 \rightarrow P_1$ shows the performance of subjects who first learned a discrimination between objects and then learned the discrimination between drawings, but for whom the actual stimulus values were changed in transfer.

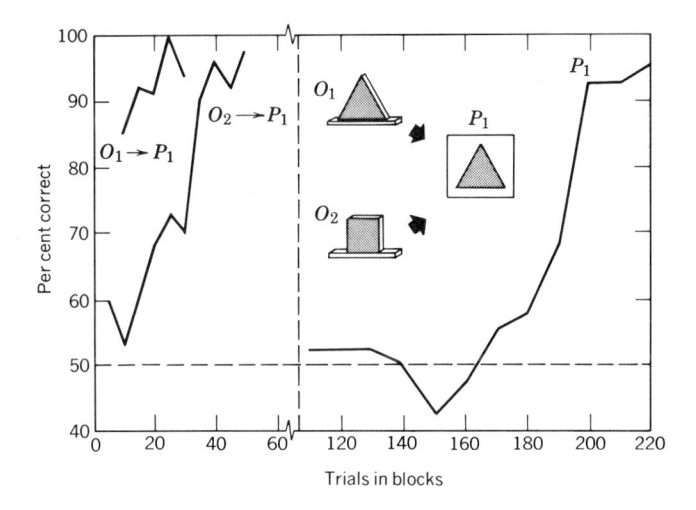

Fig. 7.1 *Object-to-pattern transfer. Backward learning curve of pattern group (far right) and two object-to-pattern transfer groups (left). (after Zeaman and House, 1963)*

Even in that case performance is greatly superior to that of subjects who start out learning to discriminate drawings. What the particular stimulus values are obviously matters little as long as a subject has learned to attend to the right stimulus dimension.

To teach a discrimination one should emphasize the relevant cue as strongly as possible in order to elicit the appropriate coding response and abbreviate the initial search process. Once the coding response is established, the emphasizer may be withdrawn. This seems to be true of discrimination learning in general, not just of concept identification. Lawrence (1952) has shown that the best way to teach a simultaneous discrimination between two shades of grey to rats is to start out with a very easy discrimination (white versus black) and then gradually shift to the test stimuli. This procedure was superior to one in which the test stimuli were used from the beginning, and it was also better than starting with the easy problem and suddenly introducing the difficult problem. Terrace (1963a) has reported a technique to teach pigeons a discrimination which employed similar principles. The best way to teach a pigeon to discriminate between a vertical and a horizontal bar, which is a rather hard discrimination for a pigeon, is to start with a simpler problem first. For instance, color discriminations are easy for pigeons, and one can train the pigeon to peck at a key if it is green and not to peck if it is yellow. Once this discrimination is established, the horizontal bar is superimposed on the green key and the vertical bar is superimposed on the yellow key. Finally, the colors are faded out gradually and the pigeon's original color discrimination is transferred to the horizontal-vertical discrimination without ever permitting it to make an incorrect peck. Indeed, Terrace (1963b) also showed that the original discrimination may be trained without errors in training by exploiting the pigeon's natural reluctance to peck at an unlighted key. He reinforced the bird with grain for pecking at the key when it was illuminated with a green light. At the same time he cautiously introduced the yellow light, at first only for very brief periods and at very dim intensities, so that the pigeon was never tempted to peck at it. In this way a discrimination can be established much more readily than with the conventional procedure which involved first establishing the pecking response to a white key and then differentially reinforcing it when the key is green and extinguishing it when the key is yellow. With the latter procedure the pigeon makes thousands of unreinforced pecks at the yellow key before learning the discrimination, and hardly ever learns the discrimination perfectly.

A maximally inefficient strategy for discrimination learning would presumably be to start with the most difficult version of the problem first. No experimental evidence apart from that of Hull (1920) which has already been discussed is available concerning this problem, but an interesting study of Bruner and Potter (1964) shows that this is true at least for the case of perceptual recognition. Bruner and Potter determined recognition thresholds either by starting with a focused picture which gradually went out of focus or by starting with an out-of-focus picture which was gradually brought into focus. Under the second condition performance was much poorer than under the first. Their results prove nothing about discrimination learning, of course, but suggest that both perceptual recognition and discrimination learning are retarded if the subject is confused initially about the appropriate stimulus analyzer or coding mechanism.

Stimulus Variability

One of the most straightforward implications of the coding theory for concept acquisition is that stimulus variability should influence the rate of concept acquisition. The more relevant cues that are added to a problem, the easier should the problem become, because the problem can be solved by attending to any one of the relevant dimensions. For instance, if all large pictures are also red and square and are classified as A's, and all small pictures are also blue and round and are classified as B's, the subject has a choice of coding size, color, or form, or any combination thereof, and should be able to solve the problem sooner than if only one of these coding responses were appropriate. On the other hand, the more irrelevant dimensions that are added to a problem the harder should concept identification become, because the subjects are more likely to respond to one of the irrelevant dimensions. Figure 7.2 from Bourne (1966) summarizes the results of experiments by Bourne and Haygood (1959, 1961) and completely confirms this expectation. Bourne and Haygood also investigated the effects of introducing irrelevant but redundant stimulus variability. To illustrate the problem, suppose that the classification to be learned is simply red vs. green, and that shape and size are irrelevant dimensions. If all shapes are combined with all sizes, the two irrelevant dimensions are independent of each other; on the other hand, if shape and size covary, i.e., all triangles are large and all circles are small, the two irrelevant dimensions are redundant. Bourne and Haygood found that introducing redundant irrelevant dimensions into a concept learning task also inhibited the rate of acquisition, but not nearly as much as when independent irrelevant dimensions were added. This result

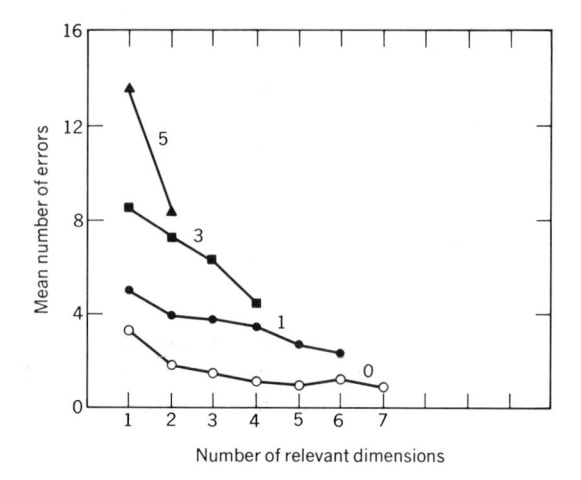

Fig. 7.2 *Mean number of errors made by subjects prior to solving a concept identification problem plotted as a function of the number of relevant dimensions for 0,1,3 and 5 irrelevant dimensions. (after Bourne, 1966)*

indicates that at least some subjects were able to notice the covariation between dimensions and were able to treat a group of redundant dimensions as one.

Increasing the number of irrelevant dimensions retards concept acquisition by increasing the set of coding responses among which a selection must be made. Keeping the number of irrelevant dimensions constant but increasing the number of values which an attribute has should also retard learning, but for a completely different reason. With a constant number of dimensions the set of coding responses which must be considered does not change, but if the number of values of each attribute is increased the process of associating these values with the experimental responses becomes more difficult. Battig and Bourne (1960) have investigated the effects of this experimental variable. Their stimulus material had either 2, 4, or 6 values per dimension, and had to be classified into two sets. For instance, with six-valued dimensions three different colors had to be associated with the same response. They found that increasing the number of values per dimension increased problem difficulty. In addition, Battig and Bourne also varied the number of irrelevant dimensions in their experiment. Performance deteriorated as more irrelevant dimensions in their experiment. Performance deteriorated as more irrelevant dimensions were added, regardless of the number of values per dimension. Thus dimensional variability and intra-dimensional variability do not interact. Adding more values per dimension simply increases the over-all difficulty of the problem. Studies which attempt to explore the possibly different causes of the inhibitory effects—produced by intradimensional variability and by increases in the number of irrelevant dimensions—have not yet been reported.

The Post-feedback Interval

If learning in a concept identification experiment takes place immediately and automatically as a function of reinforcement (informative feedback by the experimenter), delay of reinforcement should retard learning, as it does in classical conditioning. At the same time, the length of the interval between feedback and the next trial should be unrelated to learning efficiency. On the other hand, if the subject during concept learning selects and infers hypotheses, and makes decisions, then extra time after he has been told the correct solution on each trial should be quite helpful to him. A conclusive study by Bourne and Bunderson (1963) shows that the length of the post-feedback interval does indeed matter in concept learning. Performance was improved as the post-feedback interval was lengthened from 1 to 5 to 9 seconds. The improvement was bigger when the task was difficult (5 irrelevant dimensions) than when it was easy (1 irrelevant dimension), in agreement with the hypothesis that the post-feedback interval is used for processing the information just acquired. In the same study the delay of information feedback (i.e., the interval between the subject's response on each trial and the experimenter's feedback) was also varied from 0 to 8 seconds. No delay effects were obtained.

In a second experiment Bourne, Guy, Dodd, and Justesen (1965) explored even longer post-feedback intervals, from 1 through 25 seconds. For their easy task (1 irrelevant dimension) an interval of 9 seconds after the information feedback was optimal, and performance decreased somewhat for longer intervals. For the more difficult task (5 irrelevant dimensions) the optimum interval was about 17 seconds, which implies that these subjects needed almost twice as much time to perform the necessary operations after each trial than subjects who learned the easier problem.

3. HYPOTHESES AND STRATEGIES

The experimental evidence about concept learning which has been presented so far indicates that one may reasonably look at concept learning as a search process: a search is made for the relevant cue which determines the experimenter's classification. Formally this search process seems to be very close to an all-or-none process. That conclusion follows from the fact that it is often possible to describe simple concept identification data with the one-element learning model, as was shown in connection with some of Suppes' work (Suppes and Ginsberg, 1962; 1963). Of course, the one-element model can be interpreted in several ways. As will be remembered, the name one-element model comes from stimulus sampling theory where learning is conceptualized as conditioning of stimulus elements, in this case a single stimulus pattern. However, the model can also be viewed as a special case of the coding theory of discrimination learning which was discussed in the previous chapter. The conditioning probability can be interpreted as the product of two probabilities, the probability that the right coding response will be used times the probability that the stimulus-as-coded will be connected with the right response. Most of the difficulty in concept identification experiments lies in the selection of a proper coding response, and the model primarily reflects this selection process. The conditioning of the stimulus-as-coded to the correct response is almost trivial for adult subjects in the simple tasks considered here. If a subject has just been told that a red stimulus card belongs to class A and he thereupon selects color as his hypothesis, he considers only color hypotheses which are consistent with the information he has just received. Note that this is not necessarily the case when retarded children are used as subjects. The experiments of Zeaman and House described earlier have shown that once the proper coding response occurs improvement may be rapid but is by no means immediate. Other situations where the association between the stimulus-as-coded and the response is nontrivial will be discussed under the rubric of rule learning in Chapter 8.

A third interpretation of the model is in terms of hypothesis testing. Because of the importance and popularity of hypothesis testing theories of concept identification, this approach will be described in more detail before commenting further on the relationship between the one-element model and hypothesis-testing theories.

Hypothesis-testing theories assume that subjects in concept identification experiments make a guess as to the solution of the problem which is consistent with the information available to them. Such a guess is called a hypothesis. As new information is provided to the subject he modifies his initial hypothesis or, if necessary, abandons it and chooses a new one. The subject's overt responses are controlled by his hypotheses. Once he has arrived at a hypothesis which is identical or equivalent to the experimenter's classification rule the problem is solved. Hypothesis theories are reminiscent of coding theories: a hypothesis is like a coding response together with the overt response. If the experimenter presents the subject with a red object and tells him that it belongs to class A, saying that the subject formed the hypothesis "red is A" is equivalent to saying that the subject learned to code the stimulus in terms of color and associated the color red with response A. On the other hand, hypothesis theories go beyond the coding theories already discussed in stressing the constructive activity of the subject. The subject forms hypotheses, tests them and evaluates them, he doesn't just learn and is reinforced.

Some of the implications that the term hypothesis testing carries with it seem doubtful. "Hypothesis testing" suggests that subjects always have some clearly formulated plan in mind and are testing it purposefully. Some subjects, sometimes, certainly do. However, subjects do not do so all the time, as has been clearly demonstrated in one of the classical studies on concept learning by Hull (1920). Hull studied concepts defined in terms of common elements among Chinese letters. All letters which shared a certain part were assigned to a common response class. Many of Hull's subjects learned this task, in the sense of consistently responding correctly, but were unable to formulate their solution verbally. This observation led Hull to introduce the term "functional concept": a subject may respond correctly but can not tell why. Hull's finding was responsible for a methodological revolution in concept learning. While previous experimenters had relied mainly upon the introspections of subjects during concept learning, interest shifted to the subject's behavior and his verbal report was considered to be of secondary importance, or sometimes completely neglected. More recently, psychologists have rediscovered that what the subject says he does may often be quite interesting and informative after all, but certainly one can not disregard the lesson of Hull's experiment that conscious hypotheses and well-formulated rules are by no means necessary for the solution of a concept learning problem. Of course, one could treat "hypothesis" as a theoretical term and say that it does not imply all the things which we usually mean when we talk about hypotheses, but then it would probably be better to choose a more neutral term.

The most influential treatment of concept learning as hypothesis testing was published in 1956 by Bruner, Goodnow, and Austin. Their book contains a wealth of descriptive material, but no precise theory of concept learning. They suggested that the subject chooses a hypothesis which is consistent with the stimulus input and proceeds to test it. Alternatively, the subject may decide to test all possible hypotheses simultaneously, or only a subset of the possible hypotheses. Clearly, the scheme according to which the subject selects hypotheses must be specified more precisely. Once the subject has formed a hypothesis he tests it systematically. Bruner *et al.* provided some interesting descriptions of different strategies which subjects employ for this purpose. Their experimental paradigm for studying these strategies permitted the subject to select stimulus items, rather than presenting items at random. One of the strategies observed by Bruner *et al.* has been called "conservative focusing." The subject considers all possible hypotheses simultaneously and one each trial asks for a stimulus card which differs from the last in exactly one dimension. Thus he is able to tell whether the dimension tested is or is not relevant. An example will help to clarify how this selection strategy works. Suppose that the subject is told that the first item, a *large, red square*, belongs to class A. The subject now selects as his hypothesis "Large, red square is A" and asks for a *small, red square*. If the small, red square is also on A, he knows that size is an irrelevant dimension, and he can test the other dimensions one by one to see which of them is necessary for the definition of class A. Conservative focusing is obviously an excellent strategy if the solution is of the form "Square is A." It will always result in a correct solution in just as many trials as there are dimensions to test. However, there obviously are other ways to go about learning a concept. Indeed, it is only for simple concepts which are defined by the presence or absence of single attributes that this strategy works well. Obviously some problems require considerably more complex solution strategies. Different subjects as well as the same subject at different times, use different strategies. Often no particular strategy is identifiable in the behavior of a subject. In any case, the strategy which a subject uses does not explain his behavior, but it itself needs to be explained. Somehow task variables (such as stimulus complexity, manner of presentation, or time given for solution) and previous experience combine to determine a subject's strategies—but how? In order to answer this question it is necessary to provide a much more specific formulation of the hypothesis testing process.

The first precise formulation of hypothesis-testing theory is due to Restle (1962). Restle's model is much more restricted in scope than the discussion of Bruner *et al.* Indeed, it is clearly oversimplified. However, it provides us with a solid starting point around which experimental work, as well as further explanatory attempts, can fruitfully be organized.

Restle assumes that a subject takes a sample of hypotheses and tests them. Whenever a hypothesis leads to a correct classification response, or whenever it is consistent with the information feedback provided by the experimenter, the subject retains it; whenever a hypothesis leads to an error or is inconsistent with the experimenter's classification, the hypothesis is rejected.

The class of possible hypotheses can be subdivided into three subsets: correct, wrong, and irrelevant hypotheses. The problem is solved once the subject finds a correct hypothesis and eliminates all incorrect and wrong hypotheses. Three possible sampling schemes have been considered for this process of hypothesis elimination. First, suppose the subject samples only one hypothesis at a time at random from the total pool of hypotheses. If the hypothesis sampled is correct the problem is solved. If the hypothesis is not correct, it will sooner or later lead to an incorrect response. Whenever an incorrect response occurs the hypothesis upon which this response was based is discarded and the subject resamples. Resampling is again from the total pool of hypotheses, thus disallowing for memory effects. A second case arises if the subject considers all hypotheses simultaneously and on every trial eliminates those hypotheses which he does not use and which are inconsistent with the information obtained on that trial. As long as the subject holds more than one strategy, the probability that he will make a correct response on any given trial is assumed to equal the proportion of strategies which led to that response. Finally, Restle considered the possibility that subjects sample at random a subset of hypotheses and eliminate wrong and irrelevant hypotheses from it on subsequent trials. If the sample of hypotheses contains a correct hypothesis the problem will eventually be solved. If it does not contain a correct hypothesis, the subject must take a new random sample of hypothesis once all hypotheses of the first sample have been eliminated. Restle's three cases imply rather different psychological processes. The third case seems to be intuitively most appealing. However, Restle (1962) has shown that the three cases are mathematically equivalent. For simple concept learning experiments the three models make exactly identical predictions as far as the probabilities of observable response sequences are concerned. Restle's equivalence theorem is extremely important, because if one is interested in knowing which of the three procedures subjects actually use for hypothesis testing, simple concept experiments can provide no information. Experiments must be especially designed to obtain information concerning this problem.

If Restle's strategy selection model is formulated mathematically it turns out to be very similar to the one-element model; in fact, Restle's model is a member of the general class of all-or-none learning models. It has already been mentioned that such models have been applied to concept identification data with some success. Therefore it is appropriate to examine more closely the ability of these models to describe concept identification data before returning to the specific interpretation of the model in terms of a strategy selection process. There is no need to restate the all-or-none learning model here, because it has been described in detail in Chapter 2. We can start with examining some data.

4. THE CUE-SELECTION MODEL OF CONCEPT LEARNING

An experiment reported by Bower and Trabasso (1964) provides an excellent example of the good fit of the one-element model to concept identification data. The stimulus material in this experiment consisted of 5-letter words. In each of the five positions one of two possible letters appeared. The fourth position was designated as the relevant position and the response assignments were made on the basis of the letter in that position: if it was an R, response 1 was reinforced, if it was a Q response 2 was reinforced. Thus an item like JVKRZ belonged to the first response class.

The analysis of the results can be divided into two parts. First, statistics independent of parameter estimates can be considered. Response probabilities before the last error were reasonably stationary, as is shown in Fig. 7.3. It is obvious from Fig. 7.3 that subjects did not improve on trials before the last error. Statistical tests confirm this impression. The second test which has been performed concerns the independence of successes and failures on trials before the last error. The model implies that the conditional probability of a success on trials before the last error is the same whether a success or a failure had occurred on the previous trial. This independence prediction was also confirmed by the data.

Before the model can be fitted to other data statistics the parameters of the model must be estimated. The model has two parameters, q the probability of a correct response before learning has occurred, and c the probability of a transition from the initial state to the learning state on a learning trial. An informal but intuitively appealing procedure for estimating q and c has been discussed in Chapter II. It was suggested that the observed proportion of successes prior to the

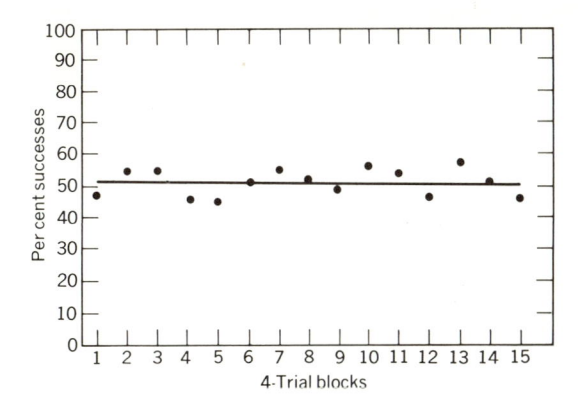

Fig. 7.3 *Stationarity data: percentage of successes prior to the last error in blocks of four trials. (after Bower and Trabasso, 1964)*

last error could be considered an estimate of q. In this case $q = .523$. The estimate for the learning rate was obtained by setting the observed mean number of errors equal to the theoretical expression and solving for c, using the previous estimate q. The expected number of trials before solution equals $1/c$, since c is the probability of learning on any given trial. The probability of an error in the unconditioned state equals $p = 1\text{-}q$, and therefore the expected number of errors equals p/c. The subjects in Bower's experiment made on the average 12.16 errors in learning the concept. Hence we obtain the estimate $c = .477/12.16 = .039$. Using these estimates one can calculate predictions for many different statistics. Some of the necessary formulas have been given in Chapter 2: for others the reader must refer to the original sources. Table 7.1 provides a comparison between the predictions of the one-element model and the Bower and Trabasso data. Evidently the one-element model describes concept identification data just as well as it describes paired-associate results.

One should not make too much of this similarity between paired-associate and concept identification data. After all, we have already reviewed several studies which showed that there were important differences between the two. The ability of the one-element model to describe both sets of data simply means that the learning process is discrete in both cases: paired-associate learning in sufficiently simple situations is all-or-none, and so is concept learning. However, one should not forget the important differences which exist in the unit of analysis in paired-associate learning and concept learning. Single

Table 7.1. *Observed and predicted statistics from the concept identification experiment of Bower and Trabasso (1964).*

Statistic	Observed	Predicted
Average errors	12.16	—
Standard deviation	12.22	12.18
Errors before the first success	.92	.89
Standard deviation	.98	1.14
Average trial of last error	25.70	24.50
Standard deviation	28.90	25.00
Probability of an error following an error	.47	.46
Runs of errors	6.44	6.57
Runs of 1 error	3.62	3.57
2 errors	1.32	1.63
3 errors	.64	.75
4 errors	.40	.35
Alternations of success and failure	12.33	12.41
Error-error pairs		
1 trial apart	5.76	5.45
2 trials apart	5.04	5.22

stimulus-response connections are acquired in the former, but a whole set of items is connected with a response in the latter. Thus, although the statistical properties of the learning data require the same formal model for the two cases, the interpretation of the model must be quite different.

Several alternative interpretations for the formal model of concept learning have already been discussed. Subjects may be learning to pay attention to the relevant stimulus dimension and connect the stimulus values on that dimension with the response alternatives. In terms of the experiment just discussed this means that the subject learns to attend to the letter in the fourth position, and to call an item a 1 if that letter is an R, and a 2 if it is a Q. This is essentially the position of Bower and Trabasso (1964). Restle's strategy selection theory is a slight variation of this position. The subject is viewed by Restle as testing various strategies. In our example the problem is solved if the subject finds the strategy "say 1 if R, say 2 if Q". In general, if the subject tests one strategy at a time until he finds the one which leads to a consistently reinforced response, a formal model is obtained which is identical with the one-element model in most ways. The more complicated versions of Restle's strategy selection theory will be considered after the simple one-strategy-at-a-time model has been explored more fully. Finally, the model has a stimulus sampling interpretation. A concept is represented by a pattern and the model describes the conditioning of the pattern.

In one respect the conditioning interpretation and the strategy selection theory have quite different implications. A conditioning interpretation suggests that learning can occur on every trial, whenever the experimenter provides informative feedback to the subject, independently of the subject's response. The strategy testing interpretation suggests that learning occurs only when the subject has made an error. If the subject is testing an incorrect strategy which per chance leads to a correct response on a trial he has no reason to reject this strategy and retains it until it leads to an incorrect response.

A semi-formal statement of this difference between the two models will help to clarify the issue, without repeating too much of the material already presented in Chapter 2. Both versions of the model are two-state models which distinguish a learning state, in which correct responses always occur, and an initial state in which correct responses occur with probability q and errors occur with probability p; in addition, both models assume that the probability of a transition from the initial state to the learning state does not change during the course of learning. The difference is that the conditioning version of the model permits transitions into the learning state on all trials on which the subject receives information feedback, while the strategy selection theory allows such transitions only when the experimenter informs the subject that he has made an error and the subject selects a new strategy. In matrix form the conditioning version can be expressed as follows:

$$
\begin{array}{cc}
 & \begin{array}{ccc} \text{Learning State} & \text{Initial State} \end{array} & \begin{array}{c} \text{Probability of a} \\ \text{correct response} \end{array} \\
\begin{array}{c} \text{Learning State} \\ \text{Initial State} \end{array} & \begin{bmatrix} 1 & 0 \\ c & 1-c \end{bmatrix} & \begin{bmatrix} 1 \\ q \end{bmatrix}
\end{array}
$$

Dividing the initial state into Initial Success and Initial Error the same model can be reformulated as follows:

$$
(1) \quad
\begin{array}{c}
\begin{array}{cccc} \text{Learning} & \text{Error} & \text{Success} & \text{Response} \\ \text{State} & \text{State} & \text{State} & \text{probability} \end{array} \\
\begin{array}{c} \text{Learning State} \\ \text{Error State} \\ \text{Success State} \end{array}
\begin{bmatrix} 1 & 0 & 0 \\ c & p(1-c) & p(1-c) \\ c & p(1-c) & q(1-c) \end{bmatrix}
\begin{bmatrix} 1 \\ 0 \\ 1 \end{bmatrix}
\end{array}
$$

Correspondingly, the strategy selection version of the model can be written as

$$
(2) \quad
\begin{array}{c}
\text{Learning State} \\
\text{Error State} \\
\text{Success State}
\end{array}
\begin{array}{cccc}
\text{Learning} & \text{Error} & \text{Success} & \text{Response} \\
\text{State} & \text{State} & \text{State} & \text{probability} \\
\begin{bmatrix}
1 & 0 & 0 \\
c & p(1-c) & q(1-c) \\
0 & p & q
\end{bmatrix}
&&&
\begin{bmatrix}
1 \\
0 \\
1
\end{bmatrix}
\end{array}
$$

As has been mentioned on several previous occasions, these two versions of the model are formally equivalent (Atkinson and Crothers, 1964; Greeno and Steiner, 1964). Thus, for every parameter pair p and c in Eq. (1) there exists a pair c' and p' in Eq. (2) which will lead to identical predictions for all data statistics. Therefore, there is no chance of deciding between (1) and (2) on the basis of goodness of fit to data from standard concept identification experiments. Some new source of information must be found by designing suitable experiments. However, since we have our problem clearly formulated we know what sort of information to look for and what kind of experiments to design. Several relevant studies have been reported by Bower and Trabasso (1964).

The first of these experiments was based upon the differential implications of (1) and (2) with respect to experimental manipulations of the number of response alternatives. Clearly, the more responses that are possible in an experiment, the less likelihood of a "chance" success exists. Chance successes, however, are nothing but excess baggage if learning occurs only on errors (Eq. (2)). The greater the probability of a chance success the fewer the opportunities to learn, and the higher the predicted trial of the last error. If learning occurs on all trials (Eq. (1)), on the other hand, increasing the number of response alternatives will have only a small effect upon the mean number of trials before the last error. This prediction, of course, presupposes an experiment in which the learning rate is constant, which means that the subjects must be faced with the same set of cues in both situations, except that in one case the stimuli are to be classified into two classes and in the other the stimuli must be classified into more than two classes. Bower and Trabasso found that the average trial of the last error increased from 18.3 for a four-response group to 26.4 for the two-response group. Thus, it appeared that increasing the number of response alternatives speeded up learning by permitting fewer chance successes, as the error learning model predicts. This result is especially interesting in that Bower (1962) has reported a paired-associate experiment in which the number of response alternatives was varied, the results of which agreed quite well with the assumption that learning occurred on all trials. Thus, paired-associate learning and concept learning seem to be different in this respect.

Bower and Trabasso also reported a reversal experiment which further discriminates between the two versions of the all-or-none model. They reversed concept assignments on every second error in a simple concept identification experiment. Color, red or blue, was the relevant dimension in their experiment. The responses were the nonsense syllables VEK and CEJ. Suppose VEK was the correct response for red. When the subject made his second error, the experimenter told the subject he was right and changed the problem, so that from now on CEJ was the correct response for red. Error learning theory predicts that the number of called errors should be the same as the total number of errors made by a control group with no reversals at all. This prediction follows from the assumption that learning occurs on errors, because only the called errors are errors for the subject. If learning can occur on all trials it follows that the total number of errors, called and uncalled, should be the same as the number of errors made by control subjects. According to incremental theory, subjects should have extreme difficulty learning the problem in the reversal condition at all.

The results were clearly in favor of the error learning model. The average number of errors made by subjects in the control group was 8.0 and the number of called errors in the reversal condition was 7.8. This result has been confirmed in later studies, so that we can pick with some assurance Eq. (2) over Eq. (1) as the more adequate model for concept learning. However, while supporting the error learning model in general, these studies also made it clear that the model is still quite inadequate. The model represents concept learning stripped of all its complexity. Our next task is therefore to define explicitly those aspects of concept identification learning which are neglected by the model, or not adequately handled.

Consider the following experiment (Trabasso and Bower, 1966) in which response assignments are changed when the subject makes an error, but in which the change is a dimensional shift rather than a reversal. If red-A and blue-B is the original concept, for instance, the experimenter changes the problem to circle-A and square-B whenever a subject makes his second error. When two errors occur with the new problem the experimenter shifts back to the color dimension. It has been found that in experiments of this type subjects make approximately as many errors in the shift condition as in the control group where the correct solution is defined in terms of either the color or form dimension but not both and is never changed during the course of the experiment. However, Trabasso and Bower pointed out that such a control group provides a biased comparison, and that the proper control group should be one in which subjects can solve the problem either on the basis of color, or on the basis of shape, or both. The reasoning was that subjects in the shift condition could solve either way, too. To see this, suppose that the experimenter defines form as the relevant variable and that an error has just occurred on the previous trial so that the subject selects a new hypothesis. If a subject selects the hypothesis "form," he will solve the problem; however, if he selects the hypothesis "color" he will also solve the problem because on his next error the experimenter will change the problem to color and call the response correct. Since only informed errors are counted, Trabasso and Bower argued that the experimental group should be properly compared with a control group solving a problem in which both color and form are relevant. Relative to such a control group subjects learning with the shift procedure performed significantly poorer, contrary to the theoretical predictions. This predictive failure points out an important deficiency in the model. The way the model is stated it is a no-memory model. Whenever an error occurs the subject samples at random a hypothesis from the total pool of hypotheses. Hypotheses which have already been tried once earlier in the process are returned to the common pool and may be tried again. Using statistical terminology we can say that subjects are sampling with replacement; psychologically this means that the theory does not permit the subject the use of memory. If subjects would sample hypotheses without replacement they would exhibit perfect memory—and frequently fail to solve shift problems at all because in that case a hypothesis once tried and rejected would presumably not be tried again. The results of Trabasso and Bower's experiment imply that subjects do use memory to some degree, hence the slower learning in the shift condition, but that memory is not perfect.

A rather different experimental approach to the problem just discussed has been taken by Levine (1966). Levine was not satisfied with inferring the kind of strategies which subjects use indirectly, but wanted to observe strategies directly. The obvious way of asking subjects what their strategies were on each trial was rejected because of the possibility of biasing the subjects through the questioning and because of the well-known observation that subjects may exhibit a strategy in their behavior but be unable to verbalize it correctly. Thus, Levine designed an experiment with special restrictions, so that the experimenter could tell by the subject's responses which hypothesis, if any, a subject was using on each trial. In this way changes in the hypotheses after errors and after successes could be observed quite directly.

In Levine's experiment subjects had to choose one of two letters on each stimulus card. The letters differed in color (black or white), form (X or T), position (right or left), and size (small or large). The subject thus could choose among 8 different hypotheses. More complex hypotheses were excluded by the instructions given to the subject, which emphasized the structure of the stimulus set and the nature of possible solutions. On the first trial of the experiment the subject was shown a stimulus card and told which of the two choices was correct. The experimenter then forced the subject to show him which of the 8 hypotheses he had selected by asking him to respond to four selected stimulus cards without receiving any feedback from the experimenter. The cards were selected in such a way that the experimenter could unambiguously infer from the subject's four responses which of the admissable hypotheses was being used, if any. Figure 7.4 shows an example of 4 such stimulus cards and the corresponding identifiable response patterns. Since the subject received no feedback during these four choices he would presumably respond on the basis of the same hypothesis on all four trials. If he changed his hypothesis an uninterpretable response pattern resulted. On the fifth trial the experimenter could predict the subject's response on the basis of the inferred hypothesis. On this trial the experimenter also told the subject "right" or "wrong" according to a pre-established scheme. Then another four blank trials were given during which the subject's new hypothesis could be inferred, and finally another reinforced trial. This cycle was repeated a third time.

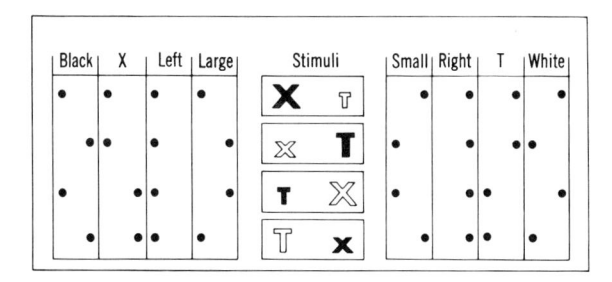

Fig. 7.4 *Eight patterns of choices corresponding to each of the eight hypotheses when the four stimulus pairs are presented consecutively without outcomes. (after Levine, 1966)*

Levine's subjects clearly did use hypotheses: 92.4 per cent of the response patterns on the blank trials were in agreement with one of the eight admissible hypotheses. Furthermore, the hypothesis inferred from a block of four blank trials could be used to predict correctly the subject's response on the fifth trial in 97.5 per cent of all cases.

Of much greater interest is the effect which a reinforced trial has upon the subject's behavior. According to the error learning model, the subject should discard his hypothesis if he is told "wrong" and try a new one, but should retain it after a "right." This is quite what Levine observed: 95 per cent of the time a hypothesis was retained after a "right," and only 2 per cent of the time after a "wrong."

Note that the very low percentage of hypothesis retention after an error means that subjects almost never picked a hypothesis which had just been called wrong. If they were sampling at random from the total pool of eight hypotheses there would be a probability of $\frac{1}{8} = .125$ of getting the same hypothesis again right after an error.

Given that subjects exclude a hypothesis from consideration if they have just been told that it is wrong, one might expect that they can remember at least some of the hypotheses which were excluded earlier in the experiment. A rational subject endowed with memory could surely do better than merely exclude one hypothesis when he makes an error. Suppose a subject was shown a card with a large black X on the left, and a small white T on the right. Further, suppose that his hypothesis on that trial was "choose X" and that he was told wrong. Clearly, the subject should exclude not only the hypothesis "choose X," but also "choose large," "choose black," and "choose left." Bruner, Goodnow, and Austin (1956) have observed such behavior in their subjects and have named it perfect focusing. We have discussed in Chapter 6 efficient information processing devices which employ this strategy. Random sampling with replacement is the opposite of perfect focusing in terms of efficiency: while the latter uses all available information, the former uses very little. Not too surprisingly, Levine's subjects operated somewhere between these extremes. Levine was able to estimate the size of the set of hypotheses from which subjects were making their choices after they were told "wrong" on each of the three reinforced trials. According to the sampling with replacement assumption this size remains at 8 throughout; perfect focusing implies that the subjects reduce their hypotheses set by one half on each trial. Both of these assumptions, along with the actual data points, are shown in Fig. 7.5. Although by no means perfect focusers, subjects do manage to reject some hypotheses which should be rejected.

While the results summarized in Fig. 7.5 show that the model

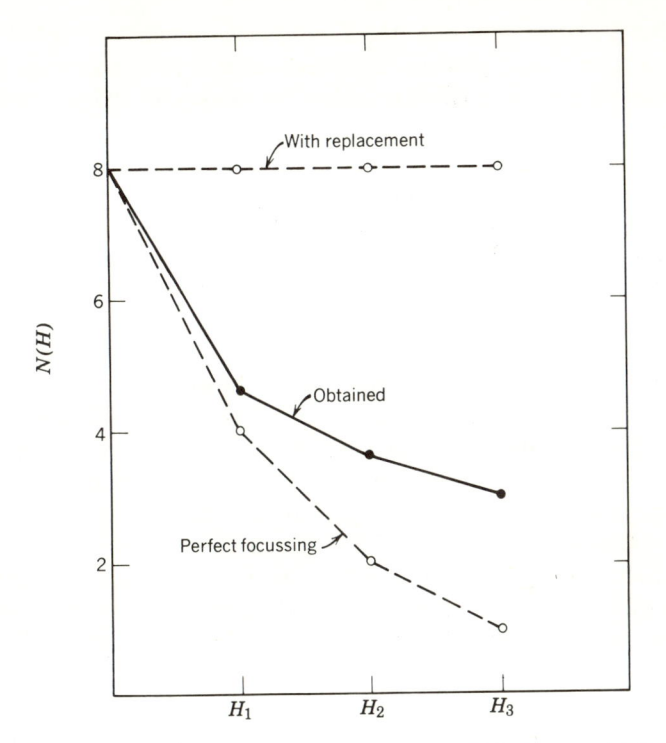

Fig. 7.5 *The size of the set of hypotheses,* N*(*H*), from which the subject is sampling immediately following a "wrong" on trials 1, 2, and 3. (after Levine, 1966)*

given by Eq. (2) is gravely inadequate in that it does not account for the use of memory in concept identification tasks, another result of Levine forces us to modify our interpretation of what "learning" means in a concept learning task. If learning means that a subject actually changes his hypothesis and tries a new one, then it is true that learning occurs only on errors, as mentioned before. But there is another kind of learning going on, in the sense that subjects may reduce the set of hypotheses under consideration. Whether an experimenter says "right" or "wrong" he always provides the same amount of information in Levine's experiment. Each reinforcement is worth exactly one bit of information, enabling a perfect focusing device to cut the set of possible hypotheses in half. Suppose that in the example described above the experimenter had said "right." Then the subject could exclude the hypotheses "small," "white," "T," and "right," thus learning something after a success. Of course, this learning would have an observable effect on his responding only after he makes an error on some later trial and selects a new hypothesis. Levine was able to show that subjects actually process information in this manner, again with less than 100 per cent efficiency, but in amounts which can not be neglected.

In another experiment using a similar procedure Levine investigated the stationarity prediction of the all-or-none model (Levine, Miller, and Steinmeyer, 1967). He found that the probability of a correct response on trials before the last error was stationary at the chance level. Furthermore, Levine's procedure permitted him to determine how often subjects used what was in fact the correct hypothesis on trials before the last error. As expected, such instances were extremely rare. The most interesting finding, however, concerns the subject's use of the complementary hypothesis, that is, the hypothesis which involves the same stimulus dimension as the correct hypothesis (e.g., "white" if "black" is correct). During the presolution period the complementary hypothesis is hardly ever used (.02). Only on the trial immediately before the last error was there a tendency to select the complementary hypothesis (.16). During the presolution period subjects were simply not responding to the correct stimulus dimension, i.e., they were not using the appropriate stimulus coding, rather than choosing among all 8 hypotheses at random. Once they found the right coding response, the problem was solved rapidly.

Levine's work provides both a confirmation and a refutation of Restle's and Bower and Trabasso's model. Subjects do respond according to identifiable strategies, they do employ a win-stay, loose-shift policy, and the data are generally in good accord with the model. On the other hand, the no-memory assumption of the model is clearly wrong, and secondly, subjects learn on successes in the sense that they adjust the set of possible hypotheses in accordance with the information provided by the experimenter. Both of these problems which arose in the Levine study have to do with the use of memory in concept learning. Further studies concerned with this issue, as well as some tentative solutions, will be considered below.

5. EXTENSIONS AND MODIFICATIONS OF THE MODEL FOR CONCEPT LEARNING

Additivity of Cues

The model for concept learning being discussed here is a model for the structure of the learning process. The specific predictions which the model makes depend upon the values selected for the parameters of the model, the conditioning rate, and the probability of a correct response on presolution trials. Although the latter is often restricted by the characteristics of the stimulus material—e.g., in a two-choice situation with binary stimulus material this value should be around one half—the model tells us nothing about the value of the conditioning rate which could be expected in any particular experiment. The general model defines a whole class of specific models, one for each parameter value. Most theories are general in this sense, i.e., they do not attempt to account for the specific values which parameters assume in various situations, but estimate these values from the data. The distinction between a general theory and specific parameter values is by no means a weakness peculiar to psychology. First of all, most scientific theories are general in the sense that they do not have a theory of parameters. As an example take Kepler's laws of planetary motion. Kepler treated the exact values of the planetary orbits as parameters of the process, which need not be specified by the theory. Kepler himself still regarded this as a weakness of his theory, but today physicists feel that the restriction of the explicable to the structure of the system was necessary, and a step in the right direction (Wigner, 1964). Which brings us to our second point, namely, that one can not be sure that the necessity of estimating parameters is always a weakness of a theory. A mature science must learn to distinguish between those problems which have solutions, and those which are not to be explained.

One subproblem of the theory of parameters which offers much promise to investigations with currently available methods concerns the way in which learning rates in concept identification experiments combine. To illustrate the nature of the problem, suppose one group of subjects is learning a concept identification problem with Cue 1 relevant and a second group is learning a problem with Cue 2 relevant. We have no means of predicting *a priori* what the learning rates will be for the two groups of subjects, although we can make some guesses such as that a perceptually striking cue will be picked up faster than a cue which is not easily noticed. However, suppose a third group of subjects learns a problem with both cues relevant. Given that we have estimated the learning rates from the data of the subjects learning with either cue separately, we can now ask how cues combine.

This problem has been thoroughly discussed by Restle (1957). Learning in concept identification tasks is a problem of cue selection. In order to obtain an expression for the probability of selecting any particular cue Restle associated with each cue i a weight w_i, and assumed that the probability of selecting cue i is given by the ratio of the weight of cue i, w_i, to the sum of all cue weights. Or, in general, when there is more than one relevant cue in a problem,

$$(3) \qquad c = \frac{\displaystyle\sum_{\text{all relevant } i\text{'s}} w_i}{\displaystyle\sum_{\text{all } j\text{'s}} w_j}$$

Thus, if a cue is introduced, the change in the learning rate can be calculated by adding the weight of the new cue to both the numerator and denominator, if the new cue is relevant, or by adding its weight to the denominator only, if the new cue is merely a distractor.

Equation (3) is called the additivity of cues assumption. It is actually a very strong and powerful assumption; it is the simplest one that can be made mathematically. Cues could combine in many other ways, and it would be foolish to assume that they always combine according to Eq. (3). Rather, the task is one of investigating under what conditions cues combine additively, if at all. Consider the following example for non-additive combination of cues (after Luce, 1959). Imagine a gourmet making a selection from a menu which offers a choice between hamburger and steak only. Our gourmet may be twice as likely to pick hamburger than steak from such a menu. Now suppose we add a new "cue" to the menu, say Lobster Thermidor, and let us also make the unrealistic assumption that the gourmet greatly dislikes lobster, and would never consider ordering it. If the new cue combines additively with the two previous items, the preference of hamburger over steak can not change, because adding a weight of zero to the denominator of Eq. (3) does not affect the equation. However, one could easily imagine how adding lobster thermidor to the menu could have a quite different effect: The gourmet may have chosen hamburger over steak only because he would not trust the restaurant with a steak, but seeing a demanding item like lobster thermidor on the menu might reassure him as to the competence of the kitchen, and he might dare to order the steak. Thus, it is not hard to imagine how cues could combine non-additively, but only experimental work can show how subjects actually combine cues.

Restle first tried out the additivity of cues assumption on a problem in animal learning. It has long puzzled psychologists whether rats learned a T-maze by acquiring a "cognitive map", or whether they simply learned a turning response. Experimental demonstrations of place learning as well as response learning were both available. Imagine a T-maze in the form of a cross as shown in Fig. 7.6. Either the right or the left arm of the maze is designated as correct by the ex-

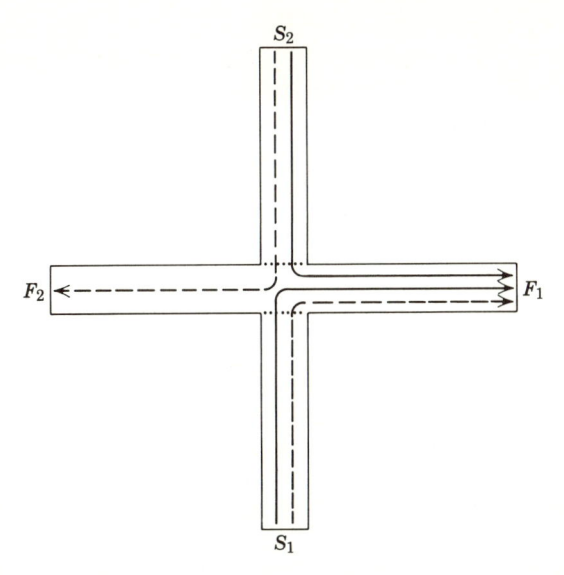

Fig. 7.6 *Plan of a T-maze to study response learning and place learning.*

perimenter, i.e., the rat finds food at the end of this arm of the maze. In the usual T-maze experiment the animal always starts from the same place, say S_1, and the upper arm of the maze is locked. If the rat learns to go to the right arm of the maze (F_1), it is then not clear whether it has learned a turning response (right turn) or whether it has learned to go to a particular place in the maze. However, if the rat sometimes starts from S_1 and sometimes starts from S_2, one can distinguish between the learning of a turning response and place learning. If food is always at F_1 and the starting position alternates between S_1 and S_2, the animal must learn to go to a particular place, which involves a right-turn on one side and a left turn on the other side. On the other hand, if food is at F_1 if the rat starts at S_1, and at F_2 if the rat starts at S_2 the problem can only be solved if the subject learns to turn right at the choice point. Rats can learn the task in both ways and Restle pointed out that their learning rates appeared to depend upon how many place and response cues the subjects were given. With strong and reliable place cues the rats responded primarily to them, but without place cues they could solve the problem merely on the basis of kinesthetic cues. Restle estimated the weight of the place cues and the weight of the response cues from the learning rates of two separate groups of rats which learned the T-maze with either place or response cues, and then used Eq. (3) to predict the learning rate of a group of rats for which both sets of cues were relevant. This prediction was strikingly successful.

The additivity of cues assumption has also been tested repeatedly in concept identification experiments. A study reported by Trabasso (1963) will serve as an illustration. The stimulus materials in Trabasso's experiment were flower designs which varied in several ways, such as number and form of leaves, color of the angle, etc. One (or sometimes two) of these attributes were selected for each group of subjects and a binary concept was defined along this dimension. The learning rate c was estimated from the mean number of errors made in learning the concept by setting it equal to the theoretical expression derived from Eq. (2) and solving for c. Since not all of Trabasso's subjects reached criterion, the usual expression for the mean number of errors has to be slightly adjusted. According to Eq. (2) the mean number of errors equals $1/c$. This expression is easily derived. It is apparent that the learning state can be entered only from the error state. Whenever an error occurs it will be the last one with probability c. Hence the probability of obtaining exactly k errors is

$$P(T = k) = c(1 - c)^{k-1} \qquad k = 1,2,3, \dots \quad .$$

The expected number of errors during training is therefore

$$E(T) = \sum_{k=1}^{\infty} k \, c(1 - c)^{k-1} = 1/c,$$

and

$$c = 1/E(T).$$

If an experiment is terminated before all subjects have reached criterion, it can be shown that

$$(4) \qquad c = \frac{p^*}{E(T) - (1 - p^*)},$$

where p^* is the proportion of subjects who solved the problem. Equation (4) will henceforth be used to estimate c.

In Table 7.2 three of Trabasso's experimental conditions are shown, together with the mean number of errors for each group and the corresponding c-estimates. In Group 1 the size of the angle between leaves and stem provided the relevant cue; there was no color, and other cues such as flower, leaf position, and leaf shape were irrele-

Table 7.2. *Additivity of cues: experimental conditions and results from Trabasso (1963).*

Group	Condition	Mean number of errors in learning	Estimate of c	Equation for c
1	Angle relevant, no color	19.50	.035	$\dfrac{w(A)}{2w(A)+w(I)}$
2	Angle relevant and colored red for emphasis	12.45	.067	$\dfrac{r.w(A)}{2rw(A)+w(C)+w(I)}$
3	Color relevant, angle fixed	4.05	.190	$\dfrac{w(C)}{2w(C)+w(I)}$

vant. In Group 2 the angle cue was relevant again, but the angle was painted red for emphasis. This led to a considerable improvement in performance. In Group 3, the angle was fixed, but it was colored either green or red, and this color was the relevant cue. This last condition proved to be by far the easiest to learn.

The equations for c, also shown in Table 7.2, represent applications of Eq. (3) to the present problem. For example, in the Group 1 problem $w(I)$ is the weight of the irrelevant cues from flower, leaf shape, and leaf position, as well as other unknown irrelevant sources. The angle cue has weight $w(A)$. The extra $w(A)$ in the denominator has been added for those relevant cues which were sampled and led to wrong hypotheses. When a cue is emphasized, its weight is multiplied by a constant, r for red; $w(C)$ is the weight of the color cue. By solving the three expressions given in Table 7.2 one can obtain the cue weights for angle and color, and for the effect of emphasis in terms of $w(I)$:

$$w(A) = .038\, w(I)$$
$$w(C) = .306\, w(I)$$
$$r = 2.03.$$

The fact that color is a more noticeable cue than the angle between stem and leaves is represented by the much larger cue weight for color.

Now consider a group which can solve the problem both on the basis of angle and color: the size of the angle is a relevant cue and, in addition, the angle is colored red or green, correlated with angle size.

The additivity of cues assumption leads to the following prediction for the learning rate in this condition:

$$c = \frac{r.w(A) + w(C)}{2r.w(A) + 2w(C) + w(I)} = .217.$$

The observed value of c for this group was .225 which is encouragingly close to the prediction.

To another group of subjects Trabasso gave the same stimulus material as in the combined group described above, except that he made the angle color an irrelevant cue. Angle size was thus the correct cue, and the angle was again emphasized by color except that the emphasizer was not neutral (always red, as in Group 2) but was distracting (sometimes green, sometimes red, but not correlated with angle size). In the prediction of the learning rate for this group the weight of the angle color cues must therefore be added to the denominator but not in the numerator:

$$c = \frac{r.w(A)}{2r.w(A) + w(C) + w(I)} = .053.$$

A group of subjects run under these conditions learned with c = .055.

Trabasso studied several other combinations, but the examples reported here will suffice to illustrate the principle of his work. His evidence, as well as evidence from other studies, offers strong support for the additivity of cues hypothesis. However, the exact range of applicability for this hypothesis has not yet been determined. Zeaman and Denegre (1967) have reported conditions under which cues do not combine additively but are compounded in a more complex way. It remains as an important task for future research to specify precisely when the additivity of cues hypothesis applies and when it does not. Right now it seems to apply rather widely, but the boundary conditions are not yet clear.

Transfer after Concept Learning

Geometric figures varying along clearly specifiable dimensions have been the stimuli in most experiments to which the cue selection model has been applied so far. In this section we shall return to the somewhat more complex experimental paradigm described in the beginning of this chapter. The paradigm is exemplified by the Underwood and Richardson (1956) study. Their stimuli were words belonging to different conceptual categories, and the subjects learned to identify these categories. The conceptual categories differed in their dominance level. For instance, it is quite obvious that BEAR, LION, and COW belong to the category ANIMALS, but that FLEA, MOUSE, and GERM are all SMALL is much harder to notice. Concept acquisition experiments with such stimulus material involve two separate problems: concept learning itself, and recognition of an item as an instance once the concept has been learned. The cue selection model can be extended to account for both of these processes.

Consider an experiment which consists of two parts, a training phase and a test phase. During training subjects learn to associate the instances of a concept with a common response. This may happen in two ways: subjects may learn each item separately and independently as in a paired-associate experiment (say with probability c) or they may learn the concept. Let the probability that a subject acquires the concept when studying an individual item be a. During the transfer phase of the experiment subjects are given new instances of the concept. If the correct concept has not been learned, no transfer will occur. If the concept has been learned transfer will occur if the subject recognizes an item as an instance of the concept. Call the recognition probability b. The value of b will vary according to the dominance level of the concept.

The main problem which still remains unspecified concerns the nature of the transfer. Greeno and Scandura (1966) proposed that transfer in this situation, if it occurs at all, is perfect, and they reported an extensive experimental test of this assumption. Their model for all-or-none transfer is a two-state model, similar to the one-element model for paired-associate learning. However, there are now two ways of entering the learning state: an item may be in the learning state already at the beginning of the test phase of the experiment through transfer, or it may enter the learning state through learning during the test phase itself.

Greeno and Scandura represented each of the concepts WHITE, ROUND, and SOFT by a nonsense syllable with which the subject had been familiarized. During the training phase of their experiment subjects learned a 7-item list which consisted of instances of these concepts paired with the appropriate nonsense syllable. Four instances of one concept, two of the other, and one of the third were used. Subjects were asked to attend to possible concept relationships among the words. The test list consisted of one new item for each concept (experimental items) and three unrelated control items. The subjects were reminded that some of the items in the test list would be related to the syllables in the same way as the items in the training list. The test list was presented repeatedly until the subject reached a criterion of 5 consecutive correct trials. Positive transfer was obtained in that the experimental items were learned faster than the control items. The amount of transfer was a function of the number of items which were presented during training. The most transfer was obtained when four training items were given and the least with one training item. In addition, Greeno and Scandura also investigated the effects of dominance level upon learning and transfer, but we can neglect this aspect of their experiment here since the relevant findings with respect to dominance level have already been discussed.

The hypothesis that transfer is all-or-none was confirmed by the results of Greeno and Scandura. Consider only those experimental items for which the subject made no errors in the transfer phase of the experiment. According to the model no errors will be made if transfer occurs, or if transfer did not occur but the subject learned the item without errors during the transfer phase itself. The rest of the experimental items, which are the items with at least one error during the test stage, are items for which no transfer occurred and are thus exactly comparable to control items under the assumption of all-or-none transfer. Greeno and Scandura compared experimental items having at least one error with control items for which at least one error had occurred and found that the two groups of items were indistinguishable with respect to a number of data statistics. Furthermore, the learning of the experimental items was, in general, in accordance with the predictions from the one-element model.

The only difference between experimental and control items is then that some of the experimental items are already in the learning state at the beginning of the test phase because of transfer of training. Suppose that at the beginning of the test a proportion t of the experimental items is in the learning state, and a proportion of $(1 - t)$ is in the initial state, i.e., let the starting vector of the model be $[t, 1 - t]$. Then $t = 0$ for the control items, and $0 \leq t \leq 1$ for experimental items. Greeno and Scandura estimated t from the data of the two experimental groups. The t-estimate for all experimental items was .402, which was significantly different from the t-estimate for the control items, which, in turn, did not differ significantly from 0. The authors also provided a significance test for the hypothesis that the learning rates are equal for control and experimental items. This hypothesis was accepted, indicating that there were no partial transfer effects in the sense of an increase in the learning rates for the experimental items.

The t-values, as an index of the amount of transfer, varied systematically among the three types of experimental items. The largest value (.538) was obtained for the item with the four training instances, an intermediate value was obtained for the item with the two training instances (.349), and the smallest value was obtained for the item with only one training instance (.281). These values could be accounted for by a quite simple argument. The amount of transfer is a function of two parameters, a, the probability of concept acquisition, and b, the probability of recognizing an item as an instance of that concept during the test phase of the experiment. The probability that a concept will not be learned is $(1 - a)$, and that it will not be learned when k instances are presented is $(1 - a)^k$. Therefore, $1 - (1 - a)^k$ is the probability of concept acquisition with k training instances. The probability of transfer, t, is then given by the product of the probability that the concept has been learned and the probability b of recognizing an item as an instance of the concept: $b[1 - (1 - a)^k]$. Thus function corresponds quite well to the observed t-values.

Thus the cue selection model can be extended in a natural way to incorporate those experimental situations where the stimuli are words and the concepts which are to be learned are superordinate terms. However, Greeno and Scandura not only provided us with an extension of the model to a new area, but, in addition, they also made an interesting psychological discovery: that transfer, under the conditions of their experiment, is all-or-none. It remains to be seen, of course, how general this finding is. There is at least one experiment which confirms Greeno and Scandura's results. This is a study by Polson (1967), in which a design similar to that of Greeno's experiment was employed. Polson's subjects learned five 8-item paired-associate lists according to an A-B, A'-B, A''-B, ... design. For instance, suppose the first list contained the item BEAR $-$ 7. A second list item might then be CAT $-$ 7, etc. As long as the subject merely learns separate paired-associates, the learning of BEAR $-$ 7 and CAT $-$ 7 should be identical according to Greeno's theory, except for learning-to-learn effects. However, if the subject acquires the concept ANIMAL along with BEAR, and if he recognizes CAT as an instance of that concept, he knows that 7 is the correct response for CAT, i.e., there will be perfect transfer of training. Polson's results were quite in agreement with this prediction. He found strong transfer effects between lists, both of a specific and a nonspecific kind. Nonspecific transfer was evaluated by means of a control group which learned 5 paired-associate lists in which the stimulus terms were unrelated from list to list (A-B, C-B, D-B, . . .). The learning rates (c in Eq. (2)) increased

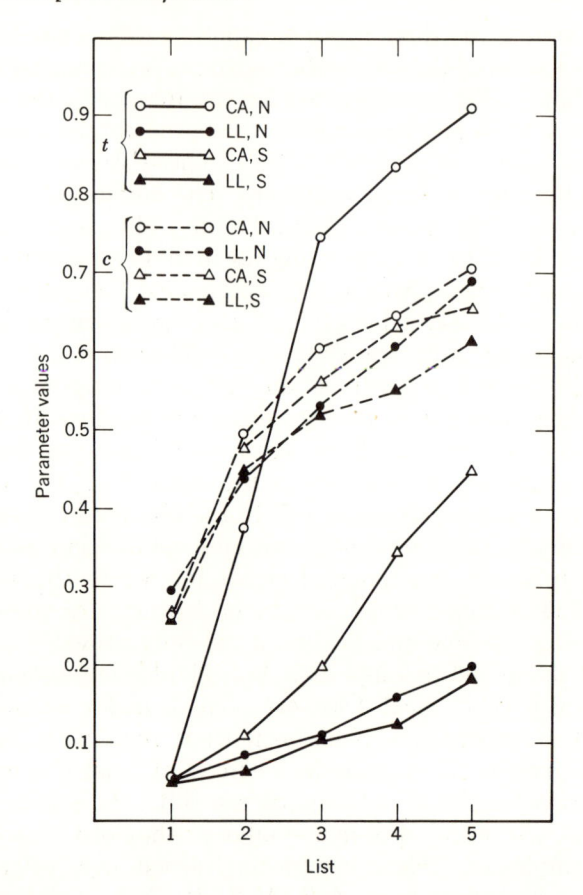

Fig. 7.7 *The observed values of the transfer probability* t *and the learning rate* c *plotted as a function of successive lists for each of the four combinations of training conditions (concept acquisition, CA, and learning-to-learn control, LL) and concept type (NOUN or SENSE). (after Polson, 1967)*

over the five lists, but they were not significantly different for experimental and control lists. The learning rate was subject only to a learning-to-learn effect, as it has been described before on several occasions. Figure 7.7 shows this increase over successive lists in Polson's experiment. The experimental condition is indicated by CA (concept acquisition) and LL stands for the learning-to-learn control group. Separate curves are shown for two kinds of experimental material, nouns (N) and sense impressions (S). Note that the learning-to-learn effect more than doubles learning rates within 5 lists. Relative to this increase the differences between the experimental and control groups are small indeed. Thus, Polson could conclude that specific transfer does not affect learning rates. Instead, specific transfer occurs because more and more items are in the learning state already at the beginning of training, as is shown by the t-estimates given in Fig. 7.7. After learning the first four lists, subjects immediately classified correctly about 90 per cent of the items of the fifth list in the case of nouns belonging to a superordinate category. There was much less concept learning of the more difficult sense impressions, but still a significant amount compared with the small increases of the t-estimates in the control group. Thus, the results of Greeno and Scandura were fully confirmed. When a concept is learned and items are recognized as belonging to it, transfer is perfect; otherwise the item is treated just like a control item.

There was another fascinating finding in Polson's experiment which is worth mentioning. It brings up a problem of great importance which has as yet received little attention. Suppose one asks when each of the eight concepts was acquired during learning—in the first, second, third, or fourth list. According to the theory, concepts are learned very much like paired-associates. There exists some probability a of learning a concept which is independent of learning the other concepts. However, this was not what Polson observed. Subjects seemed at first to be slow in acquiring concepts, but once the first concept was learned, the other seven followed rapidly. In other words, learning of the eight concepts was not independent. It is as if the subjects first had to understand that there were conceptual relationships between the lists which could be exploited before concept acquisition could start. In effect, there were two learning rates in Polson's experiment: one very small one before subjects realized the nature of the experiment, and a larger one thereafter. The best manner to treat this change in the subject's set formally in terms of the model has not yet been explored sufficiently. Note that this problem did not arise in the experiment of Greeno and Scandura because they induced a set to learn concepts in their subjects by means of instructions.

The Number of Cues in the Subject's Sample

The model thus far discussed in this chapter assumed that subjects work with one cue at a time in concept formation experiments. Two comments need to be made concerning this assumption. First, it is certainly not generally valid. The general problem of cue selection in discrimination learning has been described previously. It has been shown that subjects do not always select cues, but may respond to the total stimulus pattern instead. Furthermore, even if cue selection occurs, subjects may very well select more than one cue. Secondly, the reader should remember that there were good theoretical reasons for considering in detail here the case of selecting one cue at a time. Although this is surely an oversimplification Restle (1962) has shown that this case is formally equivalent to other more complex assumptions. In particular, as long as one assumes that subjects are choosing cues or strategies at random from the total pool of strategies, it does not matter whether the subject picks one strategy at a time, all at once, or a subset of strategies.

If the subject considers all strategies at once, Restle assumes that he then starts to eliminate incorrect strategies. When he makes a response, he sets aside all the strategies which he did not use (i.e., strategies which would have predicted the opposite response). In this way, of course, the correct strategy may sometimes be eliminated, too, and the subject will eventually run out of strategies to test. When this happens, he must begin over again with the whole set of strategies. This all-at-once model predicts exactly the same response sequences as the one-at-a-time model. The proof is easy, though not intuitively obvious, and will not be reproduced here. Restle's third case, where the subject is permitted to take a sample of s strategies at a time, is also formally equivalent to the earlier two cases. These models are equivalent, of course, only in so far as sequences of correct and incorrect responses are concerned. Should one design an experiment which goes beyond that, so that one can tell not only how fast a concept is learned, but also which cues were used in learning it, the three models of Restle (1962) make differential predictions.

Before turning to such experiments, Case III of Restle will be discussed in some more detail, as it is obviously the most reasonable case psychologically. Suppose the subject picks a random sample of s hypotheses. The proportions of correct, wrong, and irrelevant cues in that sample determine the probability that the response which the subject makes on the basis of the sample will be correct or incorrect. Suppose the response is correct. The subject can now eliminate all strategies from his sample which would have led to the opposite response, that is, all wrong strategies and some proportion of the irrelevant strategies. This process of elimination goes on until either only correct strategies are left in the subject's sample, or until an error occurs. In this case the subject takes a new sample and starts the whole process all over again. Note that this is still a no-memory model. Once the subject has eliminated a strategy he cannot recover it.

Experiments which can discriminate among the three versions of Restle's model employ redundant relevant cues. Suppose in an experiment on concept acquisition using the familiar geometric stimulus material two redundant cues are used to specify a concept, say shape and color. Through suitable transfer tests after concept learning one can determine whether subjects had learned the problem on the basis of the shape cue, the color cue, or both. If there are subjects who learned both cues the one-strategy at-a-time model is contraindicated. Whether any of the other versions of the model can fit the data in this case, is of course an empirical question.

The problem of what the subject learns in concept acquisition experiments with redundant relevant cues has been extensively studied by Trabasso and Bower (1968). One of their studies will be reported in some detail here to illustrate their approach. Trabasso and Bower used geometric figures with 5 binary attributes as stimulus material. Two of the attributes, shape (circle versus triangle) and dot (above or below figure), were used to define the concept to be learned. For one group of subjects $(S+D)$ both shape and dot were relevant. Group S learned the problem with shape as the relevant cue and dot irrelevant. Group D learned the problem with dot relevant and shape irrelevant. Finally, there were two control groups: S', which learned the shape problem in the absence of dots, and D' for which dot was the relevant cue and shape was held constant (all figures were squares). Subjects learned these problems to criterion and where given post-criterion training during which both dot and shape were relevant cues. Finally, subjects were given single-cue tests to determine which of the two cues had been learned.

The results obtained in the training phase of this experiment are summarized in Table 7.3. Note that the position of the dot was a more salient cue in this experiment, and that combining the two cues produced the fewest number of errors in training, just as one would expect. Comparing the number of errors in Groups S and D with Groups S' and D', respectively, one can see that making the second cue irrelevant depressed performance somewhat compared with the conditions where the second cue was totally absent. This is, of course, what the additivity of cues hypothesis predicts: if the second cue is absent its weight need not be considered at all, but if it is irrelevant its weight must be added to the denominator of Eq. (3). The theoretical expressions for the learning rates according to Eq. (3) are also shown in the Table. The estimated learning rates in Table 3 have been obtained

Table 7.3. *Training conditions and results in the redundant relevant cue experiment of Trabasso and Bower (1968).*

Group	Training Shape	Dot	Mean number of errors in training	Estimated learning rate	Theoretical learning rate	Predicted learning rate
$S+D$	Rel.	Rel.	4.1	.24	$\dfrac{w(S)+w(D)}{w(S)+w(D)+w(I)}$	.25
S	Rel.	Irrel.	10.1	.09	$\dfrac{w(S)}{w(S)+w\,(D)+w(I)}$	.10
D	Irrel.	Rel.	5.9	.16	$\dfrac{w(D)}{w(S)+w(D)+w(I)}$	.16
S'	Rel.	Absent	8.4	.11	$\dfrac{w(S)}{w(S)+w(I)}$	–
D'	Absent	Rel.	5.5	.17	$\dfrac{w(D)}{w(D)+w(I)}$	–

from the mean number of errors in training, as discussed earlier (Eq. (4)). Estimates for the cue weights of shape and dot ($w(S)$ and $w(D)$) may be obtained in terms of $w(I)$ from the theoretical expressions for the learning rates in Groups S' and D', and can then be used to predict the learning rates in the remaining three groups on the basis of the additivity of cues hypothesis. As Table 7.3 shows, these predictions come quite close to the obtained values, thus providing further support to the additivity of cues hypothesis.

So far the experiment has not provided new information, but has confirmed several earlier results. But now consider the results of the single cue tests which were administered to the subjects learning the two-cue problem $S+D$ after they reached criterion. All subjects were asked how they had solved the problem and on the basis of their responses were subdivided into three groups, subjects who had solved on the basis of shape alone, subjects who had solved on the basis of the dot cue alone, and subjects who had solved on the basis of both cues. Table 7.4 shows the number of subjects in each of these groups, as well as their performance on the single cue tests. First note that the subject's verbalizations and their performance agreed extremely well: They performed almost perfectly on the cues they said they had worked with and were at chance level on the cues they said they had not noticed. Secondly, note that there were indeed subjects who had learned both cues in this problem, as evidenced both by their verbal report and their performance on the single cue tests. Thus, the one-cue version of Restle's model is clearly inadequate. Trabasso and Bower (1968) have further explored that version of Restle's model which assumes that subjects are working with a sample of s cues. In this model, s is a new parameter, in addition to the learning rate c. From everything that has been said before about the equivalence of

Table 7.4. *Solution types in the Bower and Trabasso (1968) experiment.*

Number of subjects	Predicted number of subjects ($s=2$)	Verbal report	Proportion of correct sorts on single cue tests:	
			Shape	Dot
31	29	Shape	1.00	.50
45	49	Dot	.52	.99
13	11	Both	.95	.97

the various versions of Restle's model, it should be obvious that the parameter s does not enter any of the expressions which have to do with the subject's learning rate. However, s becomes important in the prediction of "solution types," i.e., the number of subjects who solved the problem on the basis of each cue separately or on the basis of both cues. If $s > 1$, learning about both cues occurs with a frequency depending upon the size of s, as well as the relative weights of the two relevant cues. For any given value of s one can calculate the probability that, if a subject has solved the problem, he has done so on the basis of Cue 1, Cue 2, or both. Trabasso and Bower found that a sample size $s = 2$ gives a fairly accurate account of the solution types in their experiment. The predicted number of subjects solving on the basis of shape, dot, and both cues are also shown in Table 7.4.

The subjects who learned only a single cue were given further training on the two-cue problem after reaching criterion on their original problem. Trabasso and Bower found that this training had absolutely no effect on their subjects in Groups S and D: none of the 86 subjects showed any learning when the second cue was made relevant during overtraining. On the other hand, 8% of the subjects in Groups S' and D' learned the newly introduced redundant cue during overtraining. When a cue is newly introduced into a problem which the subject has already solved it arouses an orienting reaction, which apparently led some subjects to resample and thus produced some learning of the redundant cue. However, resampling can not be simply equated with noticing a cue, because in another study reported in their book Trabasso and Bower made subjects verbalize all cues during overtraining, but still obtained no learning of redundant relevant cues which were present but irrelevant during original learning.

Cue selection, overlearning, and transfer certainly present many problems which have not yet been adequately solved. However, from the studies reported above it appears that the simple model for concept learning summarized by Eq. (2) can be extended in natural and interesting ways to incorporate the principal phenomena in these areas. The strategy of approaching one complexity at a time seems to pay off.

The Use of Memory in Concept Identification

All versions of the concept learning model considered so far assume that subjects do not use their memory in concept learning. When they make an error, they resample a new set of hypotheses which may include hypotheses that had already been rejected before. Subjects sample with replacement. Any model that does not concede memory to subjects is probably wrong, simply on *a priori* grounds. A considerable body of research has been concerned with the role of memory in concept learning.

Some results have already been reported which implicated memory processes in concept identification. The first was the experiment by Trabasso and Bower (1966) in which response assignments were shifted on every second error. The results of that experiment disagreed with the predictions derived from the model but they could be understood if the assumption was dropped that subjects sample hypotheses with replacement. Instead, it appeared that subjects did not resample hypotheses which were inconsistent with information already received, or at least were biased against such hypotheses. The second experiment which clearly demonstrated memory processes in concept identification was that of Levine (1966). Levine's subjects did not sample with replacement, but they progressively reduced the set of hypotheses from which they made their choices (Fig. 7.5). Their memory was imperfect, and they did not reduce the hypotheses set as much as would have been possible, but by no means could their behavior be characterized as sampling with replacement. In the present section the evidence which is available concerning the use of memory in concept identification will be discussed more systematically, and some modification will be discussed more systematically, and some modifications of the no-memory models of Restle (1962) and of Bower and Trabasso (1964) will be described which take into account this evidence.

The study of memory in concept learning poses some interesting experimental problems. The first experimental approach which has been tried consisted of giving subjects access to previous stimuli and their classifications. Bruner, Goodnow, and Austin (1956) report a representative experiment ("Information in the Head versus on the Board"). Experiments of this type will be neglected here, because their relevance to the present problem is not clear. It is true that whenever subjects receive information about what happened on previous trials, they use this information, and their performance improves. However, this says nothing about how subjects learn under normal conditions, when they are not given additional information.

A second rather direct approach has been tried by Trabasso and Bower (1964). These authors showed subjects 6 stimulus items, together with their correct classification, and then asked subjects to state the rule upon which the classification was based, and in addition to recall all 6 items together with their classification. The main result of this experiment was that subjects' recall was very poor. On the average they could recall only one of the 6 items correctly. Thus, it would seem that, if what subjects are recalling is specific item information, models which minimize the role of memory may not be far off. Levine (1969) has reported a related observation. Using his hypothesis-tracking procedure described earlier he checked whether the hypothesis selected by the subject after being told "wrong" was consistent with the particular stimulus items previously presented. The stimulus material in this study was more complex than that of the earlier study, so that the consistency of a hypothesis with up to 8 previous items could be determined. There was some but by no means perfect consistency with the immediately preceding item, as well as lesser consistency with the next to the last item and the first item, but the items in between were apparently forgotten and not used in the selection of a new hypothesis. Thus, one may conclude that there is some short-term memory for specific items in concept formation tasks, but surprisingly little, whether this memory is measured by asking for direct recall or indirectly in terms of consistency of new hypotheses with the information provided by earlier items.

A more indirect approach involving misinformative feedback has been tried by Levine (1962) and others. Subjects in misinformative feedback experiments are given some trials with random reinforcement, and after that, without informing the subjects, the experimenter starts to reinforce some particular classification consistently. If subjects were sampling at random and with replacement, the misinformative feedback would not delay solution once the regular problem is begun. On the other hand, if subjects remember which hypotheses have already been tried and rejected, misinformative feedback will retard performance. Indeed, if subject's memory were perfect and if subjects never tried a rejected hypothesis again, at least some subjects should never solve the problem at all. The experimental finding is that even brief periods of misinformative feedback severely retard concept acquisition. Interestingly, it is the experimenter's reinforcement of whatever hypotheses the subject was working with initially which retards later performance, rather than the elimination of hypotheses because of non-reinforcement. Merryman, Kaufmann, Brown, and Dames (1968) ran three groups of subjects, one a control group and three with misinformative feedback. In one group subjects received 6 noncontingent reinforcements (the experimenter said "right") and in the other group the experimenter said "wrong" six times, again independently of the subjects' responses. The mean number of errors in learning the experimental problem was almost identical for the control group and the group with the noncontingent "wrong" trials, but it was twice as high when noncontingent "rights" preceded the problem proper. Thus one can draw two conclusions from the misinformative feedback studies: first, that subjects certainly do use memory, and second, that success trials are remembered and interfere with the subject's later efforts to find a solution.

The most successful experimental design so far for the study of memory in concept identification involves giving subjects several problems concurrently. It was inaugurated by Restle and Emmerich (1966). If concept formation is a pure trial-and-error process, concurrent problems should be no more difficult than single problems. On the other hand, if subjects make use of the information which they remember, the interference introduced through concurrent problems should reflect the size of the subject's workable memory. Restle and Emmerich gave subjects either 1, 2, 3, or 6 concept identification problems concurrently. The subjects in the four groups averaged 4, 5, 8, and 7 errors per problem, respectively. Thus, making subjects remember back more than three stimuli significantly retarded performance. In another experiment the authors repeated stimuli after errors in order to obtain an indication of the subject's memory. According to the sampling with replacement assumption, the probability of a correct response when a card is repeated after an error should be strictly $\frac{1}{2}$. With perfect memory for at least one trial this probability should be 1. The authors obtained a value of .95 when subjects were working only on one problem. When subjects were working on 6 problems concurrently, the probability of a correct response to a repeated stimulus decreased to .72, but was still significantly above chance.

Erikson has investigated response latencies in concept identification experiments in order to assess the use of memory (Erikson, Zajkowski, and Ehrmann, 1966). He argued that response latencies should be related to the size of the set of hypotheses from which a subject makes his selection. The more hypotheses must be considered the more time the sampling process takes. With this additional assumption a number of obvious predictions regarding response latencies can be derived from the Bower and Trabasso model:

1. Latencies after errors are larger than latencies after successes,
2. Latencies are constant on trials before the last error,
3. Latencies after the last error are constant and equal to latencies after successes before the last error,
4. Error latencies are equal to success latencies,
5. Latencies after an uninformed error equal latencies after a success.

In an experimental test of these assumptions predictions 1, 4, and 5 were confirmed. However, as Fig. 7.8 shows, predictions 2 and 3 were clearly incorrect. The latencies after the last error were not constant, but decreased to a value much lower than success latencies before the last error. This observation may merely reflect an increase in the subject's confidence, however, an aspect of behavior which the model neglects. A trend to decrease latencies was also observed on trials before the last error when long success runs occurred (> 4), which fits in with the explanation that confidence affects latencies, in addition to whatever other factors that must be considered. The more important result of the Erikson *et al.* experiment is the failure of Prediction 2: latencies after errors decreased considerably on trials before the last error, although they remained at least as large as latencies after successes. This suggests that subjects were excluding hypotheses, that is, memory effects. Early in the experiment there were many hypotheses from which subjects had to make their selection, and hence latencies were large when subjects resampled after errors. As the experiment progressed the hypothesis pool became smaller because subjects excluded some of the hypotheses they had already tried before, and resampling after errors took less time. The error data in the Erikson *et al.* experiment were found to be in complete agreement with the

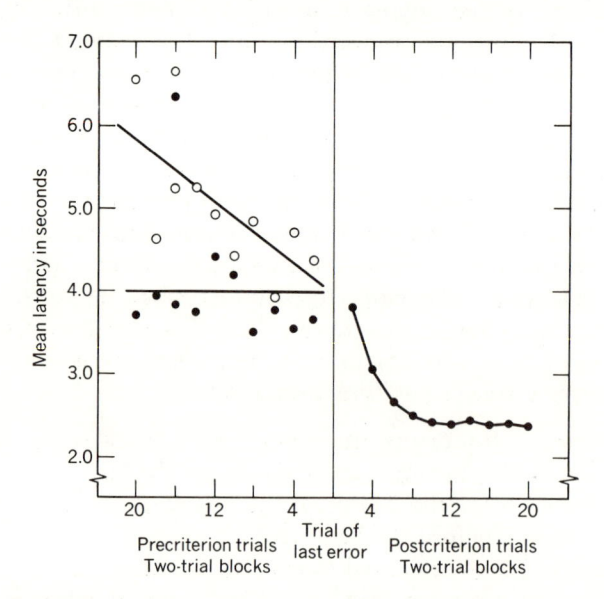

Fig. 7.8 *Mean latency on trials preceding the last error. The precriterion trials show latencies on trial* n *following errors (open circles) and following correct responses (closed circles) on trial* n-1. *(after Erikson* et al., *1966)*

Bower and Trabasso model: presolution responses were stationary and independent, and the detailed predictions of the model fit the data reasonably well. The memory effects observed in the response latencies had no noticeable effect on the learning data.

In a follow-up experiment Erikson and Zajkowski (1967) showed that if subjects are given three concurrent concept identification problems no evidence of memory is obtained. The latencies after errors in this case remained constant, indicating that the subject's hypothesis pool did not decrease. Overloading memory led to sampling with replacement.

One can summarize the experimental results on the use of memory in concept identification by saying that the subject's working memory depends upon the experimental conditions. Under optimal or near optimal conditions—one problem only, enough time to process information—memory plays a significant role. In this case the sampling with replacement assumption of Restle (1962) and Bower and Trabasso (1964) is wrong. Subjects retain information which enables them to sample from a reduced set of hypotheses. However, under conditions of stress subjects rely less and less upon memory, and their behavior approaches sampling with replacement as a limiting case.

There seem to be two major alternatives for theories of memory use in concept identification. Subjects may remember particular stimulus values and their classification and select only such hypotheses which are in agreement with the remembered stimulus response pairs. Trabasso and Bower (1966) call this a consistency-check. They assumed that subjects remember k items, and choose only among those hypotheses which pass a k-item consistency-check. In this way memory may be introduced into the framework of the Bower and Trabasso (1964) model, which now becomes a special case for $k = 1$. This leaves the earlier model quite intact; the modification that samples of size s are taken rather than one hypothesis at a time can also be incorporated within this model without difficulty.

However, all the data indicate that subject's memory for specific items is quite poor, and it is by no means sure that memory is really used for making consistency-checks. An alternative conception of the use of memory would be that subjects remember the hypotheses which have been tried before. Levine (1966) suggested such a process, and Chumbley (1967) has formulated a specific model for it. Suppose that a subject samples a set H of hypotheses in a concept identification experiment with two responses classes A and B. Call the subset of hypotheses which predict an A-response on the next trial H_A, and the subset of hypotheses which lead to a B-response H_B. Suppose the A-

response is made. If the experimenter calls it correct, the subject keeps the set H_A and discards all hypotheses in H_B. On the next trial only the hypotheses in H_A are considered. So far this model is identical with that of Trabasso and Bower (1968) where subjects are assumed to sample s hypotheses at once. However, Trabasso and Bower assumed that when a response A was made and it was called wrong the subject could not recover the hypotheses in H_B and had to start again with a new random sample. Chumbley proposed instead that subjects can recover the rejected hypotheses in case of an error with some probability m. With probability $(1-m)$ the subject forgets the hypotheses which he had not used and starts all over again, as in the Trabasso and Bower model. Thus, the subject works like a perfect focusing device, except that he is occasionally reset to zero because of memory failure. An example will make this argument clearer. Imagine stimulus materials with four binary dimensions, such as Levine's (1966, Fig. 7.4). The total set of hypotheses will then consist of 8 members if instructions ensure that more complex hypotheses are excluded. Given any particular stimulus item, four of these hypotheses will predict that the item belongs to class A and the other four will predict that it belongs to class B. If the subject chooses to say A and was correct he has now narrowed down the total set of hypotheses from 8 to 4, since only the hypotheses predicting an A need to be considered. If the subject said A, but was incorrect, we now assume that he can recall the four hypotheses which predicted the opposite response with probability m. Since the probability of being correct or incorrect is $\frac{1}{2}$ in this situation, the subject can reduce the number of hypotheses with probability $(1/2 + m/2)$, the probability that he is correct plus the probability that he is wrong but remembers the hypotheses which would have been right. With probability $\frac{1}{2}(1-m)$ he is wrong and can not remember the right hypotheses and has to start all over again.

In an experiment which was patterned after that of Levine (1966) Chumbley (1967) tried to distinguish between the two models for memory in concept learning. Trials without feedback were given in order to permit tracking of the actual hypotheses which the subject was using. The proportion of subjects working with the correct hypotheses was the dependent variable of interest. Without discussing Chumbley's experiment in detail, one can say that the model which assumed memory for hypotheses fared generally better than the consistency-check model. As a minimum modification of the latter one would have to assume that consistency-checks may sometimes be imperfect, and that giving subjects more time and reducing their memory load increases the probability of a correct check.

Chumbley provided some interesting estimates of the memory parameter m when subjects were learning one concept identification problem and when they were learning three problems concurrently. In the latter case the best estimate of m turned out to be zero, thus confirming earlier results that subjects are essentially sampling with replacement under conditions of memory overload. On the other hand, under more suitable conditions memory estimates as high as .63 were obtained. Chumbley also showed that his model provided a solution to a rather puzzling problem concerning the value of the estimates of the learning rate in many concept identification experiments. The problem is this. When subjects learn an n-dimensional concept identification problem, there are $2n$ simple hypotheses which can be formed. If subjects are sampling hypotheses at random from this set, the probability of getting the right one should be about $c = \dfrac{1}{2n}$. Some variation around this value would be expected because of differential cue saliency. In general, however, estimates of the learning rate in concept identification experiments have been appreciably higher than $\dfrac{1}{2n}$. For instance, in the experiment of Erikson and Zajkowski (1967) which was discussed earlier, $c = .25$ for the one problem condition, and $c = .15$ for the three-problem condition, while $\dfrac{1}{2n} = .125$. It seems likely that these c-estimates are inflated by memory effects. Chumbley estimated $m = .35$ for the one-problem condition of Erikson *et al.*, and $m = .09$ for their three-problem condition. These values agree quite well with those obtained in his own experiment. Chumbley also reports some unpublished data by Clayton which bear on this issue. With 6-dimensional stimulus material Clayton had six groups of subjects learning a classification problem, one group for each stimulus dimension. Since for each dimension two hypotheses can be formed $2 \sum_{1}^{6} c_i$ should equal 1, and c_i is the estimated learning rate for the i-th group. This follows because the summation goes over all possible cues. Instead, Clayton observed a sum of 1.6, which presents quite a puzzle if the c-estimates are to be proportions of relevant cues. However, if Chumbley is right, these proportions are artificially high because of memory effects which are not otherwise accounted for in the model. If unconfounded estimates could be obtained, they would presumably sum to one. Finally, we note that in a series of studies Bower and Trabasso (1964) obtained estimates of learning rates which were quite close to $\dfrac{1}{2n}$ —which means that under their experimental conditions memory played only a minimal role, and which also explains why their no-memory model fit their data so extremely well.

SUMMARY

In the simple concept identification experiments discussed in this chapter the subject's problem can be described as one of finding the relevant dimension of stimulus variability to respond to. The subject learns which dimension the experimenter uses to classify the stimuli and codes the stimuli in terms of their values on that dimension. Thus, concept identification can be regarded as a particularly simple kind of discrimination learning.

The effects of several task variables can be understood within this framework. Everything that helps to make the relevant stimulus dimension more salient perceptually improves concept identification. For instance, emphasizing the relevant cue by coloring it or the like improves learning. Once the subject responds to the right cue, the emphasizer may be withdrawn. Thus, if a problem is difficult, it is an efficient teaching procedure to introduce first a related but simpler problem in order to draw the subject's attention to the relevant aspects of the stimulus. Another experimental variable of importance in concept identification experiments is stimulus variability. Redundant relevant dimensions facilitate learning; irrelevant dimensions increase the problem difficulty, as do redundant irrelevant dimensions. Finally, the important role of the post-feedback interval was discussed: after the subject is told on a trial whether his response was right or wrong he needs some time to process this information. The optimal length of the post-feedback interval increases with problem difficulty.

The subject's responses in a concept identification experiment can be described by the all-or-none learning model. An interpretation of the model in terms of cue-selection was presented which implied that learning in the sense of trying out a new cue occurs only after an error. The model assumes that the subject selects a hypothesis at random and that this hypothesis governs his overt responses until a stimulus word is wrongly classified on the basis of that hypothesis. Then the subject discards the hypothesis and randomly selects a new one from the total pool of possible hypotheses. Experimental data were in good agreement with this model.

The model treats the learning rate, i.e. the probability that the correct cue is chosen, as a parameter to be estimated from the data. However, it was shown that if the learning rate is determined in an experiment in which one cue is relevant, and another learning rate is determined from a separate experiment in which another cue is relevant, the learning rate can be predicted if in a third condition both cues are combined. It was also shown that the model can handle the results of some transfer studies quite well with the assumption that transfer after concept-learning is all-or-none.

The cue-selection model is clearly insufficient in two respects: it assumes that subjects work with only one cue at a time, and it makes no provision for memory. Experiments with redundant relevant cues were used to investigate the first problem. A simple extension of the model was made so that more than one hypothesis may be selected at a time. A large number of experimental studies were described which demonstrate that subjects do use their memory in concept identification experiments. The importance of memory apparently depends upon experimental conditions. The data could be adequately accounted for by a further extension of the cue selection model in which the selection of hypotheses after errors may take into account information from previous trials.

RULE LEARNING AND LANGUAGE

88888888888888

Discrimination learning involves two quite distinct processes: first, the identification of the relevant stimulus attribute, or attributes, and then the association of the relevant stimulus values with the correct response alternatives. In the simplest case this second process is merely a question of paired-associate learning. For instance, in most of the studies discussed in the previous chapter, one stimulus dimension, say color, was arbitrarily designated as relevant, and a response was assigned to each value of this dimension: thus, red may be A, and blue may be B. The main problem for the subject consists in identifying which stimulus dimension is relevant; once the relevant stimulus dimension has been selected, the association between particular values and responses presents only trivial problems. For this reason, "Concept Identification" was chosen as a title for the last chapter, rather than a more general term such as concept learning. "Attribute Identification" might have been an even better descriptive title, and we shall use this term frequently from now on, following Haygood and Bourne (1965).

There are many ways to define concepts such that even if the relevant stimulus attributes are known, the problem is not yet solved. Response classes may be defined in terms of relationships among the values of the relevant stimulus dimensions so that the subject must learn the rule which specifies the correct response in terms of the attribute values. For instance, if color and size are relevant stimulus attributes, a rule defining a concept may specify that A-items are either red and small or blue and large, while all items which are red and large or blue and small belong to category B. Obviously, such rules may be quite complex and it may take subjects many trials to learn them, even if they know which attributes are relevant. Attribute identification and rule learning may thus be regarded as two distinct subprocesses of concept learning. The identification problem

398

has been discussed in considerable detail in Chapter 7. In contrast to the large number of studies concerned with concept identification, the problem of rule learning has received only little attention. Relatively few empirical studies of rule learning are as yet available, and the conceptual problems concerning rule learning are still insufficiently explored. Nevertheless, it seems worthwhile to discuss the attempts which have been made by psychologists to understand this important problem. Interesting developments in this area may be anticipated in the near future, so that much of what can be said at this time about rule learning is only tentative. Rule learning also introduces us to the fascinating problems of language and language learning, which are beginning to interest learning-psychologists.

1. THE LEARNING OF LOGICAL RELATIONSHIPS

With two relevant binary dimensions one can form 16 distinct partitions of the stimulus items. Suppose the first dimension has values R and $\bar{R}$ (which may be red and nonred) and the second dimension has values S and $\bar{S}$ (square and nonsquare, for instance). Thus, all stimulus items can be categorized as (R,S), $(R,\bar{S})$, $(\bar{R},S)$, or $(\bar{R},\bar{S})$, irrespective of the values of irrelevant attributes. In defining a concept on this stimulus set each of the four categories may be called an instance of the concept or not and hence 2^4 different concepts can be obtained in this way. Two of these concepts are trivial (all items are members of the concept, or none of them is a member) and several more are identical, except that the relevant attributes are interchanged. The 10 remaining distinct concepts are shown in Table 8.1 where they are subdivided into two complementary classes. Each rule defining a concept has a counterpart which is identical with it except that positive and negative instances are interchanged. Thus, there are only five different concepts which must be considered. The assignments of items to positive and negative categories is further illustrated for each of the five basic rules in Table 8.2. The rules differ greatly in complexity. The first rule partitions the stimulus set simply on the basis of the presence or absence of one particular attribute. This is the kind of rule which has been employed in the attribute identification studies discussed in the previous chapter. The Level II rules take into account the values of both attributes. Conjunction requires positive instances to be both red and square, and corresponds to the set-theoretic operator "intersection." Disjunction corresponds to the operator "union" and classifies all items which are either red or square or both as positive instances. The conditional rule is somewhat less

Table 8.1. *Conceptual rules describing partitions of a population with two relevant attributes (after Haygood and Bourne, 1965).*

	Basic Rule		Complementary Rule		
Name	Symbolic description	Verbal description	Name	Symbolic description	Verbal description
Affirmation	R	All red items are examples	Negation	$\overline{R}$	All not red items are examples
Conjunction	R∩S	All red and square items	Alternative denial	$\overline{R}∪\overline{S}$	All items either not red or not square
Inclusive disjunction	R∪S	All items red or square or both	Joint denial	$\overline{R}∩\overline{S}$	All items neither red nor square
Conditional	R→S	If the item is red then it must be square	Exclusion	R∩$\overline{S}$	All items red and not square
Biconditional	R↔S	Red items if and only if they are square	Exclusive disjunction	R$\overline{∪}$S	All items which are red or square but not both

familiar: if an item is red, then it must be square to be classified as a positive instance. This rule assigns positive membership to all non-red items. This is the "material implication" of logic which, as students of introductory logic know very well, is quite at variance with the everyday sense of "implication." All Level II rules involve a 1:3 split of the item categories (R,S), $(R,\overline{S})$, $(\overline{R},S)$, and $(\overline{R},\overline{S})$. The Level III rule, the biconditional, divides the categories into subsets of equal size. Thus, there is more uncertainty in the sense of information theory in this case. One can do better just guessing with a Level II rule than with the biconditional, since ¾ of all items belong to the same class in the former case, while no such frequency bias exists in the latter case.

Of the rules based upon logical relationships, as described in Tables 8.1 and 8.2, conjunction and disjunction have been studied most thoroughly. Bruner, Goodnow, and Austin (1956) observed that subjects generally used quite efficient strategies to solve conjunctive problems, but that they had great difficulty with disjunctive concepts. The problem appeared to be that naive subjects used methods which worked very well with conjunctive problems, but not with disjunctive problems. In particular, the positive focusing strategy described earlier, which is quite suitable for learning conjunctive problems leads to inefficient performance when the concept is defined by a disjunctive rule. Hunt and Hovland (1960) gave subjects a problem which could be learned either by a conjunctive or by a disjunctive rule. After reaching criterion subjects were tested to see which rule they had actually acquired. A strong bias in favor of conjunctive rules was found. However, this probably reflects the greater familiarity which subjects have with conjunctive rules. When subjects were trained on a series of disjunctive concepts before they were given a test problem which could be treated either as a conjunction or a disjunction, they were more likely to offer a disjunctive solution (Wells, 1963).

Learning of the rules shown in Table 1 has been studied systematically by Neisser and Weene (1962), Haygood and Bourne (1965), and Hunt, Marin, and Stone (1966). As a representative experiment, Experiment I of Haygood and Bourne will be described. Conjunction, disjunction, joint denial, and conditional were the rules studied in this experiment. Three different training conditions were used: Attribute Identification—the rule was described and illustrated with examples before learning began; Rule Learning—subjects were told which attributes were relevant; and Concept Learning—both attribute identification and rule learning were required. Each subject learned five problems in succession, each with the same rule, but with

Table 8.2. *The mappings of the stimulus items implied by the five rules of Table 8.1.*

Partitioning of the item set on the basis of color and form:	Rules				
	Level I	Level II		Level III	
	Affirmation	Conjunction	Disjunction	Conditional	Biconditional
Red Square	+	+	+	+	+
Red Nonsquare	+	−	+	−	−
Nonred Square	−	−	+	+	−
Nonred Nonsquare	−	−	−	+	+

different relevant attributes. The stimulus values were geometric designs with four trinary dimensions (size, color, form, and number). The construction of the items was explained to subjects so that they were familiar with the stimulus dimensions and values. Subjects worked on each problem until they reached a criterion of 16 successive correct responses. Mean trials to solution are shown in Fig. 8.1 for the three experimental conditions. Subjects learned the rule-learning and attribute-identification problems significantly faster than the concept-learning problems, which shows that the partial knowledge given to them was indeed used and did facilitate learning. The rules differed significantly in difficulty, at least initially. In the rule-learning condition subjects made almost no errors on conjunctive concepts, indicating that they were familiar with such problems. Disjunction and joint denial were difficult in the beginning, but subjects soon mastered these rules. The conditional rule was most difficult and subjects did not reach a facility with it comparable to that with the other three rules. However, one may suppose that had they been given more conditional problems they would have learned this rule eventually, just as the other rules were learned. In a follow-up experiment, precisely this was demonstrated (Bourne, 1967, Experiment

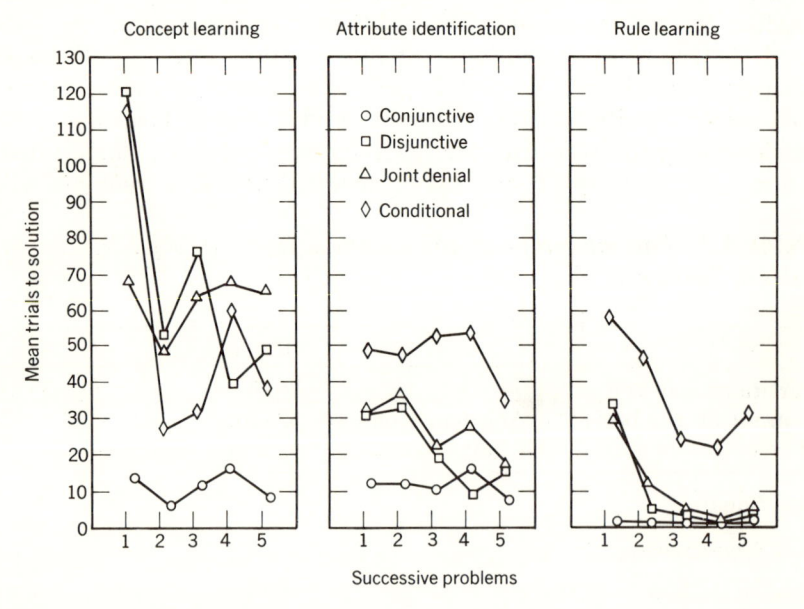

Fig. 8.1 *Mean trials to solution of problems based upon four different rules. (after Bourne, 1967)*

III). Attribute identification always takes longer than rule learning, even after considerable practice. This, of course, lies in the nature of the task. Subjects must be able to observe enough instances of each category before they can decide which attributes are relevant. Haygood and Bourne have shown that subjects operated with almost maximal efficiency on the fifth problem, with exception of the conditional concept, where performance still was relatively inefficient.

The ordering of the various rules in terms of difficulty that was obtained in the Haygood and Bourne (1965) study has been generally confirmed in the other studies mentioned above. When a biconditional rule is included, it is more difficult to learn than any other rule. The problem of how experimental variables influence the learning of the various rules remains largely unexplored. An exception is a study by Haygood and Stevenson (1967) on the effects of the number of irrelevant dimensions on the learning of conjunctive, disjunctive, and conditional concepts. With 0, 1, or 2 irrelevant dimensions these authors reported increases in the number of errors made during learning for all types of rules, with disproportionally large increases for the more difficult rules. As one would expect, practically all the difficulty introduced by increasing the number of irrelevant dimensions was caused by making the attribute identification process more complex. Rule learning was virtually unaffected by the number of irrelevant dimensions.

An interesting problem concerning rule learning which has been studied experimentally concerns the nature of transfer between rules. In the experiment reported above, subjects were given practice on the same type of problem and showed rapid improvement. In a second experiment Haygood and Bourne (1965) gave subjects practice on several types of rules and then investigated how subjects could utilize these rules. Subjects were first trained to sort items on the basis of four different types of rules: conjunctive, disjunctive, conditional, and biconditional. Then they were asked to identify which of these rules determined the solution in two final problems. The relevant attributes were named and the subjects were told that one of the four previously learned rules was relevant to the solution. The results of the training phase of this experiment confirmed the ordering of the rules in terms of difficulty to learn which was obtained earlier, with biconditional being much more difficult than conditional. The rule-identification task, like attribute-identification problems, requires a certain minimum number of exposures for solution. The subject must see at least one instance of each class of items in order to identify the rule. Table 2 shows the manner in which the concepts were defined by the experimenter, and it makes clear that there were four classes of stimuli which had to be observed in order to identify a rule. These classes were obtained by combining the factors red and nonred and square and nonsquare. Thus for efficient solution, subjects had to code the stimulus set into four subsets (R,S), $(\overline{R},S)$, $(R,\overline{S})$, and $(\overline{R},\overline{S})$. Even a maximally efficient subject could not have solved the problem before the experimenter had presented at least one instance of each of these four classes. In Table 8.3 the mean number of trials to solution (T) and the mean number of trials necessary to present at least one instance of each stimulus class are shown (TP). First note that subjects took many more trials to identify conditional and biconditional rules than conjunctive and disjunctive rules. While they performed efficiently when the rules were simple (T and TP are almost equal), they needed much more than the minimum number of trials for conditional and biconditional rules.

Also shown in Table 8.3 are the mean numbers of errors for each condition. If subjects were guessing on presolution trials about $\frac{1}{2}$ of all presolution trials should be errors, i.e., $E = \frac{1}{2}T$. In fact, E is considerably less than that. Obviously, subjects are not learning the rules all at once, but have partial information before a rule is fully identified. If subjects are using the coding scheme of Table 8.2 it seems reasonable that they would learn some classes before others and that the discrepancy between the total number of errors made and the mean trials to solution arises because some classes are learned before others. Haygood and Bourne have shown that this is indeed the case. The rules are learned as four separate, though interdependent problems. For instance, in the most difficult problem, the biconditional,

Table 8.3. *The mean number of trials (T) and errors (E) to solution and the number of trials necessary to present at least one instance of each stimulus class (TP) in rule identification (Expt. II of Haygood and Bourne, 1965).*

Rule	E	T	TP
Conjunction	2.5	6.9	6.5
Disjunction	1.9	5.7	5.0
Conditional	5.1	12.5	6.5
Biconditional	7.3	29.0	7.0

subjects learn very rapidly that (R,S) items are positive instances. The average number of examples in this category before subjects make the last error on this subproblem is .7. On the other hand, the subproblems $(\overline{R},S)$, $(R,\overline{S})$, and $(\overline{R},\overline{S})$ are considerably more difficult, with 5.2, 3.8, and 5.0 examples to the last error, respectively. Thus it is clear why so few errors are made on presolution trials if one looks at the problem as a whole: subjects practically always respond correctly on (R,S) items, and errors are made only in the difficult classifications, especially $(\overline{R},S)$ and $(\overline{R},\overline{S})$ in the case of the biconditional rule. It is interesting that if the problem is broken down into its four subparts, the error rate on presolution trials for each subpart is quite close to $\frac{1}{2}$. In terms of the example just discussed, about $\frac{1}{2}$ of the .7 presolution trials on the (R,S) subproblem were errors, $\frac{1}{2}$ of the 5.2 presolution trials on the $(\overline{R},S)$ problem were errors, etc. The error rate on presolution trials averaged over all rules and all subproblems was .53. Thus, it would appear that each subproblem was learned like the simple concept identification problems discussed in the previous chapter, i.e., by searching for the appropriate coding response. For instance, once a subject has learned to assign a common code to all items which are red and nonsquare and the appropriate response connection is made, that particular subproblem is solved. Solution of the problem as a whole, of course, depends upon the learning of all four subproblems. Thus, it would seem to be a straightforward task to extend the strategy selection model of the preceding chapter to the present situation. However, this is not the case, because the four subproblems are not learned independently of each other. The nature of the interdependence is not yet clearly understood. All that is known is that some categories are very hard to learn because they involve unfamiliar and "unnatural" response assignments. For example, much of the difficulty of the biconditional rule arises because the subject, once he has learned that items which are red and squares are members, hesitates to assign nonred and nonsquare items to the same response class, since no common cues are shared by the two subsets of items.

If the description of how subjects learn logical relationships given above is substantially correct, it follows that the more different rules subjects learn, the better they should be able to master the coding scheme upon which these rules are based, and the easier it should be for them to learn new rules. Bourne (1967) has reported an experimental test of this hypothesis. He gave subjects six practice problems. In Group I these were all of the same type (conjunctive, disjunctive, and conditional). In Group II three problems on each of two different rules, and in Group III two problems on each of three different rules were given. A control group received no pretraining. Two biconditional problems were used to evaluate the effectiveness of the pretraining. A rule identification procedure was used in both pretraining and test, i.e., the experimenter named the relevant attributes for each problem. The experimental hypothesis was confirmed. All three groups which were pretrained showed substantial transfer compared with the control group, and in addition, the more different rules were learned, the more positive transfer was obtained. However, only 9 of the 48 subjects used in the experiment solved the biconditional problem in the possible minimum number of trials. Most subjects needed from three to 10 times as many trials as absolutely necessary.

Thus it appears that positive transfer between different rules can be largely attributed to learning to use the appropriate coding scheme more effectively. Bourne (1967) has shown that this reasoning is correct in a further experiment in which he trained the subjects to sort the experimental items into four classes on the basis of the relevant stimulus dimensions. After three such sorting tasks, subjects learned either a conjunctive, disjunctive, conditional, or biconditional problem. A control group which learned the same problems was not given the sorting training. The subjects who had been familiarized with the relevant coding procedure performed much better than the control subjects. Indeed, these subjects solved conjunctive and disjunctive problems in about as many trials as were needed to present at least one instance of each of the four stimulus categories. Clearly, these subjects were making use of the coding scheme that they had learned before.

The work on rule learning which has just been discussed fits quite well into the general framework of our discussion of discrimination learning and concept learning. The subject learns to code the stimulus input in a particular way (here the four contingencies exemplified by Table 8.2) and then learns to connect the stimulus-as-coded with the proper response alternatives. Thus, the learning of logical relationships is closely related to discrimination learning and concept identification, except that both the category-response relationships and the coding process itself are more complex (two attributes and their relationship to each other must be considered in the experiments discussed here). The output of the coding system—the four stimulus categories (R,S), $(\bar{R},S)$, $(R,\bar{S})$, and $(\bar{R},\bar{S})$—is connected with the response alternatives by a paired-associate learning process, although one with complicated and as yet unspecified dependencies among the pairs learned. This is essentially the position of Bourne (1967). Neisser and Weene (1962), who also studied the learning of the various rules in Table 8.1, offered the hypothesis that the higher level rules are more difficult to learn because they presuppose the availability of components which themselves are constructed according to lower order rules. For instance, in order to learn the biconditional rule one must have available the conjunctions (R,S) and $(\bar{R},\bar{S})$. Bourne's interpretation is obviously similar to that, if one takes as the components which must be available the often-mentioned stimulus categories which are obtained by the two-dimensional classification. Hunt, Marin, and Stone (1966) interpret rule learning somewhat differently. They too work with the fourfold categorizations which are obtained by combining two relevant attributes, as anyone must since the concepts to be learned are defined in terms of these categories. However, they postulate that the subject imposes a hierarchical organization upon the stimulus material. A hierarchical coding scheme is a much stronger theory than that advanced by Bourne. In order to appreciate the difference between the two, consider the four stimulus categories in Table 8.2. There is no sense in which one of these is more important or prior to the others. Yet, as Bourne has shown, some classes are much easier to learn than others, the difficulty of any particular category depending upon the rule under consideration. This differential difficulty can not be explained within Bourne's framework other than *ad hoc*. Hierarchical organization of attributes permits one to account for this differential difficulty in a natural way, at least in principle. The model of Hunt *et al.* (1966) has already been discussed in Chapter 6 in the section on pattern recognition. Hunt *et al.* assumed that logical relationships are learned by establishing decision trees; for instance, the rule conditional can be defined by the following decision tree:

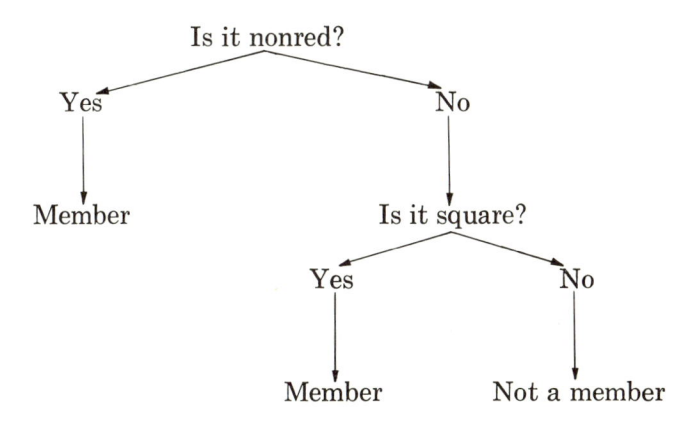

Rule learning, then consists in learning to ask a series of questions in a fixed order. A more involved example has been discussed in Chapter 6, and there is no need here to review again the various rules of thumb which Hunt *et al.* employ to construct their decision trees. These procedures were not selected because Hunt thought that they simulated human behavior, but rather because they seemed to be the most efficient problem solving strategies available. Hunt's model, it will be remembered, was developed as an artificial intelligence project. However, it is clear that in constructing decision trees some questions will be asked sooner and some later, some will be asked exactly the right way, and some not. Thus some types of items will be classified correctly by a growing tree while others will be missed. It is possible that the subject's behavior resembles a hierarchical coding process of this type. The interdependence of learning the various classes of stimulus items could then be represented in a more natural way.

Although the model of Hunt *et al.* (1966) was not primarily designed for the simulation of human behavior, the authors found that the model actually described several aspects of human rule learning quite well. In Fig. 8.2 the mean number of errors are shown which were made in learning several rules by human subjects and by Concept Learning System 1, which is the computer program embodying

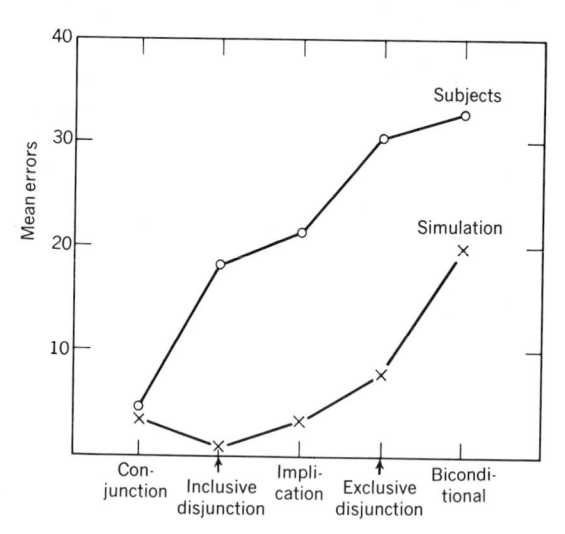

Fig. 8.2 *Mean errors to solution of problems based upon five different rules for human subjects and computer simulation. (after Hunt, Marin, and Stone, 1966)*

essentially the principles of sequential decision making described in Chapter 6. First note that Hunt *et al.*'s human subjects performed quite like the subjects of Haygood and Bourne (1965, Fig. 8.1). Exclusive disjunction is the complementary rule to biconditional, and hence the difficulty of learning this rule is not surprising. The computer program learned in a way which was at least roughly similar to human subjects. The ordering of the difficulty of the rules was the same, except for conjunction. The computer apparently does not have the strong bias in favor of conjunctive solutions which is so characteristic of people.

The over-all agreement of human subjects and the model as to the difficulty of learning the various rules is encouraging, but in itself this is a relatively weak test of the model. Therefore, Hunt *et al.* have investigated the trial by trial agreement between the responses made by the computer and the human subjects learning the same problem. Since both human subjects and computer eventually learned all problems, trials after the last error were excluded from this analysis: agreement on such trials would be spurious. The computer in this way "predicted" 70% of the responses made by the subjects, which is clearly a statistically significant figure. In order to obtain some kind of evaluation of how good these predictions are Hunt *et al.* chose a subject at random in each experimental condition and then treated the responses of these subjects as "predictions" of the responses of the other subjects in the same group. The randomly chosen subject was a less accurate predictor of his fellow subjects' responses than the computer. On the average, only 59% of the responses were predicted correctly in this manner. Thus, if one wanted to predict the responses of a subject in this experiment trial by trial and could obtain as a hint either the output of the computer or the responses of another randomly chosen subject, one would do better observing the program. This is a version of Turing's test (Turing, 1950) who suggested such a procedure for determining whether a computer successfully simulates human behavior: if one only looks at responses, can one tell whether they are the responses of a human or of a machine? In the present case the records of man and machine could not be discriminated, and hence the program passed this version of Turing's test.

Before leaving the discussion of how logical relationships are learned another important problem must be mentioned, which is, however, not directly related to the principal topic of this section. This is the long-standing observation that positive and negative instances do not convey the same amount of information to subjects in concept learning. Most of the work concerning this topic has been done within the framework of simple concept identification experiments, but its general significance can be better appreciated after the more complicated rule learning paradigms have been discussed.

The problem is the following: subjects learn a concept faster when they are given positive instances than when they are given negative instances of the concept (Smoke, 1933); do human subjects have some deep-seated bias for dealing with positive information, rather than with negative? Hovland (1952) argued that in the experiments showing a bias for positive instances there were several confounding factors. Most importantly, the amount of information transmitted by positive and negative information was different. For example, with stimulus material varying along four binary dimensions a conjunctive concept with three relevant dimensions can be specified by two positive stimulus items: if color, size, and form are the relevant dimensions and border is the irrelevant dimension, the two items with the right color, size and form and with both types of borders completely define the concept. On the other hand, at least 10 different items are necessary to define the concept by means of negative instances only. With more dimensions and more values per dimension this asymmetry between the information content of negative and positive instances becomes even more pronounced. Therefore, Hovland maintained that the faster learning with positive instances is an artifact of the way concepts are defined. However, he soon found out that even with information content of positive and negative items equalized subjects still did worse with negative items (Hovland and Weiss, 1953). For some reason human subjects are better adept at handling positive information than negative information. Freiberg and Tulving (1961) showed that this was so because of transfer from preexperimental experience. They constructed problems in such a way that either 4 positive or 4 negative instances were logically sufficient to identify the solution. Solution time was taken as the dependent variable. Subjects were given 20 problems in succession, either all based upon positive instances, or all based upon negative instances. At first, subjects were much better with positive instances than with negative instances. However, as training progressed this difference disappeared. The greater facility which subjects have with positive instances is therefore not an inherent characteristic of their information processing, but appears to be caused simply by greater familiarity with problems defined in terms of positive instances. The same factors in the human environment which are responsible for the preference of many subjects for a "positive focusing" strategy are probably also at work in shaping the bias for positive instances. Subjects obviously have a great deal of preexperimental experience with inferring conjunctive concepts from positive instances.

That the preference for positive instances is merely a result of greater familiarity with such instances and the ease with which they can be used to learn conjunctive concepts is further demonstrated by Bourne (1967) who extended the investigation of positive and negative instances to other types of rules. Three factors were studied in Bourne's experiment: rule type (conjunction, disjunction, and conditional), training conditions (positive instances only, negative instances only, or mixed) and task (attribute identification and rule learning). When the task was attribute identification and the concept conjunctive, positive instances were best, in agreement with earlier results. However, this was the only condition where positive instances were preferred. In general, the usability of a category was determined by the degree of stimulus variation within it, but there certainly was no evidence for a bias for positive information as some kind of inherent feature of human information processing.

Note, however, that there exist classes of very important rules which are learned almost entirely by induction from positive instances. These are the rules of language, which will be discussed below. Whatever the role of learning in language training, it is quite obvious that a child does not learn the rules of language through explicit training with positive and negative instances. The child is exposed almost exclusively to positive instances, i.e., to well-formed sentences or acceptable speech. Similarly in second-language learning, training with negative instances seems to be of little help, and is merely a further source of confusion (Crothers and Suppes, 1967, Expt. XVI). The same holds true for the learning of artificial languages, which will be discussed below (Braine, 1963).

2. RULE LEARNING AND ARTIFICIAL LANGUAGES

There are, of course, many different kinds of rules other than those shown in Table 8.1. The rules of Table 8.1 are important in psychological research, both historically and also because they are especially well suited to explore transfer relationships between rules, since they are all defined in the same way. They are all represented as functions of a set of simple properties. This is frequently a natural way to define concepts, but sometimes it is more convenient to describe concepts by other kinds of rules. What kind of rule description is used depends upon the type of problem under investigation.

Therefore, the characteristics of rule learning itself are intimately related to problem structure. More precisely, there are two distinct factors which must be considered in rule learning: the capabilities which the learner brings to the task (immediate memory, various processing abilities such as those required to code the experimental stimuli appropriately and to associate the stimulus-as-coded with the overt responses) and the requirements posed by the problem structure. The problem structure determines the language that is used, and this in turn determines what the subject does and learns in rule acquisition. We have already discussed how rules are learned which are expressed in terms of simple logical relations. Two other rule-types will be considered in this chapter. First, we shall briefly describe the induction and use of some rules which are stated in information processing language. Next, we shall be concerned with rewriting rules. Rewriting rules are employed in the description of natural languages, and we shall discuss in some detail how such rules are used in understanding and remembering language material.

As a part of many intelligence tests subjects are often given a letter series completion task. They are shown brief series of letters such as *atbataatbat-* and are asked to continue the series. Simon and Kotovsky (1963) have presented an interesting investigation of the behavior involved in this task. In order to solve such tasks, subjects clearly must be able to abstract somehow from the given series a rule which specifies how to generate the series, and furthermore they must be able to use this rule to continue the series. It is not necessary for subjects to be able to state these rules and operations explicitly but they must have a functional knowledge of that sort. Clearly, before one can ask how subjects induce and use the necessary rules, one must specify exactly what rules are involved. This means that one must select some kind of "language" (i.e., some kind of formalism) for the description of the rules. Simon and Kotovsky have chosen an information processing language for this task. This language has two advantages: it is very well suited to the description of the rules in question and it has been employed successfully in other studies of problem solving (Newell and Simon, 1962). It assumes that subjects come to the task outfitted with some basic knowledge. In this case, subjects must know the alphabet, forwards and backwards, the two relations *equal* and *next*, and the concept *cycle*. These primitive terms suffice to describe the rules involved in letter series completions. Several examples are shown in Table 8.4. In every case the rule description specifies a cycle of the corresponding series. For instance, in series (i) a cycle consists of an *a*, followed by a *t*, followed by either an *a* or

Table 8.4. *Letter series completion problems and their rule descriptions from Simon and Kotovsky (1963).*

	Test Sequence	Rule Description
(i)	*atbataatbat-*	$[a,t,(b,a)]$
(ii)	*aaabbbcccdd-*	Initialization: $[M1 = \text{Alphabet}; a]$ Sequence iteration: $[M1,M1,M1,\text{Next}(M1)]$
(iii)	*wxaxybyzczadab-*	Initialization: $[M1 = \text{Alphabet};\text{w}.M2 = \text{Alphabet};a]$ Sequence iteration: $[M1,\text{Next}(M1),M1,M2,\text{Next}(M2)]$
(iv)	*urtustuttu-*	Initialization: $[M1 = \text{Alphabet}; r]$ Sequence iteration: $[u,M1, \text{Next}(M1), t]$

a b. For the description of rule (ii) the concept of a variable is needed; variables are designated here by the letter M. The rule description is in two parts: the first part says that there is a variable $M1$, which is the alphabet starting with the letter a. The second part specifies the cycle: produce three times the letter specified by the variable $M1$, and then go to the next value of the variable and recycle. Series (iii) is a little more complex, because it is necessary to keep track of two variables, one starting with w and the other with a. The rule is read as follows: produce the letter specified by the variable $M1$, go to the next letter of $M1$, produce it, produce the letter specified by $M2$, go to the next letter of $M2$, and recycle.

It should be clear now how to arrive at rule descriptions in this system. The basic assumption which Simon and Kotovsky make is that to obtain a letter series concept implies generating and fixating a rule description. Once this much has been specified one can ask how the subject learns these rules. Simon and Kotovsky suggest a simple procedure: first the subject looks for cycles in the series, i.e. for a repeated letter, alphabetical progressions, or for interruptions of a regular pattern (as in series (i)). Once a cycle has been identified the relationships among the letters within the cycle are determined in terms of *equal* and *next*. If the subject is successful the result is expressed in the form of a rule description as shown in Table 8.4. The next question is how series are generated once the rule is known. In order to generate the corresponding series subjects must have available in memory a program capable of interpreting and executing rule descriptions. That is, the subject must be able to perform a few basic operations, as for instance those which are involved in the production of series (iv):

1. *Hold* the letter *r* on the list named *alphabet* in *immediate memory*.
2. *Produce u.*
3. *Produce* the letter that is in *immediate memory*.
4. *Put the next* letter on the list *alphabet* into *immediate memory*.
5. *Produce t.*
6. *Return* to step 2 and repeat the cycle as often as desired.

The reader should compare this program for the production of a series with the rule description of the series. The program is simply a step-by-step translation of the rule description into operational terms, such as *hold in immediate memory, produce, put the next letter on the list into immediate memory*, and the like.

Note how specific this theory of rule learning and rule utilization is to the rules for completing letter series, or more precisely, to the formalism which Simon and Kotovsky have chosen to express these rules. It is very important to keep this task-specific component of rule learning in mind. In the same way, the work reported in the previous section on the learning of various classifications was task specific. However, the same task independent psychological factors enter into the learning of various types of rules, such as the capacity of immediate memory.

Simon and Kotovsky have stated their theory as a computer program and they have evaluated it by comparing the performance of real subjects on series-completion tasks with the performance of their program. There was considerable correspondence between the two in that the difficulty which subjects had with various series tended to be correlated with the performance of the simulation program. Perhaps more interesting than that, the theory made it possible to locate precisely where subjects have difficulties with letter series of this type. The length of the rule description correlated with the difficulty of a series, but this correlation was only apparent. Underlying it was the factor of immediate memory: those rules which made the heaviest demands upon immediate memory were the hardest to learn!

It has been mentioned before that information processing language is very well suited for the investigation of problem solving in general. One can assume therefore that other studies of rule learning using this kind of approach will come forth in the near future. However, we shall turn to a different kind of formalism for the description of rules, where there exists an active interest today because these rules figure in the analysis of natural language. The rules in question are called rewriting rules.

Consider first an experiment reported by Suppes (1965). This experiment could be called an experiment on rule utilization. The subjects were given the four rules shown in Fig. 8.3 and had to learn to employ them in proving elementary mathematical theorems. The subjects in this experiment were first-graders, but before describing the actual experimental set-up, it is useful to discuss the problem in general terms. The theorems in Suppes' experiment were short strings of 0's or 1's. The subject's task was to show how a given string could be produced through application of the rules 1-4, starting from the symbol 1, which in formal language, is called the axiom of the system. In Fig. 8.3, S stands for any nonempty string. Thus, rules 1-4 mean that one can either add two 0's or two 1's to a string, or that one can delete a terminal 1 or 0. An example of how the string 101 (Theorem 101) can be generated by means of these rules is also shown in Fig. 8.3. The procedure takes 5 steps. The axiom of the system gives us a 1 to start with. Next two 0's are added (Rule 1), a 0 is deleted (Rule 3), two 1's are added (Rule 2), and finally a 1 is removed (Rule 4), producing the desired string 101. These are quite trivial operations, and adults would have little difficulty learning them. However, the task was challenging to Suppes' first graders. The first graders were, of course, not told to prove theorems from axioms and rules. Instead of 1's and 0's they worked with red and green lights, so that a theorem was represented by a row of lights. In the present example, the lights would be red-green-red. Below these lights was a second panel of matching lamps, the first of which was illuminated red, corresponding to the axiom of the system. The subject was told to make the second

Rules of Inference				Theorem 101	
R 1	S	⟶	$S00$	(1)	1	Axiom
R 2	S	⟶	$S11$	(2)	100	R 1
R 3	$S0$	⟶	S	(3)	10	R 3
R 4	$S1$	⟶	S	(4)	1011	R 2
				(5)	101	R 4

Fig. 8.3 *Rules of inference and a typical proof in the rule learning experiment of Suppes (1966).*

panel look like the first by pressing four buttons below the lighted panels. These buttons corresponded exactly to the rules described above, i.e., one button could be used to add two green lights, the other added two red lights, one removed a green light, and the last one removed a red light.

In this manner each subject was given 17 theorems to prove. Another group of subjects was run on a system utilizing five rules. Presolution performance for both groups is shown in Fig. 8.4. Trials before reaching criterion (five successive correct responses) were divided into quartiles and Vincent learning curves were constructed. Performance on presolution trials was constant for subjects who learned the four-rule system, but it improved somewhat during the last quartile for subjects who learned the 5-rule system. Thus, learning in this case appears to be a discrete process—just as in many other simple experimental situations that have been examined. It is worth dwelling on this result for a moment: Vincent learning curves are stationary or near-stationary on presolution trials in many different situations, ranging from paired-associate learning (Chapter 2) and recognition learning (Chapter 4) to concept learning (Chapter 7), and rule learning. It can hardly be an accident that one finds such data whenever one looks at a simple learning situation. This kind of convergence on the data level is quite encouraging to the learning theorist, because it supports the conclusions that simple learning events are quite alike in these situations. Rote learning and rule learning apparently have much in common, which makes it difficult to insist on a strict dichotomy between "conditioning" and "cognitive processes."

The Rules learned in Suppes' experiment are recursive rewriting rules. Recursion means that a symbol may refer to itself. Take for instance Rule 1 in Fig. 8.3. This rule says that one can rewrite any string as S-plus-00: $S \rightarrow S00$. The symbol S appears on both sides of the rewriting rule. One can apply this rule repeatedly and generate as long a string of 0's preceded by an S as one wants. Therefore, the property of recursiveness gives rules great generative power. How people use and induce such rules is an extremely important psychological problem.

Before turning to this problem, however, the standard terminology for rewriting rules must be explained. Two kinds of symbols must be distinguished, a set of terminal symbols, the alphabet $A = (a, b, c, \ldots)$, and a set of nonterminal or intermediate symbols $I = (S, X, Y, \ldots)$. In the preceding example, the alphabet consisted of the letters a and b, and only one nonterminal symbol was used, S. A rewriting rule is to be understood as an instruction to substitute for

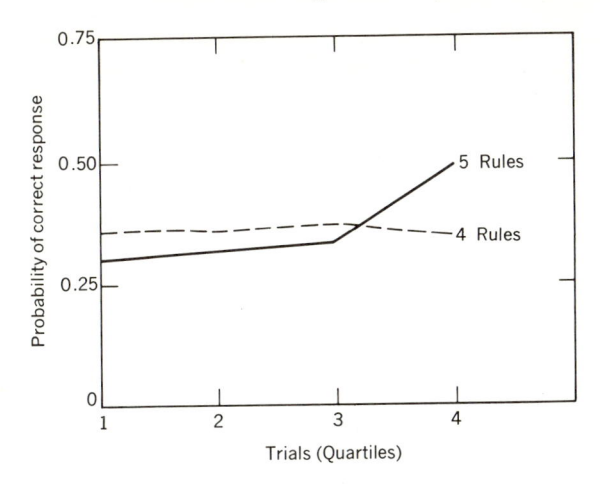

Fig. 8.4 *Vincent learning curves in quartiles in the proof experiment. (after Suppes, 1966)*

the symbol on the left side of the arrow the expression on the right side of the arrow. A set of rewriting rules is called a grammar. The set of strings containing only terminal symbols which can be produced by the grammar is called the set of well-formed strings, or the language. In the example of Suppes (1966) this is the set of theorems which can be proven.

The problem for the psychologist is the following. If subjects are presented with a subset of the well-formed strings generated by a grammar they are able to induce the rules of the grammar, at least under certain conditions. Conversely, if subjects are given rules, they can learn how to use them. What are the experimental conditions which make rule learning difficult or easy, and what is involved in rule learning? The problem is obviously closely related to that of concept identification, except that in concept identification the problem was mostly one of determining the relevant stimulus dimension. Here, the problem concerns the form of the rules. This may be quite a formidable task itself, even without any irrelevant stimulus dimensions. Nevertheless, the similarity between the two problems, and such results as those of Suppes (1966) who showed that the course of learning to utilize simple rules is quite similar to the course of learning in simple concept-identification tasks, suggest looking for similar processes in rule learning and in concept learning. Primarily, it appears worthwhile to look for something like hypothesis-testing or strategy-selection in rule learning.

What was done for concept identification by Bruner, Goodnow, and Austin (1956) was attempted for rule learning by Shipstone (1960) and Miller (1967). Bruner *et al.*, provided us with a careful description of the strategies used in solving concept-identification problems; Shipstone and Miller tried to determine the strategies used by subjects in rule learning. They made up strings of letters according to several artificial grammars. These strings were printed on cards and then given to subjects with instructions to sort the cards into several categories according to whatever principle seemed most appropriate to them. No feedback was given to the subjects. After the sorting, the experimenter attempted to determine the principles followed by the subject in sorting the cards. The grammars used varied in structural complexity, as well as in the size of the alphabet. The results of this experiment are actually quite disappointing: no definite strategies of an interesting nature could be determined from the subjects' sortings. Subjects started out sorting according to such principles as lengths of the strings, they then tended to alphabetize according to the first or last letter, but after that every subject seemed to do something different. Some invented their own rules and modified them as new evidence became available, but nothing like Bruner's general cognitive principles appeared. Subjects were actually quite good in discovering the hidden patterns in the test material, but each subject did it in his own way. Asking subjects to "think out loud" while sorting provided interesting protocols, but still no general insights. The character of the rules themselves appeared to be much less important in Shipstone's experiment than general memory factors. The size of the alphabet was the most conspicuous factor determining performance; if size of the alphabet and word length were kept constant, variations in the number and complexity of rules did not yield markedly different results.

It is not clear why Shipstone could not identify general strategies in rule learning. Perhaps there are none; but perhaps Shipstone's experimental design was not suited to detect them, or perhaps the strategies in rule learning are so different from the behavior patterns described by Bruner *et al.*, that Shipstone and Miller simply failed to identify them, in spite of their very considerable efforts. Whatever the eventual answer, further experimental work on this problem is certainly needed. However, it may be necessary to approach the problem somewhat differently. Suppose we ask how we would construct a "rule learner," following the example of the concept learner of Hunt, Marin, and Stone (1966). The problem which this "rule learner" would have to solve would be that of inducing the rules which were used to generate a given subset of strings of an artificial language. For a start, natural language would surely be too complicated to tackle. In constructing such a rule learner, many subproblems would have to be solved. For instance, one would have to think about how one could simplify the alphabet by exploiting redundancies. Then there is the question which and how many intermediate symbols are to be introduced? Perhaps a hypotheses-testing procedure could be developed, trying out plausible and likely rules. If so, the problem of sampling-with-replacement versus memory arises again. Suppose all or some of that could actually be done; one might then look again at human rule learning and—with the newly acquired experience about the nature of rule learning—consistent and meaningful behavior patterns might become apparent where none could be seen before. In any case, one could probably learn a great deal about the induction of rules from such an approach.

There are several other artificial language experiments in the psychological literature which are not concerned directly with subjects' strategies in learning rules, but which do provide some information concerning the experimental conditions affecting rule learning. A particularly simple but instructive experimental design is that of Esper (1925). It has been used most recently by Foss (1968). Figure 8.5 illustrates this artificial language. There are 36 stimuli, obtained by combining 6 shapes and 6 colors. The responses are constructed from two sets of syllables, one corresponding to colors, and one to shape. In this language each stimulus has a name which is a two-syllable combination. The first syllable refers to the color, and the second to the shape of the stimulus item. For instance, a green heart would be

		-Tep ◯	-Fub △	-Piv ☐	-Gom ♡	-Tul ☆	-Leb ♣
Zin-	Red	a	a				
Jor-	Yellow		a	a			
Kes-	Blue			a	a		
Nid-	Green	a			a		
Mof-	Grey					a	b
Ruk-	Violet					b	a

Fig. 8.5 *An illustration of the miniature linguistic system used in the experiment of Foss (1968).*

called *Nidgom*. Esper (1925) showed that if two cells of such a matrix are omitted during learning, subjects could respond correctly on a test and often did not even notice that the items had never been shown before. There are two interpretations of this finding. One is that subjects learned the rule "first syllable stands for color, second for shape," plus the shape-syllable and color-syllable paired-associates; a second interpretation holds that subjects were simply learning to associate those parts of the stimulus and response which were consistently paired (e.g., all red items were paired with the syllable *Zin*). According to this second interpretation, it is not necessary to talk about rule learning in this experiment. Foss (1968) demonstrated that subjects were indeed learning a rule in addition to the paired-associates by an ingenious modification of Esper's procedure. He taught his subjects all the stimulus-response pairs marked *"a"* in Fig. 8.5. The large 4 × 4 submatrix provided essentially a replication of Esper's experiment: after training, subjects could respond correctly to, say, a yellow heart, but this has no bearing on the question of whether subjects were really learning a rule, as we have just seen. However, only two of the items of the 2 × 2 submatrix in Fig. 8.5 were presented. Thus, both "grey" and "star" were paired exactly once with the response syllables *mof* and *tul*, and subjects had no basis for correctly responding on the basis of frequency alone to the two other items of the matrix marked "b" which recombine the colors and shapes of the two learning items. Since subjects had no difficulty in responding correctly to the *"b"* items, we must suppose that they had learned the simple rule for concatenation of response syllables in addition to the associations between particular stimulus properties and syllables.

The acquisition of artificial languages has also been studied in cases where there were no stimulus dimensions correlated with the responses. The prototype of these studies is one by Miller (1958) which has been described in some detail in Chapter 2. Miller generated strings of letters from a simple grammar and then compared how well subjects could recall these strings with random strings composed from the same letters and equated in length. Miller's rules were represented graphically in Fig. 1.2 (Chapter 1). He found that subjects learned to recall the structured strings much better than the unstructured strings. Miller concluded from these results that the structured strings were easier to learn because less information about them had to be remembered; some could be reconstructed from a knowledge of the rules. Before Miller's experiment, Aborn and Rubenstein (1952) had come to similar conclusions, working within the framework of information theory. Reber (1967) also studied free recall of strings generated by rules similar to the ones used by Miller. He, too, found that the rules facilitated recall, and that the more experience a subject obtained with these rules the better his performance became. Reber's subjects were able to tell which of a set of new items belonged to the rule-generated set and which did not. However, they did this with little explicit knowledge of the rules involved. Again, no simple strategies could be detected which determined the performance of any one subject on generalization tests. Introspectively, subjects seem to go by a vague feeling of familiarity, which is no great help to our understanding.

Braine (1963) has reported a series of artificial language experiments which show that subjects can learn rules that assign certain words to certain positions in a "sentence." In his principal experiment Braine used "sentences" of the form $S \to AP$, where A could be either one of two nonsense syllables, and P could be one of two different syllables. Learning was by means of a sentence completion test; an A-syllable was presented plus two choices for the position behind it, one of which was an A-syllable and the other a P-syllable; alternatively a P-syllable was presented together with two corresponding choices for the position in front of it. When a subject made a wrong response, he was corrected. After the initial learning, four generalization tests were given to discover whether the subjects were using position as a cue. New syllables were shown, and the subject had to fill in the position either before or behind the new syllable. He could choose from two alternatives, a previously learned A- or P-syllable. If, during original training, subjects had learned more than just associations between syllable pairs, that is if they registered the position of the words, they should always choose a P-syllable when the second position was to be filled in, and an A-syllable when the first position was to be filled in. The subjects in this experiment were 10-year-old children. They learned the problem rapidly and performed quite well on the generalization test. However, when they were asked why they responded as they did they could not verbalize the rule which their performance manifested.

In further experiments Braine showed that phrases as well as words could become associated with the sentence positions in which they recur and generalized to a new context. This was done by letting the A and P terms of the previous experiment become in themselves phrases consisting of several syllables structured according to positional rules. In this way, a hierarchical structure of elements could be obtained. Position within a sentence would be itself defined through a hierarchical scheme. Subjects learned not the absolute position of a word in a sentence, but its position relative to other words.

We have not yet considered differences among rewriting rules up to now. Rewriting rules may be classified according to their power, i.e., according to the complexity of the expressions which can be produced by them. The problem then arises whether rules of different kinds are learned differently, or at least whether some kinds of rules are easier to learn than others. Equivalently, one could ask whether, given an alternative, subjects are biased in favor of a particular class of rules. This is a fascinating problem, and although we shall be unable to offer an answer in the following, at least we shall state the problem.

For the present purposes we need to distinguish four classes of rewriting rules following, in general, the classification introduced by Chomsky (1963). The most restrictive grammar is called a finite-state or one-way linear grammar. It has only rules of the form

$$\text{(1a)} \qquad X \rightarrow aY$$
$$\text{(1b)} \qquad X \rightarrow a$$

where, as before, a, b, c, ... are elements of the terminal vocabulary of the language and X, Y, Z, ... are nonterminal symbols. Finite-state rules generate strings of elements from left to right. The X's and Y's are "states" of the system, and the rules specify transitions between states: from state X go to state Y and write out an a; next, go from Y to Z, producing a b, and so forth. An example has been given in Fig. 1.2 (Chapter 1).

A little more powerful are two-way linear grammars, which have rules of the form

$$\text{(2a)} \qquad X \rightarrow aY$$
$$\text{(2b)} \qquad X \rightarrow Za$$
$$\text{(2c)} \qquad X \rightarrow a$$

The additional power comes from the fact that strings can be built both from left to right and from right to left. In other words, one can add symbols not only at the end of the string, but also in front.

At the next higher level of complexity are context-free grammars. A context-free grammar permits the building of strings both to the left and to the right, and in addition it contains rules with more than one nonterminal symbol on the right-hand side:

$$\text{(3a)} \qquad X \rightarrow WYZ$$
$$\text{(3b)} \qquad X \rightarrow a$$

The rules of the form (3a) give rise to the property of embedding: a string Y with a structure of its own can be embedded within another string. Several illustrative examples of embedding will be discussed later.

The most powerful grammar to be considered here is the context-sensitive grammar. Its rules are of the form

(4a)
$$\phi X \psi \rightarrow \phi WYZ\psi$$
(4b)
$$\phi X \psi \rightarrow \phi a\psi$$

where ϕ and ψ are arbitrary strings of symbols which specify the context in which each particular rule applies.

The more powerful a rule is, the more calculations can be performed with it. A context-free grammar can do everything a finite-state grammar can do and it can do more than that. Note that since all these rules may be recursive, strings of any desired length can be produced. However, in any actual rule-learning experiment subjects are given a relatively small number of strings to work with, most of which are quite short. Although the rules can generate strings of infinite length, this is quite irrelevant for actual experimentation. The subject always has to infer a grammar from a set of examples which is finite and, in fact, very restricted. This produces a problem which is as yet incompletely explored but which may provide some insight into the nature of rule learning. Suppose that the language L is generated by the context-free grammar G. A finite subset $\{A \subset L\}$ of words is given to a subject and the subject is asked to infer the rules of the grammar G from the examples in A. The subject may come up with the correct context-free grammar G, or some other context-free grammar which is equivalent to G as far as the subset A of items is concerned. However, any finite set of items can always be described by a less powerful grammar, e.g., by a finite-state grammar. This description may be less elegant than the proper description—it even may be rather cumbersome. But such a description is possible and there is nothing to prevent the subject from using it. An example will clarify this point. Suppose a subject is asked to infer the grammar which produced the following four artificial words:

$$ab$$
$$aabb$$
(5)
$$aaabbb$$
$$aaaabbbb$$

These are the first four "words" of a language which is often used as an example of embedding. A comparable sentence of the natural language with this type of structure is, for instance, *The girl whom my friend dates walked up the stairs.* There is a dependency in this sentence between *the girl* and *walked up the stairs*, and an independent embedded phrase with the same structure: *whom my friend dates.* The structure of the sentences as a whole is *aabb*: *my friend cor-*

responds to *the girl,* and *dates* corresponds to *walked up the stairs.* A context-free grammar which produces these strings can be quite easily inferred. The grammar has two rules, which shall be written as

$$(6) \qquad\qquad S \to ab \quad | \quad aSb$$

using the vertical bar to denote "or" so as to make our notation a little more efficient. Note that this grammar will generate not only the strings in (5), but all strings which consist of a sequence of a's followed by equally many b's. This is, of course, completely in agreement with our intuitions about the strings in (5). But suppose a subject is only concerned with the four strings actually presented. Equation (6) is of course still an acceptable solution, but there are other possibilities. A trivial solution from the standpoint of rule learning would be a grammar which simply enumerates the four examples. This would not even be such a bad solution in this case, as four items are readily listed. In psychological terms this is pure rote learning. The subject does not rely at all upon rules.

However, the subject has the option of learning rules, though he may learn rules other than the experimenter intended. For instance, in the present case the subject might learn finite-state rules. Although we know that embedding cannot in general be accounted for by finite-state rules, this is true only if we insist upon embedding of an arbitrary degree. In the present case, the degree of embedding is quite limited and it is very easy to write down finite-state rules which will produce the items shown in (5):

$$\begin{aligned}
X_0 &\to aX_1 \\
X_1 &\to b \quad | \quad aX_2 \\
X_2 &\to bX_3 \quad | \quad aX_4 \\
X_3 &\to b \\
X_4 &\to bX_5 \quad | \quad aX_6 \\
X_5 &\to bX_3 \\
X_6 &\to bX_7 \\
X_7 &\to bX_5
\end{aligned}$$

(7)

A little calculation, or the drawing of the state diagram corresponding to these rules, will convince the reader that they indeed produce the strings in (5) and none other. It is quite obvious that a subject would not be well advised to learn finite-state rules in this case. The rules in (6) are certainly much more elegant and much easier to handle. In fact, it would be better to memorize the four items outright rather than learn 11 rules! Also, note that if we would add a new item, say *aaaaabbbbb,* a subject who has learned rules (6) will have no difficulty with it. A subject who had learned rules (7) would have to learn two additional rules to be able to handle the new item. Obviously, the finite-state system has little to recommend it. However, one cannot *a priori* assume that subjects will aways choose the most efficient and reasonable approach. One must at least consider the possibility that subjects may be learning something different from what the experimenter is trying to teach them.

An experiment on artificial language learning by Braine (1965a, b; also Gough and Segal, 1965, and Braine, 1965b) exemplifies some of the problems just discussed. Braine taught college students rules for forming three-word sentences. Twenty-two nonsense words constituted the terminal vocabulary in Braine's experiment. The rules for the concatenation of these words can be written in the present notation as

(8)
$$S \rightarrow ab_ic, \quad i = 1, 2, \ldots 12,$$
$$S \rightarrow db_je, \quad j = 1, 2, \ldots 6; 13, 14, \ldots 18,$$

where the letters stand for unusual words. Thus, there were two types of frames, *a-c* and *d-e* plus several center words, 6 of which appeared in both frames, and 6 were specific to each frame. Subjects listened to 72 strings formed according to these rules, and repeated each string as it was presented. Then they were given several kinds of tests. They were asked whether they recognized old items or items in which the center term appeared in the wrong frame, or items in which the frame itself was disturbed. Subjects accepted all items, except when the frame was incorrect, such as ab_id, or ab_ib_j. Apparently, they had learned that there were two kinds of frames, but they used center items indiscriminately. This conclusion was confirmed by a recall test and a frame-completion test in which subjects were given the frames plus the *b*-vocabulary and were asked to construct sentences.

What rules did Braine's subjects learn? At first it seems obvious that they learned rules as in (8), except that they failed to make distinctions between the *b*-terms. However, it is very easy to write a finite-state grammar for Braine's sentences, and one cannot be sure beforehand that subjects were not doing something like this, too. A finite-state grammar which may have been learned is

(9)
$$s \rightarrow aY$$
$$Y \rightarrow b_iX$$
$$X \rightarrow c$$
$$S \rightarrow dZ$$
$$Z \rightarrow b_iW$$
$$W \rightarrow e \qquad i = 1, 2, \ldots 18$$

Intentionally no distinction between the *b*-terms has been made in (9). It is obvious that the context-free grammar is much simpler than the finite-state grammar and that subjects should learn the former, but it is not easy to decide what they actually did. The finite-state grammar is unnecessarily complex. There are three rules in (9) for every one in (8). Furthermore, (9) assigns an unnatural structure to strings by insisting on some kind of division between *a* and *bc*. Intuitively, this division does not seem justified. However, clear experimental demonstrations of exactly what subjects are doing in cases like this have not yet been reported. What rules subjects learn, and how they go about it will need a great deal more study.

3. GRAMMATICAL RULES AND VERBAL LEARNING

Although very little is known about how people learn rules, a fair amount of empirical work has recently been performed on how rules are used once they have been acquired. The rules which govern the use of natural language are ideal for this purpose. Every normal adult knows these rules in the sense that he can use them freely. The rules themselves are extremely complex and although linguists are not yet able to write down the system of rules which generates all the grammatical sentences of the English language, or any other natural language, enough is known about the general characteristics of such a system of rules that psychological research concerning their utilization becomes feasible. At this time, there is considerable disagreement among linguists about several important issues in grammatical theory. As psychologists, we shall try to stay away from unsolved linguistic problems and controversies. We take from linguistics the concepts of a generative grammar, i.e., a system of rewriting rules which generates the grammatical sentences of a language and none other. Among linguists, Chomsky (1957, 1965) has been the most outspoken advocate of generative grammars. Furthermore, most linguists seem to agree that *phrase structure* rules must play an important rule in any generative grammar. Chomsky's own proposal also includes *transformational* rules. In our discussion of the psychological aspects of rule utilization we shall treat separately phrase-structure rules and transformational rules.

The topic of language acquisition will not be discussed here. Language acquisition appears to be a learning process sufficiently different from those described in this book. Maturational processes and learning interact in ways which are as yet poorly understood, and it is clear that the application of the principles of learning to first language acquisition is not straightforward (Lenneberg, 1965). Thus, the role of learning processes in the development of the child, and in particular in language acquisition, will not be considered here.

There are two ways in which one can approach psychological experiments on grammatical rules. First, one can hope to find out something by means of experiments on the nature of the grammatical rules themselves. This is a very complex question, which touches a raw nerve in the relationship between psychology and linguistics. Consider the goals and methods of these two sciences: language for the linguist is a corpus, and his task, or one of his tasks, is to describe this corpus and its structure, that is, to infer the rules which could be used to generate such a corpus. He is under no obligation to say how actual people can produce this corpus; he is interested in competence, not in production. The rules which he infers are based upon linguistic criteria only; psychological experiments have no relevance for this linguistic system. The psychologist approaches language from considerations of performance. The rules which the linguist finds useful may be relevant for him, but they need not be. It is conceivable that there could be a very elegant way of describing the rules of grammar linguistically which has no psychological counterpart. People may be producing sentences in ways which the linguists would consider nonoptimal or even outrageous as far as the systematic description of sentences is concerned.

While one must insist upon a certain amount of independence between approaches with different methods and goals, most linguists would probably be quite disturbed if psychologists told them that their system lacks psychological reality altogether. Certainly, the psychologist would be extremely misguided who would want to study language without listening to what the linguist has to say. The distinction between competence and performance notwithstanding, we do believe that linguistic principles and the psychology of language will turn out to be intimately related. They may not be identical, but it appears to be a sound research strategy to assume that the rules whose use we want to study are those identified by linguists, at least to a first approximation.

Actually, we shall not be much concerned with the precise characteristics of the rules of the grammar of natural languages. Closer to the main topic of this book is the question of how, when, and for what purpose subjects use grammatical rules if they are given a chance to do so in verbal learning experiments. We have seen before that whenever there is some kind of structure in the learning material, verbal learning is facilitated. Performance is improved if items are associatively interconnected, or if subjects have had much experience with the item-to-item transition frequencies, to name just two examples. The interitem associations or the transition probabilities are already known and the subject's learning task is thereby reduced. A similar observation has been made in the previous section on the learning of artificial languages. Once a subject has learned the rules of the language, he does not need to learn as much by rote. Knowledge of rules can thus be used to reduce memory load. The same is true if the rules are those of natural language. The rules of grammar provide a natural structure to sentence-type material, and hence a ready way for segmenting it into "chunks" for storage in memory. Not all of the information needed to regenerate these chunks must be stored in memory each time; much of it is already available to the subject in the form of general rules. However, before anticipating more of the conclusion, we must consider some of the experimental work upon which it is based.

The Retention of Sentences

The earliest experiments on the role of grammar in verbal learning have simply attempted to demonstrate that grammatically organized material is easier to learn and to perceive than material without this organization. Miller, Heise, and Lichten (1951) had discovered that content words heard over noise could be perceived more accurately in the context of sentences than when heard in isolation as separate items on a list. Sentence contexts, they concluded, facilitate intelligibility by narrowing down the set of alternative words a listener can expect to hear. Miller (1962a) observed that under time pressure subjects were able to perceive words more easily in the context of grammatical sentences than in the context of ungrammatical sentences. Miller rejects the theory that people organize the flow of speech on a word-to-word basis on the grounds that this involves too many separate decisions to keep up with the speed of speech. He argues that the listener analyzes a larger amount of information than the single word. Presumably when the words are presented in grammatical context, the listener is able to use his knowledge of language to organize the sequence of words into familiar and distinctive patterns. However, in this experiment there is no indication what these underlying patterns or decision units might consist of.

To investigate more specifically what types of constraints the sentence context imposes on the successive words in an utterance, Miller performed two experiments in which the semantic and syntactic rules could be violated independently. In Miller and Isard (1963) and

Marks and Miller (1964) five-word sentences were constructed as follows: (a) grammatical sentences (e.g., "pink bouquets emit fragrant odors"); (b) semantically anomalous sentences in which the syntactic structure was retained but the meaning destroyed (e.g., "pink accidents cause sleeping storms"); and (c) ungrammatical strings (e.g., "around accidents country honey the shoot") for the first experiment (1963). For the later experiment (1964) there were two final groups: (d) anagram strings, the original grammatical sentences with scrambled word order in which the semantic components were retained but the syntactic structure was destroyed (e.g., "bouquets pink odors fragrant emit"); and (e) word lists in which both the semantic and the syntactic components were destroyed (e.g., "accidents pink storms sleeping cause"). The first experiment (1963) was a perception task in which the sentences were presented over noise. The second experiment was a learning task. The results confirmed the prediction that disruption of semantic and syntactic rules would hinder learning and perception. The anagram strings and semantically anomolous strings had fewer errors than the strings with both disrupted syntax and meaning (i.e. ,the word lists). In the learning experiment (1964) certain characteristic errors occurred: most errors in the semantically anomalous strings were of a semantic nature (intrusions, i.e., misplacing words from one string to another), while the anagram strings were characterized by syntactic errors (inversions, i.e., incorrect word order, and morpheme errors, i.e., omitting or supplying wrong affixes). The authors conclude that both syntactic and semantic rules are involved in language processes and must be taken into account. As will be seen in the studies of grammatical transformation, these factors interact in a complicated manner, and it is often impossible to separate their respective functions.

A study reported by Epstein (1961) has shown that syntactic structure also facilitates the recall of lists of nonsense syllables. Three types of lists of nonsense sentences were presented to subjects in an ordered recall task. The first list (*A*) was composed of sentences in which English function words and bound morphemes were combined with nonsense syllable stems (e.g., "a vapy koobs desaked the citar molently um glox nerfs;" "a" and "the" are the function words, "vap," "koobs," "desak," "citar," "molent," "um," "glox," and "nerf" are the stems, and "-y," "-ed," "-ly," and "-s" are the bound morphemes). In the second list (*B*) the same items were given in a scrambled order. In the third list (*C*) the word order was retained but the bound morphemes were deleted, thus reducing the number of syntactic cues available to the subjects. The *A*-lists of pseudo-English sentences were found to be easiest to recall, the C-lists lacking bound morphemes were intermediate in difficulty, and the B-lists with ungrammatical word order were most difficult. In an extension of the Epstein study Forster (1966) hypothesized that the facilitative effect in the A-list is due to the fact that subjects need not store information concerning the order in which the nonsense syllables appear; whereas, the B-lists are most difficult to recall because full information concerning the order of the items must be stored in addition to the items themselves. In the C-lists the reduced number of syntactic cues makes it more difficult to perceive and make use of the structure than was the case with the A-lists. If subjects are not required to produce the items in order, Forster predicted, then this facilitation should disappear. However, he found that the presence or absence of syntactic structure was significant. Syntactic structure clearly did influence the recall of the items and thus its effect cannot simply be explained in terms of an inbuilt ordering function. Further investigation did not indicate that the English function words aid recall. Instead the facilitative effect appears to be centered in the nonsense syllable-bound morpheme combinations. Forster suggests that it is increased item differentiation which facilitates learning.

The facilitative effect of syntactic structure was not observed by Epstein (1962) in serial anticipation learning. Therefore, he concluded that the facilitative effect of sentence context lies in the fact that it constitutes a psychological unit or pattern. The sentence structure enables the series of elements to be perceived as a generalized linguistic form rather than as sequential or semantic associations.

That the facilitation of grouping or chunking is the crucial factor in this kind of experiment was further shown by O'Connell, Turner, and Onuska (1968). O'Connell, *et al.*, also investigated the effects of grammatical structure on the recall of nonsense material, but they presented the material orally and controlled for intonation. Word sequences were read either in a monotone voice, or with a normal English sentence intonation. Epstein (1962) had found that grammatical structure facilitated the organization of the material for recall only if the words in a sentence were presented simultaneously. Therefore, it follows that the perception of a sentence as a whole is necessary to suggest to subjects a learning strategy which involves the inherent structure of the sentence. Thus, if the material is presented orally in a monotone voice, perception of the sentence as a whole should be inhibited and the grammatical structure should have no effect upon retention. This is the result actually obtained by O'Connell *et al.* On the other hand, normal sentence intonation permitted the subjects to perceive the stimulus list under one complete intonational contour, and recall was facilitated if there was a sufficiently high level of grammatical organization in the string.

Phrase-structure Rules

While the studies so far reviewed show that grammatical structure facilitates verbal learning, they tell us little about the nature of the grammatical rules involved. In this section we shall be concerned with the psychological effects of phrase-structure rules. First, we shall briefly describe what phrase-structure rules are, using as examples the two sentences from Johnson (1965) shown in Fig. 8.6.

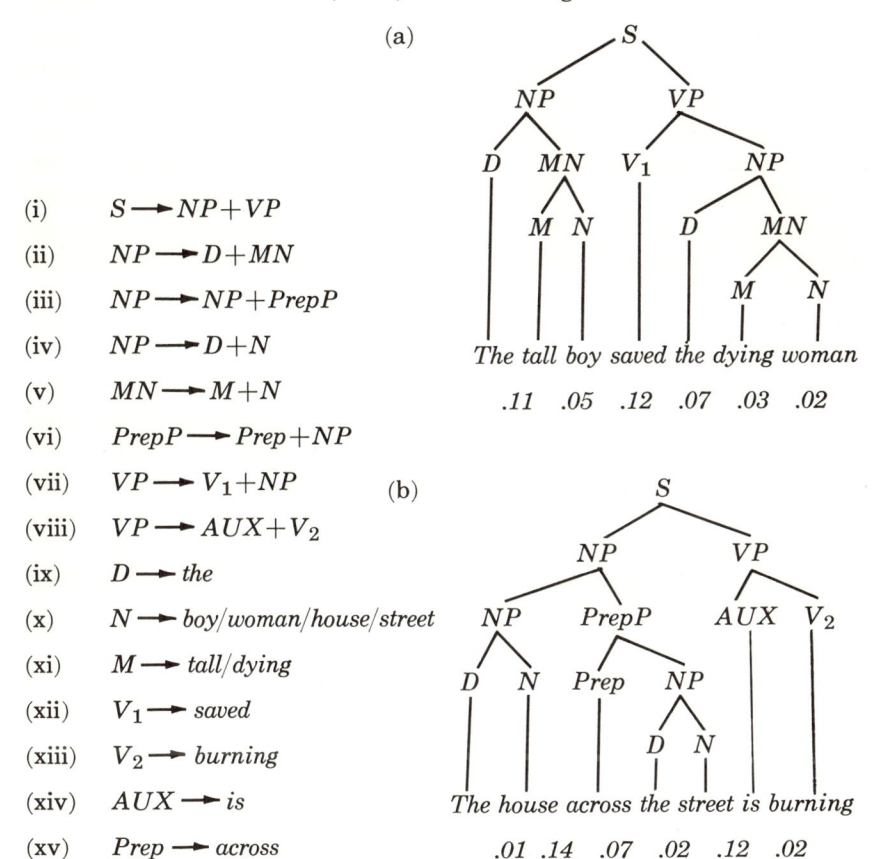

(i) $S \longrightarrow NP+VP$

(ii) $NP \longrightarrow D+MN$

(iii) $NP \longrightarrow NP+PrepP$

(iv) $NP \longrightarrow D+N$

(v) $MN \longrightarrow M+N$

(vi) $PrepP \longrightarrow Prep+NP$

(vii) $VP \longrightarrow V_1+NP$

(viii) $VP \longrightarrow AUX+V_2$

(ix) $D \longrightarrow the$

(x) $N \longrightarrow boy/woman/house/street$

(xi) $M \longrightarrow tall/dying$

(xii) $V_1 \longrightarrow saved$

(xiii) $V_2 \longrightarrow burning$

(xiv) $AUX \longrightarrow is$

(xv) $Prep \longrightarrow across$

Fig. 8.6 *A fragment of the rules for a generative grammar of English and phrase structure trees for two sentences which can be produced by these rules; below each sentence are shown the transition errors obtained in the recall experiment of Johnson (1965).*

Phrase-structure rules are context-free rewriting rules. Starting with the initial symbol S phrase-structure rules elaborate S in terms of an intermediate vocabulary (which consists of terms such as noun phrase, verb, preposition, and the like) and specify how English words as the terminal symbols of the system can be substituted once the desired phrase structure of a sentence has been developed. For instance, the first rule which has been used in both examples in Fig. 8.6 is (*i*) $S \rightarrow NP$ (noun phrase) plus VP (verb phrase). The noun phrase itself can then be broken down into determiner plus modifier plus noun (rules (ii) and (v)) or, in Example (b), necessarily into noun phrase plus prepositional phrase (iii). The rules which introduce the terminal vocabulary are of the form (ix) $D \rightarrow the$, (*x*) $N \rightarrow boy$ / *woman* / *house* / *street*, etc. The examples given are clearly oversimplified; for instance, we have not shown how the past tense of the verb in (a) is obtained, and similarly the progressive form of the verb in (b), but they suffice to illustrate how phrase-structure rules work. In the present context it is most important to realize that phrase-structure rules quite naturally organize a sequence of words into groups or chunks. For instance, sentence (a) is divided into two parts: ((*The* (*tall*(*boy*))) (*saved*(*the*(*dying*(*woman*))))); sentence (b) has major breaks after *house* as well as after *street*.

Johnson (1965) reasoned that if subjects are asked to memorize such sentences they will use the natural grouping provided by the sentence structure for chunking. The material within a chunk should be relatively coherent and there should be a tendency to recall chunks defined in this manner as a whole. Errors should be most likely in the transition from one chunk to the next, hence at the major syntactical breaks. Johnson performed an experiment to test this hypothesis. His subjects learned sentences such as (a) and (b) as responses in a paired-associate experiment in which the stimulus terms were digits. The results of principal interest are the conditional error probabilities in learning the sentences which are also shown in Fig. 8.6. Given that the first word of the sentence was recalled correctly, the probability of making an error in recalling the second word (*tall*) was .11; given the correct recall of *tall*, the probability of not recalling *boy* was .05, etc. The probability of a transition error was highest at the major grammatical subdivisions in both sentences, in agreement with the experimental hypothesis. A further finding was quite unexpected. Initially it was assumed that subjects would use a fairly stable encoding unit throughout, roughly equivalent to short phrases. However, considerable variation in the within-phrase transition errors was found, which suggests that there may be a within-phrase structure as well as a between-phrase structure. In fact, the transition errors were directly related to the linguistic level of the transitions in the phrase-structure tree. Thus to a considerable degree it is possible to predict the probability of a transition error from the phrase structure of a sentence.

The relatively high error probability for the first transition in sentence (a) shows that learning depends not only upon syntactic structure. There is no large syntactic break between *the* and *tall*, but the high error rate here is understandable if one considers the meaning of the sentence. The meaningful core of the sentence is clearly something like *Boy saves dying woman*. The word *tall* is not very closely related to the main theme of the sentence, and hence it is not remembered as well as it should be.

Johnson (1968) reported some follow-up studies which lend further support to his thesis that phrase-structure rules are an important help in memorizing sentences. In a study by Odom the experiment just reported was repeated with 17-year-old deaf subjects. These subjects could read and had a reasonable knowledge of words, but no grammar. Their utterances were an ungrammatical, unorganized "word salad." They learned ungrammatical sentences as well as grammatical sentences, and there was no correlation between transition error probabilities and the phrase structure of the sentences. In a second study Mathews observed how children between the ages of 6 and 9 learned sentences, and the kinds of errors which they made. He found that as the children became older, the more closely the pattern of transition errors resembled that of adult subjects. However, even 6-year-olds made most errors at transitions which crossed syntactic boundaries. Since by age 6 a child has learned almost all the grammatical rules of his language (although he does not use them as well as an adult), this result is exactly what should be expected.

Johnson's explanation of his findings rests on a model for the production of phrase-structure trees which has been proposed by Yngve (1960). Yngve's model contains a context-free grammar plus the assumptions that derivations are produced from the top down and from left to right. Rules are applied in such a way that always the leftmost nonterminal symbol in the last line of the already constructed derivation will be expanded. All symbols to the right of it are postponed and must be kept in memory until the time comes to develop them. Postponed symbols therefore constitute a load on memory, and given the finite capacity of short-term memory, this mechanism will severely limit the kind of grammatical constructions which can be achieved. Thus, in example (a) of Fig. 8.6, the rule $S \rightarrow NP$ plus VP would be applied first; NP would then be expanded into $D + MN$, while VP

is stored in memory; next *the* would be substituted for *D*, while *MN* is stored; once *the* is available, the process moves over to the next symbol, which is *MN* and expands that into *M* plus *N*, substitutes *tall* for *M* and *boy* for *N*, and then takes up the verb phrase. Johnson assumes that the probability of an error in recall is a function of the size of the unit which the subject starts to process. For instance, the next unit after *tall* has size one (*boy*), but after *boy* the next unit has size 4 (*saved the dying woman*). Therefore, the transition after *boy* should be much more difícult than the transition after *tall*, which is of course exactly what Johnson had observed. The assumption that transition error probability increases as a function of the size of the next syntactic unit is motivated by the observation that subjects tend to recall units as wholes or not at all.

An artificial language learning experiment also reported by Johnson (1968) supports the explanation of the phrase-structure effects in terms of Yngve's model. Johnson first showed that if one presents random sequences of letters which are spatially grouped, such as *SB JFX LZ*, subjects will group the letters into corresponding units of memory. That is, the transition error probabilities in the sequence just mentioned are highest in going from *B* to *J* and *X* to *L*, while if the sequence is printed as *SBJ FXLZ* transition errors are highest for the transition between *J* and *F*. If a sequence is not grouped at all, subjects will make their own ideosyncratic units in memorizing it. This is by no means a new finding, of course (Müller and Schumann, 1894), but it provides an easy means of studying the effects of variations in the size of subunits. Consider the following strings:

(*i*)	*NBJ*	*FQZ*	*LT*
(*ii*)	*NBJ*	*FQZLT*	
(*iii*)	*NBJ*	*FQZL*	
(*iv*)	*NBJ*	*FQZ*	
(*v*)	*NBJ*	*FQ*	
(*vi*)	*NBJ*		

Each type of string was given to a separate group of subjects as responses in a paired-associate experiment. The first result of interest concerns the probability that subjects correctly recall *B*, given that they have recalled *N*. According to Johnson's hypothesis, this should be most difficult for the first type of string, and it should be easiest for the last string. For strings (ii) − (v) the *N-B* transition error should be equal and at an intermediate level, because the size of the second subunit is irrelevant for a transition within the first subunit. The obtained transition errors were .20 for string (i) .09, .12, .09, and .13 for strings (ii) − (v), respectively, and .003 for string (vi).

This is a rather striking confirmation of the prediction that the size of a "chunk" is unimportant for short-term memory. On the other hand, the probability of correctly recalling the first letter of the second chunk (the *F*), given correct recall of the last letter of the first chunk (*J*), decreased as a function of the size of the second chunk.

There is another obvious prediction which follows from Yngve's system: the more symbols that are being postponed for processing in the construction of a sentence, the heavier the load on memory, and the harder it should be to memorize the sentence. The left-to-right processing assumption which Yngve makes implies that left-branching and embedded constructions should be difficult, because many symbols are being postponed in such constructions, while right-branching sentences should impose no stress on memory. Linguistic intuition in this matter is not entirely clear, as some examples taken from Miller and Chomsky (1963) show. People obviously have no trouble understanding a right-branching sentence such as *He watched the boy catch the ball that dropped from the tower near the lake*, even if we would add a little more after *lake*. But rather long left-branching sentences are not hard to understand either: *All of the men whom I told you about who were exposed to radiation who worked half time are still healthy*. Embedded constructions are clearly more difficult: *That the fact that he left was unfortunate is obvious*. One can improve intelligibility if this doubly embedded sentence is transformed to a right-branching form: *It is obvious that it was unfortunate that he left*. Miller (1962b) and Miller and Isard (1964) have experimentally compared the learning of right-recursive and self-embedded sentences. Their subjects found it much easier to learn a sentence with right-recursive structure than the self-embedded version of the same sentence. In the first experiment, judging from their intonation, some subjects seemed to treat the embedded sentences like a list of unrelated phrases, switching after two or three trials to a normal sentence intonation. In the more recent experiment, 22-word sentences with from one to four degrees of self-embedding were used and contrasted with equally long strings of words in random order. The number of errors was found to increase with the degree of self-embedding: subjects could handle one degree (some even two degrees) of self-embedding with about the same ease as right-recursive sentences. However, sentences with three to four degrees of self-embedding were much more difficult to learn, though they were still easier than the random strings of words. The point of difficulty with the heavily self-embedded sentences appeared to coincide with the long string of seemingly unrelated verbs towards the end. When dealing with a nested construction (or grammatical onion, as Miller graphically terms it) the subject must hold in memory the still unresolved portion of one or more constituents while he is processing the others. The human capacity to do this is extremely limited due to the fact that short-term memory has only a small, fixed capacity. Unlimited self-embedding may be perfectly acceptable from the grammatical standpoint, but psychological processes impose a severe restriction on its use.

The difficulty which people have with embedded constructions is, of course, in agreement with Yngve's hypothesis, but it does not prove it since many other assumptions about the way sentences are processed would predict this effect. More decisive support for Yngve would be a demonstration that similar difficulties occur with left-branching sentences. However, the example just given does not indicate that left-branching structures are particularly hard to understand. Relevant experiments on retention have not yet been reported. It has been shown, however, that recall is affected by the memory load defined as the average number of symbols postponed in the generation of a sentence according to Yngve's model (Martin and Roberts, 1966). Martin and Roberts gave subjects sentences for recall which differed in sentence depth, i.e., in the number of grammatical promises that must be kept track of in constructing the sentence. Two levels of sentence depth were used, and sentences of several syntactic types were studied (simple active declarative sentences, two types of passive, negative, and passive-negative). Out of 6 sentences with a low depth measure, subjects recalled on the average 3.9 sentences correctly; recall was 3.1 sentences when sentence depth measures were high. Interestingly, there were no recall differences between sentences of different syntactic types. We shall return to this finding later. Martin and Roberts also asked subjects to judge the sentences for ease of recall. Again, sentence kind was irrelevant, and sentences of lesser mean depth were judged easier to remember than sentences of a greater mean depth. The Yngve model is clearly supported by these results.

Although the few relevant psychological studies are in general agreement with Yngve's hypothesis, its status is still undecided. Miller and Chomsky (1963) point out that not all natural languages exhibit a left-to-right asymmetry. Yngve's hypothesis works quite well for English, which does show a predominance of right-branching structures. However, there are languages—Turkish and Japanese—where left-branching predominates, and there are examples of right-branching, left-branching and self-embedded constructions in every known language. At this point our information about and understanding of these structures is very incomplete, but Yngve's hypothesis in its application to all languages does not hold up.

Miller and Chomsky also raise theoretical objections to Yngve's language model on the grounds that it is a model which functions only for the ease of the speaker but not for the hearer. In fact, Yngve's model is unreasonable as a description of what the hearer does. We shall illustrate this contention with an example taken from Rohrmann (1968). Suppose a subject listens to the sentence *The new club member came early*. According to the model the hearer expects, and must keep track of, two things when he hears *the*: a continuation of the noun phrase as well as a verb phrase; thus *the* is assigned a depth measure of 2. For the same reason *new* and *club* are also assigned a depth of 2. After *member* only a verb phrase is expected, so that the measure is 1. *Came* is also assigned a measure of 1, because sentence intonation tells the hearer that something more is to come. Pitch and stress of *early* indicate that this word is the terminal word of the sentence, and hence it receives a measure of 0. The problem with this account is that it is by no means clear why the hearer should "expect" all of this: why should *club* be assigned a measure of 2—after all, the sentence might have been *The new club burned down*, in which case *club* would receive a measure of 1! Or why should the hearer expect two things after hearing *new*—how does he know that the sentence is not *The gnu died?* The point of all this is simply that it is not clear how the hearer can "expect" any particular continuation of the sentence, rather than another one, given the almost limitless possibilities of language. For such reasons Miller and Chomsky prefer to explain the difficulty with self-embedding as resulting solely from the fact that both speaker and hearer have finite memories.

However, even if there is reason to doubt that people process phrase-structure rules in the manner hypothesized by Yngve, there seem to be no questions concerning the psychological reality of those rules. All the experiments so far discussed have shown that the syntactic breaks indicated by phrase-structure rules determine the way and the ease with which sentences are grouped and organized in memory. The same is true for the perception of sentences: syntactic phrases form perceptual units.

In studies by Ladefoged and Broadbent (1960) and Fodor and Bever (1965), subjects listened to sentences with superimposed auditory clicks. They were then asked to indicate where the clicks occurred in each sentence. The prediction was that subjects would tend to hear the noise not where it actually occurred but in such a way that it would not interrupt a perceptual unit, hence between the boundaries marking off these units. The magnitude of errors in displacing the clicks could then be used as a measure of the size of the perceptual unit. The results of both experiments indicated that subjects were processing more than one word at a time. In addition, Fodor and Bever found that significantly more click displacement occurred at major syntactic boundaries than within segments, thus providing evidence for the hypothesis that the perceptual units correspond to the segments marked off by formal phrase-structure analysis. In a follow-up experiment, Garrett, Bever and Fodor (1966) showed that this effect did not depend upon acoustic correlates of the phrase structure of a sentence. For instance, consider the following sentences in which the common part can be made acoustically identical by using the same tape recording in both cases:

> (a) (*In her* hope of marrying) (Anna was surely impractical)
> (b) (*Your* hope of marrying Anna) (was surely impractical).

By placing the same acoustical material into a different linguistic context the major syntactic break can be made to occur either before or after *Anna*. Clicks which coincided with *Anna* appeared to subjects displaced either before or after *Anna*, depending upon the location of the syntactic break. Since the two passages were acoustically identical, this displacement cannot depend wholly upon the intonation and stress pattern of the sentence, but implies that in some sense the subject reconstitutes the phrase structure of a sentence to which he is listening.

Deep Structure and Transformational Rules

Not all grammatical rules are phrase-structures rules. Chomsky (1957, 1965) has argued forcefully that an efficient grammar must include transformational rules in addition to phrase-structure rules. Although not all linguists concede that transformational rules are necessary, or even desirable, the idea of grammatical transformations has been influential among psychologists interested in the effects of grammatical structure upon learning and perception. Therefore, we shall briefly explain the concept of a grammatical transformation and discuss some of the experiments concerned with the psychological reality of transformational rules.

Consider the following two sentences:

1. *They are feeding pigeons.*
2. *They are traveling salesmen.*

One needs no linguistic training to draw a phrase-structure tree for these two sentences and to see that the sentences differ in their phrase structure. In particular, it is obvious that *are feeding* is a unit in the first sentence, but *are traveling* is not in the second one. Instead, *traveling salesmen* belongs together in the second sentence. The phrase structure reflects these differences between sentences (1) and (2). These sentences differ in surface structure. Not all sentences which are obviously different syntactically differ in surface structure. Take, for instance, the following pair of sentences:

3. *They are wonderful to see.*
4. *They are eager to come.*

These two sentences have identical phrase-structure trees. Nevertheless, they are not alike. One can paraphrase (3) as *It is wonderful to see them*, but one cannot turn (4) into *It is eager to come them*. *They* in (3) is the object of the sentence; in (4) *they* is the subject. This important difference is not reflected in the phrase structures of (3) and (1). The sentences are identical in surface structure, but they differ in deep structure. The distinction between surface structure and deep structure is crucial in Chomsky's transformational grammar. Chomsky uses phrase-structure rules to arrive at the deep structure of a sentence; then he introduces transformational rules which operate on the deep structure of the sentence and produce its surface structure. Several surface structures may be related by different transformations to the same deep structure. For instance, another transformation which retains the meaning of (3) would be *To see them is wonderful.*

Formally, transformational rules differ from rewriting rules in that they take as input a whole phrase-structure tree, while rewriting rules always apply only to the last line of a derivation. In the expansion of a phrase-structure tree the rule which can be applied at any point depends only upon the symbol just under consideration. It is not important by what path this symbol has been obtained. Transformational rules, on the other hand, apply to whole phrase-structure trees. With such rules one can permute a string of symbols, an operation which is impossible with rewriting rules alone. In this way transformational rules express relationships among sentences which cannot be adequately represented in their phrase-structure trees.

For the psychologist the interesting question is whether evidence exists or can be obtained that people use transformational rules. One cannot argue that the linguistic facts alone are sufficient to demonstrate that they do—even if linguists were unanimous as to what these are. It is certainly conceivable that people achieve the same results for which linguists need transformational rules in a different way. As the discussion of artificial languages has shown, the mere fact that a certain rule applies does not guarantee that people will actually learn and use it, rather than a perhaps less elegant alternative.

That deep structure has an effect upon the recognition of sentences under noise has been demonstrated by Mehler and Carey (1966). Mehler and Carey worked with sentences of the same type as (3) and (4) which are alike in surface structure but differ in deep structure. By presenting several sentences of either type (3) or type (4) in succession they developed a set in their subjects to expect a sentence of a particular deep structure. Sentences conforming to that structure were recognized more easily than sentences with a different deep structure. This effect was even stronger when sentences differing in both deep and surface structure were used. The recognition errors which occurred tended to be compatible with the expected syntax of the sentence, rather than with its phonetic characteristics.

Several experiments have demonstrated that the transformational complexity of a sentence determines the ease with which the sentence can be recalled. It is a common experience that people are often able to give the general sense of a verbal remark or message without being able to repeat the exact words. This would seem to indicate that the syntactic and semantic components of a sentence are learned relatively independently. Mehler (1963) devised an experiment to explore how semantic and syntactic features of sentences are learned. He read to his subjects lists of 8 sentences which differed in transformational complexity. Seven sentence types were represented in addition to simple, active, declarative sentences, negative, passive, question, passive-negative, negative-question, passive-question and passive-negative-question. The sentences were presented for five trials with the order scrambled each time. After each trial, the subject attempted to write down the sentences. The results were scored in terms of types of errors made and are shown in Fig. 8.7. By far the most errors were syntactic ones; the number of omissions, though initially large, decreased rapidly as learning progressed; other errors were few and fairly constant in number. This seems to reflect the fact that subjects remembered the content of the sentences but altered the form. The error scores for the various sentence types indicate that simple active sentences were remembered with much greater ease than other forms and more errors were made in the direction of simple active sentences than in the opposite direction. In other words, there was a strong tendency to simplify the syntactic structure. Mehler hypothesized that a sentence is encoded as a simple active sentence with a kind of mental tag or footnote about its syntactic structure. Rather than store

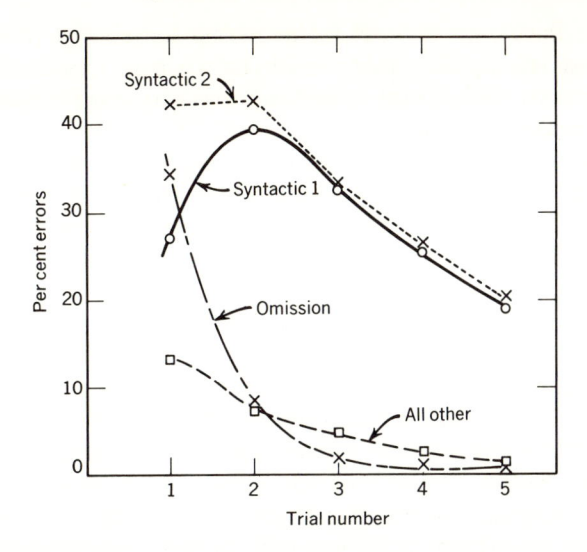

Fig. 8.7 *Errors in free recall of sentences. The curve labeled* Syntactic 1 *gives the proportion of all sentences that are syntactic errors.* Syntactic 2 *shows the same proportion of actual responses that are syntactic errors.* Omission *gives the proportion of all sentences that were completely omitted.* All other *gives the proportion of miscellaneous errors (e.g., inventions). (after Mehler, 1963)*

the sentence verbatim, the subject seems to analyze it syntactically and recode it in terms of its semantic content and syntactic form. This, then, would explain (at least in part) why the general meaning of an utterance is easier to recall than the exact wording.

Mehler's interpretation of his results has been questioned by Martin and Roberts (1966), who argued that the effects which had been attributed to transformational processes could be explained more plausibly in terms of a structural index such as Yngve's sentence depth. In effect, Martin and Roberts maintained that transformational complexity and structural complexity were confounded in Mehler's experiment. The experiment which Martin and Roberts performed has been discussed above in connection with Yngve's hypothesis. Martin found that recall depended upon the structural complexity of the sentences as measured by Yngve's depth measure, but was independent of sentence kind. In fact, simple active sentences and some passive sentences showed the lowest recall scores! The types of errors made were most frequently sentences of the same kind as the stimulus sentences but with a lesser mean depth. Martin and Roberts also reanalyzed Mehler's own data in terms of the sentence depth measure and found a strikingly close relationship between structural complexity and recall scores. Structural complexity was as good a predictor of Mehler's results as sentence kind.

In turn, the Martin and Roberts study has been severely criticized by Rohrmann (1968). It seems that in trying to vary sentence type and in controlling for structural complexity and sentence length Martin and Roberts were forced to insert adjectives and adverbials into some of their sentences, especially the simple active declarative sentences. Such insertions do not change appreciably the complexity of the surface structure of the sentence, but they have a tremendous effect upon their deep structure. Suppose one tries to make a four-word sentence out of the simple sentence *They are lions* by inserting a modifier: *They are growling lions*. The deep structure of this expanded sentence looks something like (*They are lions; lions growl*) — that is one must distinguish two underlying "ideas"! Several transformational rules which did not apply to the original sentence are necessary to arrive at the surface structure of the expanded sentence. Thus Martin and Roberts complicated the deep structure of their "simple" sentences, so that their failure to find relationships between recall and sentence type can hardly be accepted as conclusive evidence.

It is not at all clear how this controversy will be settled eventually. Nevertheless, there are several other studies which do show that syntactic information is remembered at least in part independently from the meaning of the sentence, somewhat like a footnote. Mehler and Miller (1964) studied retroactive interference as a function of semantically and syntactically similar interpolated learning material. Their subjects were first given a set of eight sentences of different syntactic types to learn, then an interpolated learning (IL) task, and finally a retest of the original eight sentences. Three kinds of interpolated tasks were used in order to determine whether differences in the amount of retroactive interference would reflect the existence of separate semantic and syntactic components. A syntactic IL task required subjects to change the syntactic form of the original sentences, but not the meaning; a semantic IL task required subjects to change the meaning of the sentence while retaining the same syntax; a digit-adding task was used as a control. One group of subjects was given two trials, the other group received four trials. The results showed greater retroactive interference for the syntactic aspects than for the semantic aspects of the sentences, which agrees with the hypothesis, except for the first two trials in both groups where the syntactic interference facilitated learning. The authors interpret this to mean that subjects first learn the content of a sentence and then the syntactic details. During the first two trials subjects are concentrating on the content and thus the syntactic IL task, which uses the same content though in different grammatical form, helps. However, during the last two trials subjects are concentrating on memorizing the syntactic form and hence the syntactic interference causes confusion.

What the preceding studies suggest is that syntactic form and meaning are remembered relatively independently of each other. Indeed, there is rather direct evidence for this in a recent study by Sachs (1967). Sachs read subjects a paragraph of normal English text. One of the sentences in the paragraph was selected as the test sentence. Subjects were given a recognition test after listening to the paragraph with either the sentence in its original form, a formally changed sentence, a syntactically changed sentence, or a semantically changed sentence. The subject was asked to tell whether the test sentence was the same as one in the original passage or not. For instance, suppose the original sentence was *He sent a letter about it to Galileo, the great Italian scientist*. A formal change of this sentence consisted merely in a permutation of the word order: *He sent Galileo, the great Italian scientist, a letter about it*. A syntactic change involved a passive transformation: *A letter about it was sent to Galileo, the great Italian scientist*. A semantic change touched upon the meaning of the sentence: *Galileo, the great Italian scientist, sent him a letter about it*. Sachs' results were quite clear: when the test sentence was embedded somewhere in the middle of the paragraph, subjects' memory for both syntactic changes and formal changes was minimal; at the same time, they were still very good at detecting changes in meaning. Her subjects obviously did not transfer to memory inessential information about the form of the sentences. Interestingly, if the test sentence was the last sentence in the paragraph all kinds of changes could be detected. Presumably subjects still retained the sentence in primary memory, which means that they still had available the sounds of the words and therefore sufficient information to detect any kind of changes.

Sachs' conclusion is that inessential information about the form of the sentences is not normally remembered. However, information about the sentence form is not always inessential. For example, there are subtle differences in the meaning of corresponding active and passive sentences. The passive serves to stress the logical object of the sentence, whereas the active stresses the subject. Very frequently the logical subject is in fact deleted from a passive sentence, as in *He was given a ticket*; it is not specified in this sentence who gave the ticket. Slobin (1968) has studied the recall of such passives and found that they are infrequently changed into active sentences probably because changes affect the semantic content of the sentences. Similarly, in studying the relationship between active declarative sentences and negations it is most important to be aware of the plausibility of the negation (Wason, 1965). Negations may be harder to understand if the sentences used are *Diamonds sparkle* and *Diamonds do not sparkle*, simply because the negation is not plausible; this relationship, however, may be reversed with another pair of sentences such as *Horses talk* and *Horses do not talk*, where the statement is made plausible only through the negation. Bregman and Strasberg (1968) have shown in an ingenious sentence recognition experiment that remembering the meaning of a sentence often implies something about its syntax. For instance, a subject may remember that a sentence was true (*The opal reflects the light*), or that it was something bad (*The boy abandoned the dog*—not a question, not a negation!*).

The semantic content of a sentence, rather than its syntactic form, is certainly primary in memory. However, psychologists have concentrated almost exclusively upon syntactic factors up to now. There is an excellent reason for this strategy, however much promise semantic investigations may hold: syntactic theory has been developed very well by linguists, so that psychologists have something to work with; as yet there has been no corresponding development in semantic theory. Therefore, we shall return to the question of how syntactic rules are handled in memory—keeping in mind the limitations of a purely syntactic approach.

Savin and Perchonok (1965) used an interesting device to study memory for syntactic information. Their study is based on the fact that short-term memory has only a very limited capacity. Thus, the authors proposed to measure the amount of memory storage taken up by a given sentence type by seeing how much material a subject could remember in addition to the sentences. If the syntactic features are encoded separately, then each should occupy a characteristic amount of space. The sentences used were in the form of simple active sentences and ten transformations: passive, negative, question, negative-question, emphatic (E) (e.g., "the boy DID hit the ball"), negative-passive, passive-question, passive-negative-question, emphatic-passive and wh-question (wh) (e.g., "who has hit the ball?"). The subject was given a sentence followed by a string of words and was then asked to recall the sentence verbatim and as many of the words as possible. It was predicted that sentences with more transformations would be more difficult to remember and, hence, fewer words would be recalled after them. The results showed this to be the case: significantly more words were retained after simple active sentences than after any of the other versions and likewise more words were recalled after single-step transformations than after the more complex ones (i.e., N > NP; P > NP, PQ, PQN, EP; Q > PQ; E > EP; also QN > PQN). No predictions were made about the relative difficulty of the individual single-step transformations. An additive relationship was found in the more complex transformations whose distance from the simple active sentence could be computed from additive combinations of the distance A-E, A-P, A-N, A-Q and A-QN. This, then, would seem to indicate that the various transformations do occupy a characteristic amount of space in the short-term memory dependent upon their relative complexity, which in turn agrees with the hypothesis that transformations are stored independently from the content of the sentence. The authors point out that the length of the sentence in number of words was not a factor since neither the Q transformation nor the E transformation lengthens the sentence; yet both increased the difficulty of remembering the sentence.

Savin and Perchonok may have developed a potentially useful technique for the study of memory processes, if other investigators are able to replicate their results. Garrett and Fodor (1968), in discussing the study, have mentioned an unsuccessful attempt at replication which involved only minor procedural changes. Further work is needed to explore this discrepancy.

To date, the most convincing evidence in favor of the hypothesis that the deep structure of a sentence is important in recall comes from two experiments by Blumenthal (Blumenthal, 1965; Blumenthal and Boakes, 1967). Blumenthal showed that the effectiveness of a prompt depends upon the function of the prompt specified by the deep structure of the sentence. He used sentences which were similar in surface structure, but differed in deep structure, as for instance this sentence pair:

1. *Gloves were made by tailors.*
2. *Gloves were made by hand.*

In the first sentence *tailor* is the logical subject and thus related to the whole phrase. In the second sentence *hand* is merely a part of an adverbial phrase and does not relate to the rest of the sentence as a whole, but acts as a verb modifier. Subjects were given ten sentences of each type to read. The experimenter then read a prompt word for each sentence and the subjects attempted to recall the corresponding sentence for each word. In the control group, the prompt was always the first noun of the sentence. In the experimental group, the prompt was always the second noun. There was no difference in the grammatical function of the first nouns in the sentences (initial nouns in both types of sentences always functioned as logical objects). However, there was a vital difference in the function of the second nouns, as described above. The results of the experiment are shown in Table 8.5. The difference in grammatical function was obviously very important in determining the effectiveness of a word as a memory prompt. Sentences of type (1) were recalled significantly better than sentences of type (2) when the final word was given as a prompt. When the first word was used as prompt there was no difference in recall between the two types of sentences. Blumenthal argued that it is not only the segmentation into units according to the surface structure of a sentence which determines its psychological organization, but that in addition the relations among words and phrases at the level of its deep structure must be considered.

There have been several attempts to measure the psychological distance between sentences of different types (e.g., Miller and McKean, 1964; Clifton and Odom, 1966). Since there exists considerable uncertainty about both the empirical results of these studies and their theoretical relevance, this work will not be reviewed here. Garrett and Fodor (1968) have recently discussed these studies and stressed the difficulty of their interpretation, which is partly caused by the unsettled state which the linguistic theory of transformation still is in.

The discussion of the psychological aspects of deep structure and transformational rules must necessarily remain open ended at this time. Too little work has yet been done. There are some interesting phenomena which must be accounted for—but in which way this ultimately will be done one can hardly tell. Even though adequate answers have not been found so far, learning theorists must not lose sight of

Table 8.5. *Mean number of sentences recalled out of ten possible (after Blumenthal, 1967).*

Prompt word	Sentence structure	
	Standard passive	Replaced-agent passive
Final noun	7.2	3.9
Initial noun	7.1	6.9

these problems, because they represent the most challenging test for their theories and their methods yet.

4. RULE LEARNING, LANGUAGE, AND LEARNING THEORY

In concluding this chapter it is appropriate to comment on the role which learning theory plays in the investigation of complex phenomena such as language. Some psychologists and many linguists feel that learning theory has been irrelevant to the study of complex psychological processes and that it must remain irrelevant by its very nature. They believe that animal learning experiments, or for that matter experiments with humans on binary prediction, paired-associate learning, or even discrimination and concept learning are so far removed in complexity from language learning that the results obtained from such experiments as well as the methods used simply have no bearing on the "higher mental processes." A second argument is directed against the behavioristic language which learning theorists frequently employ. The basic terms of S-R theory, reinforcement, stimulus and response, have clear referents in the simple animal learning experiments where these terms were originally used. Their identification is already less clear in some of the verbal learning experiments discussed in this book. With more complex problems, such as those described in Chapter 5, or in the present chapter, the relevance of S-R theory is indeed not always apparent. Instead of using the language of conditioning theory, it is argued, a cognitive language, one which deals directly with the subject's information processing, must be used.

It is certainly true that the large bulk of the work on learning has been concerned with exceedingly simple situations. To the outsider—the linguist, the educator, the computer scientist, and even to some of our fellow psychologists—the experiments done in the learning laboratories may appear too simple, or even trivial. One may concur with this criticism in part. Learning theorists should devote more of their energy to more complex issues and problems of greater general interest and of potential usefulness to society. However, the gap between the problems studied by psychologists interested in learning, especially verbal learning, and the "higher mental processes" is not as wide and unbridgeable as it is sometimes made to appear. The reader who has studied the material presented in this book will surely be in a position to form his own opinion on this point. At issue is not the fact that learning experiments have been overly simple in the past, but whether the methods and concepts developed by learning theorists can be applied to complex information processing problems *in principle*. Learning experiments have been simple because it was (and is) the conviction of many investigators that complex problems are best studied initially by abstracting from them simple, manageable subproblems, following the lead of the physical sciences. Once one knows how a list of paired-associates is learned in the laboratory, this should help us understand how a child learns in the classroom, or how a language is learned. Whether this belief will be justified, only history can tell, but it is hardly an outrageous proposition. Thus, one may admit that learning experiments often are greatly oversimplified, but one must take issue with the argument that the concepts which are adequate for simple verbal learning experiments are irrelevant to problems of greater complexity.

It is not important in which language a theory is expressed. This point was first made in Chapter 2 in connection with the one-element model of stimulus sampling theory and the hypothesis-testing model. Since then, the same problem turned up in many variations. It is not the S-R terminology nor the cognitive vocabulary which determines the character of a theory, but its formal structure. One of the principal virtues of mathematical models lies in the fact that models force the theorists to specify their formal structure explicitly, thus making especially obvious the conventional character of the theorist's language. Alternative interpretations for simple Markov models have so often been discussed here that the reader surely can provide his own examples by now. There is, however, a different example which is worth mentioning specifically. This concerns the decision mechanisms which have been shown to be an important factor in determining performance in several different learning tasks. Most of the time an information processing language has been used to describe decision processes. But this does not mean that S-R theory is incapable of describing such processes. The scanning model of Estes (1962) which was discussed in Chapter 3 provides a good example of how decision processes can be handled within the framework of stimulus-sampling theory. Which terminology is used is a matter of convention and convenience. A language is not inherently primitive because it uses terms like stimulus and response, and it is not inherently superior because it talks about cognitive processes. Of course, the same argument can be turned around: cognitive theories are not *eo ipso* mentalistic, mystic, or unscientific.

Many critics of learning theory might agree with these arguments, but maintain that the examples just given concerned relatively simple learning processes. The deficiency of *S-R* theory might not be apparent in such simple situations. Only when one looks at really complex problems can the greater power of an information processing or cognitive language be detected. For instance, Miller, Galanter and Pribram (1960) in a stimulating and influential book have argued that the basic units of behavior are not S-R connections, but must be represented as TOTE units: a TOTE unit is a sequence which consists of a *test*, an *operation*, a *test* again, and eventually an *exit*. These units permit one to describe the hierarchical structure, the branchings and loops which are characteristic of behavior sequences in man. By rearranging TOTE units *plans* are formed which govern behavior. Thus, the psychologist's task is to describe plans, and to analyze plans into their units, rather than to investigate stimulus-response contingencies.

Figure 8.8 gives an example of a plan for hammering nails, which consists of two TOTE units, both under the control of *Test Nail*. The two subunits are *Test Hammer—Lift* and *Test Hammer—Strike*. Although the example is simple enough, it illustrates some of the interesting features of plans. A behavior sequence of tests and actions is shown to have an underlying hierarchical structure with subunits which may be arranged in loops (the hammering operations will be performed repeatedly, until the outcome of *Test Nail* is satisfactory).

Plans and TOTE units are certainly a convenient means of describing behavior. However, precisely the same can be achieved by using S-R language, as has been pointed out by Millenson (1967) and Suppes (1969). We shall take up Suppes' more formal argument later and consider first Millenson's translation of the "plan for hammering" into the terminology of operant conditioning. His basic point is that responses and operations are equivalent terms, and that tests correspond to discriminations. The plan of Fig. 8.8 can be translated into S-R language without in any sense improving or modifying basic S-R notions. Figure 8.9 is drawn after Millenson. The bracket

$$\begin{bmatrix} S_i \\ R_j \end{bmatrix} \rightarrow$$

may be read as "in stimulus situation S_i response R_j is performed which leads to succeeding situation and stimulus-response contingency . . ." With this interpretation, Figure 8.9 should be self-explanatory. There may be different ways to draw this figure, which would make the hierarchical character of the contingencies more obvious, but an S-R organism acting according to Fig. 8.9 will clearly achieve the same ends as an information-processing device with the plan shown in Fig. 8.8.

The formal proof that every TOTE hierarchy can be represented

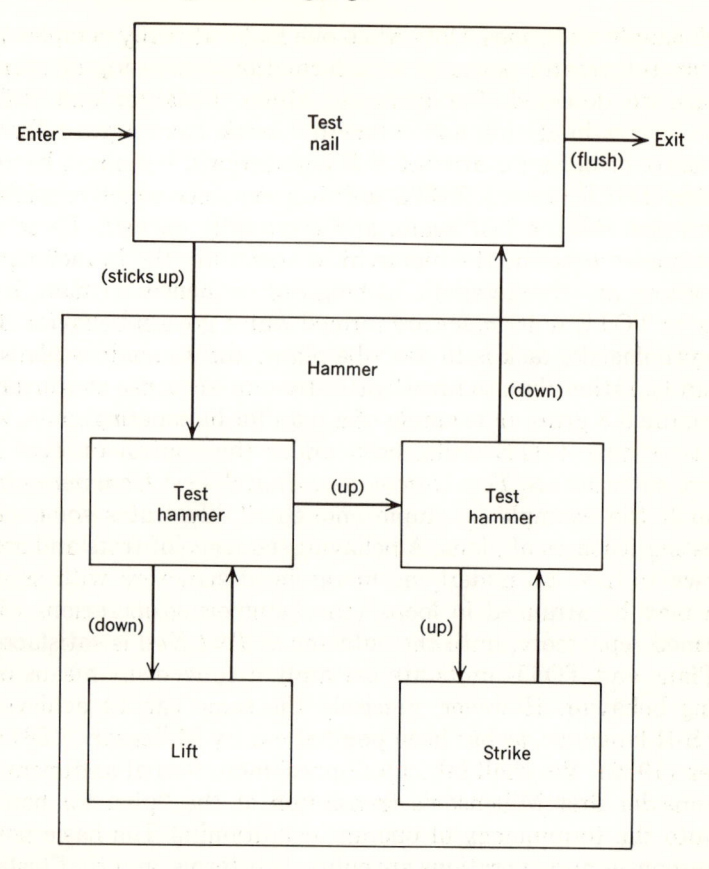

Fig. 8.8 *A hierarchial plan for hammering nails. (after Miller, Galanter, and Pribram, 1960)*

within stimulus-sampling theory is due to Suppes (1969) and goes something like this. Suppes first uses a result by Miller and Chomsky (1963) that a TOTE unit can be defined as an oriented graph and as such is equivalent to a finite automaton. A finite automaton is a device

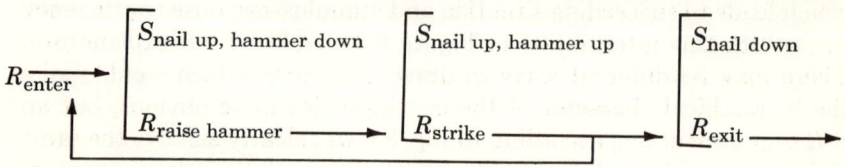

Fig. 8.9 S-R *representation of the TOTE-hierarchy for hammering nails (after Millenson, 1967).*

which generates an output characterized by what was called earlier a linear one-sided grammar. Each finite automaton uniquely specifies such a grammar, and for each grammar there is exactly one corresponding automaton. Suppes has proven a representation theorem for finite automata which says that for every finite automaton there is a stimulus-response model that asymptotically becomes isomorphic to it. The proof will not be given here, since many readers may lack the necessary background in automata theory. Suffice it to say that the isomorphism is established by identifying the internal states of the automaton with the responses of the organism; the letters of the input alphabet correspond naturally to stimulus elements; and each state of conditioning specifies a different automaton. For details and examples the reader is referred to the original source (Suppes, 1969).

Although it is possible to specify complex cognitive processes in terms of stimuli and responses, it would not always be wise to do so. Some illuminating analogies to this problem have been discussed by Crothers and Suppes (1967) and Suppes (1969). We shall repeat two of their examples. It has recently been shown that all of mathematics can be reduced to the concept of set and set membership. Procedures to perform this reduction exist even for the most complex problems of mathematics. However, in actually working on complex problems the mathematician uses concepts which are more appropriate for the level at which he is working. Reduction of his language to statements about sets, although possible, will be of no use to him in thinking about his problems. Computer languages provide an even more compelling example. The computer performs extremely complex operations with a basic language consisting of finite sequences of 0's and 1's. For the programmer it would be very inconvenient if he had to express all his commands in actual machine language. Instead he uses a more complex language such as FORTRAN or IPL, depending upon his problem. However, these languages are for the benefit of the user, not of the computer. Before the computer can understand FORTRAN it must translate it into basic machine language. Similarly with human behavior, the basic units may indeed be stimulus-response contingencies, but it would be impractical and even undesirable to insist upon an analysis of complex behavior into these units.

We have up to now avoided the topic of learning theory and language, which we started out with. This topic is clearly at the heart of all these discussions, but we have intentionally first taken up the problem in general terms. The preceding remarks should help to state the problem more precisely than is often done.

The most forceful attack on S-R theory in recent years is Chomsky's famous review of Skinner's book on verbal behavior (Skinner, 1957; Chomsky, 1959). Since the position taken in the present book on language and verbal behavior is greatly different from that of Skinner, no detailed account of either Skinner's book or Chomsky's review will be given here. Chomsky's arguments have since been repeated and elaborated by several authors (e.g., Miller, Galanter and Pribram, 1960; most recently by Garrett and Fodor, 1968, and Bever, 1968, where references may be found to other publications taking sides in this controversy). Two principal arguments are being used to show the irrelevance of S-R theory to learning. First, it is argued that *S-R* theory cannot possibly account for the complex structure of language, and secondly, even if it could, it would be impossible to learn a language in the manner S-R theory conceives of learning.

We first turn to the contention that the rules of language are too complex for the capabilities of learning theory. There has been an inordinate amount of confusion about this argument which we shall try to avoid by relying heavily upon the results established earlier, in particular the classification of rule types described in Section 2. Suppose that an adequate grammar of natural language must be a transformational grammar of the type Chomsky (1957, 1965) advocates. Such a grammar contains a system of context-free rewriting rules, plus transformational rules which operate on the deep structure of sentences. *S-R* theory (for concreteness sake one may take the stimulus sampling theory of Estes (1951; Neimark and Estes 1967) as a prototype) is indeed unable to deal with such structures. However, Chomsky's grammar is a theory of competence, not a theory of performance, and a theory of performance might look quite different from a theory of competence. This is the context in which the question of the psychological reality of grammatical transformations becomes important. We have reviewed this literature in Section 3 without coming to a conclusive answer. Certainly, the evidence available at this time in favor of transformational rules is not strong enough to support any major theoretical decision. The next question then concerns the rules which are necessary to derive the phrase-structure trees of sentences. These are, in general, context-free rewriting rules. We know from Suppes' (1969) theorem that *S-R* theories are isomorphic to finite-state grammars, but, without at least some modifications, they are apparently too weak for a context-free grammar. However, context-free rather than finite-state rules are needed primarily to allow for self-embedded constructions of arbitrary length. In actual language there are no infinite sentences, and, in fact, as we have seen, people have great difficulty with self-embedded sentences with more than two or three degrees of embedding. We have also shown (Section 2) that a few degrees of self-embedding can be handled by a finite-state grammar—not in a very elegant way, but it can be done. This is not to argue that people cannot learn context-free rules. We only want to reiterate the point made before that if people are given a rule with certain formal characteristics, they may learn these characteristics, or they may learn some other rule which, for the finite sample of items to which they have been exposed, produces the same results in a different way.

In conclusion, it is not clear whether a theory of performance will need rules that are stronger than finite-state rules, though a theory of competence certainly does. A finite-state rule, however, is equivalent to an *S-R* model at asymmptote (Suppes, 1969). Secondly, we cannot be sure at this time that it is impossible to extend S-R theory in a natural way so as to account for context-free grammars.

Arguments intended to show the inherent inadequacy of S-R theory for dealing with language have usually dealt with an impoverished version of *S-R* theory. The assumption has often been made that an *S-R* theory corresponds to a rewriting system which employs no intermediate vocabulary. In a behavioristic theory, it has been maintained, all terms must be directly observable, so that the only rules which are permitted are associational rules defined in terms of the terminal vocabulary of the theory. Lashley (1951) has shown that if this stipulation is made, a theory cannot possibly account for the orderliness of complex sequences of behavior and their hierarchical structure. The problem of the organization of language is a special case of the more general problem of the structure of behavior sequences, as Lashley has correctly perceived. Lashley's argument has been restated in a recent paper by Bever, Fodor, and Garrett (1968) on the formal limitations of associationism. However, it is important to note that these severe limitations exist only if the unreasonable restriction mentioned above is imposed upon S-R theory. In fact, behavior theory has freely used constructs which are not directly defined in terms of environmental events or responses. There was occasion a short while ago to refer to the scanning model of Estes (1962), and this model may serve as a good example in the present context as well. Hullian concepts such as habit strength, reaction potential, or reactive inhibition provide other obvious counterexamples. Suppes' representation theorem shows that actual *S-R* theories are much more powerful formally than the emaciated versions of conditioning theory against which Lashley, *et al.*, have directed their criticism.

A further argument against *S-R* theories of learning maintains that even if all the necessary grammatical constructions could be produced through simple conditioning, it would be impossible to learn the language in that way. Miller, Galanter and Pribram (1960) made some interesting calculations in this respect. Again, they assumed—incorrectly, as has been shown above—that only rules permitted by an *S-R* theory are transition rules from one word to the next. On this basis, they argue that in order to learn a sentence and be able to produce it a child must have heard the sentence at least once. Supposing that a child should be able to talk in 20-word sentences, at least, they calculate that the child must listen to something like 10^{30} 20-word sentences before it could be said to have mastered the English language. This, of course, is utterly impossible because a childhood, or even a whole life, is much too short to hear that many sentences even once. They point out the ridiculousness of this suggestion by noting that a century only has about 3.5×10^9 seconds!

Obviously, the argument of Miller, *et al.*, depends upon an incorrect conception of *S-R* mechanisms. A model which learns sentences by means of word-to-word transitions is indeed ridiculous; however, the argument is irrelevant to an S-R theory which can describe behavior of the same complexity as a linear grammar!

It is important to reject these arguments against learning theory explicitly, even though they are directed not against the kind of theory discussed here, but against a very much more primitive version of conditioning theory. However, these attacks on a strawman have produced the impression among some psychologists of having devastated the claim of learning theorists that their work is relevant to anything but the most simple laboratory experiments. But even if the counter-argument presented here is accepted, the problem of language learning remains largely unsolved. Learning theorists have very little to say about this topic, as is obvious from a perusal of the present chapter; but one cannot maintain that learning theory is in principle irrelevant to problems concerned with the acquisition and use of language.

The main problem we are now faced with is to improve our understanding of the relationship between the linguistic theory of competence and psychological theories of performance. There are several insightful discussions of this problem. For example, Miller and Chomsky (1963) and Crothers and Suppes (1967) have taken different sides on this issue. Miller and Chomsky believe that concepts such as deep structure and transformational rules have a place in both linguistic and psycholinguistic theory; Crothers and Suppes maintain that many of the devices employed in linguistic theory have no psychological reality. They argue by analogy with the theory of games and actual game playing: in a game like bridge, or chess, there exist optimal mixed strategies for each player (von Neumann and Morgenstern, 1944); however, the existence of optimal strategies is completely irrelevant to the person learning to play the game. Even the largest computer could not calculate analytically such strategies, simply because of the magnitude of the problem. Obviously, people learn to play these games in a completely different manner—which is a worthy subject for psychological investigation and quite independent of the results of game theory. The psychological theory of language is similarly independent from the linguistic theory of competence, because it must consider primarily the limitations of human memory and information processing capacities and the kind of strategies people use in discrimination learning and concept learning—problems which the linguistic theory of language competence does not have to worry about.

Most of the problems concerning learning processes in complex human behavior are still unsolved. However, there is no reason to be overly pessimistic as far as the future extension of learning theory to such processes is concerned. Such extension is in principle possible, and one may expect to see more and more work in this direction in the near future. This extension will not be in the form of a straightforward extrapolation of the results obtained in simple learning situations, as has sometimes been attempted. Language learning is not simply instrumental conditioning, or paired-associate learning, or anything like that. However, the results obtained in such laboratory situations will be relevant to the study of complex processes in that they provide the basic conceptual and methodological framework in terms of which higher level concepts can be defined. Thus, what we envisage is a solid base of psychological research, formed by the laboratory experiments which have been the main topic of this book, upon which the future investigation of language and problem solving can be built.

SUMMARY

If one is concerned with reasonably complex learning tasks, such as the rule learning problems treated in this chapter, the structure of the learning task becomes very important for understanding the subject's behavior. What and how the subject learns is largely determined by what there is to be learned. Subjects bring certain capacities to rule learning tasks, such as the ability to form associations, to hold items in immediate memory, or to code stimulus attributes. How these elementary learning operations are employed depends upon the structure of the rule learning task. Thus, rule learning may be regarded as a higher level process in which the elementary operations discussed earlier interact in new ways. The appropriate language to talk about rule learning is a higher order language which is suited to the characteristics of the particular task. We have described three types of rule learning problems, each requiring its own "language."

The first involved a fairly straightforward extension of the material on simple concept identification discussed in Chapter 7. Instead of concepts defined in terms of a single stimulus attribute, classifications in terms of the relationship of two (or conceivably more) attributes are considered. The "language" to describe such classifications employs as its basic terms logical relationships such as conjunction, disjunction, implication, and so on. These relationships are defined in terms of the values of the relevant stimulus attributes. Once the rule structure is characterized in this way the salient features of rule learning follow: in order to learn the problem subjects must code the stimulus items in terms of the categories which are obtained by combining the relevant stimulus attributes and then learn to associate these categories with the appropriate response classes.

The second type of rules which were considered are the rules which specify the operations involved in a letter-series completion test. In order to describe the structure of such problems an information processing language was used which employs such basic terms as *cycle, next, same,* and *alphabet.* A theory of rule learning which assumed that subjects operate with the same basic terms in letter-completion tests can explain performance on such tasks.

The rules which are used in forming grammatical sentences in natural language are called rewriting rules. Rewriting rules take as input an expression which is well-formed in the language under consideration and rewrite it in another permissible form. Depending upon the restrictions which are placed upon this rewriting process various types of rewriting rules are distinguished. We have briefly considered the difficult problem of how subjects induce rewriting rules from a finite set of exemplars in artificial language experiments. The problem of how the rules of natural language are acquired was not considered. Instead a number of psycholinguistic experiments were described which are concerned with the use of these rules in understanding and remembering sentences by normal speakers of the language. Reasonably clear evidence was presented that the phrase-structure of a sentence is an important factor in determining the perception and recall of it. Finally, the psychological reality of the concept of deep structure was discussed. Deep structure is something like the core meaning of a sentence including the basic grammatical relationships among the terms. Some suggestive evidence for the usefulness of the term was presented.

REFERENCES

Aaronson, D. (1967), Temporal factors in perception and short-term memory, *Psychological Bulletin*, *67*, 130–144.

Aborn, M. and Rubenstein, H. (1952), Information theory and immediate recall, *Journal of Experimental Psychology*, *44*, 260–266.

Ach, N. (1910), *Über den Willensakt und das Temperament*, Quelle und Meyer, Leipzig.

Adams, J. A. and Dijkstra, S. (1966), Short-term memory for motor responses, *Journal of Experimental Psychology*, *71*, 314–318.

Adelson, M., Muckler, F. A. and Williams, A. C., Jr. (1955), Verbal learning and message variables related to amount of information. In H. Quastler (Ed.) *Information theory in psychology*, Free Press of Glencoe. New York, pp. 291–303.

Anderson, N. H. (1960), Effect of first-order conditional probability in a two-choice learning situation. *Journal of Experimental Psychology*, *59*, 73–93.

Anderson, N. H. (1964), An evaluation of stimulus-sampling theory. In A. W. Melton, (Ed.) *Categories of human learning*, Academic Press, New York, pp. 129–144.

Anisfeld, M. and Knapp, M. (1968), Association, synonymity, and directionality in false recognition, *Journal of Experimental Psychology*, *77*, 171–179.

Arbib, M. A. (1964), *Brains, machines, and mathematics*, McGraw Hill, New York: 1964.

Archer, E. J. (1960), A re-evaluation of the meaningfulness of all possible CVC trigrams, *Psychological Monographs*, *74*, Whole No. 497.

Atkinson, R. C. (1962), Choice behavior and monetary payoff: strong and weak conditioning. In J. H. Criswell, H. Solomon and P. Suppes (Eds.) *Mathematical Methods in Small Group Processes*, Stanford University Press, Stanford.

Atkinson, R. C., Bower, G. H., and Crothers, E. J. (1965), *An Introduction to Mathematical Learning Theory*, Wiley, New York, pp. 23–34.

Atkinson, R. C. and Crothers, E. J. (1964), A comparison of paired-associate learning models having different acquisition and retention axioms, *Journal of Mathematical Psychology*, *1*, 285–315.

Atkinson, R. C. and Estes, W. K. (1963), Stimulus sampling theory. In R. D. Luce, R. R. Bush and E. Galanter (Eds.) *Handbook of Mathematical Psychology*, Vol. 2, Wiley, New York; pp. 121–268.

Atkinson, R. C. and Shiffrin, R. M. (1968), Human memory: a proposed system and its control processes. In K. W. Spence and J. T. Spence (Eds.), *The Psychology of Learning and Motivation: Advances in Research and Theory*, Vol. II, Academic Press, New York, pp. 89–195.

Averbach, E. and Sperling, G. (1961), Short-term storage of information in vision. In C. Cherry (Ed.) *Information Theory*, Buttersworth, London; pp. 196–211.

Baddeley, A. D. (1966), Short-term memory for word sequences as a function of acoustic, semantic, and formal similarity. *Quarterly Journal of Experimental Psychology*, *18*, 362–365.

Baddeley A. D. and Dale, H. C. A. (1966), The effects of semantic similarity on retroactive interference in long- and short-term memory. *Journal of Verbal Learning and Verbal Behavior*, *5*, 417–420.

Bahrick, H. P. and Bahrick, P. D. (1964), A re-examination of the interrelations among measures of retention, *Quarterly Journal of Experimental Psychology*, *16*, 318–324.

Barnes, J. M. and Underwood, B. J. (1959), "Fate" of first-list associations in transfer-theory, *Journal of Experimental Psychology*, *58*, 97–105.

Bartlett, F. C. (1932), *Remembering*, Cambridge University Press, Cambridge.

Bartz, W. H., Satz, P., Fennel, E. and Lally, J. R. (1967), Meaningfulness and laterality in dichotic listening, *Journal of Experimental Psychology*, *73*, 204–210.

Battig, W. F. (1962), Paired-associate learning under simultaneous repetition and nonrepetition conditions, *Journal of Experimental Psychology*, *64*, 87–93.

Battig, W. F. (1966), Evidence for coding processes in "rote" paired-associate learning. *Journal of Verbal Learning and Verbal Behavior*, *5*, 177-181.

Battig, W. F., and Bourne, L. E. Jr., (1955), Concept identification as a function of irrelevant information and instruction, *Journal of Experimental Psychology*, *49*, 153-164.

Battig, W. F. and Montague, W. E. (1969), Category norms for verbal items in 56 categories: a replication and extension of the Connecticut norms, *Journal of Experimental Psychology*, *80*, Part 2, 1-46.

Baum, M. H. (1954), Single concept learning as a function of intralist generalization, *Journal of Experimental Psychology*, *47*, 89-94.

Bernbach, H. A. (1967a), Stimulus learning and recognition in paired-associate learning, *Journal of Experimental Psychology*, *75*, 513-519.

Bernbach, H. A. (1967b) The effect of labels in short-term memory for colors with nursery school children, *Psychonomic Science*, *7*, 149-150.

Bever, T. G. (1968), Associations to stimulus-response theories of language. In T. R. Dixon and D. L. Horton (Eds.) *Verbal behavior and general behavior theory*, Prentice Hall, Englewood Cliffs, N.J., pp. 478–494.

Bever, T. G., Fodor, J. A., and Garrett, M. (1968), A formal limitation of associationism. In T. R. Dixon and D. L. Horton (Eds.) *Verbal be-*

havior and general behavior theory, Prentice Hall, Englewood Cliffs, N. J., pp. 421–450.

Bilodeau, E. A. and Bilodeau, I. McD. (1958), Variation of temporal intervals among critical events in five studies of knowledge of results, *Journal of Experimental Psychology*, *55*, 603–612.

Bilodeau, I. McD. and Schlosberg, H. (1951), Similarity in stimulating conditions as a variable in retroactive inhibition, *Journal of Experimental Psychology*, *41*, 199–204.

Binder, A. and Estes, W. K. (1966), Transfer of response in visual recognition situations as a function of frequency variables, *Psychological Monographs*, *80*, Whole No. 631.

Binder, A. and Feldman, S. E. (1960), The effect of experimentally controlled experiences upon recognition responses, *Psychological Monographs*, *74*, Whole No. 496.

Binford, J. R. and Gettys, C. (1965), Nonstationarity in paired-associate learning as indicated by a second-guess procedure, *Journal of Mathematical Psychology*, *2*, 190–195.

Bjork, R. A. (1966), Learning and short-term retention of paired-associates in relation to specific sequences of interpresentation intervals. *Technical Report No. 106*, Institute for Mathematical Studies in the Social Sciences, Stanford University, Stanford.

Blumenthal, A. L. (1967), Promoted recall of sentences, *Journal of Verbal Learning and Verbal Behavior*, *6*, 203–206.

Blumenthal, A. L. and Boakes, R. (1967), Prompted recall of sentences, *Journal of Verbal Learning and Verbal Behavior*, *6*, 674–676.

Boring, E. G. (1950), *A history of experimental psychology*, Appleton Century, New York.

Bourne, L. E., Jr. (1966), *Human conceptual behavior*, Allyn and Bacon, Boston.

Bourne, L. E., Jr. (1967), Learning and utilization of conceptual rules. In B. Kleinmuntz, (Ed.) *Concepts and the structure of memory*. Wiley, New York, pp. 1–32.

Bourne, L. E., Jr. and Bunderson, C. V. (1963), Effects of delay of informative feedback and length of postfeedback interval on concept identification, *Journal of Experimental Psychology*, *65*, 1–5.

Bourne, L. E., Jr., Guy, D. E., Dodd, D. and Justesen, D. R. (1965), Concept identification: the effects of varying length and informational components of the intertrial interval, *Journal of Experimental Psychology*, *69*, 624–629.

Bourne, L. E., Jr., and Haygood, R. C. (1959), The role of stimulus redundancy in the identification of concepts, *Journal of Experimental Psychology*, *58*, 232–238.

Bourne, L. E., Jr. and Haygood, R. C. (1961), Supplementary report: effect of redundant relevant information upon the identification of concepts, *Journal of Experimental Psychology*, *61*, 259–260.

Bousfield, W. A. (1953), The occurrence of clustering in the recall of randomly arranged associates, *Journal of General Psychology*, *49*, 229–240.

Bousfield, W. A. and Cohen, B. H. (1953), The effects of reinforcement on the occurrence of clustering in the recall of randomly arranged associates, *Journal of Psychology*, *36*, 67–81.

Bousfield, W. A., Cohen, B. H., and Whitmarsh, G. A. (1958), Associative clustering in the recall of words of different taxonomic frequencies of occurrence, *Psychological Report*, *4*, 39–44.

Bousfield, W. A., Puff, C. R., and Cowan, T. M. (1964), The development of constancies in sequential organization during repeated free recall, *Journal of Verbal Learning and Verbal Behavior*, *3*, 489–495.

Bower, G. H. (1961), Application of a model to paired-associate learning, *Psychometrika*, *26*, 255–280.

Bower, G. H. (1962), A model of response and training variables in paired-associate learning, *Psychological Review*, *69*, 34–53.

Bower, G. H. (1967), A multicomponent theory of the memory trace. In K. W. Spence and J. T. Spence (Eds.) *The Psychology of Learning and Motivation: Advances in Research and Theory*, Vol. I., Academic Press, New York: pp. 299–325.

Bower, G. H. (1968), *Organization and Memory*, Paper presented at the Western Psychological Association Meetings, San Diego, California, April, 1968.

Bower, G. H. and Ciark M. C. (1969), Narrative stories as mediators for serial learning, *Psychonomic Science*, *14*, 181-182

Bower, G. H., Clark M. C., Lesgold, A. M., and Winzenz, D. (1969), Hierarchical retrieval schemes in recall of categorized word lists, *Journal of Verbal Learning and Verbal Behavior*, *8*, 323-343.

Bower, G. H., Lesgold, A. M., and Tieman, D. (1969), Grouping operations in free recall, *Journal of Verbal Learning and Verbal Behavior*, *8*, 481-493.

Bower, G. H. and Theios, J. (1964), A learning model for discrete performance levels. In R. C. Atkinson (Ed) *Studies in Mathematical Psychology*, Stanford University Press, Stanford. pp. 1–31.

Bower, G. H. and Trabasso, T. R. (1964), Concept identification. In R. C. Atkinson (Ed) *Studies in Mathematical Psychology*, Stanford University Press, Stanford. pp. 32–94.

Bradley, R. A. and Terry, M. E. (1952), Rank analysis of incomplete block designs. I. The method of paired comparisons. *Biometrika*, *39*, 324–345.

Brain, M. D. S. (1963), On learning the grammatical order of words. *Psychological Review*, *70*, 323–348.

Brain, M. D. S. (1965a), The insufficiency of a finite-state model for verbal reconstructive memory, *Psychonomic Science*, *2*, 291–292.

Brain, M. D. S. (1965b), Inferring a grammar from responses: discussion of Gough's and Segal's comments, *Psychonomic Science*, *3*, 241–242.

Bregman, A. S. (1966), Is recognition memory all-or-none? *Journal of Verbal Learning and Verbal Behavior*, *5*, 1–6.

Bregman, A. S. and Chambers, D. W. (1966), All-or-none learning of attributes, *Journal of Experimental Psychology*, *71*, 785–793.

Bregman, A. S. and Strasberg, R. (1968), Memory for the syntactic form of sentences, *Journal of Verbal Learning and Verbal Behavior*, 7, 396–403.

Broadbent, D. E. (1958), *Perception and Communication*, Pergamon Press, New York.

Broadbent, D. E. (1963), Flow of information within the organism, *Journal of Verbal Learning and Verbal Behavior*, 2, 34–39.

Brown, J. A. (1958), Some tests of the decay theory of immediate memory, *Quarterly Journal of Experimental Psychology*, 10, 12–21.

Brown, J. A. (1965), A comparison of recognition and recall by a multiple response method, *Journal of Verbal Learning and Verbal Behavior*, 4, 401–408.

Brown, J. S. (1965), Generalization and discrimination. In D. I. Mostofsky (Ed.) *Stimulus Generalization*, Stanford University Press, Stanford. pp. 7–23.

Brown, J. S., Bilodeau, E. A., and Baron, M. R. (1951), Bidirectional gradients in the strength of a generalized voluntary response to stimuli on a visual-spatial dimension, *Journal of Experimental Psychology*, 41, 52–61.

Brown, R. and McNeill, D. (1966), The "tip of the tongue" phenomenon, *Journal of Verbal Learning and Verbal Behavior*, 5, 325–337.

Bruce, D. and Cofer, C. N. (1967), An examination of recognition and free recall as measures of acquisition and long-term retention, *Journal of Experimental Psychology*, 75, 283–289.

Bruce, R. W. (1933), Conditions of transfer of training, *Journal of Experimental Psychology*, 16, 343–361.

Bruner, J. S., Goodnow, J. J., and Austin, G. A. (1956), *A Study of Thinking*, Wiley, New York.

Bruner, J. S. and Potter, M. C. (1964), Interference in visual recognition, *Science*, 144, 424–425.

Buchwald, A. M. (1967), Effects of immediate versus delayed outcomes in associative learning, *Journal of Verbal Learning and Verbal Behavior*, 6, 317–320.

Bugelski, B. R. and Cadwallader, T. C. (1956), A reappraisal of the transfer and retroaction surface, *Journal of Experimental Psychology*, 52, 360–365.

Bühler, K. (1908), Tatsachen und Probleme zu einer Psychologie der Denkvorgänge, *Archiv für die gesamte Psychologie*, 12, 1–123.

Burke, C. J. and Estes, W. K. (1957), A component model for stimulus variables in discrimination learning, *Psychometrika*, 22, 133–145.

Buschke, H. (1968), Input-output, short-term storage, *Journal of Verbal Learning and Verbal Behavior*, 7, 900–903.

Buschke, H. and Lim, H. (1967), Temporal and interactional effects in short-term storage, *Perception and Psychophysics*, 2, 107–114.

Bush, R. R. and Mosteller, F. (1955), *Stochastic Models for Learning*, Wiley, New York.

Buss, A. H. (1953), Rigidity as a function of reversal and nonreversal shifts in the learning of successive discriminations, *Journal of Experimental Psychology, 45*, 75–81.

Caird, W. K. (1964), Reverberating activity and memory disorder, *Nature, 201*, 1150.

Calfee, R. C. (1966), How learning is affected by a change in subject matter: sources of interference in verbal learning, Technical Report, University of Wisconsin, 1966.

Carmicheal, L., Hogan, H. P., and Walter, A. A. (1932), An experimental study of the effect of language on the reproduction of visually perceived forms, *Journal of Experimental Psychology, 15*, 73–86.

Cattell, J. McK. (1885), Über die Zeit der Erkennung und Benennung von Schriftzeichen, Bildern und Farben, *Philosophische Studien, 2*, 635–650.

Cieutat, V. J., Stockwell, F. E., and Noble, C. E. (1958), The interaction of ability and amount of practice with stimulus and response meaningfulness (*m,m'*) in paired-associate learning, *Journal of Experimental Psychology, 56*, 193–202.

Cimbalo, R. S. and Laughery, K. R. (1967), Short-term memory: effects of auditory and visual similarity, *Psychonomic Science, 8*, 57–58.

Chomsky, N. (1957), *Syntactic structures*. Mouton, The Hague; 1957.

Chomsky, N. (1959), A review of *Verbal Behavior* by B. F. Skinner. *Language, 35*, 26–58.

Chomsky, N. (1963), Formal properties of grammars. In R. D. Luce, R. R. Bush, and E. Galanter (Eds.), *Handbook of Mathematical Psychology*. Vol. II. Wiley, New York. pp. 323–418.

Chomsky, N. (1965), *Aspects of the Theory of Syntax*, MIT Press, Cambridge.

Chumbley, J. (1969), Hypothesis memory in concept learning, *Journal of Mathematical Psychology, 6*, 528–540.

Clifton, C., Jr. and Odom, P. (1966), Similarity relations among certain English sentence constructions, *Psychological Monographs, 80*, Whole No. 613.

Cofer, C. N. (1965), On some factors in the organizational characteristics of free recall, *American Psychologist, 20*, 261–272.

Cofer, C. N. (1967), Does conceptual organization influence the amount retained in immediate free recall? In B. J. Kleinmuntz (Ed) *Concepts and the Structure of Memory*, Wiley, New York: pp. 181–214.

Cofer, C. N., Bruce, D. R., and Reicher, G. M. (1966), Clustering in free recall as a function of certain methodological variations, *Journal of Experimental Psychology, 71*, 858–866.

Cohen, B. H. (1966), Some-or-none characteristics of coding behavior, *Journal of Verbal Learning and Verbal Behavior, 5*, 182–187.

Cohen, B. H., Bousfield, W. A., and Whitmarsh, G. A. (1957), Cultural norms for verbal items in 43 categories, Technical Report No. 22, University of Connecticut, 1957.

Coleman, E. B. (1963), Approximations to English, *American Journal of Psychology, 76*, 239–247.

Conrad, R. (1964), Acoustic confusion in immediate memory, *British Journal of Psychology, 55,* 75–84.

Conrad, R., Freeman, P. R., and Hull, A. J. (1965), Acoustic factors versus language factors in short-term memory, *Psychonomic Science, 3,* 57–58.

Conrad, R. and Hille, B. A. (1958), The decay theory of immediate memory and paced recall, *Canadian Journal of Psychology, 12,* 1–6.

Conrad, R. and Hull, A. J. (1964), Information, acoustic confusion, and memory span, *British Journal of Psychology, 55,* 429–432.

Cross, D. V. and Lane, H. L. (1962), On the discriminative control of concurrent responses: the relations among response frequence, latency, and topography in acoustic generalization. *Journal of the Experimental Analysis of Behavior, 5,* 487–496.

Crothers, E. J. and Suppes, P. (1967), *Experiments in Second-language Learning,* Academic Press, New York.

Crovitz, H. F. (1969), Memory loci in artificial memory, *Psychonomic Science, 16,* 82–83.

Dale, H. C. A. (1964), Retroactive interference in short-term memory, *Nature, 203,* 1408.

Dale, H. C. A. (1967a), Response availability and short-term memory, *Journal of Verbal Learning and Verbal Behavior, 6,* 47–48.

Dale, H. C. A. (1967b), Familiarity and free recall, *Quarterly Journal of Experimental Psychology, 19,* 103–108.

Dale, H. C. A. and Baddeley, A. D. (1962), Alternatives in testing recognition memory, *Nature, 196,* 93–94.

Dale, H. C. A. and Gregory, M. (1966), Evidence of semantic coding in short-term memory, *Psychonomic Science, 5,* 75–76.

Dallett, K. M. (1962), The transfer surface re-examined, *Journal of Verbal Learning and Verbal Behavior, 1,* 91–94.

Dallett, K. M. (1964), Effects of a redundant prefix on immediate recall, *Journal of Experimental Psychology, 67,* 296–298.

Dallett, K. M. (1965), Primary memory: the effects of redundancy upon digit repetition. *Psychonomic Science, 3,* 237–238.

Das, J. P. (1961), Mathematical solutions in the acquisition of a verbal CR, *Journal of Experimental Psychology, 61,* 376–378.

Davis, R., Sutherland, N. S., and Judd, B. R. (1961), Information content in recognition and recall, *Journal of Experimental Psychology, 61,* 422–429.

Deese, J. (1957), Serial organization in the recall of disconnected items, *Psychological Reports, 3,* 577–582.

Deese, J. (1959), On the prediction of occurrence of particular verbal intrusions in immediate recall, *Journal of Experimental Psychology, 58,* 17–22.

Deese, J. (1961), From the isolated verbal unit to connected discourse. In C. N. Cofer, (Ed.) *Verbal Learning and Verbal Behavior,* McGraw-Hill, New York: pp. 11–31.

Deese, J. (1962), On the structure of associative meaning, *Psychological Review, 69,* 161–175.

Deese, J. (1965), *The Structure of Associations in Language and Thought,* The Johns Hopkins Press, Baltimore.

Doll, J. J. and Thomas, D. R. (1967), Effects of discrimination training on stimulus generalization for human subjects, *Journal of Experimental Psychology, 75,* 508–512.

Dufort, R. H., Guttman, N., and Kimble, G. A. (1954), One trial discrimination reversal in the white rat, *Journal of Comparative and Physiological Psychology, 47,* 248–249.

Ebbinghaus, H. (1885), *Über das Gedächtnis,* Duncker, Leipzig, Translation by H. Ruyer and C. E. Bussenius, *Memory,* Teachers College, Columbia University, New York: 1913.

Ebbinghaus, H. (1902), *Grundzüge der Psychologie,* Veit & Co., Leipzig.

Edwards, W. (1961), Behavioral decision theory. In P. R. Farnsworth, O. McNemar, and Q. McNemar (Eds.) *Annual Review of Psychology,* Annual Reviews Inc., Palo Alto: pp. 473–498.

Egan, J. P. (1958), Recognition memory and the operating characteristic, Technical Note AFCRC-TN-58-51, Indiana University Hearing and Communication Laboratory, 1958.

Egan, J. P., Schulman, A. I., and Greenberg, G. Z. (1959), Operating characteristics determined by binary decisions and by ratings, *Journal of the Acoustical Society of America, 31,* 768–773.

Elliott, P. B. (1964), Tables of *d'*. In J. A. Swets (Ed.) *Signal Detection and Recognition by Human Observers,* Wiley, New York: pp. 651–684.

Epstein, W. (1961), The influence of syntactic structure on learning, *American Journal of Psychology, 74,* 80–85.

Epstein, W. (1962), A further study of the effect of syntactic structure on learning, *American Journal of Psychology, 75,* 121–126.

Erdmann B. and Dodge R. (1898), *Psychologische Untersuchungen über das Lesen,* M. Niemeyer, Halle.

Erikson, J. R. and Zajkowski, M. M. (1967), Learning several concept-identification problems concurrently: a test of the sampling-with-replacement assumption, *Journal of Experimental Psychology, 74,* 212–218.

Erikson, J. R., Zajkowski, M. M., and Ehrmann, E. D. (1966), All-or-none assumptions in concept identification: analysis of latency data, *Journal of Experimental Psychology, 72,* 690–697.

Esper, E. A. (1925), A technique for the experimental investigation of associative interference in artificial linguistic material. *Language Monographs,* 1925, No. 1.

Estes, W. K. (1950), Toward a statistical theory of learning. *Psychological Review, 57,* 94–107.

Estes, W. K. (1955a), Statistical theory of spontaneous recovery and regression. *Psychological Review, 62,* 145–154.

Estes, W. K. (1955b), Statistical theory of distributional phenomena in learning, *Psychological Review, 62,* 369–377.

Estes, W. K. (1959a), The statistical approach to learning theory. In S. Koch (Ed.) *Psychology: A Study of a Science*, McGraw-Hill, New York: Vol. II, pp. 380–491.

Estes, W. K. (1959b), Component and pattern models with Markovian interpretations. In R. R. Bush and W. K. Estes (Eds.) *Studies in Mathematical Learning Theory*, Stanford University Press, Stanford: pp. 9–52.

Estes, W. K. (1962), Theoretical treatment of differential reward in multiple-choice learning and two-person interactions. In J. H. Criswell, H. Solomon, and P. Suppes (Eds.) *Mathematical Methods in Small Group Processes*, Stanford University Press, Stanford: pp. 133–149.

Estes, W. K. (1964), Probability learning. In A. W. Melton (Ed.) *Categories of Human Learning*, Academic Press, New York: pp. 90–128.

Estes, W. K. (1965), A technique for assessing variability of perceptual span, *Proceedings of the National Academy of Sciences, 54*, 403–407.

Estes, W. K. (1967), *Reinforcement in Human Learning*, Technical Report No. 125, Institute for Mathematical Studies in the Social Sciences, Stanford, Calif., 1967.

Estes, W. K. and Burke, C. J. (1953), A theory of stimulus variability in learning. *Psychological Review, 60*, 276–286.

Estes, W. K. and DaPolito, F. (1967), Independent variation of information storage and retrieval processes in paired-associate learning, *Journal of Experimental Psychology, 75*, 18–26.

Estes, W. K. and Straughan, J. H. (1954), Analysis of a verbal conditioning situation in terms of statistical learning theory, *Journal of Experimental Psychology, 47*, 225–234.

Estes, W. K. and Suppes, P. (1959), Foundations of linear models. In R. R. Bush and W. K. Estes (Eds.) *Studies in Mathematical Learning Theory*, Stanford University Press, Stanford: pp. 137–179.

Estes, W. K. and Taylor, H. A. (1966), Visual detection in relation to display size and redundancy of critical elements, *Perception and Psychophysics, 1*, 9–16.

Evans, R. B. and Dallenbach, K. M. (1965), Single trial learning: a stochastic model for the recall of individual words, *American Journal of Psychology, 78*, 545–556.

Feigenbaum, E. A. (1963), The simulation of verbal learning behavior. In E. A. Feigenbaum and J. Feldman (Eds.) *Computers and Thought*. McGraw-Hill, New York: pp. 297–309.

Feldman, J. (1963), Simulation of behavior in the binary choice experiment. In E. A. Feigenbaum and J. Feldman (Eds.) *Computers and Thought*, McGraw-Hill, New York. pp. 329–346.

Field, W. H. and Lachman, R. (1966), Information transmission (*I*) in recognition and recall as a function of alternatives (*k*). *Journal of Experimental Psychology, 72*, 785–791.

Fischer, A. (1909), Über Reproduzieren und Wiedererkennen bei Gedächtnisversuchen. *Zeitschrift für Psychologie, 50*, 62–92.

Fodor, J. A. and Bever, T. G. (1965), The psychological reality of linguistic segments. *Journal of Verbal Learning and Verbal Behavior, 4,* 414–420.

Forster, K. I. (1966), The effect of syntactic structure on nonordered recall, *Journal of Verbal Learning and Verbal Behavior, 5,* 292–297.

Foss, D. J. (1968), An analysis of learning in a miniature linguistic system, *Journal of Experimental Psychology, 76,* 450–459.

Freiberg, V. and Tulving, E. (1961), The effect of practice on utilization of information from positive and negative instances in concept identification, *Canadian Journal of Psychology, 15,* 101–106.

Friedman, M. P. (1966), Transfer effects and response strategies in pattern-vs-component discrimination learning, *Journal of Experimental Psychology, 71,* 420–428.

Friedman, M. P., Burke, C. J., Cole, M., Estes, W. K., Keller, L., and Millward, R. B. (1963), Two-choice behavior under extended training with shifting probabilities of reinforcement. In R. C. Atkinson (Ed.) *Studies in Mathematical Psychology,* Stanford University Press, Stanford. pp. 250–291.

Friedman, M. P., Trabasso, T. R. and Mosberg, L. (1967), Tests of a mixed model for paired-associates learning with overlapping stimuli, *Journal of Mathematical Psychology, 4,* 316–334.

Galanter, E. H. and Smith W. A. (1958), Some experiments on a simple thought-problem, *American Journal of Psychology, 71,* 359–366.

Gannon, D. R. and Noble, C. E. (1961), Familiarization (n) as a stimulus factor in paired-associate verbal learning, *Journal of Experimental Psychology, 62,* 14–23.

Garner, W. R. (1962), *Uncertainty and Structure as Psychological Concepts,* Wiley, New York.

Garrett, M., Bever, T., and Fodor, J. A. (1966), The active use of grammar in speech perception. *Perception and Psychophysics, 1,* 30–32.

Garrett, M. and Fodor, J. A. (1968), Psychological theories and linguistic constructs. In T. R. Dixon and D. L. Horton (Eds.) *Verbal Behavior and General Behavior Theory,* Prentice-Hall, New York. pp. 451–477.

Gelb, A. and Goldstein, K. (1925), Psychologische Analysen hirnpathologischer Fälle.X. Über Farbenamnesie. *Psychologische Forschung, 6,* 127–199.

Gibson, E. J. (1940), A systematic application of the concepts of generalization and differentiation to verbal learning, *Psychological Review, 47,* 196–229.

Gibson, E. J. (1942), Intralist generalization as a factor in verbal learning, *Journal of Experimental Psychology, 30,* 185–200.

Gibson, E. J. (1965), Learning to read. *Science, 148,* 1066–1072.

Gibson, E. J., Bishop, C. H., Schiff, W., and Smith, J. (1964), Comparison of meaningfulness and pronounceability as grouping principles in the perception and retention of verbal material, *Journal of Experimental Psychology, 67,* 173–182.

Gibson, E. J. and Yonas, A. (1966), A developmental study of the effects of visual and auditory interference on a visual scanning task, *Psychonomic Science, 5*, 163–164.

Glanzer, M. and Clark, W. H. (1963), Accuracy of perceptual recall: an analysis of organization, *Journal of Verbal Learning and Verbal Behavior, 1*, 289–299.

Glanzer, M. and Cunitz, A. R. (1966), Two storage mechanisms in free recall, *Journal of Verbal Learning and Verbal Behavior, 5*, 351–360.

Glaze, J. A. (1928), The association value of nonsense syllables, *Journal of Genetic Psychology, 35*, 255–269.

Goldstein, K. and Scheerer, M. (1941), Abstract and concrete behavior. An experimental study with special tests, *Psychological Monographs, 53*, Whole No. 239.

Goodnow, J. J. (1955), Determinants of choice distribution in two-choice situations, *American Journal of Psychology, 68*, 106–116.

Gorman, A. M. (1961), Recognition memory for nouns as a function of abstractness and frequency, *Journal of Experimental Psychology, 61*, 23–29.

Gough, P. B. and Segal, E. M. (1965), Comments on "The insufficiency of a finite state model for verbal reconstructive memory". *Psychonomic Science, 3*, 155–156.

Grant, D. A., Hake, H. W., and Hornseth, J. P. (1951), Acquisition and extinction of a verbal conditioned response with different percentages of reinforcement, *Journal of Experimental Psychology, 42*, 1–5.

Green, D. M. and Swets, J. A. (1966), *Signal Detection Theory and Psychophysics*, Wiley, New York.

Greeno, J. G. (1964), Paired-associate learning with massed and distributed repetitions of items, *Journal of Experimental Psychology, 67*, 286–295.

Greeno, J. G. (1967), Paired-associate learning with short-term retention: mathematical analysis and data regarding identification of parameters. *Journal of Mathematical Psychology, 4*, 430–472.

Greeno, J. G. and Scandura, J. M. (1966), All-or-none transfer based on verbally mediated concepts, *Journal of Mathematical Psychology, 3*, 388–411.

Greeno, J. G. and Steiner, T. E. (1964), Markovian processes with identifiable states: general considerations and application to all-or-none learning. *Psychometrika, 29*, 309–333.

Guthrie, E. R. (1935), *The Psychology of Learning*, Harper, New York.

Guthrie, E. R. (1959), Association by contiguity. In S. Koch (Ed.) *Psychology: A Study of a Science*, Vol. II, McGraw-Hill, New York. pp. 158–195.

Guttman, N. and Kalish, H. I. (1956), Discriminability and stimulus generalization. *Journal of Experimental Psychology, 51*, 79–88.

Haber, R. N. and Erdelyi, M. H. (1967), Emergence and recovery of initially unavailable perceptual material, *Journal of Verbal Learning and Verbal Behavior, 6*, 618–628.

Hake, H. W. and Hyman, R. (1953), Perception of the statistical structure of a random series of binary symbols, *Journal of Experimental Psychology*, *45*, 64–74.

Hall, J. F. (1954), Learning as a function of word frequency, *American Journal of Psychology*, *67*, 138–140.

Hanawalt, N. G. and Demarest, I. H. (1939), The effect of verbal suggestion in the recall period upon the reproduction of visually perceived forms, *Journal of Experimental Psychology*, *25*, 159–174.

Harlow, H. F. (1949), The formation of learning sets. *Psychological Review*, *56*, 51–65.

Harrow, M. and Friedman, G. B. (1958), Comparing reversal and non-reversal shift in concept formation with partial reinforcement controlled, *Journal of Experimental Psychology*, *55*, 592–598.

Haygood, R. C. and Bourne, L. E., Jr. (1965), Attribute- and rule-learning aspects of conceptual behavior, *Psychological Review*, *72*, 175–195.

Haygood, R. C. and Stevenson, M. (1967), Effects of number of irrelevant dimensions in nonconjunctive concept learning, *Journal of Experimental Psychology*, *74*, 302–304.

Hebb, D. O. (1949), *The Organization of Behavior*, Wiley, New York.

Hebb, D. O. (1961), Distinctive features of learning in the higher animal. In J. F. Delafresnaye (Ed.) *Brain Mechanisms and Learning*. Oxford University Press, London.

Heidbreder, E. (1946), The attainment of concepts: I. Terminology and methodology. *Journal of General Psychology*, *35*, 173–189.

Heidbreder, E. (1949), The attainment of concepts: VIII. The conceptualization of verbally indicated instances, *Journal of Psychology*, *27*, 263–309.

Hellyer, S. (1962), Frequency of stimulus presentation and short-term decrement in recall, *Journal of Experimental Psychology*, *64*, 650.

Herman, L. M. and Bahrick, H. P. (1966), Information encoding and decision time as variables in human choice behavior, *Journal of Experimental Psychology*, *71*, 718–724.

Herrnstein, R. J. and Loveland, D. H. (1964), Complex visual concept in the pigeon. *Science*, *146*, 549–551.

Hilgard, E. R. (1956), *Theories of Learning*. Appleton-Century Crofts, New York, Third Edition by E. R. Hilgard and G. H. Bower, 1966.

Hintzman, D. L. (1968), Exploration with a discrimination net model for paired-associate learning, *Journal of Mathematical Psychology*, *5*, 123–162.

Höffding, H. (1891), *Outlines of Psychology*, Macmillan, London.

Hollingworth, H. C. (1913), Characteristic differences between recall and recognition, *American Journal of Psychology*, *24*, 532–544.

Horowitz, L. M. (1961), Free recall and ordering of trigrams. *Journal of Experimental Psychology*, *62*, 51–57.

Hovland, C. I. (1937), The generalization of conditioned responses. I. The sensory generalization of conditioned responses with varying frequencies of tone, *Journal of General Psychology*, *17*, 125–148.

Hovland, C. I. (1952), A "communication analysis" of concept learning, *Psychological Review*, *59*, 461–472.

Hovland, C. I. and Kurtz, K. N. (1952), Experimental studies in rote learning theory:X. Pre-learning syllable familiarization and the length-difficulty relationship, *Journal of Experimental Psychology*, *44*, 31–39.

Hovland, C. I. and Weiss, W. (1953), Transmission of information concerning concepts through positive and negative instances, *Journal of Experimental Psychology*, *45*, 165–182.

Howe, M. J. A., (1967), Consolidation in short-term memory as a function of rehearsal, *Psychonomic Science*, *7*, 355–356.

Hubel, D. H. and Wiesel, T. N. (1962), Receptive fields, binocular interaction, and functional architecture in the cat's visual cortex, *Journal of Physiology*, *160*, 106–154.

Hull, C. L. (1920), Quantitative aspects of the evolution of concepts, *Psychological Monographs*, *28*, Whole No. 123.

Hull, C. L. (1943), *Principles of Behavior.* Appleton-Century-Crofts, New York.

Humphreys, L. G. (1939), Acquisition and extinction of verbal expectations in a situation analogous to conditioning, *Journal of Experimental Psychology*, *25*, 294–301.

Hunt, E. B. (1962), *Concept Learning: An Information Processing Problem*, Wiley, New York.

Hunt, E. B. and Hovland, C. I. (1960), Order of consideration of different types of concepts, *Journal of Experimental Psychology*, *59*, 220–225.

Hunt, E. B., Marin, J., and Stone, P. J. (1966), *Experiments in Induction.* Academic Press, New York.

Izawa, C. (1966), Reinforcement-test sequences in paired-associate learning, *Psychological Reports*, *18*, 879–919.

Jakobson, R. and Halle, M. (1956), *Fundamentals of Language*, Mouton & Co., The Hague.

James, W. (1890), *Principles of Psychology*, Holt, New York.

Jarvik, M. E. (1951), Probability learning and a negative recency effect in the serial anticipation of alternative symbols, *Journal of Experimental Psychology*, *41*, 291–297.

Jenkins, J. G. and Dallenbach, K. M. (1924), Obliviscence during sleep and waking, *American Journal of Psychology*, *35*, 605–612.

Jenkins, J. J., Mink, W. D., and Russel, W. A. (1958), Associative clustering as a function of verbal association strength. *Psychological Reports*, *4*, 127–136.

Jenkins, J. J. and Russell, W. A. (1952), Associative clustering during recall. *Journal of Abnormal and Social Psychology*, *47*, 818–821.

Johnson, N. F. (1965), The psychological reality of phrase-structure rules, *Journal of Verbal Learning and Verbal Behavior*, *4*, 469–475.

Johnson, N. F., Sequential verbal behavior. (1968), In T. R. Dixon and D. L. Horton (Eds.) *Verbal Behavior and General Behavior Theory.* Prentice-Hall, New York. pp. 421–450.

Johnson, P. J. (1967), Nature of mediational responses in concept indentification problems, *Journal of Experimental Psychology, 73*, 391–393.

Johnson, R. C. (1962), Reanalysis of "Meaningfulness and verbal learning". *Psychological Review, 69*, 233–238.

Jost, A. (1897), Die Assoziationsfestigkeit in ihrer Abhängigkeit von der Verteilung der Wiederholungen. *Zeitschrift für Psychologie, 14*, 436–472.

Kalish, H. I. (1958), The relationship between discriminability and generalization: A re-examination. *Journal of Experimental Psychology, 55*, 637–644.

Kaplan, G. A., Yonas, A., and Shurcliff, A. (1966), Visual and acoustic confusability in a visual search task. *Perception and Psychophysics, 1*, 172–174.

Karrush, W. and Dear, R. E. (1966), Optimal stimulus presentation strategy for a stimulus sampling model of learning, *Journal of Mathematical Psychology, 3*, 19–47.

Kelleher, R. T. (1956), Discrimination learning as a function of reversal and nonreversal shifts, *Journal of Experimental Psychology, 51*, 379–384.

Keller, L., Cole, M., Burke, C. J., and Estes, W. K. (1965), Reward and information values of trial outcomes in paired-associate learning, *Psychological Monographs, 79*, Whole No. 605.

Kendler, H. H. and Kendler, T. S. (1962), Vertical and horizontal processes in problem solving, *Psychological Review, 69*, 1–16.

Kendler, T. S. and Kendler, H. H. (1959), Reversal and nonreversal shifts in kindergarten children, *Journal of Experimental Psychology, 58*, 56–60.

Kendler, T. S., Kendler, H. H., and Wells, D. (1960), Reversal and nonreversal shifts in nursery school children, *Journal of Comparative and Physiological Psychology, 53*, 83–88.

Kent, G. H., and Rosanoff, A. J. (1910), A study of association in insanity, *American Journal of Insanity, 67*, 37–96.

Kimble, G. A. (1961), *Conditioning and Learning*, Appleton-Century-Crofts, New York.

Kintsch, W. (1963), All-or-none learning and the role of repetition in paired-associate learning, *Science*, 1963, 140, 310–312.

Kintsch, W. (1965), Habituation of the GSR component of the orienting reflex during paired-associate learning before and after learning has taken place, *Journal of Mathematical Psychology, 2*, 330–341.

Kintsch, W. (1966), Recognition learning as a function of the length of the retention interval and changes in the retention interval, *Journal of Mathematical Psychology, 3*, 412–433.

Kintsch, W. (1967), Memory and decision aspects of recognition learning, *Psychological Review, 74*, 496–504.

Kintsch, W. (1968a), An experimental comparison of single-stimulus tests and multiple-choice tests of recognition memory, *Journal of Experimental Psychology, 76*, 1–6.

Kintsch, W. (1968b), Recognition and free recall of organized lists, *Journal of Experimental Psychology, 78,* 481–487.

Kintsch, W. and Buschke, H. (1969), Homophones and synonyms in short-term memory, *Journal of Experimental Psychology, 80,* 403-407.

Kintsch, W. and McCoy, D. F. (1964), Delay of informative feedback in paired-associate learning, *Journal of Experimental Psychology, 68,* 372–375.

Kintsch, W. and Morris, C. J. (1965), Application of a Markov model to free recall and recognition, *Journal of Experimental Psychology, 69,* 200–206.

Koffka, K. (1935), *Principles of Gestalt Psychology.* Harcourt, Brace, New York.

Köhler, W. (1941), On the nature of associations, *Proceedings of the American Philosophical Society, 84,* 489–502.

Kopp, J., and Lane, H. L. (1968), Hue discrimination related to linguistic habits, *Psychonomic Science, 11,* 61–62.

Koppenaal, R. J. (1963), Time changes in the strength of *A-B, A-C* lists; spontaneous recovery? *Journal of Verbal Learning and Verbal Behavior, 2,* 310–319.

Krechevsky, I. (1932), Antagonistic visual discrimination habits in the white rat, *Journal of Comparative Psychology, 14,* 263–277.

Kuhlmann, F. (1907), On the analysis of the memory consciousness for pictures of familiar objects, *American Journal of Psychology, 18,* 389–420.

LaBerge, D. (1959), A model with neutral elements. In R. R. Bush and W. K. Estes (Eds.), *Studies in Mathematical Learning Theory,* Stanford University Press, Stanford. pp. 56–63.

Ladefoged, P. and Broadbent, D. E. (1960), Perception of sequence in auditory events, *Quarterly Journal of Experimental Psychology, 12,* 162–170.

Lane, H. L. (1965), The motor theory of speech perception: A critical review. *Psychological Review, 72,* 275–309.

Lane, H. L. (1967), A behavioral basis for the polarity principle in linguistics. In K. Salzinger and S. Salzinger (Eds.) *Research in Verbal Behavior and Some Neurophysiological Implications,* Academic Press, New York.

Lashley, K. I. (1951), The problem of serial order in behavior. In L. A. Jeffres (Ed.) *Cerebral Mechanisms in Behavior.* Wiley, New York. pp. 112–135.

Lashley, K. S. and Wade, M. (1946), The Pavlovian theory of generalization, *Psychological Review, 53,* 72–87.

Laughery, K. R. and Pinkus, A. L. (1968), Recoding and presentation rate in short-term memory, *Journal of Experimental Psychology, 76,* 636–641.

Lawrence, D. H. (1949), Acquired distinctiveness of cues: I. Transfer between discriminations on the basis of familiarity with the stimulus. *Journal of Experimental Psychology, 39,* 770–784.

Lawrence, D. H. (1952), The transfer of a discrimination along a continuum, *Journal of Comparative and Psychological Psychology*, *45*, 511–516.

Lawrence, D. H. (1963), The nature of a stimulus: some relations between learning and perception. In S. Koch (Ed.) *Psychology: A Study of a Science*, Vol. V. McGraw-Hill, New York. pp. 179–212.

Lawrence, D. H. and DeRivera, J. (1954), Evidence for relational discrimination, *Journal of Comparative and Physiological Psychology*, *47*, 465–471.

Lenneberg, E. (1967), *The biological basis of language*, Wiley, New York.

Lettvin, J. Y., Maturana, H. R., McCulloch, W. S., and Pitts, W. H. (1959), What the frog's eye tells the frog's brain, *Proceedings of the Institute of Radio Engineers*, *47*, 1940–1951.

Levine, M. (1962), Cue neutralization: The effects of random reinforcements upon discrimination learning, *Journal of Experimental Psychology*, *63*, 438–443.

Levine, M. (1966), Hypothesis behavior by humans during discrimination learning, *Journal of Experimental Psychology*, *71*, 331–338.

Levine, M., Miller, P. I., and Steinmeyer, H. (1967), The none-to-all theorem of human discrimination learning, *Journal of Experimental Psychology*, *73*, 568–573.

Lewin, K. (1917), Die psychologische Tätigkeit bei der Hemmung von Willensvorgängen und das Grundgesetz der Assoziation, *Zeitschrift für Psychologie*, *77*, 212–247.

Liberman, A. M., Harris, K. S., Kinney, J. A., and Lane, H. L. (1961), The discrimination of relative onset time of the components of certain speech patterns, *Journal of Experimental Psychology*, *61*, 379–388.

Lieberman, B. (1960), Human behavior in a strictly determined 3 × 3 matrix game. *Behavioral Science*, *5*, 317–322.

Lieberman, B. (1962), Experimental studies of conflict in two-person and three-person games. In J. H. Criswell, H. Solomon, and P. Suppes (Eds.) *Mathematical Methods in Small Group Processes*, Stanford University Press, Stanford. pp. 203–220.

Lorente de Nô, R. (1938), Analysis of the activity of the chains of internuncial neurons. *Journal of Neurophysiology*, *1*, 207–244.

Lovejoy, E. (1968), *Attention in discrimination learning. A point of view and a theory*, Holden-Day, San Francisco.

Luce, R. D. (1959), *Individual choice behavior: A theoretical analysis*, Wiley, New York.

Luce, R. D. (1963), A threshold model for simple detection experiments, *Psychological Review*, *70*, 61–79.

Luce, R. D. and Raiffa, H. (1957), *Games and decisions*, Wiley, New York.

Mackintosh, N. J. (1965), Selective attention in animal discrimination learning, *Psychological Bulletin*, *64*, 124–140.

Mackworth, J. F. (1963), The relation between visual image and post-perception immediate memory, *Journal of Verbal Learning and Verbal Behavior*, *2*, 75–84.

Mackworth, J. F. (1965), Presentation rate, repetition, and organization in auditory short-term memory, *Canadian Journal of Psychology*, *19*, 334–315.

Mandler, G. (1962), From association to structure. *Psychological Review*, *69*, 415–427

Mandler, G. (1967a), Verbal learning. In G. Mandler and P. Mussen (Eds.) *New Directions in Psychology. III.* Rinehart and Winston, New York. pp. 1–50.

Mandler, G. (1967b), Organization and memory. In K. W. Spence and J. T. Spence (Eds.) *The Psychology of Learning and Motivation: Advances in Research and Theory*, Vol. I. Academic Press, New York. pp. 328–372.

Mandler, G. and Pearlstone, Z. (1966), Free and constrained concept learning and subsequent recall, *Journal of Verbal Learning and Verbal Behavior*, *5*, 126–131.

Marks, L. E. and Miller, G. A. (1964), The role of semantic and syntactic constraints in the memorization of English sentences, *Journal of Verbal Learning and Verbal Behavior*, *3*, 1–5.

Marks, M. R. and Jack, O. (1952), Verbal context and memory span for meaningful material, *American Journal of Psychology*, *65*, 298–300.

Marley, A. A. J. (1965), The relation between the discard and regularity conditions for choice probabilities, *Journal of Mathematical Psychology*, *2*, 242–253.

Marshall, G. R. (1967), Stimulus characteristics contributing to organization in free recall. *Journal of Verbal Learning and Verbal Behavior*, *6*, 364–374.

Martin, E. (1965), Transfer of verbal paired associates. *Psychological Review*, *72*, 327–343.

Martin, E. (1967a), Stimulus recognition in aural paired-associate learning, *Journal of Verbal Learning and Verbal Behavior*, *6*, 272–276.

Martin, E. (1967b), Relation between stimulus recognition and paired-associate learning, *Journal of Experimental Psychology*, *74*, 500–505.

Martin, E. (1968), Stimulus meaningfulness and paired-associate transfer: An encoding variability hypothesis, *Psychological Review*, *75*, 421–441.

Martin, E. and Roberts, K. H. (1966), Grammatical factors in sentence retention, *Journal of Verbal Learning and Verbal Behavior*, *5*, 211–218.

McGeoch, J. A. (1929), The influence of degree of learning upon retroactive inhibition, *American Journal of Psychology*, *41*, 252–262.

McGeoch, J. A. (1930), The influence of associative value upon the difficulty of nonsense syllable lists, *Journal of Genetic Psychology*, *37*, 421–426.

McGeoch, J. A. (1932), Forgetting and the law of disuse, *Psychological Review*, *39*, 352–370.

McGeoch, J. A. (1942), *The Psychology of Human Learning*, Longmans, New York.

McGovern, J. B. (1964), Extinction of associations in four transfer paradigms, *Psychological Monographs*, *78*, Whole No. 593.

McLean, R. S. and Gregg, L. W. (1967), Effects of induced chunking on temporal aspects of serial recitation, *Journal of Experimental Psychology, 74*, 455–459.

McNulty, J. A. (1965a), Short-term retention as a function of method of measurement, recording time, and meaningfulness of the material, *Canadian Journal of Psychology, 19*, 188–195.

McNulty, J. A. (1965b), An analysis of recall and recognition processes in verbal learning, *Journal of Verbal Learning and Verbal Behavior, 4*, 430–435.

Mehler, J. (1963), Some effects of grammatical transformations on the recall of English sentences, *Journal of Verbal Learning and Verbal Behavior, 2*, 346–351.

Mehler, J. and Carey, P. (1967), Role of surface and base structure in the perception of sentences, *Journal of Verbal Learning and Verbal Behavior, 6*, 335–338.

Mehler, J. and Miller, G. A. (1964), Retroactive interference in the recall of simple sentences, *British Journal of Psychology, 55*, 295–301.

Melton, A. W. (1963), Implications of short-term memory for a general theory of memory, *Journal of Verbal Learning and Verbal Behavior, 2*, 1–21.

Melton, A. W. and Irwin, J. M. (1940), The influence of degree of interpolated learning on retroactive inhibition and the overt transfer of specific responses, *American Journal of Psychology, 53*, 173–203.

Merikle, P. M. and Battig, W. F. (1963), Transfer of training as a function of experimental paradigm and meaningfulness, *Journal of Verbal Learning and Verbal Behavior, 2*, 485–488.

Merryman, C., Kaufmann, B., Brown, E., and Dames, J. (1968), Effects of "rights" and "wrongs" on concept identification, *Journal of Experimental Psychology, 76*, 116–119.

Millenson, J. R. (1967), An isomorphism between stimulus-response notation and information processing flow diagrams, *Psychological Record, 17*, 305–319.

Miller, G. A. (1956), The magical number seven, plus or minus two: Some limits on our capacity for processing information, *Psychological Review, 63*, 81–97.

Miller, G. A. (1958), Free recall of redundant strings of letters, *Journal of Experimental Psychology, 56*, 485–491.

Miller, G. A. (1962a), Decision units in the perception of speech, *Institute of Radio Engineers Transactions on Professional Group Information Theory*, IT-8, 81–83.

Miller, G. A. (1962b), Some psychological studies of grammar, *American Psychologist, 17*, 748–762.

Miller, G. A. (1967), *The Psychology of Communication*, Basic Books, New York.

Miller, G. A., and Chomsky, N. (1963), Finitary models of language users. In R. D. Luce, R. R. Bush, and E. Galanter (Eds.) *Handbook of*

Mathematical Psychology. Vol. II. Wiley, New York. pp. 419–492.

Miller, G. A., Galanter, E., and Pribram, K. H. (1960), *Plans and the Structure of Behavior*, Holt, New York.

Miller, G. A., Heise, G. A. and Lichten, W. (1951), The intelligibility of speech as a function of the context of the text materials, *Journal of Experimental Psychology*, *41*, 329–335.

Miller, G. A. and Isard, S. (1963), Some perceptual consequences of linguistic rules, *Journal of Verbal Learning and Verbal Behavior*, *2*, 217–228.

Miller, G. A. and Isard, S. (1964), Free recall of self-embedded English sentences. *Information and Control*, *7*, 292–303.

Miller, G. A. and McKean, K. O. (1964), A chronometric study of some relations between sentences, *Quarterly Journal of Experimental Psychology*, *16*, 297–308.

Miller, G. A. and Nicely, P. E. (1955), An analysis of perceptual confusion among some English consonants, *Journal of the Acoustical Society of America*, *27*, 338–352.

Miller, G. A. and Selfridge, J. A. (1950), Verbal context and the recall of meaningful material. *American Journal of Psychology*, *63*, 176–185.

Miller, N. E. (1967), Memory and learning. *Proceedings of the American Philosophical Society*, *111*, 315–325.

Millward, R. (1964), Latency in a modified paired-associate learning experiment, *Journal of Verbal Learning and Verbal Behavior*, *3*, 309–316.

Milner, B. (1967), Amnesia following operation on the temporal lobes. In O. L. Zangwill and C. M. W. Whitty (Eds.) *Amnesia*, Butterworths, London.

Moray, N. (1959), Attention in dichotic listening: Attentive cues and the influence of instructions, *Quarterly Journal of Experimental Psychology*, *11*, 56–60.

Müller, G. E. (1913), Zur Analyse der Gedächtnistätigkeit und des Vorstellungsverlaufes, III. Teil. *Zeitschrift für Psychologie, Ergänzungsband 8.*

Müller, G. E. and Pilzecker, A. (1900), Experimentelle Beiträge zur Lehre vom Gedächtnis, *Zeitschrift für Psychologie, Ergänzungsband 1.*

Müller, G. E. and Schumann, F. (1894), Experimentelle Beiträge zur Untersuchung des Gedächtnisses, *Zeitschrift fur Psychologie*, *6*, 81–190, 257–339.

Murdock, B. B., Jr. (1961), The retention of individual items, *Journal of Experimental Psychology*, *62*, 618–625.

Murdock, B. B., Jr. (1962), The serial position effect in free recall, *Journal of Experimental Psychology*, *64*, 482–488.

Murdock, B. B., Jr. (1963a), Short-term memory and paired-associate learning, *Journal of Verbal Learning and Verbal Behavior*, *2*, 320–328.

Murdock, B. B., Jr. (1963b), An analysis of the recognition process. In

C. N. Cofer and B. S. Musgrave (Eds.) *Verbal Behavior and Learning*, McGraw-Hill, New York. pp. 10–22.

Murdock, B. B., Jr. (1963c), Interpolated recall in short-term memory, *Journal of Experimental Psychology*, 66, 525–532.

Murdock, B. B., Jr. (1964), Proactive inhibition in short-term memory, *Journal of Experimental Psychology*, 68, 184–189.

Murdock, B. B., Jr. (1965a), Effects of a subsidiary task on short-term memory, *British Journal of Psychology*, 56, 413–419.

Murdock, B. B., Jr. (1965b), Signal detection theory and short-term memory, *Journal of Experimental Psychology*, 70, 443–447.

Murdock, B. B., Jr. (1966), The criterion problem in short-term memory, *Journal of Experimental Psychology*, 72, 317–324.

Murdock, B. B., Jr. (1967a), Distractor and probe techniques in short-term memory, *Canadian Journal of Psychology*, 21, 25–36.

Murdock, B. B., Jr. (1967b), Recent developments in short-term memory, *British Journal of Psychology*, 58, 421–433.

Nahinski, I. D. (1967), Statistics and moments-parameter estimates for a duoprocess paired-associate learning model, *Journal of Mathematical Psychology*, 4, 140–150.

Neimark, E. D. and Estes, W. K. (1967), *Stimulus Sampling Theory*. Holden-Day, San Francisco.

Neimark, E. D., Greenhouse, P., Law, S., and Weinheimer, S. (1965), The effect of rehearsal preventing tasks upon retention of CVC syllables, *Journal of Verbal Learning and Verbal Behavior*, 4, 280–285.

Neisser, U. and Weene, P. (1962), Hierarchies in concept attainment, *Journal of Experimental Psychology*, 64, 640–645.

Neumann, J. von (1956), Probabalistic logics and the synthesis of reliable organisms from unreliable components. In C. E. Shannon and J. McCarthy (Eds.) *Automata Studies*, Princeton University Press, Princeton. pp. 43–98.

Neumann, J. von and Morgenstern, O. (1944), *Theory of Games and Economic Behavior*, Princeton University Press, Princeton.

Newell, A. and Simon, H. A. (1962), Computer simulation of human thinking, *Science*, 134, 2011–2017.

Noble, C. E. (1952), An analysis of meaning, *Psychological Review*, 59, 421–430.

Norman, D. A. (1966), Acquisition and retention in short-term memory, *Journal of Experimental Psychology*, 72, 369–381.

Norman, D. A. and Wickelgren, W. A. (1965), Short-term recognition memory for single digits and pairs of digits, *Journal of Experimental Psychology*, 70, 479–489.

O'Connell, D. C., Turner, E. A., and Onuska, L. A., (1968), Intonation, grammatical structure, and contextual association in immediate recall, *Journal of Verbal Learning and Verbal Behavior*, 7, 110–116.

Olson, G. M. (1969), Learning and retention in a continuous recognition task, *Journal of Experimental Psychology, 81*, 381–384.

Osgood, C. E. (1949), The similarity paradox in human learning: A resolution, *Psychological Review, 56*, 132–143.

Paivio, A. (1969), Mental imagery in associative learning and memory, *Psychological Review, 76*, 241–263.

Palermo, D. S., and Jenkins, J. J. (1964), *Word Association Norms: Grade School through College*, University of Minnesota Press, Minneapolis.

Parks, T. E. (1966), Signal-detectability theory of recognition-memory performance, *Psychological Review, 73*, 44–58.

Pavlov, I. P. (1927), *Conditioned Reflexes: An Investigation of the Physiological Activity of the Cerebral Cortex*, Oxford University Press, London.

Pavlov, I. P. (1928), *Lectures on Conditioned Reflexes*, Translated by W. H. Gantt. International Publishers, New York.

Peters, W. (1910), Über Ähnlichkeitsassoziationen, *Zeitschrift für Psychologie, 56*, 161–206.

Peterson, L. R. (1967), Search and judgment in memory. In B. J. Kleinmuntz (Ed.) *Concepts and the Structure of Memory*, Wiley, New York. pp. 153–180.

Peterson, L. R., Hilner, K. and Saltzman, D. (1962), Time between pairings and short-term retention, *Journal of Experimental Psychology, 64*, 550–551.

Peterson, L. R. and Peterson, M. J. (1959), Short-term retention of individual items, *Journal of Experimental Psychology, 58*, 193–198.

Peterson, L. R., Wampler, R., Kirkpatrick, M., and Saltzman, D. (1963), Effect of spacing presentations on retention of paired-associates over short intervals, *Journal of Experimental Psychology, 66*, 206–209.

Pick, A. D. (1965), Improvement of visual and tactual form discrimination, *Journal of Experimental Psychology, 69*, 331–339.

Pillsbury, W. B. and Sylvester, A. (1940), Retroactive and proactive inhibition in immediate memory, *Journal of Experimental Psychology, 27*, 532–545.

Pollack, I. (1953), The assimilation of sequentially encoded information, *American Journal of Psychology, 66*, 421–435.

Pollack, I., and Decker, L. R. (1958), Confidence ratings, message reception, and the receiver operating characteristic, *Journal of the Acoustical Society of America, 30*, 286–292.

Pollack, I., Johnson, L. B., and Knaff, P. R. (1959), Running memory span, *Journal of Experimental Psychology, 57*, 137–146.

Polson, P. G. (1967), A quantitative study of the concept identification and paired-associates learning processes in the Hull paradigm, Unpublished Ph.D. dissertation, Indiana University, Bloomington, Indiana.

Polson, M. C., Restle, F., and Polson, P. G. (1965), Association and discrimination in paired-associate learning, *Journal of Experimental Psychology, 69*, 47–55.

Posner, M. I. (1964), Rate of presentation and order of recall in immediate memory. *British Journal of Psychology, 55*, 303–306.

Posner, M. I. and Konick, A. F. (1966), Short-term retention of visual and kinesthetic information, *Organizational Behavior and Human Performance*, *1*, 71–86.

Posner, M. I. and Rossman, E. (1965), Effect of size and location of informational transforms upon short-term retention, *Journal of Experimental Psychology*, *70*, 496–505.

Postman, L. (1950), Choice behavior and the process of recognition, *American Journal of Psychology*, *63*, 576–583.

Postman, L. (1961), The present status of interference theory, In C. N. Cofer (Ed.) *Verbal Learning and Verbal Behavior*, McGraw-Hill, New York. pp. 152–178.

Postman, L. (1963), One-trial-learning. In C. N. Cofer and B. S. Musgrave (Eds.) *Verbal Behavior and Learning: Problems and Processes*, McGraw-Hill, New York. pp. 295–321.

Postman, L. (1964), Short-term memory and incidental learning. In A. W. Melton (Ed.) *Categories of Human Learning*, Academic Press, New York. pp. 146–201.

Postman, L. and Phillips, L. W. (1965), Short-term temporal changes in free recall, *Quarterly Journal of Experimental Psychology*, *17*, 132–138.

Postman, L. and Postman, D. L. (1948), Changes in set as a determinant of retroactive inhibition, *American Journal of Psychology*, *61*, 236–242.

Postman, L. and Riley, D. A. (1959), Degree of learning and interserial interference in retention, *University of California Publications in Psychology*, *8*, 271–346.

Postman, L. and Schwartz, M. (1964), Studies of learning to learn: I. Transfer as a function of method of practice and class of verbal materials, *Journal of Verbal Learning and Verbal Behavior*, *3*, 37–49.

Postman, L. and Stark, K. (1969), The role of response availability in transfer and interference, *Journal of Experimental Psychology*, *79*, 168–177.

Postman, L., Stark, K., and Fraser, J. (1968), Temporal changes in interference. *Journal of Verbal Learning and Verbal Behavior*, *7*, 672–694.

Premack, D. (1965), Reinforcement theory. In M. R. Jones (Ed.) *Nebraska Symposium of Motivation*, University of Nebraska Press, Lincoln. pp. 123–188.

Raffel, G. (1936), Two determinants of the effects of primacy, *American Journal of Psychology*, *48*, 654–657.

Rapoport, A. and Orwant, C. (1962), Experimental games: A review, *Behavioral Science*, *7*, 1–37.

Reber, A. S. (1967), Implicit learning of artificial grammars, *Journal of Verbal Learning and Verbal Behavior*, *6*, 855–863.

Reed, H. B. (1946), Factors influencing the learning and retention of concepts. I - IV, *Journal of Experimental Psychology*, *35*, 71–87; 166–179; 252–261.

Restle, F. (1955), A theory of discrimination learning, *Psychological Review*, *62*, 11–19.

Restle, F. (1957), Discrimination of cues in mazes: A resolution of the "place versus response" question, *Psychological Review, 64,* 217–228.

Restle, F. (1961), *The Psychology of Judgment and Choice.* Wiley, New York.

Restle, F. (1962), The selection of strategies in cue learning, *Psychological Review, 69,* 329–343.

Restle, F. (1964), Sources of difficulty in learning paired-associates. In R. C. Atkinson (Ed.) *Studies in Mathematical Psychology,* Stanford University Press, Stanford. pp. 116–172.

Restle, F. and Emmerich, D. (1966), Memory in concept attainment: Effect of giving several problems concurrently, *Journal of Experimental Psychology, 71,* 794–799.

Restorff, H. von (1937), Über die Wirkung von Bereichsbildung im Spurenfeld, *Psychologische Forschung, 18,* 297–342.

Riley, D. A. (1962), Memory for form. In Postman, L. (Ed.) *Psychology in the Making,* Knopf, New York. pp. 402–465.

Rock, I. (1957), The role of repetition in associative learning, *American Journal of Psychology, 70,* 186–193.

Rohrmann, N. L. (1968), The role of syntactic structure in the recall of English nominalizations, *Journal of Verbal Learning and Verbal Behavior, 7,* 904–912.

Rose, R. M. and Vitz, P. C. (1966), The role of runs in probability learning, *Journal of Experimental Psychology, 72,* 751–760.

Rosenblatt, F. (1958), The preceptron: A probabalistic model for information storage and organization in the brain, *Psychological Review, 65,* 386–401.

Rothkopf, E. Z. and Coke, E. U. (1961), The prediction of free recall from word association measures, *Journal of Experimental Psychology, 62,* 433–438.

Rumelhart, D. E. (1967), The effects of interpresentation intervals on performance in a continuous paired-associate task, Technical Report No. 116, Institute for Mathematical Studies in the Social Sciences, Stanford University, Stanford.

Sachs, J. D. S. (1967), Recognition memory for syntactic and semantic aspects of connected discourse, *Perception and Psychophysics, 2,* 437–442.

Saltzman, I. J. (1951), Delay of reward and human verbal learning, *Journal of Experimental Psychology, 41,* 437–439.

Savin, H. B. and Perchonock, E. (1965), Grammatical structure and the immediate recall of English sentences, *Journal of Verbal Learning and Verbal Behavior, 4,* 348–353.

Schoonard, J. W. and Restle, F. (1961), Analysis of double alternation in terms of stimuli and responses, *Journal of Experimental Psychology, 61,* 365–367.

Schwartz, F. and Rouse, R. D. (1961), The activation and recovery of associations, *Psychological Issues, 3,* Whole No. 1.

Selfridge, O. G. (1959), Pandemonium: A paradigm for learning. In *Proceedings of a Symposium on the Mechanization of Thought Processes,* London: H. M. Stationary Office.

Selfridge, O. G. and Neisser, U. (1960), Pattern recognition by machine, *Scientific American, 203,* 60–68.

Selzer, L. K. and Wickelgren, W. A. (1963), Number of items presented and recalled as determinants of short-term recall, *Nature, 200,* 1239–1241.

Shannon, C. E. (1948), A mathematical theory of communication, *Bell Systems Technical Journal, 27,* 379–423; 623–656.

Shepard, R. N. (1967), Recognition memory for words, sentences, and pictures, *Journal of Verbal Learning and Verbal Behavior, 6,* 156–163.

Shepard, R. N. and Chang, J. J. (1963), Stimulus generalization in the learning of classifications, *Journal of Experimental Psychology, 65,* 94–102.

Shepard, R. N., Hovland, C. I., and Jenkins, H. M. (1961), Learning and memorization of classifications, *Psychological Monographs, 75,* Whole No. 517.

Shepard, R. N. and Tegtsoonian, M. (1961), Retention of information under conditions approaching a steady state, *Journal of Experimental Psychology, 62,* 302–309.

Shepp, B. E. and Zeaman, D. (1966), Discrimination learning of size and brightness by retardates, *Journal of Comparative and Physiological Psychology, 62,* 55–59.

Shipstone, E. I. (1960), Some variables affecting pattern conception, *Psychological Monographs, 74,* Whole No. 504.

Siegel, S. (1961), Decision making and learning under varying conditions of reinforcement, *Annals of the New York Academy of Science, 89,* 715–896.

Siegel, S. and Goldstein, D. A. (1959), Decision making behavior in a two-choice uncertain outcome situation, *Journal of Experimental Psychology, 57,* 37–42.

Simon, H. A. and Feigenbaum, E. A. (1964), An information processing theory of some effects of similarity, familiarization, and meaningfulness in verbal learning, *Journal of Verbal Learning and Verbal Behavior, 3,* 385–396.

Simon, H. A. and Kotovsky, K. (1963), Human acquisition of concepts for sequential patterns, *Psychological Review, 70,* 534–546.

Skinner, B. F. (1938), *The Behavior of Organisms,* Appleton-Century-Crofts, New York.

Skinner, B. F. (1957), *Verbal Behavior,* Appleton-Century-Crofts, New York.

Slamecka, N. J. (1966), Differentiation versus unlearning of verbal associations, *Journal of Experimental Psychology, 71,* 822–828.

Slobin, D. I. (1968), Recall of full and truncated passive sentences in connected discourse, *Journal of Verbal Learning and Verbal Behavior, 7,* 876–881.

Smoke, K. L (1933), Negative instances in concept learning, *Journal of Experimental Psychology, 16,* 583–588.

Sokolov, E. N. (1963), *Perception and the conditioned reflex,* Pergamon, New York.

Spence, K. W. (1937), The differential response in animals to stimuli varying within a single dimension, *Psychological Review, 44*, 430–444.

Spence, K. W. (1942), The basis of solution by chimpanzees of the intermediate size problem, *Journal of Experimental Psychology, 31*, 257–271.

Sperling, G. (1963), A model for visual memory tasks, *Human Factors, 5*, 19–30.

Stern, W. (1938), *General Psychology from the Personalistic Standpoint*, McMillan, New York.

Sumby, W. H. (1963), Word frequency and the serial position effect, *Journal of Verbal Learning and Verbal Behavior, 1*, 443–450.

Suppes, P. (1966), Mathematical concept formation in children, *American Psychologist, 21*, 139–150.

Suppes, P. (1969), Stimulus-response theory of finite automata, *Journal of Mathematical Psychology, 6*, 327–355.

Suppes, P. and Atkinson, R. C. (1960), *Markov Models for Multiperson Interactions*, Stanford University Press, Stanford, 1960.

Suppes, P. and Ginsberg, R. A. (1962), Application of a stimulus-sampling model to children's concept formation with and without correction of responses, *Journal of Experimental Psychology, 63*, 330–336.

Suppes, P. and Ginsberg, R. (1963), A fundamental property of all-or-none models, binomial distribution of responses prior to conditioning, with application to concept formation in children. *Psychological Review, 70*, 139–161.

Suppes, P. Groen, G. and Schlag-Rey, M. (1966), A model for response latency in paired-associate learning, *Journal of Mathematical Psychology, 3*, 99–128.

Suppes, P. and Schlag-Rey, M. (1962), Test of some learning models for double contingent reinforcement, *Psychological Reports, 10*, 259–268.

Sutherland, N. S. (1959), Stimulus analyzing mechanisms. In *Proceedings of a Symposium for the Mechanization of Thought Processes*. Vol. II. London: H. M. Stationary Office. pp. 575–609.

Terrace, H. S. (1963a), Errorless transfer of a discrimination across two continua. *Journal of the Experimental Analysis of Behavior, 6*, 223–232.

Terrace, H. S. (1963b), Discrimination learning with and without errors, *Journal of the Experimental Analysis of Behavior, 6*, 1–22.

Terwilliger, R. F. (1962), Note on familiarity and verbal learning, *Psychological Reports, 10*, 409–410.

Theios, J. (1963), Simple conditioning as two-stage all-or-none learning, *Psychological Review, 70*, 403–417.

Theios, J. and Brelsford, J., Jr. (1966), Theoretical interpretations of a Markov model for avoidance conditioning, *Journal of Mathematical Psychology, 3*, 140–162.

Thomas, D. R. and DeCapito, A. (1966), Role of stimulus labelling in stimulus generalization, *Journal of Experimental Psychology, 71*, 913–915.

Thorndike, E. L. (1931), *Human Learning*, Appleton-Century-Crofts, New York.

Thorndike, E. L. and Lorge, I. (1944), *The Teacher's Word Book of 30,000 Words*, Columbia University Press, New York.

Thurstone, L. L. (1927), A law of comparative judgment, *Psychological Review, 34*, 273–286.

Tinbergen, N. (1951), *The study of instinct*, Oxford University Press, Oxford.

Tolman, E. C. (1932), *Purposive Behavior in Animals and Men*, Century, New York.

Trabasso, T. R. (1963), Stimulus emphasis and all-or-none learning in concept identification, *Journal of Experimental Psychology, 65*, 398-406.

Trabasso, T. R. and Bower, G. H. (1964), Memory in concept identification, *Psychonomic Science, 1*, 133–134.

Trabasso, T. R. and Bower, G. H. (1966), Presolution dimensional shifts in concept identification: A test of the sampling with replacement axiom in all-or-none models, *Journal of Mathematical Psychology, 3*, 163–173.

Trabasso, T. R. and Bower, G. H. (1968), *Attention in Learning: Theory and Research*, Wiley, New York.

Treisman, A. (1964), Selective attention in man, *British Medical Bulletin, 20*, 12–16.

Tulving, E. (1962), Subjective organization in free recall of unrelated words, *Psychological Review, 69*, 344–354.

Tulving, E. (1964), Intratrial and intertrial retention: Notes toward a theory of free-recall verbal learning, *Psychological Review, 71*, 219–237.

Tulving, E. (1966), Subjective organization and effects of repetition in multitrial free-recall learning, *Journal of Verbal Learning and Verbal Behavior, 5*, 193–197.

Tulving, E. and Arbuckle, T. Y. (1963), Sources of intertrial interference in immediate recall of paired-associates. *Journal of Verbal Learning and Verbal Behavior, 1*, 321–324.

Tulving, E. and Arbuckle, T. Y. (1966), Input and output interference in short-term associative memory, *Journal of Experimental Psychology, 72*, 145–150.

Tulving, E. and Osler, S. (1968), Effectiveness of retrieval cues in memory for words, *Journal of Experimental Psychology, 77*, 593–601.

Tulving, E. and Pearlstone, Z. (1966), Availability versus accessibility of information in memory for words, *Journal of Verbal Learning and Verbal Behavior, 5*, 381–391.

Turing, A. M. (1950), Computing machinery and intelligence, *Mind, 59*, 433–460.

Underwood, B. J. (1948), "Spontaneous recovery" of verbal associations, *Journal of Experimental Psychology, 38*, 429–439.

Underwood, B. J. (1953), Studies of distributed practice: VIII. Learning and retention of paired nonsense syllables as a function of intralist similarity. *Journal of Experimental Psychology, 45,* 133–142.

Underwood, B. J. (1957), Interference and forgetting, *Psychological Review, 64,* 49–60.

Underwood, B. J. (1961), An evaluation of the Gibson theory of verbal learning. In C. N. Cofer (Ed.) *Verbal Learning and Verbal Behavior.* McGraw-Hill, New York. pp. 197–216.

Underwood, B. J. (1963), Stimulus selection in verbal learning. In C. N. Cofer and B. S. Musgrave (Eds.) *Verbal Behavior and Learning: Problems and Processes,* McGraw-Hill, New York. pp. 33–48.

Underwood, B. J. and Ekstrand, B. R. (1966), An analysis of some shortcomings in the interference theory of forgetting, *Psychological Review, 73,* 540–549.

Underwood, B. J. and Freund, J. S. (1968), Errors in recognition learning and retention, *Journal of Experimental Psychology, 78,* 55–63.

Underwood, B. J. and Goad, D. (1951), Studies of distributed practice: I. The influence of intralist similarity in serial learning, *Journal of Experimental Psychology, 42,* 125–135.

Underwood, B. J., Ham, M., and Ekstrand, B. R. (1962), Cue selection in paired-associate learning, *Journal of Experimental Psychology, 64,* 405–409.

Underwood, B. J. and Postman, L. (1960), Extraexperimental sources of interference in forgetting, *Psychological Review, 67,* 73–95.

Underwood, B. J., Rehula, R., and Keppel, G. (1962), Item selection in paired-associate learning, *American Journal of Psychology, 75,* 353–371.

Underwood, B. J. and Richardson, J. (1956a), The influence of meaningfulness, intralist similarity, and serial position upon retention, *Journal of Experimental Psychology, 52,* 119–126.

Underwood, B. J. and Richardson, J. (1956b), Verbal concept learning as a function of instructions and dominance level, *Journal of Experimental Psychology, 51,* 229–238.

Underwood, B. J., Runquist, W. N., and Schultz, R. W. (1959), Response learning in paired-associate lists as a function of intralist similarity, *Journal of Experimental Psychology, 58,* 70–78.

Underwood, B. J. and Schultz, R. W. (1960), *Meaningfulness and Verbal Learning,* Lippincot, Philadelphia.

Wald, A. (1950), *Statistical Decision Functions,* Wiley, New York.

Wason, P. C. (1965), The contexts of plausible denial, *Journal of Verbal Learning and Verbal Behavior, 4,* 7-11.

Watson, J. B. (1925), *Behaviorism,* Norton, New York.

Waugh, N. C. and Norman, D. A. (1965), Primary memory. *Psychological Review, 72,* 89–104.

Waugh, N. C. and Norman, D. A. (1968), The measure of interference in primary memory, *Journal of Verbal Learning and Verbal Behavior, 7.* 617–626.

Wells, H. (1963), Effects of transfer and problem structure in disjunctive concept formation, *Journal of Experimental Psychology, 65,* 63–69.

Whitman, J. R. and Garner, W. R. (1962), Free recall learning of visual figures as a function of form of internal structure, *Journal of Experimental Psychology, 64,* 558–564.

Wickelgren, W. A. (1964), Effects of different terminal sounds on short-term memory for initial consonants sounds, *Nature, 203,* 1199–1200.

Wickelgren, W. A. (1965a), Acoustic similarity and retroactive interference in short-term memory, *Journal of Verbal Learning and Verbal Behavior, 4,* 53–61.

Wickelgren, W. A. (1965b), Acoustic similarity and intrusion errors in short-term memory, *Journal of Experimental Psychology, 70,* 102–108.

Wickelgren, W. A. (1965c), Distinctive features and errors in short-term memory for English vowels, *Journal of the Acoustical Society of America, 38,* 583–588.

Wickelgren, W. A. (1966), Distinctive features and errors in short-term memory for English consonants, *Journal of the Acoustical Society of America, 39,* 388–398.

Wickelgren, W. A. (1967), Exponential decay and independence from irrelevant associations in short-term memory for serial order, *Journal of Experimental Psychology, 73,* 165–171.

Wickelgren, W. A. and Norman, D. A. (1966), Strength models and serial position in short-term recognition memory, *Journal of Mathematical Psychology, 3,* 316–347.

Wickens, D. D., Born, D. G. and Allen, C. K. (1963), Proactive inhibition and item similarity in short-term memory, *Journal of Verbal Learning and Verbal Behavior, 2,* 440–445.

Wigner, E. P. (1964), Events, Laws of Nature, and Invariance Principles, *Science, 145,* 995–999.

Williams, J. P. (1961), A selection artifact in Rock's study of the role of repetition, *Journal of Experimental Psychology, 62,* 627–628.

Wimer, R. (1964), Osgood's transfer surface: Extension and test, *Journal of Verbal Learning and Verbal Behavior, 3,* 274–279.

Woodworth, R. S. and Schlosberg, H. (1961), *Experimental Psychology,* Holt, Rinehart, and Winston, New York.

Wulff, F., (1922), Über die Veränderung von Vorstellungen *Psychologische Forschung, 1,* 333–373.

Wundt, W. (1905), *Grundriss der Psychologie,* Engelmann, Leipzig.

Yates, F. A. (1966), *The Art of Memory,* University of Chicago Press, Chicago.

Yngve, V. H. (1960), A model and a hypothesis for language structure, *Proceedings of the American Philosophical Society, 104,* 444–466.

Young, J. L. (1966), Effects of intervals between reinforcements and test trials in paired-associate learning, Technical Report No. 101, Institute for Mathematical Studies in the Social Sciences, Stanford.

Zeaman, D. and Denegre, J. (1967), Variability of irrelevant discriminative stimuli. *Journal of Experimental Psychology*, *73*, 574–580.

Zeaman, D. and House, B. J. (1963), The role of attention in retardate discrimination learning, In N. R. Ellis (Ed.) *Handbook in Mental Deficiency*, McGraw-Hill, New York. pp. 159–223.

Zinnes, J. L. and Kurtz, R. (1968), Matching, discrimination, and payoffs, *Journal of Mathematical Psychology*, *5*, 392–421.

AUTHOR INDEX

SUBJECT INDEX